T0228229

MARGUERITE YOURCENAR'S HADRIAN: WRITING THE LIFE OF A ROMAN EMPEROR

PHOENIX

Journal of the Classical Association of Canada
Revue de la Société canadienne des études classiques
Supplementary Volume LXII
Tome supplémentaire LXII

KEITH BRADLEY

Marguerite Yourcenar's Hadrian: Writing the Life of a Roman Emperor

UNIVERSITY OF TORONTO PRESS
Toronto Buffalo London

ISBN 978-1-4875-4881-0 (cloth)   ISBN 978-1-4875-4889-6 (EPUB)
ISBN 978-1-4875-4890-2 (PDF)

Library and Archives Canada Cataloguing in Publication

Title: Marguerite Yourcenar's Hadrian : writing the life of a
Roman emperor / Keith Bradley.
Names: Bradley, K. R. (Keith R.), 1946– author.
Series: Phoenix. Supplementary volume ; 62.
Description: Series statement: Phoenix. Supplementary volume ; 62 |
Includes bibliographical references and index.
Identifiers: Canadiana (print) 20230525725 | Canadiana (ebook) 20230525768 |
ISBN 9781487548810 (cloth) | ISBN 9781487548902 (PDF) |
ISBN 9781487548896 (EPUB)
Subjects: LCSH: Yourcenar, Marguerite – Criticism and interpretation. |
LCSH: Yourcenar, Marguerite. Mémoires d'Hadrien. | LCSH: Hadrian, Emperor
of Rome, 76–138 – In literature.
Classification: LCC PQ2649.O8 Z64 2024 | DDC 843/.912–dc23

Cover design: John Beadle
Cover images: Marble Busts of Hadrian and Antinous. British Museum

We wish to acknowledge the land on which the University of Toronto Press
operates. This land is the traditional territory of the Wendat, the Anishnaabeg, the
Haudenosaunee, the Métis, and the Mississaugas of the Credit First Nation.

This book has been published with the help of a grant from the Federation for the
Humanities and Social Sciences, through the Awards to Scholarly Publications Program,
using funds provided by the Social Sciences and Humanities Research Council of Canada.

University of Toronto Press acknowledges the financial support of the Government of
Canada, the Canada Council for the Arts, and the Ontario Arts Council, an agency of the
Government of Ontario, for its publishing activities.

Canada Council   Conseil des Arts
for the Arts   du Canada

ONTARIO ARTS COUNCIL
CONSEIL DES ARTS DE L'ONTARIO
an Ontario government agency
un organisme du gouvernement de l'Ontario

Funded by the   Financé par le
Government   gouvernement
of Canada   du Canada

For
Diane

CONTENTS

PREFACE

Marguerite Yourcenar is best known as a novelist, and *Mémoires d'Hadrien* is her most celebrated novel. The book tells the life story of the Roman emperor Hadrian, and for good reason it is often categorized as a historical novel. It is not a novel in any ordinary sense, however, and I approach it here as a fictive historical biography. By "fictive" I mean artfully, artistically, and imaginatively contrived from identifiable evidence, and by "historical biography" I mean a genuine account of a Roman emperor's life. My purpose is to explain how and why *Mémoires* is as it is and to promote in an essentially historiographical undertaking appreciation of the biographical accomplishment it represents.

The project began from the simple thought that a succinct essay might expeditiously be written comparing Yourcenar's portrait of Hadrian with various modern scholarly treatments of the emperor. What resulted, however, was an unpredictably long engagement with the life and career of a pre-eminent literary artist and exploration of a complement of critical scholarship largely unknown in the English-speaking classical world. The putative essay has become consequently a book, whose underlying theme is the relationship between fiction and history. To exemplify which I refer in passing to both conventional studies of Roman emperors and instances of biographical literature in wider compass, raising questions about the viability of Roman imperial biography as generally practised, and, by implication, about much else that is written about the Roman past. I incorporate material from Yourcenarian experts as appropriate, and draw selectively on various preparatory studies previously published.[1]

I quote and paraphrase passages from *Mémoires* and Marguerite Yourcenar's other writings liberally throughout to make clear the basis of my observations. (I offer no apology for this.) I give quotations in French and

English, using published English translations when possible – for *Mémoires* itself the elegant rendition of Yourcenar's companion Grace Frick – but in other cases, and especially for extracts from Yourcenar's correspondence and interviews, items essential to my purpose, I have translated the passages myself, very literally, for basic purposes of communication alone. Occasionally I give no translation at all if I consider the meaning of a word or phrase obvious, nor do I usually translate statements in French from other scholars. I include extended English versions in the main text but consign short extracts to my notes.

The project began at the University of Notre Dame and concluded at the University of Victoria. I am grateful to both institutions for their support. In the early stages Notre Dame provided precious resources for travel to places associated with Yourcenar and Hadrian, and in this connection I particularly thank Joan Howard for making possible a visit to Petite Plaisance, Yourcenar's home on Mount Desert Island in the state of Maine, and especially Marc-Etienne Vlaminck for his outstanding services during an extended visit to the Centre International de Documentation Marguerite Yourcenar in Brussels. I am very grateful also to Rémy Poignault for making available the resources of the Société Internationale d'Études Yourcenariennes at Clermont-Ferrand. Notre Dame also allowed me the benefit of much practical help from two research assistants, Elisabetta Drudi and Kelly Taylor, to both of whom I extend warm thanks. At both institutions innumerable librarians have accommodated endless requests for bibliographic assistance. I am thankful to them all.

Colleagues who have promptly answered enquiries or created occasions on which to present aspects of my work in public are too numerous to mention individually; I trust that they will severally accept this blanket statement of my gratitude. I must nonetheless register two crucial obligations to friends no longer living: to the incomparable Mark Golden, with whom I shared many productive conversations concerning my book that can now, regrettably, be recalled only as fond memories; and to Anthony Birley, Hadrian's principal modern biographer, who over a long period of time supplied a steady stream of relevant materials and, more generously still, urged me without reservation or rancour to disagree with him as I saw fit. I record these obligations in sadness.

In the latter stages, the sustaining companionship of my veteran Victorian colleagues John Fitch and John Oleson has been invaluable, while Fanny Dolansky's efficiency in improving the presentation of my ramshackle pages of typescript has exceeded all reasonable expectations. In turn, Patricia Clark and John Drinkwater, remarkable friends of long standing, have given extraordinary help not only as careful readers of work in progress but, more importantly, as providers also of moral support at times of doubt and hesitation. I can scarcely thank them enough for their encouragement and commitment.

Completely inexpressible is my debt to my wife, Diane Boyle Bradley, without whose infinite patience and gentle reassurance I could never have brought the book to conclusion. Its dedication, utterly inadequate in return, is offered with love eternal.

I extend thanks finally to Jonathan Edmondson and Alison Keith for welcoming my book to the monograph series they supervise, and to my editors Suzanne Rancourt and Barbara Porter at the University of Toronto Press for again bringing my work to fruition. The enterprise continues long-held interests in Latin biography and fiction that converge and broaden now into examination of Marguerite Yourcenar's recovery of Hadrian's life story. I trust, but cannot guarantee, that both Romanists and Yourcenarians will find something of interest in its pages, but hope above all in what I have written to affirm the essential grandeur of Yourcenar's creation.

KRB

Id. Oct.

a. mmxxii

ABBREVIATIONS

Works of Marguerite Yourcenar

ACB   *En 1939, l'Amérique commence à Bordeaux: Lettres à Emmanuel Boudot-Lamotte (1938–1980)*. Édition établie, présentée et annotée par Élyane Dezon-Jones et Michèle Sarde. Gallimard: Paris 2016.

AN   *Archives du Nord*. Gallimard: Paris 1977 (cited from *EM*) = *How Many Years*. Translated from the French by Maria Louise Ascher. Farrar Straus Giroux: New York 1995.

AS   *Anna, soror* ... Grasset: Paris 1934; Gallimard: Paris 1981: *Comme l'eau qui coule* 9–75, 241–53 *Postface* (cited from *OR*) = *Two Lives and a Dream*. Translated by Walter Kaiser in collaboration with the author. Farrar Straus Giroux: New York 1987: 155–216, 227–42 *Postface*.

CA   *Les Charités d'Alcippe*. La Flûte enchantée: Liège 1956; Gallimard: Paris 1984.

CG   *Le Coup de grâce*. Paris: Gallimard 1939 (cited from *OR* with *Préface* of 1962) = *Coup de Grâce*. Translated from the French by Grace Frick in Collaboration with the Author. Farrar, Straus and Giroux: New York 1984.

CL   *La Couronne et la Lyre*. Gallimard: Paris 1979.

CNMH   *Carnets de notes de «Mémoires d'Hadrien»* (cited from *OR*).

CNON   *Carnets de notes de «L'Œuvre au Noir»* (cited from *OR*).

DAF   *Discours de réception de Madame Marguerite Yourcenar à l'Académie française et réponse de Monsieur Jean d'Ormesson*. Gallimard: Paris 1981.

DR   *Denier du rêve*. Grasset: Paris 1934; Plon: Paris 1959 (cited
          from *OR*) = *A Coin in Nine Hands*. Translated from the
          French by Dori Katz in collaboration with the author.
          University of Chicago Press: Chicago 1994.

EH   "L'Écrivain devant l'Histoire." *Société Internationale d'Études
          Yourcenariennes* Bulletin 36 (2015): 119–38.

EM   *Essais et mémoires*. Bibliothèque de la Pléiade. Gallimard:
          Paris 1991.

ER   *Entretiens radiophoniques de Patrick de Rosbo avec
          Marguerite Yourcenar*. Mercure de France: Paris 1972.

F   *Feux*. Librairie Plon: Paris 1957. Éditions Gallimard: Paris
          1974 (cited from *OR*).

FP   *Fleuve profond, sombre rivière. Les «Negro Spirituals»,
          commentaires et traductions*. Gallimard: Paris 1966.

Frick   *Memoirs of Hadrian and Reflections on the Composition of
          Memoirs of Hadrian*. Translated from the French by Grace
          Frick in Collaboration with the Author Marguerite Yourcenar.
          Farrar, Straus and Giroux. New York 1990.

HZ   *D'Hadrien à Zénon. Correspondance 1951–1956*. Texte établi
          et annoté par Colette Gaudin et Rémy Poignault. Avec la
          collaboration de Joseph Brami et Maurice Delcroix. Édition
          coordonnée par Élyane Dezon-Jones et Michèle Sarde. Préface
          de Josyane Savigneau. Gallimard: Paris 2004.

HZ II   *«Une Volonté sans fléchissement»: Correspondance 1957–
          1960. (D'Hadrien à Zénon, II)*. Texte établi, annoté et préfacé
          par Joseph Brami et Maurice Delcroix. Édition coordonnée par
          Colette Gaudin et Rémy Poignault avec la collaboration de
          Michèle Sarde. Gallimard: Paris 2007.

HZ III   *«Persévérer dans l'être»: Correspondance 1961–1963
          (D'Hadrien à Zénon, III)*. Texte établi et annoté par Joseph
          Brami et Rémy Poignault avec la collaboration de Maurice
          Delcroix, Colette Gaudin et Michèle Sarde. Préface de Joseph
          Brami et Michèle Sarde. Gallimard: Paris 2011.

HZ IV   *«Le Pendant des* Mémoires d'Hadrien *et leur entier
          contraire»: Correspondance 1964–1967 (D'Hadrien à Zénon,
          IV)*. Texte établi et annoté par Bruno Blanckeman et Rémy
          Poignault. Préfacé et coordonné par Élyane Dezon-Jones et
          Michèle Sarde. Gallimard: Paris 2019.

L   *Lettres à ses amis et quelques autres*. Édition établie,
          présentée et annotée par Michèle Sarde et Joseph Brami.
          Gallimard: Paris 1995.

MH	*Mémoires d'Hadrien*. Plon: Paris 1951 (cited from *OR*).
OR	*Œuvres romanesques*. Bibliothèque de la Pléiade. Gallimard: Paris 1982 (repr. 2011).
P	*Pindare*. Grasset: Paris 1932; Gallimard: Paris 1991 (cited from *EM*).
PCC	*Présentation critique de Constantin Cavafy 1863–1933. Suivi d'une traduction intégrale de ses poèmes par Marguerite Yourcenar et Constantin Dimaras*. Gallimard: Paris 1958 (cited from *EM*).
PE	*En pèlerin et en étranger*. Gallimard: Paris 1989 (cited from *EM*).
Plon 1951	*Mémoires d'Hadrien*. Plon: Paris (first edition).
PV	*Portrait d'une voix: Vingt-trois entretiens (1952–1987)*. Gallimard: Paris 2002.
QE	*Quoi? L'Éternité*. Gallimard: Paris 1988 (cited from *EM*).
RC	*Radioscopie de Jacques Chancel*. Éditions du Rocher: Monaco 1999 (interviews and broadcast of 1979).
Réception critique	Mémoires d'Hadrien *de Marguerite Yourcenar. Réception critique (1951–1952)*. Centre International de Documentation Marguerite Yourcenar: Brussels 2002.
SBI	*Sous bénéfice d'inventaire*. Gallimard: Paris 1962, 1978 (cited from *EM*) = *The Dark Brain of Piranesi and Other Essays*. Translated by Richard Howard in Collaboration with the Author. Farrar Straus Giroux: New York 1984.
SP	*Souvenirs pieux*. Gallimard: Paris 1974 (cited from *EM*) = *Dear Departed*. Translated from the French by Maria Louise Ascher. Farrar Straus Giroux: New York 1991.
TGS	*Le Temps, ce grand sculpteur*. Gallimard: Paris 1983 (cited from *EM*) = *That Mighty Sculptor, Time*. Translated by Walter Kaiser in Collaboration with the Author. Farrar, Straus and Giroux: New York 1992.
TP	*Le Tour de la prison*. Gallimard: Paris 1991 (cited from *EM*).
YO	*Les Yeux ouverts: Entretiens avec Matthieu Galey*. Éditions du Centurion: Paris 1980 = *With Open Eyes: Conversations with Matthieu Galey*. Translated by Arthur Goldhammer. Beacon Press: Boston 1984.

Classical Abbreviations

AE	*L'Année épigraphique*
BMC	*Catalogue of Coins in the British Museum*
BNJ	*Brill's New Jacoby*
CIL	*Corpus Inscriptionum Latinarum*

CPJ   *Corpus Papyrorum Judaicarum*
CRAI   *Comptes rendus de l'Académie des Inscriptions et Belles-Lettres*
EJ²   *Encyclopedia Judaica* (2nd edition)
IG   *Inscriptiones Graecae*
IGLS   *Inscriptions grecques et latines de la Syrie*
IGRR   *Inscriptiones Graecae ad Res Romanas Pertinentes*
IKourion   *The Inscriptions of Kourion*
ILS   *Inscriptiones Latinae Selectae*
LTUR   *Lexicon Topographicum Urbis Romae*
PGM   *Papyri Magicae Graecae*
PIR²   *Prosopographia Imperii Romani* (2nd edition)
RE   *Real-Encyclopädie der classischen Altertumswissenschaft*
RIC   *Roman Imperial Coinage*
RMD   *Roman Military Diplomas*
RP   R. Syme, *Roman Papers* I–VII
SB   *Sammelbuch griechischer Urkunden aus Ägypten*
SEG   *Supplementum Epigraphicum Graecum*
SIG³   *Sylloge Inscriptionum Graecarum* (3rd edition)
Tab. Vind. *Tabulae Vindolandenses*

Abbreviations for classical authors and works are generally those of the fourth edition of the *Oxford Classical Dictionary*. Citations for Fronto refer to the Loeb edition of C.R. Haines. Dates are AD unless otherwise indicated.

MARGUERITE YOURCENAR'S HADRIAN:
WRITING THE LIFE OF A ROMAN EMPEROR

Marguerite Yourcenar. Photograph by Yousuf Karsh.

1

Imperial Biography

Yet each man is a memory to himself.

William Wordsworth

I

Marguerite Yourcenar's *Mémoires d'Hadrien* was published in Paris in early December 1951 and has remained in print ever since. It has been translated into more than twenty languages and is the work with which Yourcenar, a prolific novelist, poet, and essayist, is most associated. It tells the life story of the Roman emperor Hadrian and is often called in consequence a historical novel. For the sake of convenience I shall refer to it as a novel throughout this book, as Yourcenar herself sometimes did. In the first instance it is a product of the creative imagination, as every novel is, and a work generally regarded as a literary masterpiece, as a great novel should be. But because it gives a portrait of a real figure from the Roman past and is based on original sources of information, it makes a claim to being in some sense a genuine work of history as well. In this regard it is distinct from Yourcenar's almost equally acclaimed *L'Œuvre au Noir*, a novel set in Europe of the early Renaissance whose chief protagonist Zénon (Zeno), unlike Hadrian, is a complete fiction.[1]

As a result *Mémoires* has produced reactions from both critics and historians. Due to its stylistic grandeur and apparent historical accuracy, the former have always held it in great esteem. From the outset it was heralded as majestic and miraculous, its beauty, poetic qualities, psychological insight, and metaphysical aspects repeatedly praised. It transcended the historical novel as conventionally understood, and could be called an unprecedented masterpiece. There was also untrammelled praise for Yourcenar's immense erudition and scrupulous research, and complete confidence in the novel's overall authenticity. That certain details had been altered was recognized, but even scholars, the critics said, were unlikely to raise quibbles in view of the explanations Yourcenar had provided in the *Note* on historical sources with which her book concluded. The portrait of Hadrian was magisterial, and comparisons were variously drawn with Flaubert, Chateaubriand, Pater, James, and Proust. Little has changed in the interval. In France, where it is now included in the *Programmes des Agrégations de Lettres*, *Mémoires* has come to enjoy almost iconic status, and the same is true elsewhere in Europe, in Belgium and Italy especially.[2]

Historians also were at first favourably impressed, with *Mémoires* sometimes cited as a genuine contribution to knowledge. Particularly high praise came from F.C. Grant, a scholar of early Christian history: "So accurate is [Yourcenar's] portrayal of the times in which the emperor Hadrian lived that the novel belongs on a shelf near the later Latin classics, if not in the same alcove, and also close to the great histories of that time, beginning with Dio Cassius and ending with Gibbon and Hermann Schiller and Rostovtzeff."[3] Subsequently, however, emphasis has fallen on the book's factual inaccuracies and speculative nature, so that in the early twenty-first century, at least in the English-speaking world, it receives little attention as a serious historical work. Indeed, to many contemporary classical historians both the book and the circumstances under which it was composed are scarcely known, and attitudes when they exist at all now tend to be dismissive, with scholars easily able to contend that the critics, less classically expert than Yourcenar herself, were, and perhaps remain, too dazzled by her erudition to appreciate the problems that lie beneath her reconstruction of Hadrian's history. The authors of a major work on Hadrian's Villa at Tibur, the modern Tivoli, offer a typical if not unsympathetic verdict: "Sensitive, deeply felt, it imaginatively constructs the character and concerns of the all-ruler whose intelligence and self-awareness are edged with cynicism and weariness and sometimes suppressed by a streak of barbarism," and yet, Yourcenar's "descriptions of Hadrian's temperament and thoughts are largely inventions – intriguing but unverifiable."[4]

My concern in this book, a sequence of soundings comprising an extended essay on the book's character, lies in assessing Yourcenar's historiographical achievement and the issues her novel raises for recovering Hadrian's life, the chief of which is the authenticity of the portrait and the means by which authenticity was conceived and realized. Underlying that concern is the assumption that history's most fundamental subject is the human subject. In attempting the assessment I introduce various details about Yourcenar herself and explain how *Mémoires* came to be written, my object being to show how and why in the novel Hadrian appears as he does. I also describe some of the intricate historical problems the portrait presents as I confront the criticisms the book has elicited. In so doing I have in mind as readers both Yourcenarian scholars who may not be fully aware of the limitations of the original sources on which knowledge of Hadrian's life depends – a factor that has ramifications for the question of the novel's historical authority – and Roman historians who either have not read the novel, or, if they have, know little about its author. My method will be expository in the main and much will be no more than synthetic. I draw, that is, principally on the researches of others in two fields of enquiry, modern Yourcenarian studies and Roman Imperial history, well aware of the perils the strategy holds. My hope nonetheless is that the results will be mutually reinforcing and together contribute to enhancing appreciation of what in the last analysis I regard as an extraordinary accomplishment: a book singular in character perhaps best defined as a prose poem.[5]

The novel itself apart, I proceed by paying special attention to a body of evidence that comes directly from Yourcenar herself. First, two items that are printed with *Mémoires*, the *Note* to which I have already alluded, which was expanded over time in new editions, and Yourcenar's reflections on the book's composition, the *Carnets de notes de «Mémoires d'Hadrien»*, a quasi-appendix included from 1953 onwards after initial publication in the journal *Mercure de France* of 1952. (A small addition was made in 1958.)[6] Secondly, the six volumes of Yourcenar's correspondence so far publicly available: *Lettres à ses amis et quelques autres* (1995), a selection extending across Yourcenar's lifetime; four comprehensive volumes under the collective title *D'Hadrien à Zénon* published between 2004 and 2019 that contain items from 1951 to 1967; and *«En 1939, l'Amérique commence à Bordeaux»* (2016), a volume of letters from 1938 to 1980 written to an early publisher and lifetime friend, Emmanuel Boudot-Lamotte.[7] W.H. Auden was of the opinion that knowledge of a writer's personal life never illuminated the writer's work and saw no reason for the publication of private correspondence. Yourcenar's letters, however, covering a wide range of subjects with many changes of tone and register, offer valuable insights into her writings, provide detailed commentaries upon them, and are especially valuable for understanding the history of *Mémoires*. In the care with which they were composed they inevitably remind a Romanist of the younger Pliny's *Letters*, although the personality that obtrudes – severe, determined, rigorous – is rather different from that of the Roman predecessor.[8] Thirdly, there are the print versions of many interviews that Yourcenar gave to the press, radio, and television throughout her years of celebrity: *Les Yeux ouverts*, the product in 1980 of conversations with the critic Matthieu Galey; *Entretiens radiophoniques avec Marguerite Yourcenar*, a volume of what were originally radio interviews by the journalist Patrick de Rosbo, also published in 1980; *Radioscopie de Jacques Chancel*, an extensive radio broadcast from 1979 published in 1999; and *Portrait d'une voix* (2002), a collection of twenty-three shorter exchanges with various commentators from 1952 to 1987. The title is taken from the *Carnets*. Again, all of this material contains much of relevance to my enquiry. Finally, I draw at times on what I shall refer to as the *Notebook*, a compilation of notes on *Mémoires* and other miscellaneous items, some in diary-like form, that Yourcenar made as her novel was coming to completion or soon afterwards. It belongs now to a large repertory of documents, her correspondence included, Yourcenar donated to the Houghton Library at Harvard University.[9] Altogether, these materials are invaluable for the task of assessment I have in mind. They reveal in addition an important development which I examine in my penultimate sounding, namely the way in which Yourcenar's portrait of Hadrian assumed a life of its own after 1951 as the assurance of her understanding of the character she had created became firmer and firmer with the passage of time. Her Hadrian, it becomes clear, was a figure not confined to the limits of the novel, but one who lived much longer in both her imagination and her admiration, with doubts about the authenticity of her creation neither long nor seriously entertained.

II

Mémoires was written between 1948 and early 1951 in the United States. Yourcenar was born in 1903 in Brussels of French and Belgian descent, but left Europe at the onset of World War II to rejoin Grace Frick, the friend who became her translator and lifetime companion; her voyage from Bordeaux to New York on the liner *Manhattan*, in all its wartime tension, is described in a sombre letter composed soon after her arrival (*ACB* 90–3). Her childhood had been spent mainly in France. But before moving to the United States, which she first visited in 1937–8, Yourcenar had lived something of a bohemian life in Europe, spending various periods as a young adult in Italy, Switzerland, Austria, and particularly Greece. In 1947, however, she became an American citizen. She was living then in Hartford, Connecticut, and teaching in Brooklyn at Sarah Lawrence College. But in 1950 she moved with Grace Frick to a house on Mount Desert Island in Northeast Harbor in the state of Maine – the couple named it, delightfully, Petite Plaisance – and this remained her home until her death in 1987. (Frick died a few years earlier in 1979.) To European critics unaccustomed to associating high culture with residence in the United States it might have seemed, and still sometimes does, that Yourcenar had chosen to live a life of exile. There were certainly initial moments when she was conscious of an intellectual isolation in the New World, as recorded for example in a letter of 7 April 1951 to the German author Joseph Breitbach – although she immediately qualified her lament by attributing her feelings in part to her working conditions and a health too frail to deal with New York's busy life. Matters might not have been all that different, she admitted, had she remained in Europe (*L* 85). Any reader of her correspondence will know, in fact, that life in America made an undeniably strong and positive impact upon her. It is impossible to imagine for instance that *Fleuve profond, sombre rivière*, her translations of what were once known, without controversy, as "Negro spirituals," begun in earnest in the early 1940s and eventually published in 1964, could have been inspired by residence anywhere else. She did not live as a recluse. In a letter written from Germany in June 1954, she explained to her correspondent that she had emigrated to the United States voluntarily for reasons of friendship and in order to pursue literary projects. She was not a wartime refugee in the true sense of the term, and if political and personal circumstances had kept her there longer than anticipated, it was not because France was closed to her. She acknowledged all the same that she knew what it was like to experience the mistrust and apprehension that arrival in a foreign country brings (*L* 110).[10]

Yourcenar's cultural identity nonetheless remained French. On 14 August 1954 she affirmed the point to an admirer of *Mémoires* who had requested personal information about her:

Je suis française de naissance, bien que née par hasard à l'étranger (en Belgique, que j'ai quittée huit jours après ma naissance). J'ai acquis en 1947 la nationalité américaine, mais suis restée totalement française d'habitudes et de culture, bien que j'aie vécu dans tant de pays que j'ai peine à me croire, par moments, une nationalité quelconque. (*L* 111)

I am French by birth, although by chance I was born abroad (in Belgium, which I left eight days after my birth). I received American citizenship in 1947, but I have remained completely French in habits and culture, although I have lived in so many countries that at times I can scarcely credit any nationality at all.[11]

She continued that her father, originally from the north of France, close to Lille where she had lived in infancy, had belonged to the minor non-titled French nobility, while her mother, who had died shortly after giving birth and of whom she had no recollection, was of aristocratic Belgian stock originally from the Meuse valley (*L* 111–12). Such details were repeated on other occasions. In 1976, she told an interviewer who spoke of her as an exile that after her peripatetic early life she had never thought it necessary to live in France, but that she felt profoundly French regardless: when in Europe she was fully at home both there and elsewhere (*PV* 176–7). The point was made again in October 1979 in a letter to the novelist and man of letters Jean d'Ormesson:

Je suis, comme vous le savez, en possession de la citoyenneté américaine depuis 1947. Auparavant, fille d'un Français et d'une Belge devenue française par son mariage, née par hasard à Bruxelles, mais de parents domiciliés dans le Nord … j'ai toujours été considérée comme française, et tous mes papiers officiels ont été français. (*L* 616)

As you know, I have held American citizenship since 1947. Previously, as the daughter of a French man and a Belgian woman who became French through her marriage, born by chance in Brussels but of parents domiciled in the North … I have always been considered French, and all my official documents have been French.

This particular letter was occasioned by Yourcenar's nomination for election to the Académie française, Jean d'Ormesson being her chief sponsor. And on 6 March 1980, she was indeed elected, the first woman so to achieve immortality and at her death still the only woman awarded such recognition. Her nomination, however, was a highly fraught affair, in part because she was a woman but also because she was an American citizen, and her statement here is notably more insistent than one given in an interview of the same year to Jacques Chancel (*RC* 23). She said there that after becoming an American citizen she had never asked her lawyer to pursue the question of dual citizenship, implying that her French citizenship had formally lapsed, which in fact it had; but reinstatement occurred on 6 December 1979 when the French consul to the United States travelled from Boston to Northeast Harbor expressly for the purpose.[12] The formal details aside, however, there is no question of Yourcenar's cultural orientation. In the tranquillity and relative detachment of Petite Plaisance, Yourcenar embarked on her later novels, poems, and essays as a French author, maintaining a voluminous correspondence with members of the European intellectual and literary community and punctuating her life in Maine with frequent travels overseas to France and Europe at large, and, late in life, much farther afield as well.[13] Petite Plaisance could evoke lyrical description, as in this extract from a letter of 1 May 1961:

Depuis 1951, j'ai, avec une amie américaine, Grâce Frick, une petite maison dans une île du Maine, qui est une province à l'est des États-Unis, près du Canada, et qui ressemble un peu, je crois, aux Ardennes, si seulement les Ardennes et leurs forêts étaient au bord de la mer! Le paysage est très beau; la maison est située près d'un village et à quelques pas de la mer; il y a un hectare de jardin, presque entièrement en bois et en prairie; nous avons une grande quantité d'oiseaux sauvages qui font leurs nids dans nos arbres et chantent du matin au soir; nous avons aussi un très joli chien épagneul tout noir que j'aime beaucoup … (*L* 155)

Since 1951, with Grace Frick, an American friend, I have a small house on an island in Maine, which is a state in the eastern United States, close to Canada, and which resembles a little, so I think, the Ardennes, if only the Ardennes and their forests were at the edge of the sea! The countryside is very beautiful; the house is located near a village and just a few steps from the sea; there's a hectare of garden, almost entirely wooded and grassed; we have a huge number of wild birds which make their nests in our trees and sing from morning till night; we have as well a very pretty spaniel, all black, of which I'm very fond …

Mémoires was not Yourcenar's first novel. But its publication became a literary event and catapulted her to fame. She claimed that its origins went back to a moment in her twenties when she had foreseen all the major works she was to compose in her life to come, and a visit to Hadrian's Villa at Tivoli had triggered immediate inspiration. She had first encountered Hadrian even earlier, as a child. In 1914 at the beginning of World War I her father, Michel de Crayencour, took her to England for safety's sake and on a visit to the British Museum she saw a bronze bust of Hadrian that had recently been recovered from the river Thames.[14] There were early attempts and drafts, but it was not until late 1948 that Yourcenar began to write the book in its present form, after the arrival of a trunk from Switzerland that contained a few of her old, forgotten pages that suddenly impelled her to renew the project. So at least she reported in the years that followed, both in the *Carnets* (*CNMH* 524–5) and frequently in her interviews and letters, creating as a result an almost mythical, and certainly contrived, version of the novel's genesis. The story is what it is.[15] Some portions of the book were composed on long train journeys across country, others during commuting rides and in whatever free time Yourcenar found while teaching at Sarah Lawrence. When she began, she and Frick were living in Hartford. But by the time she finished they had acquired Petite Plaisance and it was there, as she recorded in the *Notebook* in her distinctively undulating hand, that its final words were written:

Île de Mount Desert – 26 décembre 1950.

Aujourd'hui, le 26 décembre, j'ai écrit la dernière ligne des Mémoires d'Hadrien. Ouvrage terminé, sauf pour quelques corrections, çà et là, de deux à trois lignes, et la copie d'une trentaine de pages. Et terminée aussi ce qui fût somme toute la plus grande aventure de ma vie.

Mt Desert Island – 26 December 1950.

Today, December 26, I have written the last line of Memoirs of Hadrian. Work completed, save for a few corrections, here and there, to two or three lines, and copying of some thirty pages. Completed also what was, all in all, the greatest adventure of my life.[16]

By this time Yourcenar had long identified herself with a name that was more or less an anagram of her birth name Crayencour, concocted with her father's connivance when, in her late teens, Marguerite Antoinette Jeanne Marie Ghislaine de Crayencour set out to make a literary name for herself.[17]

In form the book is an epistolary novel but a novel of one letter only. Hadrian, sick, spent, and close to death in the Villa addresses, at length, the boy he has selected one day to succeed him, the future emperor Marcus Aurelius. Not, that is, his immediate successor, as critics often assume, the mature and reliable Antoninus Pius, but the youth who will eventually follow Pius according to arrangements Hadrian has made, as was historically the case. In the modern idiom the year in which Hadrian writes is 138. But it is not specified as such because Yourcenar, in her commitment to historical authenticity, wished to avoid dating forms that were not genuinely Roman. Instead, she has Hadrian give the year in which he is writing as "from the foundation of the city" as she believed a Roman would. (The detail is one to which modern academic historians and biographers might hardly pay attention.) His birth in 76 and death in 138 of the Christian era were matters of fact, Yourcenar once said, but for Hadrian, who scarcely knew the Christians and encountered them only towards the end of his reign, this was inconsequential; from his point of view he lived in the eighth century of the Roman era (*PV* 93–4).[18]

The choice of a letter as the form of the novel and the selection of Marcus as its addressee should not be thought capricious. The Greek historian Cassius Dio, one of the main authorities for Hadrian's history, records that Hadrian did indeed compose a letter late in life when sick expressing his wish for death to relieve his suffering, and also that he highly approved of Marcus, a youth whose character made him a figure of great promise (69.17.3; 69.21.2). They are statements that Yourcenar seemingly conjoined, as it were, as a point of departure for her enterprise. The letter begins in the month of May and continues until the following July, a few days before Hadrian's death, which in modern terms occurred on 10 July at Baiae on the Bay of Naples. As he writes, Hadrian can be visualized as he appears in a bronze portrait found in Israel in a Roman legionary camp near Tel Shalem, drawn and weary, with resignation detectable in the tensely furrowed forehead, heavy eyes,

Figure 1. Bronze statue of Hadrian, found at the Camp of the
Sixth Roman Legion in Tel Shalem (Israel). Wikimedia Commons.

and cheekbones prominent from the ravages of time, the grey- or silver-
haired man of the *Sibylline Oracles* (5.47; 8.52; 12.164). He was sixty-two
years of age when he died. Marcus on the other hand can be imagined as the
youth of the famous portrait of about 140 in the Museo Capitolino in Rome,
quietly sensitive, ready to be informed, his charmingly oval-shaped face on
the cusp of manhood – a "visage candide d'adolescent" as Yourcenar has
Hadrian describe it (*MH* 496). Marcus was born in 121, and in *Mémoires* he
is said to be seventeen years of age.[19]

Hadrian begins his letter with a set of personal reflections that contrast
the physical and sensual pleasures of his earlier days – hunting, food and
wine, sex, sleep – with the infirmities and sickness of old age. The body
is his preoccupation. He suddenly changes course, however, and decides to
tell Marcus the full story of his life in order to give Marcus instruction.
Hadrian accordingly describes his family background and birth in Italica in
the Roman province of Baetica in Spain, continues with his boyhood and

Figure 2. Young Marcus Aurelius. Capitoline Museum. Wikimedia Commons.

education, his entry into public life and the early stages of his civic and military career, his accession and his accomplishments as emperor before, finally, returning to the present and the anticipation of life's end. It remains throughout a first-person, confessional narrative in which the only voice heard is that of Hadrian himself – the "portrait of a voice" (*CNMH* 527: "Portrait d'une voix"). The letter is in effect an autobiography. It contains no chapters as such but is divided into six long segments that have as titles Latin phrases Yourcenar took from ancient classical sources: *Animula vagula blandula*, the first line of a Latin poem Hadrian is said to have composed on his deathbed, used for the opening set of reflections; *Varius multiplex multiformis*, a phrase taken from a description of Hadrian found in an anonymous late Latin source; and four words or phrases, *Tellus stabilita, Sæculum aureum, Disciplina Augusta, Patientia*, that appeared as legends on issues of the Imperial coinage during Hadrian's reign.[20]

In the narrative as a whole there are three critical moments or phases which Yourcenar called "échecs" or "fléchissements": periods of intense strain that take Hadrian almost to the point of emotional breakdown. First the moment of his accession, with the high anxiety that anticipation of the throne brings when it is never quite certain, until his predecessor Trajan is dead, that Hadrian truly will succeed. Next the mysterious death of the youth Antinous, for whom Hadrian in mid-life conceives a grand passion and whose loss causes him to collapse into despair. And finally a war against the rebellious Jews of Palestine late in the reign, which brings deep disappointment to an emperor who has spent many years promoting throughout his far-flung empire ideals of imperial peace.[21] The emotional range of the life Yourcenar constructs is consequently vast. As a young man Hadrian is an ambitious hedonist, unscrupulous in public and private life. But as the mature emperor he is a pragmatic cosmopolitanist, motivated by an ideal of service to humanity, seeking to achieve unity and peace in Rome's empire and to create a new world order grounded on commitment to principles found in Greek culture and the consequent force of Hellenism that will bind the many into the one. In mid-life his love for Antinous is all-consuming, though ecstasy is tinged with sadness as thoughts of the boy's loss of youth impinge, and once the tragedy of his death intervenes Hadrian's grief is boundless, issuing in an extravagant act of deification: Antinous becomes a god. In old age, with love lost and physical decline to be endured, all that then remains is the contemplation of death, tempered by a quiet confidence that the eternity of Rome will guarantee personal immortality and keep alive his ideals of humanity, liberty, and justice, until at the very last, as a consciousness of human sensibility persists and courage remains, he utters his final words: "Tâchons d'entrer dans la mort les yeux ouverts ..." (*MH* 515).[22]

Whether Hadrian's letter can be classified as a novel in any generally understood sense is an important question. Not simply because, as Yourcenar's *Note* informs her reader, it is based closely on original historical sources and scholarship, but because of what must at first sight seem her astonishing claim, repeatedly made, that she was not a novelist at all and not the author in particular of historical novels. The claim appears, emphatically, in an interview from late in life with Shusha Guppy that was published in an issue of *The Paris Review* for 1988.[23] Guppy had met and spoken with Yourcenar in London in April 1987, and the two had agreed to meet again the following November in Amsterdam to review Yourcenar's revisions to a draft of the initial exchange. In the event, the second meeting never took place. In October Yourcenar fell ill at Petite Plaisance, suffered a stroke in early November, and died in hospital at Bar Harbor on 17 December. She was eighty-four years of age. The interview appeared consequently without whatever final amendments Yourcenar might have made. She is unlikely, however, to have had second thoughts about her remark to Guppy. As early as 1952 she had informed the publisher Gaston Gallimard that she had no plans ever to write a novel, implying already that she did not think of

Mémoires as such, and when interviewed much later in 1984 by her biographer Josyane Savigneau, she had questioned whether it could be said that she had ever written a novel at all. To Guppy she was uncompromising: "I have never written a historical novel in my life. I dislike most historical novels."[24]

For the sake of convenience, of course, Yourcenar was prepared to term *Mémoires* a novel and to describe herself as a novelist, as she does for example in *Ton et langage dans le roman historique*, the brilliant essay from 1972 that explained some of her procedures in her two major works (*TGS* 289–311).[25] At times also she spoke and wrote of the advantages the novel held as a literary medium. It was the best contemporary means of psychological investigation available, and perhaps the only one that allowed a spontaneous understanding to establish itself between author and reader. It permitted also a superior view of historical personality in comparison with the dogmatic black and white judgments of historians. The novelist, moreover, had a special ability to communicate human truth and was the only kind of author capable of fathoming the great difference between official historical documents and the intimate truth underlying them.[26] Simultaneously, however, she was suspicious of, and resistant to, the form. In an interview from 1954 she stated that she did not like the genre at all, its historical form included, and that the novel's prominence in the twentieth century was unfortunate: all too often it was an impure mixture of realism and authorial effusiveness, intellectually undemanding, and of interest to her only to the extent that it responded to a concern for art and composition (*PV* 37–9).[27] Referring specifically to *Mémoires*, she wrote in the *Carnets*:

Le roman dévore aujourd'hui toutes les formes; on est à peu près forcé d'en passer par lui. Cette étude sur la destinée d'un homme qui s'est nommé Hadrien eût été une tragédie au xviiᵉ siècle; c'eût été un essai à l'époque de la Renaissance. (*CNMH* 535)

In our time the novel devours all other forms; one is almost forced to use it as the medium of expression. This study of the destiny of a man called Hadrian would have been cast in the form of a tragedy in the Seventeenth Century, or of an Essay, perhaps, in the period of the Renaissance.[28]

Further, she maintained, the historical novel itself was a problematic category, given the fact that by definition all novels were "historical" no matter what their chronological setting. Any past era was difficult to recover and as repositories of a naturally fallible memory they were inevitably interpretative or contemplative, as, significantly, were histories reliant on the same sources of information; it was not just that there were very few good historical novels or that novels in general caused her an allergic reaction.[29]

If, however, she sometimes acknowledged herself to be a historical novelist as conventionally understood, Marguerite Yourcenar distinguished herself from her great predecessors, from Flaubert and Zola in their obsession with realistic details, and from Tolstoy and Balzac with their propensity for the specious digression, identifying more with Proust and, again significantly, his evocation of "un temps perdu" (*HZ* 137–8).[30] Nevertheless, to isolate the historical novel was to commit an intellectual error:

Ceux qui mettent le roman historique dans une catégorie à part oublient que le romancier ne fait jamais qu'interpréter, à l'aide des procédés de son temps, un certain nombre de faits passés, de souvenirs conscients ou non, personnels ou non, tissus de la même matière que l'histoire … De notre temps, le roman historique, ou ce que, par commodité, on consent à nommer tel, ne peut être que plongé dans un temps retrouvé, prise de possession d'un monde intérieur. (*CNMH* 527)

Those who put the historical novel in a category apart are forgetting that what every novelist does is only to interpret, by means of the techniques which his period affords, a certain number of past events; his memories, whether consciously or unconsciously recalled, whether personal or impersonal, are all woven of the same stuff as History itself … In our day, when introspection tends to dominate literary forms, the historical novel, or what may for convenience's sake be called by that name, must take the plunge into time recaptured, and must fully establish itself within some inner world.

Yourcenar insisted in turn that she was not a historical specialist and that despite its historical grounding *Mémoires* was not a work of scholarship. The *Note*, she informed her Italian translator Lidia Storoni Mazzolani, had been necessary because a public increasingly ignorant of classical literature had to be made aware of the work's firm foundation (*L* 148).[31] In the spirit, however, of what she wrote in the *Carnets*, she often spoke of the book not as a novel at all but in seventeenth-century terms as a "historical essay" or a "récit," a term referring to a modest work limited in scope, or else as "un discours," or a "traité-monologue," or an "essai monologue": the monologue, that is, of a man scrutinizing his life as Hadrian could have seen it. This indeed is what she thought an ancient Roman would actually have written: a formal discourse on the model of Seneca's essays addressed to a single recipient but intended for a larger readership.[32]

She also sometimes spoke of *Mémoires* in biographical terms, calling it a historical biography or a cradle-to-grave biographical novel. In a long letter to F.C. Grant, the scholar who so admired her book, she wrote that she had not intended to compose a historical biography properly speaking, still less to give a comprehensive picture of life and manners in the Roman Empire of the second century. Rather, she had wanted to use knowledge of the past to create a work reminiscent of historical compositions from poets of the past, and to reveal thereby the human poetry of history. She was conscious nonetheless of its biographical nature, as also when elsewhere she expressed some hesitation over whether to call the work a historical biography written in the first person or, quite simply, a novel; and again when observing that Hadrian's clairvoyance, as she had portrayed it, was not suitable strictly speaking for historical biography, as opposed to her poetic compositions.[33] Yet the statement of intentions she gave in the letter mentioned earlier to Joseph Breitbach might easily be construed as a list of the rudiments of a biographical enterprise. It had been her intent, she fulsomely said there, to reveal a figure who was a great agent of peace, for whom words alone were never enough, a multicultured man of letters and the most energetic of statesmen, an individualist who was both a great legislator and a reformer, a voluptuary and a citizen, a lover obsessed by his memories, and someone variously engaged with other people but who to the end was one of the most self-controlled spirits ever. None of this, however, was to be hagiographical: she wished to capture the narrow limits by which Hadrian's rich individuality was bound, the subtle mistakes of calculation, the imperceptible errors, and the final enigmatic agony of his life's end (L 83). Similar thoughts are implicit in another definition of her goal: the composition as she understood it from the historical record of a portrait of a life that had been lived only once – its biographical uniqueness, that is – including what she termed the work of a man's spirit. Elsewhere she could boldly assert that the letter changed in form as Hadrian wrote it, gradually becoming a political testament and a set of memoirs that would have exceeded his capabilities had he considered such a project from the outset, pointing at least on one occasion to a concern with a full life history.[34] The book can scarcely be considered anything else. The autobiographical conceit was a means of distancing its author from the content of the work and enhancing thereby its apparent authenticity; and in the last analysis *Mémoires* must always, I think, be deemed sui generis, generically indeterminate. But a life story it remains, and it is above all as a biography that I shall understand it in all that follows.[35]

Critics have certainly approached it in this way. A prominent view is that *Mémoires* is a "literary biography," an artfully arranged sequence of life events as opposed to a traditional womb-to-tomb account, in which Yourcenar elaborates the historical basis of the narrative in order to emphasize certain features of Hadrian's personality in the pursuit of authenticity.[36] The autobiographical character is in turn often acknowledged and advanced in light of Philippe Lejeune's well-regarded definition of autobiography: "Un récit rétrospectif en prose qu'une personne réelle fait de sa propre existence, lorsqu'elle met l'accent sur sa vie individuelle, en particulier sur l'histoire de sa personnalité."[37] It can be said therefore that a fine distinction is perceptible between an objective personality and a personality entirely controlled by the narrative; or else that Yourcenar's reader is allowed to understand Hadrian as he has finally become at the moment he composes his memoirs, revealing his true identity to Marcus through his reliance on a selective and even faulty memory of past events; or else that the need is foreclosed for excessive historical details with which Marcus could be expected already to be familiar (full-scale battle descriptions for instance), increasing as a result the narrative's impressionistic quality.[38] Whether *Mémoires* should be judged a "manual for princes," or its author categorized as a colonialist writer intent on promoting a patriarchal ideology, I rather doubt; but whatever the literary effects postulated, the essence of *Mémoires* remains Hadrian's life story.[39] The question that consequently presents itself is whether a true biography of Hadrian can actually be written.

III

By "true biography" I mean a contemporary work such as Richard Ellmann's biography of Oscar Wilde – a figure of considerable interest to Yourcenar – which due to the availability of documentary evidence of a sort unknown to ancient historians allows for a thoroughly detailed account of Wilde's everyday life from birth to death, together with a sensitive study through analysis of his poetry, plays, and essays of the evolution of Wilde's views on art and aesthetics. Not merely a record therefore of the life lived, but also an intellectual biography and, through its careful examination of Wilde's constant struggles with his religious and sexual identity, a penetrating psychological study as well. Biography on this example emerges as a literary form in which the personality and individuality of a historical subject can be comprehensively portrayed. Comparably, to take a more recent illustration, A.N. Wilson's biography of Charles Darwin, the work pertinently of a novelist as well as a biographer, can tell not only an absorbing life story, but provide an equally fascinating account firmly set in its sociocultural context of the emergence of a scientific principle, the result being both biography and intellectual history.[40] Many other modern examples could be brought forward. Kay Redfield Jamison, a practising psychiatrist who brings to her project a specialist's expertise and empathetic understanding, has set out the lifelong history of the American poet Robert Lowell and the bipolar disease from which he suffered, drawing on a huge volume of Lowell's medical records and of his personal notebooks and correspondence with family members and friends. The result is a comprehensive, multi-dimensional biography that allows its reader to see precisely how Lowell's illness dominated his adult life: how he lived with the constant fear of madness and coped with recurrent episodes of mania and depression, how his familial and other personal relationships were impacted, and how closely bound up his illness was with the creativity that brought him lasting literary distinction. The complex life of the Bostonian patrician and quintessential New Englander is rendered accessible to a degree unimaginable for a Roman emperor thought by contemporaries to be mad such as Caligula. Nor is this an example due solely to the subject's relative modernity. In the nineteenth century, England's peasant poet John Clare may also have suffered from the same illness, and while the materials from which Jonathan Bate has written his biography are insufficient to allow a definitive medical statement, they are voluminous enough to permit understanding of Clare's mid-life decline, his gradual descent into depression and delusion, and his eventual confinement to various mental institutions. A mass of correspondence and an autobiography have survived to allow the course of Clare's life to be charted in detail: his impoverished rural origins, his astonishing emergence as a poet of sudden but ephemeral celebrity, his perpetual struggle to avoid poverty, his personal and professional relationships, and the onset of his "madness." The account of his escape from a mental asylum in Essex and his return, on foot, to his home in Northamptonshire richly exposes the means by which Clare survived the journey and his delusory, pitiable belief that he was married simultaneously to two women, one of whom was never his wife and was long since dead. Ancient historians have nothing at their disposal even remotely comparable with which to work.[41]

This does not mean that Roman emperors lack biographers. Conventional imperial biography, however, bears little resemblance to the modern works to which I have referred. Caligula indeed is a case in point. A standard procedure is to open with a list of facts from the end of the reign of Rome's first emperor Augustus and that of his successor Tiberius, the period of Caligula's early life, with the few objectively known details of his childhood inserted at appropriate chronological points.[42] Reports then follow of events that occurred, or may have occurred, through the course of Caligula's adulthood, no matter what the degree of direct involvement concerned, with their biographical significance – what they meant for Caligula's development as an individual – largely unstated or, as in this illustration, set out in tentative, conditional terms: "The first six months of Caligula's reign was [sic] a period of near-euphoria. But it exacted an exhausting toll on the young emperor. The strain of being at the centre of power and attention, and the adulation of the masses, would have made enormous demands on his nerves and stamina, coming after a life spent almost totally out of the public view. Hardly was the summer over [sc. 37], when he fell seriously ill."[43] In turn, assumptions are made that stories of Caligula's unusual behaviour preserved by ancient authors are inherently fallacious and must be rationalized according to contemporary notions of what is thought rational. A directive to troops to pick up seashells on the French coast can be attributed for example not to Caligula's apparent instability, but to a desire to instil in his soldiers military discipline; or else plans to make a favourite horse a Roman consul and to build a bridge of ships across the Bay of Naples, signs of aberration in antiquity, become elements of a conscious policy to humiliate the Roman aristocracy. Such constructs are preferred over the evidence of men close to Caligula's lifetime, with little offered about Caligula as a human subject or about the social conditions and cultural realities in which his life was lived.[44]

Consequently, a widely adopted expedient in dealing with any number of Roman rulers is to accommodate the limited amount of evidence available to a form of imperial life writing called political biography, which typically involves adding to catalogues of attestable or hypothesized public events discussion of relations between emperor and senate, Rome's body of elite office holders and administrators, in which putative developments are inferred from the investigative technique of prosopography: examination, that is, of senatorial recruitment and career patterns over time. But even this is subject to a severe stumbling block. At no time in Imperial history can the full 600 members of the Roman senate be identified, a fact that by definition renders suspect the basic foundation of political biography as commonly understood, while "the senate" in any case never constituted a monolithic bloc, as any reader of Tacitus will know. Advances in overall historical knowledge might well be made this way, but anything close to "true biography" remains elusive, especially when awareness of the modern "biographical turn" in historical writing that ultimately stretches back to Lytton Strachey and emphasizes subjectivity and individual experience is at a premium, when the nature, history and requirements of biography as promulgated and discussed by theorists of the genre go unnoticed. A biography of Constantine can duly regard the psychology of the emperor's religious conversion as unfathomable, yet simultaneously, and paradoxically, credit him with a deceitful and duplicitous comportment said to be universally characteristic of all politicians. The result is to leave undisclosed the distinctiveness of both the subject and the world in which he lived, its political disposition included.[45]

I take as a further illustration a section of the outstanding biography by Donald R. Howard of Geoffrey Chaucer, a figure from an era almost as remote as that of Roman antiquity, and one that has at its core a similarly minimal amount of hard evidence from which to proceed. The section concerned is a description of a journey Chaucer made in the winter of 1372–3 from England to Italy on court business. It begins with a straightforward statement on the route across the Continent taken by Chaucer and the party with which he travelled as far as the Alps. The physical hardships confronted in crossing the mountains and their psychological consequences are then enumerated: the severity of the weather, which necessitated dense layers of protective clothing, the difficulties of the terrain and absence of maps, which meant reliance on guides, the travellers' inability to progress at anything more than snail's pace, the dangers of attack from brigands, of losing their way, of dying from exposure, all of which are contrasted with the modern reality: "What we do in two comfortable hours by plane took a laborious month for mediaeval travelers." Next, and more subtly, the mediaeval mental picture of the journey is explained, not a downward expedition as the reader might anticipate, but the exact opposite, because in view of a cosmography that placed the Garden of Eden at the top of the world, Asia immediately below and Europe and Africa side by side farther below still, an initially surprising result obtains: "when Chaucer traveled from England to Italy, he would have supposed himself moving *up*: up toward Rome, toward Jerusalem at the center of the earth, and beyond that … up the mainland of Asia toward the Earthly Paradise at the 'end of the East,' closest to Heaven." Lastly, Howard moves to environmental factors, making astute observations on the mediaeval lack of time zones and national boundaries, evoking the travellers' response to changing landscapes and the "exquisite delight" taken in safely finding food and shelter, and against this backdrop a final, cosmic image of Chaucer himself is presented, descending from the harsh mountains to the temperate spring-like lowlands, free from all the perils of the previous weeks. The effect is to captivate, and to convince, completely:

Coming then into this wintertime oasis, having seen from the mountaintops the valleys and houses and towns below as a soaring bird might see them, Chaucer found that here, near Turin, trees and shrubbery to a surprising extent remain green in winter. There were not just evergreens with needles but trees and shrubs like the holly familiar to Englishmen, strange and lovely nondeciduous plants along the wayside that he could stoop to touch and admire, and ask their names of his Genoese companions, plants having lush red berries and crisp pointed leaves, and here and there even winter flowers of bright yellow and winter roses of white. He would have looked back at the forbidding snowcapped promontories his party had just negotiated: they seemed distant and inscrutable, a world of ice suspended in the sky. Of the geology behind such a landscape, medieval man knew nothing; it was because of "untamed" nature, the decay of the world attendant on the Fall of Man, that man's place on the Island of the Earth was so far less hospitable than the Garden of Eden

had been, and this hostile world could be tamed and inhabited only by human inge-
nuity, by the arts of civilization.[46]

I know of no conventional Roman imperial biography that meets this
standard of imaginative explanatory excellence, that evokes mentality and
opens up psychological insight with so much success, or that appreciates the
advantages of historical particularity that biography affords. In the summer
of 43 the emperor Claudius made a similar journey to that of Chaucer, but
this time from Italy to Britain following a route that may have taken him
by sea from Ostia, Rome's port, to Massilia (Marseilles) and then by road
and river to Gesoriacum (Boulogne), before crossing the Channel into Kent
and Essex and culminating at Camulodunum (Colchester).[47] It was a journey
that allowed Claudius to claim personal participation in Rome's conquest of
a new province, but also a journey to the end of the earth, since to Romans
Rome was the centre of the world, as Augustus's Golden Milestone in the
Roman Forum declared, and a journey into the more or less geographically
unknown. Some years earlier, in 39–40, Caligula had similarly travelled
from Italy to northern Europe intent on invading Britain, notoriously to no
effect. Conventional biography, however, has little to offer on the magnitude
of such undertakings and does little to communicate the realities of lived
historical experience or to bring the past to life in the manner of Howard on
Chaucer. The result is a biographical vacuum.[48]

A further model might be sought in Jonathan Bate's *Soul of the Age*, a
book with the provocative subtitle, *A Biography of the Mind of William
Shakespeare*.[49] Documentation for Shakespeare's life is as exiguous as, if
not worse than, for many Roman emperors, which is what makes the book
attractive as a potential Roman guide. Bate's procedure is to draw from the
corpus of Shakespeare's plays and poems a picture of the world in which
their author lived, recreating life experience by historically contextualiz-
ing what little is factually known about Shakespeare through clues provided by the literary corpus. The threads of the sociocultural context woven
include contemporary medical information, with special attention to plague
and syphilis; demographic factors, including conventional ages of marriage;
Elizabethan educational institutions, with examination of curriculum and
the types of books children read in schools; literary and theatrical history –
the general availability and range of books, the importance and character of
acting companies; contemporary legal practices and court records; European
geography and geopolitics; and leading contemporary currents of thought.
What is deduced about the biographical subject from this rich panorama
is often audaciously and admittedly speculative. But the factual substrate is
vividly brought to life all the same, and to my mind this is rather better as

an evocation of the past than the inconclusive discussions of source criticism (*Quellenforschung*) with which conventional Roman imperial biography often preoccupies itself. An attempt to fill the vacuum has been made.

With Caligula again, therefore, concepts and definitions of mental illness in Roman antiquity should be potentially far more illuminating for assessing the evidence of his instability than modern notions of what "ought to" or "must have been" the case as far as his erratic behaviour is concerned. As Zvi Yavetz once observed, "One does not have to be a trained psychologist in order to establish the fact that a hard pressed childhood is bound to leave its mark on the adult. And Caligula's childhood and adolescence were anything but normal." In which connection, it can be noted that the novels of Charles Dickens now emerge in the grasp of a seasoned biographer as vehicles by which the legacy of a whole sequence of their author's childhood traumas is said to have been expunged.[50] And yet the cogency of Yavetz's remarks is offset by the assumption that what constituted a "normal" childhood and adolescence for an upper-class Roman boy in first-century Rome is identical with what their author took to be normal in his late twentieth-century environment. Instead, the notion that madness was understood in antiquity less as a clinical state than a departure from prevailing norms, with rich materials and studies at hand to investigate, could perhaps produce a more credible biographical result.[51] Not to mention consideration of the altogether different childrearing regime in which Caligula's childhood was spent, account of which has been taken, in contrast, in a compelling study of the emperor Nero that shows the value of drawing on the patterns of childrearing among Rome's upper classes in order to understand and evaluate the early life of a ruler often still judged in stereotypical terms. Likewise in this case, with Nero another ruler sometimes regarded as deranged, pursuit of the ramifications of the Apolline, Solar, and Herculean imagery so prevalent in the ancient sources of information for his reign has allowed a convincing, self-consciously constructed image of the emperor to emerge as a superhuman "Roi-Soleil" that his subjects could easily recognize and appreciate.[52]

Recovery of the sociocultural conditions under which the lives of Roman emperors were lived is crucial then in the biographical enterprise. And it is an irony of course that in the foremost specimen of Roman imperial biography from antiquity, written by a courtier in the age of Trajan and Hadrian, there is much that does evoke lived historical experience. The purpose of Suetonius's *Caesares*, a work still too often regarded as trivializing and sensationalistic, remains debatable given the absence of any programmatic statement of authorial intent.[53] I continue to believe, however, that a standard of evaluation formed from expectations of imperial performance dominant in the early second century underlies Suetonius's choice and organization of subject matter, the project as a whole constituting a history of the rise of autocracy at Rome with Julius Caesar and of the exercise of absolute power by Caesar's first-century successors.[54] It must in any case be accepted that the rubrics into which Suetonius arranges his material reflect contemporary sociocultural values and matters of importance in assessing how an emperor's life was lived. There is also a strong interest in the biographies in the essence of their subjects. Caesar is said to have been naturally lenient in avenging wrongs (*Iul.* 74.1), Claudius naturally bloodthirsty (*Claud.* 34.1), Nero monstrously cruel (*Ner.* 7.1), comparable to his boon companion Otho (*Oth.* 2.2); and although Suetonius gave him the benefit of the doubt Vespasian, he records, was similarly thought to have been naturally covetous (*Vesp.* 16.3). A concern with the subject's inner life (*Aug.* 61.1: *interior vita*) allows therefore emotional and at times psychological details to emerge that fuse character with personality. The vignette of Caesar hesitating to cross the Rubicon, his decision impelled by a supernatural apparition and sealed with an unforgettable aphorism, is a prime example (*Iul.* 31.2–32: *alea iacta est*), the illustration of Nero's panic and vacillation in the crisis that drove him to suicide another (*Ner.* 47.1–2). Nor is there any shortage of simply striking details: weeping soldiers kiss the hands and feet of Otho's corpse, moved by an unexpectedly noble suicide (*Oth.*11–12); Vespasian, foiled by misfortune, tries at the last minute to forestall the execution of his enemy Helvidius Priscus (*Vesp.* 15); Domitian, practising his archery skills, selects a slave for target practice and attempts to pinpoint his arrows between the wretched man's outstretched fingers (*Dom.* 19). Suetonius fully understood biography's capacity to bring the past, in all its particularity, to life, a point that was not lost on Marguerite Yourcenar who very much admired him. In an essay from 1959 she called him one of Rome's great historians and a great portraitist, commending his lives for their psychological perspicacity, realism, and long-lasting cultural influence (*SBI* 5; 16). In the essay of 1972, moreover, she similarly described him as the literary counterpart of Rome's veristic sculptors (*TGS* 291). (He duly appears as a minor character in *Mémoires* [*MH* 383–4)].)[55]

It is not too much to say therefore that Suetonius anticipated the belief of the much later pioneer of "new biography" Lytton Strachey that life history should be governed by a careful selection of relevant material, psychological inference, and the lively animation of his subjects through the interplay of imagination and literary artistry. Strachey's goal was to create verbal portraits of credible human beings with a painter's verisimilitude, a goal realized both in *Eminent Victorians* and in the later images he created of Queen Victoria and those close to her: Prince Albert above all, but a succession of formidable British prime ministers as well (Melbourne, Peel,

Gladstone, Disraeli).[56] Academic cradle-to-grave chronographers of Roman emperors cannot perhaps be held to the same aesthetic standards. But modern examples of biography from other historical fields such as those to which I have referred, written in the mould established by Strachey, prove that at a minimum accessible communication is possible and sheer impenetrability avoidable.[57]

The essential question accordingly is whether Marguerite Yourcenar was able in her novel to achieve a comparable level of biographical plausibility by locating the bare record of events known of Hadrian's life in a narrative that adequately captures, as far as was possible at the time of composition, the texture of antiquity in which the emperor's life was lived, together with something of his inner life that carries a degree of authority or conviction. Was the biographical vacuum filled, and if so how was this done? The approach might be to consider *Mémoires* an a priori experiment in biographical writing whose success is to be determined by examination of its sources and methods and the context in which it came into being.

IV

Hadrian – P. Aelius Hadrianus – was born in 76 and ruled the Roman Empire from 117 until 138. He came to power at the age of forty-one and occupied a position that had existed for almost a century and a half: the emperorship was long since a deeply entrenched institution. Augustus, Rome's first emperor, died in 14 after a reign of more than forty years, and at the accession of his successor Tiberius scarcely anyone, so Tacitus later reported (*Ann.* 1.3), could remember the earlier Republican form of Roman government that Augustus's new order had replaced and that in the minds of nostalgic Romans quickly became idealized. From the outset the *novus status* was defined in formal terms, unsurprisingly in view of Rome's cultural inclination to the legalistic, but to all intents and purposes the ruler was subject to little restraint. Already under Augustus, as Marguerite Yourcenar well knew, the unfortunate poet Ovid had experienced the capricious exercise of imperial power, when what he repeatedly termed "Caesar's wrath" drove him from a life of elegant ease in the city of Rome to a miserable exile in the barbarous lands of the Black Sea from which he never returned.[58] Half a century later, when the young Nero became emperor – in the event the last of the first ruling dynasty – his mentor Seneca addressed a treatise to him advocating the exercise of mercy (*clementia*) in the years to come, a plea that was predicated on the fear that its opposite might be more apparent, as earlier reigns had given cause to expect.[59] The quality of mercy was a virtue that only an autocrat could display, and as Seneca's nephew Lucan put it in his politically confrontational *Pharsalia*, Caesar was indeed everything (3.108). So too Pliny in reference to Hadrian's predecessor Trajan: everything was in his sway (*Ep.* 3.20.12).

The absolutist character of the emperorship was beyond question therefore when Hadrian came to power. The decisions the emperor made had the force of law. He controlled almost limitless resources both public and private – the distinction was blurred – which allowed him to meet the material needs of individuals and communities throughout his empire. And to the mass of his subjects he was the ultimate source of redress and relief in times of crisis, a figure who transcended ordinary mortals both in his omnipotence and in the way he was venerated in cult. To those, moreover, who aspired to careers in government and the administration of empire, men the emperor needed but who needed him more, he was the patron par excellence, controlling access to office and the prestige office afforded. The formal grants of authority delegated to him when he acceded were not unimportant, and comportment was valued when it displayed *civilitas* – the attributes of a citizen as opposed to raw naked power: he was not a royal monarch, given that kingship, both in concept and terminology, had for centuries been abhorrent to Romans. Yet his authority was all-embracing and was recognized as such.[60] In 69, during a brief period of civil war, the general Vespasian had seized and quickly consolidated power, inaugurating what became a new regime, the dynasty of the Flavians. The following year the senate passed a resolution that conferred on him his predecessors' powers and included in a sweeping blanket clause the sanction to do whatever he thought fit for the good of the empire.[61] Vespasian's actions had indeed revealed openly what everyone had known from the beginning, that the emperor's authority resided ultimately in his control of Rome's military forces, the legions and auxiliary troops that protected the empire's borders and the praetorian guard that in Rome and Italy served as his special security force. The Roman emperor was a military potentate, and it is no surprise that the Latin word for military commander, *imperator*, was part of his official nomenclature or that one of the two principal visual modes in which he displayed himself to his subjects was in military dress as Rome's commander-in-chief; and if the other presented him in civilian clothing, it was as no ordinary citizen but as Rome's chief priest, the *pontifex maximus* who presided over Rome's entire religious apparatus. In every aspect the emperor was supreme, and in the eastern regions his Greek subjects, less sensitive than Romans of the Latinate west, spoke of him without compunction as a king (*basileus*). Hadrian himself was indeed celebrated in a decree from the city of Thyatira in Lydia, unknown when Yourcenar wrote *Mémoires*, in extravagantly divine terms as "the greatest of kings of all time, Emperor Caesar Trajan Hadrian Olympios Zeus Hellenios." The only effective recourse for those who might have reason to oppose him was revolution.[62]

Marguerite Yourcenar fully understood the nature of the position Hadrian held as the first man in Rome: "Nous avons du mal aujourd'hui à imaginer la toute-puissance d'un homme qui parlait en maître à Alexandrie comme en Angleterre, à Athènes comme à Rome. Aucun souverain, aucun dictateur de notre époque n'a régné sur tant de peuples, n'a eu l'occasion de comparer des mœurs si diverses" (PV 30).[63] She was categorical in her Note, however, that there was no good modern biography of Hadrian to which she could, in 1951, refer her reader, a statement that remained unchanged in the definitive Pléiade edition of 1982 (OR 548). She had read The Life and Principate of the Emperor Hadrian by B.W. Henderson from 1923, a work for long the only relevant biography in English, but she had found it superficial despite its length, observing that it offered an incomplete picture of Hadrian's thought and the problems of his reign, and had not made use of all the available historical evidence. The book is now completely out of date and almost forgotten. Yet it has a certain interest as an illustration of how historical interpretation is always determined by the historian's own time and place, in this instance early twentieth-century Oxford, where Henderson was a fellow of Exeter College and tutor in ancient history. The work was published six years before his death at what now seems the tragically early age of fifty-seven, the last of a series on Rome's early emperors. His view that Hadrian was a humane, cosmopolitan ruler driven by a desire to foster peace throughout his empire even as he maintained strict discipline among the Roman legions and kept them ready for action, is one with which many ancient historians will still agree. The manner, however, in which he presented his views is remarkable. For his Roman Empire is really the British Empire of his own day, and as he wrote about his prince of peace he can be seen looking out from Exeter, or rather looking down, on a world made up of largely inferior and uncivilized peoples quite unlike the British. Even Italy, for which an Edwardian gentleman's affection is much in evidence, had to rank among the lesser nations, labouring as it did under the oppressive weight of the Catholic Church – Cardinal Newman has an unflattering cameo – while the United States, given its oddly fabricated name, was deemed incapable of inspiring the sort of patriotism known to Englishmen.

Predictably, therefore, Hadrian turns out to be the epitome of what Henderson thought an Oxford-educated Englishman at the turn of the twentieth century should be: someone who as an undergraduate had read great books and played sports and thereby equipped himself for a lifetime of service in British imperial governance. It was a scheme of education outlined in an earlier book, The Study of Roman History (1920), and in his biography

Henderson evidently regarded Hadrian as one of its prime products. His image of the emperor commending his troops in North Africa for their military efficiency is more or less that of an Englishman discharging the same function in India, where an ideal Viceroy was to mirror a Roman official who had been well trained in the law. The vantage point is clearly attributable to Britain's place in the world in the early 1920s, and the author's attitudes a reflection of his standing in British society; even in the mother country the trades unions were expected to know their place.[64] At the same time, the book expresses a contemporary enervation that had followed the Great War with a world-weariness striking in a man, writing of the 1890s as a lost Golden Age, who today would be considered still in his prime. Yourcenar's view that in 1951 a definitive biography of Hadrian was yet to be written is perfectly understandable.[65]

Henderson's "great man" approach to writing history was soon to be swept away in Oxford by Ronald Syme, a prodigy from New Zealand who arrived two years after Henderson's biography appeared and gradually promoted what was then the new method of prosopography, the decisive impact of which became clear with The Roman Revolution of 1939. In time, Syme was to become highly distinguished, "universally acknowledged" as Roman history's "greatest practitioner in the twentieth century."[66] But despite the new methodological emphasis – he called prosopography "the indispensable science and art" – he was also to develop a strong biographical interest in Hadrian, composing an array of studies in which there was little reluctance to pronounce on the emperor's comportment and the features of his personality.[67] He was not to write a conventional life of Hadrian – biography itself was a literary form he disdained – but in many ways his studies give him a claim to being one of Hadrian's principal modern students. Born in 1903, it happens that he was an exact contemporary of Yourcenar, and although they were never to meet or to have any contact he was to develop a profound interest in her novel.[68] Of necessity he will figure prominently in this study as a foil to her.

It was impossible of course for Yourcenar to know the current standard biography of Hadrian, Anthony Birley's Hadrian: The Restless Emperor of 1997, a major achievement of wide influence and the essential starting point for all contemporary research.[69] But again necessarily it likewise receives much attention here. Its pre-eminent quality is its insistence on facts. Hadrian's personal characteristics are brought forward from time to time – his insatiable curiosity, his passions for hunting and architecture, his desire to excel in all areas of knowledge, his sense of history – but by and large Birley finds Hadrian's personality baffling and he concentrates instead on what Hadrian did: where he went and with whom and who held office under him.

He reconstructs Hadrian's great imperial journeys of inspection across the empire in scrupulous chronological and geographical detail, and he introduces and situates every identifiable office holder of the period. In turn, conclusions on policy and governance follow: administrative adjustments made to Roman civilian and military life were relatively few; Hadrian's commitment to Hellenism was mistakenly excessive and led eventually to the bloody war against the Jews; but like Augustus before him he set the borders of empire at practicable limits, his imperial tours formed part of a program to raise the provinces to the level of the Italian heartland, and consolidation and safeguarding of empire were guiding principles throughout his reign. On this conception, therefore, Hadrian is the sum of what Hadrian did, and Birley's book emerges as a classic illustration of W.H. Auden's apophthegm, "In the case of a man of action – a ruler, a statesman, a general – the man is identical with his biography."[70] Inevitably Birley was aware of Yourcenar's *Mémoires*, but in line with current scepticism he firmly rejected her presentation: "The book has received enormous acclaim and its literary merits are unquestioned. Yet the personality there portrayed seems to have been accepted by not a few scholars as an authentic representation of the 'real Hadrian.' Whether Yourcenar's Hadrian is in fact so close to the real man is another matter."[71] Nevertheless, whether the factual record is truly strong enough to justify the historical conclusions Birley offers soon emerges as an unsettling issue when his book is studied closely, leading to a legitimate question of where the line is to be drawn between what turn out to be a historian's ubiquitous speculations and the imaginative evocations of a supreme artist.[72]

For Marguerite Yourcenar Hadrian was unquestionably a great figure, a man liberal in disposition and highly cultured: "libéral et lettré" as she expressed it. It is not impossible that a Roman autocrat should or could have been liberal and cultured. But this particular characterization heightens the essential issue that *Mémoires* raises. Is the biographical portrait of Hadrian Yourcenar paints fact or fiction? Is Hadrian in any way really "biographable"?[73] Difficult enough in themselves, such questions are rendered still more problematic by two complicating factors: first, Yourcenar's lifelong presentation of herself once she had become a public figure as having opposed the European totalitarian regimes of the 1930s that in their day had drawn a certain inspiration from Imperial Rome; and second, the description, given in March 1952, some months before publication of *Mémoires*, of her objective in writing the book in which the phrase just quoted appears: "Il s'y agit d'une reconstruction par le dedans des motivations et des pensées du grand empereur libéral et lettré du IIe siècle" (*HZ* 27).[74] How might the interior life of Hadrian, his motives and thoughts, ever be known? The question is unanswerable, it would seem, and perhaps this makes it fruitless to think that a definitive solution to the problem of authenticity can ever be found. Yet in pursuing the question there is much of interest to ponder: the sources of knowledge at the disposal of anyone who tries to write the life of Hadrian, whether novelist, biographer, or historian; the complex issue of how the Roman past, and especially the biography of a central figure from that past, might be recovered; the related question, rendered acute by the examples of conventional imperial biography to which I have alluded, of how the results of investigation might best be communicated; and the justification of implicitly assuming, as I shall do throughout, that Yourcenar's novel continues a tradition from antiquity itself in which literature responded continually, creatively, and provocatively to the exercise of absolute power. These are the themes with which my essay is concerned and which make the enquiry worthwhile. My hope is that it will be of interest to those concerned with distinguishing between fact and fiction in the practice of history.

2

Authenticity Pursued

I cannot see how one can pass judgement on events
about which we are so inadequately and contradictorily informed.

A.D. Momigliano

I

Hadrian is in many respects a familiar figure. He is easily remembered as the
builder of the Wall in Britain, the Castel Sant'Angelo in Rome, and the great
Villa at Tivoli, as a military disciplinarian and devotee of Greek culture, as the
first emperor to wear a beard who spent much of his reign travelling across his
vast empire, and, perhaps most memorably of all, as the lover of the Bithynian
boy Antinous. He readily excites the imagination, and there is little about his
biography that seems to be problematic. Yet nothing could be further from
the truth. Much is known about Hadrian but little of him. For as Royston
Lambert said in his as yet unsurpassed book on Antinous, if "every schoolboy
knows the name and some of the achievements of one of the greatest emperors of Rome … what we do know is frequently the subject of irreconcilable
controversy: from the place of Hadrian's birth to the poem which he wrote or
did not write on his deathbed."[1] Such inclarities and ambiguities do indeed
fill Hadrian's whole life history. Was he born in Rome or in Spanish Italica?
There is evidence for both possibilities. Did he compose a deathbed poem? The
only testimony comes from a highly controversial source. The situation does
not improve with time. Hadrian can no longer be credited with initiating the
rebuilding at Rome of the Pantheon. That award now goes to Trajan.[2]

I describe here the limits and limitations of the primary evidence for
Hadrian's life, ultimately as an aid to increasing appreciation of Yourcenar's

novel but in the first instance to show, to both critics unfamiliar with the details and historians who tend to underestimate them, that any reconstruction of Hadrian's biography rests on very fragile foundations. It is safe to say that there is a historical tradition about Hadrian that has reached the modern world from antiquity; but in itself it brings no guarantee of historical truth. In considering how Yourcenar responded to the tradition, I shall give examples in later chapters of what I consider to be her success in achieving biographical authenticity in her novel. But as a prelude, the difficulties of seeing through a glass darkly have to be fully exposed. It is impossible otherwise to understand how, or whether, a comprehensive portrait of Hadrian might ever be realized, by biographer, historian, or novelist. To set the topic in perspective, I note that A.N. Wilson's major biography of Queen Victoria lists in its bibliography thirty-two sets of manuscript collections and 275 printed sources from which the story of the monarch's life is reconstructed.[3] The manuscript collections include a wide array of correspondence, diaries, journals, papers, and other items from the principal personnel involved, not least the Queen herself, while the printed sources include collections of contemporary letters, memoirs, and other personal items. Comparably, Diarmid MacCulloch opens his mammoth political biography of Thomas Cromwell by inviting his reader to find his "true" subject in "the maze of his surviving papers," a trove comprising "thousands and thousands of individual documents."[4] By the standards of early modern and modern historical writing such masses of evidence are unexceptional. But in ancient history they are unfathomably unmatchable. Hadrian cannot be known in the way that the lives and careers of Victoria and Cromwell are known; and it is not the absence of contemporary personal materials alone that is so troubling. The risible reality is that there are just two substantial narrative accounts of Hadrian's life that remain from antiquity, each a third-party account and each, as Yourcenar made clear in her *Note*, an account that is inherently defective (*OR* 546). I begin my description with them.

II

Yourcenar tells in the *Carnets* of opening two particular books that she found among the remnants of her earlier collection when the trunk of her effects arrived from Switzerland in December 1948: "C'étaient Dion Cassius dans la belle impression d'Henri Estienne, et un tome d'une édition quelconque de *L'Histoire Auguste* … achetés à l'époque où je me proposais d'écrire ce livre" (*CNMH* 525).[5] I assume that these two books are those still to be seen on Yourcenar's shelves at Petite Plaisance, an edition of the Greek historian Cassius Dio printed by Henricus Stephanus, from which the first page with the date of publication is unfortunately missing, and the first of the three volumes of the Latin work known as the *Historia Augusta* in David Magie's edition from the Loeb Classical Library.[6]

The *Historia Augusta* is a collection of Latin biographies of the many actual and aspirant rulers of Rome's empire of the second and third centuries. The life of Hadrian opens the collection and is the earlier of the two extant narratives. It is roughly 5,000 words in length and covers some twenty-six pages in the standard Teubner edition of Ernst Hohl.[7] It is followed by biographies of Lucius Aelius Caesar, Hadrian's first choice to succeed him (he died prematurely), and of Antoninus Pius and Marcus Aurelius who in the event ruled successively after him. The work as a whole is broadly modelled on the *Caesares* of Suetonius, but everything it contains is of lesser quality and altogether it is shrouded in mystery. It presents itself as the product of not one but six authors, men who seem to be writing in the late third and early fourth centuries in the reigns of the emperors Diocletian and Constantine (285–337). The biographies of Hadrian and Lucius appear to have been composed by a figure named Aelius Spartianus, the lives of Antoninus Pius and Marcus Aurelius by a certain Julius Capitolinus. These individuals, however, as the four others, are otherwise unknown, and whether they ever really existed is part of a wider question about the authorship and nature of the *Historia Augusta* at large. Despite slight variations, all six biographers write in a generally comparable manner, and what they offer is full of inventions, errors, strange names, repetitions, and questionable, if not fictitious, documents, all of which led the late nineteenth-century German scholar Hermann Dessau to propose that the collection is a forgery, the product of a single individual who concocted a cluster of false identities and wrote, as some of the work's mannerisms and inventions suggest, not at the beginning but at the end of the fourth century. Precisely, in fact, towards the year 395. The theory was long regarded as controversial. In the second half of the twentieth century, however, in a corpus of four books and numerous scholarly papers, it was vigorously reaffirmed by Ronald Syme and has now become widely, though not universally, accepted. Most scholars today believe the *Historia Augusta* to be a hoax, the creation of an author Dessau characterized as a *Fälscher* and Syme as an impostor.[8]

Nevertheless, exactly when the *Historia Augusta* was composed remains a matter of dispute. On technical grounds some scholars believe that the collection cannot be earlier than the year 361, and while many follow the late fourth-century ascription, others posit an earlier fourth-century date and others still a date in the early fifth century, or even later.[9] What the putative impostor was trying to accomplish is equally unclear. The work has been associated with a renaissance of Latin literature in a late fourth-century Golden

Age, when eminent *littérateurs* looked to the accomplishments of the Roman past for models on which to ground their new creations, the consequence being that the author of the *Historia Augusta* is thought to have written imperial biographies in emulation of Suetonius, but as a parody rather than as a serious contribution to Latin letters. On the other hand, the very notion of a late fourth-century Latin literary revival has been unequivocally dismissed.[10] Some scholars have suggested that evidence of contemporary religious or political struggles is detectable in the collection, one for instance confidently characterizing it as an anti-Christian tract written in the early 390s by a militant pagan aristocrat named Nicomachus Flavianus, a figure known from the *Saturnalia* of Macrobius, and identifying it with the supposedly lost work of history with which Flavianus is credited.[11] Another specialist, however, acerbically rejects this suggestion altogether and asserts a counter view: the author was "a frivolous person of decadent literary tastes and a weird sense of humour, with no agenda worthy of the name at all." He was nothing but "a fully fledged forger," and people in the know knew exactly who he was. In turn, a third contender restores as the culprit an anti-Christian aristocrat, but a figure now named Tascius Victorianus, known from Sidonius Apollinaris, who produced nothing more than a mediocre effort that he put together in fits and starts, and perhaps never completed.[12] While in total contrast, another investigator proposes that the work is not a forgery or a hoax at all, but the playful contrivance of an early fifth-century writer addressing a small circle of *érudits* interested in the nature of biography and alert to the collection's all-pervasive literary allusiveness. It is a work primarily of fiction and has no concern with religious or political controversies, its key feature being the numerous allusions that challenge readers to solve the many puzzles of recognition and appreciation its author creates.[13] Debate is endless.

The result, it follows, is that the extent to which any ideological posture controls the *Historia Augusta* is impossible to determine. There is general agreement nonetheless that the lives become increasingly fanciful as they progress through time, either because the author ran out of reliable materials on which to base his work, or because he no longer cared about maintaining even a charade of authenticity. Even so, the theory of single authorship provides no answer to the crucial question Arnaldo Momigliano raised in 1954 of why an impostor, whoever and if such the author was, should have wanted to perpetrate a hoax in the first place, an idea which on the surface was, and remains, preposterous.[14] One detail concerning Hadrian illustrates the consequent dilemma historians and biographers always have to face. In the life of the third-century emperor Alexander Severus, Hadrian is passingly said to have considered building a temple to Jesus Christ and enrolling him among the Roman gods (*HA Sev. Alex.* 43.6). It is a report that can be taken seriously and traced to a putative earlier Christian source, or else deprived of all historical significance on the grounds that the life concerned is a meritless fabrication illustrating a rogue biographer's conception of an ideal prince.[15] How therefore to distinguish fact from fiction, at any juncture in the work, is far from obvious.

The life of Hadrian itself is chaotically organized and far less polished than a true Suetonian life. It proceeds in the main chronologically, but shows signs at times of topical interest as well. To determine its value one approach has been to examine its arrangement of material and to test all of its statements *seriatim* against whatever other evidence is available – to apply, that is, the methods of source criticism – the result being that the life appears to many to be one of the more trustworthy items in the *Historia Augusta* as a whole and to contain relatively little that is fictional.[16] It names as one authority on which it drew Marius Maximus, an individual known to have flourished about the year 220 and to have composed biographies, now lost, of Rome's emperors from Nerva to Elagabalus (96–222). Reports are attributed to him in the life that Hadrian was naturally cruel, that he behaved kindly but only to avoid comparison with the tyrannical Domitian, and that some miraculous cures he effected were simulated (*HA Hadr.* 20.3; 25.4). For Anthony Birley, Marius Maximus was a serious author who provided the writer of the biography with most of the sound information the life is believed to contain, and he can suggest for instance that on a set of administrative measures Hadrian took early in his reign Maximus "must have supplied copious detail."[17] For Syme, on the other hand, Marius Maximus was a scurrilous gossip interested only in scandalous anecdotes, while the origin of the life's reliable material lies in a purely hypothetical set of earlier imperial biographies written in the third century by an otherwise unattested author Syme simply called "Ignotus."[18] The reason for such diametrically opposed views is that the overall character and trustworthiness of Marius Maximus's biographies cannot be determined given that they no longer exist.[19] It may be that Syme was correct to identify four sources of information in the life of Hadrian in total: not only the compositions of Marius Maximus and his Ignotus, but also, as will appear, the autobiography Hadrian is known to have written, together with contributions from the compiler considered responsible for the biography as it finally came into being. But when consensus is unattainable on this question, views of the viability of its each and every statement will evidently be subjective and vulnerable. One solution is to ignore the problems involved and to take everything at face value.[20]

What makes this situation more confusing still is a layer of complexity seldom in my view given adequate attention. I call it "the Bardon factor." The first volume of Henry Bardon's *La Littérature latine inconnue* (1952), a work that Marguerite Yourcenar knew and relished, opens with a startling statement: "Il faut en convenir: nous ne connaissons pas la littérature latine." It goes on to offer some remarkable statistics: of 772 known Latin authors, 276 are mere names; no more than fragments of works survive from 352 of them; and it is only from the remaining 144 that one or more compositions remain.[21] The figures may be arguable – Bardon took them from an older work – but their overall import is not: no more than a fifth of identifiable classical Latin literature exists today, and, worse, no one has any idea what portion of everything that was ever written is represented by what can be identified by title, fragment, or author's name, since nothing can be known of works that have left no trace at all. Exactly what the full sources of the life of Hadrian were, it follows, is anyone's guess, and the prospects of proving which authors provided the author-compiler of the life of Hadrian with reliable information are virtually nil. As Fergus Millar has said, "Hopeless uncertainties prevail in the field of source-criticism."[22]

Altogether, therefore, the conclusion is inescapable that the Augustan life of Hadrian is a highly dubious source on which to base definitive biographical statements. The problems that envelop it are legion, and the temptation to trust it simply because it exists have to be resisted. This should not surprise historians (though some may need a reminder: even if Marius Maximus was a reliable writer, he was writing a century after Hadrian). But Yourcenarian critics who for understandable reasons may not be aware of the technical issues involved and continue to refer to the Latin biography unhesitatingly as the composition of "Spartianus" may find it disturbing.[23] Written at the earliest more than two hundred years after Hadrian's death, its reliability is inherently dubious on chronological grounds alone, not to mention those of authorial identity and purpose. To make the point I ask what credence could be placed, for the composition today of a historical biography of Queen Victoria, who died in 1901, in a brief account still to be composed for an unknown reason by an unknown writer drawing on indeterminate prior accounts some time before the approximate year 2155. The answer is pitifully plain.

As illustration, consider the following extract:

Ergo conversis regio more militibus Brittaniam [sic] petit, in qua multa correxit murumque per octoginta milia passuum primus duxit, qui barbaros Romanosque divideret. (HA Hadr. 11.2)

Accordingly after he had dealt with military matters in the manner of a king he set out for Britain, where he resolved many issues and was the first to begin an eighty-mile-long wall intended to separate barbarians and Romans.

The passage refers obviously enough to the construction of Hadrian's Wall in Britain. And as soon as it is read it is almost impossible not to associate with it the physical remains that can still be seen and to assume that the text conveys accurate information. A glance at any handbook confirms that the Wall was, indeed, more or less eighty Roman miles in length. What the passage does not convey, however, is more notable. There is no indication of when the Wall was built, where it was located, how long it took to build, who was responsible for its design and construction, or what it looked like. Archaeology and epigraphy have long since shown that it stretched from Wallsend to Bowness-on-Solway, that it was built partly of stone and partly of turf by Roman soldiers stationed in Britain, and that it had a series of features that included mile-castles, turrets, forts, and gates as well as the ditch customarily called the Vallum. It was begun as such, in all likelihood, when Hadrian arrived in Britain from Lower Germany in 122 and was completed several years later. But none of this can be known from the *Historia Augusta*.[24] Hadrian's presence in Britain is understood in the text, but strictly speaking it does not prove that he was ever in the north of England where the Wall was eventually built, and while a reason for its construction is expressed, it means very little given that there were as many native inhabitants in Britain to the south of the Wall as there were to the north (if not more), very few of whom were Roman citizens. (The widely held belief of a generation ago that Britain saw a military irruption in the 120s requiring severe retaliation has now been discarded.) How in any case could a fourth-century compiler be expected to know Hadrian's purpose, two centuries earlier, in erecting a barrier that was soon replaced by the so-called Antonine Wall in Scotland? As for the many other corrective measures he took, what were they? The passage, famously the only reference in all of classical literature to the Wall, is typical in its frustrating brevity and indeterminacy.[25]

In 1951, Marguerite Yourcenar did not know the "problem" of the *Historia Augusta*. A peripheral awareness is just possible, but there is no indication of which I know that in her preparations for writing *Mémoires* she had ever read Dessau's revolutionary work or any other pertinent items of scholarship.[26] In her *Note* she spoke of the Latin life as one of the better items in the *Historia Augusta,* implying that she understood the later lives, written by other hands, to be less authoritative; and taking Spartianus to be its author – a chronicler as she called him – she dated the life of Hadrian roughly towards 300 (*OR* 546). Obviously enough she was familiar with the passage on the Wall, and from what she had learned from archaeology she was able to have Hadrian speak in *Mémoires* as follows:

En même temps, l'érection d'un mur coupant l'île en deux dans sa partie la plus étroite servit à protéger les régions fertiles et policées du sud contre les attaques des tribus du nord. J'ai inspecté moi-même une bonne partie de ces travaux engagés

partout à la fois sur un glacis de quatre-vingt lieues: j'y trouvais l'occasion d'essayer, sur cet espace bien délimité qui va d'une côte à l'autre, un système de défense qui pourrait ensuite s'appliquer partout ailleurs. (*MH* 393)

At the same time the erection of a wall cutting the island in two in its narrowest part served to protect the fertile, guarded areas of the south from the attacks of northern tribes. I myself inspected a substantial part of those constructions begun everywhere at the same time along an earthwork eighty miles in length; it was my chance to try out, on that carefully defined space running from coast to coast, a system of defense which could afterward be applied anywhere else.

The assurance Yourcenar displayed here in Hadrian's presence in the north depended, I suspect, on her reading of R.G. Collingwood's works on Roman Britain from the 1930s. She did not see the Wall herself until 1953. Nonetheless, Hadrian's words reflect the interpretative leap of faith she made from her source, like many historians and biographers before and since, in order to accommodate the demands of the type of historical composition she had chosen for her biographical purpose. It is a typical, and understandable, example of how she responded to the historical tradition.[27]

The second narrative of Hadrian's reign comes from the comprehensive history of Rome, in eighty books, composed in the early third century by the Greek historian and Roman senator Cassius Dio of Nicaea in Bithynia. Dio was well read in history and experienced in government, and his father, he notably remarks, had been in office as provincial governor of Cilicia when the emperor Trajan died and had passed on to him some recollections of Hadrian's accession (69.1.3). Even so, the events of Hadrian's reign took place a century before the record Dio made of them, and, more disconcertingly, while composed earlier than the *Historia Augusta*, perhaps in 217 or 218, his account does not survive intact. Much of his history has in fact been lost, and all that is left for Hadrian is a series of excerpts and fragments from a process of culling and summarizing carried out centuries later in the Byzantine age. Hence my designation of it as the later narrative. Hadrian's reign was treated in Dio's Book 69. But practically all that can now be read are uneven portions of an *Epitome* made by the monk Ioannes Xiphilinus of Trapezus in the late eleventh century, together with a few scraps from other hands also writing many centuries later.[28] "Cassius Dio's" narrative therefore is again a very brief item, and the apparent advantage of its original earlier date of composition is offset by its truncated form and whatever purpose Xiphilinus may have had in excerpting it. Clear goals and interests have been attributed to him. But little can be certain and caution is obviously required: P.A. Brunt tellingly observed, for instance, that Xiphilinus was less interested in imperial administration than was Dio himself.[29] The material the fragments contain is of course important, and it is generally assumed that Xiphilinus was a reliable copyist. Yet Dio himself was not a historian of the first rank, and in his accounts of emperors as a whole he tends to write in narrow focus, concentrating on events in a manner akin to Suetonius's method of measuring emperors in terms of public expectations of imperial performance, with little aptitude for psychological penetration. His attitude to Hadrian is generally critical, the result, it is often said, of a long-standing "senatorial tradition" of hostility to the emperor that influenced his record, a notion I regard as valueless.[30] This is Millar's sympathetic but frank assessment of his account:

What Dio records of Hadrian is largely a collection of anecdotes, from a variety of sources, centred round the Emperor and the leading men of his time. Some chronological structure is preserved, but it is vague and uncertain. Hadrian is seen from the point of view of the Roman aristocracy, and while his military reforms are praised there is no indication that his philhellenism, which led him, among many other things, to benefit Nicaea, seemed to Dio either important or praiseworthy.[31]

One item related to Hadrian's philhellenism included in Xiphilinus's excerpts is the statement that Hadrian "allowed the Greeks to build in his honour the shrine which was named the Panhellenion, and instituted a series of games in connection with it" (69.16.2). The context shows that a benefaction to the city of Athens is involved, but little detail is provided and precisely what the text means is far from straightforward. From ancillary materials, especially inscriptions, it is known that a league of Greek city-states based at Athens and called the Panhellenion was instituted during Hadrian's reign, with member cities sending delegates to a Panhellenic council and a Panhellenic religious festival being periodically celebrated complete with athletic contests. Even so, while religious, cultural, and political elements were involved, the full reasons for the league's establishment are unknown, an explanation for why admission was open to some but not all Greek cities remains elusive, and whether it was founded at Hadrian's initiative or that of the Greeks themselves is a matter of unresolved debate. Dio's statement evidently lies at the core of these issues. His notice is too elliptical, however, to permit definitive answers to emerge; and although many scholars accept that the league was inaugurated in the year 131/132, the notice again gives no firm guidance on this equally fundamental question.[32] It is preceded by another statement concerning Athens, namely that Hadrian completed the building there of the Olympieion, the grand temple to Olympian Zeus in the southeast of the city begun centuries earlier near the river Ilissos and whose remains can still be seen (69.16.1). As independent testimony allows, Hadrian subsequently presided over a ceremony of dedication that included an honorific speech from the sophist Polemo of Laodicaea. It does not automatically follow that the foundation of the Panhellenion and the dedication of the temple were conjoined events. But the inference has certainly been drawn, and for present purposes it illustrates a key point: because of its epitomated, minimalist character, Dio's evidence is always open to dispute, and inference is the order of the day in the reconstruction of Hadrian's history. The loss of Dio's original text is in fact the single most important reason why recovery is impossible of a detailed chronology for Hadrian's reign in any way comparable to that taken for granted in true biography.[33]

As it happens, *Mémoires* refers to the Panhellenion no more than indirectly (*MH* 460), although as her recreation of the dedication of the Olympieion shows, Yourcenar was certainly aware of the significance of the imperial cult with which it is sometimes associated. Hadrian recalls Polemo's speech in an emotive, transporting passage that emphasizes a union between Rome and Greece historians have similarly recognized, and, importantly, that relies on the same assumptive method historians necessarily adopt. A response to the historical tradition again displays itself:

Ce fut là que la Grèce me décerna ces appellations divines où je voyais à la fois une source de prestige et le but le plus secret des travaux de ma vie: Évergète, Olympien, Épiphane, Maître de tout. Et le plus beau, le plus difficile à mériter de tous ces titres: Ionien, Philhellène. Il y avait de l'acteur en Polémon, mais les jeux de physionomie d'un grand comédien traduisent parfois une émotion à laquelle participent toute une foule, tout un siècle. Il leva les yeux, se recueillit avant son exorde, parut rassembler en lui tous les dons contenus dans ce moment du temps. J'avais collaboré avec les âges, avec la vie grecque elle-même; l'autorité que j'exerçais était moins un pouvoir qu'une mystérieuse puissance, supérieure à l'homme, mais qui n'agit efficacement qu'à travers l'intermédiaire d'une personne humaine; le mariage de Rome et d'Athènes s'était accompli; le passé retrouvait un visage d'avenir; la Grèce repartait comme un navire longtemps immobilisé par un calme, qui sent de nouveau dans ses voiles la poussée du vent. (*MH* 422)

It was at this time that Greece granted me those divine appellations wherein I could recognize both a source of prestige and the most secret aim of my life's work: Evergetes, Olympian, Epiphanios, Master of All. And the most beautiful of all these titles, and most difficult to merit, Ionian and Friend of Greece. There was much of the actor in Polemo, but the play of features in a great performer sometimes translates the emotion shared by a whole people, and a whole century. He raised his eyes to the heavens and gathered himself together before his exordium, seeming to assemble within him all gifts held in that moment of time: I had collaborated with the ages, and with Greek life itself; the authority which I wielded was less a power than a mysterious force, superior to man but operating effectively only through the intermediary of a human person; the marriage of Rome with Athens had been accomplished; the future once more held the hope of the past; Greece was stirring again like a vessel, long becalmed, caught anew in the current of the wind.

Four other narratives of Hadrian's reign exist, all briefer still and all very late. They belong to handbooks of emperors' lives written in the second half of the fourth century in an age apparently eager for summary historical information. They are the *Liber de Caesaribus* of Sex. Aurelius Victor, a senator of African origin who was appointed to the prefecture of the city of Rome under Theodosius I; the *Breviarium ab urbe condita* of Eutropius, a functionary who held the important administrative post of *magister memoriae* under Valens; an anonymously authored *Epitome* of Victor's work, which at the relevant stage differs considerably from the *Liber de Caesaribus* itself; and the *Breviarium rerum gestarum populi Romani* of Festus, another eminent official who produced a compilation of historical events, also in the reign of Valens, from the beginning of Rome's history until his own day. Yourcenar could refer to these works, together with the *Historia Augusta* itself, as "chronicles" she thought comparable to the works of poorly informed journalists, not without reason (*PV* 241). All four are intricately connected to some degree, and they share discernible associations with the *Historia Augusta* as well. But precisely how they are connected is another unanswerable question. Their investigators commonly believe that there was once a no longer extant history of Roman emperors written in the mid-fourth century from which the chronicles' composers variously drew material, the so-called *Kaisergeschichte* of the German scholar A. Enmann, who, in 1884, advanced the theory of a basic lost source from the hand of another "Ignotus": an anonymous author, that is, of a hypothetical work that exists only in the academic imagination and whose authority is beyond calculation.[34] When they write of the Julio-Claudians and Flavians, the chroniclers can sometimes be seen to be copying verbatim from Suetonius's *Caesares*, but this does not help with what they say of Hadrian. Their evidence altogether occupies no more than a few pages, and at times it provokes extreme scepticism.

The *Epitome* records, for instance, that Hadrian's wife Vibia Sabina vowed never to allow herself to become pregnant because, well aware of Hadrian's cruelty, she wanted to save the human race from destruction (14.8); Festus in turn alleges that the reason for Hadrian's abandonment of the eastern provinces Trajan had acquired through warfare against Parthia was his jealousy of Trajan's reputation for glory (*Brev.* 20). How such personally petty anecdotes, late and unsubstantiated, can be taken as historically meaningful is an obvious imponderable, and they simply have to be noted as ingredients of the general tradition of which every biographer of Hadrian has to be aware.[35] As of course was Yourcenar. She took from the *Epitome*, recall, the words *varius multiplex multiformis* as a title for the second segment of her book, a phrase, one of the few descriptions to survive from antiquity of Hadrian's character, not in itself as prejudicial as its context in the *Epitome* implies (14.6): the younger Pliny used similar language of an associate in a highly complimentary sense (*Ep.* 1.16.1: *quam varium, quam flexibile, quam multiplex*).[36] It was not intended, however, to flatter Hadrian, who, it is said, had a propensity to conceal his true nature by dissimulating, a view with which the Latin life agrees in its longer statement of Hadrian's competing, contrary characteristics (*HA Hadr.* 14.11).[37] Yourcenar was sympathetic to the complexity as she saw it of Hadrian's personality, and took pains to reveal its development over time. But the fourth-century writers, in contrast, give no more than static impressions of their subject, to biographical disadvantage. Ultimately, in view of its long remove from the events recorded, the import of their evidence is highly debatable and the verdict expressed by an expert on Aurelius Victor – "his account of Hadrian's reign is flimsy and superficial" – is one that can safely be applied to all of their accounts.[38]

Finally in this rubric, Hadrian is mentioned purely in passing in many other literary works, including many earlier writings and in many settings. A generation after his death the courtier M. Cornelius Fronto, who had known Hadrian personally, offers a suggestively cool opinion of the emperor in a letter to Marcus Aurelius (1.110), while later in the century the Greek antiquarian Pausanias gives in his *Description of Greece* invaluable eyewitness information on the building projects for which Hadrian had supposedly been responsible in Athens and other Greek cities (e.g. 1.5.5, 1.36.3, 1.18.6–9). Much later, at the turn of the fourth century, Eusebius of Caesarea in his revolutionary *Ecclesiastical History* quotes a passage from a second-century predecessor, Hegesippus, that identifies Antinous as a slave (*doulos*) once owned by Hadrian (4.8.2); and later still the historian Ammianus Marcellinus records that the emperor had once blocked up the Castalian spring at Antiochene Daphne, fearing that someone might receive a prophecy of rule from its waters as he himself had once done (22.12.8); the belief lived on into the next century, reappearing in the *Ecclesiastical History* of the Greek historian Sozomen (5.19).

No one would choose to lose such incidental items, of which this is a mere sample. Their individual merits, however, must always be carefully evaluated. Fronto's remark is no more than a momentary thought, whereas Pausanias's evidence opens up an important question of whether something that can be called Hadrianic policy in, or an underlying grand design for, the Greek world can be established, and if so how it is to be conceptualized. Likewise, the designation of Antinous as a slave also seems important, safely attesting his juridical status. Yet Hegesippus's text does not survive independently, Eusebius's accuracy in transmitting it is beyond scrutiny, and allowance has to be made for the religious position from which the designation is made: Christian authors hostile to the paederastic association they thought the emperor enjoyed with Antinous may have led to the invention of servile status as a means of denigrating Hadrian (and of course Antinous). What emerges, especially perhaps from Sozomen, is that by late antiquity there was a multifaceted set of beliefs about Hadrian – a tradition – that was transmitted from generation to generation, and that by the time of the emperor Julian could easily lend itself to caricature (*Caes.* 311D).[39] How securely rooted in historical reality its various elements are is anyone's guess, and collectively the elements underline how unfortunate it is that an authoritative, comprehensive, contemporaneous narrative of Hadrian's life and reign has not survived. A special case in point arises with Tertullian's famous description of Hadrian as "the explorer of every curiosity" (*Apol.* 5.7: *omnium curiositatum explorator*), a phrase often taken at face value to mean that inordinate curiosity was a prime feature of Hadrian's character. The description, however, follows a patently absurd story about the emperor Tiberius sending to the Roman senate news received from Palestine of the divinity of Jesus, with a threat of reprisal against anyone who failed to accept the news as genuine (*Apol.* 5.2). The implications for other historical statements in the treatise, a virulent, anti-establishment tract composed for ideological reasons some sixty years after Hadrian's death, are self-evident.[40]

This difficult situation is compounded by discrepancies that sometimes appear among the scraps of information the literary record contains. The question of Hadrian's birthplace mentioned at the outset is a classic example. Eutropius (*Brev.* 8.6.1) was confident that Hadrian was born at his ancestral home of Italica in southern Spain. The Latin biography on the contrary asserts that he was born in Rome (*HA Hadr.* 1.3). The matter is significant for any consideration of Hadrian's early life and formation, as historians of childhood will especially understand, and for any modern writer's conception of the eventual personality Hadrian became. Scholars who believe that the evidence of the *Historia Augusta* is attributable to a sober source are adamant in their preference for Rome as Hadrian's birth-place, referring to the statement of Eutropius as an inadvertent error.[41] The weakness of this view is obvious. Meantime, a horoscope of Hadrian, compiled by a certain Antigonus of Nicaea and preserved in the *Apoteles-matica* of Hephaestion of Thebes (2.18), contains astrological information that allows the geographical latitude for which the horoscope was cast to be calculated, promising thereby a safe solution to the issue. But whether the horoscope has any historical weight is a real conundrum. Antigonus is no more than a shadowy second-century figure, and when, where, and on what basis he produced the horoscope no one knows. Moreover, what happened to the horoscope until it was apparently copied by the equally shadowy Hephaestion at the turn of the fifth century (perhaps) is likewise a mystery. All of which suggests that the horoscope is of minimal help in determining Hadrian's birthplace. Scholars from both camps have claimed that it supports their rival views.[42] In contrast, Yourcenar's response to the informational discrepancy was ingenious. She followed Eutropius on birth in Italica, and accounted for the version in the Latin life as an official pronouncement appropriately made for a man who later became emperor (*MH* 310). For Yourcenar, indeed, Hadrian was always a child of the Anda-lusian plain, spending his first twelve years in Spain until on his father's death he was sent to Rome to be educated; the Spanish bias, strikingly displayed in her essay of 1952, *L'Andalousie ou les Hespérides*, has not always been appreciated by her admirers:

Italica, patrie de Trajan, d'Hadrien, de Théodose, est plus qu'aux trois quarts enfouie sous la terre, mais ses mosaïques et ses quelques statues attestent une splendeur due aux efforts de l'artisan local hellénisé, ou au luxe des importations de Grèce et de Rome. Chez le noble poète espagnol du xviiᵉ siècle, Rodrigo Caro, Italica reste l'emblème de la solitude mélancolique, le lit desséché laissé par l'immense écoule-ment d'une vie disparue. Les Sévillans aiment à citer la phrase de Hume, rappelant que deux empereurs andalous, se succédant à Rome, assurèrent un des ses rares siè-cles à l'humanité: Séville a sa rue Trajan, sa rue Hadrien. (*TGS* 382)[43]

Italica, the birthplace of Trajan, Hadrian, and Theodosius, is more than three-quar-ters buried, but its mosaics and its few statues attest to a splendor which is the result of the efforts of Hellenized local artisans or else of the luxury of importations from Greece and Rome. For the noble Spanish poet of the seventeenth century, Rodrigo Caro, Italica remains the symbol of melancholy solitude, a dry riverbed left by the vast flood of a life that is gone. The people of Seville are fond of quoting that phrase of Hume which states that the two Andalusian emperors who succeeded each other in Rome made possible one of the rare beautiful centuries humanity has known: Seville has its Trajan Street and its Hadrian Street.

III

As the *Note* once more shows, Yourcenar was well aware that the literary narratives of Hadrian's life have to be supplemented by documents and material evidence, the volume of which, in contrast to the paltry literary record, is great. Coins, inscriptions and papyri, legal sources, art and archaeology all contribute to knowledge of Hadrian. The result is a paradox. In a sense there is both too little and too much from which to recover his life, far more than anyone might ordinarily hope to control. Ancient historians accordingly might balk at the claim Yourcenar made to have read everything recorded of Hadrian (*PV* 35). But she did not exaggerate. There is scarcely a page in the novel that does not somehow depend upon, or reflect her exploitation of an ancient source, as above all the grand *thèse* of Rémy Poignault brilliantly illustrates.[44] Here I want only to emphasize that the paradox leads to another kind of reconstructional hazard, one due not to the wealth of evidence available but to the difficulties of interpretation intrinsic to its several categories. In doing so, I shall refer at times to various items that were unknown in Yourcenar's day, since inevitably new discoveries constantly add to and refine Hadrian's history.

1. *Coins.* As the titles of the novel's segments show, Yourcenar had an intimate knowledge of Hadrianic coin issues and was alert to the historical implications of their designs and legends. In keeping with the Roman Imperial coinage generally, Hadrian's coins either commemorate actions he took, or express programmatic principles with which he presumably wished to be associated; his coins, that is, were vehicles of communication as well as of economic exchange. Surprisingly, however, while the process by which the coins were physically produced and minted can readily be reconstructed – the workforce was often made up of slaves and former slaves – the issue of how their designs and legends were selected is one to which there is no incontrovertible answer. Who was responsible for the choices made is unknown, a fact historians and critics alike might on the face of it find baffling, but such is the reality.[45] It is often assumed, with reason, that emperors themselves were responsible. Augustus is known to have struck a coin displaying his birth sign of Capricorn, Nero the *artifex* issued an image of himself as a lyre player, and Constantine much later had his portrait displayed in an attitude of Christian prayer. These instances, however, were exceptions rather than the rule. Images and legends were

normally the work of Roman administrative officials: the moneyers (*mon-etales*) who presided over the Imperial mint, its superior administrator, the *procurator monetae*, and its apparent chief supervisor, the *a rationibus*, men who followed emperors' general directives or those of figures close to them, or else merely assumed what an emperor's wishes were. So at least it is thought. I know of no Roman instance analogous to that of Queen Victoria in 1860, who repeatedly, and indignantly, turned down images of herself presented by a modeller at the Royal Mint because she found them all unsatisfactory.[46]

Yourcenar attached a special importance to the Hadrianic legend TELLUS STABILITA, repeatedly affirming in her interviews and correspondence that stability was an all-important ideological axiom of Hadrian's regime. She was justified in so doing: the legend was "a new creation ... in the imperial coinage."[47] Its choice, however, cannot be directly connected to Hadrian himself and this is true of all the legends and images that appeared in his reign, with one possible exception. At a late date four series of coins were issued that seem tied to Hadrian's grand provincial tours. One commemorated the provinces visited, a second the emperor's arrival in each location, a third his achievements in restoring local prosperity, and the fourth his provision of regional military security. "This explosion of regional motifs," Richard Duncan-Jones has written, "stands out as quite exceptional and essentially different from the main run of coin-types of the Principate. At least in its scale, this initiative was unlike anything that had come before, and it seems that it must reflect policy at a high level." The initiative, in other words, was that of Hadrian himself.[48] In *Mémoires*, Yourcenar makes Hadrian personally responsible for the coin designs that celebrate Rome's provinces – he speaks for instance of a personified female Britannia sitting on a throne of rocks, and of a Dacia with her predictable scimitar (*MH* 381) – and perhaps she was right to do so.[49] But there is no reason to think that this was general practice. It is certainly an arresting moment in the novel when the emperor declares on his deathbed that he had the day before met with Domitius Rogatus and given instructions for a new coin issue bearing the legend PATIENTIA: "j'ai choisi cette légende qui sera mon dernier mot d'ordre" (*MH* 505): a L. Domitius Rogatus is recorded as procurator of the mint close to, if not actually during, Hadrian's last years, and the legend is genuine enough.[50] It was introduced, however, many years before Hadrian's last illness among emissions of the years 131–2, when the term cannot have signified the quasi-Stoical fortitude Yourcenar attributes to Hadrian at his life's end so much as the patient endurance with which he freely bore the burdens of empire on behalf of his people. Yourcenar, I think, based her idea on an entry in the standard numismatic work of reference she had consulted, the second volume of the *Roman Imperial Coinage*, where in a comment on a coin issued by Antoninus Pius to commemorate Hadrian, the editors defined *patientia* as "the heroic endurance shown by Hadrian in his last illness."[51] Most importantly, however, the degree to which the imagery of coins permits historical conclusions about Hadrianic programs and policies in any modern sense is a matter of controversy, and the value of coins for biographical purposes consequently enigmatic.[52]

This is confirmed by the fact that coins were issued not by the Imperial mint alone but also, spontaneously and at their own discretion, by local city mints throughout the empire. The coinage of Hadrian's wife Sabina offers telling illustration. In the literary tradition Sabina is virtually invisible, yet she was given unusual prominence on coins both at Rome and in the provinces. For political and dynastic reasons, Hadrian may have systematically promoted her image through the Roman mint in the last decade of his reign; but this does not satisfactorily explain the provincial activity. More than eighty local mints, an extraordinary number, are known to have issued coins displaying Sabina's portraits, many in the eastern half of Rome's empire, the explanation perhaps being that local communities intended to honour her during what was to be the last of Hadrian's great provincial tours, on the entirely reasonable assumption that she accompanied her husband as a member of his entourage.[53] Local practices, however, were inconsistent. Some cities did not portray Sabina at all, and the volume of issues concerned appears to have increased after the final tour. Results therefore are again inconclusive. Yourcenar nonetheless was well aware of the overall phenomenon. As her Hadrian pointedly remarks, "J'aimais assez qu'un profil d'impératrice figurât sur les monnaies romaines, avec, au revers, une inscription, tantôt à la Pudeur, tantôt à la Tranquillité" (*MH* 418).[54]

2. *Documents*. One of the most celebrated epigraphical items from Hadrian's reign is an inscription known as the *Laudatio Matidiae* ("The Eulogy of Matidia"). It preserves fragments of a speech Hadrian made in honour of his mother-in-law Salonia Matidia following her death in December 119.[55] It celebrates Matidia's many virtues: her daughter-like devotion to and affection for her uncle Trajan right up until his death; her success in inspiring her husband's love; and her chaste mode of life through a long widowhood. Her beauty, her deference to her mother, and her own motherly kindness are also commemorated, as too her dutifulness to relatives, her cheerfulness and modesty, and her goodwill towards her son-in-law. Although incomplete, the document conveys a sense of genuine emotion and deep loss, especially in the designation of Matidia as the best of mothers-in-law and in Hadrian's reference to the cries of mourning for her heard from his female relatives. It is almost as if the emperor's voice can be heard and his sentiments truly

understood, and as a record of words Hadrian once actually spoke the document is vitally important, raising a biographical potential which Yourcenar evidently appreciated. In a passage that seemingly echoes the laudation, she has Hadrian speak of caring for Matidia when she returned from Trajan's Parthian campaign, fatally ill, having made the long journey to and from the eastern frontier in his entourage: "Ma belle-mère Matidie avait rapporté d'Orient les premiers symptômes d'une maladie mortelle: je m'ingéniai à la distraire de ses souffrances à l'aide de fêtes frugales, à enivrer innocemment d'un doigt de vin cette matrone aux naïvetés de jeune fille" (*MH* 368).[56]

Difficulties nonetheless obtrude. The precise occasion of Hadrian's speech is unknown. It is usually understood as a eulogy delivered when Matidia was consecrated on 23 December 119. She was indeed deified, and an imposing temple complete with a cult statue was later built for her worship at Rome in the Campus Martius.[57] Alternative contexts, however, are possible: either at her funeral earlier, or some weeks later when Hadrian sought permission from the senate for her formal deification, or later still at Tibur in association with the erection of a statue locally authorized there. (It was at Tibur that the inscription concerned was discovered; sixteenth-century drawings of it are all that now remain.)[58] It cannot be known, moreover, whether Hadrian was the author of the speech, or whether his words were written by a court attendant to whom the task of compiling a list of the ideal Roman woman's conventional characteristics had been delegated, the *simplicitas, moderatio*, and *modestia*, for instance, attributed to Trajan's wife Plotina in the panegyrical speech Pliny some years earlier addressed to Hadrian's predecessor (*Pan.* 83–4).[59] In his remarks to Marcus in *Mémoires* on the contemporary condition of Roman women, Hadrian astutely stresses the stereotypical character of funerary commemoration, rendering the biographical potential no more than that: "Sincères ou non, les éloges officiels et les inscriptions tombales continuent à prêter à nos matrones ces mêmes vertus d'industrie, de chasteté, d'austérité, qu'on exigeait d'elles sous la République" (*MH* 376).[60]

Similar considerations apply to other documents, both inscriptions and papyri, whether the famous records of the speeches Hadrian made to troops stationed on Rome's African borders; or the wealth of items recording his administrative decisions, such as this brief letter from 134, written to an association of Greek athletes in response to a request brought by a local delegate and subsequently preserved in inscriptional form to showcase the emperor's favour:

Imperator Caesar Trajan Hadrian Augustus, son of deified Trajan Parthicus, grandson of deified Nerva, *pontifex maximus*, holding tribunician power for the eighteenth time, three times consul, father of the fatherland, to the Athletic Association of the

Athletes Devoted to Heracles, greetings. Yes, a place where you wish I shall order to be given to you and a building to house your archives, and if you consider the alteration of your statutes necessary, that is up to you. The ambassador was Ulpius Domesticus. Farewell. May 5, from Rome.[61]

As is evident here, such items of public import were usually not initiated by the emperor but presented to him for resolution by a third party, a convention from which an authoritative petition-and-response model of Imperial government was put forward a generation ago. New discoveries continue to show the process in operation. An exceptionally full inscription from the province of Asia records a decree from Hadrian's visit in the spring and summer of 129 that responded to widespread complaints that soldiers travelling on official business were abusing their rights to requisition local facilities. It clarified the obligations of both local populations and soldiers to provide wagons, guides, meals, and accommodation, and it noted as possible complications military transportation of prisoners, of animals for the amphitheatre, and even of public moneys. An edict on a similar theme was issued from Maroneia in 132 as Hadrian returned from the war in Judaea: of concern were infractions affecting the Thracian or Macedonian coastal cities of Maroneia, Abdera, and Philippi. From the last months of his life, moreover, when ill, there is also a fragmentary letter to the citizens of the obscure Greek city of Naryka, preserved on a bronze stele now in the Louvre, that confirms the city's formal status: "I do not think that anyone will dispute that you have a *polis* and the rights of a *polis*."[62]

All such documents are written in the first person, and at first sight they seem again to convey a record of Hadrian's actual voice. But his precise role in formulating replies to requests for intervention is not as straightforward as the habit makes it seem. Every emperor had at his disposal a body of councillors from whom he sought advice on political and administrative matters, the so-called *consilium principis* (the term is a modern designation), an assemblage of leading senators and members of the equestrian order who might be formally styled the emperor's "friends" (*amici principis*), and who gathered on an ad hoc basis as circumstances permitted. Sometimes leading freedmen were included.[63] Decisions in the emperor's name followed deliberation, but as with the coinage it is impossible to specify the extent to which they express the emperor's personal views. For the practical management of communications various subordinates were available, above all the secretaries *ab epistulis latinis* and *ab epistulis graecis*, officials in charge of the emperor's formal correspondence whose responsibility it was to prepare items for his attention and to draft his responses.[64] The words of the Hadrianic documents that now remain, therefore, do not necessarily reflect the voice of Hadrian himself at all. It may be, as some scholars have urged, that a distinctive Hadrianic style of expression is perceptible; but if so his contributions to discussion and the manner in which final decisions were made remain beyond grasp. As Graham Burton has put it, "the extent to which all imperial pronouncements were substantially made by the emperor (with or without his advisers) rather than by lower ranking palatine officials whose decisions were then merely authenticated by the emperor" is a "much debated question."[65]

Marguerite Yourcenar was aware that Hadrian made administrative decisions after consultation with his advisers, and she integrated material from documents such as those just mentioned into *Mémoires*. Obviously, however, she did not know the new examples cited and the advances in factual knowledge they supply ("what happened"), the consequence being that inaccuracies in her narrative can be exposed with ramifications for biographical reconstruction.[66] Equally, however, the lacunose character of most documents, the result of environmental and human damage before reclamation, inevitably produces disputes about their contents and meaning, as initial attempts at restoration of uncertain or entirely missing sections of texts are followed by refinements and adjustments from experts. Their significance consequently can be far from plain. One view of Hadrian's letter to Naryka maintains that the city, aware of Hadrian's moribund status, tried to secure material benefits while it was still possible to do so: "Having failed to act previously out of poverty or simple inertia, Naryka may now have decided to despatch an embassy before it was too late." No basis, however, for poverty or inertia is offered to support this proposition, and another view counters that the purpose behind the document is entirely indeterminable.[67] Again, a communication addressed by Hadrian to Cyrene that seems to show the emperor "execrating Jews," as if a strongly antisemitic tendency were on display, depends on a calculated restoration of an incomplete section of text, and the attitude attributed to Hadrian is in fact a fancy of the restorer's imagination.[68] The result is that Burton's "much debated question" becomes increasingly more intractable. Certainly, to regard Rome's emperor as an essentially passive figure whose prime function was to resolve the piecemeal problems presented to him, as the petition-and-response model of governance holds, may need to be modified, and some scholars have no difficulty in identifying individual emperors' policies and programs or, specifically in Hadrian's case, in accommodating the model with personal initiative.[69] It remains true nonetheless that there is a singular absence of evidence to show emperors directly engaged in the articulation and execution of coherent, ideologically based objectives. Conclusions of this kind can be achieved only by assumption or projection, which by definition means entry into the land of invention. The only lead comes from Juvenal's (deliberately) cynical story of a consiliar debate held on the Palatine on what to do with a monstrously large fish once presented to the emperor Domitian, where the solution adopted follows the proposal of a single consiliar member with no input from the emperor at all (*Sat.* 4). The limitations for the recovery of biography are, once more, all too clear.[70] To learn from another age of the rich archives containing the personally written letters through which Toussaint L'Ouverture issued decrees and negotiated with French, British, and Spanish officials during his decade of predominance following the revolution in Saint Domingue, items that include the constitution of 1801 that Toussaint himself composed, is to throw into sobering relief the irremovable constraints by which Roman historians and biographers are bound.[71]

The reservations I have outlined apply equally to Hadrianic decisions attested in legal sources, the number of which is again relatively large. The rulings preserved in Justinian's *Digest* offer for instance a particularly important body of knowledge about a multiplicity of events on which the narrative sources are either brief, generalized, or silent.[72] Yourcenar again incorporated many of them into *Mémoires*, as with this slightly adapted detail that Hadrian once exiled a well-to-do woman who had excessively abused her female slaves: "On s'est récrié quand j'ai banni de Rome une patricienne riche et considérée qui maltraitait ses vieux esclaves" (*MH* 375).[73] The main point to grasp, however, is that Hadrian's legal actions cannot be assumed to express his personal views without comparable consideration of the deliberative mechanics of governance from which the actions followed. A strong argument has been made that signs of individuality, of Hadrian's "personal temperament," can be detected in the legal texts – "occasional outbursts of impatience and anger," especially "at any hint of corruption of justice," and "a confidence in his own ability to assess a witness' character from face to face questioning" – and admittedly it is tempting to think that Hadrian's voice can really be heard in decisions where first-person words are quoted, as in this example on the transfer to children of the property of a father under condemnation: "The number of Albinus' sons has made a favorable impression on me, since I prefer the empire to be increased by the children of men rather than by an abundance of money; and therefore I wish them to be granted their paternal property, which will very little enrich so many possessors, even if they take the whole" (*Dig.* 48.20.7.3).[74] Nevertheless, whether such quotations are genuinely authentic remains contentious – denial is strong in some quarters – and the degree of personal independence they reflect remains ambiguous given the context to which the rulings belong. Excerpted from earlier juristic writings chiefly of the Severan era, they are by definition selective, preserved by and within an altogether different cultural climate from that of Hadrian's era. The *Digest* was presented to an incipiently mediaeval world dominated by the New Rome of Constantinople in December, 533, and it has with reason been described, in culturally appropriate terms, as "a Christian lawbook, inspired by God, aided by God, and promulgated in the name of Christ."[75] The biographical value of its contents is again necessarily affected.

As for the evidence of papyri, if the eulogy of Matidia has already shown that documentary evidence can involve much more than matters of Imperial governance, a recently published item from Karanis in the Fayum presents a further illustration. It reveals an extraordinary "community prayer," as its editors call it, in which Hadrian is invoked as "saviour and benefactor of the world," and with his deified predecessors and many other divinities is solicited for a range of earthly blessings to be conferred on his subjects.[76] The honorific phrase is a glorious testament to the monarchical power and status the emperor was thought to enjoy in Egypt, the successor not only of Rome's previous emperors but also of the Ptolemaic kings of the Hellenistic age. The document was again of course unknown to Yourcenar, although it has a certain resonance with her exploration of the psychology of an emperor believed to have godlike power and status that becomes one of the most fascinating aspects of her novel. But she did know what is perhaps for present purposes the most eye-catching papyrus of all concerning Hadrian: another item from the Fayum that reveals a portion of an apparent copy of a personal letter (no less) that Hadrian wrote late in life to Antoninus Pius. The item, fragmentary and open to interpretation, is thought to be a school handwriting exercise, consisting of fifteen lines written in a master's hand followed by a pupil's copy of the first five lines. It seems to communicate a sense of Hadrian's impending end and refers to the deaths of his parents:

The Emperor Caesar Hadrian Augustus to his most esteemed Antoninus, greeting. Above all I want you to know that I am being released from my life neither before my time, nor unreasonably, nor piteously, nor unexpectedly, nor with faculties impaired, even though I shall almost seem, as I have found, to do injury to you who are by my side whenever I am in need of attendance, consoling and encouraging me to rest. From such considerations I am impelled to write to you as follows, not, by Zeus, as one who subtly devises a tedious account contrary to the truth, but rather making a simple and most accurate record of the facts themselves ... and he who was my father by birth fell ill and passed away as a private citizen at the age of forty, so that I have lived half as long again as my father, and have reached nearly the same age as my mother. ...[77]

Evidence from the Latin life and Cassius Dio indicates that Hadrian wrote an autobiography and gave instructions for its publication under the names of certain of his educated freedmen, one of whom was a certain Phlegon. This fragment has been seen as its beginning, and the inference accordingly drawn that the autobiography was composed in epistolary form. The theory is attractive, and is supported by a tradition of Roman autobiographical letter writing stretching back to the era of the middle Republic. It is also controversial and incapable of proof. The original letter may not have been Hadrian's autobiography at all, and Yourcenar herself, it happens, was somewhat sceptical of its authenticity.[78] Inevitably, however, she found the letter's contents too enticing to pass over, and folded them into her version of Hadrian's almost final thoughts: "Si mes calculs sont justes, ma mère est morte à peu près à l'âge où je suis arrivé aujourd'hui; ma vie a déjà été de moitié plus longue que celle de mon père, mort à quarante ans" (*MH* 514).[79]

My long list of doubts and cautions extends finally into the world of Hadrianic art and architecture. Here I emphasize at once that Yourcenar had a far more extensive knowledge of Roman material culture than most conventional ancient historians of her generation. As Michèle Goslar has shown in an important study, a deep knowledge of the portraits of Antinous permeates *Mémoires*, and an equal familiarity with those of Hadrian himself and the members of his immediate family circle is attested not least by Yourcenar's seven-page list, from December 1952, of possible illustrations for the edition of the novel to be published by Le Club du meilleur livre. The care, moreover, with which illustrations were selected for the many successive editions of the novel in order to vivify its characters has been well revealed by Alexandre Terneuil.[80] As with numismatic studies, however, within specialist scholarship there are devastatingly sobering observations that promptly undermine whatever first impressions might be formed about portraiture's historical value. "We know nothing," Klaus Fittschen has said for instance, "about the workshops that produced portraits of emperors and their families, or, for that matter, those of private individuals. We know not one of the artists who designed the portrait types and nothing about the organization of the workshops in Rome and the provinces where the copies were made or their relationship to the emperor and 'court sculptor'."[81] If that judgment is even approximately true, how are historians and biographers of Hadrian then to proceed? At times, scholars have regularly taken the representations of Hadrian's beard to be material evidence of his devotion to Hellenism, but apart from the fact that he was not the first emperor to be shown with a beard at all, understanding of what his philhellenism might mean and how it might be culturally defined have become issues more freighted than they once seemed.[82]

Similar quandaries surround the Villa at Tivoli, which with its 900 rooms and connecting corridors, an enormous architectural and aesthetic complex covering perhaps 140 hectares in the Tiburtine hills, is one of the greatest monuments of and to Hadrian's reign. An inspirational visit to the site when she was just twenty years of age was one of the reasons why Yourcenar first felt herself drawn to Hadrian (*YO* 151), and it is here of course that she situates Hadrian when her novel begins.[83] The site, some 28 km from Rome, is both evocative and mysterious, its appeal impressively captured by the gifted travel writer Elizabeth Speller:

A visit to the luminous ruins of Hadrian's villa is one of the most delightful ways of spending time in or around Rome. Shady avenues between cypresses, olive groves and pools of silent water are interrupted by empty fountain bowls and vacant plinths, haunting and potent architectural echoes of magnificence. It is easy to scramble freely through empty doorways and over fallen stone to enter one small, roofless space after another. Inner courtyards contain broken brick and wild flowers, while broad steps and colonnades now lead into ploughed fields and wide views of the Campagna. Arches of long-dismantled public rooms provide shade at midday, and here and there a mosaic pavement or a still attached fragment of porphyry provides a visual echo of what once glittered on this spot. In some more restored parts of the complex, replica statues recreate the second-century environs, but mostly the remains are tantalising in what they hint at. That they are still so substantial after so long is testament to Hadrian's demands for excellence in structure as well as style.[84]

Despite its fame, however, the Villa appears in the historical literary sources only once, in a section of the Latin life stating that Hadrian gave the names of provinces and famous places to its various elements (*HA Hadr.* 26.5). It is tempting, as my quotation and the Latin text both suggest, to see in the complex the personal influence and tastes of Hadrian himself, and perhaps even the very planning of the Villa. Many academic discussions succumb, especially since Hadrian is credited in the tradition with architectural interests. To believe otherwise would seem to defy all sense. To do so, however, is again to take a leap of faith. For strictly speaking, Hadrian's role in the design, construction, and decoration of the Villa can only be a matter of speculation, and in these remarks from expert authorities, I am struck by the guardedness that accompanies their belief that the Villa must, somehow, have been due to Hadrian's initiative:

Hadrian built not so much out of self-esteem as from a lively, genuine concern for the art of architecture ... The Villa offered greater opportunities for direct expression than most of his urban monuments, and *whatever his role* in planning individual

Villa buildings, the frequent changes made during construction and the alterations made to structures thought finished were *surely* the result of his interventions and instructions. His overall concept of the Villa *may* have formed gradually as he came to envisage it as a statement of his world, a distillation in art and architecture of its culture.[85]

As much as with the modern visitor, the magic of Tivoli seduced Yourcenar's imagination, and it was natural therefore that she should see Hadrian's personal choices displayed in its every decoration: "le jaspe vert comme les profondeurs marines, le porphyre grenu comme la chair, le basalte, la morne obsidienne. Le rouge dense des tentures s'ornait de broderies de plus en plus savantes; les mosaïques des pavements ou des murailles n'étaient jamais assez mordorées, assez blanches, ou assez sombres" (*MH* 386). It is again understandable that she did so.[86]

IV

The limitations of evidence I have traced (or belaboured) are obstacles faced by every historian or biographer of Hadrian. All that exists from which to reconstitute his life are, as Marguerite Yourcenar herself put it, "des fragments de réel" (*CNOR* 866). This reality is improbably symbolized by the Tel Shalem statue, the head of which is a genuine likeness of Hadrian, but the body a recycled version of a predecessor, perhaps a Hellenistic monarch.[87] Whether therefore a true biography of Hadrian is at all a viable proposition is a formidable question. The sources that remain allow many events that occurred during his lifetime to be catalogued, but in their insufficiency, uncertainty, partiality, and even in some respects, strangely, their abundance, the sources reveal little of how Hadrian experienced those events, or of the extent to which he was engaged with, or responsible for, or otherwise affected by them. By ordinary methods and procedures, a comprehensive life history that recovers the real man is beyond reach. Hadrian cannot be known in ways the modern biographical subjects to whom I earlier referred can be known.

How do conventional classical historians respond to this dilemma? I conclude my survey by drawing attention to a number of statements that illustrate how much of what is said depends on inference and speculation. There is, in fact, no alternative but to write of Hadrian in terms of "possibles" and "probablies," with consequences that are self-evident: authorial subjectivity, disagreements over definitions of the possible, the probable and the indefinable boundaries in between, and much that is inventive. Certain details can be established without controversy – Hadrian was born on 24 January 76 and died on 10 July 138 – but they are relatively few. Consider for the sake of illustrating reactions the following quotations:

1. Then presently Hadrian cast loose the shackles which fastened him to Rome. Whether in some spirit of joyous adventure, or in a mood of reaction from the monotony of administration, or again in the faithful discharge of his duty to the Empire as he realized this, the Emperor left Rome and Italy, and began his long series of travels round the many lands which owned his sway.
2. Très classique, mais révélatrice pour la sensibilité d'Hadrien, la *laudatio* suit le partage "cicéronien" et traditionnel entre l'éloge des *fortuita* et l'éloge des *virtutes*.
3. [Hadrian] wished to be seen as a new Augustus. Such a notion had clearly been in his mind for some time.
4. Pictorially, Hadrian expressed his ecumenical view of the Empire through the personification of provinces. Towns, landscapes and rivers were also admitted to this gallery, the idea being that every member is important in the organization of the new nation state.
5. [Hadrian] was driven by a desire to establish his family permanently as the third imperial dynasty of Rome, worthy successors of the earlier Julio-Claudians and Flavians.
6. Hadrian and he may have met when Antinous was a youthful teenager when the emperor toured the area in 123 AD, by now in his mid forties. If so, their relationship would have lasted for several years. Hadrian will doubtless have been attracted by Antinous' lushly sensual features.[88]

Evidently enough, scholars have never hesitated to identify aspects of Hadrian's thinking and personality that motivated the accomplishments with which he is credited. The policies he initiated and his innermost thoughts can be detailed without compunction. As stated at the beginning of this chapter, Hadrian seems to be easily accessible. (Hundreds of other examples could be listed.) And yet all of these statements are problematic. The first posits three possible motives that may have governed Hadrian's decision to undertake the last of his provincial tours; but as far as I am aware there is no evidence for the first two, while the third is an interpretative inference from slender hints detectable in the two main narrative sources. That Hadrian may have found Rome "shackling" is impossible to know. The second statement concerns the *Laudatio Matidiae*. It takes Hadrian's authorship of the speech for granted and its content as a reflection of his character. The vulnerability of both assumptions goes unrecognized. The third item is a confident statement on Hadrian's thinking at a time when a change was made in his titulature on the coinage from IMP[ERATOR] CAESAR TRAIANUS HADRIANUS AUG[USTUS] to HADRIANUS AUGUSTUS. No evidence exists, however, to show who was responsible for the change, and the thoughts attributed to Hadrian consequently have no firm authority. Likewise in the next example, an assertion concerning the "province series" of coins and representations of Rome's provinces in statuary later incorporated into a temple in Rome built in Hadrian's honour by Antoninus Pius: the presupposition that Hadrian thought in terms of a "nation state" is patently anachronistic. The fifth example again takes its reader deep into Hadrian's mind, with a motive brought forward to explain his building activities in Rome and the provinces. The logical connection between the two is far from certain, however, and the motive itself again an inference only. The final extract comes from a discussion of Hadrian's relationship with Antinous, with a first encounter posited when Hadrian was travelling through Bithynia. The uses of the subjunctive mood are enough to show its hypothetical nature, and there is in any case no indication in classical texts of what Hadrian thought of Antinous's appearance, so that any physical attraction he might have felt is irrecoverable. Altogether the statement depends on unverifiable assumptions that the extant sculptures give faithful likenesses of Antinous, and that Hadrian shared the implicit responses to them of the modern author. In all these cases, it is clear, judgment depends on imagination, and there can be no quarrel with this: conjecture is a necessary part of the ancient historian's stock-in-trade. All the same, it must be understood that conjecture comes very close to fiction, and exactly where the line between the historically plausible and the purely imaginary is to be drawn is an issue to which no all-encompassing answer can be given. Conjecture that some authorities claim as rational or legitimate may seem to other scholars completely irrational or illegitimate, and for the establishment of "facts" much depends in practice on powers of persuasion.[89]

Take for example a theory concerning a twelve-line funerary epigram found on a Greek inscription at Rome. The poem celebrates a certain Amazaspos, who is said to have been a brother of Rome's client-king Mithridates of Iberia, and to have died at Nisibis while accompanying an Italian leader on campaign against Parthia. Its final line describes him as "like unto modest maidens." The poem's author is unknown. But it has been ascribed to Hadrian due to its metrical comparability with other verses he wrote, and, in view of its last line, to what is called his "penchant … for handsome orientals" [sic]. The Italian leader accordingly must be Trajan, the campaign his war against the Parthians, and Amazaspos's death the result of military convulsions at Nisibis, if not of disease, during the military expedition. Hadrian's authorship, moreover, would account for the public display of the poem at Rome and remind its readers of the price paid for Trajan's unfortunate attempt to expand Rome's frontiers.[90] The case is clearly attractive: the number of Hadrian's extant poems is small, the temptation to find more and to untangle their topical allusiveness irresistible. And yet, equally clearly, the line here between informed speculation and total fiction has almost entirely disappeared, and whether new facts have indeed been established remains an open question.

This overall issue is particularly evident in the standard biography of Hadrian, in which wide-ranging associations are frequently introduced in order to illuminate the basic outline of Hadrian's life course. Anthony Birley suggests that Hadrian in his maturity retained childhood memories of the military victory won in Britain by the Roman general Cn. Julius Agricola at the battle of Mons Graupius in the year 83. And perhaps he did. He was seven years old at the time. He may also have taken note, when reading Cicero as a boy in school at Rome, of an aberrant provincial governor from long ago named C. Fabius Hadrianus in view of the name they shared.[91] Yet in both cases the possible has no support in any extant record – very little is known in fact of Hadrian's childhood – and reconstructive suggestions of this kind might be thought little different in effect from a novelist's imaginings: Yourcenar has her Hadrian recollect that the story of Fabius Hadrianus belonged to the dim and distant family lore to which he was exposed as a boy in Spain, which on the face of things seems just as likely (MH 309). Much indeed of what any modern imperial biographer writes has to be hedged with caveats ("possibly," "probably," "doubtless"), or be expressed in conditional language ("would have," "could have," "might have"), the consequence being that the external record of the subject's life is often patchy, uncertain, far from complete.[92] Ronald Syme's studies of Hadrian centred predominantly on public matters: politics, governance, the acquisition and exercise of imperial authority – what Syme called "the power." In many contexts, however, unambiguous pronouncements were made on Hadrian's personality and psychology that, displaying the biographer's interests, simultaneously crystallize the dilemma of how to separate fact from fiction.[93] The list that follows, select but representative, begins with quotations from the monumental *Tacitus* of 1958, at first comparing Hadrian with Trajan, and then moves to examples from the several studies cited earlier:

1. Hadrian was hampered by a tortuous character, a keen intellect, and an intensive education.
2. Hadrian comported himself with ease as any man's equal.
3. Hadrian's character was various and peculiar. Of a wondrous native aptitude, he grasped with ease and avidity all arts, all sciences.

4. Hadrian was devoured by an insatiable curiosity for strange lands and alien habits.

5. Hadrian, as his acts and journeys appear to show, had for his task to assess, codify, and regulate the world-empire.

6. Hadrian was moody and capricious, even rancorous; and in the last biennium of his life angry and erratic, broken in health, and tortured by the vexatious problem of the succession.

7. He paraded hostility to distinctions of nation or class, he took delight in converse with persons of low degree ... Above all, he disliked pomp and pretension.[94]

Once more these statements may all be true. But if so they are, I think, more intuitively than empirically true, attributable perhaps to a distinctive ability to divine – a word Syme frequently used – what lay buried in, or beneath, the historical record. In one study the "real person" discovered is an especially intriguing specimen: "not a hero or a villain, not a conventional artefact or a political projection. In short, something like a character in a modern novel."[95] The image perceived is encapsulated in this generic characterisation of a stereotypically Oxonian "intellectual":

He is curious and conceited, instable and petulant; against birth and class, authority and tradition. He dabbles in the arts, he admires the beauties of nature. A cosmopolitan by his tastes, he is devoted to foreign travel; he detests nationalism, militarism, and the cult of power; and he will defend 'les droits de l'homme' or the cause of universal peace.[96]

Syme's intuitive capacity sometimes extended to much fuller affirmations, exemplified best of all in the present context by the impostor he believed to be the author of the *Historia Augusta* as revealed in his final book on the subject.[97] The man emerges as a figure as *varius, multiplex, multiformis* as Hadrian ever was or might have been: clever, versatile, erudite, bookish, dishonest, elusive, humorous, alert, careless, cynical, gay, unscrupulous, resourceful, agile, capricious, ingenious.[98] He was a "scholar, scholiast and parodist" who claimed not to be a historian but to be writing simply to "furnish the facts of history"; and if writing in a pedestrian style, he was a "word-fancier" all the same, and a "literary gentleman" capable of rhetorical and even elegant writing with a taste for "the curious and the exotic" but "double-faced in his mockery." Above all, he was mendacious, hiding behind a mask, or several masks, which he gently lifted just once to reveal the humour that underlies all his work. He relished "invention and audacity," both of which increased as his work progressed, so that by the end he has become "a master in the art of historical fiction." He is not named, but his social rank is not in doubt: not from the top draw, but a "grammarian, librarian, or the like."[99] A figure therefore intimately knowable and an obviously living presence, yet one who to ordinary mortals might seem a figment of a fertile imagination, no matter how persuasively presented. (There is no independent evidence, recall, to prove that the rogue biographer ever existed.) A permeable barrier emerges between history and fiction, one implicit consequence being perhaps that a novelist in full control of the historical tradition might well be capable of painting a portrait of a Roman emperor as convincing as that of a percipient historian. And it happens that to correspondents and interviewers alike, Yourcenar comparably described Hadrian as "very intelligent," spoke of his "intellectual qualities," called him an "intellectualised Greco-Roman," and on one occasion at least called him simply an "intellectual" (with the word suitably placed in guillemets).[100] She observed once, commenting on the absence of detail in the historical sources on Hadrian's emotional life, how from time to time a detail from a text caught the eye and allowed her to "sense" Hadrian as he must actually have been: "il y a toujours ce moment unique où un détail quelconque accroche, et nous fait sentir le personnage tel qu'il a dû être" (*PV* 160). The divinatory convergence is striking.

V

My intention in this chapter has been not to lament the paucity of sources from which investigation proceeds, as is often the case in ancient history, but to demonstrate that recovery of the life of Hadrian depends on many items of evidence from which something can be learned, all of which in the absence of any reliable contemporary guiding narrative are far from straightforward in what they convey. (The notion, incidentally, that any source remaining from antiquity is a contemporary source and that the portrait of Hadrian therefore inherently accurate, as Yourcenarian scholarship sometimes assumes, must obviously be set aside.)[101] This means that what can be said about Hadrian objectively and incontestably is minimal. The materials available constitute a source tradition, to which historians and biographers have to respond by drawing inferences and exercising the imagination. But where the boundaries of inference and imagination should be fixed is a problem to which there is no easy, no definitive solution. The tradition in and of itself does not to my mind communicate an unquestionably clear image of Hadrian or an unquestionably clear Hadrianic vision of empire. But the examples I have given show that historians and biographers are not at all reluctant to write of both Hadrian's personality and his actions and to ascribe to him qualities, motivations and initiatives with a surprising degree of assurance.

The fragility of the source tradition cannot be overstated. Its core comprises two meagre written sources, one seemingly the work of an unidentifiable author writing at least two hundred years after Hadrian's death for reasons no longer discernible, the other an abridgment in the main of a lost historical narrative made by an obscure monk in Constantinople almost a millennium later. The supplementary materials in turn involve hypotheses about undocumented authors, disputable restorations of fragmentary documents, and even ignorance at times of how some items came into being at all. A modern biographer of Queen Victoria could hardly comprehend such a state of affairs, and might well wonder how Hadrian, "the most ambiguous figure among the last of the *principes*" as he has been called, can ever be truly found. Simply put, prospects for knowing "the real man" are dim.[102]

In describing its components, I have also wanted to give brief indications of how Marguerite Yourcenar the novelist responded to the source tradition, which as far as I can tell she knew as well as any classical scholar. She cannot have known items that have come to light since 1951, as I have said; but her claim to have read all the evidence on Hadrian up until then was not an idle boast, and in painting her portrait she was more sensitive than most scholars of her generation to the value of exploiting evidence from Roman art and architecture. She was in addition as confident as any academician that her portrait was authentic, and the reasons for her confidence, together with the ways in which she filled the biographical vacuum the source tradition leaves, will become increasingly apparent as the content of her novel is further explored. At this juncture, however, it is not evident to me that in the project of recovering Hadrian the findings of historians, even the most reputable and most admired historians, should by definition be privileged over those of an accomplished prose-poet. Given the inescapable weakness of the foundations, any attempt to present a life of Hadrian is necessarily an exercise in invention – the fictive – an exercise Yourcenar likened to the art of the mosaicist who reassembles a portrait from scattered *tesserae* (*AN* 1031). The only measure of success is whether the assemblage created is complete and colourful enough to be convincing.

3

Authenticity Filtered

L'authenticité est une chose, la véracité en est une autre.

Marguerite Yourcenar

I

Lytton Strachey understood what Plutarch had long since proved, that biography does not have to follow the rigid cradle-to-grave format of much modern biography. The life story can be told, and character be illustrated, in diverse and chronologically creative ways. By and large, however, biographers of Roman emperors have tended to ignore the organizational choices available to them, preferring in all its predictability the mechanical womb-to-tomb model as a matter of course.[1] In Hadrian's case, the question of structure requires a particularly decisive response to the far from adequate base of materials from which the biographical attempt is to be made, and, a challenging prospect, a compelling strategy on how to bring the biographical subject to life. It bears repeating that there is a difference between cataloguing a succession of events that occurred during Hadrian's lifetime with which he can be associated, and portraying a personality both impacted by and having an impact upon those events, especially for the years of his reign when the disclosure of underlying impulses and motives for actions taken might be considered essential. It cannot be assumed that Hadrian was responsible for every development attributed to him in the source tradition, or that every personal anecdote the tradition contains is accurate.

Yourcenar knew the historical tradition for what it was, signalling its deficiency when once referring to Antinous with the qualifying phrase, "tel que la tradition nous le présente" (*HZ* 158), and wondering despondently on another occasion, irked by the mistakes a publicist had made in the details of her own biography, about the reliability of the chroniclers on whom the tradition depends (*HZ* 495).[2] The perennial problem had to be confronted that the shortcomings of the sources preclude provable connections between the actions recorded and the mind of the individual associated with them, to which her response was to choose autobiography as her biographical mode, a move that brought several advantages. It allowed Hadrian to speak through the filter of memories as hazy and partial as the tradition itself, with events recounted imprecisely but not necessarily inaccurately (memory, after all, is inherently selective and prone in later life to deteriorate). It short-circuited the problem of how decisions of imperial governance were made, permitting Hadrian to claim all the successes of his reign as his own. And it eliminated any possibility of reproach for errors in the story as he told it, since his perspective alone was all that mattered. The choice reflects the insight Yourcenar implicitly attributed to him that no biographer will ever fully know his subject any more than Plutarch had fully known Alexander (*MH* 303).[3]

From the outset, as he dwells on what he perceives to be the shapeless trajectory of his life, Hadrian is sensitive to memory's deceptiveness. Memory, he suggests, can give form to life, especially to the heroic life; but within his own non-heroic past he finds no clear and understandable pattern, only a chaotic lurching from one extreme to another. He can barely identify or define himself, and what he sees is due solely to the influence of contingency. To some degree his past actions signify who he is, both in his own and others' perception; but there is an unfathomable disconnect between his actions and his true self, as a constant need for self-examination and self-accountability proves. Accomplishments have occupied only a fraction of his life, vague wishes and desires the rest, and making sense of it all is illusory (*MH* 304–6).[4] Such thoughts reflect in effect the indeterminacy of the historical tradition, and as Hadrian tells his story there are frequent reminders of memory's fallibility: time dims or erases recollections altogether, or, in the case of Antinous, suffuses many memories into a fresco-like composite as the experiences of many years become uncontrollably intermingled. Memories in their evanescence are like "des boucles de fumée" or "les bulles d'air irisées d'un jeu d'enfant" (*MH* 335).[5] In which of course there is an essential plausibility for any epoch. In antiquity, Roman education duly placed a heavy premium on the training of memory, and the historical Hadrian could well in early life have been schooled in the use of a device such as the memory palace the expert Quintilian describes in his educational treatise. (Hadrian's memory was reputed to have been keen.) Yet as Quintilian well knew, individual capacities varied, and with age degradation was to be expected (*Inst.* 11.2.6–51).[6]

If then Yourcenar's autobiographical strategy turned the source tradition's imperfections to novelistic advantage, rendering precision of detail less important than an overall impression of the course of Hadrian's life, at the same time she was preoccupied with accuracy, claiming in the *Note* faithfulness to the facts of Hadrian's life (*OR* 543: "fidélité aux faits"). As noted earlier, she explained her purpose in her letter to F.C. Grant, addressing the criticisms of *Mémoires* he had raised despite his overall admiration for her book. She had conducted the fullest research possible to prepare for her book, but it had not been her intention to write a historical biography in the conventional sense of the term, and still less to use Hadrian as a vehicle for offering a comprehensive picture of second-century life and manners in any academic sense:

Mon désir au contraire était de profiter de nos connaissances historiques d'aujourd'hui pour tenter, *mutatis mutandis*, l'équivalent de certaines grandes reconstructions poétiques de l'histoire faites par des poètes du passé; pour retrouver en somme, s'il se pouvait, la poésie humaine de l'histoire, que nous risquons d'ensevelir de nos jours sous nos fac-similés et nos fiches. Tous les faits historiques utilisés dans les *Mémoires d'Hadrien* avaient donc été, non certes altérés ou changés, mais soumis à cette particulière perspective. (*HZ* II 57)

On the contrary, my wish was to benefit from modern historical knowledge in order to attempt, *mutatis mutandis*, the equivalent of certain great poetic historical reconstructions carried out by poets of the past; in sum, to rediscover if possible the human poetry of history, which we risk burying today under our facsimiles and index cards. All the historical facts used in the *Memoirs of Hadrian* have accordingly been, not indeed altered or changed, but subjected to this particular perspective.

What emerges is a commitment to historical truth, but a distinctive kind of truth, a poetically inspired human truth imaginatively recovered that transcends the constraints of both the historical tradition and the conventional practices of history. Here I consider certain sociocultural aspects of that truth, by which I mean elements of the novel clearly consistent with cultural idioms and patterns of social behaviour in the high Imperial age, that together constitute a first order of authenticity. It may not have been Yourcenar's intent to offer a comprehensive picture of Roman life and manners in Hadrian's era, but there is much in the novel regardless that contributes to its biographical success through evocation of the particularities of a lost age. I begin with some remarks on the type of language the novel adopts, move next to topics of relevant affirmation, but stress throughout the singularity of Yourcenar's reconstruction.[7]

II

Peu à peu, cette lettre commencée pour t'informer des progrès de mon mal est devenue le délassement d'un homme qui n'a plus l'énergie nécessaire pour s'appliquer
longuement aux affaires d'État, la méditation écrite d'un malade qui donne audience
à ses souvenirs. Je me propose maintenant davantage: j'ai formé le projet de te rac-
onter ma vie. À coup sûr, j'ai composé l'an dernier un compte rendu officiel de mes
actes, en tête duquel mon secrétaire Phlégon a mis son nom. J'y ai menti le moins possible. L'intérêt public et la décence m'ont forcé néamoins à réarranger certains faits.
La vérité que j'entends exposer ici n'est pas particulièrement scandaleuse, ou ne l'est
qu'au degré où toute vérité fait scandale. (*MH* 301)

Little by little this letter, begun in order to tell you of the progress of my illness, has
become the diversion of a man who no longer has the energy required for continued
application to affairs of state; it has become, in fact, the written meditation of a sick
man who holds audience with his memories. I propose now to do more than this: I
have formed a project for telling you about my life. To be sure, last year I composed
an official summary of my career, to which my secretary Phlegon gave his name. I
told as few lies therein as possible; regard for public interest and decency forced me
nevertheless to modify certain facts. The truth which I intend to set forth here is not
particularly scandalous, or is so only to the degree that any truth creates a scandal.

Yourcenar clearly knew the evidence attributing an autobiography to
Hadrian apparently made public under the name of his freedman Phlegon.
Her compositional method has by definition therefore something of the
inherently realistic about it. Criticism that the form of *Mémoires* lacks
validity because Hadrian did not write an autobiography is impermis-
sible.[8] The work is attested by the *Historia Augusta* and the epitome of
Cassius Dio, and seems to have comprised at least two books that contained information on Hadrian's Italic ancestry, provided the detail that
he followed at one stage of life the example of Trajan's heavy drinking,
and included a record of predictions when tribune of the *plebs* that he
would one day rise to the emperorship. There are also two overtly political
assertions: Hadrian was not responsible for the deaths of four consulars
who were executed at the beginning of his reign, while the emperor Titus,
much earlier, had poisoned his father Vespasian.[9] Scholars agree that the
work was apologetic in nature and belongs to the last portion of Hadrian's
life, especially if identified with the papyrus fragment from the Fayum
to which earlier reference has been made.[10] The details here on Hadrian's
minimal obfuscation of the truth and regard for propriety are consistent
with this presumption.

One feature that requires special notice is the absence of direct speech in the autobiography Hadrian composes. In her essay *Ton et langage dans le roman historique*, Yourcenar stated her strong belief that any attempt to replicate the manner of everyday diction in Roman antiquity was impossible, given that the formality of extant Latin literature allows little of what ordinary conversational language was like to be known. In the interests of accuracy, therefore, the novel avoids direct speech altogether, except that Hadrian himself "speaks" through his writing in a carefully cultivated form to which Yourcenar gave the name *"oratio togata."* She meant by this a dignified style – "mi-narratif, mi-méditatif" – that allowed the emperor both to tell his life story and to meditate upon it, but a style, or voice, that excluded immediate reactions to events. It was derived from her study of Greek and Latin prose authors and the putative remains of Hadrian's own words, and was meant to validate the content of Hadrian's composition. She recognized that she had not succeeded in capturing the tone and timbre of Hadrian's voice consistently, and that French idioms inevitably obtruded; but authenticity of expression in securing "the portrait of a voice" was her aim despite the difficulties involved.[11] The kernel of the essay had been expressed much earlier in a letter from February 1953 in which Yourcenar, casting herself in the role of Hadrian's amanuensis, assumed that the man whose memoirs she was transcribing would have dictated them to her, and that the bilingual emperor would sometimes have addressed her in Greek and sometimes in Latin (*HZ* 226–7). In the essay itself, she was straightforward about her intent: "Il ne s'agissait pas, bien entendu, d'imiter ici César et là Sénèque, puis plus loin Marc Aurèle, mais d'obtenir d'eux un calibre, un rythme, l'équivalent du rectangle d'étoffe qu'on drape ensuite à son gré sur le modèle nu" (*TGS* 294).[12]

The degree to which success was, or is, achieved, is a matter of taste and judgment. A commentator who regards the historical novel as a completely fallacious enterprise has dismissed Yourcenar's venture as an exercise in futility because *oratio togata* is a form of speech accessible only in writing.[13] But to believe that toga'd speech is a genuinely historical type of Latin discourse is an error, and to take *Mémoires* as representative of the historical novel at large trivializes its classical source foundations. The epistolary form of *Mémoires* demands in any case a written character, and the good sense of the decision to avoid dialogue is easily demonstrable. The contrast presented by Gore Vidal's acclaimed *Julian* (1962), in which conversations appear with expressions that no Roman, even in the fourth century, could ever have uttered, is self-evidently more than enough to prove the wisdom of Yourcenar's strategy. ("He's got an herb the Persians use" is not how I imagine Julian or anyone close to him can ever have actually spoken.)

Yourcenar rightly perceived that Latin literature has left nothing uncontroversially imitable from which to reproduce conversational speech, and she was as sensitive to the danger of vocal anachronism as she was to that of having his accomplishments construed in contemporary terms of liberalism or pacificism (*HZ* III 280).[14] She came to believe, however, that his voice could indeed be heard: "Si j'ai choisi d'écrire ces *Mémoires d'Hadrien* à la première personne, c'est pour me passer le plus possible de tout intermédiaire, fût-ce de moi-même. Hadrien pouvait parler de sa vie plus fermement et plus subtilement que moi" (*CNMH* 527).[15] Historians might well be sceptical about the claim, but as it is Hadrian's voice convinces if only for its consistency and regard for propriety.

Historians might equally wonder about the immense elaboration *Mémoires* represents of the information now remaining from the original autobiography associated with Phlegon. Two discussions that again inject issues of the fictive give reason for pause. Ronald Syme understood Hadrian's work to be not merely apologetic but deliberately mendacious. No Roman emperor ever told the truth in an autobiography, and because Suetonius described Tiberius's earlier, no longer extant, specimen as brief and succinct, so was that of Hadrian. It included details moreover in the *Historia Augusta* other than those already cited (they could be divined): an astrologer's prediction that Hadrian would become emperor; a report that Hadrian was not responsible for the death of the exiled senator C. Calpurnius Crassus Frugi; a story that his brother-in-law L. Julius Servianus attempted to sabotage Hadrian when delivering news of the death of Nerva to Trajan in Germany; and a statement on Trajan's lukewarm support of the marriage to Sabina (recorded supposedly by Marius Maximus but originally given in the autobiography). In addition, Hadrian's mental state was at times detectable: the anecdote concerning Julius Servianus was malicious, and so revealed "the condition of Hadrian's mind towards the end." All of which, I think, is breathtaking in its confidence.[16] In turn, Anthony Birley maintained that details in the Latin life on his Italic origins register a response by Hadrian to criticism that he was a provincial parvenu who owed his rise to power only to his connection to Trajan; that its story of Hadrian's loss of his tribune's cloak, an omen somehow of his future accession, illustrates anxieties he felt regarding the prospect of attaining supreme power; and that the reason given for the execution of the four consulars – they had plotted against him – was due to Hadrian's need to guarantee the senate's approval of the arrangements made for the succession late in the reign. All three propositions share a comparable assumption that Hadrian's state of mind at any point of his life can be discovered, the troublesome nature of the Latin life notwithstanding.[17]

In this context of imaginative speculation, where fact and fiction are indistinguishable, and no matter whether the Fayum papyrus was its immediate inspiration, Yourcenar's decision to create an autobiography in epistolary form is inherently defensible, and at a minimum her construction of *oratio togata* as a suitable style of Roman speaking is testimony to her pursuit of historical authenticity. A conscious effort was made to capture Hadrian's manner of speech from close examination of historical evidence, and the character of what she contrived converges particularly well with the recollection of Cornelius Fronto that in his formal speech Hadrian had affected an old-fashioned eloquence (2.138). She was pleased, unsurprisingly, to receive compliments on her solution to the stylistic problems composition of her book had presented.[18]

III

Je suis descendu ce matin chez mon médecin Hermogène, qui vient de rentrer à la Villa après un assez long voyage en Asie. L'examen devait se faire à jeun: nous avions pris rendez-vous pour les premières heures de la matinée. Je me suis couché sur un lit après m'être dépouillé de mon manteau et de ma tunique. Je t'épargne des détails qui te seraient aussi désagréables qu'à moi-même, et la description du corps d'un homme qui avance en âge et s'apprête à mourir d'une hydropisie du cœur. Disons seulement que j'ai toussé, respiré, et retenu mon souffle selon les indications d'Hermogène, alarmé malgré lui par les progrès si rapides du mal, et prêt à en rejeter le blâme sur le jeune Iollas qui m'a soigné en son absence. Il est difficile de rester empereur en présence d'un médecin, et difficile aussi de garder sa qualité d'homme. L'œil du practicien ne voyait en moi qu'un monceau d'humeurs, triste amalgame de lymphe et de sang. (*MH* 287)

Today I went to see my physician Hermogenes, who has just returned to the Villa from a rather long journey in Asia. No food could be taken before the examination, so we had made the appointment for the early morning hours. I took off my cloak and tunic and lay down on a couch. I spare you details which would be as disagreeable to you as to me, the description of the body of a man who is growing old, and is about to die of a dropsical heart. Let us say only that I coughed, inhaled, and held my breath according to Hermogenes' directions. He was alarmed in spite of himself, by the rapid progress of the disease, and was inclined to throw the blame on young Iollas, who has attended me during his absence. It is difficult to remain an emperor in presence of a physician, and difficult even to keep one's essential quality as a man. The professional eye saw in me only a mass of humors, a sorry mixture of blood and lymph.

So the letter begins. The medical examination to which Hadrian refers is a prelude to his reflections on the body to come. It is of immediate interest, however, in the way it encapsulates a crucial aspect of comportment of the high Imperial age, a preoccupation among the socially elite with matters of physical health and well-being. The most striking, or most notorious, illustration of the disposition comes in the record of Aelius Aristides in his *Sacred Tales* of the multifarious symptoms that from the 140s onwards caused him, for almost thirty years, intermittent periods of pain both physical and mental. Aristides describes the anguish of illness in immense detail, offsetting his descriptions with expressions of the relief provided by the healing intervention of Asclepius, whose instructions, received through the technique of incubation in the god's temple at Pergamum, he scrupulously followed – until a further onset of distress eventuated in an incessant cycle of torment and recovery. His complaints, chiefly respiratory and intestinal, it seems, defy precise definition. But this relatively brief extract shows the typical grimness of his afflictions:

And shortly thereafter my intestines swelled, I trembled with cold, shivering ran through all my body, and my breath was impeded. And the doctors produced purges, and I was purged for two days, by drinking squirting cucumber, until finally there was a bloody discharge. And fevers attacked me, and now everything was despaired of, and there was not any hope even for my survival. And finally the doctors made an incision, beginning from my chest all the way down to the bladder. And when the cupping instruments were applied, my breathing was completely stopped, and a pain, numbing and impossible to bear, passed through me and everything was smeared with blood, and I was excessively purged. And I felt as if my intestines were cold and hanging out, and the difficulty in my respiration was intensified. And I did not know what to do, for in the midst of taking food and of talking, there was an attack, and I thought that I must choke. And my other physical debilities were in proportion to these things. Antidotes and various other things were given in vain. (2.62–4)[19]

The physical maladies apart, Aristides's record also itemizes the many strange dreams he experienced during incubation, and in view therefore of what could be regarded as psychosomatic illness and hypochondria, his case history figured prominently in E.R. Dodds's influential assessment of the high Imperial age as "an age of anxiety." In turn, he has been thought to provide evidence of a second-century cultural shift, encouraged by theories of self-fashioning, that induced individuals to construct images of themselves as suffering patients in discourses of highly subjective self-representation; and a new interest in the body and in medicine has been advanced, perhaps more convincingly, as a defining feature of the now prominent intellectual movement commonly called the Second Sophistic. In *Mémoires*, notably, Hadrian happens to characterize Favorinus of Arelate, one of the movement's most flamboyant exemplars, as a hypochondriac as obsessed with his health as a besotted lover (*MH* 383).[20] Plutarch, it happens, had judged it worthwhile to provide advice to the educated on how to keep well, counselling moderation in eating, working and sexual activity, with two facts recalled: Titus brought on his own death when ill by insisting on bathing before dining, and Tiberius understood that doctors were of no avail to the elderly (*Mor.* 122b–137e).

Rampant disease was of course one of the elemental conditions of second-century life, as of every other period of classical history. If the great plague that struck Rome's empire in Marcus's reign was an exceptional event it was exceptional in degree not in kind.[21] Among ancient populations, unlike their counterparts in the modern developed world, the end of life did not arrive predictably in generational sequence, but could be expected at almost any age, a reality to which Yourcenar's Hadrian frequently alludes. He recalls a former mistress who died prematurely on a fever-infested island, in exile following a scandalous divorce (*MH* 336). He mentions the death from fever one winter of the servant woman Arete at the Villa: it affected him, he says, more than the loss of Sabina, who beforehand suffers severe intestinal pains (*MH* 488).[22] He tells of his efforts to relieve the symptoms of a fatal disease afflicting Matidia when she returned from Trajan's disastrous eastern expedition (in a manner that aligns with his praise of her in the extant *elogium* [*MH* 368]), and not unlike Aristides he describes the early death of his adopted son and successor Lucius in a grand set piece that well conveys the tragedy of Lucius's last long year. There are symptoms first during spring-time exercise at Rome of breathlessness and spitting up of blood, to relieve which Lucius is duly despatched to the more healthful climate of Pannonia; but a year later he is urgently brought back once unnerving bulletins have arrived detailing fits of coughing and bouts of fever. Treatment from Rufus of Ephesus, a specialist in phthisis, and Hermogenes (both incidentally historical figures) is of no help: the pulmonary condition brings long afternoons of pain, torpor, fever, sweat and emaciation, and nights of rattled breathing. A haemorrhage, finally, brings the end. Lucius was not even forty years of age (*MH* 491–5; cf. 369).[23]

The preoccupation at large is diversely expressed. The *Letters* of Pliny, Hadrian's exact contemporary, document his own illnesses (an issue with his eyes for instance), those of his wife Calpurnia (the ill health that followed a miscarriage), and of any number of men and women in his social circle. He advised two friends how to cope with their complaints from experiences of his own, while the condition of another reminded him of how sickness drives away all immediate concerns other than the desire to recover and to avoid death. His fear that the revered Fannia might die when taken ill while tending an ailing Vestal can seem palpable; and if he does no more than politely acknowledge the loss of a correspondent's pupil, extreme circumstances provoked moving obituary notices for his mentor Q. Corellius Rufus and the poet Silius Italicus, both of whom committed suicide due to intolerable medical conditions, the former in his late sixties, after suffering an incurable complaint for more than thirty years, the latter at the age of seventy-five, when unable any longer to withstand the pain his illness brought. Most dramatically of all, Pliny tells of an individual terminally ill who was prompted to end his life by the example of a devoted wife, a couple who literally bound themselves together and plunged into Lake Como. Like the Hadrian of *Mémoires*, he can even admit to anxiety brought on when members of his household staff were taken ill, or, worse, when one of them died.[24]

The essays of Aulus Gellius likewise display concern for the body's vulnerability. Gellius describes how he once listened to a discourse on the Stoic conception of pain from the Platonist philosopher L. Calvenus Taurus, with whom he and other pupils were studying in Greece in the 140s: it took place in Boeotian Lebadia at the house of a friend of the philosopher bedridden from agonizing stomach cramps (*NA* 12.5). He also gives an eyewitness account of the visit Taurus and his acolytes made to another sick individual confined in the heat of summer within the villa of the unsavoury Herodes Atticus at Cephisia that led to a memorable discussion on the difference between veins and arteries – a situation unlikely, I should think, to have brought much relief to the individual in distress (*NA* 18.10).[25] Later, in the 160s, the rhetorician Apuleius of Madauros, in a speech of thanks made at Carthage for the award of an honorific statue, tells, in meticulous detail, of a painful accident he suffered while preparing to give a recital of his literary work: "I twisted my ankle so badly in training that I came close to sundering the joint from the leg. However, the joint slipped out of place and is still weak as a result of the dislocation. And then in realigning it with a violent blow, I had a momentary spasm and broke out in quite a sweat. Next an acute pain of the intestines began, which eased off just before it finished me off." He has managed now, Apuleius self-consciously tells his listeners, to hobble along to give his speech, on the mend at last following a spa treatment (*Flor.* 16. 20–4).[26]

The correspondence between Cornelius Fronto and his pupil the young Marcus also, appositely enough, supplies exhaustive evidence of how the bodily fixation was experienced in the heart of the Antonine court. Its contents are highly personal, indicative of an affectionate friendship if not a closer bond, with many details on matters of health passing back and forth, voluminously so on Fronto's part.[27] The complaints from which he suffered were numberless. He writes of recurrent pains in all his limbs and joints – neck, shoulders, elbows, hands, groin, knees, ankles, feet, toes – as well as of peri-odic coughs and colds, respiratory infections, episodes of fever, gastric distur-bance, diarrhoea and nerve pain. In one particularly severe crisis he lost his voice, had difficulty with his circulation, fell into unconsciousness, and sup-posedly almost died. Marcus was not so chronically afflicted but he too had coughs, colds, and sore throats, mentioning once a protracted ulcerous chest illness. Others in the family similarly suffered, his mother, his sister, and in due course his children. (Milk was the best remedy, Fronto said.) All in all, the letters suggest rather more than a decorous interest in the health of the court's members. Sickness, real or anticipated, produced an all-pervasive social malaise often intensely felt, especially in moments of acute distress such as that once experienced by Marcus's later co-ruler Lucius Verus: extensive bloodletting was involved.[28]

Hadrian himself, recall, was sixty-two when he died, a relatively advanced age in Roman antiquity. He is said by Cassius Dio to have uttered on his deathbed the familiar aphorism that many physicians have killed a king (69.22.4), an example of sardonic humour that controls almost everything Yourcenar's Hadrian has to say about doctors. He is aware at the beginning of Hermogenes's questionable trust in medica-tions that will have no real impact (*MH* 287–8); and at the end, refusing any longer to quarrel, he recognizes his doctors' need to lie about their remedies in view of their patients' fears of pain, asserting in unflattering terms, in anticipation of Dio, that it is their foolish medicines that have in fact killed him (*MH* 513–14). An anecdote from a late Christian writer preserves a convergent tradition: Hadrian suffered late in life from an injury a multitude of doctors found incurable; his response was to mock them and to compose an abusive letter castigating the ignorance of the medical profession as a whole. If relief was provided and remedies were sometimes effected by medical practitioners, human exposure to early mortality was an unavoidable reality of which no reader of *Mémoires* is ultimately left unaware.[29]

Altogether, an authentic context can safely be established for the novel's opening scene. A particular aspect of contemporary sociocultural comport-ment is effectively evoked. It draws on the tradition's immediate record of Hadrian's late decline, its specificity brought out by the carefully inserted sentence referring to humoral theory that alerts the reader at once to the inadequacies of medical knowledge in antiquity. But when considered in wider compass it has a superordinate value attributable to what I consider to be Yourcenar's sensitivity to second-century social and cultural conditions in general. If entirely fictive, the episode is a realistically auspicious point of departure for appreciation of the authenticity of Hadrian's life story to come.

And an aspect of his personality is perhaps discoverable: "Intérêt d'Hadrien pour la médecine" (*CNON* 866).[30]

Before the late decline, the tradition is consistent that Hadrian throughout his life was physically robust, devoted to exercise, and remembered for setting an example of manliness to his troops with twenty-mile marches while carrying his own military equipment, for avoiding the use of a carriage, and for never covering his head whatever the extremes of weather.[31] Yourcenar followed the tradition unswervingly. Her Hadrian is unequivocal: "Mais la grande resource était avant tout l'état parfait du corps: une marche forcée de vingt lieues n'était rien, une nuit sans sommeil n'était considérée que comme une invitation à penser" (*MH* 381).[32] Justification for the portrait of a figure who enjoys until his final years a body free from the perils that rendered longevity in his world exceptional is obvious.

One of the forms of exercise involved, to which Hadrian almost immediately adverts, is a passion of which his illness has now deprived him, the sport of hunting: "Je ne chasse plus" (*MH* 289). He ruminates nonetheless on the benefits the pursuit has given him through the course of his life, benefits rather more than the merely physical. In boyhood, hunting taught lessons of how to command and to confront danger, and brought his first encounters with death and courage, even if in Spain an excessive enthusiasm for the sport met with reproof from Trajan. Simultaneously he had experienced the mixed emotions of pity for the victims and enjoyment of their suffering in expeditions that had been violent. Later, in manhood, clean and fair contests had offered relief from the deviousness of human struggles: in Tuscany he had tested the mettle of those in his retinue; and in Bithynia and Cappadocia he had made the hunt an occasion for festival, at least until the premature loss of his favourite companion intervened. At Tivoli, the sudden sound of a stag can still stir a bestial instinct – he becomes leopard as well as emperor – and enjoyable memories of lions killed in Mauretania are recalled. An unanswerable question nonetheless lingers: had he been able to spare men who might otherwise have become his victims by shedding the blood of so many animals often secretly preferred to them (*MH* 289)?

Again there is a validating context into which to locate these thoughts. In the classical Greek tradition, hunting of large quarry with horses and dogs required skills and expert marksmanship consistent with the pursuit of what Plato's Athenian Stranger calls "godlike manliness" (*Leg.* 824a–b). For Xenophon in the *Cynegeticus* it was an essential component of the young man's education, physically preparing him for military service and leading ethically to "excellence in thought and word and deed" (1.18–19; 12.1–19); indeed, it was a source of virtue, the acquisition of which included the valuable knowledge of how to obey commands and to obey laws, views later to be adopted by Hadrian's friend Arrian of Nicomedia.[33] Already in the era of Trajan and Hadrian, however, the orator Dio Chrysostom had brought this tradition to the fore in a speech on kingship, specifying the hunt as the perfect form of recreation for the good monarch: "It makes his body stronger, his heart braver, and affords a field for the practice of every military activity. For he must ride, run, in many cases meet the charge of the big game, endure heat and withstand cold, often be tortured by hunger and thirst, and he becomes habituated to enduring any hardship with pleasure through his passion for the chase" (*Or.* 3.135–6).[34] In which connection it is of more than passing interest that when describing Hadrian's measures for instilling discipline in Rome's legions, the Latin life cites Scipio Aemilianus as one of the exemplars on whom Hadrian based his comportment (*HA Hadr.* 10.2), for long ago in the Roman past, in the aftermath of Pydna, the great hero had learned the arts of hunting in Macedonia as a young man, unusually for a Roman it was thought, but with the outcome of an exceptional reputation for courage (*andreia*).[35] If, moreover, Hadrian had heard, or later read, Pliny's speech to Trajan, mentioned earlier in connection with Matidia, he will have known that Trajan himself was credited with embodying the militaristic, courageous tradition of the huntsman, and so was in his own person another model to follow (*Pan.* 81.2–4). The remark was perhaps self-referential since Pliny himself was a committed boar hunter (so he said), as was his friend Tacitus: the sport created an opportunity for intellectual stimulation as well as physical exercise (*Ep.* 1.6; 9.10). The often brilliantly portrayed hunting scenes in Roman mosaics, in paintings, and on sarcophagi confirm beyond any doubt the centrality of the hunt in Roman aristocratic culture of the early second century, and it is no surprise therefore that an image of Hadrian in pursuit of a lion appeared on the coinage with the legend VIRTUTI AUGUSTI.[36]

The evidence on which Hadrian's devotion to the hunt is built is once more relatively abundant. The main narratives speak of the avocation as a lifetime fixation, indulged as frequently as possible. Trajan did supposedly recall him from early military training in Spain due to his overenthusiasm for the sport, and soon after his accession he is said on one occasion to have narrowly avoided a plot against his life. At times he suffered injuries, breaking a collarbone and a rib in Bithynia, elsewhere damaging a leg; and in Mysia he founded the city of Hadrianotherae to commemorate the killing of a bear with a single blow.[37] In Egypt, moreover, he once supposedly killed a lion with his own hand, as the Greek miscellanist Athenaeus records (15.677d–f).

Also relevant are the hunting scenes of the eight circular sculptural reliefs known as the Tondi Adrianei that decorate the Arch of Constantine in Rome, a series of medallions portraying Hadrian on horseback attacking a lion or a bear, and two inscriptions, one a commemoration from Hadrian himself of his favourite horse Borysthenes, the other, from Thespiae, dedicating to Eros the spoils of a bear Hadrian killed that is also believed to be the emperor's own composition.[38] The former, it has been said, "gives a vivid picture of the ruler of the world racing across the fields of Tuscany, chasing boars from Pannonia, astride a stallion bred on the steppes of Russia, exulting in the strength and bravery of the animal he rode." There may in fact have been a second poem honouring a horse named Samis, known from a marble stele found close to Tivoli and brought to the healing springs of Albula after suffering a wound from a boar in Etruria.[39]

This collocation of material is more than enough to account for the way in which Hadrian's reminiscences of his hunting adventures are subsequently folded into Yourcenar's narrative at large: in Arcadia and the valley of the Helicon with Antinous; in the forests of Mysia, where the murderous plot had been foiled and Hadrianotherae later founded; in the Libyan desert, the site of the great lion hunt which later prompted nightmares; and in Umbria and close to Rome as advantage was taken of the new resources of the Villa. Yourcenar took a hint from Cassius Dio to identify the emperor's hunting chief as the figure Mastor, and allowed the sound of Borysthenes's hoofs to be heard as Hadrian lay on his deathbed.[40] And she notably informed a correspondent that it was the Boeotian inscription that was the direct source for the passage on hunting in the valley of Helicon (*HZ* 120), a version of which she produced for *La Couronne et la Lyre*, her anthology of poetry adapted from the Greek (*CL* 403).[41] Precisely what happened with the alleged attempt to kill Hadrian soon after his accession, no more than possibly involving Hadrian's enemy Lusius Quietus as Yourcenar has it, is unknown. But a generation or so later, readers of Apuleius's *Metamorphoses*, enthralled by the story of the gory death of his Tlepolemus, might well have wondered about the event: the wickedly jealous Thrasyllus, rejected as a suitor by the beautiful Charite in favour of Tlepolemus, contrived his rival's death during a hunt that involved an attack from a ferocious boar, with the villainous Thrasyllus himself supplying the *coup de grâce* (*Met.* 8.4-5).[42] Any biographer might well assume that there were many other hunting expeditions now lost to the tradition: in Greece with Arrian when a pupil of the philosopher Epictetus, or in Britain when organizing construction of the Wall, where wild boar was the target of choice.[43]

Marguerite Yourcenar herself was a staunch opponent of hunting. It might have been a coincidence that Rachel Carson was a nearby Maine resident, but

Yourcenar was ecologically minded regardless long before environmentalism entered the mainstream liberal consciousness. Together with Grace Frick, she adopted all kinds of conservationist measures at Petite Plaisance, and actively supported public environmental causes.[44] Frick was an accomplished horse-woman and at her behest Yourcenar learned to ride, with a certain sense of mature satisfaction. Her opposition to hunting, however, was unmitigated. A description of an occasion when she had witnessed a pigeon shoot in Belgium in 1929 is clinically appalling, while two late essays strongly condemn the wearing of female clothing made from the furs and skins of slaughtered animals.[45] I cannot imagine therefore that she would ever have regarded Hadrian's avocation as sport. The opening of Maine's hunting season in 1958 brought a torrid critique in a letter to her friend Élie Grekoff – disgust with seeing men decked out in red hunting jackets, hulking butchers as she called them, proudly tying onto their vehicles a year-old deer that half an hour earlier had been grazing peacefully in the woods, its carcass destined to be trashed for the most part because it had no consumptive use; and exasperation that 40,000 animals had been killed in the state the year before. It was traumatic to have seen during an October camping trip another freshly killed animal (*HZ* II 279–80).[46] In an essay from 1955 on the *Cynegetica* attributed to the Antonine Greek poet Oppian, she was categorical that every hunting expedition in the civilized world represented regression to a world of barbarism:

Née du besoin d'une nourriture carnée et de la nécessité de se défendre contre les grands fauves, la chasse est devenue un art, le plus ancien de tous, une passion aussi. L'homme a trouvé à y satisfaire son goût du risque et des prouesses physiques, sa vanité et sa jactance, et surtout sa férocité innée. Promu citadin, il y a vu la chance de se replonger périodiquement dans l'habitat barbare qu'il n'a pas au fond cessé de regretter. Il a enrichi ces jeux violents des plaisirs savants du dressage; il y a associé des chevaux, des chiens, parfois des oiseaux de proie. Il en a fait une école de ruse, une épreuve d'endurance, souvent une occasion de faste. Il n'a jamais cessé d'y mêler le sentiment du sacré. (*TGS* 392)

Born out of the need for a meat diet and the necessity of defending oneself against wild animals, hunting became an art, the most ancient of all, and a passion as well. Man found that it satisfied his liking for risks and physical feats, his vanity and his boastfulness, and above all his innate ferocity. Once he became a citizen, he saw in it a chance to reenter periodically the barbarian world he basically never ceased to miss. He embellished that violent sport with the learned pleasures of dressage; he brought to it horses, dogs, and sometimes birds of prey. He created a school of stratagem out of it, a test of endurance, and often an occasion for ostentatious display. And he never ceased to include in it the sentiment of the sacred.

Yourcenar later reiterated to Matthieu Galey that the hunter who turned up in the autumn carrying a rifle with telescopic sights and a bottle of whisky in his pocket, prepared at the end of the day to carry off his bloody kill on the hood of his car, had lost all right to the designation of *homo sapiens* (*YO* 313). Hadrian's identification with the leopard at the moment of intense emotion induced by the climax of the hunt might well be the product of authorial sentiment.

It was the classical tradition, however, and the associations of hunting with militarism, courage, and manliness that mattered. In the introduction to her renditions from Oppian in *La Couronne et la Lyre* – both Oppian and his imitator – she cites the technical treatises of Xenophon and Arrian as evidence of the devotion to hunting with hounds on the part of great landowners in antiquity, and referring to the emperors Commodus and Caracalla speaks of the enormous popularity of hunting in second-century Asia Minor in particular (while revealing as always her sympathy for slaughtered animals through a reference to the legend of the martyrdom of St. Blaise). It is Hadrian furthermore who is correctly credited with having been the first emperor to have himself represented in the act of hunting, a figure who was, she says, surrounded as much by beaters and grooms as poets and scholars. Contemporaries alert to the advertisement of virtue and godlike courage will not have forgotten that Alexander of Macedon was once said to have slain a lion, a feat full of monarchical, and even mystical, overtones.[47] I conclude accordingly that in the hunting events of the source tradition and the cultural context to which they belong, Yourcenar found a way to show Hadrian, in his reflections and reminiscences, as a biographical subject continually engaged in self-examination. This was the product of the creative artist at work in the enterprise of bringing Hadrian fully to life.[48]

Je ne m'attends pas à ce que tes dix-sept ans y comprennent quelque chose. Je tiens pourtant à t'instruire, à te choquer aussi. Tes précepteurs, que j'ai choisis moi-même, t'ont donné cette éducation sévère, surveillée, trop protégée peut-être, dont j'espère somme toute un grand bien pour toi-même et pour l'État. Je t'offre ici comme correctif un récit dépourvu d'idées préconçues et de principes abstraits, tiré de l'expérience d'un seul homme qui est moi-même. J'ignore à quelles conclusions ce récit m'entraînera. Je compte sur cet examen des faits pour me définir, me juger peut-être, ou tout au moins pour me mieux connaître avant de mourir. (*MH* 301–2)

I do not expect your seventeen years to understand any of it. I desire, all the same, to instruct you and to shock you, as well. Your tutors, whom I have chosen myself, have given you a severe education, well supervised and too much protected, perhaps; from it I hope that eventually great benefit will accrue both to you and to the State. I offer you here, in guise of corrective, a recital stripped of preconceived ideas and of mere abstract principles; it is drawn wholly from the experience of one man, who is myself. I am trusting to this examination of facts to give me some definition of myself, and to judge myself, perhaps, or at the very least to know myself better before I die.

As the passage earlier quoted from *Animula vagula blandula* shows (*MH* 301), Hadrian changes course in his narrative after his initial reflections and decides to tell Marcus his full life story. If self-concern is unmistakable, the didactic intent of the reconsidered project emerges clearly in this new extract: Hadrian intends both to inform and to instruct Marcus, even to shock him. In this Yourcenar engages with a distinctive idiom of Roman social life, the belief that a father should personally prepare his son for adulthood by providing appropriate instruction and education. For upper-class Romans literature sometimes offered a means by which this could be done, as when Cicero addressed the *De officiis* to the young Marcus to school him in the moral qualities required for leadership in statecraft. But engagement could be much more direct. Cato was said to have taught his son reading, swimming, athletics, law, and military exercises, and Augustus was to teach his grandsons Gaius and Lucius, his adoptive sons, to read, to take notes, and to copy his own handwriting. The idiom applied at every social level. Artisans passed on skills to their sons, or apprenticed them to master craftsmen to learn trades by which they might in due course earn their daily bread. It also applied in every age. As Horace's freedman father insisted that his son be taught in Rome, far from the family home, no matter what the sacrifice involved, so centuries later Augustine's father found the means despite straightened circumstances to advance his son's education by sending him to study in Carthage. It was what had always been expected of a Roman *paterfamilias*.[49] It does not matter in Yourcenar's reconstruction that the relationship between Hadrian and Marcus is one of grandfather to adoptive grandson, as the case of Augustus shows. His father died when Marcus was a boy, and it had been his paternal grandfather, M. Annius Verus, a relative of Hadrian's, who had had primary responsibility for raising him. The childless Hadrian is said always to have been especially fond of Marcus, who when fifteen was betrothed to the daughter of Lucius Aelius Caesar, Hadrian's intended successor by adoption, a closeness Yourcenar conveys now by using the familiar form of address, the *tutoiement*, the English translation conceals. After Lucius's premature death, Hadrian adopted and marked out for the succession Antoninus Pius. But he also simultaneously required Pius to adopt Marcus and the son of Lucius, thereby identifying both young men as potential future rulers.[50] Here, Hadrian's claim to have chosen Marcus's teachers in the past, the references to the public domain, and the emphasis on instilling in the young man the lessons drawn from experience combine to suggest that Hadrian, in Yourcenar's conception, is to continue to fulfil traditional expectations by equipping Marcus, in both statecraft and character, one day to become Rome's emperor. As he narrates his rise to power and recounts his imperial accomplishments, his object is to teach Marcus life's lessons as only a father can, even as he hopes simultaneously better to understand himself.

Marcus is addressed in the letter no more than sporadically, but enough to keep the didactic purpose in view. To Hadrian, no advocate of asceticism, the boy is full of youthful austerity and gravity, given to philosophical interests. Yet from his habit of entering quotations into his notebooks, Marcus can be imagined to have absorbed any number of items of practical advice by the time he reaches the letter's end: how not to cause offence by carrying books into the imperial box when attending the public games, seeming thereby not to enjoy the predilections of the populace, or how not to accept gifts on his accession from cities scarcely able to afford them (*MH* 367, 377). He will know the importance of maintaining the fifteen years of peace with Parthia Hadrian has achieved, of avoiding violent confrontations with personal rivals, as once happened with Pius and the arrogant Herodes Atticus, and the need to complete the building of the Odeon Hadrian has begun at Rome (*MH* 397, 458, 462). Hadrian's close companion Celer is a man to be trusted, and the young lawyer Fronto will likely become a loyal servant (*MH* 471, 508). Marcus will have a sense of the godlike ascendancy to which power may one day uniquely raise him, bringing the capacity, so it seems, to work miracles of healing (*MH* 399). And above all, perhaps, Marcus will be able to compare the wisdom Hadrian believes himself to have attained with the knowledge Marcus will come to acquire himself in the fullness of time. An especially crucial lesson is conveyed when Hadrian ends the account of his rise to power: "l'essentiel est que l'homme arrivé au pouvoir ait prouvé par la suite qu'il méritait de l'exercer" (*MH* 357).[51]

As *Disciplina Augusta* comes to a close, such incidental remarks give way to an extended address that makes especially vivid Hadrian's father-like devotion to Marcus. He has brought the boy into the public spotlight by admitting him to the College of Arval Brethren, by having him in close attendance at a public sacrifice, by arranging his adoption by Pius; he has watched over Marcus's education, and, certain misgivings aside, has observed his intellectual development, taken notice of his philosophical and ascetic tastes, and anticipates that he himself has given his subjects their one chance of seeing

Plato's dream realized of a pure-hearted philosopher rule over them. Marcus is present now at the Villa, and Hadrian is able to watch him as he writes. He knows that Marcus feels more filial regard towards Pius than to himself; there is a difference of temperament between them; but Hadrian has met his responsibility, and the letter will be there to give direction (*MH* 495–8).[52]

It seems inescapable here that Yourcenar is prompting her reader to think of Marcus as the eventual author of the *Meditations*, the collection of private philosophical reflections that give rare insights into a Roman emperor's mind.[53] The work is exceptional in showing how an emperor late in life remembered his earliest years, for in its opening book some seventeen individuals are catalogued from whom Marcus, even as a child, learned ethically beneficial lessons, and to whom he expresses debts of gratitude. They comprise both kin and non-kin members, illustrating the paradigmatic cultural diversity of informal personal influences to which a boy of his station was exposed. Hadrian, however, is not included in the list. As Yourcenar's Hadrian hints, it was Antoninus Pius who was to exert the more formative influence, and Marcus indeed speaks of him in the *Meditations* in almost panegyrical terms (1.16).[54] Strictly, therefore, authorial omniscience has led here to anachronism. That does not diminish the validity, however, of Yourcenar's recourse to an unquestionably characteristic pattern of Roman behaviour. Support was available in a brief entry in the Augustan life of Marcus: he was brought up under the watchful care of Hadrian (*HA Marc.* 4.1: *Educatus est in Hadriani gremio*).

It is a matter of accident that far more is recoverable about Marcus's upbringing than that of Hadrian. Many names of those who were his teachers, from boyhood to maturity, are on record, with the survival of Fronto's correspondence a particularly important resource for revealing aspects of Marcus's educational formation in his late teens and early adulthood.[55] The education of older boys and young men in the upper sector of Roman society was heavily based on the study of rhetoric, its purpose being to provide pupils with full command of the arts of persuasion and thereby to prepare them for adult roles as leaders of the civic communities, in contexts both civil and military, to which they belonged. Rhetoric was taught through close scrutiny of language and literature, with rigorous practice in speechmaking. Assuming the identities of historical characters confronting crisis, or else presented with daunting, often fanciful, legal problems, pupils learned how to make decisions on matters of moment and, ideally, to become capable of resolving any issue put before them. As they learned from the past for the sake of the future, they absorbed through their years of study the traditional, highly moralistic and patriarchal ideology of the Roman establishment, which in due course was passed on to succeeding generations. The system replicated the conservative structures of Roman society from one age to another, instilling in the young habits of authority and command.[56] Rome's ruling class, not a hereditary aristocracy but a body constantly changing its sources of recruitment, never seems to have wavered in its commitment to traditional methods of instruction for its members and their sons. The ideal template had been set out by Quintilian. It began in infancy with carefully selected child minders, nurses who were tellers of tales and singers of songs, and pedagogues responsible for basic instruction in reading and writing, continued with the literary curriculum of the grammarian (*grammaticus*), and ended with oratorical training from the rhetorician (*rhetor*). The ages at which the boy progressed from one stage to the next were not rigidly defined, but the major shifts occurred at roughly ages seven and thirteen. Quintilian favoured the idea that when the boy was ready for the grammarian he should attend a public school and engage with fellow pupils rather than be taught by private tutors. But the grooming of a future emperor was a special case. Fronto duly took his imperial pupil through one exercise after another – verse composition, the use of similes and epigrams, translations between Latin and Greek, the composition of rhetorical exercises – the components of a regimen intended to culminate in the fully formed, and morally perfected, consummate Latin orator.

The Hadrian of *Mémoires* has just a few passing memories of childhood, inevitably of a childhood spent in Spain (*MH* 511). On the family estate he carved his name on chestnut trees, and there were visits to Cadiz, which brought the first sights of Spanish dancing girls (*MH* 445, 463). He can say little about his relationship with his father because the man, made out to be a self-effacing figure of many virtues but minimal accomplishments, died when Hadrian was still a boy (*MH* 309). There is a hint, however, of a legacy of scrupulous attention to detail in practical matters and of a general scepticism in demeanour, and an image of him, sedated in his sick room in Italica as death approached, haunted the elderly Hadrian's dreams as he in turn sought relief from his own suffering (*MH* 512).[57] In very early life, predictably enough, Hadrian had had a Spanish nurse, a tall, grim woman he remembers for her devotion to Epona and, literally, her singing of the goddess's praises (*MH* 478). She is a Yourcenarian invention, but one as it happens authenticated by the fortuitous discovery of a tombstone identifying the historical Hadrian's real nurse. Her name was Germana, a slave woman who outlived Hadrian and was eventually buried on the confines of the Villa. A prevailing connection might be presumed, particularly since Hadrian set her free. The woman, however, is known only from the chance discovery of her tombstone, and nothing more of her can be said. She does not appear in *Mémoires*.[58]

Hadrian also has memories of those who educated him, especially once in Rome in the establishment of Terentius Scaurus, where learning was more rigorous in every sense than in the schools of Spain. Scaurus appears in *Varius multiplex multiformis*, and it is here that Yourcenar, fully familiar with the methods of Roman education, has Hadrian connect the conventional rhetorical training he describes with the complex character he ultimately becomes:

L'école de Térentius Scaurus, à Rome, enseignait médiocrement les philosophes et les poètes, mais préparait assez bien aux vicissitudes de l'existence humaine: les magisters exerçaient sur les écoliers une tyrannie que je rougirais d'imposer aux hommes; chacun, enfermé dans les étroites limites de son savoir, méprisait ses collègues, qui tout aussi étroitement savaient autre chose. Ces pédants s'enrouaient en disputes de mots. Les querelles de préséance, les intrigues, les calomnies, m'ont familiarisé avec ce que je devais rencontrer par la suite dans toutes les sociétés où j'ai vécu, et il s'y ajoutait la brutalité de l'enfance. Et pourtant, j'ai aimé certains de mes maîtres, et ces rapports étrangement intimes et étrangement élusifs qui existent entre le professeur et l'élève. (*MH* 310)

Terentius Scaurus' school, in Rome, gave mediocre instruction in the philosophers and the poets but afforded rather good preparation for the vicissitudes of human existence: teachers exercised a tyranny over pupils which it would shame me to impose upon men; enclosed within the narrow limits of his own learning, each one despised his colleagues, who, in turn, had equally narrow knowledge of something else. These pedants made themselves hoarse in mere verbal disputes. The quarrels over precedence, the intrigues and calumnies, gave me acquaintance with what I was to encounter thereafter in every society in which I have lived, and to such experiences was added the brutality of childhood. And nevertheless I have loved certain of my masters, and those strangely intimate though elusive relations existing between student and teacher.

Q. Terentius Scaurus is a genuinely historical figure who according to the *Historia Augusta* was indeed Hadrian's teacher (*HA Verus* 2.5). Aulus Gellius applauded him as the most distinguished grammarian of the age (*NA* 11.15.3).[59] Yourcenar attributes to him withering criticism of Hadrian's poetic ambitions but also, more positively, credits him with having introduced Hadrian to the study of Greek and inspired his enduring love of the language, with appropriate mention of his childhood writing exercises (*MH* 311–12). An entry in her *Notebook* admits that this could not be confirmed: Scaurus was a historical figure, and his school is described from what is known of schools at the time, but there is no evidence that he did, or did not, encourage Hadrian in the study of Greek. What matters, however, is the overall plausibility of what is said, and the record of Scaurus's now lost writings offers in fact circumstantial support for the assumptions Yourcenar made. Scaurus produced commentaries on both Virgil and Horace, the former perhaps mythologically oriented, the latter dealing at least with the *Ars poetica*. A critical interest in poetry is thereby assured. There was also an *Ars grammatica*, of great later influence, which is thought to have covered among other topics spelling errors and their correction, and differences between Greek and Latin grammatical constructions. A separate treatise on spelling, *De orthographia*, can still be read. A connection with Greek instruction is therefore also indicated. How well Yourcenar knew Scaurus's history is an open question. But the associations made are more than suggestive, while the disputes alleged concerning fine points of philology seem to echo in turn much to be found in Fronto and Gellius.[60]

Hadrian has more to offer on his memories of the rhetorical curriculum to which he was exposed:

Les méthodes des grammairiens et des rhéteurs sont peut-être moins absurdes que je ne le pensais à l'époque où j'y étais assujetti. La grammaire, avec son mélange de règle logique et d'usage arbitraire, propose au jeune esprit un avant-goût de ce que lui offriront plus tard les sciences de la conduite humaine, le droit ou la morale, tous les systèmes où l'homme a codifié son expérience instinctive. Quant aux exercices de rhétorique où nous étions successivement Xerxès et Thémistocle, Octave et Marc-Antoine, ils m'enivrèrent; je me sentis Protée. Ils m'apprirent à entrer tour à tour dans la pensée de chaque homme, à comprendre que chacun se décide, vit et meurt selon ses propres lois. (*MH* 311)

The methods of grammarians and rhetoricians are perhaps less absurd than I thought them to be during the years when I was subjected to them. Grammar, with its mixture of logical rule and arbitrary usage, proposes to a young mind a foretaste of what will be offered to him later on by law and ethics, those sciences of human conduct, and by all the systems wherein man has codified his instinctive experience. As for the rhetorical exercises in which we were successively Xerxes and Themistocles, Octavius and Mark Antony, they intoxicated me; I felt like Proteus. They taught me to enter into the thought of each man in turn, and to understand that each makes his own decisions, and lives and dies according to his own laws.

The link is once more culturally sound. Hadrian's acknowledgment of his adult ability to think proteanly, to enter the mental world of any figure with whom he must contend, is Yourcenar's intuitive acknowledgment of the acculturative character of Roman education, at work here through the particular medium of the *suasoria*, the rhetorical exercise in which the student, adopting the role of a historical or mythological character, learned to deliver a deliberative set of arguments bringing a moment of crisis to resolution. The *suasoriae* of the elder Seneca illustrate the kind of topics assigned. Should Alexander set sail on the open ocean or enter Babylon? Should Agamemnon sacrifice Iphigenia? Should Cicero beg Antony to spare his life or destroy his writings as Antony insists?[61] Classical Greek history was an especially rich source of subject matter. The satirist Lucian advised the aspirant orator to have at his disposal every purple patch possible from the history of the Persian Wars, and some two centuries later Libanius presents Neocles and Themistocles still opposing each other on the issue of the father's attempt to nullify the disowning of the son after Themistocles's success at Salamis.[62] Altogether the mode of presentation is a further indication of the way *Mémoires* puts flesh on the bones of the tradition by drawing on a realistic feature of Roman practice, with a suitably Orbilian reminder conveyed by the word "assujetti" of the harsh discipline associated with Roman methods of instruction (already signalled in the previous passage cited). The outcome of the process of the upper-class Roman boy's social formation – unattainable from a simple list of political and military events from Hadrian's boyhood years – is appositely reflected at a later stage when Hadrian thinks of himself in conversation with his one-time guardian, Acilius Attianus, as a pupil reciting a difficult exercise to a grammarian (*MH* 364). The historical Hadrian's admiration for the eminent rhetorician T. Castricius, praised by Gellius as the greatest declaimer and teacher of his day, is a suitably corroborative gem (*NA* 13.22.1).[63]

IV

Given the examples outlined, no knowledgeable reader can doubt that *Mémoires* astutely recovers any number of threads from the texture of life in Hadrian's second-century world, achieving what I have called first-order authenticity: facets of socio-historical reality imaginatively evoked.[64] Others will appear in due course. This should induce no surprise in view of Yourcenar's extensive classical learning. Under her father's tutelage she began to learn Latin at about age ten and Greek two years later, at a time when classical languages were considered unsuitable academic subjects for girls and access in schools was prohibitive.[65] A lifelong interest in the Greco-Roman past followed, with results reflected not least today in the contents of the library at Petite Plaisance, where hundreds of classical volumes are still to be seen. (A visitor is immediately struck by the complete *Dictionnaire des Antiquités grecques et romaines* of Charles Daremberg and Edmond Saglio.)[66] Already at the age of twenty-six, she could write with authority, in the precocious essay *Diagnostique de l'Europe*, of the era from Antoninus Pius to Romulus Augustulus as an "époque de décadence" (*EM* 1652–5). Her knowledge of antiquity was profound, and critics have always marvelled at her "érudition." *La Couronne et la Lyre* is one illustration of her breadth of knowledge: it opens with extracts from the Homeric epics, ends with selections from authors of the Byzantine era, and provides historical and critical background throughout. Published in 1979, it occupied much of Yourcenar's attention during the mid- to late 1940s, and was a project undertaken in part, she said, to understand when writing *Mémoires* the library that Hadrian would have read (*CL* 9–10). Its preface alone, as Achmy Halley has noted, leaves no question about the importance of the classical literary heritage in her imagination.[67]

There is every reason therefore to believe that *Mémoires* is rather more than pure fiction, especially when the contents of the *Note* are observed, the multiplicity of classical references the text contains discovered, and evidence for the correction of errors brought forward.

As discussion of the historical tradition will have intimated, the *Note* lists original sources of every kind, literary, epigraphical, papyrological, numismatic, iconographic, archaeological (*OR* 543–55). It also gives an extensive bibliography of historical works consulted that begins with Gibbon and ends with materials published as late as 1950. In between there are dozens of references to general histories and specialist studies in all the major European languages. A special debt is acknowledged to the German historian Wilhelm Weber, the authority responsible for the chapter on Hadrian in the eleventh volume of the first edition of the *Cambridge Ancient History* from 1936. Some of the preparations were carried out in 1937–8 at Yale University, where Grace Frick was then a doctoral student and at whose invitation Yourcenar made her first visit to the United States.[68] She claimed to have destroyed her records of that year's work. But it cannot all have been forgotten, and once the decision was made a decade later to resume the project her research became intense, with reading in libraries in New York, Hartford, Yale and elsewhere, as her personal circumstances changed.[69] The reason for the *Note*'s existence was obviously to substantiate the assertion that *Mémoires* was historically valid: "on travaille sur une réalité" (*PV* 60) – and by any standard it shows an impressive command of the foundations of Roman history in the high Imperial age.[70]

That is well proven by the profusion of allusions to classical authors found throughout the novel, both canonical and lesser known. In the opening pages of *Animula vagula blandula* alone, three authors are passingly introduced as Hadrian speaks to Marcus of food, physical love, and sleep: first Apicius, the Tiberian author of a Latin book of recipes; finally Isocrates, through a Greek commonplace equating sleep with death; and in between the Stoic philosopher Posidonius, who is credited with a clinical description of the sexual act that Marcus has copied into his student's notebook (*MH* 292, 301, 295). The description belongs in fact to Marcus's *Meditations* (6.13).[71] But familiar, I imagine, with the fragments of Posidonius that remain, Yourcenar assumes that Hadrian would have read him, and introduces the philosopher in a context that allows her subject again conveniently to show a paternal interest in the boy, and her knowledge of the true source of the allusion indirectly to reveal itself. Such a strategy is liberally deployed throughout, grounded on both the reasonable belief, as Quintilian's grand curriculum would suggest, that in the course of his education Hadrian had been exposed to many of the authors whose works can still be read, and on that element of the tradition likewise identifying Hadrian as a devotee of literature with a taste for the archaic and an author in his own right (*HA Hadr.* 14.8–9; 15.10; 16.5–6). Discoursing on his love of the Greek language, he duly puts on display the results of his education in Greek history and philosophy (*MH* 312); and as he contemplates building a Pantheon at Rome, and aligning himself thereby with the peaceful regime of Augustus, he expresses his desire to have acknowledged a link both with his immediate predecessors Nerva and Trajan, and with all the earlier Caesars whose biographies the courtier Suetonius had composed. In spite of some unfairness, he maintains, Suetonius's lives permitted valuable aspects of the emperors' personalities to emerge that Hadrian finds exemplary for the continuation of Roman imperial rule (*MH* 415–16). Hadrian was on Yourcenar's own admission to be the cultivated representative of second-century Greco-Roman culture (*RC* 66).

Once *Mémoires* had been published, friends and correspondents raised questions that Yourcenar addressed in reprints and new editions, fixatedly correcting errors and inconsistencies and sometimes seeking professional advice for the purpose. Reading the work before publication, her friend Constantin Dimaras wondered if it was possible for a stack of Roman coins to stand upright in a column like modern coins, as Yourcenar had written. In Switzerland at the time, she at once conducted an experiment at a museum in Avenches, and finding that she was able to stack some gold and bronze Trajanic coins on top of one another left her text unchanged (*HZ* 110).[72] Similarly, when in March 1955 she was asked whether Hadrian was the first Roman officially to apply the epithet "eternal" (*aeterna*) to Rome, as she had Hadrian remark (*MH* 371), she sent letters of enquiry from France to three experts – Marcel Durry at the Sorbonne, Cornelius C. Vermeule at the University of Michigan, Walter Hatto Gross in Germany – and citing references to numismatic evidence received from Durry was soon able to reply, triumphantly, that she had been correct (*HZ* 467–8).[73] Matters were rather different, however, despite his overall admiration of the novel, with queries raised by the ancient historian Julien Guey, to whom Yourcenar wrote in May 1953. Yes, she said, the original version contained some Anglicisms, the result of her long residence in an Anglo-Saxon country, but corrected new printings were in process; she had also already rephrased a misleading sentence concerning Hadrian's attitude to the city of Antioch, and she granted that the word "Sénat" was inappropriate for the local council of Alexandria in Egypt, confessing her inability to find one better. (In the Pléiade "le conseil local" is substituted.) She acknowledged further that her references to Rome's walls were ambiguous – Servian or Aurelian? – but this was part of a strategy to engage her readers, while a phrase concerning the Colosseum had now been rewritten even though the late name "Colisée" had been retained: to have used the formal "Flavian Amphitheatre" would have been too obscure for her readers: there was a limit on how precise to be.[74] And yet, as she unequivocally stated at the beginning of her letter, her intention overall had been to give as faithful an account of Hadrian's life as possible, the enormity and encumbrances of the task notwithstanding. At a minimum, the commitment to authenticity, both generally and on points of detail, was never in question: "Personne ne sait mieux que moi qu'on n'arrive jamais qu'à une approximation, mais j'ai fait ce que j'ai pu pour rester fidèle à la lettre et à l'esprit de l'histoire, tout en cherchant à retrouver par-delà les textes toujours plus ou moins figés cette réalité obscure et changeante qui est celle de la vie même" (*HZ* 268).[75]

There are times, however, as implied by the comment just mentioned on Suetonius, when for all the ways in which Yourcenar's achievement seems authentically successful, her reader may suspect that the voice being portrayed is less that of Hadrian than the voice of his biographer. Take for example the way in which Hadrian constantly describes to Marcus the varied characteristics of the many lands through which he had travelled and the impact made upon him. Often this is done through brief suggestive touches: the breezes from the Propontis fanning the rooms of the ancient palace of King Nicomedes, the streams splattering the Vale of Tempe before reaching blond Euboea and wine-rose Attica, the gardens of a merchant's house in Sidon carpeted already in March with roses (*MH* 404, 407, 480). But at other times description is fuller and overtly conjoined with emotional response, as when dawn on Mt. Casius inspires in Hadrian a sense of total exhilaration (*MH* 428). The topographical and the psychological can indeed become intricately intertwined, as in this moving excerpt on the winter lands of the Danube with which the young Hadrian contrasts the more familiar temperate regions of the Mediterranean:

Notre sol grec ou latin, soutenu partout par l'ossature des rochers, a l'élégance nette d'un corps mâle: la terre scythe avait l'abondance un peu lourde d'un corps de femme étendue. La plaine ne se terminait qu'au ciel. Mon émerveillement ne cessait pas en présence du miracle des fleuves: cette vaste terre vide n'était pour eux qu'une pente et qu'un lit. Nos rivières sont brèves; on ne s'y sent jamais loin des sources. Mais l'énorme coulée qui s'achevait ici en confus estuaires charriait les boues d'un continent inconnu, les glaces de régions inhabitables. Le froid d'un haut-plateau d'Espagne ne le cède à aucun autre, mais c'était la première fois que je me trouvais face à face avec le véritable hiver, qui ne fait dans nos pays que des apparitions plus ou moins brèves, mais qui là-bas s'installe pour de longues périodes de mois, et que, plus au nord, on devine immuable, sans commencement et sans fin. Le soir de mon arrivée au camp, le Danube était une immense route de glace rouge, puis de glace bleue, sillonnée par le travail intérieur des courants de traces aussi profondes que celles des chars. Nous nous protégions du froid par des fourrures. La présence de cet ennemi impersonnel, presque abstrait, produisait une exaltation indescriptible, un sentiment d'énergie accrue. On luttait pour conserver sa chaleur comme ailleurs pour garder courage. À certains jours, sur la steppe, la neige effaçait tous les plans, déjà si peu sensibles; on galopait dans un monde de pur espace et d'atomes purs. Aux choses les plus banales, les plus molles, le gel donnait une transparence en même temps qu'une dureté céleste. Tout roseau brisé devenait une flûte de cristal. (*MH* 321–2)

Our Greek and Latin lands, everywhere supported by bone-structure of rock, have the trim beauty of a male body; the heavy abundance of the Scythian earth was that of a reclining woman. The plain ended where the sky began. My wonder never ceased in presence of the rivers: that vast empty land was but a slope and a bed for their waters. Our rivers are short; we never feel far from their sources; but the enormous flow which ended there in confused estuaries swept with it the mud of an unknown continent and the ice of uninhabitable regions. The cold of Spain's high plateaus is second to none, but this was the first time that I found myself face to face with true winter, which visits our countries but briefly. There it sets in for a long period of months; farther north it must be unchanging, without beginning and without end. The evening of my arrival in camp the Danube was one immense roadway of ice, red at first and then blue, furrowed by the inner working of currents with tracks as deep as those of chariots. We made use of furs to protect ourselves from the cold. The presence of that enemy, so impersonal as to be almost abstract, produced an indescribable exaltation, and a feeling of energy accrued. One fought to conserve body heat as elsewhere one fights to keep one's courage. There were days when the snow effaced the few differences in level on the steppes; we galloped in a world of pure space and pure atoms. The frozen coating gave transparency to the most ordinary things, and the softest objects took on a celestial rigidity. Each broken reed was a flute of crystal.

The notion conveyed of the immensity of Rome's empire apart, this feeling for landscape and seasonal atmosphere could be said to assist, compellingly, the purposes of authentification, with Hadrian placed in specific settings that elicit from him profound human responses. And as Anne-Yvonne Julien has shown, the appeal of lands beyond the borders of empire is an important element of the personality portrayed.[76] The descriptions, reminiscent of Donald Howard's account of Chaucer's crossing of the Alps, impart a true sense, I think, of what it was like to be there, of life as Hadrian may well have experienced it. Yet far from the merely academic, they project onto him what I equally suspect must be the responses of a writer who herself had travelled extensively in Hadrian's world in her formative years. His memories of eating on a Greek beach from a menu of resin-filled wine, bread sprinkled with sesame seeds, and fish grilled and charred on an open fire (*MH* 292) must surely derive, for example, from memories of her own Greek travels during the 1930s with her fellow poet André Embiricos, travels that once included a voyage into the Black Sea and allowed her to linger in the shade if not of a beech at least of trees where she could read from Hesiod and Theognis (*SP* 874). In her own voice, she was to write in the *Préface* to *La Couronne et la Lyre* of Greece's low spreading plains beyond the folds of its mountains, the lofty places, the valleys bottle-necked with rocks, the capes separated into long fingers dipping into the sea and the wind-driven expanse between them, the islands each one a world to itself (*CL*13). There is little difference in the mode of expression.[77]

The issue consequently presents itself of authorial transference, the attribution to the biographical subject of opinions that are those of the biographer and reflect the biographer's own experience and disposition.[78] Its impact is to my mind unquestionably felt in a brief passage in which Hadrian compares and contrasts Roman and Greek portraiture, where something close to editorializing appears. His views are those Yourcenar herself had come to hold as herself a connoisseur of ancient art:

Nos portraits romains n'ont qu'une valeur de chronique: copies marquées de rides exactes ou de verrues uniques, décalques de modèles qu'on coudoie distraitement dans la vie et qu'on oublie sitôt morts. Les Grecs au contraire ont aimé la perfection humaine au point de se soucier assez peu du visage varié des hommes. (*MH* 388)

Our Roman busts have value only as records, faces copied to the last wrinkle, with every single wart; stencils of figures with whom we brush elbows in life, and whom we forget as soon as they die. The Greeks, on the contrary, have loved human perfection to the point of caring but little for the varied visages of men.

The same is true of rather more complex remarks Hadrian makes in *Tellus stabilita* when considering the state of Rome's empire once he has become its emperor. They concern the institution of slavery. After expressing his distrust of law as an instrument of social control, Hadrian refers to an assault once made against him by a mining slave near Tarraco in Spain, and tells of how he had refused to execute the slave, as the law allowed, but through kindly treatment, including medical attention, converted the man from a violent enemy into a loyal retainer (*MH* 373–4).[79] Admitting next to doubts that it could ever be abolished, he proceeds to list the regulations on slavery for which he had been responsible, observing that his intention had been to use the law carefully. The regulations specified follow items in the historical tradition and so have an inherent validity; a ban for instance on sales of slaves to brothel owners and gladiatorial schools closely follows an item in the Latin life (*HA Hadr.* 18.8). The record of Hadrianic legislation on slavery is in fact extensive, and it is often taken to indicate a sympathetic attitude on Hadrian's part to the servile element of Rome's population, erroneously in my view.[80] The examples here end with a reference, dependent on evidence from Justinian's *Digest* (1.6.2) to his once sentencing a female slave owner to exile for excessively punishing one of her slaves (*MH* 375). They are meant as a whole to illustrate Hadrianic *humanitas*.

The measures concerned, however, can be offset by legal texts not incorporated into *Mémoires* that suggest a different attitude. The context of one such item is a lengthy exposition of the extent to which slaves might be legitimately tortured for information in situations where their owners had died in suspicious circumstances. At issue was the application of an enactment of the early Principate, the *Senatus Consultum Silanianum*, that, in the event of a slave owner's murder or the murder of an immediate member of his family, required all the slaves in the household to be tortured in order to discover the murderer's identity. Hadrian is not mentioned here, but in a later section, a verbatim ruling from him is given in which insistence is laid on observing the traditional rule: when owners were under physical attack their slaves were to subordinate all considerations of personal safety, including threats to their lives, and to render their owners all necessary assistance on penalty of execution. The ruling was given in part for the sake of the law's exemplary import to other slaves. It depended on a specific case in which a female slave had failed to assist her mistress when the woman was attacked in her chamber and killed. The slave had not intervened physically, nor had she cried out for help. (Her explanation was that the assailant had threatened to kill her too.) Hadrian's words exhibit no sympathy for the human quandary in which the slave woman presumably found herself at the moment when her mistress was assaulted. They adhere instead to conservative Roman slave-owning norms. Whether Hadrian formulated the ruling himself or followed consiliar advice cannot be determined.[81]

The significance of the extract concerned is that any attempt to portray the distinctive features of Roman society in the Imperial age must necessarily at some point include reference to its slave-owning practices. Authenticity requires this. Yet the way in which Hadrian introduces his humanizing measures betrays the unease with which the novelist responded to the institution that produced them. These are Hadrian's opening words:

Je doute que toute la philosophie du monde parvienne à supprimer l'esclavage: on en changera tout au plus le nom. Je suis capable d'imaginer des formes de servitude pires que les nôtres, parce que plus insidieuses: soit qu'on réussisse à transformer les hommes en machines stupides et satisfaites, qui se croient libres alors qu'elles sont asservies, soit qu'on développe chez eux, à l'exclusion des loisirs et des plaisirs humains, un goût du travail aussi forcené que la passion de la guerre chez les races barbares. À cette servitude de l'esprit, ou de l'imagination humaine, je préfère encore notre esclavage de fait. (*MH* 375)[82]

I doubt if all the philosophy in the world can succeed in suppressing slavery; it will, at most, change the name. I can well imagine forms of servitude worse than our own, because more insidious, whether they transform men into stupid, complacent machines, who believe themselves free just when they are most subjugated, or whether to the exclusion of leisure and pleasures essential to man they develop a passion for work as violent as the passion for war among barbarous races. To such bondage for the human mind and imagination I prefer even our avowed slavery.

The overt problem here is the presumption that Hadrian should ever have thought about the suppression of Roman slavery at all. Nothing could be more historically unrealistic. Because for all the discussions of slavery of the mind and soul to be found in the Greco-Roman philosophical tradition, even in expounders close in time to Hadrian such as Dio Chrysostom, a world without slavery of the body in antiquity was scarcely imaginable, and certainly never seriously advocated. Hadrian's words are in truth those of a writer conditioned by the liberal tendencies of modern Western societies to regard slavery as a moral evil, a concept alien to Roman antiquity. This was certainly Yourcenar's standpoint, for Hadrian's words can be correlated with what she has to say in the early pages of *Fleuve profond, sombre rivière*, a study of the origins of the Negro spirituals she translated for her French audience that includes a brief but rigorous history of the transatlantic slave trade and contemporary race relations (*FP* 7–30). The collection of what she saw as expressions of a masterful poetic form was published in 1964. But Yourcenar's interest in them was aroused when she first visited the United States, and already in the 1940s she was producing her own versions, the response, I think, of an immigrant beginning to understand at first hand the history of racial tensions in the society into which she had chosen to place herself, especially when travelling in the southern states.[83] Her study contains references to the political movement led by Martin Luther King Jr and to the civil rights legislation of 1964, and was evidently completed shortly before the volume's publication. It is accurate in factual detail, but in tone it is rancorously indignant in view of the human misery caused by the slave trade, the aftermath of America's Civil War, and the then present-day struggle for equality of civil rights. No holds are barred in the description of events. Yourcenar did not hesitate to expose the hypocrisies of the materialism on which American slavery had been based or the virulence of the current racism to which it had led. An allusion from a decade later shows well enough that the strength of her feelings did not dissipate with the passage of time: the humiliation of people of colour had been perpetuated after emancipation in innumerable new ways (*SP* 852).

At the same time, Yourcenar was well aware of the antecedents of the African slave trade. Her study opens with remarks on the exploitation of sub-Saharan Africa across the millennia from Pharaonic Egypt to the Arab caliphates and necessarily includes Roman practices: "des rafles opérées par des marchands maurétaniens procuraient aux Romains la denrée de luxe qu'était pour eux l'esclave à peau de bronze ou d'ébène, porteur de litière, majordome ou gladiateur" (*FP* 8).[84] But if the ancient history of African enslavement was thoroughly understood, slavery in its Hadrianic moment could not be registered in *Mémoires* dispassionately, or even fully, due to the pressure of the moral position inherited from the modern abolitionist movement so evident in her study and the challenges of contemporary racism keenly expressed there.[85] Perhaps therefore the humanity of Hadrian in which Yourcenar had come so firmly to believe precluded any comprehensive incorporation of the measures historically attributed to him that preserved and strengthened the Roman slavery system. His definition of slavery, "l'horrible état qui met l'homme à la merci d'un autre homme" (*MH* 375), is understandable enough to the modern reader, but whether Hadrian could actually have said those words is debatable. His world was one in which concepts of human rights were nonexistent and slavery itself was ineradicable.[86] Indeed, in an interview from

1971 Yourcenar acknowledged the sense of historical anticipation her interviewer had detected in the words she had Hadrian speak, confessing to a certain licence: "Je ne suis pas sûre si Hadrien aurait pu le dire. Il n'y avait pas encore ce problème-là qui lui aurait permis d'y penser et là je me suis donné certaines libertés" (*PV* 120).[87] Like many other commentators, she found it difficult, if not impossible, to remain emotionally disengaged and intellectually detached in view of the inextricable, unavoidable connections between slavery in antiquity and its later New World forms.

The result is that from time to time seeping anachronism is detectable in the narrative. It is a special, even foreseeable, complication, explicitly visible in two final passages to which I want to draw attention, each of which concerns a similarly elemental feature of Roman culture. In the first, which involves Hadrian's almost final words, Yourcenar engages with the Roman fixation with defeating death in a world where, as already emphasized, life was relatively short and the moment of its end beyond calculation. The cultural consequence was a panoply of death rituals and monumentalization that included in the Imperial age the ubiquitous habit, at all social levels, of commemoration by epitaph.[88] It is appropriate, therefore, that Yourcenar's Hadrian is always conscious of the need to confront and withstand the uncertainty of life: it controls his impulse as emperor to construct new buildings and cities, to carve his name on the colossal statue of the god Memnon in Egypt, and to compete as an author with poets from the past (*MH* 384–7, 445, 454–5). It also inspires this prediction, when with his mighty mausoleum almost ready to receive his ashes, he speaks of his unyielding belief in the eternity of Rome and Rome's legacy to future ages:

Nos livres ne périront pas tous; on réparera nos statues brisées; d'autres coupoles et d'autres frontons naîtront de nos frontons et de nos coupoles; quelques hommes penseront, travailleront et sentiront comme nous: j'ose compter sur ces continuateurs placés à intervalles irréguliers le long des siècles, sur cette intermittente immortalité. Si les barbares s'emparent jamais de l'empire du monde, ils seront forcés d'adopter certaines de nos méthodes; ils finiront par nous ressembler. Chabrias s'inquiète de voir un jour le pastophore de Mithra ou l'évêque du Christ s'implanter à Rome et y remplacer le grand pontife. Si par malheur ce jour arrive, mon successeur le long de la berge vaticane aura cessé d'être le chef d'un cercle d'affiliés ou d'une bande de sectaires pour devenir à son tour une des figures universelles de l'autorité. Il héritera de nos palais et de nos archives; il différera de nous moins qu'on ne pourrait le croire. J'accepte avec calme ces vicissitudes de Rome éternelle. (*MH* 513–14)

Not all our books will perish, nor our statues, if broken, lie unrepaired; other domes and other pediments will arise from our domes and pediments; some few men will think and work and feel as we have done, and I venture to count upon such continuators, placed irregularly throughout the centuries, and upon this kind of intermittent immortality. If ever the barbarians gain possession of the world they will be forced to adopt some of our methods; they will end by resembling us. Chabrias fears that the pastophor of Mithra or the bishop of Christ may implant himself one day in Rome, replacing the high pontiff. If by ill fate that day should come, my successor officiating in the vatical fields along the Tiber will already have ceased to be merely the chief of a gang, or of a band of sectarians, and will have become in his turn one of the universal figures of authority. He will inherit our palaces and our archives, and will differ from rulers like us less than one might suppose. I accept with calm these vicissitudes of Rome eternal.

The passage once more succeeds in expressing something authentically Roman. Yet in its prospect of the fall of Rome's empire and the decline of Latin literature Hadrian's vision is self-evidently over-determined and too infused with authorial omniscience to be thoroughly convincing – not in the sense that any novelist must know and control everything her novel's plot contains, but in that Yourcenar had historical knowledge of a kind that Hadrian himself can never have had. The distorting Christianizing details – "l'évêque du Christ," "la berge vaticane" – make far too great a demand on the reader to be fully credible; and the vision as a whole seems to depend on a view of decline and fall that disallows any concept of late antiquity as a transitional era or an era of high attainment in its own right. In the age of Oppian, Yourcenar thought, a barbarian wind, "Un soufflé déjà barbare," was already blowing through a civilization that had exhausted itself, and, as she once put it, one feature of the metaphysical complex of her book was the contrast between the open world of Hadrian and the closed worlds of the ages to come.[89] Composing his memoirs in his dying days, Hadrian was quite literally waiting for the barbarians.

Correspondents, even admiring correspondents, sometimes pointed to the issues involved. A Norwegian lawyer wrote to say that it was impossible for Hadrian to have known about Christian bishops and to have anticipated their replacement of him on the Vatican. To which Yourcenar replied that there were valid grounds for assuming Hadrian to have been familiar with the organization of the early Christian church, and that the Vatican had a pre-Christian history as a Roman religious site despite its present-day Catholic associations. Crediting him moreover with visionary power was justified by sources suggesting, rightly or wrongly, that at least towards the end of his life Hadrian was thought to have had mystical or prophetic gifts.[90] In this, Yourcenar was elaborating what she had already stated in a passage of the *Carnets*: Hadrian's clairvoyance was meant to illustrate the Faustian aspect of his character and followed the suggestive evidence not only of the *Sibyllines*, but of Aelius Aristides and Cornelius Fronto as well (*CNMH* 530). Her procedure was comparable to that of Shakespeare in allowing Macbeth a vision of the future kings of Scotland, or of Racine, in whose *Athalie* Joad has a vision of future Jewish history. It was permissible in a work defined not on this occasion as a historical biography but as a poem. In both aspects, however, Yourcenar appears to have been conscious of the extent to which her novel strained the limits of the factual record.

Such cases of a more or less clear authorial presence encouraged correspondents and interviewers to ask at times whether the Hadrian of *Mémoires* was not really Yourcenar herself, whether, that is, subject and author were not one and the same. Critics in turn regularly brought this as a charge against her. Her response was always a robust denial: it was not she who had built the Pantheon, stabilized the world, and maintained peace on Rome's frontiers.[91] It is easy nonetheless to see why the question was raised. It becomes more intense still when, to take the final example, Hadrian describes his initiation into the mystery cult of the god Mithras, an event for which, in contrast to everything discussed so far, there is no basis in the source tradition at all and an act of authorial imagination alone must be accepted. This is Hadrian's description of how while serving in Trajan's campaigns in Dacia he was admitted to the cult:

Je fus initié dans un donjon de bois et de roseaux, au bord du Danube, avec pour répondant Marcius Turbo, mon compagnon d'armes. Je me souviens que le poids du taureau agonisant faillit faire crouler le plancher à claire-voie sous lequel je me tenais pour recevoir l'aspersion sanglante. J'ai réfléchi par la suite aux dangers que ces sortes de sociétés presque secrètes pourraient faire courir à l'État sous un prince faible, et j'ai fini par sévir contre elles, mais j'avoue qu'en présence de l'ennemi elles donnent à leurs adeptes une force quasi divine. Chacun de nous croyait échapper aux étroites limites de sa condition d'homme, se sentait à la fois lui-même et l'adversaire, assimilé au dieu dont on ne sait plus très bien s'il meurt sous forme bestiale ou s'il tue sous forme humaine. (*MH* 326–7)

My initiation took place in a turret constructed of wood and reeds on the banks of the Danube, with Marcius Turbo, my fellow officer, for sponsor. I remember that the weight of the bull in its death throes nearly brought down the latticed floor beneath which I lay to receive the bloody aspersion. In recent years I have reflected upon the dangers which this sort of near-secret society might entail for the State under a weak ruler, and I have finally restricted them, but I admit that in presence of an enemy they give their followers a strength which is almost godlike. Each of us believed that he was escaping from the narrow limits of his human state, feeling himself to be at the same time himself and his own adversary, at one with the god who seems to be both the animal victim and the human slayer.

One of the most difficult tasks that confront ancient historians conditioned by monotheistic traditions is to comprehend and explicate the polytheistic world of Roman antiquity. This is particularly true of the so-called mystery cults and the presumably complex psychology of those who were initiated into them. What was it like in the second century to participate in the secret mysteries of Dionysus or Isis or Cybele? Yourcenar offers one answer here in her evocation of Hadrian's transcendental experience. The rite to which allusion is made is that of the *taurobolium*, a baptism of the worshipper in the blood of a bull sacrificed above a grille covering an underground chamber occupied by the candidate for initiation. It reappears when Hadrian later tells of Antinous's initiation at Palmyra (*MH* 425). The rite is ghoulish yet transporting, repulsive but liberating, or so it seems as Hadrian recounts an experience in which pleasure and pain, joy and disgust are simultaneously, confusingly felt.[92] Intensity of emotion is convincingly expressed. Yet while according to the tradition Hadrian was initiated into the Eleusinian mysteries in Greece, there is no evidence that he became a Mithraic devotee; and Yourcenar has drawn in any case on a rite belonging to the mysteries of Cybele, not those of Mithras, which is known chiefly from a highly tendentious and controversial description given by the late Roman poet Prudentius (*Perist.* 10.1006–50). Mystery cult initiates are well attested epigraphically from the second century onwards, and some were worshippers of both Mithras and Cybele. But this is not true of Hadrian. It was not the case, however, that Yourcenar wilfully misled her reader. She explained in the *Note* that the Mithraic episode was her own contrivance (*OR* 543), a startling admission of which most first-time readers of *Mémoires* could hardly be aware, and an admission that discloses a paradox, if not a bewildering contradiction: Yourcenar's narrative is avowedly faithful to the historical record but simultaneously incorporates episodes that are pure invention. What claim to biographical authority therefore does the overall portrait of Hadrian have, when fact and fiction are rendered indistinct?[93]

V

Through the filter of memory that lies at its poetic heart, *Mémoires* can be said in numerous ways to communicate a realistic sense of how life was lived in the Roman world of Hadrian and to fill the biographical vacuum as a result far more fully than conventional accounts. First-order authenticity is not in doubt, and that is the central point I have wanted in this chapter

to establish. Yet the issues of authorial transference and free invention latterly outlined have led to a problem, one formulation of which might be
to ask exactly how Yourcenar conceived of a historically faithful portrait
of Hadrian and how such a portrait was to be realized. She remarked in an
interview from the late 1980s that it is impossible ever to give a completely
precise description of any moment in anyone's life, but that approaching
the moment, which I take to mean drawing closer and closer to the reality of the moment, could continue indefinitely (*PV* 369). To examine the
methods deployed in approaching the moments of Hadrian's life becomes
accordingly the essential means by which to comprehend the nature of Yourcenar's response, imaginative and even experimental as it is, to the imperfect
historical tradition of the second century in which, incontestably, she had
fully immersed herself.

4

Authenticity Invented:
The Rules of the Game

To tell the whole story of a life the autobiographer must devise some means by which the two levels of existence can be recorded – the rapid passage of events and actions; the slow opening up of single and solemn moments of concentrated emotion.
Virginia Woolf

I

Marguerite Yourcenar was a combative person. Her truculence is a major theme of Josyane Savigneau's biography and is particularly evident in the letters that document confrontations with her publishers: she was never reluctant to threaten, or actually to take, legal action against any one of them. If a single aphorism from her writings were required to epitomize this aspect of her personality the choice would be simple: "Il faut toujours lutter." Comparable perhaps to a Roman coin legend, the phrase appears in several contexts where Yourcenar was faced with difficulties, and appropriately enough it became the title of the preface Savigneau contributed to *D'Hadrien à Zénon*. I begin this chapter, in order to illustrate further the commitment to historical fidelity, with accounts of two challenges made by informed readers to the historicity of *Mémoires* and of Yourcenar's reactions to them. I then show in contrast that the degree of fabrication in the novel is far more extensive than indicated so far, and the problem identified in the preceding chapter correspondingly more perplexing, but suggest finally that examination of Yourcenar's methods of composition resolves the tension between fidelity and fabrication, rendering comprehensible the overall conception of her biographical project. In all aspects, her characteristic strongmindedness is of the essence.[1]

II

Les Blazius et les Vadius existent, et leur gros cousin Basile est encore debout. Il m'est une fois, et une fois seulement, arrivé de me trouver en présence de ce mélange d'insultes et de plaisanteries de corps de garde, de citations tronquées ou déformées avec art pour faire dire à nos phrases une sottise qu'elles ne disaient pas, d'arguments captieux soutenus par des assertions à la fois assez vagues et assez péremptoires pour être crus sur parole par le lecteur respectueux de l'homme à diplômes et qui n'a ni le temps ni l'envie d'enquêter lui-même aux sources. Tout cela caractérise un certain genre et une certaine espèce, heureusement fort rares. (*CNMH* 538)

The pedants of comedy, Vadius and Blazius still exist, and their fat cousin Basil is ever about. Once and once only have I happened to be confronted with that mixture of insults and coarse jokes; with extracts truncated or skillfully deformed, so as to make our sentences say some absurdity which they do not say; with captious arguments built up by assertions both vague and peremptory enough to win ready credence from the reader respectful of academic trappings and lacking the time, or the desire, to look up the sources for himself. Characteristic, all of it, of a certain species which, fortunately, is rare.

So a notorious illustration of Yourcenar's distemper from the *Carnets*. It opens, as Grace Frick's gloss "pedants of comedy" makes clear, with a reference to carping characters from the classical French theatre who symbolized for Yourcenar academic critics of her book, or rather one critic in particular. This was Charles Picard, an eminent specialist in Greek and Roman art who published a sharp review of the first edition of *Mémoires* in the *Revue archéologique* of 1954.[2] Sarcastic and condescending, Picard was piqued by Hadrian's childhood recollection that no Greek statues were to be seen in Spain – "il n'y avait pas, je crois, une seule statue grecque dans toute la péninsule" – and by how little Hadrian knew about his native city of Italica. He suggested that the emperor who spoke "par cette voix féminine" should have been familiar with the material remains still to be seen onsite and in the archaeological museum at Seville nearby, supplying as they did ample evidence of the presence of Greek art in southern Spain in Hadrian's day. He asked whether Italica was not one of the cities to which L. Mummius long ago had sent statues and other artworks after his destruction and looting of Corinth, as Theodor Mommsen had once conjectured; he pointed to Hadrian's failure, in declaring that the great temple to Zeus Olympios at Athens, begun by the Pisistratids, had been almost immediately abandoned and left incomplete, to realize that centuries later the Seleucid king Antiochus IV had employed the Roman architect D. Cossutius when renewing the project; and he wondered why the "mosaïques des murailles" in the Villa at Tivoli could be given the strange description "dorées": what did this gilded word mean? Noting various misspelled names and significant gaps or infelicities in the *Note*'s references, he concluded that Yourcenar's claim to be hewing close to "la fidélité aux faits" was altogether disturbing. The absence, moreover, of illustrations from the book, none even of Antinous, elicited a stinging question: "Qui donc disait que les dames aimaient les photographies de beaux hommes?" And in final withering remarks the historical novel at large was condemned as an offence against history.[3]

Yourcenar's immediate reaction to the review is known from three letters written in mid-August and September 1954 during a twenty-two-month visit to Europe. They express outrage at Picard's insulting manner and make clear her intention of the moment to write a rejoinder. To the poet Alexis Curvers she said that in so doing she planned to use the resources of the library of the Institute of Archaeology in Munich, anticipating what she called a "grotesque duel." But the reason was unequivocally straightforward: "il faut toujours lutter" (*HZ* 369). She duly sought advice from her lawyer Jean Mirat, asking whether, and if so how, she could legally demand publication of her response in the *Revue*, and also whether it would matter that her reply was longer than Picard's review. A postscript noted that the journal had a correspondence section, so that publication should be considered routine. But she was worried because Picard was its "directeur" and would want to avoid public criticism. She feared being told that her reply had never been received.[4]

The enormous effort preparation of the response involved, as also the intensity of feeling Picard's assault had aroused, is revealed by a dossier of materials in the Houghton Library at Harvard University. It comprises a typed but incomplete draft, with a copy for Yourcenar's lawyer, of a cover letter to the director of the *Revue* (strongly worded, critical of Picard's tone, insistent on publication of a response); typed copies of the review itself; many notes made on hotel stationery and scraps of paper by Yourcenar and Frick dealing, chaotically, with numerous inscriptional, papyrological, textual, and bibliographical points of detail; and several typed pages and one handwritten page of drafts of the eventual response composed in the form of a letter from Munich dated 26 July 1954. The letter refutes Picard's objections one by one, systematically cites scholarly chapter and verse (complete with footnotes), uses the same phraseology of victimized outrage that appears in the correspondence, and confirms use of the resources of the library in Munich. It concedes nothing of substance, acknowledges no more than printing errors in the novel, and ends with a polite but firm apology for the letter's length, some 4,000 words in the fullest version, four times as long as Picard's review.

A single word, Yourcenar said, may give a false impression of a book or of its author's intentions, so that at times, unfortunately, whole pages were required to set the record straight.[5]

A four-page handwritten item from Yourcenar's *Notebook*, undated and (to me) illegible in places, supplies further information on the emotional toll the review exacted. In effect it is a preliminary version of the Blazius-Vadius entry in the *Carnets* and must be later than the letters and materials in the Houghton dossier, all of which evidently belong to the late summer of 1954. Full of anger still, a self-absorbed and self-pitying Yourcenar laments that she has tried to reply to Picard's absurd critique, but has been overcome by the demands of other work, fatigue, and disgust for his quibbling incomprehension of her procedures. Several drafts notwithstanding, she has abandoned the effort in the face of a Keatsian *taedium vitae* – "Je comprends mieux le dégoût mortel d'un Keats" – although a reply censuring Picard's objectionable methods will be necessary one day if only for the sake of protecting younger, less well-known writers more easily discouraged from their work. From all his prattling misrepresentation, all that has emerged is the discovery of three printing errors.[6]

Indignation extended well into the following year. In a letter from Northeast Harbor of 15 August 1955 to Alexis Curvers and his wife Marie Delcourt, in what was clearly an ongoing exchange on the subject, Yourcenar excoriated Picard as duplicitous and malicious, unworthy to be considered a scholar, and typically ignorant of literature; yet to engage with his pedantry, she said, was to risk looking as publicly myopic and ridiculous as he (*HZ* 481–2). In the event therefore no rejoinder was published in, or as far as I know submitted to, the *Revue archéologique*, nor was any legal action taken. Yourcenar's distress nonetheless lingered. She was unforgiving, and in time made the dyspeptic addition to the *Carnets*.

More positively, however, a long process soon began of gathering photographs from museums all over the world with which to illustrate future editions of *Mémoires*. And in subsequent printings changes were made to accommodate the questions Picard had raised. The line seen earlier concerning the Villa's mosaic decoration now became "les mosaïques des pavements ou des murailles n'étaient jamais assez mordorées" (*MH* 386). A sentence was amended to settle the issue of Greek statues in Spain: "une seule statue grecque" became "une seule bonne statue grecque" (*MH* 310) And in *Sæculum aureum* Hadrian when in Alexandria was made to have Italica in his thoughts and to act accordingly: "J'achetai chez un bon sculpteur tout un lot de Vénus, de Dianes et d'Hermès pour Italica, ma ville natale, que je me proposais de moderniser et d'orner" (*MH* 434).[7]

That this was due to Picard is clear from a letter Yourcenar wrote several years later, in June 1960, to Lidia Storoni Mazzolani:

On m'avait reproché de n'avoir pas mentionné l'existence des statues d'Italica, les plus belles et même les seules belles statues hellénistiques qui aient jamais jusqu'ici été trouvées en Espagne, dans la description dédaigneuse faite par l'Empereur du lieu de sa naissance, et j'ai essayé de donner ce qui est mon hypothèse, c'est que ces deux ou trois œuvres furent un don d'Hadrien lui-même à son pays natal. (*L* 148)

I had been criticized for not having mentioned the existence of statues from Italica, the most beautiful and indeed the only beautiful Hellenistic statues that have ever been found in Spain until now, in the scornful description of his place of birth given by the Emperor, and I have tried to give what is my hypothesis, namely that these two or three works were a gift from Hadrian himself to his natal land.

The critic's name goes unmentioned but is hardly in doubt, and the Houghton draft of Yourcenar's response to Picard shows exactly where the idea of a gift originated. She said there, quoting her own first version, "une seule statue grecque," that she intended the remark about the absence of Greek statues in Spain to consist with the impression that Hadrian's family was relatively indifferent to literature and art, thereby dramatizing Hadrian's later conversion to Hellenism. She had not meant to make a general statement on the character of high culture in Roman Spain, only to capture the mixed feelings she imagined Hadrian to have experienced when speaking late in life of a Spain he had left when very young. An article she had recently published demonstrated well enough her knowledge of the remains of Rome's presence in Spain. And no one in any case could say definitively whether there were any Greek statues in Italica for Hadrian to have seen in childhood, since precisely when the Hellenistic statues from Italica still visible arrived was unknown: she had consulted the relevant authoritative work on Spanish sculpture. In the spring of 1951, however, when in Seville, the director of the Archaeological Museum, Don Juan Lafitte, had suggested to her that some of the statues could well have been gifts from the Spanish emperor to the city of his birth, and it was this suggestion apparently that became the "hypothesis" underlying the new sentence.[8]

In the Picard episode at large Yourcenar's aggressiveness cannot be missed. For present purposes, however, two other features are more important: her self-assurance, first, that her portrait of Hadrian in *Mémoires* was historically justifiable, and her openness, secondly, to amendment of details no matter how painful the source of correction. The passage from the *Carnets*, splenetic at the outset, mercifully closes on a much milder note with a statement of gratitude to those scholars whose interventions had led to improvements in what she called her literary effort to reconstruct the past, and a similar remark was included in the letter of August 1955 to Curvers and Delcourt (*HZ* 482).[9] The commitment to historical accuracy was never in question:

Trop d'entre eux ont bien voulu spontanément se déranger pour rectifier après coup une erreur, confirmer un détail, étayer une hypothèse, faciliter une nouvelle recherche, pour que je n'adresse pas ici un remerciement amical à ces lecteurs bénévoles. Tout livre republié doit quelque chose aux honnêtes gens qui l'ont lu. (*CNMH* 539)

Too many of them have graciously, and of their own accord, taken trouble to rectify some error already in print, or to confirm a detail, support a hypothesis, expedite new research, for me not to express here a word of gratitude to such well-disposed readers. Each book which sees a new edition owes something to the discriminating people who have read it.

In July 1956 Yourcenar received from F.C. Grant the text of an address on *Mémoires* he had recently given at Union Theological Seminary in New York. She promptly acknowledged receipt but did not reply in detail. There were other obligations.[10] By early February 1957, however, she had discovered that Grant's unaltered address had been published in the *Anglican Theological Review* of 1956 as a de facto review of Frick's translation of the novel. Paul Minear, a local friend and theology professor at Yale had alerted her to the situation. The essay contained much praise, recall, but Grant asked many challenging questions as well, which together Yourcenar took to be another direct assault against her book. A second episode of determined resistance ensued.[11]

The origins of the affair are recoverable from two letters Yourcenar drafted to Grant that were never finished or despatched. The first is dated 6 February 1957 and occupies twelve and half pages in its modern printed format (*HZ* II 57–69). It apologizes for its tardiness in following up the initial acknowledgment of receipt, but then expresses surprise, and chagrin, that the address had been published without her knowledge. She would have written much sooner, she said, had she known that it was to be printed. She gave the statement of her aims in writing *Mémoires* to which I referred early in the previous chapter, and then systematically refuted some of the objections Grant had raised, those mainly concerning mystery cults and Hadrian's clairvoyance. The Greek and Latin authorities and the scholarly resources from which she had drawn material are cited – Cato, Numenius, the Suda, Lucian, Ovid, Hyginus, Catullus, Martial, Celsus – and individual scholars are named on whose views she had relied: Henry Bardon on the date of Juvenal's exile, Henri Grégoire on Christian persecutions. Some of Grant's questions remain unanswered, certain sentences are not in final form, and no conclusion is reached. The second draft, a more general letter little more now than two printed pages, belongs to later in the same year but is undated (*HZ* II 202–4). It states that Yourcenar had learned that Grant was to attend a meeting in late January 1958 at the Bangor Theological Seminary, and it issued a polite, even enticing invitation to visit Petite Plaisance for purposes of discussion. The invitation is accompanied, however, by a litany of complaints far from welcoming and cannot, I should think, have elicited a warm response had it ever been received. Grant is upbraided for not having forewarned Yourcenar of his intent to publish his essay, for not having waited to hear from her before doing so, for not having sent her a copy once it had appeared. After learning of its publication she had begun a point-by-point response to his questions, but the project had become too enormous and had been set aside because of more pressing work. In any case, due to his hasty and incomplete reading of the novel, some of the issues he raised were irrelevant, while others showed that he had failed to read her *Note*. His apparent praise for the book was undercut by his sceptical tone towards the scholarly foundations of the work and some of his remarks were insulting. Wishing nonetheless to avoid acrimony (so indeed she said), and anxious to resolve matters, she thought that face-to-face conversation would be profitable. There was much at stake: "Je tiens trop à la question de la vérité historique pour laisser la chose constamment sans réponse et je me sens moralement obligée de faire quelque chose pour corriger votre attaque implicite si vous n'entreprenez pas de le faire vous-même" (*HZ* II 203–4).[12]

The similarities between the drafts and Yourcenar's response to Picard are obvious. But because they were never finished, the invitation to Grant did not materialize and no meeting ever took place as far as I know. Their defiant character, however, is enough to illustrate Yourcenar's insistent urge to counter any perceived affront, and to some degree her attitude was merited. Grant may not have meant his essay to cause offence, but what would now be regarded as its sexist bearing is glaring – he constantly refers to her as "Miss Yourcenar" – and the manner in which he wrote of her treatment of Hadrian's relationship with Antinous, which as an Episcopalian minister he found abhorrent, is from a contemporary perspective both sexist and blatantly prejudicial: "I am amazed that the inner, emotional side of this type of erotic behavior is so well understood by a woman writer, and equally surprised that she does not let fall even a hint of her agreement with the "moralists" who disapproved the emperor's conduct. One expects a woman to protest this waste of affection by those who should normally devote it to the opposite sex. Perhaps it is due to her instinctive French understanding of human love and tenderness, even in grotesque and unnatural forms; or to her restraint as a novelist, writing strictly and objectively from the point of view of the Epicurean emperor." Yourcenar did not advance in her principal draft to the subject of Hadrian and Antinous. But it requires little effort to imagine the insult felt and the distress caused.[13]

The principal draft is in fact soberly written, with Yourcenar, as she says in the second letter, responding point by point to Grant's enquiries. "Was there a persecution of Christians in Antioch under Trajan?" She had drawn on the evidence of Ignatius of Antioch, aware that it was open to scholarly dispute but confident that it contained a kernel of truth. "Or did 'milk-fed serpents' glide about the Cave of Trophonius?" This was an unattested detail, to be sure, but it derived from evidence in Aristophanes's *Wealth* that gave reason to attribute a curative power to the snake during the ritual of incubation associated with Asclepius. "Were the rites of Mithras 'barbarous' during the first two centuries?" She knew that the rite of the *taurobolium* was not Mithraic – a reference to Prudentius occurs – but the influence of the cults of Cybele and Attis had led to a common perception that it was; iconographically Mithras was indistinguishable from Attis (and Paris), so that to Romans, conservative in matters of religion, Mithraism must at first have seemed a suspicious foreign cult (*HZ* II 61–4).[14] As much as any historian, it seems, Yourcenar knew the source tradition's weaknesses and the differing views of Hadrian that could consequently flow from any element within it. The sparse, fragmentary records of his involvement with mystery cults allowed him variously to be regarded as a figure who was simply curious, as a mystic and almost a visionary, or as a skilful politician who exploited religious practice for his own purposes. As she saw it, her decision to portray Hadrian's initiation at Eleusis as the central religious experience of his life lay in its essential likelihood, since it provided a unifying point of concentration for Hadrian's devotion to Hellenism, his political views, his concern as a cultured antiquarian to preserve and renew historical traditions, and perhaps also a genuine religious fervour. In turn, although the details of the experience could never be directly known because of the veil of secrecy that had always overhung Eleusinian ritual, imaginative deductions could be made from Cicero's *Somnium Scipionis*, cosmological details in Virgil, and even an epigram in the *Palatine Anthology* (*HZ* II 57–9). Further, Hadrian's clairvoyant description of Rome's doomed future was fully defensible. The sense of a world coming to an end, with an Edenic Golden Age lost for ever, could be strongly felt in Plutarch, Tacitus, and Juvenal, among others; and despite the risk of idealization, it did not seem impossible that a man of genius should have been able to feel cracks in the machine of empire whose weight he bore, and which was soon rapidly to break down. The great minds of the classical age were raised on the idea of the instability of all human affairs, the promise of Rome's eternity notwithstanding. Crude optimism was a rarity, and the tradition credited Hadrian in his old age with virtually superhuman powers: the Latin life, Aelius Aristides, the author of the *Sibylline Oracles*, Fronto – all could be summoned in support (*HZ* II 66–7).[15]

Yourcenar's rebuttal of Grant again illustrates an inherent combativeness – it betrays also perhaps a certain self-defensiveness – but more importantly it again gives evidence of the unassailable fact that a rational foundation underlies the manifold aspects of the portrait of Hadrian *Mémoires* presents. The deductions made might be contestable, and at times perhaps demonstrably wrong. But an inherent plausibility can be asserted in much of what the portrait contains given the command of sources and accompanying scholarship Yourcenar could easily, when required, put on display. She knew those sources far better in fact than those she took to be her adversaries, both Picard and Grant, and far better than most readers of her novel today might realize (classicists included). Her commitment to and pursuit of "la vérité" can scarcely therefore be impugned, and this indeed she always passionately, palpably defended. What distinguishes her biographical practice is the far from conventional approach of simultaneously undertaking to disclose "la poésie humaine de l'histoire" (*HZ* II 57). It is in this, not least, that complication lies.

III

La lutte contre la brutalité judiciaire continue: j'ai dû réprimander le gouverneur de Cilicie qui s'avisait de faire périr dans les supplices les voleurs de bestiaux de sa province, comme si la mort simple ne suffisait pas à punir un homme et à s'en débarrasser. (*MH* 506)

The struggle goes on against brutal misuse of judiciary power: I have had to reprimand the governor of Cilicia who took it into his head to execute under torture the cattle thieves in his province, as if simple death were not enough to punish a man and dispose of him.

In letters from the mid-1950s to the Greek author Constantin Coukidis and the Italian legal scholar Atanazio Mozzillo, Yourcenar acknowledged that in this extract from *Patientia* she had allowed herself a certain liberty. The evidence on which the passage was based identified the governor's province as Baetica, not Cilicia, but she had deliberately introduced the change – it was not a mistake – because Cilicia was more recognizable to her readership and made her narrative more accessible without compromising its integrity. The alteration was justifiable (*HZ* 522; *HZ* II 40 [Mozillo had written an appreciative essay on the novel for the Italian legal journal *Labeo*]).[16] The evidence concerned was a legal ruling in which the historical Hadrian stated that the standard penalty for cattle rustling, execution by decapitation, was not applied in all circumstances: if for instance the crime were not habitual, the lighter sentence of condemnation to hard labour, sometimes for a specified period of time, was imposed.[17] Yourcenar obviously understood the import of the ruling, and although she was aware that Hadrian did not in this instance write to the governor of Baetica but to Baetica's provincial council, to include the detail was irrelevant. The novel in the end was a work of literature not of scholarship. As she said to the sympathetic Ghislain de Diesbach in the summer of 1963, speaking of her career as a writer up until that date: "J'ai abordé des thèmes qui touchent au domaine de l'érudition, ou même qui y rentrent tout à fait, et que la plupart de nos contemporains ne fréquentent guère, les seuls spécialistes exceptés; d'autre part, ces spécialistes, quand il en est, n'ont pas toujours qualité pour juger d'une œuvre qui reste avant tout du domaine de la création littéraire, et ne prend l'érudition que comme un point de départ" (*HZ* III 424).[18] There was a difference, she added, between "l'interprétation poétique de l'histoire et l'histoire tout court," one that evidently permitted a certain manipulation of the source tradition (*HZ* III 425).[19]

Such interventions were indeed extensive. The early paragraphs of the *Note* provide a long catalogue of examples that illustrate Yourcenar's conception of how to write a literary life history (*OR* 543–5). She focuses first on twenty-three names of characters who appear in *Mémoires*, most of whom, she makes clear, are historically attested. She points at times to the sources that identify them, reporting that Isaeus, the instructor of the young Hadrian in Athens, is known from an inscription, and that the poet Strato of Sardis is an author known from the *Palatine Anthology*. But she admits that the roles they play in her narrative far exceed the information the sources contain, observing for instance that Hadrian's presence in Athens with Isaeus as she presents it is unverifiable. Some characters moreover have very weak origins: the name of Arete, the servant at the Villa whose death Hadrian found affecting, is taken from one of his poems, that of the courier Menecrates from a no more than legendary source, and the names of the servants Veronica and Theodoros she adapted from names in Marcus's *Meditations*. Some characters, however, are purely fictional: Hadrian's body slave, Euphorion, the tragic actor Olympos and the dancer Bathyllus, Leotychides, a Greek doctor with whom Hadrian studies in Athens, and his Caucasian guide Assar. There is no obfuscation here.[20]

The same is true, secondly, with the events Yourcenar itemizes. The gift of astrological prophecy attributed to Hadrian's grandfather Marullinus comes from the historical tradition, but as the gift of an uncle, not a grandfather. In turn, while Pompeius Proculus is known to have governed the province of Bithynia, whether he was in office when Hadrian arrived there, as the novel has it, is not. The conviction of the secretary Gallus for peculation, meant to bring out the emperor's rancour, is one of many fabrications that include the manner of Marullinus's death, and the cultic activities at Palmyra of three individuals, the merchant Meles Agrippa, the functionary Castoras, and Marcius Turbo.[21] She is explicit that nothing is known of the characters Chabrias, Celer, and Diotimus other than a notice in Marcus's *Meditations* of their exceptional loyalty to Hadrian's memory. Nonetheless, she has used them to suggest something of the flavour of Hadrian's court in his last years: Chabrias, as a philosopher, to represent the Stoics and Platonists who supposedly surrounded Hadrian, Celer the military element, and Diotimus, the young courtiers in whom Hadrian had an erotic interest. Other elements are equally contrived but again suggestively defensible: Hadrian's encounter with a gymnosophist, his early love affairs, Lucius's presence in Alexandria prior to Antinous's death. Magical practices imaginatively described at Canopus and an accident suffered by a small child draw on Egyptian documents, though attribution of the architect Apollodorus's execution to discovery of a plot against Hadrian is pure hypothesis. Finally, Hadrian's engagements with sorceresses do no more than elaborate hints in the sources, while the names he sees on the Colossus of Memnon at Thebes are taken from records of visitors to the site.[22] Yourcenar's conception of historical life writing, it emerges, permitted enhancement or embellishment of materials found defective in the interests, as it were, of filling in some of the gaps the materials exposed, but without in her well-informed mind unreasonably straining their limits. She granted herself considerable leeway, but did not indulge in absolute fiction for its own sake and certainly not in sensationalistic or extravagant fiction. Her overriding aim, as she reaffirmed at a late date, was to achieve biographical authenticity through unforgettable impressions (*AN* 1037).[23]

The scale of enhancement, however, is far greater than the *Note* suggests. The changes or adaptations seem to be relatively few – "assez peu nombreux" (*OR* 543) – but they are far more numerous than the unsuspecting reader can appreciate.[24] To some extent this was a practical matter. Some months before publication, in July 1951, Yourcenar told Constantin Dimaras that Plon had allotted just five or six pages for a printable version of the *Note*, which was clearly insufficient to cover the material she had at hand. The remainder she hoped to publish elsewhere (*L* 89–90). Later, in an important letter of 15 March 1953 to her friend Hortense Flexner, she explained that what the *Note*'s seven pages contained was a mere sample selected from an original dossier of thirty-six single-spaced typed pages listing and discussing the sources on which her novel was based (*HZ* 238).[25] Those pages can now be found, allowing for an inaccurate page count, in Yourcenar's *Notebook*, one section of which is headed "Faits historiques modifiés ou Faits imaginés (i.e. sans source historique directe)."[26] The pages are indeed typed in single space, they contain many handwritten annotations and emendations, and they give Yourcenar's reasons for composing as she did in some ninety-two passages of the novel. Any thought that she may have intended to conceal her procedure is obviously inadmissible.

Entries in the *Note* were sometimes adapted from the preliminary versions of the *Notebook*. On Mithraic initiation, for instance, the Pléiade, its text unchanged from the first edition, reads: "L'épisode de l'initiation mithriaque est inventé; ce culte était déjà, à cette époque, en vogue aux armées; il est possible, mais nullement prouvé, qu'Hadrien, jeune officier, ait eu la fantaisie de s'y faire initier" (*OR* 543). The *Notebook* has this entry: "Tout l'épisode de l'initiation d'H. au culte de Mithra pendant les guerres daces est sans fondement historique; la supposition s'appuie seulement sur le fait que ce culte s'était propagé avec rapidité dans les cercles militaires, sans toutefois y avoir déjà acquis l'immense importance qu'il allait avoir au IIIe siècle. Il n'est pas absurde de supposé [*sic*] qu'H. à vingt ans se laissa prendre aux appâts de ce culte étranger, et pendant une campagne." A handwritten marginal note adds: "'contamination' entre le culte mithriaque et celui de la Grande Mère (sacrifice et baptême), plus que debatable, mais à la limite du possible."[27] (The *Note* similarly introduces the corrupting influence of the cult of the Syrian goddess on the Mithraic ritual of baptism: "à cette époque où les religions du salut «contaminaient»" [*OR* 544]).[28]

Like the *Note*, however, the *Notebook* emphasizes throughout the historical foundations of the passages to which its contents refer or the reasoning behind them. History, Yourcenar writes, in an entry crossed out by hand, does not tell us that Hadrian met Epictetus at Rome, as the novel has it, but he could have done so and a reference to Spartianus is inserted as if proving the point [cf. *HA Hadr.* 16.10]). His relations with practitioners of the occult are drawn from what the chroniclers teach us about his appetites for the curious, and although he probably knew Philo of Byblus and Numenius, we do not know if he did or did not meet Satyrus, a doctor of the time. A scene furthermore in the Museum of Alexandria is authentic, except for the presence of Hadrian's court musician, Mesomedes of Crete, which history does not affirm; a handwritten note adds "pas probable." The episode of a Libyan hunting expedition depends heavily on a poem from a certain Pancrates known from a papyrus, while an episode in which an enraged Hadrian blinds an unfortunate slave is taken directly from Galen. Scenes of Dacian prisoners burned alive, of advisers to king Decebalus committing suicide, and of other atrocities of war are inspired by the reliefs of Trajan's Column.[29] And again there are pure inventions: a meeting with Plutarch is unattested but plausible, one with Acilius Attianus at Brindisi follows the spirit of history alone, Hadrian may or may not have met the philosopher Demonax, his admiration for the poetry of Theognis and taste for the female dancers of Gades are pure suppositions. Again, however, the intent is not to falsify but to augment the sparse record in historically credible fashion. Accordingly, a sorcerer's prediction that Hadrian would not die by drowning is based on his frequent consultation of such a figure; whether Neratius Priscus helped Hadrian in the study of law is unknown, but he was Hadrian's friend and legal adviser; an affair with a senator's wife can be deduced from what is known about his private life.[30]

Indisputably, therefore, *Mémoires* is not an ordinary academic biography and cannot now be read as a precisely positivist record of Hadrian's life. But this is not to say that it cannot be read as a realistic evocation of Hadrian's life on its own terms, which are those of a fictive autobiography reliant on the subject's memory-challenged recollections in which fidelity to facts or the spirit of history – the facts of history generally speaking – is arguably maintained in a manner consistent with the explanations prospectively produced for Picard and Grant. Yourcenar proceeded in her enterprise from the same starting point as academic historians, assessing the evidence available and making decisions about the meaning of its various constituents, and chose for her reconstruction the medium of a retrospective biography that allowed her to avoid the unrealizable goal of a prosaic linear factual narrative, but that by proceeding within the boundaries of plausibility made it possible to locate and to define the individual figure in a world whose cultural contours were perceptible. The medium also had, and still retains, the attractive advantage of making unnecessary the ubiquitous "possiblies and probablies" of academic discourse. Instead, it brings the past to life through an author's carefully prepared imagination, as if drawing on the rhetorical figure deployed by orators and historians in antiquity to bring before their audiences' or readers' eyes a vivid picture of actual events, with details enhanced, or even invented, for the sake of an immediacy that would provoke an emotional, sympathetic response. This was what Greeks called *enargeia*, and Romans *illustratio*, *evidentia*, or *demonstratio*.[31] To Atanazio Mozzillo, Yourcenar admitted that scholars might well be shocked by what she termed her light modifications: they caused her pangs of conscience, and amending in one edition after another she tried to keep them to an absolute minimum. The grand object of her book nevertheless was to capture the human reality of Hadrian. To do so in a literary narrative that was integrated, comprehensible, and full of life, punctilious details had sometimes to be suitably accommodated without sacrificing their significance (*HZ* II 39–42).

IV

In all of this much more was involved than a narrative of events alone, no matter how credibly situated in time, place, and mentality they were. Yourcenar also set out to disclose Hadrian's inner life, his emotions, his reactions and responses to events (and personages) – the workings of his personality. She adverted to this ambitious aspect of her project frequently once *Mémoires* had been published: "Refaire du dedans ce que les archéologues du XIXe siècle ont fait du dehors," she stated in the *Carnets* (*CNMH* 524), and in almost identical words in an interview from 1954, "il s'agissait de refaire du dedans ce que les archéologues avaient fait du dehors avant moi" (*PV* 36).[32] How was this to be done? As Bernard Crick was to write much later in his celebrated biography of George Orwell, "None of us can enter into another person's mind; to believe so is fiction."[33] And Yourcenar herself could acknowledge that there was a certain rashness to her enterprise, allowing on one occasion that the thoughts she had attributed to Hadrian could not be proven genuine (*PV* 103). But the goal, she said, was to show Hadrian in all his complexity and uniqueness regardless, with the wrinkles of Roman veristic art as her guide, in what was an almost religious belief that the external record contained significant details from which the interior life could be successfully discovered (*PV* 123). There was always that revelatory moment when a detail disclosed the person as he must have been (*PV* 160). Arnaldo Momigliano was later to specify that the biographer had an "additional task" that a historian never had to face, namely the obligation "of inferring from external details the mental state of the individual about whom he is writing."[34] It was an obligation that Yourcenar had already recognized and accepted. As she simply, but unobjectionably, said, "Mais aucune existence ne peut se juger du dehors" (*AN* 1004).[35] Importantly, therefore, what she presented of Hadrian's personality was not from her viewpoint fiction in any usual sense; it was as historically authentic as anything communicated of Hadrian's external world and has to be regarded as such in any assessment of her achievement.

Three elements were identified in the method of recovery: disciplined academic research, sensitivity to historical and cultural context, and recourse to the constancy of human nature over time (*CNMH* 528–9). These "rules of the game" as Yourcenar called them are set out in a long passage of the

Carnets that complements an earlier entry identifying as prerequisites for success exacting scholarship ("érudition") and something Yourcenar called *"magie sympathique,"* an ability to enter in thought the biographical subject's inner world – "à se transporter en pensée à l'intérieur de quelqu'un" (*CNMH* 526).[36] The first rule is uncontroversial. Yourcenar's academic preparation needs at this stage no further corroboration. The two that remain are interrelated and, in the third case especially, more demanding. I consider them in inverse order.

To posit an unchanging human nature as a means of historical reconstruction may provoke surprise at first blush and perhaps unease. It is an aspect of investigation that conventional Roman biography tends to avoid. Yourcenar's position, however, was firm, explicable, and cogent. In her discussions with Patrick de Rosbo she compared human feelings and emotions, the constituents of human nature, to the seven notes of a musical scale that were more or less changeless and therefore identifiable, but capable at the same time of immense variation and combination, the result being that they manifested themselves in thousands of different ways over time from one epoch to another and from one milieu to another (*ER* 44). If, for instance, methods of warfare in the modern world were materially different from those used by Attila – and here Yourcenar depressingly referred to what was then the current use of napalm and herbicides in Vietnam – this was a matter of technological change alone, not of the psychological underpinning involved: in both cases deployment stemmed from immutable human needs and instincts (*ER* 57–8). Accordingly, as the long passage from the *Carnets* had made clear, those needs and instincts, once acknowledged, offered a point of contact between past and present: just like us, people in the past crunched their olives and drank their wine, smeared their fingers with honey and struggled against the bitter wind and blinding rain, sought the summer shade of a plane tree, took their pleasures and thought their thoughts, and eventually grew old and died. The essence of the human condition was eternally fixed, and perceptible therefore across time (*ER* 63; *CNMH* 529).[37]

Such views were long held. Yourcenar once stipulated, for example, birth, death, love, and sickness as the most significant aspects of human existence, constants, but constants that presented across time and place in particularist ways, and it was the past's connections to, and differences from, the present that interested her in writing a historical novel (*PV* 59 n.2).[38] On another occasion, she cited suicide as an example of what this meant: to the Japanese the decision to take one's life was heroic, the supreme proof of the triumph of courage and free will, whereas for Christians the decision was far more contentious, given that it was God's will that life was to be lived to its natural end (*PV* 109–10).[39] Later still, she wrote that although history might bring majestic changes, the fundamentals of human nature were always the same: generosity, kindness, intelligence, and a certain desire to see things realistically were countered by cupidity, stupidity, ignorance, brutality, and an inordinate preoccupation with the self that demanded the imposition of one's own views on others (*HZ* IV 329; *PV* 179–80).[40] Affected by time and place, these features manifested themselves differently due to culturally specific idioms and the extraordinary plasticity of human nature, but overall they showed little variation in themselves and the effects they produced. Human essentialism, therefore, as Yourcenar conceived it, transcending the historically contingent, provided the means of entry into Hadrian's inner life, with time no more than an illusory irrelevance: "Le temps ne fait rien à l'affaire. Ce m'est toujours une surprise que mes contemporains, qui croient avoir conquis et transformé l'espace, ignorent qu'on peut rétrécir à son gré la distance des siècles" (*CNMH* 527).[41] The point was easily explained by imagining a succession of two dozen pairs of skeletal hands (no more), or a sequence of twenty-five long-lived persons, lugubrious images to be sure, but images that gave the right perspective (*CNMH* 520–1): the immanence of the human condition allowed construction of a bridge between past and present, between one's ancestors and oneself, and between Marguerite Yourcenar and the emperor Hadrian. At issue was "a consciousness beyond the temporal, knowledge of a timeless reality."[42]

Yourcenar offered no objective criteria for these views. They were either intuitive, or the result of reflection on her own life experience and of her profound knowledge of world history, or a combination of both. In effect she was a cultural relativist, writing *Mémoires* at a moment when the anthropological school of Franz Boas held a certain intellectual prominence. Ruth Benedict had remarked in her enormously successful *Patterns of Culture* (1934) on the widely divergent attitudes to suicide found in differing cultures, and notably included in her late work *Chrysanthemum and the Sword* (1946) observations on Japanese views of suicide very much in line with those of Yourcenar.[43] Benedict's concern was with cultural disparities in societies at the macro-level and the distinctive dominant values that emanated from what she called "the raw materials of existence." She said little of human nature itself or of what she called "human temperament" or referred to simply as human "instincts." But her "raw materials" encompassed any number of what can only be taken as absolute states of emotion universally experienced by human subjects: anger, love, grief, fear, suspicion, despair, humiliation, jealousy, disgrace, shame, affection, some of which Yourcenar herself will have known from her encounters with Picard and Grant. Alluding in the mid-1970s to ethnology, a discipline barely a hundred years old, Yourcenar was certain that the religious sentiments of anguish and fervour felt by the prehistoric sorcerer and the Christian of any age were identical (*AN* 958–9). To all intents and purposes she subscribed to the crisp summary of the Boas doctrine, "Cultures are many; man is one."[44]

The connection can be no more than tentative. But Yourcenar certainly knew the Polish émigré Bronislaw Malinowski, whose study of the Trobriand Islanders, *The Argonauts of the Western Pacific* (1922), had earlier opened a new chapter in the history of anthropology. It was in his apartment in New York that Yourcenar listened in June 1940 to news on the radio of the fall of France, calling him in a later memoir of a visit to Poland "le grand ethnologue."[45] In November 1941, she and Frick entertained him prior to a lecture Malinowski gave at Hartford Junior College where Frick was then the college's dean.[46] And in a letter to Emmanuel Boudot-Lamotte of October 1945, she spoke of him as one of her best friends in the United States, remarking that while she had not yet read his newly published book, *The Patterns of Cultural Change*, she expected to recommend it for publication in France, on the assumption that it would be as important as its predecessors (*ACB* 121).[47] The book's correct title is in fact *The Dynamics of Cultural Change: An Inquiry into Race Relations* (1945), and a copy can be found at Petite Plaisance, as can a second posthumous publication, *A Scientific Theory of Culture and Other Essays* (1944), where Malinowski defines human nature as "the biological determinism which imposes on every civilization and on all individuals in it the carrying out of such bodily functions as breathing, sleep, rest, nutrition, excretion and reproduction."[48] A universalizing construct, that is, whose organizational forms and institutions he described as multifarious and differing from society to society. The extent of any putative connection is obviously indeterminable, but the letter to Boudot-Lamotte implies some familiarity on Yourcenar's part with his and similar theories. At a minimum the confluence of anthropological circumstances apparent is suggestive.

In any case Yourcenar's views were hardly revolutionary. She might be presumed to have known that Gibbon had long ago regarded human emotions as a vital resource when historical sources were in short supply – "knowledge of human nature and of the dire operation of its fierce and unrestrained passions, might, on some occasions, supply the want of historical materials" – and that in his record of even the relatively well-documented life of the emperor Julian, he had taken account of a plethora of sentiments, hope and fear, gratitude and revenge, duty and ambition, love of fame and fear of reproach, no matter how impossible it was to measure their impact.[49]

Criticism has of course been offered. Yourcenar's concept of timelessness negates that of the historical, it is said, because the historian's subject matter is change, not similarity, and the very viability of the historical novel is consequently undermined.[50] Yet the elementary fact has to be registered that change cannot be identified until the past has first been fully recovered on its own terms. Yourcenar's position, it happens, now finds new support from Ramsay MacMullen's illustration of a scientifically documented global and cross-cultural human nature that may indeed, as Gibbon believed, function as a legitimate tool of historical analysis: emotions such as anger, sadness, shame, pride, and guilt, known to the historians of classical antiquity but equally evident in the progression of modern American history, vary in expression across time and place but in essence are universal. They crystallize, MacMullen shows, in the concept of a "pancultural" human nature, a view strikingly similar to that of Yourcenar, and one moreover available as much to the novelist as to the historian, the result being that as authorities on the past the distinction between the two may well altogether disappear.[51]

As for the all-important "sympathetic magic," Yourcenar meant by this a communion-like experience between author and literary character, whether historical or fictional, achieved when distinctions between past and present were erased and prolonged concentration created a sense of intimacy that permitted her to sense her character's affecting presence and influence.[52] She explained the experience to Matthieu Galey in terms that connote the quasi-mystical or transcendent:

Quand on passe des heures et des heures avec une créature imaginaire, ou ayant autrefois vécu, ce n'est plus seulement l'intelligence qui la conçoit, c'est l'émotion et l'affection qui entrent en jeu. Il s'agit d'une lente ascèse, on fait taire complètement sa propre pensée; on écoute une voix: qu'est-ce que cet individu a à me dire, à m'apprendre? Et quand on l'entend bien, il ne nous quitte plus. Cette présence est presque matérielle, il s'agit en somme d'une «visitation». (*YO* 238–9)

When one spends hour upon hour with an imaginary character or a character who lived in the past, one's conception of that character ceases to be a product of the intelligence alone; emotion and affection also come into play. Little by little you withdraw from the world and silence your own thoughts. You listen to a voice and ask, What does this person have to tell me, to teach me? And once you have heard that voice well, it will never leave you. The character's presence is almost physical: in a word it's a "visitation."

I construe this as having much in common with what Keith Hopkins opportunely termed "empathetic imagination," the capacity to escape the confines of the present and the clinical modes of thought by which all are bound as victims of time and place, to penetrate the past by emotively imagining what people in antiquity "thought, felt, experienced, believed," and to exploit a sense of "empathetic wonder" in order to discover what it was like to be there.[53] A generation earlier, the historian of Victorian England G.M. Young had similarly written of total immersion in pertinent documents and chronological blocking in the pursuit of an imaginative realization of "three-dimensional" and "stereoscopic" historical scenes: "Go on reading," Young had said, "until you can hear people talking. Then you will understand why things happened as they did," one outcome being the claim that his celebrated essay "Portrait of an Age" was written "wholly from the inside," with an ability "to think Victorian" long maintained.[54] It is a strategy in fact that can be traced back at least to the nineteenth-century German philosopher Wilhelm Dilthey, which means that Yourcenar's practice belongs to a long tradition culminating for contemporary Romanists in Hopkins's formulation, "history is, or should be, a subtle combination of empathetic imagination and critical analysis."[55] The parallels are plain, although for Yourcenar the historical biographer the pertinent question became twofold: not only what it was like to be there, but also what it was like to be Hadrian. The answer lay in following all the rules of the game, but especially in the exploitation of sympathy or empathy. (The terms were more or less synonymous: Yourcenar used both when explaining to Patrick de Rosbo her ability to access the inner world of the past and its protagonists [ER 61].)[56] Wonderment was what the novelist writing true biography could bring to the enterprise, asking what it would be like to see the Parthenon as the Greeks saw it, shining, full of gold and colour, or how a whole day of Hadrian's life could be fully restored from a momentary detail in an obscure historical source (YO 56, 61).[57]

Even so, Yourcenar's experience of sympathetic magic was rather different from what I take to be the imaginative working experience of ordinary academic historians. The experience is called in the Carnets "une méthode de délire," a phrase Yourcenar glossed as "une participation constante, et la plus clairvoyante possible, à ce qui fut" – "a method akin to controlled delirium," in Frick's translation, "a constant participation, as intensely aware as possible, in that which has been" (CNMH 526). To Matthieu Galey, she said that it meant the attainment of what seems to the observer a trance-like state, in which through deep, Hindu-like contemplation the mind is cleared of all pre-existing ideas and thoughts, and the character of the historical subject fully absorbed: a kind of self-willed identification between author and historical subject which leads to a state that could be called "le comble de la sagesse" (*YO* 153–4).[58] A connection seems evident with the opening of the long passage on "the rules of the game" where Yourcenar refers to drawing on Ignatius of Loyola's *Spiritual Exercises* and Hindu asceticism in order to gain understanding through meditation (*CNMH* 528). As she informed the neuropsychiatrist Humphrey Osmond, her practice was the result of extensive reading not only in psychology and philosophy, but also in mystical literature both Christian and Eastern (*HZ* II 306–8).[59]

The *Notebook* leaves little doubt of Yourcenar's ability to achieve a state of mind that in her understanding produced a sense of intimate identification with her characters and a deep immersion into the settings she created for them. It refers to her once being found in a trance when she was writing a passage in *Mémoires* that describes Hadrian's ascent of Mt. Etna with Antinous (*MH* 412), and to once willing herself to feel Hadrian's tears on her face – the tears, I think, that she has Hadrian shed when Antinous died (*MH* 440, 443). The record it gives of the writing of the novel's final scene at Baiae is remarkable (*MH* 515): she felt the weight of the bed covers on Hadrian's swollen arms, stood up the better to see between his pillows, wept with Diotimus, identified with both the distressed Chabrias and the dying Hadrian who consoled him, as if she herself were the aged emperor conscious of the sweetness of flesh still left in his fingertips. Words then follow almost identical to those of the later version of the *Carnets* – "j'ai essayé d'aller jusqu'à la dernière gorgée d'eau, le dernier malaise, le dernier regard. L'empereur n'a plus qu'à mourir" – and acknowledgment is made of the tears she finally shed not only for Hadrian, but for his creator and everyone else as well. This was all attributable, it seems, to the combination of a magical art with an intellectual operation that allowed Yourcenar to communicate across the great interval of eighteen centuries separating her from her subject, and gave access to both the inner and outer dimensions of the scene she was creating. To establish human constancies across such a vast interval was the work of the magician, and the creative phenomenon itself, dependent on deep emotional absorption, was the result of empathetic application.[60]

Such evidence consists with a pronouncement Yourcenar made in 1957 on the technique of emotional identification Josyane Savigneau quotes in her biography, to the effect that sympathy in its true meaning was essential for understanding a character's inner life, and that sympathy itself required the exercise of imagination.[61] Yet to adopt the suggestion of defining Yourcenar's experience as "metempsychosis" seems to me to take a step too far. The term is taken from Philippe Lejeune, who used it allusively of Yourcenar's description of her birth in the first instalment of her novel-like family history, *Souvenirs pieux*. A bold theory then follows: Yourcenar's self-identification with Hadrian is an expression of a pathological narcissism impelled by a quest for the mother she had never known and mediated through an obsession with homosexuality.[62] I do not question that Yourcenar the creative artist worked at a level of both emotional concentration and intellectual perception of a rare order, or that she believed that the presence of her characters could at times be sensed. As she explained to Humphrey Osmond, however, French "délire" has a much more figurative meaning than English "delirium" (*HZ* II 307); and her remarks in the *Postface* of 1981 to her early novella *Anna soror* ... illustrate well enough the belief that she was one of many novelists who knew what it was to experience intimate encounters with their characters during moments of literary composition, sensations of loss or possession (*AS* 936).[63] Ultimately, the method of undeviating contemplation appears to have been as deliberate in the moment as it was an extraordinary, keenly intuitive, means by which to increase the prospects of success in the endeavour of recovering the reality of the past.[64]

"The drama, the human interest of the individual life will always retain its hold on the general public. Historians will demand larger views." So again Ramsay MacMullen.[65] Immediate thoughts return to Lytton Strachey and *Eminent Victorians*, where a sequence of individual lives uncovers aspects of an era allegedly too complex for its history to be written. Instead, representative life stories are the sources of true, and perennially valuable, historical knowledge, their form of art constrained by obligations to privilege the significant over the redundant and critical truth over panegyric. A careful selection of relevant material is required, with psychological insight into personality and the vivid animation of subjects secured through artistic imagination. The historical truth duly, and notoriously, exposed in this instance is the hypocrisy of the Victorian age and the pernicious consequences of Victorian Christianity its celebrated adherents exemplified: lust for ecclesiastical power, neurotic pursuit of "abnormal" feminine influence, dogmatism and disdain for the lower classes, fanaticism and overweening ambition. In every case, the facade of commitment to Christian principles is shattered by conflicting factors of class and status, so that English gentility emerges as a barrier to any genuine application of the Gospel. A supreme ironist, Strachey illustrated his subjects' weaknesses in mortifying manner, his most flagrant example being Cardinal Manning's support for an item of canon law in 1870 that rendered faith superfluous for reception into the Catholic Church. On any count, biography reveals itself as a subtle literary form, rich and provocative, yet completely capable of capturing the historical currents of an age without recourse to crude chronography.[66]

For Yourcenar, however, it was not biography but history itself that aroused her scepticism. Her *Notebook* contains a three-page handwritten list of thirty-one facts deliberately omitted from *Mémoires*, as if Strachey's principle of biographical selectivity were clearly understood. They include references to figures of whom she was clearly aware (Platorius Nepos), social customs (the types of napkin used at the imperial table), and anecdotes from the source tradition (stories recounted by Phlegon). But her preference for the biographical over the historical was more significantly expressed through the distrust she displayed towards the practice of history at large. She told Patrick de Rosbo that she found the rigid ideological preconceptions or theories of historians rebarbative: they "hardened" and "purged" the past, falsely systematizing it, by which she can only have meant distorting it. It was a mistake to align historical facts on a Marxist or structuralist or any other ideological axis, to arrange events in order to show the progress of capitalism or technology. This was to emaciate the past, and not a contemporary problem alone: Christianizing history as far back as the seventeenth century had been just as misdirected (*ER* 56). As she pointed out moreover to Atanazio Mozzillo, historians could never free themselves from their present: Mommsen was the product of Prussian militarism and rigour, Gibbon of Enlightenment anticlericalism (*HZ* II 43–4). Not surprisingly, Hadrian shared her judgment, with an outcome already seen: "Les historiens nous proposent du passé des systèmes trop complets, des séries de causes et d'effets trop exacts et trop clairs pour avoir jamais été entièrement vrais; ils réarrangent cette docile matière morte, et je sais que même à Plutarque échappera toujours Alexandre" (*MH* 302–3).[67]

Yourcenar gave a synoptic statement of her views in a lecture originally delivered in Paris in February 1954 and later revised. It is entitled *L'Écrivain devant l'Histoire*.[68] It begins by tracing History's long trajectory in the West from antiquity onwards, showing many points of correspondence with her other statements. Positing that a personified History is essentially a form of human memory whose first pre-literate manifestation took the form of myth, she distinguished in the Western tradition four historical attitudes: legendary history, exemplary history, humanist history, and modern scientific history. The first two belonged to the mediaeval world and were concerned respectively with the noble and the ethically edifying. They had no need of historical accuracy in any modern sense. A major shift came with the Renaissance and the development of an attitude that sought the universal and unchangeable in the past. History became a humanistic means of individual self-improvement, with a belief in human dignity and a human ability to use reason in judging problems that allowed instruction by example (*EH* 125, 152). In a subsequent phase, Romanticism brought a reactionary taste for the exotic and the primitive, encouraging both nationalist identities and individual rebelliousness even as interest in *realia* was maintained, until finally in the modern age a complete rejection of history had occurred due to the emergence of popularization, the seclusiveness of specialist academic enquiry, and the abuse of history for ideological purposes. The intrusion of propaganda, the burdens of massive documentation, and history's very complexity had shattered all hopes of achieving historical truth, the result being an alienation from the past, a popular disaffection exacerbated by the catastrophic events of the 1930s and 1940s.[69]

Positioning herself not as an academic historian but a literary author of a work on a historical subject, Yourcenar then set out the principles she had adopted in writing *Mémoires* in this moment of isolation. As in the *Carnets* and her remarks to Patrick de Rosbo, thorough knowledge of the basic source material, in all its heterogeneity, came first, together with knowledge of specialist research; but with the supplement now of the benefits brought by travel to the regions of concern.[70] Historical truth could be approached, if at times remaining finally inaccessible, but a distinction was needed between hard facts (the battle of Waterloo of June 1815) and plausibilities, confidence in which was especially difficult when the inner life of historical actors was at issue. She gave a telling illustration. In the absence of definitive evidence, it would never be known whether Hadrian had forged Trajan's will to allow him to succeed to the emperorship, as there was reason to believe, or whether Trajan's wife Plotina had influenced Trajan to choose Hadrian as his successor. Even if new evidence were found, it would be unreliable, coming from either a friend or an enemy, while a genuine confession from Hadrian himself could never be expected: "Nous sommes là dans un domaine où pour de bonnes raisons nous ne saurons jamais la vérité parce que trop de gens avaient intérêt à la cacher" (*EH* 132).[71] There was much therefore that could be a matter of hypothesis alone: Hadrian's state of mind while serving in Trajan's Dacian wars or his real feelings for Sabina.

There were nonetheless other steps to be taken. The writer had consciously to set aside all contemporary ideas and to understand the past on its own terms, one strategy in Hadrian's case (again) being to read everything that Hadrian himself had read. This allowed the writer to understand the moral and intellectual ethos in which he had lived and to think of his life as he himself thought of it (*EH* 134, 161).[72] A "system of equivalences" had next to be established, by which Yourcenar meant uncovering the ways in which human emotions, constant across time, expressed themselves in specific historical contexts. She used this time the example of St. Francis, who, in choosing an ascetic life, withdrew from the world of commerce, casting his luxurious clothes before his father's feet in what at the time had been an act of religious import, but that today could be compared to a son's rebellion against his father's wishes in which religious sentiment was inconsequential: the mystical impoverished vagabond wandering across Italy shared the feelings of the young contemporary poet who rejected the security of a profession and turned instead to the world of ideas or sentiment. Cultural context differed, but in both cases the human emotions at work were identical (*EH* 134–5, 162). Similarly, if the historical subject were a tyrant – Genghis Khan, Timour, Hitler, Stalin – the writer had to paint as accurate a portrait as possible of his unique individuality; he was a figure regardless who condensed in one form or another the violence and greed that were timeless aspects of the human condition (*EH* 163).

The task that finally remained was for the writer to decide on the best manner of communicating what had been learned. How could historical figures be made to speak? The idioms and tones of the past were irrecoverable, those of the present unsuitable. Compromise was required, minimizing offence to the past but permitting appreciation of both its cultural distinctiveness and the constancy of the human condition (*EH* 163–4). Yourcenar had made Hadrian speak in the first person accordingly not as a novelist's fantasy, but in the hope that he would express himself in terms of his own life and destiny, in other words authentically. Equally, she had wanted to present human life in all its fluidity before it became entrenched in a noble but congealed system too often called "History"; and she had chosen a protagonist whose world in its "structures mentales" had something in common with the contemporary world, if, she feared, increasingly less so: "un monde dans lequel l'homme jouit des bénéfices d'une longue culture, a derrière lui un passé et croit avoir un avenir, croit à la possibilité de réformer certaines choses, de maintenir certaines autres, peut voyager de pays à pays, peut se faire une idée globale de l'humanité" (*EH* 164).[73] Hadrian's intellectual disposition resembled ours in matters that counted, and he was to be an intermediary between past and present. Her project consequently had been to create a neo-humanist history that privileged above all what she called "l'éternelle fluctuation des choses humaines" (*EH* 165).[74] And for the sake of her audience's self-knowledge and, more importantly still, its knowledge of others, she had aspired to make a small advance in knowledge of the human being in what, at a minimum, had been a learning experience for herself.

A compelling feature of the lecture is the number of historical authorities introduced to substantiate its views. They range, in one more indication of erudition, from Suetonius and Plutarch in antiquity to the more recent giants Gibbon and Mommsen, and now the contemporary Toynbee.

She omitted the pioneering *Annalistes* of the early twentieth century, Marc Bloch and Lucien Febvre, whose methods had made such a radical impact on French historical scholarship in the era of *Mémoires'* gestation. But in his vote of thanks the presiding official of the occasion alluded to an earlier presentation from Febvre himself in which, he said, there had been much in common with Yourcenar's presentation, and it was now of enormous interest to see the past reimagined and made to live again despite the practical difficulties involved (*EH* 139). Singular though her approach might have been, Yourcenar's insistence on recovering Hadrian's world on its own terms could readily be taken to consist with *Annaliste* objectives. Notably, the telling phrase "structures mentales" had not appeared in the original version of the lecture.[75]

A final methodological statement occurs in *Les Yeux ouverts*. Explaining to Matthieu Galey why she had written of Hadrian in a novel rather than a historical essay, Yourcenar again shared her misgivings about history as a discipline, referring to historians' tendency to systematize, to give no more than subjective views about the past, to pervert historical truth through adherence to faddish theories, to conceal their standpoints, to fail to free themselves from bias: a nineteenth-century bourgeois, a German militarist and admirer of Roman imperialism, a Marxist preoccupied with communism – whether they knew it or not all were victims of theory (*YO* 62). In contrast, she had set out in *Mémoires* to show the past from a certain angle, to give a certain image of the world, and, on the principle that there could be no history of France without the French, a portrait of the human condition that could be achieved only through concentrating on an individual or a group of historical actors, an operation in which what she called the "rythme de la condition humaine" was all important (*YO* 215, 62). To have Hadrian tell his story in his own name had solved the problems that faced historians; and if the sources were too meagre for all phases of his life to be recovered, the attempt had to be made and the evidence brought to life (*YO* 155). The tactics were clear: "on se met à la place de l'être évoqué; on se trouve alors devant une réalité unique, celle de cet homme-là, à ce moment-là, dans ce lieu-là. Et c'est par ce détour qu'on atteint le mieux l'humain et l'universel" (*YO* 62).[76]

The consistency of Yourcenar's views over time and the confidence with which she expressed them are self-evident. Her characteristic self-assurance threatened perhaps to obliterate her own subjectivity as she propounded them, although she was more than alert to the impact of the moment on the composition of *Mémoires*, as will soon be seen.[77] The goal nonetheless of fully recovering and revivifying the life of a Roman emperor remains distinctive. It could be said in 1956 that academic biographers of the emperor Tiberius, "sober and diligent" as they were, had "washed most of the colour off the picture."[78] Yourcenar's method of immersing herself in the full panoply of the Roman past was to produce a portrait of a far different kind, and it is worth observing that a literal sensitivity to colour contributed to its distinctiveness. In her essay of 1954, *Le Temps, ce grand sculpteur*, Yourcenar commented on the impossibility in her modern world of knowing exactly how statues looked to the men and women of antiquity who first saw them, since the paint with which they were originally adorned had long since disappeared (*TGS* 312–16). Yet to bring Hadrian back to life in *Mémoires* with, as it were, the colours of his time and place in history restored, was to create a true likeness of him; and in accomplishing that design, as earlier intimated, the introduction of sculpture and other forms of artistic accomplishment assumed a real importance.[79] A lengthy passage in *Tellus stabilita* allows the emperor to reflect on contemporary tastes and his role as a patron of art, itemizing works he has collected for the Villa – copies of the Hermaphrodite and the Centaur, the Niobid and the Venus – and recollecting images seen in distant regions as he travelled: colossal statues of the gods and kings of Egypt, the wrist bracelets of Sarmatian prisoners incised with images of galloping horses and devouring serpents. He describes to powerful effect the many representations of Antinous, which he has imposed upon the world, giving a careful and sometimes critical commentary on the results but speaking always, like his creator, with precise, technical control: "Il y a ce bas-relief où le Carien Antonianos a doué d'une grâce élyséenne le vendangeur vêtu de soie grège, et le museau amical du chien pressé contre une jambe nue. Et ce masque presque intolérable, œuvre d'un sculpteur de Cyrène, où le plaisir et la douleur fusent et s'entrechoquent sur ce même visage comme deux vagues sur un même rocher (*MH* 390)."[80] Once more, and extraordinarily, the biographical void is filled.

V

The opening sentence of the *Note* not only includes the crucial phrase "la fidélité aux faits" but also describes *Mémoires* as a work that "touche par certains côtés ... à la poésie" (*MH* 543). From the beginning, the novel was conceived as work poetic in character, comparable as Yourcenar said to F.C. Grant to accomplished poetic reconstructions of history achieved by poets from the past, and one that would reveal the human poetry of history (*HZ* II 57). The theme was repeatedly stressed, as in the letter of June 1963 to Ghislain de Diesbach, where Yourcenar defined *Mémoires* as a poetic interpretation of history rather than a work of history in a strict sense, which I take to mean history of the kind repudiated in her Paris lecture (*HZ* III 425). What she considered the poetic to be is of course the essential, and difficult, question. Professionally and formally she could describe herself as an essay-ist, novelist, and poet.[81] Yet in practice Yourcenar did not regard essays, nov-els, and poetry as rigidly distinct categories. To Matthieu Galey she said that all her literary compositions were poems, and whether she was writing verse or prose, a poet, as she understood the term, is what in the first instance she was, someone who was "switched on" ("«en contact»"), through whom a "current" ("courant") passed, so that with a creative electrical charge as it were running through her, distinction of form was inconsequential: the reason was that rhythm, implicitly taken to be poetry's defining feature, was as much an aspect of prose as of verse. Differences there were, since the rhythms of verse were more obvious than those of prose, but there was an element of musicality within prose and its rhythms were there for readers to discover (*YO* 209–11). In this, evidently, technical issues were uppermost in Yourcenar's thinking. On other occasions, however, her explanations were more abstract. In the *Préface* to her early novel, *Denier du rêve*, a story of a failed assassination attempt against a dictator in the Rome of 1933, she contended that realism and poetry were, or ought to be, one and the same (*DR* 162), and to an interviewer's bald question in 1971 of what poetry rep-resented to her, she similarly replied that it was an attempt to draw near to "l'essence de la réalité" (*PV* 128–9).[82] As the novelist was equipped to translate human truth, she wrote to one correspondent, the poet's respon-sibility was to express an eternal truth, while to another she stated that her poetry and her prose writings dealt with the same subjects and themes, observing that Hadrian's meditation on death in *Mémoires* took up a topic that had occupied her in what she referred to as the "metaphysical" son-nets she had written when very young. She simultaneously described her early book *Feux*, the result, she said, of a love crisis, as a prose-poem, and firmly concluded that poetry described any account of reality presented in unconventional terms (*L* 346, 420).[83] To Patrick de Rosbo, drawing again on the electrical metaphor, she remarked that the novel had to pass through the magnetic field of a character, as if she herself had to be a conduit for the force that came from her protagonists (*ER* 28); while to Galey she clarified that it was the German definition of the poet that she preferred, a figure who relied on the use of imagination and emotion (*YO* 147). I distil these state-ments to mean that her object in *Mémoires* was to capture the essence of the individual life in all its complexity in a rich, even rhythmical, literary composition, guided above all by the fixed elements of human nature and the universally identifiable emotions of the human condition. To portray, that is, the real man.[84]

In this enterprise, two debts, or influences, may be posited. First to, or of, C.P. Cavafy, whose poetry Yourcenar discovered in Greece in the late

1930s through the critic and scholar Constantin Dimaras. They met in 1936 through their mutual friend André Embiricos, when in the aftermath of Cavafy's death three years earlier Dimaras was engaged in promoting his work. The poems immediately captivated Yourcenar, and just as immediately she conceived the idea of translating them. Unable, however, to read modern Greek adequately, she was forced to rely on Dimaras for explication and, predictably, a series of disputes soon erupted. Dimaras complained that her versions were inaccurate and misleading. But inflexible as always, Yourcenar resisted correction and stubbornly insisted on having the final word on all aspects of what nominally became a joint publishing project. Versions of individual poems began to appear in journals in the 1940s, but the culmination was a volume in 1958 containing what was considered at the time renditions, in prose, of the full Cavafy canon.[85] "There exist other translations, in French, that are more faithful," Dimaras eventually said of the book, "but that are far from being of the same literary value … I still see it more as the work of a great French stylist than the work of a Greek poet." His judgment supports what has been otherwise suggested, that in effect Yourcenar saw herself as the virtual co-author with Cavafy of a new set of compositions.[86] She and Dimaras maintained a long-standing friendship, however, and their volume became important in disseminating knowledge of Cavafy's poetry broadly in France and elsewhere in Europe.[87]

Cavafy had said of himself: "I am a *poietes historikos*; I would never be able to write a novel or a play, but I feel 125 voices inside me telling me I could write history."[88] Yourcenar quoted the remark, slightly changed, in the critical introduction to her volume, drawing on it as a kind of preface to her discussion of Cavafy's Greek historical poems – poems on topics not from classical Greek history but from the Hellenistic, Roman, and Byzantine eras, which on a traditional view are, or were, seen as periods of Greek decline (*PCC* 137). They present, as Yourcenar astutely observed, a succession of glimpses of historical moments in which characters appear as vividly as the elaborately painted faces of Egyptian mummy portraits (*PCC* 140):

Cavafy dédaigne délibérément les grandes perspectives, les grands mouvements de masse de l'histoire; il n'essaie pas de ressaisir un être dans ses profondeurs d'expérience, dans ses changements et dans sa durée … Il se limite intentionnellement ou non à l'aperçu rapide, au trait net et nu. Mais ce champ de vision étroitement restraint est presque toujours d'une stricte justesse; ce réaliste ne s'encombre guère de théories, anciennes ou modernes, repoussant ainsi cette pâtée de généralisations, ce ragoût de grossiers contrastes et d'épais lieux communs scolaires qui fait vomir l'histoire à tant de bons esprits. (*PCC* 137–8)

Cavafy does not care for broad perspectives, the great movements of history; he makes no attempt to grasp a human being in his deepest experience, his changes, his duration ... Intentionally or not, he confines himself to the swift glimpse, to the naked, sharply etched feature. Yet this narrowly limited field of vision is almost always of the strictest accuracy. This realist never burdens himself with theories, ancient or modern, thereby discarding that stew of generalizations, clumsy contrasts, and clotted scholarly commonplaces that give so many minds indigestion at the feast of history.

Issues of form aside, there is a clear, if partial, correspondence here with Yourcenar's views of history and historical theory, and, together with devotion to Hellenism, an indication of the appeal Cavafy had for her. Conventionally his poems are divided into three, often overlapping categories, historical, sensual, and philosophical. Yourcenar, however, arranged the historical poems into various cycles, and noting their contemporary resonances proceeded to collapse in what is now a familiar way the chronological distance between antiquity and the present, stressing that the poems were all historical due to their dependence on what she again perceived to be the crucial importance of memory (PCC 152).[89] Her discovery of him in Greece in early life was to some degree ironic, given that Cavafy's views of Greek culture were not shaped by any deep familiarity with Greece the country.[90] But it was in this period that she began consciously to integrate poetic elements into her prose writings, and critics have justifiably seen that Mémoires bears many traces of an impact, especially in the cosmopolitan conception of Hellenism the novel attributes to Hadrian.[91]

The Notes that accompany Yourcenar's translations illustrate the range of classical sources that inspired Cavafy's historical poems, as also Yourcenar's own familiarity with them. The poems vary from superficially plain accounts of past moments to allegorical and mythical narratives, at times with commentary on the events depicted. Their protagonists are sometimes genuine figures – Julian is perhaps the most celebrated example (Cavafy despised him) – but the contexts evoked can be totally imaginary. Thus the grand procession in Antioch conjured up to memorialize Julian's death has no basis in fact, but seems to be as authentic an event as the murder of Julius Caesar or the battle of Actium, both subjects of other poems. Likewise the thoughts and feelings attributed to historical figures far exceed the limits of the material exploited.[92] Two examples explore the interior world of Nero. "The Steps" pictures him peacefully asleep, oblivious to the shaking of his ancestral Lares announcing the imminent arrival of the Furies, his fate sealed by the murder of his mother, while "Nero's Deadline" plays on the young emperor's certainty that Delphi's warning to fear the number seventy-three can be safely ignored; long life is assured, except that in Spain the seventy-three-year-old Galba is already initiating the revolt that will soon drive Nero to suicide. In both cases, the distance between source and poetic contrivance is plain to see.[93]

Cavafy is a historical poet, therefore, who in an Aristotelian sense recounted events as they might have been in terms of probability or necessity rather than the actual events of history themselves. This allowed for both the invention of plausibly fictional actors and the extrapolation of actors' inner thoughts and feelings unknown and unknowable to the conventional historian. And arguably it is in this that Cavafy's influence on Yourcenar was most substantially felt, his poems fully in her mind as she was writing *Mémoires*.[94] She too became a poet-historian, but one whose preoccupation in *Mémoires* was not random glimpses of many characters' lives, but a sustained narrative of a single subject's whole life – a "human being in his deepest experience, his changes, his duration" – reconstituted through the filter of his memories. It was, and remains, an elaborate illusion, but as with Cavafy's poems an illusion grounded on the foundation of historical sources. Proceeding from mastery of an objective evidentiary substrate, Yourcenar created through her belief in a universal human nature and recourse to *magie sympathique* an account of both the external particulars of her subject's life and his inner responses to them, in which the Aristotelian probable or necessary gave scope for creating what she repeatedly called "plausibilities." The inadequacies of the tradition could thereby be overcome, and through literary artistry a figure convincingly be portrayed with claims to truth and impervious to positivist criticism.[95]

At the same time, secondly, an influence may also be admitted from Strachey's "new biography" and the critique of traditional life writing, with its advocacy of "granite-like sociality" and "rainbow-like intangibility," that followed from Virginia Woolf.[96] Yourcenar knew Strachey's biographies of course, and her prefatory remarks to the translation she made in 1937 of Woolf's *The Waves* reveal an awareness of the strong biographical tradition in the English novel in general and in Woolf's novels in particular.[97] The medium, however, through which influence was transmitted may well have been André Maurois's *Aspects de la biographie*, the Clark lectures given in Cambridge in 1928 and subsequently published in both English and French. The principles it establishes are revealing. Maurois emphasized that in the wake of *Eminent Victorians*, future biographical writing was obliged to go beyond a mere documentary record of events: truth was its first and absolute requirement, but a totalizing portrait was now vital, with personality brought fully and vividly to life, if not idealized, for which in cases where sources were imperfect imaginative reconstruction was permissible.

Everything moreover was to be told from the subject's perspective, not that of a third-party narrator. This created an opportunity to expose the subject's thoughts, feelings, and emotions that lay beneath the record of events, and introduced into the enterprise a poetic element that could be guided by the biographer's own emotional experiences. Composition in turn was understood to require artistry akin to musical composition: a specific key signature was to be chosen, and a discernible rhythm maintained throughout by means of recurring motifs that led to a climactic, and again poetic, sense of destiny. Autobiography was acknowledged as a vehicle well suited for expressing psychological insight, but in view of its dependence on distorting memory it could equally be found wanting in the pursuit of truth. There was, however, a formidable stumbling block. The project of synthesizing the subject's outer life and inner life could, in the event, be fully realized only by a novelist, a figure such as Maurois's immediate predecessor as Clark lecturer, E.M. Forster, whose techniques alone permitted a character's inner life to be completely captured. Maurois duly quoted from Forster's *Aspects of the Novel* a long passage on the personality of Queen Victoria.[98]

It would be difficult to find a more apposite synopsis of the strategies that underlie *Mémoires*, a monologic autobiography full of memory-induced deficiencies, but also an illusory contrivance of a novelist in which imaginative and literary techniques are melded with a historian's command of evidence and an anthropologist's view of human nature to animate a biographical subject nourished by her own substance.[99] The correlation with the deliberative context of biographical expression Maurois's lectures represent is precise, with the novel's "valeur poétique" found in the inner life of Hadrian that *Mémoires* recovers until the destiny Yourcenar envisaged for him is met. Fidelity to facts is united with artistic sensibility to uncover the essence of its subject in a literary form Yourcenar eventually defined as a novel of a biographical type (*ER* 23).[100] Of herself at a late stage, she wrote of having tried to become in her career both "historien-poète" and "romancier" (*SP* 877).[101]

VI

When *Mémoires* appeared in English translation, Yourcenar included in the *Note* an illuminating passage that has no exact counterpart in the French version, even in the Pléiade. It sums up much of what has been exposed here of her attitudes to the past and of her uncompromising methods of biographical reconstruction:

History has its rules, though they are not always followed even by professional historians; poetry, too, has its laws. The two are not necessarily irreconcilable. The perspectives chosen for this narrative made necessary some rearrangements of detail, together with certain simplifications or modifications intended to eliminate repetitions, lagging, or confusion which only didactic explanation would have dispelled. It was important that these adjustments, all relating only to very small points, should in no way change the spirit or the significance of the incident or the fact in question. In other cases, the lack of authentic details for some given episode of Hadrian's life has obliged the writer to prudent filling in of such lacunae from information furnished by contemporary texts treating of analogous experiences or events; these joinings had, of course, to be kept to the indispensable minimum. And last, this work, which tries to evoke Hadrian not only as he was but also as his contemporaries saw him, and sometimes imagined him, could even make some sparing use of legendary material, provided that the material thus chosen corresponded to the conception that the men of his time (and he himself, perhaps) had of his personality.[102]

I move now in the three chapters that follow to investigate how Yourcenar's methods were deployed in the three moments of crisis that brought despairing reactions of collapse or shock in Hadrian's life, the moments around which Yourcenar said she structured *Mémoires*.[103] The crisis of the accession, the crisis due to Antinous's death, and the crisis attributable to the failure of the Jewish War are, a priori, perfectly reasonable as potentially pivotal points in Hadrian's history. But precisely how they were experienced is the crucial question. In view of "the Crick factor," how anyone might ever know the mind of another is an eternal hazard for both historians and historical biographers, and there is little in this case in the tradition from which Hadrian's interior life in the three episodes of concern can be indisputably recovered. Yourcenar indeed is at her most inventive when pursuing the psychological meaning of the hints that remain. Through the methods outlined, however, it becomes possible to understand how she perceived the *fléchissements* as she did, and the contribution they make to the recreation of a life history she believed, persistently, to be true. The presentation of this truth may be termed second-order authenticity. The guiding principle throughout, evident to Strachey, Woolf, and Maurois, articulated latterly by Momigliano and fully absorbed by Yourcenar herself, is that biography inherently demands revelation of the interior world that accompanies the external events of its subject's life course.[104]

5

The Accession

Hadrian went to the East with Trajan in 113. No evidence shows him active in the field or deciding policy. Various frictions or recriminations may have ensued in the high command. However, some of Hadrian's partisans were now emerging.

Ronald Syme

But it is not clear whether he was moved by prudence or envy.

J.G.A. Pocock

I

Late in the year 117 the Roman mint issued gold and silver coins showing a laureate bust of Hadrian as emperor on one side and Trajan and Hadrian standing face to face with clasped hands on the other. The accompanying legends present Hadrian as Trajan's son and successor, endowing him with titles celebrating military conquest and expansion of empire. Their key element, prominently positioned in the reverse exergue, is the word ADOPTIO, which signified, in official terms meant for contemporary public consumption, that Trajan had formally adopted Hadrian as his son and heir designate, complying with what was now an uncontroversial practice when a reigning ruler had no natural son to succeed him. The coins were issued, however, after Trajan's death. In 113, at what proved to be a late stage of his reign, Trajan embarked on a military campaign against Rome's long-standing enemy in the east, the empire of the Parthians. He met with early and spectacular success but thereafter was forced to retreat, fell ill, and in the summer of 117 died at Selinus in Cilicia on the southern coast of what is now Turkey.

According to the source tradition it was on his deathbed, at a literally last moment, that he adopted Hadrian. But Hadrian was not with him. He was instead in Antioch in Syria, where during Trajan's expedition he had served, and was still serving, as governor of the province. He received news of the transaction, and almost immediately was proclaimed emperor by the legions under his command. He was not to return to Rome, however, until the following year. The coins minted in the interim were evidently intended to prove the legitimacy of his emergence as emperor and to affirm that power had been smoothly and legitimately transferred from one ruler to another.[1]

It is from Trajan's apparent reluctance to name his successor until at death's door that Yourcenar creates in *Mémoires*, in the final, longest section of *Varius multiplex multiformis*, the first momentous crisis in Hadrian's life (*MH* 344–58). From her remarks in *L'Écrivain devant l'Histoire*, it is clear already that the circumstances surrounding the act of adoption are imperfectly known. Nonetheless, that Hadrian did indeed face a crisis at this stage of his life of some sort historians are prepared to accept, if only proleptically. Yourcenar's originality lies in artfully disclosing its nature and extent. I examine here the construction and presentation of the episode from the viewpoint of biographical credibility, with attention to the elements of the historical tradition concerned and Yourcenar's response to them, the authorities on whom she drew in the course of her preparations, and the significance of the time at which *Mémoires* was composed.[2]

The narrative Hadrian gives comes at a double remove. It belongs to the end of his life of course and draws on his memory of events from long ago. But those events, especially the details of Trajan's military operations, can be described only from recollections Hadrian has of them from what at the time had been his vantage point at Antioch. He was not involved in the expedition himself, and he does no more therefore than report indirectly to Marcus what he had learned of the expedition's course as it unfolded. His account, realistically constructed, cannot consequently be all-embracing in the manner of an empirical historical study of Trajan's war. As Yourcenar presents them, Hadrian's recollections are partial and elliptical, which I take to be a consciously contrived strategy to accommodate both the vantage point concerned, consistent with the methodology just examined, and the deficiencies of a notoriously ill-documented phase of Roman history. It also obviates any potential criticism that the account is inaccurate. At the same time, the reader of *Mémoires* might well imagine that Hadrian's record is one of events unfolding in real time, and in the synoptic sections of the chapter I use the present tense to convey something of the immediacy of his narrative. It is as if two consciousnesses are at work. A recent visit to Athens has confirmed Hadrian's desire to replace Trajan's militaristic policies with a

Greek-inspired vision, long in gestation, of empire-wide peace. Yet Trajan's failure to name him as successor creates an anxiety that increases exponentially as the war proceeds. Whether he will ever be able to realize the vision, or whether he will ever become emperor at all, Hadrian simply does not know. Uncertainty leads to inner turmoil, thoughts of suicide impinge, and it is only when news from Selinus finally reaches him that what he calls "la grande crise" is resolved (*MH* 343; cf. 411).[3]

II

The events narrated form the episode's external frame. They also raise a host of historical problems. Hadrian has been in office as governor of Syria for a year when Trajan, intent on setting in motion his long-contemplated plans for eastern expansion, joins him in Antioch, the natural hub for Roman military operations on the eastern frontier, open as it was to Parthian trade and travel routes. The kingdom of Armenia is to be invaded first before an assault against Parthia proper. Trajan duly advances northwards into Commagene, where festivals are celebrated, and then at the city of Satala he accepts the obeisance of various petty kings. His general Lusius Quietus leads troops to the shores of Lake Van, and northern Mesopotamia, abandoned by the Parthians, is easily annexed. Following the submission at the city of Edessa of Abgar, ruler of the small kingdom of Osrhoene, Trajan returns to Antioch at the end of his first campaigning season. Hadrian notes his age as then sixty-four.

During the winter, precisely in December, a terrible earthquake strikes Antioch. Trajan himself is injured, but he heroically assists the afflicted, though surprisingly acquiesces when Christians are scapegoated for the disaster. Large supplies of timber meantime are harvested to prepare for the construction of pontoons and bridges made from boats, and in the following spring campaigning resumes. Trajan rejoins his army on the river Euphrates to begin an advance across the river Tigris, and Hadrian subsequently receives a succession of reports of his progress: Babylon is conquered, the Tigris crossed, the Parthian capital of Ctesiphon falls, the prince of Arabia Characene submits, the Tigris is fully opened to Roman shipping, and Trajan sails to Charax on the Persian Gulf. There, however, so Hadrian learns much later, there is nothing but lamentation: Trajan has led Roman forces to regions previously unexplored and is confident of having gained a great victory. But India and Bactriana to the east lie far beyond his reach, if only for reasons of age, and as Hadrian well knows disaster is suddenly intervening, with resistance to Rome's imposition of taxes in Seleucia, revolts in Cyrene, Jewish zealots cutting off supplies to Roman forces in Egypt, and ethnic disturbances springing up in Cyprus. Trajan is compelled as a result to return to Babylon, sending Lusius Quietus to punish the rebellious cities of Cyrene, Edessa, and Seleucia – Hadrian later repaired the damage inflicted – as Osrhoes, the Parthian king of kings and instigator of the various revolts, now takes the offensive, with a resurgent Abgar recovering control of Edessa and Armenian allies lending support to Persian satraps. Surrounded on all sides, Trajan spends a second winter laying siege to the city of Hatra, where he remains until spring. In May, however, now seriously ill, he retires across the Euphrates to Antioch, and to avoid the heat of mid-summer decides to return to Rome and to leave Hadrian as commander-in-chief of all the Roman armies in the east. Some ten days or so later, unable to travel farther, he succumbs at Selinus and his wife Plotina immediately secures the declaration of her favoured Hadrian as his successor. The new emperor's first act is to abandon all claims to the territories his adoptive father had briefly conquered.

In essence, Hadrian's narrative follows the sole continuous source of knowledge about Trajan's expedition, a series of passages drawn by Xiphilinus from the history of Cassius Dio (68.17.1–69.2.2). The passages are at times substantial, but as excerpts they provide no more than a relatively continuous account. They are supplemented by a few fragments from a history of Rome's wars against Parthia by Arrian of Nicomedia (far fewer than generally thought), sporadic notices from Cornelius Fronto and late epitomators, and various numismatic and epigraphical items. Altogether documentation for Trajan's Parthian war is meagre, much of it is anecdotal and sensationalistic, and exactly what the episode as a whole involved is impossible to determine. Hadrian's narrative understandably resembles therefore a series of snapshots.[4]

On his telling, the expedition and his crisis seem to extend over two and a half years. Most historians argue, however, for a much longer interval, placing Trajan's departure from Rome in the autumn of 113 – some date it precisely to 27 October – and his death in early August 117. Even so, consensus on the details of what happened during the almost four years concerned is non-existent. Experts tend to assign an easy conquest of Armenia to Trajan's first campaigning season in 114 after a winter spent in Antioch (the city is attested as his wintering site in one year of the campaign); a decisive victory against the Parthians in southern Mesopotamia and the establishment of two new provinces, Armenia and Mesopotamia, to the second season of 115; and the capture of the Parthian capital Ctesiphon and an advance to the Persian

Gulf in the third season of 116. Revolt in the newly conquered territories and elsewhere then necessitated retreat. Many questions, however, remain. Did the first campaigning season see action in northern Mesopotamia after the conquest of Armenia? Was there an advance in the second season across the Tigris into the kingdom of Adiabene before the march south along the Euphrates to Ctesiphon? When exactly did Ctesiphon fall? And if, as some fourth-century sources report, a third province of Assyria was established, where precisely was it?[5]

Further, while an earthquake did indeed occur at Antioch, apparently in 115, its exact date is disputed. Some authorities assign it to December, others to January, which has implications for where Trajan spent the winter of 114/115 – at Antioch as most seem to think or, on other suggestions, at Osrhoenian Edessa or Babylon.[6] The main item at issue symbolizes the poor nature of almost all the material available. This is an entry in the *Chronicle of World History* compiled in the sixth century by the Byzantine Christian scholar John Malalas, a native of Antioch who is thought to have drawn on local records for the date he gives for the calamity, 13 December 115 (11.3–8).[7] However, the huge amount of time, some four and a half centuries, between the event and its incorporation in Malalas's chronicle immediately gives reason for pause in view of the unverifiable assumptions on which it depends, that the date was once securely recorded, safely preserved over time, and always transmitted accurately. (I pass over the *Chronicle*'s overriding ideological purpose of determining the moment of the Incarnation.) In fact, Malalas's *Chronicle* is notoriously full of erroneous information, recording for instance an enemy occupation of Antioch during Trajan's war that is sheer fantasy.[8] Scholars accordingly pick and choose what to believe from it. Malalas credits Trajan with rebuilding Antioch after the earthquake, and also with offering a human sacrifice to expiate the catastrophe the earthquake represented. One authority duly rejects the assertion of rebuilding, noting that no epigraphical or archaeological evidence supports it; but another claims that reconstruction did indeed begin under Trajan and continued into the reign of Antoninus Pius, while simultaneously dismissing the alleged act of human sacrifice as sensationalistic exaggeration. It is unsurprising therefore that the credibility of the date of the earthquake can be both accepted and rejected. Ultimately it is hard not to agree with the conclusion drawn from a meticulous analysis that Malalas's *Chronicle* as a whole is a complete fraud; and certainly its record that many senators accompanied Trajan to Antioch is hardly a reason to believe that Hadrian's succession had long been made apparent.[9] The recollection Yourcenar's Hadrian has of a Trajanic persecution of Christians might well come from its statement, following the alleged building program, that Trajan put to grisly death a number of Christians and encouraged the voluntary martyrdom of many more. But again there is a problem. One of the alleged victims was the bishop of Antioch, Ignatius, whose martyrdom most scholars date a decade or so earlier, following the evidence of the more reliable ecclesiastical historian Eusebius that Ignatius died in Rome.[10]

Altogether, an uncontroversially complete account of Trajan's expedition is (as yet) impossible to achieve, and the competing discussions of its chronology and progress provide a fine illustration of the frailty of knowledge that besets not only the present topic but much of Roman Imperial history generally. The unavoidable consequence is that when basic facts are in such short supply, historical questions of motive and objective are necessarily elusive if not illusory, and attempts to define them sometimes border on what can only be called the fictional. Any characterization of the aims of Trajan's war, and any description of its course and sequel, has to be carefully qualified, a point of some importance as a check on, or corrective to, the imprecision of Hadrian's narrative in *Mémoires*.[11]

According to the principal source, Trajan was impelled to undertake the Parthian war by a desire for glory, a notably human, emotional aspiration. Hadrian's account of the "imitateur d'Alexandre" is suffused with this idea (*MH* 352).[12] In the present context, however, what requires emphasis is that a detailed narrative of the expedition is redundant in a biography of Hadrian. Yourcenar judged correctly that a minimalist approach was the appropriate tactic to adopt in reconstructing Hadrian's memoirs, and that her portrait of him in crisis should depend on the dramatic nature of the events the record of the war preserves. That is best conveyed now not so much by the sparse literary tradition as by physical evidence. The coinage announced and celebrated Trajan's glorious successes, powerfully pictorializing the submission of the Parthian claimant to the throne of Armenia, Parthamasiris, Trajan's assignment of kingdoms to vassal rulers, his defeat of the Parthians and coronation of their king, Parthamaspates, and the acquisition of the new provinces Armenia and Mesopotamia.[13] The *cognomina* with which the senate rewarded him, *Optimus* and *Parthicus*, appeared in his nomenclature on the coins' legends, and also in the *Acts of the Arval Brethren*, the priests who during the war continually offered prayers and sacrifices for Trajan's safety and success. The *Fasti Ostienses* show moreover that the honorific *Parthicus* was bestowed when the senate received laurelled despatches announcing Trajan's victories, in response to which religious supplications for the emperor's well-being were authorized and celebratory games held.[14]

These items implicitly communicate an enthusiasm with which news of the eastern campaigns was presumably received in the Roman heartland, where few people can have had first-hand knowledge of the distant territories in which their emperor was fabulously extending empire, just as most of Yourcenar's readers past and present will hardly know in detail the topography of the regions concerned, stretching as they do from present-day Turkey into Iraq and Iran. The strange but genuine place names incorporated into her text are enough to suggest the exotically vast scope of Trajan's undertaking, which among contemporary commentators is best captured by the unconventional Elizabeth Speller's description of southern Turkey where Selinus lay: "Only small towns now lie on this length of dramatically beautiful wooded and fissured coast, although several resorts cater to tourists, but the masonry that seems randomly abandoned on its hillsides hints at a previous busier existence. In the second century it was a place of fine Seleucid towns along a coast which had traditionally been plagued by pirates and was now heavily fortified."[15] Hopes of limitless empire might well be considered to have been high after the successes of Trajan's Dacian wars a decade earlier – territory had been annexed and gold poured in – and anticipation was far from unrealistic of new triumphal celebrations displaying foreign kings in chains, captives in bonds, wagonloads of enemy arms and plunder, with a victorious Trajan following in his chariot. And while it remains moot whether Trajan's undertaking marked a critical new phase of Roman imperialism, an audacious attempt to solve a centuries-old frontier problem by direct annexation of eastern lands, the scale of the expedition was undoubtedly grandiose, so that enthusiasm quickly gave way to shock as reports of revolt and the conqueror's death reached the capital.[16]

For Yourcenar, consequently, the challenge was to uncover Hadrian's response to the sequence of events and changes of fortune perceptible. The basic record of Trajan's honours was there in the remnants of Cassius Dio's history. But she was fully aware of the importance of the documentary evidence also available. Her *Notebook* contains four pages listing more than a hundred Hadrianic coin legends culled from the standard catalogues, written in capital letters in her own hand, the very first of which happens to be ADOPTIO; and in one of her prime sources of information for the war, a contribution on Trajan's coinage from Marcel Durry (*OR* 549), the key Trajanic legends, all in a single paragraph, are impossible to miss: PROFECTIO AUGUSTI, REX PARTHUS, OPTIMUS, REGNA ADSIGNATA, PARTHIA CAPTA, REX PARTHIS DATUS.[17] Hadrian is able as a result to inform Marcus of Trajan's new titles and triumphal prospects, the former during the first winter of the war – "une série de titres nouveaux décernés par le Sénat" (*MH* 346) – the latter when Trajan is on the Persian Gulf: "Le Sénat vota cette fois à l'empereur le droit de célébrer, non pas un triomphe, mais une succession de triomphes qui dureraient autant que sa vie" (*MH* 351). The connections are clear.[18]

Yourcenar drew of course, as the *Note* shows, on any number of second-ary studies in her preparations. One was the first volume of *L'Histoire de l'Asie* by René Grousset of 1921 (*OR* 548), a work that gives only a very brief notice of Trajan's campaigns, assigning everything to the year 115 and showing little interest in problems of chronology and military operations. The second volume of R. Paribeni's *Optimus Princeps* of 1927 (*OR* 549) will have been more rewarding, as also a work not listed in the *Note* but still to be seen in Yourcenar's library, N.C. Debevoise's *A Political History of Parthia* (1937).[19] Grousset was concerned to promote an economic explanation of Trajan's expedition, maintaining that the annexation of new provinces was prompted by a need to establish direct trade connections between Rome and India, and, through securing access to the silk route, ultimately between Rome and China. He was not alone. R.P. Longden, the author of the chapter on Trajan's wars in the first edition of the *Cambridge Ancient History* (1936), another of Yourcenar's authorities (*OR* 549), was more sober in his estimate but likewise thought an economic motive important.[20] The impact can be seen in a set of reflections Yourcenar attributes to Hadrian as he speaks of Trajan's thinking during the winter of the earthquake at Antioch:

Le problème de l'Orient nous préocccupait depuis des siècles; il semblait naturel d'en finir une fois pour toutes. Nos échanges de denrées avec l'Inde et le mystérieux pays de la soie dépendaient entièrement des marchands juifs et des exportateurs arabes qui avaient la franchise des ports et des routes parthes. Une fois réduit à rien le vaste et flottant empire des cavaliers Arsacides, nous toucherions directement à ces riches confins du monde; l'Asie enfin unifiée ne serait pour Rome qu'une province de plus. Le port d'Alexandrie d'Égypte était le seul de nos débouchés vers l'Inde qui ne dépendît pas du bon vouloir parthe; là aussi, nous nous heurtions continuellement aux exigences et aux révoltes des communautés juives. Le succès de l'expédition de Trajan nous eût permis d'ignorer cette ville peu sûre. (*MH* 347–8)

The problem of the Orient had preoccupied us for centuries; it seemed natural to rid ourselves of it once and for all. Our exchanges of wares with India and the mysteri-ous Land of Silks depended entirely upon Jewish merchants and Arabian exporters who held the franchise for Parthian roads and ports. Once the vast and loosely joined empire of the Arsacid horsemen had been reduced to nothingness we should touch directly upon those rich extremities of the world; Asia once unified would become but a province more for Rome. The port of Alexandria-in-Egypt was the only one of our outlets toward India which did not depend upon Parthian good will; there, too, we were continually confronted with the troublesome demands and revolts of the Jewish communities. Success on the part of Trajan's expedition would have allowed us to disregard that untrustworthy city.

These were views Hadrian comes firmly to discard, appreciating the futility of military success in a vast and uncontrollable portion of the earth: "il ne s'agissait pas seulement de vaincre, mais de vaincre toujours, et nos forces s'épuiseraient à cette entreprise" (MH 348).[21] Which is reasoning that seems to come straight from another authority Yourcenar held in high esteem, the *Social and Economic History of the Roman Empire* (1926) of M.I. Rostovtzeff (OR 549), who labelled Trajan's eastern campaigns disastrous and applauded Hadrian's decision to abandon the territories Trajan had annexed: "If he desisted from the aggressive policy of Trajan, it was because he realized that such a policy could not be carried out, that the resources of the Roman Empire were not ample enough to support a policy of further conquests. The first task of a prudent ruler of the Empire was to establish strong and true foundations before proceeding on to embark on far-reaching military conquests, and that was Hadrian's policy."[22] It is credible enough therefore that once the great crisis is over Hadrian should feel satisfaction at seeing the caravans of merchants reforming on the banks of the Orontes and trade with eastern lands resuming (MH 359). This is the natural emotional corollary of the way events have unfolded. His reflections stem from the judgments found in Yourcenar's researches, and in this instance it is of more than incidental interest that the notion of an overland trade route between Rome's empire and China, long dismissed as a romantic aberration, has now found new arguments in its favour. Inescapably, however, the primary materials on Trajan's war have virtually nothing to say of Hadrian: Cassius Dio mentions him only once, when on Trajan's departure for Italy he is left in charge of Rome's forces in the east (68.33.1), while the Latin life merely refers to his appointment as legate of Syria (HA Hadr. 4.1). Yourcenar accordingly has him observe that during the accession crisis his was not the rank of even the second man in Rome (MH 348). The result is that any reconstruction of his views of, and reactions to, the external frame of the war must necessarily be conjectural. Yet as this example suggests, once Yourcenar's account is assessed with attention to the resources at her disposal, understanding emerges not only of her conception of the war's events, but also of her discovery of Hadrian's reactions to and commentary upon them. The inner world disclosed is not mere fiction.[23]

III

With the first season's military events efficiently summarized, Hadrian dwells at length in the winter of discontent at Antioch on the wisdom of Trajan's ambitions. Conscious of widespread resentment of and opposition to them among the provincial populations, he nervously awaits the sporadic attentions of an emperor already ill, given to drink, and privy to the counsels of his enemies (*MH* 346–9). The succession is still crucially in doubt, and he is unable therefore to indulge an heir's luxury of choosing to obey, reject, or accommodate Trajan's misguided plans, powerless even to secure an audience with Trajan for local leaders. His allies lose all influence, and palace freedmen block his access to Trajan's private apartments. All seems lost as desperation overtakes him: "Je me cherchai des alliés où je pus; je corrompis à prix d'or d'anciens esclaves que j'eusse volontiers envoyés aux galères; j'ai caressé d'horribles têtes frisées" (*MH* 349).[24] The confession draws on a rumour from the Latin life that before his accession Hadrian habitually bribed Trajan's freedmen, corrupting his favourites at court for reasons of self-advancement (*HA Hadr.* 4.5), just as the tradition of Trajan's habitual heavy drinking is conveniently brought into play.[25] Court intrigue is indeed front and centre in the narrative from the very beginning (*MH* 345), and various figures, all fixated on the succession, are introduced to illustrate an intense factionalism. Those concerned, both enemies and allies, are all historically attested as either having served in the east with Trajan or having belonged to his retinue. By and large, that is, the empirical basis from which Yourcenar creates her image of the anxiety-laden Hadrian is sound. The interplay among the personnel allows recovery in the moment of Hadrian's varying emotions.

From the outset three military men, Celsus, Palma, and Nigrinus, prominent members of the emperor's *consilium* and high command, are identified as Hadrian's long-standing enemies (*MH* 344). A fourth, Lusius Quietus, is soon added (*MH* 345). Celsus, Palma, and Lusius Quietus have already been described as supporters of Trajan's expansionist policies and opponents of Hadrian in a passage where Hadrian, shortly before the commencement of the expedition, assesses his political position (*MH* 342). The most threatening by far is Lusius Quietus:

Le plus dangereux de mes adversaires était Lusius Quiétus, Romain métissé d'Arabe, dont les escadrons numides avaient joué un rôle important dans la seconde campagne dace, et qui poussait sauvagement à la guerre d'Asie. Je détestais tout du personnage: son luxe barbare, l'envolée prétentieuse de ses voiles blancs ceints d'une corde d'or, ses yeux arrogants et faux, son incroyable cruauté à l'égard des vaincus et des soumis. (*MH* 342)

The most dangerous of my adversaries was Lusius Quietus, a Roman with some Arab blood, whose Numidian squadrons had played an important part in the second Dacian campaign, and who was pressing fiercely for the Asiatic war. I detested everything about him, his barbarous luxury, the pretentious swirl of his white headgear bound with cord of gold, his false, arrogant eyes, and his unbelievable cruelty toward the conquered and to those who had offered their submission.

Lusius Quietus was indeed a Moor who commanded a contingent of his own African cavalry in Trajan's second war in Dacia before playing a significant role in the Parthian expedition, notably, once revolts broke out, recovering Nisibis in Adiabene, destroying Edessa, and butchering the Jews of Cyrene. His strong military reputation is attested well into late antiquity. Trajan adlected him to the senate at the praetorian rank and awarded him a consulship, held seemingly in 117. Soon after Hadrian's accession, however, he was alleged to have conspired against the new emperor and was executed. In the late fourth century the orator Themistius, who knew of Lusius's African origin, claimed when addressing the emperor Theodosius that Trajan had designated him his successor (*Or.* 16. 205a), a scarcely credible assertion but one that together with other allegations of conspiracy underlies Yourcenar's characterization of him here and in the sequel. (His murderous hunting plot against Hadrian has already been remarked.) He has been identified in two monuments: on Trajan's Column in a panel that depicts the Moorish cavalry he led in the Dacian fighting, and on Trajan's Arch at Beneventum in a panel where the submission of Mesopotamia is represented during the Parthian war. The identifications cannot be certain, but the panels may well have contributed to Yourcenar's representation of him. Equally controversial is the supposition that Quietus is "the man from Qwrnyn" who appears in a passage describing a plot against Hadrian in the *Physiognomica* of the sophist Polemo preserved in a mediaeval Arabic translation. It occurs in a context in which small, deep-set eyes are interpreted as signs of evil character. This too may have influenced Yourcenar. Altogether the few scraps of information that remain are fashioned into a frightening, formidable figure.[26]

A. Cornelius Palma and L. Publilius Celsus also achieved eminence under Trajan, holding second consulships respectively in 109 and 113. Palma, from Volsinii, was responsible as legate of Syria for the annexation of Arabia. But the record on "le consulaire Celsus" as Hadrian once calls him is sparse (*MH* 349), and his particular achievements, origins, and family connections are all unknown – "presumably Italian" is the best that can be determined – although as alleged conspirators, both he and Palma fell with Lusius Quietus.[27] There can be little elaboration here, therefore, and the preparation for establishing Hadrian's exposure to the mistrust of Palma or Celsus's hatred is altogether minimal (*MH* 342). It is their eventual execution that again controls their designation now as enemies. So too with C. Avidius Nigrinus, suffect consul in 110, the fourth apparent conspirator who was also put to death after Hadrian's accession. Interestingly, he receives no earlier attention in *Mémoires*, as if Marcus is simply expected to know all about him. Like Lusius Quietus, he is said to have enjoyed influence and wealth, and even again to have been marked out by Hadrian for the succession. He was executed in his home town of Faventia.[28]

As the narrative unfolds, the four men are frequently in Hadrian's mind. They are the adversaries to whom his conversations with Trajan during the first winter in Antioch are reported by members of the court (*MH* 346). He fears supersession by Palma or suppression by Quietus when Trajan is ready to proceed with the expedition's next stage (*MH* 349). He is almost bereft of hope for the future after an hours' long secret meeting one evening that Trajan holds with Celsus (*MH* 349). And he suspects a secret arrangement with Quietus's faction when Trajan returns from the Persian Gulf with the matter of the succession still unresolved (*MH* 355). The account constantly moves between the events of the outer frame and Hadrian's inner reactions to them, drawing on impressionistic memories of shadowy men long since dead at the time Marcus is told about them. They are no less believable for that.

As for allies, two men only are brought on stage, Latinius Alexander and P. Acilius Attianus. The latter, once Hadrian's guardian, has passingly been met in the novel as a devoted friend (*MH* 325, 340); and he comes to play a pivotal role as the succession is eventually secured. The former appears in Hadrian's account of the earthquake at Antioch, his sole appearance, when the influence of Palma and Quietus is especially alarming. Hadrian's insecurity is in no way quelled: "Mon ami Latinius Alexander, qui descendait d'une des vieilles familles royales de l'Asie Mineure, et dont le nom et la fortune pesaient d'un grand poids, ne fut pas davantage écouté" (*MH* 349).[29] The detail given here is intriguing. Latinius Alexander is once more a genuine figure, but there is no indication in Yourcenar's *Note* or *Notebook* of how she knew of him. He is attested by a single piece of testimony, an inscription from Ancyra in Galatia that was set up on a statue base by the city's tribal leaders to honour his daughter Latinia Cleopatra. The inscription describes the woman as being of royal descent, as her father must have been too, enumerates in detail Latinius Alexander's offices within and services to the city, and speaks of an occasion when he supplied provisions as Hadrian and his "sacred armies" once passed through Ancyra.[30] Experts now generally date this incident to the autumn of 117, when, as emperor, Hadrian was en route from Antioch to the Danube. And already in the *Social and Economic History*, quoting the relevant part of Latinius's inscription and taking him to be a "member of the royal Galatian family," Rostovtzeff had written: "It is evident that the city was so exhausted by the passage of the 'holy army' that Alexander came to her rescue with distributions of food," adding a reference to a volume by Wilhelm Weber on chronology.[31] Yourcenar was familiar with this work as well as that of Rostovtzeff (*OR* 549), and her knowledge of Latinius Alexander and his inscription, I imagine, is likely to have come from one or the other if not both. Her use of the information in the inscription, however, is bold: she has invented Latinius's friendship with Hadrian and his location in Antioch during the Parthian war, preserving his name, royal ancestry, and reputation for wealth, but disregarding the record of Hadrian's later journey through his home city. It is a telling illustration of how an aspect of Hadrian's inner life can be imaginatively drawn from a fortuitous item of evidence.

More anomalous is the case of Trajan's doctor Crito, who while not named as such might also be considered an ally despite his lesser social status. He is a peripheral figure, but appears in the Parthian narrative several times. He is alarmed after the Armenian campaign when Trajan suffers from liver complaints (*MH* 346); with Matidia he assists the feeble emperor as Trajan returns to Antioch after abandoning his expedition (*MH* 354); and fearing there the ill effects of summer heat, he advises retreat to Rome (*MH* 356). Hadrian in turn alludes to a rumour once Trajan is dead that it was Crito, in collusion with Plotina, who had clandestinely impersonated Trajan at Selinus, seemingly dictating the emperor's dying wishes in order to guarantee Hadrian's succession (*MH* 357). Implicitly present at Trajan's cremation, he is understood to return to Rome with Plotina (*MH* 358).

Crito certainly was Trajan's doctor. But Yourcenar's *Note* gives no indication of how she knew of him, nor does her *Notebook*.[32] His full name was T. Statilius Crito, but it is his last name alone that appears in *Mémoires*. In late literary notices he is said to have attended the emperor during the earlier Dacian campaigns and to have written a history of them entitled *Getika*, a few fragments of which remain. Four inscriptions give his full name and identify a wife and son. They also show his origin to have been the city of Heraclea Salbace in Caria, record that other physicians honoured him at Ephesus, and name him as Trajan's chief doctor, procurator, and friend.[33] Three of the inscriptions were published before 1951, that revealing his wife and son coming to light later. Yourcenar, however, seems to have known none of them. Which is important because one inscription that on technical grounds belongs at latest to 114/115 refers to a testamentary disposition Crito had made, meaning that he was by that time dead; and the later item, a dedication from his wife and son, confirms this. It is scarcely possible therefore that Crito was ever a member of Trajan's retinue during the Parthian expedition. An ambiguous entry in the Byzantine *Suda*, quoting from the *Getika*, could be pressed to mean that he was with Trajan until the acquisition of Armenia in 114 – it speaks, in two separate but possibly related sentences, of Trajan having settled Parthian affairs and of Crito having accompanied him in war – but the balance of specialist opinion is against this.[34] In any case, he cannot have been alive in the late stages of the expedition or present at Trajan's death and cremation. I suspect that Yourcenar came across his name when reading of Trajan's wars and perhaps knew of the *Getika*, the relevant fragments included, and unaware of the epigraphical record assumed that it was legitimate to include him in the Parthian narrative. It was entirely reasonable to do so. In the event, however, Crito's role in the episode must be judged, at best, largely invented. His concern over Trajan's failing liver takes up the tradition that the ruler was a heavy drinker, while his name has been substituted in Trajan's deathbed scene for the anonymous figure suborned by Plotina in a story of impersonation that appears in the Latin life (*HA Hadr.* 4.10). Whether Yourcenar knew the medical collection for which Crito was remembered is an open question. Its chief item, discernible especially from allusions in Galen's writings, was the *Cosmetics*, "a solid collection of many recipes for plasters, hair dyes, and similar concoctions that had known and beneficial properties."[35]

Hadrian's remaining, and principal, ally is a woman, namely Trajan's wife Plotina, a character whose role in the accession crisis is vital and who receives considerable attention in *Mémoires* as a whole.

Yourcenar follows the historical record in including both Plotina and Matidia in Trajan's eastern entourage, with Hadrian fittingly observing their initial arrival in Antioch (*MH* 344–5). In the critical winter following the first campaigning season, Plotina is then briefly seen as the object of her husband's respect, and, with Matidia, as the purveyor of counsel, though a counsel that Trajan, already in incipient decline and overly dependent on the two women, increasingly resists and resents (*MH* 346). If the real Plotina did indeed offer words of advice to her husband they are, in Yourcenar's idiom, lost to history, and Yourcenar wisely made no attempt to fill the silence: the problem of recreating authentic Roman conversation apart, the tradition preserves nothing directly from her, which to Yourcenar reflected the reality of women's subsidiary status in antiquity. She commented on this both in the *Carnets* (*CNMH* 526) and when responding to questions on the apparent absence from her novels of major female protagonists. It was not that there were no great women in the past, she explained, but their experiences lacked the scale of men's lives, remembered as they were only as appendages to men – lovers, mothers, or domestic heads of households – and it would have been impossible consequently to include the political and military elements of the story had she made Plotina its narrator, a possibility she had initially contemplated. No woman had sufficient access to power to make a comprehensive female view of the world viable, and even women who were socially well placed could not become central literary subjects.[36] Michèle Sarde, in contrast, has ascribed the literary absence to a misogyny born of a self-depreciation attributable to the pernicious influence of two men, Yourcenar's father, and her sometime editor André Fraigneau, who was the object of an early, unrequited infatuation. To my mind, however, this disregards the limitations of the sources, to which Yourcenar was always sensitive, and the reality that ancient Roman culture was undeniably patriarchal, no matter how off-putting to modern sensibilities this may be. The passing reference once made to "le sens austère et patriarcal de la famille" at Rome is proof enough of Yourcenar's awareness of this (*TGS* 383).[37] The result was that Plotina, in a collection of personal memories, like several other important figures, could be seen only through the eyes of Hadrian, which inevitably meant imperfectly, from a certain angle (*CNMH* 531).[38]

It is authenticity and technique in combination therefore that control Yourcenar's presentation, a prime illustration coming from a crucial passage in which Hadrian expresses the relief he feels from knowing that he has Plotina's support against his powerful adversaries:

Et c'est alors que m'apparut le plus sage de mes bons génies: Plotine. Il y avait près de vingt ans que je connaissais l'impératrice. Nous étions du même milieu; nous avions à peu près le même âge. Je lui avais vu vivre avec calme une existence presque aussi contrainte que la mienne, et plus dépourvue d'avenir. Elle m'avait soutenu, sans paraître s'apercevoir qu'elle le faisait, dans mes moments difficiles. Mais ce fut durant les mauvais jours d'Antioche que sa présence me devint indispensable, comme plus tard son estime le resta toujours, et j'eus celle-ci jusqu'à sa mort. Je pris l'habitude de cette figure en vêtements blancs, aussi simples que peuvent l'être ceux d'une femme, de ses silences, de ses paroles mesurées qui n'étaient jamais que des réponses, et les plus nettes possible. Son aspect ne détonnait en rien dans ce palais plus antique que les splendeurs de Rome: cette fille de parvenus était très digne des Séleucides. Nous étions d'accord presque sur tout. Nous avions tous deux la passion d'orner, puis de dépouiller notre âme, d'éprouver notre esprit à toutes les pierres de touche. Elle inclinait à la philosophie épicurienne, ce lit étroit, mais propre, sur lequel j'ai parfois étendu ma pensée. Le mystère des dieux, qui me hantait, ne l'inquiétait pas; elle n'avait pas non plus mon goût passionné des corps. Elle était chaste par dégoût du facile, généreuse par décision plutôt que par nature, sagement méfiante, mais prête à tout accepter d'un ami, même ses inévitables erreurs. L'amitié était un choix où elle s'engageait tout entière; elle s'y livrait absolument, et comme je ne l'ai fait qu'à l'amour. Elle m'a connu mieux que personne; je lui ai laissé voir ce que j'ai soigneusement dissimulé à tout autre: par exemple, de secrètes lâchetés. J'aime à croire que, de son côté, elle ne m'a presque rien tu. L'intimité des corps, qui n'exista jamais entre nous, a été compensée par ce contact de deux esprits étroitement mêlés l'un à l'autre. (*MH* 349–50)

And it was then that the wisest of my good geniuses came to my aid: Plotina. I had known the empress for nearly twenty years. We were of the same circle and of about the same age. I had seen her living calmly through almost as constrained an exist- ence as my own, and one more deprived of future. She had taken my part, without appearing to notice that she did so, in my difficult moments. But it was during the evil days at Antioch that her presence became indispensable to me, as was always her esteem in after times, an esteem which I kept till her death. I grew accustomed to that white-clad figure, in garments as simple as a woman's can be, and to her silences, or to words so measured as to be never more than replies, and these as succinct as pos- sible. Nothing in her appearance or bearing was out of keeping with that palace more ancient than the splendors of Rome: this daughter of a race newly come to power was in no way inferior to the Seleucids. We too were in accord on almost everything. Both of us had a passion for adorning, then laying bare, our souls, and for testing our minds on every touchstone. She leaned toward Epicurean philosophy, that narrow but clean bed whereon I have sometimes rested my thought. The mystery of gods, which haunted me, did not trouble her, nor had she my ardent love for the human body. She was chaste by reason of her disgust with the merely facile, generous by determination rather than by nature, wisely mistrustful but ready to accept any- thing from a friend, even his inevitable errors. Friendship was a choice to which she devoted her whole being; she gave herself to it utterly, and as I have done only to my loves. She has known me better than anyone has; I have let her see what I carefully concealed from everyone else; for example, my secret lapses into cowardice. I like to think that on her side she has kept almost nothing from me. No bodily intimacy ever existed between us; in its place was this contact of two minds closely intermingled.

At first blush, much of this might be considered novelistic extravagance. In fact it scarcely exceeds the limits of the tradition. Plotina's origins are strictly speaking unknown, and Yourcenar avoids wild speculation about them. Her full name was Pompeia Plotina to judge from a solitary refer- ence in a late source, an item that has been interpreted to mean that Plotina was the daughter of a senatorial Pompeius whose *praenomen* Lucius can be recovered from inscriptions commemorating some of Plotina's freedmen.[39] Her family home is commonly taken to be Nemausus (Nîmes) in Gallia Narbonensis, because the Latin life reports that in what can be determined as the winter of 122/123 Hadrian paused there, when crossing from Britain to Spain, to dedicate a basilica to her (*HA Hadr.* 12.2). She may by then have been dead.[40] It is no more than a deduction, but, together with her marriage to the Spanish Trajan, it allows her properly to be described as "the daughter of a race newly come to power" – Frick's gloss of Yourcenar's "parvenus" – a member, that is, of the Gallo-Spanish nexus that came to prominence in the early Antonine era as Yourcenar noted in her observations on Roman Spain in *L'Andalousie ou les Hespérides*.[41] Plotina's date of birth can only be estimated: somewhere between 62 and 72, with marriage between 74/76 and 84/86 to a husband, born in 53, perhaps a decade and a half older.[42] The record is absurdly inadequate. But Yourcenar clearly understood that Plotina and Hadrian, born in 76, were close in age.

Plotina's exemplary comportment all through Trajan's reign is the theme of remarks in Cassius Dio (68.5.5), with modesty assumed in the *bon mot* attributed to her on first entering the imperial residence on the Palatine: she hoped, she said to the crowd assembled there, to leave the palace the same woman as when she entered. Her reputation is indeed unsullied in the source tradition. In Pliny's *Panegyric* (83.5–6) she is commended for the deference, respect, and obedience shown to her husband, whose formative influence has made her a model of Roman womanhood, and with whom a mutuality of attitude is acknowledged in their response to Trajan's rise to the emperorship. The tradition was emphatic that she increased the glory of Trajan.[43] On the coinage, meantime, she was associated with the goddesses Vesta and Pudicitia, symbols of chastity; and from a documentary text she appears to have had influence with her husband in matters of public consequence, once favouring the Jews of Alexandria in their dispute with local Greeks.[44] None of this can have been unknown to Yourcenar, whose familiarity moreover with Plotina's portraiture supported the cogency of Hadrian's memory of the consort's simple, white clothes, a variation on the modesty of self-presentation Pliny extolled (*Pan.* 83.7).[45] Her habits of speech cannot be verified. But her friendship with Hadrian, signalled here by the rare usage of the first person plural, is drawn from another notice in the principal source where the ambiguous phrase "loving friendship" is used of their association at the moment of Hadrian's accession (Cass. Dio 69.1.2; cf. 69.10.3[1]). The words might be taken as evidence of a sexual relationship, or of a suspicion of such emanating from contemporary rumours in court circles, but Yourcenar clearly rejected such an interpretation and preferred to construe in terms of Platonic intimacy alone.[46] In which connection, given the clear Epicurean reference, she must be presumed also to have known of Plotina's later request to Hadrian to rescind the requirement of Roman citizenship for the headship of the Epicurean school at Athens, together with her letter to the Athenians informing them, once Hadrian had agreed, that she had gained her request. Yourcenar seems never to have referred directly to the inscriptions that record this exchange; but it is difficult to believe she did not know them. They are discussed in items of scholarship she had read and surely underlie the philosophically spiritual bond envisaged.[47] I conclude that the passage altogether can be taken as a typical example of the exercise of empathetic imagination, blending objective elements of the tradition with inferences concerning their human significance to create a convincing evocation of the woman Hadrian once knew.

As Hadrian speaks of her, Marcus can have no doubts of her importance to him as counsellor and friend. He knows already that Plotina's intervention and their shared literary interests had been responsible at an early stage of his career for Hadrian's appointment as Trajan's speech writer, a task Hadrian had come to relish. It was the first of her good services for him (*MH* 330). The second had been her contrivance of his marriage to Trajan's grandniece Sabina, the daughter of Matidia. Her insistence on the union had overcome the emperor's opposition (*MH* 331). She is a woman of considerable skill and influence, her "beau visage" having been Hadrian's only source of pleasure in the tight imperial circle into which his marriage had brought him (*MH* 332). Marcus will have understood, therefore, that when Trajan arrives in Antioch to prosecute his war, Plotina's "prudente approbation" of Hadrian was assured, the bond between them firmly fixed (*MH* 342). A small detail serves as a reminder. From his stay in Greece en route, Hadrian has brought books to share with her (*MH* 343) – a final touch of fabrication, but one perhaps indebted to Pliny's testimony, connoting cultural interests on the consort's part, that he once agreed to forward to Plotina a letter from a literary friend (*Ep.* 9.28.1).[48] Otherwise it is extracts from the Latin life that are exploited in these recollections, admittedly with some leeway. The speech-writing detail is credited to a date after Hadrian's first consulship, and reasons for Trajan's opposition to the marriage, attributed in the life to Marius Maximus, are unstated. Yourcenar embellished the record in order to promote the justifiable characterization of Hadrian's relationship with Trajan in the pre-accession years as one constantly antagonistic.[49]

As a whole, however, the personality of the woman as Hadrian remembers her has much to commend it, the depiction illustrating well enough Yourcenar's preoccupation with representing her protagonists free from stereotype or caricature (*ER* 86). Without raising alarm, the intimacy Plotina shares with Hadrian is marked by mutual trust and the exchange of few words. In later years, Yourcenar thought of Plotina as approaching her literary ideal of female perfection, and in a variety of contexts drew attention to what she took to be her refinement, intelligence, lucidity, and loyalty, as well as to her understanding of, and tranquil indifference to, life's vicissitudes, simultaneously loving and detached, and passive through wisdom rather than weakness.[50] In the climax of the present crisis her relationship with

Hadrian becomes all-important. But for the moment her discreet political sensibility and judgment, an antidote to Hadrian's anxieties, are enough to preserve the compact as the long winter in Antioch concludes and the imperial party leaves for the new season of military activity:

Notre entente se passa d'aveux, d'explications, ou de réticences: les faits eux-mêmes suffisaient. Elle les observait mieux que moi. Sous les lourdes tresses qu'exigeait la mode, ce front lisse était celui d'un juge. Sa mémoire gardait des moindres objets une empreinte exacte; il ne lui arrivait jamais, comme à moi, d'hésiter trop longtemps ou de se décider trop vite. Elle dépistait d'un coup d'œil mes adversaires les plus cachés; elle évaluait mes partisans avec une froideur sage. En vérité, nous étions complices, mais l'oreille la plus exercée eût à peine pu reconnaître entre nous les signes d'un secret accord. Elle ne commit jamais devant moi l'erreur grossière de se plaindre de l'empereur, ni l'erreur plus subtile de l'excuser ou de le louer. (*MH* 350)

Our accord dispensed with explanations and avowals, or reticences: facts themselves sufficed. She observed these more closely than I; under the heavy braids which the fashion demanded her smooth brow was that of a judge. Her memory retained the exact impression of minutest objects; therefore, unlike me, she never had occasion to hesitate too long or to decide too quickly. She could detect at a glance my most secret adversaries, and evaluated my followers with cool detachment. In truth, we were accomplices, but the most trained ear would hardly have been able to catch the tones of a secret accord between us. She never committed the gross error of complaining to me about the emperor, nor the more subtle one of excusing or praising him.

IV

The friends and enemies who dominate Hadrian's mind through the course of the accession episode are all historical figures. Relations with them are recovered from Yourcenar's strategy of drawing from the skeletal source tradition psychological features an undeviating human nature demands. Ambition and fear are the chief personal elements brought forward: ambition to succeed to the emperorship, and fear of failure to do so, with recourse at times to calculated dissimulation or resort to the relief of trusted companionship. Which is basically comparable to attributing to Trajan a desire for glory to explain the eastern expedition. As the episode reaches its climax, ambition and fear are elaborated to show a character vacillating from moment to moment as reports are received of military events. An inner drama is exposed from the details of the war's changing fortunes, and it is in the narrative's disproportionate attention to this that the fragmentary external record is made to consist with what has been called "the Law of Biographical Relevance." The indirect vantage point from which events are recounted remains important throughout, and the chronological distance between the crisis itself and Hadrian's recollections obviates the inevitability of outcome characteristic of conventional accounts.[51]

In the palace at Antioch, alarm grips Hadrian as news arrives of Trajan's new conquests, and dissimulation notwithstanding, diffidence sets in. What will happen to him should Trajan's plans be fully realized? Has he completely misjudged the emperor's greatness? Should he arrange a return to active military service? An act of sacrifice on Mt. Casius ostensibly to celebrate Trajan's success conceals the torment. Fear of civil war is anticipated when Plotina sends word that Trajan, stricken with paralysis at Hatra in the wake of revolt Hadrian has foreseen, stubbornly refuses to name an heir. The prospect of suicide looms amid debilitating insomnia, even as prosaic administrative work continues. But the desire for power, a truly Roman *libido dominandi*, remains undiminished: "Je voulais le pouvoir. Je le voulais pour imposer mes plans, essayer mes remèdes, restaurer la paix. Je le voulais surtout pour être moi-même avant de mourir" (MH 353).[52] Close to forty years of age, the frustration of having failed to fulfil his ambitions induces in Hadrian a psychological paralysis, with desperate recourse to oracles – the Castalian spring at Daphne included – and barbaric magical rites for signs that all is not lost in a second winter of anguish. Then, with Trajan in retreat and close to death, he fretfully resumes conclave with Plotina and Attianus, the latter now, through Plotina's intervention, both adviser to Trajan as a counterweight to Celsus and commander of the praetorian guard.[53] Matidia provides support in her role as Trajan's nursemaid. No one dares, however, to raise the question of the succession, and Hadrian's fear persists that Trajan intends to die intestate or has already made secret compact with Lusius Quietus's supporters. Pity obtrudes: "Je le plaignais: nous différions trop pour qu'il pût trouver en moi ce continuateur docile, commis d'avance aux mêmes méthodes, et jusqu'aux mêmes erreurs, que la plupart des gens qui ont exercé une autorité absolue cherchent désespérément à leur lit de mort" (MH 355–6).[54] Realistically, Hadrian reassures himself, Trajan has little choice. Yet uncertainty prevails despite his appointment as military deputy, as Trajan, persuaded by Crito, sails from Antioch for Rome until finally, en route to Selinus where the imperial party has unexpectedly put in, Hadrian is met by a courier bringing news confirming a secret report from Plotina of Trajan's decease and his designation as heir in the emperor's will. Relief, and deflation, are immediate: "Tout ce qui depuis dix ans avait été fiévreusement rêvé, combiné, discuté ou tu, se réduisait à un message de deux lignes, tracé en grec d'une main ferme par une petite écriture de femme" (MH 356).[55] Cremation of Trajan's body follows. The imperial party departs for Rome. And Hadrian returns to Antioch, the legions acclaiming him along the way. The climax has passed, and the long-alternating, all-consuming doubts, hopes, fears, and insecurities give way to final resolution: "Un calme extraordinaire s'était emparé de moi: l'ambition, et la crainte, semblaient un cauchemar passé ... Ma propre vie ne me préoccupait plus: je pouvais de nouveau penser au reste des hommes" (MH 358).[56]

The inventive quality of the emotional trajectory hardly requires emphasis. Yet it is, again, firmly based on objective elements of the historical tradition. The sacrifice Hadrian makes on the summit of Mt. Casius derives from a record in the Latin life (HA Hadr. 14.3), the preparation for suicide – staining his chest with red ink to mark the entry point for a knife – follows an anecdote in Cassius Dio (69.22.3), and the detail of the Castalian spring, as seen earlier, can be found in Ammianus Marcellinus.[57] Notable also is the realism of the physical setting in which the emotional drama is played out, the Seleucid palace at Antioch (MH 346). As Yourcenar could well have known, the structure is thought to have been situated on the pear-shaped island that lay between the encircling branches of the river Orontes where in the late Imperial age Diocletian was to build a new residence – rather more therefore than a novelistic figment.[58] To some extent, however, the most convincing aspect of Hadrian's account is his admission to Marcus of his ignorance of what truly took place during Trajan's last days at Selinus. His rivals later accused Plotina, he says, of compelling the dying emperor to write some lines bequeathing the imperial power to him; and worse, recall, some said that Crito, impersonating Trajan, had dictated his final wishes while an orderly named Phaedimus (Phœdime), hostile to Hadrian and impervious to bribery, had suspiciously succumbed the day after Trajan. Hadrian continues:

Il ne me déplairait pas qu'un petit nombre d'honnêtes gens eussent été capables d'aller pour moi jusqu'au crime, ni que le dévouement de l'impératrice l'eût entraînée si loin. Elle savait les dangers qu'une décision non prise faisait courir à l'État; je l'honore assez pour croire qu'elle eût accepté de commettre une fraude nécessaire, si la sagesse, le sens commun, l'intérêt public, et l'amitié l'y avaient poussée. (MH 357)

It would not displease me that a handful of reasonable people should have proved capable of verging upon crime in my behalf, nor that the devotion of the empress should have carried her so far. She was well aware of the dangers which a decision *not* taken portended for the State; I respect her enough to believe that she would have agreed to commit a necessary fraud if discretion, common sense, public interest, and friendship had all impelled her to it.

In this Yourcenar draws together various garbled facts and rumours that appear in the Latin life and Cassius Dio. According to the former, Trajan had intended to designate L. Neratius Priscus his successor, not Hadrian, or else to follow Alexander's example of designating no successor at all – a detail, recall again, worked into Hadrian's account – if not to leave the choice to the senate from a list he left of possibilities; Trajan had died indeed before naming anyone, and it was Plotina who arranged for an impersonator to name Hadrian the adoptee (*HA Hadr.* 4.8–10). None of this is reliable.[59] The relevant extract in Cassius Dio's account seems more substantive because it reproduces information supposedly told to Dio by his father, who had been governor of Cilicia at the time: Trajan's death was kept secret for several days to allow the adoption to be announced beforehand, the proof coming from Trajan's letters to the senate which were signed not by Trajan but Plotina (69.1.3–4).[60] In fact this is simply hearsay, no more verifiable than Trajan's belief, reported in an earlier extract, that he had been poisoned (68.33.2).[61] Manipulation is in evidence in Yourcenar's identification of Crito as the anonymous impersonator of the *Historia Augusta*, but Phaedimus was indeed an imperial freedman, M. Ulpius Phaedimus, who died at Selinus within days of Trajan, as a commemorative inscription records.[62]

What becomes evident, however, is that through the autobiographical conceit of narrative indirection, Yourcenar uses the imprecision of the source tradition to advantage by recovering Hadrian's insecurities from its various discrepant elements. No attempt is made to reconcile them. Instead, the complete ignorance in which the emergence of Hadrian as emperor is historically enveloped is retained and preserved to render credible a biographical account.[63] Hadrian's final statement brings the whole episode to an end with an inarguably convincing sense of *Realpolitik* that Marcus is surely meant to remember ever afterwards, that the holder of power should prove himself worthy of it.[64] In sum, the range of human sentiments attributed to Hadrian in the reconstitution of this first major crisis of his life is due to Yourcenar's article of faith that human nature from age to age produces predictable responses in analogous situations; and from a sterile tradition a dynamic inner life is recovered through the medium of the poetically plausible in a manner academic imperial biography normally evades. André Maurois wrote that a great biography is a work in which "two enemy sisters Erudition and Poetry are united to create the image" of its subject, and a work that "places a man ... at the centre of the tableau and arranges the events in relation to this hero."[65] This is surely the case here. The reconstitution cannot be verified by conventional means. But it achieves authenticity in terms of the rules of the game with which Yourcenar operated, and at a minimum explanation of why the account is as it is becomes apparent. Consideration of the time at which *Mémoires* was written refines, amplifies, and complicates.

V

It is a commonplace that all history is contemporary history. Paribeni saw the Parthian empire as the Ottoman empire of his day, Henderson compared the outset of Hadrian's reign to the aftermath of World War I – the Roman world was "weary" from the wars Trajan had waged – and the Wall now evokes thoughts of Berlin and the West Bank.[66] It is a commonplace of which Yourcenar herself was well aware, as already seen, but what makes this interesting at this stage is that Yourcenar is herself the best witness of how her present affected her conceptualization and execution of the accession crisis. In the *Carnets de notes, 1942–1948*, included now in the collection of essays *En pèlerin et en étranger*, she wrote that like everyone whose imagination was nourished on and formed by history, she had often tried to place herself in other centuries and to cross the barrier of time, to make voyages for which the passports required were study of ancient literatures, philology, and archaeology (*PE* 531). Her remarks have an obvious correspondence with the rules of the game she was later to set out in the *Carnets de notes de «Mémoires d'Hadrien»*. What attracts attention, however, is the date at which the remarks were made: at some point during World War II, or soon thereafter, after her migration to the United States. (It had been a matter of choice, I emphasize, to leave Europe when war broke out.)

Recall in this connection the entry in the *Chronologie* recording Yourcenar's experience in 1940 of listening to the news of the fall of France with Bronislaw Malinowski: they wept together, she movingly writes, at what seemed to be the absolute end of their world (*OR* XXI). But in the same entry she speaks also of a short article she had written in an official publication of the French Consulate in New York, in which she attacked a book widely read in the United States that she characterized as a work of Nazi propaganda (*OR* XXII). This was Anne Morrow Lindbergh's *The Wave of the Future*.[67] Precisely when the article was published is an unanswerable question. But *Forces du passé et forces de l'avenir*, scarcely five pages in its modern printed format, can now be read in *En pèlerin et en étranger* (*PE* 460–4).[68] It seems to react against what Yourcenar took to be Lindbergh's provocative plea in 1940 for socio-economic change and moral regeneration in order to forestall in the United States a tyrannous cataclysm of the kind then destroying Europe. Lindbergh had written: "I cannot see this war, then, simply as a struggle between the 'Forces of Good' and the 'Forces of Evil.' If I could simplify it into a phrase at all, it would seem truer to say that the 'Forces of the Past' are fighting the 'Forces of the Future.' The tragedy is, to the honest spectator, that there is so much good in the 'Forces of the Past,' and so much that is evil in the 'Forces of the Future.'"[69] Yourcenar took issue with what she regarded as the simplistic linear historical development that underlay Lindbergh's argument, replacing it with a cyclical conception intended to show that past catastrophes were not necessarily fatal to civilization. The fall of the Roman Empire was a prime example. A few generations after the great invasions, the barbarians – the forces of the future – had retreated to their forests and steppes, or else had been assimilated or overcome; and it was Roman law that subsequently directed civil life, bishops authorized by Rome who baptized the last Germanic or Slavic pagans, and Latin, not the language of the Goths or the Huns, that schoolchildren learned in the countries of Europe from Spain to the Baltic. The forces of the past were not annihilated. Seizing, moreover, on the metaphor used to signal potential devastation, Yourcenar observed that if waves sometimes ravage the shore at high tide, they eventually and inexorably recede.[70]

Yourcenar had the better of the exchange. It is difficult, however, as Bérengère Deprez has observed, to see how *The Wave of the Future* could be thought a work of extreme political propaganda.[71] It does no more than call for a quasi-isolationist, self-protective stance on the part of the United States vis-à-vis Europe, one ungenerous and shortsighted but not inflammatory. What stands out in Yourcenar's essay, however, is a riveting paragraph that catalogues the constituents of Hitlerian totalitarianism and brings out its full contemporary horror: war, rampant nationalism, extermination of inferior races, torture, secret police forces, monopolizing of power by military faction, palace revolutions and massacres, moral and religious intolerance, forced labour, a fanatical leader cult. None of this of course was historically new. But the privileged Lindbergh, Yourcenar implied, had no conception of its present-day impact, and there was every reason, especially in moments of despair, to think that the savagery that had been unleashed on the world was the true future of humanity and perhaps its sole reality. Civilization itself was in peril:

Déjà, la Pologne se voit ramenée, non seulement à l'état où elle se trouvait lors des fameux partages, mais dans l'affreux chaos qui suivit les grandes invasions tartares, et la France, abattue et humiliée, revit les temps désastreux de la guerre de Cent Ans. Non seulement les pays où les libertés civiques avaient donné leurs plus beaux fruits, la Hollande, la Belgique, les États baltes et certains des États scandinaves se trouvent ramenés à leur ancienne situation de provinces vassales, mais l'Allemagne victorieuse elle-même, reniant son XVIIIe siècle, et toute une partie de son XIXe siècle, n'a pas désormais d'idéal plus actuel que de ressembler de son mieux à la Germanie

préchrétienne. Si telle est la direction où s'engagent les Forces de l'Avenir, symboli-
sées par les tanks des trois dictateurs, encore quelques tours de roue, et l'humanité se
retrouvera en plein âge de pierre. (*EM* 461)

Already Poland sees itself reduced, not only to the state in which it was before the
notorious partitions, but into the frightful chaos that followed the great Tartar invasions, and France, beaten and humiliated, is reliving the disastrous times of the Hundred Years War. Not only do the countries where civil liberties had borne the finest
fruit, Holland, Belgium, the Baltic states and certain Scandinavian states, find themselves reduced to their former condition of vassal provinces, but victorious Germany
itself, renouncing its eighteenth century and a large part of its nineteenth century,
has from now on no more current ideal than to resemble as best it can pre-Christian
"Germania." If such is the direction on which the Forces of the Future, symbolised
by the tanks of the three dictators, are embarked, a few turns of the wheel more and
humankind will again find itself in the midst of the Stone Age.[72]

Two generations later, it is impossible, I think, for Western readers fully to
absorb the immensity of the threat as Yourcenar palpably described it. Once
war ended, however, she was able to write in the *Carnets* that having lived
through a period when the world seemed to be falling apart she had come
to learn the importance of the Prince (*CNMH* 525). By this she meant the
importance of a leader who was not a despot of the type that had taken
the world to the brink of destruction, but an enlightened figure able to
use the opportunity of the postwar period to restore the world and, perhaps,
to create a completely new world order. In subsequent interviews and correspondence, she explained that Hitler and Mussolini had caused her to think
deeply about the nature of a national leader, and about how what she called the
"monomanie du prince" could be avoided (*RC* 75). She believed that immediately after the war a mood of euphoria had encouraged high expectations of
political leadership, with candidates available, as it were, to whom the world
could look for enlightened governance. The foundation of the United Nations
had offered a further inducement to think of the future optimistically, a current in which she had found herself implicated but one, in the event, that was
short-lived. The 1950s brought a series of political and other deceptions, not
least the Suez crisis and the rise to power in France of a dictatorial Charles de
Gaulle, so that ten years on her postwar faith in the future had completely
evaporated: "J'avais perdu cette foi" (*PV* 324). A letter of 1959 in which she
speaks of her aims in *Denier du rêve* captures this sense of disillusion: the
pessimistic mood of 1934 that she had wanted to evoke in a story set for
all intents and purposes in Mussolini's Rome had sadly returned; it was a
mood of political inertia, dishonest compromise, sheer ignorance, unrealistic

initiatives, and aspirations conceived in isolation.[73] Her rewriting of the novel in 1958 and 1959, with its even greater stress on "political evil" ("mal politique"), symbolizes the personal development (*DR* 164). The bleakness of the fifties, recalled from her travels in Europe at the time, long remained in her mind (*SP* 736–7).[74]

It was in the euphoric interval of 1948 to 1951, however, that Hadrian became in Yourcenar's mind the model Prince, conceptually fashioned by the hopes of the moment she shared for a better future. Her goal, she claimed, was to recover what she perceived to be the classical serenity of the world to which Hadrian had brought stability, and to examine the extent to which he was formed by a Greco-Roman culture whose foundations differed from those of her own world. This was where his appeal lay. At the same time, if mercifully sensitive to the dogmatism of theory, she believed that contemporary experience would help her to understand the effort required of Hadrian to reform Rome's finances, reinvigorate its culture, and govern its provinces effectively.[75] She said to Matthieu Galey that she had been directly influenced in this by the example of Winston Churchill, a figure who was both a statesman and an author of memoirs (*YO* 159). Extracts from a letter of 1968 and an interview of 1969 leave no doubt about the connection between past and present:

le livre sur Hadrien s'accroche à l'image d'un homme de génie qui serait en quelque sorte l'idéal anti-Hitler ou anti-Staline, et présuppose que ce génie humaniste pourrait pour quelque temps, et jusqu'à un certain point recréer autour de lui cette «terre stabilisée» qui est celle des monnaies hadrianiques. (*L* 291)[76]

the book on Hadrian clings to the image of a man of genius who would be somehow the ideal anti-Hitler or anti-Stalin, and presupposes that this humanist genius could, for some time and up to a certain point, recreate around him the "stabilised world" of the Hadrianic coinage.

À l'époque où j'écrivais *Hadrien*, c'est-à-dire vers 1950, on pouvait encore se dire qu'un certain nombre d'esprits bien constitués se mettraient d'accord pour établir un *modus vivendi* mondial. Je me souviens qu'un critique italien disait qu'Hadrien, à ce moment-la, était un mélange d'André Gide et de Trygve Lie, alors secrétaire général de l'ONU. (*PV* 76–7)

At the time when I was writing *Mémoires*, towards 1950, it could still be said that a certain number of sound intellects might reach agreement on establishing a *modus vivendi* for the world. I remember that an Italian critic said that Hadrian, at that moment, was a blend of André Gide and Trygve Lie, then Secretary-General of the United Nations.

The potential danger here inevitably was one of anachronism. But if, as has been suggested, the age of gold Yourcenar took Hadrian's reign to be reflected the prospective new composure of her own postwar world, there was an element in the historical tradition that could justify the conception of Hadrian she formed, namely his reputation as a champion of peace.[77] The record is relatively strong and consistent. It extends from statements made by the more or less contemporary Fronto all the way to (the egregious) Malalas. Enthusiastic in his pursuit of peace, Hadrian is said to have provoked no war at all and never to have gone to war willingly, subduing the Jews beyond Syria only after they had rebelled. Although alert to the need for military preparedness, he sought to establish universal peace, sometimes paid subsidies to foreign rulers for the purpose, and could boast as a result that he had accomplished much more than other emperors. Complementing the tradition is the unsurprising fact that the legend PAX was prominently displayed on his coinage.[78]

Yourcenar presented Hadrian therefore not only as a "prince" of the sort for whom, *mutatis mutandis*, expectations in her own postwar world were high, but as a leader whose desire for peace was programmatic, a matter of policy. Recounting in an earlier section of *Varius multiplex multiformis* his participation in Trajan's first campaign against the Dacians, Hadrian confesses to Marcus his enjoyment of the military life, but with two important qualifications: it had always been his nature to oppose policies based on war, and despite loyal service he had come to harbour objections to Trajan's expansionist goals (*MH* 325–6). Then, he continues, as his influence grew in the year of his first consulship, he had begun to politic against what he calls the Trajanic military party, believing it important for an anti-expansionist voice to make itself heard (*MH* 340); and later still, when visiting Greece, his objections to war had assumed an idealistic cast as the notion emerged of Hellenizing the world: the achievements of the classical past were only a harbinger of what still might come, the objectives of Hellenizing barbarians, and even of Atticizing Rome, presented themselves as attainable possibilities; but for the full flowering of the Greek genius peace was essential (*MH* 343–4):

J'acceptais sans irritation les complaisances un peu hautaines de cette race fière; j'accordais à tout un peuple les privilèges que j'ai toujours si facilement concédés aux objets aimés. Mais pour laisser aux Grecs le temps de continuer, et de parfaire, leur œuvre, quelques siècles de paix étaient nécessaires, et les calmes loisirs, les prudentes libertés qu'autorise la paix. La Grèce comptait sur nous pour être ses gardiens, puisque enfin nous nous prétendons ses maîtres. Je me promis de veiller sur le dieu désarmé. (*MH* 344)

I accepted without irritation the slightly haughty condescension of that proud race, according to an entire nation the privileges which I have always so readily conceded to those I loved. But to give the Greeks time to continue and perfect their work some centuries of peace were needed, with those calm leisures and discreet liberties which peace allows. Greece was depending on us to be her protector, since after all we say that we are her master. I promised myself to stand watch over the defenseless god.

Equally, there was no lack of the pragmatic in Hadrian's thinking. The abandonment of Trajan's provinces had been a strategic decision made to avoid engagement in unfavourable military conditions and did not signify a putative decline of interest in furthering Roman interests in the east. (It had been worthwhile to retain Dacia.) Peace there had been forced – Hadrian fully understands the extent of the emperor's power – just as later victories following unavoidable actions in Mauretania and Britain had led to similar results. Peace was not an idol, therefore, but a state of non-belligerence to be secured by decisive action as needed, including the personal settlement of disputes between Greeks and Jews in Alexandria (*MH* 359–62). A break with the immediate past, nonetheless, there had been, with the public funeral afforded the governor of Dacia, Julius Bassus, a symbolic final demonstration of his opposition to Trajan's expansionism (*MH* 361). Despite the intrigue suspected, and the ferment that followed with the execution of the four consulars, Hadrian had soon been ready to leave Rome to carry out his mission – *Tellus stabilita* had begun – with the cleavage between the old and the new starkly stated: "Mes prédécesseurs, jusqu'ici, s'en étaient surtout absentés pour la guerre: les grand projets, les activités pacifiques, et ma vie même, commençaient pour moi hors les murs" (*MH* 369–70).[79] Much later still, he speaks rhapsodically of what his twelve years of travel across the empire have meant, leaving Marcus in no doubt of the essence of the mission: social order and economic prosperity for his subjects guaranteed by a strong and disciplined army stationed on the frontiers for the preservation of peace within:

Je voulais que l'immense majesté de la paix romaine s'étendît à tous, insensible et présente comme la musique du ciel en marche; que le plus humble voyageur pût errer d'un pays, d'un continent à l'autre, sans formalités vexatoires, sans dangers, sûr partout d'un minimum de légalité et de culture; que nos soldats continuassent leur éternelle danse pyrrhique aux frontières; que tout fonctionnât sans accroc, les ateliers et les temples; que la mer fût sillonnée de beaux navires et les routes parcourues par de fréquents attelages; que, dans un monde bien en ordre, les philosophes eussent leur place et les danseurs aussi. (*MH* 390–1)

I desired that the might and majesty of the Roman Peace should extend to all, insensibly present like the music of the revolving skies; that the most humble traveller might wander from one country, or one continent, to another without vexatious formalities, and without danger, assured everywhere of a minimum of legal protection and culture; that our soldiers should continue their eternal pyrrhic dance on the frontiers; that everything should go smoothly, whether workshops or temples; that the sea should be furrowed by brave ships, and the roads resounding to frequent carriages; that, in a world well ordered, the philosophers should have their place, and the dancers also.

The Wall in Britain and a diplomatic settlement with Parthia were just two of the measures taken to achieve what Hadrian calls, addressing Marcus directly, his modest ideal (*MH* 393, 397). The Jewish War admittedly was a setback for a ruler passionate for peace (*MH* 473). Yet even on his deathbed, as in patient endurance he looks to Rome's future, he is confident that while no longer his concern – the future is in the lap of the gods and catastrophe may yet befall – the ideal will nonetheless outlive him: "La paix s'installera de nouveau entre deux périodes de guerre; les mots de liberté, d'humanité, de justice retrouveront ça et là le sens que nous avons tenté de leur donner" (*MH* 513).[80]

Clearly enough, an irremovable devotion to peace bringing basic human rights in its train is one, and perhaps the most fundamental, feature of the Hadrian Yourcenar brought to life, with the pull of the present always in play. It is as if she anticipated a critical verdict soon to be rendered: "The popularity of the biographical form in the present-day historical novel is due ... to the fact that its most important exponents wish to confront the present with great model figures of humanist ideals as examples, as resuscitated forerunners of the great struggles of today."[81] One contemporary event that cannot have been missed was the adoption in Paris on 10 December 1948 by the General Assembly of the United Nations of *The Universal Declaration of Human Rights*, core items of whose opening clause are the seemingly Hadrianic virtues of freedom, justice, and peace.[82] In *Disciplina Augusta*, Hadrian tells of his organization of an annual assembly in Athens of delegates from various Greek cities whose purpose was to administer the affairs of the Greeks at large; he had wished also by this act to restore to his favoured Athens its ancient position of Greek pre-eminence (*MH* 460). The foundation of the Panhellenion is evidently meant, an institution whose precise origins, as already seen, remain matters of debate. It was an easy step, however, to associate a league of Greek cities whose representatives were to celebrate a renewed and reinvigorated Hellenism with the peace-promoting tradition surrounding Hadrian, and just as easy to draw an analogy between the ancient body and the new international institution. The convergence surely occurred to Yourcenar, no matter that theories of universal rights, impossible in a slave-owning society, were unknown to classical antiquity. It is here, if not already, that issues of presentational distortion come plainly into view.

From the world of scholarship, the influence can be detected of J.M.C. Toynbee's grand analysis of the "province series" of coins that were issued late in Hadrian's reign, a "bel ouvrage" that merited special mention in Yourcenar's *Note* (OR 552–3).[83] The coins concerned show female personifications of Italy, twenty-three provinces and the city of Alexandria, together with the slightly anomalous (if mythically appropriate) male representation of the river Nile. Their images have distinctive emblems or attributes: ears of grain for Alexandria, a spear and shield for Germania, the sistrum of Isis for Egypt, an elephant-skin headdress for Africa. One type includes as legends the names of the female figures; a second shows Hadrian meeting them at scenes of sacrifice, sometimes clasping or preparing to clasp their hands in symbolic commemoration of a visit; another shows them kneeling before him, waiting to be raised up by their restorer as, in civilian dress, he holds their hands in his. Together they bear some relationship to Hadrian's imperial tours and his conferment of benefits upon the provinces visited. But for Toynbee they showed the full development of an ideal of world unity conceived centuries earlier: "The imperial, or oecumenical, idea of the world as a unity was introduced into the Greek East by Alexander the Great. Augustus turned that idea into fact by making it, for the first time in Greek history, a historical and organic reality. Hadrian worked out the Imperial idea to its logical conclusions and brought its historical realisation in the living organism of the Empire to full maturity."[84] For Toynbee, that is, the province series completed a Hadrianic policy announced long before the provincial tours began on a coin type of 119–21 that bore the legend RESTITORI ORBIS TERRARUM ("to the restorer of the world"). From all of which the logical inference might be drawn that a project of imperial unification was conceived from the beginning much as Yourcenar conveyed it.[85] If the correlation is clear, however, it can hardly now be justified.

Peace had long been a notion to endorse at Rome, and with the advent of autocracy it became a concept to be associated directly with the emperor: PAX AUGUSTA. In Roman ideology, however, peace meant above all the absence of war, of civil war especially, together with unthreatened military domination of the Mediterranean world that empire brought. Not peace in our time, as a permanent state of being among a comity of nations, but uncontested dominion over a multiplicity of peoples, abandoned, as they might have perceived it themselves, in a wasteland of impotence. In 123 or so the title HADRIANUS AUGUSTUS appeared on Hadrian's coinage, a motif that has been associated with the senate's conferment of the name "Augustus" on Rome's first emperor and first proponent of imperial peace. It proclaimed thereby a new pacific dispensation. No one, however, could have failed to remember that the original conferment came at the conclusion of a terrible conflict between Romans themselves, in which the prize had been mastery of empire and the outcome uncertain almost to the end. (The story of the two ravens ready to announce the victory, one for Octavian, the other for Antony, still circulated in the fifth century.) Nor could Hadrian himself have ever been unaware of the long sequence of localized provincial revolts against Roman rule that had occurred since the inception of the Augustan peace. They continued into his reign.[86]

It is a message of Roman domination that the coins of the province series indisputably express. They capture the rich individuality of each region, but communicate also a sense of the vast extent of Rome's Mediterranean dominion, commemorating Hadrian's ostensibly welcome arrival in its every corner but simultaneously reflecting the omnipotence of an autocrat who alone is able to raise up his subjects from the posture of humble submission to which they have been reduced. Rome's cultural disposition had of course always been quintessentially militaristic, its mission always to war down the proud and to build a limitless empire, to fulfil the prophecy that its sons were destined to see the world beneath their feet. No emperor consequently could sensibly ignore or afford to break with tradition, and as Claudius's invasion of Britain proves, war at a minimum was sometimes a political necessity. Threats to peace may well have seemed remote by Hadrian's day to the inhabitants of the empire's inner core, with fighting confined to remote frontiers.[87] Every emperor nonetheless was obliged to display military authority, publicly presenting himself with appropriate trappings of power. He was accompanied when travelling by an escort that included detachments of the praetorian guard; he and his male relatives monopolized the ancient practice of assuming honorific names that signified the conquest of foreign peoples – *Germanicus, Britannicus, Dacicus, Parthicus* – and that were graphically publicized at every opportunity. He received the acclamations of the legions when victories were won in battle, their number being included in his titulature. The spectacular ceremony of the military triumph, during which the godlike victor rode through the City in a golden chariot, was likewise by Hadrian's day his alone to celebrate, completing the emperor's appropriation of all the military honours once competitively open to men of Rome's ruling class. Far and wide, monuments to his successes were erected – arches particularly showed scenes of enemies reduced to slavery – and everywhere statues portrayed him in battle dress as a conquering hero, his brow adorned with the civic crown, his foot trampling down a subjugated enemy. The complementary image of the *civilis princeps* notwithstanding, it was as *Imperator Caesar* that most of Rome's subject populations "saw" their ruler, a figure far different from any modern conception of a prince of peace.[88]

It happens that Hadrian took no new names commemorating military victories. From Trajan he inherited the epithets *Germanicus, Dacicus, and Parthicus,* and they are visible on his very early coins, including those celebrating his adoption. They appear also in a grandiosely worded document announcing his accession from the Prefect of Egypt, Q. Rammius Martialis: "Be it known that for the salvation of the whole race of mankind the imperial rule has been taken over from the god his father by Imperator Caesar Traianus Hadrianus Optimus Augustus Germanicus Dacicus Parthicus. Therefore we shall pray to all the gods that his continuance may be preserved to us for ever and shall wear garlands for ten days."[89] The names were soon abandoned. But after the Jewish War an acclamation was accepted, and a victory arch suitably built south of the city of Scythopolis in Judaea. Another triumphal arch was dedicated in 130 (seemingly) when Hadrian became the first emperor to visit the city of Gerasa in Arabia.[90] Through the medium of statuary, moreover, Hadrian was prominently displayed to his subjects all across the empire as the military ruler. Perhaps the most vivid illustration is a statue now in Istanbul from Hierapytna in Crete that shows him victorious, with wreathed head, breastplate, and *paludamentum,* his left foot firmly trampling down a fallen barbarian victim, a blatant illustration of sheer force all the more remarkable because the statuary form itself is rare. Its breastplate has a statue of Athena crowned by Victories to left and right standing on the back of a she-wolf suckling the infants Romulus and Remus, a common Hadrianic motif visible on the torso of a statue still standing in the agora of Athens. Symbolizing the "triumph of Greco-Roman civilization over the barbarian world," it indicates that the well-being of the cities of the empire, Athens included, rested on the strong support of Roman military might and the invincible emperor who commanded its legions. Notably, Hadrian was the first emperor to be represented in sculpture in heroic nudity with shield and helmet as the war god Mars.[91] (The detail is gracefully folded into Hadrian's recollections [*MH* 421]). Altogether, therefore, there was no reluctance to propagate a militaristic image of him fortifying the frontiers of the empire, maintaining military discipline, and, as circumstance permitted, recording military success. Coins from the last years present him indeed in military dress, severally addressing the troops stationed across the empire's frontiers or else riding with them in the field.[92] And yet, occasions for the celebration of victories were relatively rare, and it is because his military activities contrasted so sharply with those of Trajan that Hadrian could be thought not to have met imperial expectation. Criticism is undisguised for instance in Fronto's far from complimentary allusion to his passion for peace – it kept Hadrian from undertaking justifiable military endeavours and rendered him alone of Rome's emperors comparable to the pacific king of old Numa – and in the contempt displayed for the abandonment of Trajan's new provinces and the military enervation that followed: the Syrian legions, especially, had subsequently sunk into degeneracy. To some contemporaries, it appears, Hadrian's pursuit of peace was disturbing.[93]

VI

In 1963, when deprecating the possibility of a stage version of *Mémoires*, Yourcenar stated firmly that no direct equivalence could be made between modern and ancient conceptions of liberalism and pacifism: "il serait erroné de réduire les politiques complexes d'Hadrien à une forme con-ventionelle de «libéralisme» ou de «pacifisme»" (*HZ* III 281).[94] Roman ideology, it can be added, did not admit morally principled resistance to warfare of a kind that gave rise in the modern world to the conscientious objector. It remains true regardless that her personal views and aspirations in the aftermath of World War II were projected onto the Roman past and created an inevitably time-bound portrait of Hadrian's accession, a small but I think telling indication of which is the use of the word "partisans" of Hadrian's enemies and allies. The term is redolent of the 1930s, and as the first epigraph to this chapter shows it was not unique to the novelist.[95] It has been said, perhaps rightly, that Yourcenar's novels do not express political opinions, but the moment of *Mémoires'* composition encouraged a distinctive reimagining of an episode inspired by hopes for deliverance under inspired leadership from the nightmare of the recent totalitarian past.[96] Yourcenar was never reluctant to explain to the uninformed that the truth cannot be known of what transpired while Hadrian waited in Antioch for Trajan's return from the Persian Gulf and for news from Seli-nus. Nevertheless, by proceeding from what she believed to be the eternal verities of the human condition, she reconstituted the emotional history of the man whose accession was quickly heralded as a messianic promise for "the salvation of the whole race of mankind" (*P.Oxy.* 378); and in dis-closing Hadrian's all-too-human ambitions and fears, she likewise gave dramatic substance, and authority, to the impoverished factual framework that remains of Trajan's eastern crusade. The account consequently can be comprehended in both conception and design. It is one that does not abuse the privilege of the novelist, and in which a contrast emerges, a biographi-cal contrast, between "a mere character in public events" and a character who is marked by a "vibrant humanity."[97]

6

Antinous

It is symptomatic of the constricting specialisms and the oppressive burden of fact of our time that it has been left to the imagination of a novelist, Marguerite Yourcenar, to create the broadest, the most balanced and in many ways the most authentic interpretation of the affair.

Royston Lambert

I

In the late summer of the year 130 Hadrian was in Alexandria. In the autumn he spent several weeks sailing along the river Nile before return-ing to the metropolis for the winter. With him on the excursion was his companion Antinous. Their departure followed soon after the hunting expedition in the Egyptian desert where a dangerous lion had threat-ened Antinous's life. Antinous, however, did not return to Alexandria. In late October he died by drowning in the river at a moment, the day of Athyr, when the similar death of the Egyptian god Osiris was tradition-ally commemorated. Yourcenar chose to make this event the cause of the second, and perhaps the most consequential, of the three critical turning points in Hadrian's life, and in her reconstruction it is Hadrian himself, accompanied by the faithful Chabrias, who finds Antinous's lifeless body in the Nile's muddy waters. The discovery brings to a tragic climax a story that occupies the whole of *Sæculum aureum*, a title that refers less to Hadrian's aspirations or accomplishments as emperor than to the personal happiness to which his relationship with Antinous, as Yourcenar imagined it, led. This is her description of the moment of fatal discovery and of Hadrian's response:

Il ne nous restait plus qu'à explorer la berge. Une série de réservoirs, qui avaient dû servir autrefois à des cérémonies sacrées, communiquaient avec une anse du fleuve: au bord du dernier bassin, Chabrias aperçut dans le crépuscule qui tombait rapidement un vêtement plié, des sandales. Je descendis les marches glissantes: il était couché au fond, déjà enlisé par la boue du fleuve. Avec l'aide de Chabrias, je réussis à soulever le corps qui pesait soudain d'un poids de pierre. Chabrias héla des bateliers qui improvisèrent une civière de toile. Hermogène appelé à la hâte ne put que constater la mort. Ce corps si docile refusait de se laisser réchauffer, de revivre. Nous le transportâmes à bord. Tout croulait; tout parut s'éteindre. Le Zeus Olympien, le Maître de tout, le Sauveur du monde s'effondrèrent, et il n'y eut plus qu'un homme à cheveux gris sanglotant sur le pont d'une barque. (*MH* 440)

There was no longer anything for us to do but to search the shore. A series of reservoirs which must once have served for sacred ceremonies extended to a bend of the river; on the edge of the last basin Chabrias perceived in the rapidly lowering dusk a folded garment and sandals. I descended the slippery steps; he was lying at the bottom, already sunk in the river's mud. With Chabrias' aid I managed to lift the body, which had suddenly taken on the weight of stone. Chabrias hailed some boatmen who improvised a stretcher from sail cloth. Hermogenes, called in haste, could only pronounce him dead. That body, once so responsive, refused to be warmed again or revived. We took him aboard. Everything gave way; everything seemed extinguished. The Olympian Zeus, Master of All, Saviour of the World – all toppled together, and there was only a man with greying hair sobbing on the deck of a boat.[1]

Attention to historical accuracy is evident here as always. The last sentence draws on the inflated language of emperorship that Hadrian historically came to enjoy, an example of which was just seen, and of which, as implied here, he can be presumed to have been conscious himself. It draws also on the *Sibylline Oracles* for the minor detail of the colour of his hair. There is little in the source tradition, however, to explain precisely how Antinous met his end and what Hadrian's personal reaction to it was. An ambiguous excerpt of Cassius Dio's history states that Antinous died either by accidentally falling into the river, which is what Hadrian is said to have said of it in his autobiography; or else deliberately, the purpose being to satisfy a superstitious prediction that an act of sacrifice was needed for Hadrian to continue to accomplish his imperial aims. This was the truth, the extract asserts, but whether Antinous committed suicide or died involuntarily it leaves unclear (69.11.2–3). Aurelius Victor reports that the death was voluntary and followed the stipulation of certain *magi* that a human offering was needed to prolong Hadrian's life (*Caes.* 14.8); and the Latin life likewise alludes to the possibility of devotional suicide, though detail is minimal and other explanations are vaguely raised (*HA Hadr.* 14.6). On the other hand, the Latin life provides the strongest evidence for Hadrian's immediate response, recording that the emperor wept for Antinous like a woman (*HA Hadr.* 14.5: *quem muliebriter flevit*), a brief statement that offers a point of departure for the image of Hadrian sobbing in the passage quoted and the emotional breakdown Yourcenar attributed to him. Her description of his discovery of Antinous's corpse, however, is an invention, and as her *Notebook* acknowledges, the account she gives of his funeral is one of her many "developed scenes." How valid therefore was Yourcenar's choice of Antinous's death as Hadrian's second crisis? Any attempt at an answer requires examination of her construction of the story of Antinous as a whole.[2]

At once a problem arises. Antinous is simultaneously one of the most and one of the least familiar figures from classical antiquity. Most because of the great number of extant portraits in statuary, coinage, and other visual forms that from a physical perspective make him immediately recognizable (or so it seems); least because very few details of his life have been preserved. His origins lay in Claudiopolis in Bithynia, he became what is often euphemistically called the "favourite" of Hadrian, and he died in Egypt. Nothing is known, however, of his family history and social background. And when and where Hadrian met him, how long their association lasted, and what the nature of their relationship was are questions to which there are no definitive answers. It is his afterlife, ironically, that is better documented. Hadrian deified Antinous after his death, rendering him across the Roman Mediterranean the object of what became a remarkable cult, celebration of which included festivals, games, and artistic competitions. In time, Christian dogmatists vilified Antinous as Hadrian's catamite. But his image was broadcast far and wide, and his popularity as a figure of religious attraction long endured. This was especially true at Antinoopolis, the city in Egypt named after him that Hadrian built near the site where Antinous died.[3]

Yourcenar was alert obviously to the deficiencies of the sources, although confusion could easily arise. Explaining to a correspondent in 1953 her objections to the presentation of Antinous in an earlier novel by Roger Peyrefitte, she stated that there were just two serious chronicles with information on Antinous's death, neither of which was a contemporary record. One indicated that Antinous was understood to have voluntarily sacrificed his life for Hadrian, while the other made two statements: first, that Antinous sacrificed himself when certain magical procedures involving the emperor demanded a human offering on Hadrian's behalf, and secondly that Hadrian had done no more in his semi-official memoirs than to write that drowning was the cause of death. This was all, she affirmed, that could be said with assurance about an event that had caused the emperor to weep so much. The chronicles to which she (obliquely) referred were evidently the excerpt from Cassius Dio and the Latin life, with the notice from Aurelius Victor overlooked. The misprision that concerned her was the earlier author's belief that Antinous's apotheosis glorified an act of sacrificial devotion necessary for Hadrian to leave Egypt. But no contemporary inscription, she insisted, no coin, no monument of any kind mentioning Antinous referred to what she termed, notably, such a heroic act. Which did not mean that the idea of devotional death itself was false, only that the sources' silence more likely meant that Antinous's loss had been too unsettling and too personally affecting for Hadrian to permit any official announcement about it ever to be made. He seemed to have given imperial fiat alone as the reason for the deification, and Antinous himself had revealed nothing (*HZ* 245–6).[4]

The awkward summary apart, Yourcenar was correct to stress the limitations of any "tradition authentique" relating to Antinous's demise (*HZ* 245). But more important still is the implication of her letter that for the full story of Antinous to be told there were non-literary materials that had to be considered as well as the meagre literary texts; and already in her *Note* of 1951 she had referred to papyrological, epigraphic, numismatic, and art-historical sources, together with various secondary discussions, a list that was much longer in the *Note*'s final form due not least to the impact of the Picard affair. The material evidence was vitally important, she affirmed in the *Note*, and she was committed to producing from it an authentic narrative that contained both physical and psychological features, no matter that the uncertainty surrounding Antinous's death, doubtless there from the beginning, had to be preserved.[5] A dazzling early passage illustrates the extent to which, to give one example, the physical descriptions of Antinous depend on, and reflect, Yourcenar's deep knowledge of his portraiture. As Michèle Goslar has shown, it readily displays the influence of three specific artworks: the bust of Antinous in the Sala Rotunda of the Musei Vaticani in Rome, the Farnese Antinous of the Museo Archeologico Nazionale in Naples, and the Braschi Antinous also in the Vatican:[6]

Je retrouve une tête inclinée sous une chevelure nocturne, des yeux que l'allongement des paupières faisait paraître obliques, un jeune visage large et comme couché. Ce tendre corps s'est modifié sans cesse, à la façon d'une plante, et quelques-unes de ces altérations sont imputables au temps. L'enfant a changé; il a grandi. Il suffisait pour l'amollir d'une semaine d'indolence; une après-midi de chasse lui rendait sa fermeté, sa vitesse athlétique. Une heure de soleil le faisait passer de la couleur du jasmin à celle du miel. Les jambes un peu lourdes du poulain se sont allongées; la joue a perdu sa délicate rondeur d'enfance, s'est légèrement creusée sous la pommette saillante; le thorax gonflé d'air du jeune coureur au long stade a pris les courbes lisses et polies

d'une gorge de bacchante. La moue boudeuse des lèvres s'est chargée d'une amer-
tume ardente, d'une satiété triste. En vérité, ce visage changeait comme si nuit et jour
je l'avais sculpté. (*MH* 406)

I see a head bending under its dark mass of hair, eyes which seemed slanting, so long
were the lids, a young face broadly formed, as if for repose. This tender body varied
all the time, like a plant, and some of its alterations were those of growth. The boy
changed; he grew tall. A week of indolence sufficed to soften him completely; a single
afternoon at the hunt made the young athlete firm again, and fleet; an hour's sun
would turn him from jasmine to the color of honey. The boyish limbs lengthened
out; the face lost its delicate childish round and hollowed slightly under the high
cheekbones; the full chest of the young runner took on the smooth, gleaming curves
of a Bacchante's breast; the brooding lips bespoke a bitter ardor, a sad satiety. In truth
this visage changed as if I had molded it night and day.

Goslar's important study is replete with other examples of descriptive reliance on sculptural portraits, rendering irrefutable Yourcenar's proposition
that Antinous's iconography was key to recovering his full history. Her belief
furthermore that portraits were produced before as well as after Antinous's
death is explicit in Hadrian's expansive, and affecting, description in *Tellus
stabilita*, the description of a connoisseur, of how his sculptors had executed
their commissions and shown Antinous between the ages of fourteen and
nineteen with the attributes of a panoply of gods (*MH* 389–90).[7] Nevertheless, Yourcenar's *Note* confirms and extends the reference to invention of her
Notebook. Much of what she wrote was acknowledged as fictive, as it had
to be, far more so than with the narrative of the accession. The brief details
given on Antinous's family origins – son of a lowly imperial factotum, raised
by a grandfather, sent to school in Nicomedia – were based on social conditions prevalent in Bithynia at the time. Her attribution to the sculptor
Aristeas of a portrait in the Museo Nazionale in Rome followed a scholarly
hypothesis, whereas the attribution of the Farnese Antinous in Naples to
the sculptor Papias was her own conjecture. The episode, moreover, of Antinous's Mithraic initiation at Palmyra, like the initiation of Hadrian himself,
was no more than a possibility, and Hadrian's intense grief on Antinous's
death was due in part to what she deemed useful in otherwise questionable Christian sources. The hopeless inadequacies of the tradition made the
opportunity for imaginative reconstruction greater than ever, and Yourcenar
accordingly embellished the factual skeleton immensely.[8]

How then were accuracy and invention to be reconciled? The answer lay
not so much in dealing with prosaic details of a kind that positivist historians might endlessly debate, but, as the rules of the game required, in the

formulation of a narrative controlled by sociocultural realities on the one hand and recourse to fundamental human emotions on the other. These are the constituents therefore to which attention must turn in order to appreciate how Yourcenar fashioned and substantiated her account as she did. As with the crisis of the accession, the constraints of Hadrian's indirect, if impassioned, vision have to be kept in mind, and so too the moment in which the account came into being. In addition, the particular question arises of how Yourcenar conceptualized homoeroticism in classical antiquity, since the inevitable assumption was made, as by almost everyone before and since, that the story of Hadrian and Antinous that had long been of interest to her was in the first instance a love story. A photograph of a statue of Antinous bought in Florence in 1926 was one of the few items she carried to the United States in 1939 (*CNMH* 522).[9]

II

Sæculum aureum contains seven sections of varying length. All have as their backdrop journeys Hadrian had once made across his empire that he now recalls in telling Marcus of his life's golden years. He begins at Nicomedia in Bithynia, in the palace of the erstwhile king Nicomedes, where he first encountered Antinous, a youth of unspecified age perhaps in his early teens. (A proleptic thought of Caesar is sparked.) Hadrian is struck at a literary soirée by Antinous's shepherd-like appearance and detains him in a conversation from which an intimacy immediately develops. An unlettered Asiatic Greek, Antinous captivates Hadrian with his beauty and the pet-like attention he at once begins to display. Storybook years follow, in which Hadrian comes to enjoy absolute mastery of the boy – the only imperial subject, he remarks, of which that can be said – as the two become virtually inseparable. They travel first to Thrace and mainland Greece (Athens is included), then westwards to Italy and Rome, and later to North Africa. A second visit to Athens opens a journey farther east to inland Asia culminating in Palmyra and Samosata, while a lengthy stay in Antioch as they return precedes visits to Jerusalem and Alexandria. Antinous is constantly at Hadrian's side, and never far removed from his thoughts and feelings. Their intimacy has an erotic dimension, but Hadrian touches no more than delicately upon it. Coarseness is avoided. Of more importance is the passionate bond between the two, and for Hadrian himself the liberating power it unleashes to simplify his life, enhance all sensory experience, and bestow upon him pure happiness (*MH* 404–6, 412–14).[10]

At the same time, the allusions Hadrian makes to the temples that will one day be built to Antinous, to the coins that will bear his image, and to

Antinous's distress and thoughts of death, leave no doubt of the high tragedy to come. Ecstasy is recalled, but Hadrian equally tells Marcus of the intimations of the youth's death of which he had been completely unaware in the moment, writing remorsefully of occasions on which he had exposed Antinous to unsavoury experiences and wistfully recalling an inscrutability in the boy that had concealed a carefully planned, self-inflicted death. And so, on the anniversary of the death of Osiris, Antinous slips quietly into the Nile in order to fulfil a prophecy that Hadrian's reign will continue only through the offering of a human sacrifice. The tradition of suicide, that is, is purposefully followed, as Antinous literally gives his life for Hadrian. The body is discovered, interment follows, and a decision is made to build the memorial city. Marcus is assumed to have perfect understanding of all that is involved (*MH* 419–21, 423–4, 428–9, 438–51).[11]

Into this narrative, historical facts and personages are seamlessly incorporated as authenticating devices. The world of the sophists, symbols of historical enervation as Yourcenar well knew, is invoked by the literary setting of Hadrian's initial encounter with Antinous and the introduction in turn of the powerful Herodes Atticus and his son (*MH* 404, 409–10). (Aulus Gellius's reminiscences of his student days at Athens come to mind, with visiting dignitaries and the pretentious Italian young clustering around the philosopher Calvenus Taurus.) The architectural rejuvenation of Athens with which Hadrian is traditionally credited is inserted into the description of the first visit he and Antinous make to the city (*MH* 409); Hadrian's speeches to the Roman troops of Africa Proconsularis underlie a heavily allusive passage on their visit to Lambaesis (*MH* 421–2); and the sporadic comments on the socially disordered and religiously varied condition of Alexandria recall aspects of Dio Chrysostom's Alexandrian discourse (*MH* 434–5). The narrative is realistically grounded throughout, with the journeys themselves, instruments of governance as Rémy Poignault has well called them, the prime example of the firm historical underpinning of the personal story.[12] Predictably, however, time and place are recalled solely in general terms, and only hazily does it emerge that the journeys, and the companionship between Hadrian and Antinous, occupy several years. In the *Carnets*, Yourcenar placed Hadrian's first meeting with Antinous in Asia Minor in 123–4 (*CNMH* 531), and to Matthieu Galey she indicated that their association lasted five years, beginning when Hadrian was aged forty-seven (*YO* 75, 164). But there is nothing so specific in *Mémoires* itself, and it is something of a surprise that Antinous is said at his death to have been a little less than twenty years of age. Dependence on memory makes chronological and geographical precision both impossible and irrelevant.[13]

As an illustration of "realistic" technique, an entirely fictitious episode set in Egyptian Canopus is especially indicative. Threatened by court intrigue and incipient ill health, Hadrian visits a sorceress to learn his future. Antinous and Lucius accompany him. The woman utters fateful prophecies, to avert the fulfilment of which she proposes a sacrifice, and a falcon that Hadrian had once given Antinous as a gift is soon ritually drowned in water from the Nile (*MH* 437–8). A reference in the *Note* to A.-J. Festugière's *L'Idéal religieux des Grecs et l'Évangile* (1932) makes explicit the episode's basis (*OR* 552). Yourcenar learned from Festugière of a ritual known from the *Greek Magical Papyri*, the "divinization" of an animal by a practitioner of magic. It drew on the myth that Osiris was once drowned by his enemy Seth and interred in a coffin that was consigned to the sea and eventually washed up in Phoenicia, where Osiris's sister-wife Isis was able to restore him to life. The sacrificial creature in the ritual was assimilated to Osiris by becoming *esiès*, an Egyptian word meaning "praised," often used of the god, and thereby acquired his *pneuma* which then allowed the magician to cast spells as requested. Festugière gave four examples of animals attested in the procedure, the last of which, a falcon, was to be killed by immersion in the milk of a black cow, mummified, sacrificed, and addressed with a spell.[14]

This was the material Yourcenar adapted to fit the sacrificial aspect of Antinous's death included in the tradition, dispelling in one particular its obscurity. Her sorceress hypnotizes and drowns the bird in water from the river in which Antinous will end his life, its entranced state permitting the semblance of a voluntary death that is to bring relief to Hadrian. It is then deposited in a casket and buried in an abandoned graveyard at the edge of the canal connecting Canopus to the Nile. The episode ends with the departure of Hadrian and his attendants, though as Hadrian now informs Marcus, unknown to him at the time Antinous had later, and enigmatically, returned to the sorcerer's house alone. Completely fabricated, the episode consists nonetheless with a genuine form of ancient religious practice that, much later, Yourcenar confirmed to a German reader of her novel who had raised a question about the extent of falconry in Roman antiquity (*HZ* IV 332–3).[15] She agreed that the activity was rare, but added that this was one reason why in her narrative the sacrificial bird, which Hadrian had originally received from Abgar of Osrhoene before giving it to Antinous (*MH* 426), was to be considered an offering of great value: the falcon was understood to be a symbol of the sun, and often appeared in the magical papyri as an object of sacrifice, which is indeed the case. She cited Festugière again, noting his reference to a ritual that Hadrian had actually witnessed involving the prophet of Heliopolis Pachrates, who could cause death and sickness and induce dreams.[16] She explained finally that her adaptation made it natural, and much more dramatic, that it should be Antinous's precious gift that was offered up on Hadrian's behalf, with the sacrifice prefiguring his death in the river and conversion into a solar symbol a few weeks later. Her reader now can hardly miss the point of the death and apotheosis soon to come.[17] The episode is a telling illustration of how plausible invention once more fills the void of the tradition through recourse to cultural history. The same is true, but far more significantly, of the way in which the intimate relationship between Hadrian and Antinous is presented.

III

In Hadrian's memories of his halcyon years, Antinous is a creature totally devoted to the emperor, but a figure who undergoes a metamorphosis from uneducated schoolboy to young sophisticate. If puppy-like in his submissiveness from the beginning, a familiar spirit, he is not altogether infantilized: his searching eyes could make Hadrian feel judged, and his capacity for independent thought and action leads eventually to the act of suicidal dedication. In Syria, an oblation is required on Mt. Casius, but in a violent thunderstorm the officiant and the sacrificial animal, a fawn, are both struck dead, and it is Antinous alone who perceives what was portended, one of the signs of change in the youth. He had come to Nicomedia as an unlettered boy, but during the years of travel he acquires knowledge and expertise in a variety of fields. In Athens he plays the lyre among a group of musicians and forms an attachment to the Platonist Chabrias. He finds Latin difficult, but has an interest in mathematics. In Phrygia, he races horses, dances, and sings, in Arcadia and the valley of the Helicon he hunts, his prize at first no more than a hare but later a bear, and in the Egyptian Oasis of Ammon he is experienced enough to accompany Hadrian when the prey is a lion. An unmistakable maturation, a growth in sophistication, is in evidence, which Hadrian captures as the young shepherd, now an eighteen-year-old absorbed in recondite, sensuous Greek poetry and certain works of Plato, can be taken for a young prince (*MH* 405, 429, 409, 411, 421, 413–14, 431–2, 419).[18] Acculturation to the rarefied world of Hadrianic aestheticism and sensuality is multifaceted and comprehensive, with the emperor's role in the process explicitly drawn when instruction in sexual matters is described. The motives are far from congenial:

Et il y eut cette nuit de Smyrne où j'obligeai l'objet aimé à subir la présence d'une courtisane. L'enfant se faisait de l'amour une idée qui demeurait austère, parce qu'elle était exclusive; son dégoût alla jusqu'aux nausées. Puis, il s'habitua. Ces vaines tentatives s'expliqent assez par le goût de la débauche; il s'y mêlait l'espoir d'inventer une intimité nouvelle où le compagnon de plaisir ne cesserait pas d'être le bien-aimé et l'ami; l'envie d'instruire l'autre, de faire passer sa jeunesse par des expériences qui avaient été celles de la mienne; et peut-être, plus inavouée, l'intention de le ravaler peu à peu au rang des délices banales qui n'engagent à rien. (*MH* 423–4)[19]

And there was that night in Smyrna when I forced the beloved one to endure the presence of a courtesan. His conception of love had remained austere because it was centered on but one being; his disgust now verged on nausea. Later he got used to that sort of thing. Such idle experiments on my part are explained well enough by a taste for dissipation; there was also mingled therein the thought of inventing a new kind of intimacy in which the companion in pleasure would not cease to be the beloved and the friend; there was the desire to instruct him, too, giving him some of the experiences which had been those of my own youth. And possibly, though less clearly avowed, there was some intention of lowering him slowly to the level of routine pleasures which involve no commitments.

Such a fulsome record has no historical justification. It derives from Yourcenar's preconception that the relationship between emperor and favourite was, by definition, an example of a male same-sex relationship well attested in classical Greek history in which an idealized form of heroism between friends and comrades was an all-encompassing ingredient. The association, that is, was to be understood again in distinctly cultural terms. Proof is immediately forthcoming from a letter that Yourcenar wrote in 1953 to the poet Hortense Flexner, a long, carefully composed statement responding to the shock felt on reading *Mémoires* by Martha Gellhorn, the celebrated war correspondent and one-time wife of Ernest Hemingway, who, as Flexner had reported to Yourcenar, was disturbed by the Hadrian–Antinous relationship, not so much for its sexual as for its implicitly exploitative character. The letter duly accommodates Gellhorn's misgivings. Marriage ages among Greeks and Romans had first to be understood, Yourcenar said, noting, as if a modern demographic historian, the considerable age difference between spouses typical of antiquity: a young woman of fourteen or fifteen, or even younger, could be matched to a husband ten or fifteen years older. She posited next a special interest on the part of mature Greek men in the beauty of both male and female adolescents, and explained the age interval in both cases, not altogether logically, as a means of coping with the travails of emergent sexuality: relationships were created in which the older and more experienced male initiated a partner, whether male or female, into a sexual union that created the opportunity for entry into the social world of adulthood at large, which meant that the convention was not exploitative at all but quite the opposite. It provided a mechanism for successfully nurturing the development of the young that contrasted with the modern tendency to ignore the role of sexuality in adolescent life. This was the basis of male-male relationships in pre-classical and classical Greece, as also later at Rome, although in Hadrian's day the Greek ideal of what Yourcenar saw as heroic love had disappeared, rendering such relationships comparable to heterosexual relationships with courtesans. Hadrian was perhaps exceptional, she maintained, in seeking through his commitment to Antinous, especially after his death, a return to the erotic ideals of the Greek past. But Romans were not offended by dalliances such as those alleged of Trajan, any more than were some moderns – she cited Eleanor Clark as an example – even if some were scandalized by the way Hadrian expressed his deep and lasting passion for Antinous. She suspected in the end a touch of the puritanical in Gellhorn (*HZ* 236–41).[20]

Yourcenar's reasoning might not be fully accepted today. But her sensitivity to the distinctive patterns of Greco-Roman culture is notable, and illustrates the crucial point she made to Atanazio Mozzillo, that an ancient social phenomenon had to be assessed on its own terms, as free as possible from the influence of personal subjectivity (*HZ* II 44).[21] Three details can be added. First, remarks from Yourcenar's essay of 1930, *La Symphonie héroïque*, where heroic friendship is symbolized by the sublime examples of Achilles and Patroclus in the *Iliad* and Nisus and Euryalus in the *Aeneid*: its origins lay in military companionship but extended far beyond, and as the mark of free men it surpassed all conventional relationships, transcending mere sensuality, achieving grandeur through facing danger with mutual courage, and finding its ultimate distinction in an exalted notion of sacrifice (*EM* 1656–67). Secondly, a strong objection to a proposal for a female dancer to play the role of Antinous when plans for staging a ballet of the love story were in progress in Paris in 1953: the heroic and athletic character of the adventure, she insisted, would be completely lost (*HZ* 249). Thirdly, the gloss of "Greek love" Yourcenar gave in the introduction to *La Couronne et la Lyre*: a mixture of admiration for an adolescent boy flowering in beauty, carnal desire, and, in principle at least, a protective tenderness on the part of the older man; of fidelity from the adolescent to the older partner; and again of heroic friendship between comrades of the same age (*CL* 20).[22]

It is no accident, therefore, that during the visit to Antinous's genuinely ancestral Arcadia, Hadrian records his restoration of the tomb of the classical Theban general Epaminondas, buried long ago with the young love companion who fell with him in battle at Mantinea. The event depends on Pausanias's notice of an inscription Hadrian composed for a stele dedicated at Epaminondas's tomb (8.11.8), and Plutarch's notice of the death in battle and subsequent burial with Epaminondas of his companion Caphisodoros (*Mor.* 761d). Nor is it an accident that in Phrygia, on a visit to the tomb of Alcibiades, where according to Athenaeus Hadrian erected a statue of him (13.574), Hadrian should recall, in one of Yourcenar's "developed scenes," his reflections of the night spent there as he does. Or that he remembers the exact terms in which his close friend Arrian had behaved towards Antinous in Athens. The three passages are revealingly consistent:

Sur la route, non loin de Mantinée, je fis rénover la tombe où Épaminondas tué en pleine bataille, repose auprès d'un jeune compagnon frappé à ses côtés: une colonne, où un poème fut gravé, s'éleva pour commémorer ce souvenir d'un temps où tout, vu à distance, semble avoir été noble et simple, la tendresse, la gloire, la mort. (*MH* 408)[23]

On the road not far from Mantinea I restored the tomb where Epaminondas, slain in the heat of battle, is laid to rest with the young companion struck down at his side; a column whereon a poem is inscribed was erected by my order to commemorate this example of a time when everything, viewed at a distance, seems to have been noble, and simple, too, whether tenderness, glory, or death.

J'aime à m'étendre auprès des morts pour prendre ma mesure: ce soir-là, je comparai ma vie à celle du grand jouisseur vieillissant qui tomba percé de flèches à cette place, défendu par un jeune ami et pleuré par une courtisane d'Athènes. Ma jeunesse n'avait pas prétendu aux prestiges de celle d'Alcibiade: ma diversité égalait ou surpassait la sienne. J'avais joui tout autant, réfléchi davantage, travaillé beaucoup plus; j'avais comme lui l'étrange bonheur d'être aimé. (*MH* 414)[24]

I like to measure myself alongside the dead; that night I compared my life with the life of that great artist in pleasure, no longer young, who fell pierced by arrows on this spot, defended to the end by a beloved companion and wept over by an Athenian courtesan. My young years made no pretension to the prestige of Alcibiades' youth, but my versatility equalled or surpassed his own. I had tasted as many delights, had reflected more, and had done far more work; I knew, like him, the strange felicity of being loved.

Ce lecteur assidu des dialogues socratiques n'ignorait rien des réserves d'héroïsme, de dévouement, et parfois de sagesse, dont la Grèce a su ennoblir la passion pour l'ami; il traitait mon jeune favori avec une déférence tendre. (*MH* 411)

This assiduous reader of Socratic dialogue treated my young favourite with tender deference, for he knew full well the rich stories of heroism, devotion, and even wisdom, on which Greece has drawn to ennoble love between friends.

Without question, Yourcenar cast the relationship between Hadrian and Antinous in terms of a classical Greek paederastic ideal of *erastes* and *eromenos* according to which an aristocratic male (especially) courted and cultivated a favoured boy as a socializing means of preparing him for eventual entry into the adult world of civic comportment.[25] Its influence is most detectable as Hadrian, whose goal of stabilizing Rome's empire had depended above all, recall, on the programmatic promotion of Hellenism, tells nostalgically of the deep emotion shared with Antinous at the feast that followed the lion hunt in the Libyan desert. Antinous's display of bravery had led to near disaster averted only by Hadrian's intervention:

On but en son honneur du vin de palme. Son exaltation montait comme un chant. Il s'exagérait peut-être la signification du secours que je lui avais porté, oubliant que j'en eusse fait autant pour n'importe quel chasseur en danger; nous nous sentions pourtant rentrés dans ce monde héroïque où les amants meurent l'un pour l'autre. La gratitude et l'orgueil alternaient dans sa joie comme les strophes d'une ode. (*MH* 432)

In his honor we drank palm wine. His exultation mounted like song. Perhaps he exaggerated the significance of the aid which I had given him, forgetting that I would have done as much for any hunter in danger; we felt, nevertheless, that we had gone back into that heroic world where lovers die for each other. Pride and gratitude alternated in his joy like the strophes of an ode.

Significantly, however, Hadrian draws on one occasion a striking contrast between the devotion shared by gloried Greeks from the distant past and the far from noble pleasures enjoyed between men and boys in his contemporary Roman world. He tells of a visit to Troy undertaken to assess damage from a flood, during which he piously paid tribute at the tomb of Hector, but failed to recognize in Antinous, dreamily standing over the grave of Patroclus, a successor to the friend of Achilles:

Je trouvai quelques moments pour me recueillir sur la tombe d'Hector; Antinoüs alla rêver sur celle de Patrocle. Je ne sus pas reconnaître dans le jeune faon qui m'accompagnait l'émule du camarade d'Achille: je tournai en dérision ces fidélités passionnées qui fleurissent surtout dans les livres; le bel être insulté rougit jusqu'au sang. La franchise était de plus en plus la seule vertu à laquelle je m'astreignais: je m'apercevais que les disciplines héroïques dont la Grèce a entouré l'attachement d'un homme mûr pour un compagnon plus jeune ne sont souvent pour nous que simagrées hypocrites. Plus sensible que je ne croyais l'être aux préjugés de Rome, je me rappelais que ceux-ci font sa part au plaisir mais voient dans l'amour une manie honteuse: j'étais repris par ma rage de ne dépendre exclusivement d'aucun être. (*MH* 424)

I took a moment to pay homage at the tomb of Hector; Antinous stood dreaming over Patroclus' grave but I failed to recognize in the devoted young fawn who accompanied me an emulator of Achilles' friend: when I derided those passionate loyalties which abound chiefly in books the handsome boy was insulted, and flushed crimson. Frankness was rapidly becoming the one virtue to which I constrained myself; I was beginning to realize that our observance of that heroic code which Greece had built around the attachment of a mature man for a younger companion is often no more for us than hypocrisy and pretence. More sensitive to Rome's prejudices than I was aware, I recalled that although they grant sensuality a rôle they see only shameful folly in love; I was again seized by my mania for avoiding exclusive dependence on any one being.

The vignette can be taken to represent a moment in the evolution of Hadrian's sensibilities. But the cultural precision Yourcenar evokes is sharp, and the conceptualization of Roman homoeroticism involved is a key aspect of her commitment to historical propriety. Whether it is an accurate conceptualization is an open question. Attitudes at Rome to male same-sex relationships were invariably multifaceted and diverse, constantly changing over time.[26] What can be appreciated, however, is the importance placed on understanding antiquity free from modern encumbrances and the resolve with which Yourcenar held to this position. To Matthieu Galey, comparing the Zeno of *L'Œuvre au Noir* with Hadrian – and here she spoke of Hadrian not as a fictive character – she was firm about historical context:

Un type humain purement homosexuel existe très peu dans l'Antiquité; c'est même une chose tellement rare que je ne pourrais pas en fournir un exemple, en tout cas pas dans le monde grec; le latin peut-être, vers l'époque de la décadence. Tous ces gens-là se marient, tous ces gens-là ont des maîtresses; ils ont le sentiment de la liberté de choix et ce n'est pas du tout le fait de l'obsession ou d'une compulsion, comme c'est le cas de nos jours, où l'homme de goûts «minoritaires» tend à se créer une espèce de mythologie d'hostilité envers la femme, de crainte envers la femme. C'est très frappant à l'époque actuelle. (*YO* 182)

There are very few examples of pure homosexuality in antiquity. In fact, it was such a rare thing that I can't cite a single example, at least not from the Greek world. From the Latin world in the period of decadence, perhaps. Men married and had mistresses. They felt they had freedom of choice; their homosexuality had nothing of an obsessive or compulsive quality about it, unlike today's homosexuality, in which one occasionally observes a tendency for men of "minority" tastes to create around themselves a mythology of hostility toward women or fear of women. This is very striking nowadays.

A decade earlier, in a trenchant letter to Simon Sautier, a student who had written a thesis on her work and had unwisely sought her reaction, she had been equally firm: to speak of homosexuality in antiquity was anachronistic (*L* 365).[27] She made the point again to Jacques Chancel: it was better to think of Hadrian as bisexual in a context where the man who loved life, or sufficiently loved love itself, loved to some extent everything that he found seductive and beautiful. Hadrian would never have thought in the chauvinistic and isolationist terms surrounding homosexuality in the twentieth century (*EC* 127–8). To Mozzillo, she allowed that in antiquity Stoics and other rigorists had decried certain aspects of sensuality; but in contrast to contemporary practice Hadrian's same-sex comportment would not have required a claim of self-justification or breached the general social ethos as long as – and here again her perception is keen – social sensitivities were not compromised (*HZ* II 44). To Shusha Guppy latterly, as earlier to Galey, she expressed irritation with the word "homosexual": it was tiresome and dangerous if not absurd because of its prejudicial implications; a slight preference for the emergent "gay" could be grudgingly admitted (*PV* 384; *YO* 66: "fâcheux").[28] Altogether Yourcenar's views were well and objectively formed long before same-sex relationships in antiquity became, from the 1970s onwards, a subject of mainstream academic interest. For present purposes, it is the long-standing commitment to recover and portray antiquity as it was that is so prominent and pertinent.[29]

How Yourcenar came to form her views is a difficult question. But her letter to Hortense Flexner offers a clue (*HZ* 240), drawing as it does for support of her exposition on the authority of the nineteenth-century historian, essayist, and poet John Addington Symonds (1840–1893), two of whose works she named in her *Note* as sources on which she had drawn in her researches: an essay on Antinous published principally in Symonds's *Sketches and Studies in Italy*, and a monograph, or pamphlet, entitled *A Problem in Greek Ethics*. Yourcenar regarded both as unusually important, distinguishing them from other discussions of Hadrian and Antinous she had consulted (*OR* 550).[30] Symonds himself died in Rome at the age of fifty-three of complications from influenza, and was buried under the cypresses of the Protestant Cemetery close to Shelley and Keats. His Latin epitaph, composed by the redoubtable authority on Plato and one-time master of Balliol, Benjamin Jowett, celebrates a friend and former pupil as a man full of the light of learning and a figure of exceptional industry, whose mind, despite a frail body, had always burned with a zealous passion for literature and history. Weathered now and scarcely legible, the stone immortalizes Symonds as a man of high intellectual accomplishment, but gives no indication of the personal crises he had endured as a homosexual in an age hostile to such an identity; nor does it communicate anything of the homoerotic culture in which, under Jowett's tutelage, he had spent his years at Oxford, a culture fostered by the Platonic "homosociety" promoted in Jowett's Oxford classical syllabus. Sexual identity is obviously the key to Symonds's interest in Antinous. Yourcenar was alert in recognizing the value of what resulted from it.[31]

The interest first appears in Symonds's poem "The Lotos-Garland of Antinous," composed in 1868 but published only a decade later. Anxious about its reception, he described it in a letter of February 1878 to Edmund Gosse as "an Euripidean sort of affair (not dramatic but narrative) about [Antinous's] death."[32] Its almost four hundred lines imagine the event as a sacrificial suicide, with the lotus flower of its title taken from an anecdote recorded by Athenaeus: the poet Pancrates suggested to Hadrian at Alexandria that a rose-like flower that had sprung from the blood of a Libyan lion the emperor had killed should be named after the favourite; Hadrian approved, and Pancrates subsequently wrote a poem on the lion hunt mentioning "the flower named for Antinous." This, Athenaeus explains, quoting four of Pancrates's verses, was the origin of the garland known to him as *Antinoeios* (15.677d–f).[33] Symonds's poem opens with a tableau of Hadrian sailing along the Nile in a luxuriously appointed barge with Antinous lying languorously beside him. At sunset, a revel is prepared for the accompanying party. Antinous appears as Bacchus, wearing a crimson lotus garland trimmed with ivy. He knows that he is soon to die, since a seer has prophesied that Hadrian's imminent death can be averted only by a human sacrifice, and Antinous has secretly determined to end his life before his garland's flowers lose their dew. As cupbearer, he grandiloquently declares his devotion to the emperor, wishing him good health and long life, and Hadrian keeps a blossom that falls from the garland. Antinous spends the night in the prow of the barge preparing the rituals of death, aware that the blush of youth is fading and anticipating the fame his sacrificial act will bring. At the tower of Besa, he slips into the river unseen and next morning his body is found surrounded by lotus flowers that burn miraculously in a pool as Antinous himself, gleaming as a star in the night-time sky, looks down smiling "like a god," the "martyr and the miracle of love." The image is based on a report from Cassius Dio: Hadrian took a star he himself observed to be the star of Antinous, favouring a story told by friends that Antinous's soul was reflectingly embodied there (69.11.4). The flowers are presumably meant to symbolize memory of the loved one, not Homeric oblivion.[34]

It is natural to ask whether Yourcenar knew Symonds's poem. She certainly knew Symonds as a poet. In the summer of 1951, she wrote two letters to the publisher Jean Ballard concerning initial publication of some of her translations of Greek poetry that would eventually appear in *La Couronne et la Lyre*. Ballard had raised some objections because of the poems' homosexual content, to which there was a typically indignant reaction. In her first, no more than mildly sarcastic, letter Yourcenar cited Symonds as a poet who, if confronted with a stance of this sort, would have replied that his choice of materials for a project such as hers would depend solely on the pleasure they gave – a very simple response, she said, and one that would be her last word on the matter (*HZ* 32–3). But of course it was not. In the second letter, still promoting her cause, she referred to Symonds as an authority on Greek lyric poetry and praised his version of "The Garland Seller," a poem by Hadrian's contemporary Strato of Sardis, who, she wrote, was a poet remembered for the *Mousa Puerilis*, a collection of paederastic epigrams of which Symonds thought highly, as did the scholars Croiset and Edmunds [*sic*]. If they were little known to the public in France, this was not the case in England: "The Garland Seller" was one of the nineteenth century's great translation successes, if too much of a paraphrase for her taste (*L* 90–3).[35] Her verdict is something of a surprise, given that Symonds's version is a very free adaptation – Strato's eight lines become his thirty-six – but it is Yourcenar's familiarity with Symonds as a poet, and one she could place in very elevated company, that is relevant: she named him with Ronsard and Shelley. As for the scholars, by "Croiset" she meant Alfred and Maurice Croiset, authors of the standard French history of classical Greek literature that first appeared in the late nineteenth century, and by "Edmunds" she meant J.M. Edmonds, whose three Loeb volumes of Greek lyric poetry from the first half of the twentieth century were basic works of reference at the time.[36]

"The Garland Seller" can now be read in the chapter on the *Greek Anthology* in the second series of Symonds's *Studies of the Greek Poets* (1877).[37] It is preceded by remarks on the indelicacy of Strato's poetry – "there are few readers who, even for the sake of his pure and perfect language, will be prepared to tolerate the immodesty of his subject-matter" – and by a statement that Symonds had "paraphrased" Strato's poem, a significant item in view of Yourcenar's use of the same term in her second letter to Ballard.[38] It does not follow that Yourcenar knew "The Lotos-Garland" because she knew "The Garland Seller." But when Strato appears in *Mémoires* as Hadrian's one-time guide to the brothels of Sardis, Hadrian speaks of him in a way suggestive of the "immodesty" Symonds found in his poetry: "Ce Straton, qui avait préféré à ma cour l'obscure liberté des tavernes de l'Asie, était un homme exquis et moqueur, avide de prouver l'inanité de tout ce qui n'est pas le plaisir lui-même, peut-être pour s'excuser d'y avoir sacrifié tout le reste" (*MH* 423).[39] More notably, while Symonds's revel in "The Lotos-Garland," with its chorus of boys and girls, is complete fantasy, Antinous's death in *Mémoires* also follows a historically unattested festive episode, if one less elaborate than that of Symonds.[40] Lucius has invited Hadrian to dine with him on the river; Antinous at first refuses to accompany Hadrian, but subsequently changes his mind and arrives amid the company's applause for a dancing girl, with the wild gaiety of the evening captured by the garland Lucius immediately tosses to him. Yourcenar describes his appearance carefully, with attention to the torso that Symonds, very familiar with Antinous's iconography, found captivating – "But oh! What tongue shall tell the orient glow / Of those orbed breasts, smooth as dawn-smitten snow" – and in both contexts Antinous makes his sacrifice as a nineteen-year-old.[41] Yourcenar's account is clearly of a different order. But Symonds's postulate that Antinous's suicide was an act of heroic self-sacrifice clearly consists with her conception of idealized Greek homoerotic relationships. A peripheral influence there might have been.[42]

With Symonds's essay on Antinous the case is stronger. His correspondence from early 1878 shows that he had by then decided to compose what he termed "a monograph upon that most romantic personage," and that he was heavily invested in gathering information for it from all possible sources, one result being a certain regret for the earlier poem. As he said to Gosse, "I think I might have ventured on a far more heroic treatment than I then thought possible." The phraseology – "romantic personage," "heroic treatment" – is indicative of the presuppositions brought to bear. The outcome was the essay that appeared the following year in two instalments in the *Cornhill Magazine* and later in *Sketches and Studies in Italy*.[43] It is not an academic product of the modern kind, with source citations and footnotes; its intended audience was an educated reading public, not a narrow circle of scholars. It is based nonetheless on a thorough knowledge of all the sources available in the late nineteenth century from which an attempt to write Antinous's history could be made, as also of previous investigations, and has been called "the first modern scholarly study of Antinous in English."[44] It was written when Symonds had moved for health reasons to Davos Platz in Switzerland, and his letters show the lengths to which he went to secure material, importuning friends in England to consult references in "Spartianus" and to send him books (Dessau's revolutionary paper on the *Historia Augusta* was not to appear for another ten years), asking the British Museum for details on coin issues that bore Antinous's portrait (the results were alarming), and commissioning a translation of an earlier study by a Danish enthusiast.[45] The limitations of the sources are not evaded, and to a large extent the essay, like a modern historical study, is a statement of possibilities and probabilities only. The reader is alerted to the issues stemming from the tradition's indeterminate accounts of Antinous's death and the impossibility of ever knowing the truth of how his life ended, although the notion of a sacrificial death so prominent in "The Lotos-Garland" is, in the end, the preferred option. An essential assumption regardless is that Antinous was a historical figure whose character is best perceived from the realistic evidence of statuary, the subject with which the essay opens. All sense of mythologizing is dismissed, and in what he takes to be "a failing age," Symonds defines Antinous as a symbol of a decadent paganism, his physical features, combining "Greek beauty" with "something of Oriental voluptuousness," revealing a person authentically individualized: "A prevailing melancholy, sweetness of temperament overshadowed by resignation, brooding reverie, the innocence of youth touched and saddened by a calm resolve or an accepted doom – such are the sentences we form to give distinctness to a still vague and uncertain impression."[46]

The relationship with Hadrian is discreetly addressed. If the essay contains a homoerotic leitmotif detectable to those who shared Symonds's disposition, many contemporaries could have read it free from any thought that emperor and favourite shared a physical intimacy.[47] The relationship is one of love and dedication – "Hadrian had loved Antinous with a Greek passion" – set predominantly in terms of friendship and comradeship of a decidedly sociocultural type: Zeus and Ganymede, Achilles and Patroclus, Alexander and Hephaestion are brought forward as precedents, admittedly perhaps with a certain ambiguity; but it is only when the perspectives are introduced, as they must be, of Christian commentators, neatly styled "gladiators of the new faith," that hints of the disreputable appear, with attention focused on the cult that was instituted after Antinous's apotheosis: "all inveigh, in nearly the same terms, against the emperor's Ganymede, exalted to the skies, and worshipped with base fear and adulation by abject slaves." Much is made instead of the evidence of the Ildefonso statuary group in the Prado of Madrid, that was believed in Symonds's day to portray Hadrian and Antinous in an attitude of mutual devotion. The relationship, however, is not as idealized as its Greek pedigree might suggest – "the love between them had been less than heroic" – and the final summary paragraphs, where Symonds returns to the portraits of Antinous on which he relied heavily for his view of Antinous's personality, are sober and sensible, their florid flights notwithstanding: "Could a more graceful temple of the body have been fashioned, after the Platonic theory, for the habitation of a guileless, god inspired, enthusiastic soul? The personality of Antinous, combined with the suggestion of his self devoted death, made him triumphant in art as in the affections of the pious." Despite later refinements to, and increases in, the iconographic evidence, the conclusion is one hardly controversial: "The utmost we can do is to indulge our fancy in dreams of greater or less probability, and to mark out clearly the limitations of the subject." Ultimately, Antinous remained a mystery for Symonds, as he always must.[48]

Two points of correlation between the essay and *Mémoires* stand out, apart from the coincidence, if that is what it is, that Yourcenar also thought of Antinous as a Greek in whose veins flowed Oriental blood (*MH* 405). In Shelley's prose fragment "The Coliseum" (1817), the face of a young stranger makes an indelible impression on the story's other protagonists – "a face, once seen, never to be forgotten" – a face like that of Hadrian's companion: "The mouth and the moulding of the chin resembled the *eager and impassioned tenderness* of the statues of Antinous; but instead of the *effeminate sullenness* of the eye, and the narrow smoothness of the forehead, shone an expression of profound and piercing thought." Symonds refers to Shelley early in his essay when describing Antinous, quoting the words I have italicized: "The undefinable expression of the lips, together with the weight of the brows and slumberous half-closed eyes, gives a look of sulkiness or voluptuousness to the whole face. This, I fancy, is the first impression which the portraits of Antinous produce; and Shelley has well conveyed it by placing the two following phrases, 'eager and impassioned tenderness' and 'effeminate sullenness,' in close juxtaposition."[49] Yourcenar, in turn, also knew Shelley's description: "Tout ce qu'on peut dire du tempérament d'Antinoüs est inscrit dans la moindre de ses images. *Eager and impassionated tenderness, sullen effeminacy:* Shelley, avec l'admirable candeur des poètes, dit en six mots l'essentiel, là où la plupart des critiques d'art et les historiens du xixᵉ siècle ne savaient que se répandre en déclamations vertueuses, ou idéaliser en plein faux et en plein vague" (*CNMH* 531).[50] Here, however, confusion has occurred in the transmission of the crucial six words: "impassioned" has become "impassionated," and "effeminate sullenness" has become "sullen effeminacy."[51] To account for which one authority has proposed that Yourcenar drew Shelley's words not from Shelley directly but from Symonds's essay, ascribing the errors to Yourcenar's inability to check the quoted phrases when composing *Mémoires*, the reason being that *Sketches and Studies in Italy* was a rare book difficult of access. The repetition, more or less, of the same six words alone makes the suggestion attractive, although simple inadvertence, frequently detectable in Yourcenar's references, should be kept in mind.[52]

More substantively, when rejecting the view, a falsehood as he saw it, that Hadrian was somehow responsible for Antinous's death, Symonds quotes and places considerable emphasis on the key words from the *Historia Augusta* that speak of Hadrian weeping like a woman: "Spartian's own words, *quem muliebriter flevit*, as well as the subsequent acts of the Emperor and the acquiescence of the whole world in the new deity, prove to my mind that in the suggestion of *extispicium* we have one of those covert calumnies which it is impossible to set aside at this distance of time, and which render the history of Roman Emperors and Popes almost impracticable."[53] As indicated at the beginning, these words are vital for Yourcenar's reconstruction of the second crisis. Their impact is evidenced by the remarks she made in a letter of March 1952 to Christian Murciaux when commenting on the comparison Murciaux had made in an admiring article between Hadrian and the Alexis of her novel, *Alexis ou le Traité du vain combat* (1929). Her attraction to Hadrian, she wrote, was due to the complexity of a subject who was both man and emperor, one striking aspect of which, together with his dreams of the gods and his love of Greece, was his emotional response to Antinous's death; and as she described the magical process of composing the passage of lament in *Mémoires* Murciaux especially admired, the all-important words came naturally, if not quite accurately, to mind: composition had been possible only on condition of first listening in absolute silence to, or perhaps for, the sob of which the chroniclers spoke: "*flevit muliebriter*" (*HZ* 137–8). There is of course only one such chronicler. But the literal value attached to his words cannot be missed. This may be due to Yourcenar's independent judgment as she laboured to understand Hadrian; but the attention the words drew from Symonds is self-evident, and both authors were prepared to accommodate for their respectively comparable purposes the critical reproach inherent in them: given the almost natural assumption in antiquity that men were in all respects stronger than women, any description of a man's actions as woman-ish could only signify weakness.[54]

Most significant of all is what I take to be a further correspondence between Symonds and Yourcenar in the distinction each drew between the idealized paederastic relationships of the classical Greek era and Hadrian's decadently Roman relationship with Antinous. As seen a moment ago, Symonds had written that "the love between them … had been less than heroic," a brief mention that might be thought inconsequential. Except that it was derived from the history of Greek love Symonds had produced six years earlier in his treatise *A Problem in Greek Ethics*. This was, and remains, a learned study of Greek paederasty from Homer to the high Imperial age, in which evidence from a wide array of literary sources is deployed. It glorifies classical Greek civilization in a perhaps predictable Victorian manner. But it is an objective investigation all the same, especially cogent in its analysis of the two key Platonic dialogues, *Symposium* and *Phaedrus*. At first privately printed in just ten copies, and ten years after composition, it was distributed more widely in a still privately printed edition of 1901 under the auspices of the Areopagi-tiga [sic] Society. A copy of a 1908 reprint remarkably made its way at some point into Yourcenar's library at Petite Plaisance.[55] Symonds defined Greek love in the treatise as "a passionate and enthusiastic attachment subsisting between man and youth, recognized by society and protected by opinion, which, though it was not free from sensuality, did not degenerate into mere licentiousness." A product of the post-Homeric era, it took two forms, one that was "chivalrous and martial," associated with Dorian polities, the other "sensual and lustful." In its nobler aspects, it became a defining feature of classical Greece, and one that marked off Greek from later Roman culture. At Athens, it "was closely associated with liberty, manly sports, severe stud-ies, enthusiasm, self-sacrifice, self-control, and deeds of daring." Honourable comradeship and friendship were its terms of reference, with the model of ideal mutual dedication epitomized by the relationship between Achilles and Patroclus. Chaeronea, however, brought a turning point: in the long submis-sion to Macedon and Rome, Greek love in its heroic martial form disap-peared together with Greek independence. Yet its sensual form endured and coarsened, especially under the Roman dispensation: poets such as Catullus and Martial introduced a paederastic foulness into literature unknown to Greeks before the turn of the era: "It is the difference," Symonds firmly concluded, "between a race naturally gifted with a delicate, aesthetic sense of beauty, and one in whom that sense was always subject to the perturbation of gross instincts."[56]

In which context perhaps the example might be mentioned, unknown to Symonds, of Q. Vibius Maximus, a high-ranking equestrian official who governed Egypt early in the second century and who was tried on several charges before Trajan. One charge appears to have been that of *stuprum*, a controversial legal term most likely meaning sexual corruption of a freeborn person. It was the outcome of an association the prefect had pursued in Alex-andria with a seventeen-year-old youth of respectable background named Theon. The documents recording the trial give details seemingly brought forward by the prosecution, with initial reference to the devotion and desire Vibius Maximus felt for the boy:

Further, a seventeen-year-old boy used to dine with you every day. Every one of these men here ... would see the lad at your drinking-party, sometimes with his father and sometimes alone. They would see, too, the shameful glances and shameful behaviour of these male lovers ... These men testify by your genius, my Lord, that while they would be outside his door awaiting his greeting they would see the boy coming out of his bed-chamber, all but bearing the signs of his familiarity with him. For once this handsome, wealthy youth had become familiar with shame, he became more and more depraved and insolent ... And far from being innocent, he used to give an exhibition to Maximus' debtors of what he had been doing. And you, with your severe bearing and austere looks, why did you not try to stop him? ... this beardless and ... yes, handsome boy you kept in the Palace every day and would no longer send him to school or to those exercises which are proper for the young ... You travel about the whole of Egypt in this lad's company. Why, even in the seat of justice at the public Assizes this seventeen-year-old child was with you! Yes, at Memphis and Pelusium and wherever you went, he was your companion.[57]

The emphasis here falls not so much on the liaison itself as its notoriety, for which the boy's impudence and his lover's lack of decorum could be deemed responsible. The prosecution could obviously play on the prejudices of those who might think the affair shaming, and Vibius Maximus was in fact convicted and disgraced.

In any case, it is within this conceptual framework that Symonds was able to present both Alexander and Hadrian casting back, in the era of antique decadence, to an imagined age of lofty Greek heroic ideals, although Hadrian as it happens warrants no more than a footnote from him.[58] Yourcenar, for whom the dialogue *Symposium* was "le plus noble exposé de l'érotique hellé-nique" (*TGS* 348), followed suit, adopting precisely the same notion of historical development in her situation of the relationship between Hadrian and Antinous, not least as Hadrian's important words in the Troad on hypocrisy and pretence indicate (*MH* 424).[59] Indeed, in the *Carnets* that accompany *L'Œuvre au Noir*, Hadrian's disposition is placed in a tradition in which three elements are distinguished: a debauchery ("débauche") acknowledged in the Roman world, even if condemned by its moralists; a lyricism ("lyrisme") expressed by the Greek and Latin poets; and a philosophical strain ("tradi-tion philosophique"), entirely Greek and not at all Roman, that Hadrian the philhellene consciously pursues, falsifying to some extent its true character for the sake of emphasizing the poetic and the heroic (*CNON* 867–8). The correlation with Symonds's analysis seems firm, and it was surely Symonds Yourcenar had in mind when she explained to Patrick de Rosbo that she had followed the view of certain scholars ("érudits") in writing of what was evi-dently a conscious need on Hadrian's part to return to the erotic and heroic values of the Greek past in view of the way he had tried to exalt Antinous (*ER* 81). The letter to Hortense Flexner is conclusive: "Je pense que J.A. Symonds a raison de supposer que l'accent mis par Hadrien sur son attachement pro-fond (au moins *après* la mort du jeune homme) était probablement un retour conscient aux idéaux érotiques du passé" (*HZ* 240).[60] Altogether, the cumula-tive evidence for Symonds's influence on Yourcenar is persuasive and helps, I think, to account for the manner in which she portrayed the story of Hadrian and Antinous as she did. Her careful refusal to conflate ancient and modern sexual attitudes was not motivated by the overriding interest in the history of homosexuality with which Symonds is associated – her cause was imaginative but properly informed biographical reconstruction – and any suggestion of influence must be circumstantial. The high regard, however, in which she held Symonds is undeniable.

IV

Critics have sometimes regarded Hadrian's relationship with Antinous as the most important feature of *Mémoires* and, by implication, of the historical Hadrian's life as well. It is not only that Antinous's presence is felt before the main story begins; but like Plotina, he remains at the forefront of Hadrian's mind until Hadrian is close to death, in confirmation of a love once gained but tragically lost (*MH* 508–9, 510).[61] Yourcenar herself denied this verdict, but there is no doubt about the intensity of emotion the "aventure d'amour" conveys (*YO* 99–100). If the sociocultural character of the relationship is discernible, what may now be added for Yourcenar's recovery of the past from the methodological belief in an unchanging human nature? Two closely connected emotions are dominant: love and grief.

In the *Préface* of *Feux*, Yourcenar unambiguously expressed her belief that a love she called "total" is a universal human experience (*F* 1075).[62] Amplification followed in remarks made to Matthieu Galey when asked to distinguish between love and passion. The latter is aggressive, she replied, whereas the former is self-denying; both can be enduring, but men are less disposed to love because less likely to deny the self; love moreover is dangerous, like a disease, bringing an unmasculine loss of self-control – this was the fate of Hadrian when Antinous died – and as potentially harmful as beneficial (*YO* 98–101).[63] Elsewhere she allowed that falling in love is part of the human condition no one escapes (*PV* 141). But a definition of love was problematic. She had earlier said as much to Galey when dismissing the triviality of the modern sentimental notion that two people could be thought "made for one another," urging in its stead what she called "sympathetic love," a form of emotional attachment she glossed as a "sentiment profond de tendresse pour une créature ... qui partage les mêmes hasards, les mêmes vicissitudes que nous," and, simultaneously, "un lien, charnel ou non, sensuel toujours ... où la sympathie prend le pas sur la passion" (*YO* 76).[64] In turn, she held that while an element of the sacred flowed from the universality of such sensual relations, it was a feature no longer universally recognized, having been replaced by prudery or ribaldry (*YO* 76–7).[65] The Greeks, she ventured, may have known it, with pointed reference to the age differential between husbands and wives that made Greek marriage characteristically paederastic; and it could certainly be found in Hindu tradition. The sensually sacred was absent, however, from Christian and post-Christian cultures, by which Yourcenar meant, I think, the cultural traditions of contemporary Western societies, given that in Europe a variety of cultural traditions of love could be identified (*YO* 77–8).[66]

The import of these ideas, tortuous and demanding, is that emotional experience and its manifestations are subject to, or affected by, variations in individual cultural traditions; and unsurprisingly the philosophizing disquisition on love Hadrian offers in *Animula vagula blandula* owes much to them (*MH* 294–8). The passage, difficult in its own right, is built on five propositions, all of which depend on Hadrian's ineradicable memories of the unnamed Antinous: love is a unique experience, otherwise unequalled and requiring an irrational surrender to physical ecstasy on the part of the lover; its progression from love of another's body to love of the complete person is a mystery that can bring both pleasure and pain; it is also an experience that resembles initiation into a mystery cult, the immediate intensity of which can be later forgotten even as elements of the secret and the sacred are acknowledged; total obsession with its object passes in time beyond the physical to enter the sphere of the metaphysical; and all of this is distinct from mere sexual gratification.

The disquisition comes of course not from Hadrian but from his creator, a further example of authorial intrusion conditioned, I imagine, by Yourcenar's own bisexual history.[67] Its propositions nonetheless control the story of Hadrian and Antinous and explain the great weight attached to the key phrase *quem muliebriter flevit*, with all its implications of weakness to which love exposes the lover. They must be accepted or discarded according to the degree to which any reader regards them as valid constituents of human experience. Yourcenar had no doubts. In a letter from June 1952, she was emphatic that Antinous, a far from complicated individual, was the embodiment of a devotion so complete in its sensual-religious dimension that it surpassed conventional ideas and could scarcely be called love at all: it was a rare example of absolute commitment, one not confined by time and place, but presently to be found among very simple people, those least used to interrogating sentiment (*HZ* 158).[68] As for Hadrian, her all-encompassing theories allowed his erotic history to be known in full: liaisons with men as an adolescent and during his military service were to be expected, and there were also affairs with women (*YO* 74). But the encounter with Antinous was different: "Mais quand Hadrien vieilli – il a quarante-sept ans – rencontre Antinoüs, il a sans doute assez vite, avec bientôt des creux et des baisses de niveau dans l'émotion qu'il reconnaît lui-même, le sentiment d'une rencontre unique, et que la mort plus tard vient sceller" (*YO* 75).[69]

An evaluation of this kind must always be personal, subjective, and variable. Conjugal love, parental love, love of family and friends, love of country, for some love of God – the varieties and degrees of a concept utterly amorphous are manifold, ever-adapting to circumstance, and infinite. The question is whether anything from the Roman past might serve a reasonably authenticating purpose. I hazard two possibilities.

A study of the major love poets of the Augustan era has revealed the existence in contemporary Roman society of a jet-set sector, a demi-monde devoted to the pursuit of pleasure in various forms, one of which was sexual fulfilment through intense, transitory love affairs between young men and women or boys and sometimes both. The high-octane passions generated differed significantly on this view from the more restrained sentiments characteristic of formal marriage between men and women of Rome's upper classes. The value of the study here lies in its assumption that the poets' sentiments have meaning to present-day readers because they reflect universal experience: Latin literature and Roman life are not only mutually reinforcing, the emotions literature expresses are recognizable because human nature "changes very little." The ability of the Roman male pleasure seeker to gratify his appetite equally with a woman or an adolescent boy is a particularity of his historical milieu, but the emotions involved, in both range and intensity, are not limited by time or place.[70]

For upper-class Romans, marriage was frequently the result of family contrivance rather than initiative on the part of the principals concerned, and as the intricacies of familial connections are traced women can seem to be pawns devoid of personality, power, and feeling at the easy disposal of dominant males. A monumental treatment redresses the balance. From both literature and the idioms of spousal commemoration at death, the elements of success in marriage are discernible, one of which, across society broadly, was what at the simplest level can readily be understood as a mutual affection expected to endure in genuine partnership across a long interval of time. On this view, it becomes possible even to employ the vocabulary of romantic love, and, without excluding wider familial demands, sometimes to see marriage as the outcome, in the modern idiom, of a love match. If the commemorative evidence belongs to moments when feelings of loss perhaps heightened statements of marital intimacy, the assumption is again irresistible that human emotions are essentially unchanging over time despite cultural idiosyncrasy. (In this case the undeniable subordination of women.) For present purposes, the assumption is the important point.[71]

Cultural predisposition and linguistic constraint are constant barriers to historical understanding. I note, however, that shortly after the decision Hadrian makes in *Animula vagula blandula* to tell Marcus his whole life story, he alludes contemptuously to a category of contemporary writers called authors of "Milesian tales" who are likened to butchers whose pieces of meat, hung up for sale, attract flies (*MH* 303). Yourcenar presumably held a low opinion of the Greek romances, if, as it must be, it is to these works that Hadrian's allusion applies, adventurous love stories of seeming great popularity in the high Imperial age, in which the convention of the *coup de foudre* is ubiquitous and a homoerotic element sometimes found. (The stories might have figured more prominently in Hadrian's analysis of love.) In the absence of quantifiable evidence, it is impossible to say how prevalent the form of sexual engagement represented by Vibius Maximus and Theon was in the central epoch of Rome's history. But that is no obstacle to the overall plausibility of Yourcenar's construction of the emotional tenor of Hadrian's relationship with Antinous: destabilization of the self, loss of personal control, the alternation of pleasure and pain, of transcendence and despair – these are all aspects of human experience consistent with the framework of universal emotions earlier illustrated, and conveyed at times by evidence as validating as can be expected. I have to assume that when Virgil wrote of Nisus and Euryalus that they shared a mutual love – *his amor unus erat*– Roman readers knew what was meant (*Aen.* 9.182).[72]

With the discovery of Antinous's corpse, Hadrian's immediate response is to make arrangements for the body to be embalmed and Antinous's memory to be immortalized through apotheosis and the foundation, near Hermopolis, of the new city, though intermittent thoughts of a final resting place in the Villa at Tivoli intervene. Matters practical take precedence, all informed by the historical record of Antinous's cult and of Antinoopolis, yet with significant recollection of Hephaestion's obsequies in Hadrian's intention to surpass Alexander. Funerary poetry is commissioned from Mesomedes, an authentic figure on late record as a Cretan freedman and friend who did indeed compose a poem in praise of Antinous. Long thought to be lost, it has been detected in an inscription from Cyprus unknown when Yourcenar wrote *Mémoires*. In the final section of the narrative, however, as Hadrian continues his journey on the Nile, sentiment comes to the fore. The refrain of "Antinoüs était mort" tolls like a bell in his mind, and there are frequent outbursts of uncontrollable weeping. Hadrian is now less the godlike master of the world than a mere mortal with greying hair consumed with anatomizing his grief. He has encountered death before, in many situations, but never to such overwhelming effect. Aware of the interplay of resentment, loss, and guilt, he reproaches himself for Antinous's suicide. Moments of calm temporarily surface – he can be diverted by the sights of the river journey, the Colossus of Memnon above all, or by the requirements of routine governance – but memory cannot be controlled, and imagining the beloved's final self-destroying act unleashes a flood of remorse and recrimination. Recollections of past happiness generate new feelings of revulsion and self-pity, tears are never far away – they recall those of Hercules, Plato, and Alexander, all bereft from the loss of a friend – and dignitaries are forced to avert their eyes when approaching him until composure is restored, "comme s'il était obscène de pleurer" (*MH* 443). Chabrias is given his due for first noticing a new glimmering star observed night after night in the constellation of Aquila that Hadrian names the star of Antinous. He is long inconsolable, however, and his grief, violent in its intensity, seems inextinguishable until, in the fullness of time, a turning point comes with the interment of the embalmed body. The crisis subsides, and Hadrian leaves Alexandria for Greece (*MH* 442–51).[73]

Yourcenar's exploitation of the reproachful reference in the *Historia Augusta* is blatant, its meaning for the loss of masculine self-mastery cannot be missed, its impact is narratively profound: "Autour de moi, je sentais qu'on commençait à s'offusquer d'une douleur si longue: la violence en scandalisait d'ailleurs plus que la cause. Si je m'étais laissé aller aux mêmes plaintes à la mort d'un frère ou d'un fils, on m'eût également reproché de pleurer comme une femme" (*MH* 449).[74] The psychological inventiveness of these final pages is undeniable, yet the question once more has to be one of historical confirmation, of whether the grief attributed to Hadrian has a basis in Roman experience. Every Romanist will immediately recall riveting examples of sadness evoked by the death of loved ones that suggest a positive answer, of Quintilian at the successive losses of his two young sons and their mother, or earlier of Cicero at the loss of his daughter soon after childbirth.[75] From the era of concern, Juvenal's belief that the capacity to weep was the finest aspect of human sensibility will likewise come to mind (15.131–3). Poignant expressions of pain are found moreover on the tens of thousands of tombstones that survive from Roman antiquity, the special value of which is their testimony of reactions to death across a wide swathe of society. Like burial markers and funerary urns, they are a form of memorial to the dead familiar from their modern counterparts, yet also to be registered are such unique manifestations as the annual celebration of the Lemuria and Parentalia, religious rites by which families honoured the memory of their ancestors and sought to appease the spirits of the untimely dead for the safety of the living.[76] The conclusion seems obvious that the emotions expressed in the Roman past are emotions universally known. A warning admittedly might be noticed against simple elision of funerary rituals and the intensity of emotions due to divergent theories of how grief has historically made itself felt, whether variably, according to fluctuating demographic and material conditions ("cultural relativism"), or unchangingly but with distinctive forms of display ("ethological humanism"), even if the grief expressed was undoubtedly genuine.[77] Yourcenar had no such reservations at all. Hadrian's grief was inferable from an unquestionably ubiquitous experience, and could be confirmed from the evidence of the extravagant forms of commemoration to which it led. For understanding her reconstitution that is all that matters.

Among the educated one of those conventions was the composition of a literary work written to console the bereaved. Seneca's *Ad Marciam*, intended to comfort a mother on the loss of a son, and Plutarch's *Consolation to His Wife*, the result of the death of a two-year-old daughter, are straightforward examples. They belong to a long Greco-Roman tradition in which any number of assuaging thoughts might be offered, "often," in one succinct formulation, "by recalling that human beings are mortal; that we must bear the inevitable; that death frees us from the pangs of life; and that time heals all pain." Simultaneously, the bereaved are "exhorted to be grateful for having enjoyed the opportunity to know the deceased."[78] Here Hadrian specifies that he received a work of consolation from Numenius, an obscure rhetor known from a brief late source.[79] The work has not survived, but for its authenticating value Yourcenar recreates its platitudinous contents from her immersion in the tradition for Hadrian to read. He takes it up one night. Two lines of thought are present. First, that death is an unavoidable evil against which beauty, youth, and love provide no defence: the evils of life are worse than death itself and it is better to die soon than to live long. Second, that the soul is more important than the body and lives on in immortality (*MH* 448–9). The latter is a variation on one of the stock themes, especially appropriate for Antinous, enumerated by the Greek rhetor of the age of Diocletian, Menander, in his prescriptions for composing a consolatory speech: "perhaps he is living now with gods, travelling round the sky and looking down on the world … Let us therefore sing his praises as a hero, or rather bless him as a god, make paintings of him, placate him as a superhuman being."[80] The thoughts, however, have no effect. Hadrian is unable to find relief even in his creation of a new god: nothing redeems the mortal loss (*MH* 449). Re-creation is seductively effective. Realism prevails.

V

How does Yourcenar's construction of Hadrian's crucial engagement with Antinous compare with the achievements of imperial biographers and historians? The relationship, it happens, has traditionally been regarded as unpalatable as a mainstream historical subject, eliciting only brief comment; and given the weakness of the source tradition, one strategy is to abandon reconstruction altogether – there may have been no relationship at all – and to concentrate instead on the meaning of the Antinous cult; from which it emerges that Antinous was possibly much younger when he died than usually thought.[81] The sole modern study of any consequence is Royston Lambert's *Beloved and God: The Story of Antinous and Hadrian*, an outstanding work written not by a classical scholar but by a Cambridge educationalist whose interests lay in English boarding-school education, and who was also at one point headmaster of a private school. Lambert spent his last years in Greece, however, at work on his book, which when he died was not quite finished. He never saw it in print.[82] It opens with a list of basic questions. Who was Antinous? What did he look like? What sort of person was he? What was the nature of the association with Hadrian? How did he die? What happened to his remains? What effect did his death have on Hadrian? Definitive answers are of course impossible. But Lambert offered bold conclusions regardless, maintaining for instance that Hadrian first met Antinous in 123 when the youth was a member of a school of imperial pages, but dating their intimacy only from the winter of 127/128 when Antinous had joined the imperial entourage and travelled to North Africa. To find answers to his questions he drew widely on Roman religious, social, and political history, fleshing out his narrative with the richness of the Roman past; and not unlike Yourcenar he associated Hadrian's initiation into the Eleusinian mysteries with a sense of divine self-consciousness and a conception of world unity underpinned by theocracy. In his discussion of paederasty he sharply separated Roman from Greek attitudes, and he set out effectively the geographical extent and chronological duration, well into late antiquity, of the Antinous cult. Like the historians of antiquity, moreover, he told his story in dramatically fashioned episodes, instilling his account of Hadrian's arrival in Egypt with intimations of impending doom, and filling his description of the eventual destruction of Antinoopolis with real sadness. His book is a history that reads like a novel.[83]

The book's most arresting feature is one that connects Lambert more closely still with Yourcenar. This is the manner in which he explained the history of Hadrian and Antinous in terms of "psychological probabilities," or as Yourcenar put it "from the inside." His Hadrian is a lonely, insecure figure, who in early life was shown little affection and who as an adult had little affection to give. He was melancholic, self-absorbed, emotionally stunted, sexually confused, histrionic, and driven to excel by an inferiority complex. His relationship with Antinous was fraught and obsessive, ending when Antinous, keenly aware of the problems his physical maturation raised and as obsessed with

Hadrian as Hadrian was with him, offered himself as a living sacrifice to save both from danger: "Better, he may have thought, to be a dead and hallowed martyr than a living and forgotten has-been," a conclusion, Lambert argued, that fits with everything that is known from the factual record and the psychology of the protagonists that can be deduced from it. Antinous, on this view, is the Freudian son who dies for the father, with Hadrian perhaps temporarily driven out of his mind and his control of public affairs adversely affected. The description of Hadrian's possible mental state when the mummified body of Antinous is about to be buried in Egypt illustrates his psychological penetration, rhetorical effectiveness, and heavily romanticized view of the past:

Contemplating this final, harrowing moment, the Emperor, having had long months to brood on his loss and to devise a new ecumenical cult for Antinous, may have interposed. *He* had claims over Antinous, who may have died for him, stronger than those of the Egyptians. Having delivered over the body to the priests of the Nile for the violations necessary for spiritual perpetuation, was he to abandon it for ever to Egyptian soil? This may have been an ultimate separation which Hadrian found impossible to accept. The ceremonial boat on which the gilded coffin of Antinous lay may have been replaced, in the middle of 131, by a real one on which he was transported, over the seas, to his final resting place.[84]

The method is clearly controversial, and the criticism can easily be made that history should have nothing to do with extravagances of this kind. As indicated earlier, however, conventional historians are known to enter the minds of their subjects without undue difficulty and to make similar observations in other contexts, if not perhaps on such a grand scale. Lambert's procedure is not as vulnerable as it may first seem, his portrait of Hadrian is self-consistent and compelling, and his novel-like speculations are grounded on evidence interpreted with full allowance for historical contingency. His Hadrian may not be the real Hadrian, but like the Hadrian of Yourcenar he is a credible figure; and while Lambert chose not to engage with her directly, a debt to Yourcenar may be admitted from the epigraph of this chapter. Bringing to his project the insights of a social scientist, he appreciated more than most, I think, the imagination of a literary artist and the sensibility of a student of human nature, convinced as Yourcenar was convinced of the devastating effects on Hadrian of Antinous's death.[85]

VI

How then finally is Yourcenar's account of Hadrian's encounter with Antinous to be assessed? Hadrian's coinage displayed the legend SAECULUM AUREUM, "The Age of Gold," for the first time in 121. It was a move perhaps associated with an emphasis placed on the Parilia, a religious festival held annually on 21 April to celebrate the foundation of the City, and it was accompanied by representations of Aion, the personification of eternity, and the phoenix, a symbol of rebirth.[86] The phrase appealed to Romans' mythical memory of the once paradisal age in the reign of Saturn, an age of peace and innocence, natural prosperity and social equality, that was recalled every year at the winter solstice, when Saturn's own festival was held. Its most characteristic feature was the freedom, supposedly universal in the distant past, temporarily granted to slaves, a custom still maintained in Hadrian's day. I imagine that whoever was responsible for the legend intended to promote the idea that the new reign was soon to create at Rome an everlasting age of paradise.[87]

Marguerite Yourcenar converted the legend from a public to a private purpose, making it a symbol of the height of personal happiness Hadrian enjoyed through the encounter with Antinous, but a happiness that like Saturn's festival was of relatively brief duration only. A depth of despair was its sequel. She recorded in her *Notebook's Journal* that she composed the "tragedy of the first of Athyr" in March 1950 in her modest Bronxville apartment, where images of the Villa of the Mysteries alone decorated its walls, and that for several successive nights the labour reduced her to tears – tears shed not for Hadrian's friend, but for the "incommunicable human grief" Hadrian suffered from his loss, a suffering against which he struggled all alone, and later forgot before his eventual death. The remarks betray an identification with her subject that again transcends authorial transference as usually understood, and in their hyper-sensitivity help to explain why *muliebriter flevit* became the genesis of Hadrian's second great crisis.[88] Whether Antinous's death was a cardinal turning point in Hadrian's emotional life no one will ever know. But through *magie sympathique*, factual, sociocultural, and psychological strands are woven together in Yourcenar's narrative, one that in totality comes to resemble the poetic truth of the historical novel once called the "verisimilar." For Yourcenar, the techniques of the novel were the only means by which biographical truth could be attained.[89]

Altogether of course the account is a positivist's nightmare. Much, if not most, is sheer invention. Which means that it would be a dreadful mistake if it were to be taken as an authoritative "history" of the origin, progress, and conclusion of the encounter. In absolute terms, "We cannot know the details of Hadrian and Antinous's relationship."[90] Yourcenar was well aware of this, and uninformed readers might well be disappointed when reaching the end of *Mémoires* to discover from the *Note* that the story of Antinous she composed is largely an imaginative elaboration. But as I have emphasized, she cannot be accused of deception. She disclosed her inventions and revealed by her references to sources and scholarship the basis of what she had written. Much of her elaboration draws in fact on a profound knowledge of classical history, art history included, the result of which is an authentically textured story, nowhere more so than in its appreciation of the character of Roman same-sex relations. This, it seems, owes much to the influence of Symonds, and when judged in the context of current scholarship Yourcenar's perspective was formed long before sexuality in antiquity became a subject of serious modern investigation. In turn, she was able to add a psychologically convincing dimension to Hadrian's memories of Antinous by drawing on elements of human nature scarcely contestable; and in this, the story is more than structurally apposite. True biography requires a record of the subject's inner life, and as Yourcenar herself contended, while *Mémoires* without love would still have been the story of a great man, it would have been a story incomplete (*YO* 100).[91] Modern counterparts are easily found. The result, inevitably, is an illusion, but a uniquely successful illusion comparable to the "opération magique" by which Hadrian believed portraiture capable of evoking the lost face of "l'ami jamais assez pleuré" – "the friend for ever mourned" (*MH* 385). Yourcenar's unrivalled recreation realizes the potential for poetic invention the source tradition opens up, and brings its reader as close to a truth as any biography might hope to do.[92]

7

The Jewish War

Ruling the Roman Empire meant war, torture and execution.

Peter Brown

I

In what were to be the late years of his reign Hadrian was compelled to wage a war against the Jews of Judaea, who in the year 132 rose in revolt against Roman rule. Shim'on bar Kosiba, an insurgent more usually known as Bar Kokhba, led the insurrection. The war lasted approximately three and a half years and was won by Rome, with formidable consequences for those defeated: Jerusalem and Judaea were renamed as Roman entities and forfeited their historical identity. Marguerite Yourcenar presents the episode as the third of the three major turning points in Hadrian's life, although it occupies just two of the six portions of *Disciplina Augusta* and numbers fewer than twenty pages in the Pléiade (*MH* 466–82). Once more it interlaces external events with Hadrian's inner responses to them, and is marked by two features: the failure of Hadrian's aim to avoid war through the promotion of an empire-wide policy of peace – "Je ne le nie pas: cette guerre de Judée était un de mes échecs" (*MH* 472) – and a personal crisis of confidence as he considers Rome's future. As always, the evidence on which Yourcenar's narrative is based is fraught with difficulties. Her treatment of the episode, the issues of historical reconstruction it raises, and its significance for Hadrian's biography are the subject of this chapter; and again the manner in which Yourcenar reconstructs and justifies her perception of the crisis is the central theme.[1]

II

The episode begins with an allusion to Jewish disaffection that followed a decision, taken onsite shortly before the fatal visit to Egypt, to rebuild Jerusalem as a Roman city in the aftermath of the city's destruction a generation earlier by the emperor Titus. The new foundation, to be named after Hadrian himself as Aelia Capitolina, with its markets, baths, and temples for the gods of the Greco-Roman pantheon, was for Jews an abomination. (A sanctuary for Adonis was to be built on the Temple Mount.) It was no surprise, therefore, Hadrian explains to Marcus, that resentment turned with the passage of time to violent opposition (*MH* 429–30). There were more immediate irritants as well: the public exhibition of a boar, the emblem of Rome's Legion X Fretensis, offended Jewish sensibilities through the attention it drew to what Jews considered to be unclean meat; a ban placed on the public reading of a Jewish legend, thought by Rome in the context of tumultuous New Year's celebrations to foster Jewish nationalistic sentiments, was another provocation; and so too the prohibition, enacted by the provincial governor Tineius Rufus, of the distinctive Jewish practice of circumcision. All in all, when advocates of Jewish monotheistic exceptionalism encouraged resistance to the promotion of Greek culture in the city, full-scale revolt was the outcome (*MH* 467–8).

The rebel leader, Hadrian continues, was Bar-Kochba, a man of genius whose name meant "Son of the Star," and who claimed to be the Messiah the Jews had long awaited.[2] Jewish sectarianism prevented unanimity of purpose. But with support from two influential figures, the aged rabbi Akiba and the high priest Eleazar, agents with ready access to stores of weapons led assaults on Rome's troops and quickly occupied Jerusalem, the emergent new city was put to the torch, and detachments of Rome's Legion XXII led by Publius Marcellus, arriving from Egypt, were annihilated. Rome responded by summoning two more legions, Legion XII and Legion VI, and overall operations were entrusted to the command of the erstwhile governor of Britain Julius Severus, who brought additional troops with him from the far north. Understanding the need to fight a campaign of attrition against guerrillas scattered in strongholds throughout Judaea, Severus eventually recaptured Jerusalem and later still other rebel cities in what turned out to be the third year of the war (*MH* 468–70). By which time Hadrian had personally joined his forces, arriving in the autumn of the war's second year. The following spring, in appalling conditions, he supervised what was to become a year-long siege of the citadel of Bethar, where Bar-Kochba and his fanatical followers had ensconced themselves. The revolt did not extend far beyond the Jewish homeland, contrary to the rebel leader's initial expectations, and the Roman recovery of Jerusalem was followed in time by the burning of Ascalon and wholesale execution of rebels in Gaza. Meantime, however, the siege of Bethar had seemed interminable, and Hadrian concludes this first section of his account by describing how he had spent sleepless nights deep in brooding thoughts and anxious contemplation, aware of both his own physical decline and the potential decline of his whole empire (*MH* 470–8).

The beginning of the war's end had come when Akiba and nine other rebel leaders were executed for disobeying an edict issued by Tineius Rufus forbidding the study of Jewish law. From Rome's perspective such activity had been a pretext for continuing Jewish resistance, and Hadrian had approved the executions. Three months later – it was February – the citadel of Bethar finally capitulated, a vital development after a primary assault that Hadrian had watched from a nearby hilltop. From other towns vast numbers of captives were taken and sold into slavery, and those who survived were barred from returning to Jerusalem, a single day each year apart. Many were compelled to leave their homeland altogether, and Judaea, renamed Palestine, ceased to exist. Finally, after a period of recuperation in Sidon, Hadrian in late spring was able to sail back to Rome. In the four years of fighting, he specifies, fifty rebel fortresses and more than 900 rebel towns and villages had been destroyed, with close to 600,000 enemy deaths and some 90,000 Roman losses. Victory had meant, however, that Aelia Capitolina could be built (*MH* 478–82). As for Bar-Kochba, Marcus has known his fate all along: a centurion brought Hadrian the man's severed head when the war ended, a fact Hadrian ironically made clear at the outset of his recollections: it was the only time he had seen the rebel leader face to face (*MH* 468).

As he read this section of the letter, Marcus will have remembered that Hadrian had spoken of Jews on earlier occasions: those of the Near Eastern diaspora, merchants especially, who had been implicated in the events of Trajan's war against Parthia (*MH* 352), and those in Alexandria whose cantankerous disputes with local Greeks Hadrian had spent almost a whole week settling at Pelusium years before (*MH* 360–1). When in Alexandria more recently he had also had to deal with no less a character than the rabbi Akiba, who led a delegation intent on dissuading Hadrian from his plans to build a new Jerusalem (*MH* 435). The terms of reference used throughout had been notably disparaging: Hadrian had spoken of Israel's "fureurs religieuses, ses rites singuliers, et l'intransigeance de son Dieu" (*MH* 352), of Jerusalem as "la forteresse d'une race et d'un dieu isolés du genre humain" (*MH* 435).[3] His account now of the Jewish War displayed a comparable animus that

Marcus cannot have missed. The same is true for present-day readers of *Mémoires*. A disquieting question of authorial attitude arises.

III

The factual framework of the war is presented once more in broad brushstrokes, and the passage of time is no more than vaguely indicated. Many details are introduced elliptically, and Hadrian's narrative, simply put, is a sequence of discrete memories. In this, however, it reflects what his creator could, or really could not, know when she came to recover Hadrian's recollections. There are just two relatively extended accounts of the war's course in classical sources, a section of Xiphilinus's epitome of Cassius Dio's history, material subject to what are now familiar limitations, and a passage in the *Ecclesiastical History* of the Christian historian Eusebius from the late third century, a source clearly far removed in time from the events concerned. Incidental details are found in ancillary sources, often from much later still.[4]

Cassius Dio identifies Hadrian's foundation of Aelia Capitolina as the chief cause of disaffection that led to war, with the building of a temple to Jupiter on the Temple Mount. While Hadrian was nearby in Syria and Egypt open revolt was avoided. But weapons were secretly stockpiled, and once Hadrian was no longer close at hand armed resistance erupted, with rebels securing strategic sites and adopting irregular tactics rather than confronting Roman forces in open battle. Rome's initial response was minimal, which meant that rebellion spread throughout Judaea and beyond, involving it seems both Jews and non-Jews: the whole universe, Dio rhetorically claims, fell into revolt. Hadrian therefore then sent his best generals to oppose the rebels, but the only one named is the governor of Britain Julius Severus, whose policy was to wage a campaign of attrition against the insurgents. Rome suffered huge losses, but Severus eventually met with success: almost the whole of Judaea was devastated, great numbers of strongholds were captured, villages were razed, and rebels killed; fifty outposts and 985 villages were burned, 580,000 rebels died in combat and countless numbers were lost to famine, fire, and disease (69.12.1–14.4).[5]

Eusebius begins with vague reference to earlier remarks on the Jewish uprisings under Trajan and continues with reports of new outbreaks of revolt implicitly in Judaea, but without any immediate cause of war specified. Hadrian is said to have responded by sending reinforcements to the governor Rufus who carried out brutal military reprisals, with myriads of men, women, and children killed and the land enslaved. The rebel leader is identified as a murderous bandit named Barchochebas, a name explained as meaning "star," who appealed to the downtrodden as a charismatically messianic figure. Events reached a climax in Hadrian's eighteenth year when the fortress of Beththera, close to Jerusalem, was reduced by famine after a lengthy siege, and Barchochebas was put to death. Hadrian then banned the Jews from entering Jerusalem and populated the new city he called Aelia with foreigners (*Hist. eccl.* 4.6).

Both accounts are miserable. Neither has much to offer on the origins and the chronology of the war, the full military arrangements and personnel involved, or Hadrian's participation in the fighting. Scholars inevitably debate the validity of every individual detail endlessly. Yet there is little else to go on in the literary record. The Latin life has just one relevant sentence (*HA Hadr.* 14.2): the Jews initiated a war because they had been forbidden to practise circumcision, if indeed this is what the sentence truly means.[6]

Yourcenar naturally drew on the two main sources – the statistical information on war damage presumably relies on Cassius Dio, the expulsion of Jews from Jerusalem on Eusebius – but there was little in them from which to build and develop Hadrian's narrative. Numismatic evidence could be used, because Yourcenar knew that the Jewish rebels had minted coins during the war that bore legends expressing their aspirations and identified Shim'on bar Kosiba as their leader.[7] But she had no access to evidence that had begun to revolutionize the history of the war just as she was writing *Mémoires*: troves of objects discovered by archaeologists in the late 1940s and early 1950s in desert hill caves close to the Dead Sea where some of the rebels had taken refuge, evidence of how they had sustained themselves and maintained their cause, and also various letters written in Hebrew or Aramaic that provided vital information on the geographical scope of the rebellion and its political and socio-economic dimensions. Some of the letters came from Bar Kokhba himself and pointed to the exercise of a ruthlessly monarchical authority.[8] Yourcenar quickly became aware of the new finds, as her remarks in the *Note* of the English translation of *Mémoires* first indicate: "The archaeologists of Israel, too, are now steadily bringing new contributions to our still limited knowledge of the history and topography of this war."[9] But as her comments in the Pléiade show, the new knowledge had come too late: "Les découvertes archéologiques faites en Israël durant ces dernières années et concernant la révolte de Bar Kochba ont enrichi sur certains points de détail notre connaissance de la guerre de Palestine; la plupart d'entre elles, survenues après 1951, n'ont pu être utilisées au cours du présent ouvrage" (*OR* 550).[10]

The problem of establishing a reliably factual account of events is well illustrated by an enigmatic set of documents for which a clear explanation is as yet unavailable and which may have nothing to do with the Jewish War at all. Some two hundred Latin inscriptions carved on limestone rocks attest Hadrian's interest in preserving as imperial property four species of trees in

the northern Lebanon above the city of Byblus. The species are not identified, but cedar, cypress, juniper, fir, pine, and oak have been identified as possibilities. The initiative implied can be associated with Hadrian's presence in
the region in the year 130, though the inscriptions themselves date from the
end of his reign. It may be that Hadrian wished to protect timber supplies for
shipbuilding purposes, especially for ships' masts, a suggestion that cannot
be proved but that attracts attention because it was made by Ernest Renan,
the first authority to catalogue the inscriptions concerned, and an authority
whose writings had considerable influence on Yourcenar's reconstruction of
Hadrian's war. She relied on his *L'Église chrétienne* of 1879 throughout. At the
end of her narrative she has Hadrian recall the great pine trees of Bithynia's
woodlands that will be marked for felling in the fullness of time (*MH* 481), a
detail that may be no more than coincidental – the geographical anomaly is
obvious – but notable all the same given the discoveries Renan made.[11]

What had been possible, however, was to exploit a completely separate
tradition from the Greco-Roman record, the memories of Hadrian's war
preserved in Jewish rabbinical literature, which became in fact the source of
most of the Jewish elements in the narrative. This Yourcenar did in a boldly
innovative way, acknowledging her procedure in the *Note* with simultane-
ous reinforcement of her commitment to historical fidelity (*OR* 547).[12] The
importance of the material will have been understood not least from the secondary works she read in her preparations. In the original version of the
Note, unchanged in the Pléiade, she listed just three such items, but much
more had been read as the fuller English version reveals.[13]

The zeal indeed with which she had investigated Jewish sources emerges
from a typically trenchant paragraph in her principal letter to F.C. Grant,
who in his essay on *Mémoires* had questioned what he took to be Yourcenar's "exaggeration of Jewish opposition to Greek learning," represented
in the novel by the refusal of a wounded rebel named Ben Dama to receive
medical help from a Greek doctor (*MH* 468).[14] This is what she said:

Les informations sur le problème juif dans les années qui précédèrent la guerre de
Palestine sont toutes tirées de Lieberman, *Greek in Jewish Palestine*, de la traduction
anglaise du Talmud, et aussi des textes relatifs au Judaïsme de Théodore Reinach. Je
n'ai jamais dit que tout rapport d'esprit entre le judaïsme et l'hellénisme ait été à
cette époque inexistant. Les agissements et les doctrines des fanatiques ont été décrits
tels qu'on les trouve dans les ouvrages ci-dessus, en particulier l'épisode de Ben-
Dama. Pour ces exemples d'étroitesse de vue et de fanatisme, je n'avais d'ailleurs que
l'embarras du choix. Si j'ai relativement si peu insisté, c'est de nouveau qu'Hadrien
ne pouvait voir tout ce développement que d'assez loin et de très haut, et c'eût été
une erreur [*d'insister.*] (*HZ* II 65)

The materials on the Jewish problem in the years preceding the war in Palestine are all taken from Lieberman, *Greek in Jewish Palestine,* from the English translation of the Talmud, and also from texts relevant to Judaism from Theodore Reinach. I never said that intellectual relationships between Judaism and Hellenism at this time were completely non-existent. The intrigues and doctrines of the fanatics were described as found in the above works, particularly the Ben Dama episode. For these examples of narrowness of view and fanaticism, I was indeed stuck for choice. If I put such relatively little stress on them, it's again because Hadrian could only see this whole development from a distance and from above, and it would have been a mistake [to insist further].

Reinach's *Histoire des Israélites* (1884) opens with a brief resumé of the dramatic effects of Hadrian's war: the death by fire and the sword of 600,000 Jews (not counting those who perished from hunger and disease), the glut of prisoners sold into slavery, the devastation of Galilee and Judaea, the expulsion of Jews from Jerusalem, their replacement in Aelia Capitolina by Greeks, Phoenicians, and Syrians; and a chapter introducing the Talmud mentions Rabbi Akiba as an ardent patriot who fought at the siege of Bethar and became a heroic martyr. It gives no details, however, of the rabbinical materials concerned.[15] The remaining items, in contrast, introduce relevant texts from the Mishnah and Tosefta, the Midrashim and the Jewish and Babylonian Talmuds that Yourcenar incorporated into her narrative as a way of amplifying the sparse Greco-Roman record. In this, a principal element is the so-called "Bethar-complex," a congeries of interrelated tracts of differing origins and dates that emphasizes the three and a half years' duration of the war and the vast number of Jewish casualties suffered. That Yourcenar understood her strategy to be contentious is inferable from the acknowledgment in the *Note* to which I referred a moment ago, especially because the materials are far from contemporary with the events concerned, the earliest belonging to the turn of the third century and the remainder to much more distant dates.[16] This inevitably means that there is no scholarly consensus on the Jewish tradition's trustworthiness as a whole: opinions range from complete dismissal, to acceptance of specifics that although formally adopted decades and even centuries later preserve some "collective memory" of historical events and context.[17] Yourcenar evidently took the latter view. Hadrian himself is occasionally portrayed favourably in the record. But as the emperor remembered above all for the Romanization of Jerusalem and the expulsion of Jews from their ancestral homeland, he is far more frequently vilified, his name accompanied by horrific curses ("May his bones rot!"). Authorial judgment accordingly had to be exercised, and the underlying shape and nature of *Mémoires* as a project to be considered. Acknowledging an early positive review of her novel, Yourcenar made this important statement on her procedures to the Abbé Albert Vincent in January 1954, emphasizing as in her later letter to Grant that the point of departure for her narrative, as always, had been Hadrian's autobiographical perspective even while a poetic sense of destiny was in view:

Dans tout ceci, ma difficulté principale était d'essayer d'intégrer les documents rabbiniques, tout en n'oubliant pas qu'Hadrien n'a pu voir ce monde étranger que de loin et un peu en gros, quelle que fût sa bonne volonté. Il est bien difficile aussi, dans un ouvrage qui tout en se basant le plus strictement possible sur l'histoire tend à offrir une image tragique de la destinée humaine, de n'être pas amené à *composer* les faits dans un certain sens. Il est clair que l'échec ou le demi-échec d'Hadrien dans ses rapports avec ce monde fermé du judaïsme permettait de souligner à ce moment [*de*] son existence l'élément de défaite qui entre forcément dans toute vie, même la plus réussie. Il fournissait au moment voulu un thème de *démesure*, qui appartient peut-être plus, à bien y réfléchir au domaine traditionnel de la morale tragique qu'à celui de l'histoire. (*HZ* 301–2)

In all this, my chief difficulty was to try to integrate the rabbinical documents, while not forgetting that Hadrian could only see this strange world from afar and rather broadly, whatever his good intentions. It's also very difficult, in a work that while basing itself as strictly as possible on history tends to offer a tragic image of human destiny, not to be led to arrange facts in a particular way. It's clear that Hadrian's setback, or half-setback, in his relations with this closed world of Judaism allowed the element of defeat that inevitably enters into every life, even the most successful, to be brought out at this moment of his existence. It provided at the desired moment a theme of immoderation, which belongs more perhaps on reflection to the traditional domain of tragic morality than to that of history.

Hadrian's meeting with Akiba in Alexandria offers an example of Yourcenar's procedures (*MH* 435). According to Jewish sources, the great scholar visited Rome on more than one occasion, and as a member of a rabbinical delegation conceivably encountered Hadrian there in the early years of his reign. But there is no tradition of direct dialogue between Akiba and Hadrian in Rome as there is with other Jewish sages.[18] In her list of modified facts, Yourcenar wrote that the visit she describes, plausible enough in itself, was based on a supposition often made by Jewish historians.[19] And some modern scholars have indeed advanced such a supposition: Akiba, in his ninetieth year, using an interpreter because of his imperfect Greek, appealed to Hadrian in Alexandria to rescind his plans for building Aelia Capitolina, but negotiations were unsuccessful and hopes for improved relations between

Romans and Jews collapsed. The rabbi was thought to be the Jewish patriarch said to have visited Egypt in a letter of Hadrian known from the *Historia Augusta* (*Quad. Tyr.* 8.4), though one commentator identified him as Joshua ben Hananiah, and made this rabbi the ninety-year-old ambassador concerned.[20] The visit in and of itself is dubious, however, and certainly no serious scholar today is likely to accept the connection with Hadrian's putative letter. Yourcenar was inclined to trust it, even though she knew that it was suspect (*OR* 546–7), as did Ernest Renan.[21] But whoever she thought the patriarch to be, she retained the characterization of Akiba as a Greekless figure almost ninety years of age.

IV

Hadrian's decision to rebuild Jerusalem as a Roman city seems according to Cassius Dio to have preceded the Jewish War but according to Eusebius to have followed it. Both cannot be right.[22] This is another classic illustration therefore of the poverty of information available for writing the life of Hadrian. It is not an isolated issue. Despite the new information provided by archaeology, almost every aspect of the Bar Kokhba war remains a matter of controversy. In 1993, Fergus Millar baldly stated that "no narrative of the war is possible."[23] A decade later, Peter Schäfer introduced the proceedings of a conference on the war with a lengthy list of unresolved issues: Bar Kokhba's origins and political ideology; his fate; the identity of his supporters; questions of whether Jerusalem was truly captured by the rebels and whether the rebellion extended beyond Judaea into Galilee; the nature of the engagements between Jewish and Roman forces. "We are still in the dark," he concluded, "as to what finally caused the outbreak of the revolt and why Hadrian, the Emperor of peace and renewal, stumbled into such a war so devastating that he needed his full military force to crush it."[24] A second decade later, the outstanding study of William Horbury continues to reveal how tenuous knowledge of the war as a whole is, and perhaps always will be: his meticulously presented findings illustrate throughout that hardly any detail in the records that now remain, large or small, is beyond challenge, not least the moment in 132 at which revolt began: estimates vary between the middle and the end of the year.[25] Under such circumstances Yourcenar's impressionistic technique can hardly warrant censure, particularly since her principal goal was to recover something of Hadrian's human response to the war. By examining portions of the text closely, however, it becomes possible to appreciate the reasonableness with which the broad strokes were drawn and which they still convey. I examine next, therefore, section by section, two portions of text in which the various elements of the traditions on which

Yourcenar drew can be uncovered. First, Hadrian's long opening exposition of the antecedents of the rebellion (*MH* 466–7), and second, a paragraph in which he describes the outbreak of the revolt (*MH* 468–9). The commentary form adopted illustrates the factual foundation of the narrative to the degree that any such foundation is perceptible.

1.a. Les affaires juives allaient de mal en pis. Les travaux s'achevaient à Jerusalem malgré l'opposition violente des groupements zélotes. Un certain nombre d'erreurs furent commises, réparables en elles-mêmes, mais dont les fauteurs de troubles surent vite profiter. (*MH* 466)

1.a. Jewish affairs were going from bad to worse. The work of construction was continuing in Jerusalem, in spite of the violent opposition of the Zealot groups. A certain number of errors had been committed, not irreparable in themselves but immediately seized upon by fomentors of trouble for their own advantage.

The introductory sentence looks back to Hadrian's earlier visit to Jerusalem when he had set in motion plans to build Aelia Capitolina, and the subsequent encounter in Alexandria with Akiba, who had tried to dissuade him from the enterprise (*MH* 429–30, 435).[26] Yourcenar clearly took the view, following Cassius Dio, that the decision to build the new Jerusalem was made well before the outbreak of revolt, which allows her second sentence to speak of its material progress and the continuing opposition to the initiative from a radical segment of the Jewish population. Many scholars concur, associating the decision with Hadrian's visit to Jerusalem precisely in 130 or even earlier.[27] The final sentence, with its reference to troublemakers, picks up a hostile characterization of radical Jewish sectarianism evident in Hadrian's description of his engagement with Akiba that will continue in the narrative throughout. The vocabulary of Jewish extremism pervades Renan's version of events in *L'Église chrétienne*.

1.b. La Dixième Légion Expéditionnaire a pour emblême un sanglier; on en plaça l'enseigne aux portes de la ville, comme c'est l'usage; la populace, peu habituée aux simulacres peints ou sculptés dont la prive depuis des siècles une superstition fort défavorable au progrès des arts, prit cette image pour celle d'un porc, et vit dans ce petit fait une insulte aux mœurs d'Israël. (*MH* 466–7)

1.b. The Tenth Legion Fretensis has a wild boar for its emblem; when its standard was placed at the city gates, as is the custom, the populace, unused to painted or sculptured images (deprived as they have been for centuries by a superstition highly unfavorable to the progress of the arts), mistook that symbol for a swine, the meat of which is forbidden them, and read into that insignificant affair an affront to the customs of Israel.

The emblem of Legion X Fretensis, the garrison stationed in Jerusalem when the war began, was in fact a wild boar. The incident described derives from a notice in Jerome's *Chronicle* that may have been added to the record he took over from the *Chronicle* of Eusebius: "Aelia was founded by Aelius Hadrianus, and on the face of the gate by which we go out to Bethlehem a pig was carved in marble, signifying that the Jews are subject to Roman power."[28] Jerome situates the notice in the year 136, which may or may not be accurate; but scholars tend to place the incident after the conclusion of the war, not as Yourcenar's Hadrian does beforehand.[29] The choice should be attributed to Yourcenar's willingness to dispose details she thought best for securing historical plausibility, unless Hadrian's defective memory is culpable. The insult to Israel's customs refers to the Jewish designation of the pig as an unclean animal. But in Suetonian fashion, Yourcenar has generalized what Jerome's notice depicts as an incident affecting one entrance to the city, the western gate, alone. Insult is preceded by injury in Hadrian's allusion to the results of Jewish avoidance of graven images dictated by the Second Commandment, a canard that is an aspect of the anti-Jewish posture Yourcenar consistently ascribes to Hadrian.

1c. Les fêtes du Nouvel An juif, célébrées à grand renfort de trompettes et de cornes de bélier, donnaient lieu chaque année à des rixes sanglantes; nos autorités interdirent la lecture publique d'un certain récit légendaire, consacré aux exploits d'une heroïne juive qui serait devenue sous un nom d'emprunt la concubine d'un roi de Perse, et aurait fait massacrer sauvagement les ennemis du peuple méprisé et persécuté dont elle sortait. Les rabbins s'arrangèrent pour lire de nuit ce que le gouverneur Tinéus Rufus leur interdisait de lire de jour; cette féroce histoire, où les Perses et les Juifs rivalisaient d'atrocité, excitait jusqu'à la folie la rage nationale des Zélotes. (*MH* 467)

The festivals of the Jewish New Year, celebrated with a din of trumpets and rams' horns, give rise every year to brawling and bloodshed; our authorities accordingly forbade the public reading of a certain legendary account devoted to the exploits of a Jewish heroine who was said to have become, under an assumed name, the concubine of a king of Persia, and to have instigated a savage massacre of the enemies of her despised and persecuted race. The rabbis managed to read at night what the governor Tineus Rufus forbade them to read by day; that barbarous story, wherein Persians and Jews rivaled each other in atrocities, roused the nationalistic fervor of the Zealots to frenzy.

A host of repressive anti-Jewish measures taken by Hadrian during the Bar Kokhba period can be found in rabbinical sources.[30] They include interdiction of (a) the blowing of the *shofar* at Rosh Hashanah, the Feast of Trumpets (Book of Numbers 29:1); and (b) public reading of the Book of Esther, which contains the founding legend of the festival of Purim – the "legendary account" concerned – according to which the beautiful Esther, concubine of the king of Persia, saved enslaved Jews from the exterminating threat of the hostile Haman with the aid of her adoptive father Mordecai. Whether the ban was the work of Q. Tineius Rufus, a genuinely historical figure in office as governor of Judaea when the Jewish rebellion broke out, cannot be known.[31] Evidently, however, it is the rabbinical tradition on which Yourcenar has drawn, attributing to Hadrian a view of the Book of Esther with which any impartial reader might agree. Its story is indeed ferocious. Conflation of Rosh Hashanah and Purim, which belong to two very different moments of the Jewish calendar, gives astonishing pause, but conjunction of festivals and stasis should not.[32]

1.d. Enfin, ce même Tinéus Rufus, homme par ailleurs fort sage, et qui n'était pas sans s'intéresser aux fables et aux traditions d'Israël, décida d'étendre à la circoncision, pratique juive, les pénalités sévères de la loi que j'avais récemment promulguée contre la castration, et qui visait surtout les sévices perpétrés sur de jeunes esclaves dans un but de lucre ou de débauche. Il espérait oblitérer ainsi l'un des signes par lesquels Israël prétend se distinguer du reste du genre humain. (*MH* 467)

1.d. Finally, this same Tineus Rufus, a man of good judgment in other respects and not uninterested in Israel's traditions and fables, decided to extend to the Jewish practice of circumcision the same severe penalties of the law which I had recently promulgated against castration (and which was aimed especially at cruelties perpetrated upon young slaves for the sake of exorbitant gain or debauch). He hoped thus to obliterate one of the marks whereby Israel claims to distinguish itself from the rest of human kind.

The rabbinical tradition credits Tineius Rufus with issuing a decree against circumcision, which from a Roman perspective was a Jewish peculiarity that often elicited criticism.[33] The ban is frequently identified with the reference to genital mutilation in the *Historia Augusta* attributed to Hadrian (*HA Hadr.* 14.2).[34] Tineius is likewise said to have engaged in discussions with Rabbi Akiba on this and other points of Jewish belief and custom, asking why God had not created men already circumcised if circumcision was his wish, and why there was no reference to the practice in the Ten Commandments. He also enquired why God caused rain to fall and carried out other acts on the Sabbath when labour was forbidden; why he did not feed the poor if he cared for them; and why he hated Gentiles.[35] Such reports plainly underlie Hadrian's description of Tineius as a man of intelligence with an interest in Jewish culture. In contrast, Hadrian's action against castration, a practice often associated with Roman slave-holding, is known from a directive to a Spanish governor recorded in the *Digest* (48.8.4.2): extending directives from Domitian and Nerva, Hadrian made offenders liable to penalties under the *Lex Cornelia de veneficiis et sicariis*, essentially the law for murder. The date of this enactment is unknown, however, and whether it included the ban on circumcision is a matter of insoluble debate.[36]

2.a. Un aventurier sorti de la lie du peuple, un nommé Simon, qui se faisait appeler Bar-Kochba, le Fils de l'Étoile, joua dans cette révolte le rôle de brandon enduit de bitume ou de miroir ardent. (*MH* 468)

2.a. An adventurer born of the very dregs of the people, a fellow named Simon who entitled himself Bar-Kochba, Son of the Star, played the part of firebrand or incendiary mirror in that revolt.

The adventurer's formally full correct name, Shim'on bar Kosiba, has been known only since the discovery of letters, written on papyrus, providing information on the extent and course of the revolt.[37] The classical sources do not give the name Simon at all. I assume Yourcenar took it from Bar Kokhba's coinage, where the formula "Shim'on Nasi-Israel" (Simon, Prince of Israel) regularly appears.[38] That Bar Kokhba was of low social origin is a detail consistent with Eusebius's description of him as a murderous but charismatic bandit who appealed to the socially downtrodden.[39] That the second part of his name meant "Son of the Star" was an obvious inference from Eusebius's *Barchochebas*, a Greek form also found in an earlier brief notice in Justin Martyr's *First Apology* (31.6), unless Yourcenar came across the meaning of the Aramaic name in her secondary reading. It is confirmed by elements of the rabbinical tradition that characterize Bar Kokhba in messianic terms. The Book of Numbers (24:17) reads in the fourth prophecy of the evil prophet Balaam: "A Star shall come out of Jacob; a sceptre shall rise out of Israel, and batter the brow of Moab, and destroy all the sons of tumult." Rabbi Akiba is said to have identified Bar Kokhba as the fulfilment of this prophecy, taking his name to mean "son of the star" despite the fact that "kosiba," appearing in rabbinic texts as "koziba," literally means "lie."[40] The proclamation was immediately contested, leading to contradictory traditions about Bar Kokhba's leadership of the revolt and responsibility for its ultimate failure.[41] For understanding Yourcenar's procedures this distinction does not matter, but it had an impact on her overall narrative. She gave Bar Kokhba an active role in taking his special name, which presumably is the source of the concluding fiery associations, unless the influence of a fire-breathing anecdote from Jerome is at work.[42]

2.b. Je ne puis juger ce Simon que par ouï-dire; je ne l'ai vu qu'une fois face à face, le jour où un centurion m'apporta sa tête coupée. (*MH* 468)

2.b. I could judge this Simon only by hearsay; I have seen him but once face-to-face, the day a centurion brought me his severed head.

The sentence presupposes Hadrian's presence in the theatre of war, a circumstance that many historians accept despite the absence of definitive evidence.[43] The strongest indication comes from the report of Cassius Dio that during the war Hadrian wrote to the senate in Rome without including the customary formula, "If you and your children are in good health, it is well; I and the legions are in good health" (69.14.3), which, as Yourcenar noted in her letter to the Abbé Vincent, seems to attest his presence in Judaea safely enough: the report was inexplicable otherwise (*HZ* 301). As for her belief that Hadrian spent the final two years of hostilities there, an entry in her unpublished list of modified facts reads: "On s'est rangé ici à l'opinion des historiens qui estiment qu'H. passa ces deux années en Palestine," which obviously shows that she was aware of the uncertainty.[44] Indeed, in the letter to the Abbé Vincent she cited Renan as an example of nineteenth-century historians who had thought otherwise, observing his view that Hadrian had supervised the war's operations from Athens (*HZ* 301).[45] Nothing in fact in the classical sources attests direct contact between Hadrian and Bar Kokhba. The detail of the severed head – in itself not unrealistic, as Marcus was later to know directly (*Med.* 8.34) – comes from a Jewish legend according to which Bar Kokhba was killed after the surrender of Bethar and his head brought to Hadrian, with a sinister Samaritan admitting responsibility for the death. In one version, Hadrian asked to see the corpse, which was brought to him with a snake coiled around its neck, prompting the exclamation, with reference to a verse from the Book of Deuteronomy (32:30): "If his God had not killed this man, who would have been able to do so?"[46] Yourcenar clearly knew the story, but apparently replaced the questionable Samaritan with a Roman soldier.

2.c. Mais je suis disposé à lui reconnaître cette part de génie qu'il faut toujours pour s'élever si vite et si haut dans les affaires humaines; on ne s'impose pas aussi sans posséder au moins quelque habileté grossière. (*MH* 468)

2.c. Yet I am disposed to grant him that degree of genius which must always be present in one who rises so fast and so high in human affairs; such ascendancy is not gained without at least some crude skill.

The judgment, less factual, more deliberative, complements the high opinion of Bar Kokhba implicit in Hadrian's legendary words just quoted and perhaps reflects Yourcenar's own opinion. Renan had remarked on Bar Kokhba's courage.[47] While inventive, it can be associated with the extraordinary accomplishments attributed to Bar Kokhba in Jewish sources: "He is portrayed as a glorious warrior, fierce in battle. He heads an army of powerful, fearless soldiers. He catches the huge stones flung from the Roman catapults and hurls them back. One kick from his foot kills instantly. He could not be conquered by men – as Hadrian acknowledges when he declares that only God could have brought him down."[48] Bar Kokhba's administrative and organizational ability, inferable long since from the production of the rebels' coinage, is confirmed by the documentary evidence to which Yourcenar had no access. She may, however, have felt justified in her assessment after acquiring an article from the *Palestine Exploration Quarterly* of 1954, in which one of Bar Kokhba's letters was published. It reads in part, forcefully: "I call heaven to witness against me that if any of the Galilaeans who are with you is mistreated, I shall put fetters on your feet as I did to Ben Aphul."[49] Such ruthlessness is well portrayed in the documentary materials: "Shimun son of Kosibah, the prince over Israel, to Yehonathan and to Mesabalah, peace. (Order) that you should examine and seize the wheat which Hanun son of Yishmael brought and send some of it, specifically one *seah*. And place it under guard since it was found having been stolen. And if you do not do so, then recompense will be exacted from you. And as for the man, you are to send him to me under guard. And any Tekoan man who is found with you, let the houses they are dwelling in burn and from you I will exact recompense. And Yeshu son of the Palmyrene you will seize and dispatch to me under guard. And do not scorn to take the sword which is on him – send it (too)!"[50]

2.d. Les Juifs modérés ont été les premiers à accuser ce prétendu Fils de l'Étoile de fourberie et d'imposture: je crois plutôt que cet esprit inculte était de ceux qui se prennent à leurs propres mensonges et que le fanatisme chez lui allait de pair avec la ruse. (*MH* 468–9)

2.d. The Jews of the moderate party were the first to accuse this supposed Son of the Star of deceit and imposture; I believe rather that his untrained mind was of the type which is taken in by its own lies, and that guile in his case went hand in hand with fanaticism.

Jewish tradition again informs the first clause of this sentence. (Contrast Tacitus on Jewish political and military factionalism in the ethnographic prelude to his record of the war led by Titus [*Hist.* 5.12].) In response to Rabbi Akiba's proclamation of Bar Kokhba as Messiah, Rabbi Yohanan ben Torta is said to have responded: "Akiba, grass will grow up from your jaws and the son of David will not yet have come," a riposte Yourcenar subsequently folds into her narrative (*MH* 473).[51] Together with the challenge to Akiba's interpretation of Bar Kokhba's name – not "son of a star" but "son of a liar" – this is often taken to signify Jewish political rivalries that incorporated the view, consistent with Eusebius's record, that Bar Kokhba was an impostor.[52] On the latter point, Jerome wrote much later of his ability to keep a lighted straw in his mouth to make it seem as if he were breathing out flames (*Adv. Rufin.* 3.31). Comparison has been drawn with the wonder-working slave leader Eunus from centuries earlier in Sicily.[53]

2.e. Simon se fit passer pour le héros sur lequel le peuple juif compte depuis des siècles pour assouvir ses ambitions et ses haines; ce démagogue se proclama Messie et roi d'Israël. (*MH* 469)

2.3. He paraded as the hero whom the Jewish people had awaited for centuries in order to gratify their ambitions and their hate; this demagogue proclaimed himself Messiah and King of Israel.

The messianic depiction of Bar Kokhba in Jewish sources is already clear enough. That Hadrian's Roman contemporaries knew of a long-established belief that men from Judaea were fated to rule the world is evident from Tacitus (*Hist.* 5.13) and Suetonius (*Vesp.* 4.5), writing in references to the war that began under Nero. Eusebius communicates Bar Kokhba's aspirations, and cites Justin Martyr's remark that Bar Kokhba threatened dire punishment of Christians if they did not deny the messianic claims of Jesus (*Hist. eccl.* 4.6.2; 4.8.4). The coins designating him as "Prince of Israel" are pertinent to the final phrase, but Renan was also able to cite a Jewish text suggesting regal pretensions.[54]

2f. L'antique Akiba, à qui la tête tournait, promena par la bride dans les rues de Jérusalem le cheval de l'aventurier. (*MH* 469)

2.f. The aged Akiba, in a foolish state of exaltation, led the adventurer through the streets of Jerusalem, holding his horse by the bridle.

Renan's description of Akiba's so-called messianic proclamation of Bar Kokhba may be relevant here: "Il lui donna en quelque sorte l'investiture

devant le peuple, en lui remettant solennellement le bâton de commande-
ment et en lui tenant l'étrier, quand il monta sur le cheval de guerre pour
inaugurer son règne de Messie."[55] Inspiration may have come from a passage
in the Book of Esther (6.9–11): the deviously ambitious Haman, plotting to
secure the favour of the Persian king, was superseded by Esther's adoptive
father and ally Mordecai, and at the king's bidding was forced to lead Mordecai on horseback through the city square of Shushan, arrayed in a robe given
to him by the king. Mortified, Haman was compelled to utter the proclamation: "Thus shall it be done to the man the king delights to honour."[56] Akiba
has already been introduced of course as an old man in Hadrian's account of
his visit to Alexandria prior to the calamitous Nile journey.

2.g. le grand-prêtre Éléazar rededia le temple soi-disant souillé depuis que des visi-
teurs non circoncis en avaient franchi le seuil; des monceaux d'armes rentrés sous terre
depuis près de vingt ans furent distribués aux rebelles par les agents du Fils de l'Étoile;
il en alla de même des pièces défectueuses fabriquées à dessein depuis des années dans
nos arsenaux par les ouvriers juifs et que refusait notre intendance. (*MH* 469)

2.g. the high priest Eleazar rededicated the temple, said to be defiled from the time that
uncircumcised visitors had crossed its threshold. Stacks of arms hidden underground
for nearly twenty years were distributed to the rebels by agents of the Son of the Star;
they also had recourse to weapons formerly rejected for our ordnance as defective (and
purposely constructed thus by Jewish workers in our arsenals over a period of years).

As seen earlier, a priest Eleazar is named on some of the rebels' coins and is
perhaps to be identified with the Rabbi Eleazar of Modin associated in rabbinical texts with Bar Kokhba at the siege of Bethar.[57] Unknown to classical
sources, he is a figure credited with conservative pronouncements consistent
with the cleansing of the Temple mentioned here, including condemnation
of epispasm.[58] The Temple, destroyed by Titus, was depicted on the rebels'
coinage as a symbol of national identity, and perhaps also as a call to rebuilding. As for the claim that Eleazar rededicated it, Yourcenar may have noticed
Sachar's assertion that its altar was so treated.[59] She clearly drew at the end
of the extract on the report of Cassius Dio that when Rome requisitioned
arms, the Jewish population manufactured items of low quality which, on
rejection, could be kept for its own use (69.12.2).[60]

2.h. Des groupes zélotes attaquèrent les garnisons romaines isolées et massacrèrent
nos soldats avec des raffinements de fureur qui rappelèrent les pires souvenirs de la
révolte juive sous Trajan; Jérusalem enfin tomba tout entière aux mains des insurgés
et les quartiers neufs d'Ælia Capitolina flambèrent comme une torche. (*MH* 469)

2.h. Zealot groups attacked isolated Roman garrisons and massacred our soldiers with refinements of cruelty which recalled the worst memories of the Jewish revolt under Trajan; Jerusalem finally fell wholly into the hands of the insurgents, and the new quarters of Aelia Capitolina were set burning like a torch.

Cassius Dio has the Jewish rebels avoiding open military confrontations with Roman forces when rebellion broke out, and seeking good positions in the countryside that could be converted into places of refuge as needed (69.12.3, 69.13.1–2). Eusebius mentions only Tineius Rufus's merciless military response to the initial outbreak (*Hist.eccl.* 4.6.1). Whether Jerusalem, the headquarters of Rome's Legion X Fretensis, fell to the rebels is a question of eternal debate. The coin legends JERUSALEM and OF THE LIBERTY OF JERUSALEM have been understood as evidence that it did, and alternatively as evidence only of aspirations and propaganda.[61] Yourcenar may simply have followed Wilhelm Weber, who wrote unequivocally in the first edition of the *Cambridge Ancient History* that "Aelia was taken by storm."[62]

2.i. Les premiers détachements de la Vingt-deuxième Légion Déjotarienne, envoyée d'Égypte en toute hâte sous les ordres du légat de Syrie Publius Marcellus, furent mis en déroute par des bandes dix fois supérieures en nombre. La révolte était devenue guerre, et guerre inexpiable. (*MH* 469)

2.i. The first detachments of the Twenty-Second Legion Deiotariana, sent from Egypt with utmost speed under the command of the legate of Syria, Publius Marcellus, were routed by bands ten times their number. The revolt had become war, and war to the bitter end.

Legion XXII Deiotariana was stationed in Egypt in 119. But it does not appear in a list of Rome's legions on an inscription from Rome of the mid-second century (*ILS* 2288). The common assumption has been that it was ordered to Judaea to participate in suppressing the Jewish rebellion and was destroyed in the process. New evidence unavailable to Yourcenar supports this possibility, but certainty is unattainable.[63] Yourcenar turned the common assumption into a fact. She correctly identified the governor of Syria as the man put in charge of the legion, but mistook his name through all the various editions of *Mémoires*: not Publius Marcellus, but C. Publicius Marcellus (*cos. suff.* 120). An inscription from Ancyra in Galatia, known to Renan, whose account Yourcenar could again have followed, shows that he left his province with troops to assist in the Roman resistance.[64] Predictably there is no evidence for the number of rebels involved in the initial stages of the revolt, but its evolution into a full-scale war against Rome is beyond question.

The gravity of the threat the revolt represented emerges from modern assessment of Rome's unusually large military response.[65]

These two paragraphs show how Yourcenar combined classical and Jewish traditions, often supplementing the former with the latter, to recreate Hadrian's vivid and absorbing memories of the events of the Bar Kokhba war. Each section of the external frame could be analyzed in the same way, with a multiplicity of details standing out as elements taken from Jewish records: Usfa in Galilee as a centre of rabbinical study, Rome's prohibition of the study of Jewish law, the martyrdom of Akiba and nine of his colleagues, the mass sale of prisoners into slavery at Abraham's Well, the designation of the ninth day of the month of Ab as the day for admission of Jews to Jerusalem, the day supposedly on which Bethar fell (*MH* 479–80).[66] Of special interest in this regard are the various Jewish figures, Akiba and Eleazar apart, who appear in the narrative.

Before the outbreak of revolt, in connection with his wish to promote Greek culture in the new Aelia Capitolina, Hadrian recalls a long-standing personal acquaintance with a Rabbi Joshua, whose philhellenism had not been well received by his co-religionists. The opening of schools in Jerusalem where Greek could be taught was the issue of immediate concern (*MH* 468).[67] This is Joshua ben Hananiah, a pre-eminent teacher said to have once lived in poverty while working as a blacksmith, but a figure of great intellectual influence in early rabbinical history. Akiba was one of his pupils. He was reputed to have more than once travelled to Rome on diplomatic missions, as well as to Athens and Alexandria, and Jewish sources contain many reports of purported conversations or discussions he held with Hadrian on topics of religious belief and practice: the nature of the Jewish god and his creation of the world, his selection of Jews as the chosen people, Mosaic law.[68] The discussions included quasi-scientific topics, one of which, said to have taken place in Athens, considered the gestation period of the snake. Perhaps, however, the most prominent aspect of the tradition is the report that in his wisdom Joshua forestalled a potential revolt when Hadrian withdrew permission for the rebuilding of the Temple. He reappears in Yourcenar's account during the siege of Bethar when Hadrian's thoughts turn to significant Jewish individuals: "même chez le rabbin Joshua qui avait été longtemps mon conseiller dans les affaires juives, j'avais senti, sous la souplesse et l'envie de plaire, les différences irréconciliables, le point où deux pensées d'espèces opposées ne se rencontrent que pour se combattre" (*MH* 473).[69] Yourcenar creates between emperor and rabbi something of a bond that is scarcely discernible in the dispassionate evidence itself.

It cannot be independently corroborated. But the anecdotes concerned provide a rational basis for the relationship depicted, the characterization of Joshua, and the discussions in Athens Yourcenar presents as fact. She will have noted the association from a brief mention, complete with a few of the relevant Talmudic references, in Renan.[70] The dictate disavowing study of Greek at the expense of the Torah comes from anecdotes in which the question was posed whether a Jew is permitted to teach his son Greek, to which Joshua replied, "Let him teach him Greek at a time when it is neither day nor night, for it is written (Joshua I, 8), '*Thou shalt meditate thereon day and night*'" – on the Law, that is.[71]

Conjoined with Joshua are two other men, Ismaël and his nephew Ben Dama, the individual met earlier through the critique of F.C. Grant: "Ismaël, membre important du sanhédrin et qui passait pour rallié à la cause de Rome, laissa mourir son neveu Ben-Dama plutôt que d'accepter les services du chirugien grec que lui avait envoyé Tinéus Rufus" (*MH* 468).[72] The arch-conservative uncle is Ishmael ben Elisha, who in Jewish lore prohibited his nephew Eleazar ben Dama from studying Greek philosophy by uttering a firm directive similar to, if not identical with, that of Rabbi Joshua. The nephew supposedly died from a snake bite when his uncle refused to allow the intervention of an heretical doctor. The involvement of Tineius Rufus, however, is unattested.[73] Finally, two other men, one identified as a Jewish quisling, the other an advocate of appeasement: "Notre meilleur agent, Élie Ben-Abayad, qui jouait pour Rome le rôle d'informateur et d'espion, était justement méprisé des deux camps; c'était pourtant l'homme le plus intelligent du groupe, esprit libéral, cœur malade, tiraillé entre son amour pour son peuple et son goût pour nos lettres et pour nous; lui aussi, d'ailleurs, ne pensait au fond qu'à Israël. Josué Ben-Kisma, qui prêchait l'apaisement, n'était qu'un Akiba plus timide ou plus hypocrite" (*MH* 473).[74] The former is Elisha ben Abuyah, traditionally understood to be a great scholar, but also an apostate and philhellene who desecrated observance of the Sabbath and indeed adopted the role of Roman informer. The latter is Jose ben Kisma, traditionally thought to have been a political moderate who died towards the end of the war predicting Roman destruction at the hands of the Parthians: "Bury me deep in the ground; for there will be no coffin in Israel that the Parthians will not use as a horse-trough."[75] Yourcenar duly exploited the tradition: "Josué Ben-Kisma, chef des soi-disant modérés, qui avait lamentablement échoué dans son rôle de pacificateur, succomba vers cette même époque aux suites d'une longue maladie; il mourut en appellant de ses vœux la guerre étrangère et la victoire des Parthes sur nous" (*MH* 479).[76]

All in all, Yourcenar's deftness in blending Jewish evidence into the skeletal outline of the Bar Kokhba war left by Cassius Dio and Eusebius is remarkable. Much of what Hadrian has to say is far from fiction and has a firmer foundation than might at first be supposed.[77] Yourcenar's preparation was extensive, and the commitment to producing an authentic account of the war is indisputable. Inaccuracies, adjustments, and elaborations can be identified, but by and large Hadrian's memories are inherently explicable; and the construct of a genuine crisis can scarcely be contested, if only in view of the impact made by the huge losses of Roman life as passingly recalled by Fronto (2.22). Much of the Jewish material borders, undeniably, on fable or romance and issues of factual certainty remain. But judiciously deployed, especially through the attention paid to personnel, the material became a means by which to achieve both an entrée into Hadrian's experience that memory could duly recover, and *enargeia* in his description of events. The war presented is not a war against an amorphous enemy, "the Jews" of the history books, but a war against a people riven by fissures and factionalism attributable to identifiable protagonists. Years later, Yourcenar could say that it gave her a strange feeling to see the now accessible, almost tangible finds of archaeologists validating what from records sparse and dry she had tried in her novel to bring to life: "ce qu'on avait tâché de faire revivre" (*L* 297).[78]

V

A pause at this point, doubtless welcome, impelled by a palpable feature of so much of Yourcenar's text quoted so far: the provocative vocabulary often on display that together with an insistence on Jewish fanaticism has exposed Yourcenar to accusations of antisemitism. Hadrian's portrait again of Akiba in Alexandria is typical of the tendency:

Ce fanatique ne se doutait même pas qu'on pût raisonner sur d'autres prémisses que les siennes; j'offrais à ce peuple méprisé une place parmi les autres dans la communauté romaine: Jérusalem, par la bouche d'Akiba, me signifiait sa volonté de rester jusqu'au bout la forteresse d'une race et d'un dieu isolés du genre humain. Cette pensée forcenée s'exprimait avec une subtilité fatigante: je dus subir une longue file de raisons, savamment déduites les unes des autres, de la supériorité d'Israël ... L'ignorance d'Akiba, son réfus d'accepter tout ce qui n'était pas ses livres saints et son peuple, lui conféraient une sorte d'étroite innocence. Mais il était difficile de s'attendrir sur ce sectaire. (*MH* 435)

This fanatic did not even suspect any reasoning possible on premises other than those he set forth. I offered his despised people a place among the others in the Roman community; Jerusalem, however, speaking through Akiba, signified its intention of remaining, to the end, the fortress of a race and of a god isolated from human kind. That savage determination was expressed with tiresome deviousness: I had to listen to a long line of argument, subtly deduced step by step, proving Israel's superiority … The ignorance of Akiba, and his refusal to accept anything outside his sacred books or his own people, endued him with a kind of narrow innocence. But it was difficult to feel sympathy for this bigot.

One particular scholar has indeed brought a litany of charges against Yourcenar, taking Hadrian's seemingly inflammatory language, and the uncompromising tone of the whole episode of the Jewish War, as evidence of an authorial prejudice anachronistically imposed that completely vitiates the narrative's historicity. In view of Rome's long-standing familiarity with Jewish religious customs and sensibilities, Hadrian's surprise at the offence caused by the display of Legion X's standard at Jerusalem is illogical; and had he truly held conversations with Rabbi Joshua, he would not have confused the festivals of Rosh Hashanah and Purim. His recourse to derogatory tropes in characterizing Jews – devotees of wealth and world dominance, with segregation of the "enlightened" from the "fanatical" – betrays centuries' old attitudes of condescension; and Yourcenar's attribution to Hadrian of such insensitive phrases as "l'abcès juif" and "la contagion zélote," not to mention use of the word "race" with its echoes of "the final solution," is especially culpable given the time at which her novel was composed and published. The term was taken from the sole item of scholarship on the war consulted.[79]

That Yourcenar's account relied on a single secondary source is of course plainly wrong, as the *Note* proves. More importantly, however, the critical disposition towards Jews found in much classical literature generally is more than enough to justify Hadrian's harsh vocabulary; and even a cursory acquaintance with the rabbinical literature of concern supports the picture drawn of Jewish cultural and religious diversity. Nevertheless, indictments of the kind made haunted Yourcenar throughout her career, surfacing at a late stage, as pointed out earlier, in the debate about her suitability for admission to the Académie française.[80] She faced the charges head on when speaking with Matthieu Galey, arguing forcefully that it was historical accuracy alone that had controlled Hadrian's comportment in the novel, a key aspect of which was a desire to dominate he shared with all imperialists. (The implicit collapse of time and universality of behaviour are unsurprising but noteworthy.) She was not reluctant to use vocabulary she thought historically appropriate in reaffirming her view of Hadrian's fatal inability to understand Jews and Judaism:

Hadrien, lui aussi, avait beaucoup d'amis juifs, libéraux et hellénisés. Il se heurte au fanatisme du vieil Akiba, et j'avoue qu'à moi-même Akiba … n'inspire guère plus de sympathie que Khomeini. Le fanatisme juif n'est pas plus respectable qu'aucun fanatisme. Certes, Hadrien a commis une erreur; sa part d'aveuglement fut la même que celle des Anglais ou des Américains qui s'imaginaient rendre service, en les anglicisant ou en les américanisant, à des populations restées en dehors des grands courants de l'époque. Il ne comprend pas que les zélotes préfèrent camper dans les ruines de Jérusalem, naguère détruite par Titus, au profit et aux commodités d'une ville nouvelle, à la romaine. L'incapacité de se comprendre de part et d'autre produira la guerre de Palestine et avancera de quelques années la mort de l'empereur. (YO 279)[81]

Hadrian, too, had many Jewish friends: Hellenized, liberal Jews. He had to confront the fanaticism of old Akiba, and I must confess that I myself find Akiba scarcely more sympathetic than Khomeini ... Jewish fanaticism is no more respectable than any other. Admittedly, Hadrian made a mistake; his blind spot was the same as that of the English or the Americans, who thought by Anglicizing or Americanizing groups that remained apart from the mainstream of the times, they were doing them a favor. He could not understand that zealots would prefer to remain amidst the ruins of Jerusalem, destroyed earlier by Titus, rather than share in the profits and amenities of a new, Roman-style city. The inability of both sides to understand each other eventually brought on the war in Palestine and shortened the emperor's life by a few years.

Whether Yourcenar can be believed that Hadrian, fascinated by all religions, became aware of the young prophet Jesus – and here, notably, she speaks unequivocally of her Hadrian as the historical Hadrian – she was surely right to insist, in what is in effect another example of first-order authenticity, on the defining assimilative capacity of Roman polytheism and on what correspondingly seemed to Romans (and Greeks) the obstinacy and intractability to which Jewish monotheism led (YO 280).[82] The oddity of Judaism, with its keeping of the Sabbath and custom of male circumcision, was frequently remarked upon, and frequently mocked, by Romans who naturally thought of identifying the god of the Jews with Jupiter, or Dionysus, or even Iao of the Chaldaean mysteries, while Jewish traditions of sages engaging with prominent Romans in discussions and explications of their religious beliefs and cultural practices are evidence in themselves of a Jewish consciousness of difference.[83] The singularity of monotheism within the world of Greco-Roman polytheism cannot be minimized, and although to a present-day readership this may be an inconvenient truth, it is a truth that cannot be gainsaid. When understood within context, the disdainful attitude Yourcenar attributed to Hadrian is historically beyond reproach. While acknowledging, accurately, that Rome sanctioned Judaism as a licit religion, Hadrian laments, and resents, its failure to show any reciprocal acceptance of other religious practices: Dacians, Phoenicians, and

Egyptians, peoples with their own religious systems, recognized that their gods could be identified with, or assimilated to, the gods of the Roman pantheon; Jews alone refused, dogmatically, to exhibit any comparable tolerance: "Aucun peuple, sauf Israël, n'a l'arrogance d'enfermer la vérité tout entière dans les limites étroites d'une seule conception divine, insultant ainsi à la multiplicité du Dieu qui contient tout; aucun autre dieu n'a inspiré à ses adorateurs le mépris et la haine de ceux qui prient à de différents autels" (*MH* 468).[84] Roman polytheism and Jewish monotheism were hopelessly irreconcilable, as too the cultural idioms that flowed from them, and it is on this mutual antagonism that the derogatory language of factionalism and zealotry that pervades Hadrian's record of the Bar Kokhba war is based. To Marcus, as to any Roman, such an explanation will have seemed superfluous. But it was consistent, as Yourcenar well knew, with the statement in the Latin life that Hadrian despised foreign rites and scrupulously followed Roman conventions (*HA Hadr.* 22.10). It also served the purpose, and continues to do so, of instructing unaware readers in the realities of the historical background.[85]

And yet. The matter is not quite so simple. Writing as late as June 1974 to Jeanne Carayon, a close friend, Yourcenar could speak uninhibitedly of present-day Jews in a manner that while superficially complimentary arouses now a certain consternation, given the stress placed on Jewish distinctiveness and the sense of "otherness" conveyed. From her own past and present friendships, she speculated, something of an essential Jewishness could be identified, its features being a basic kindness, a taste for a gentleness of life, and often an intellectual enthusiasm and intensity she found overwhelming, a warm admixture that altogether made for living life well. But it was difficult to generalize because, the Holocaust apart (curiously glossed as "l'espèce de sacre"), her sensitivity to the need to combat racism, of every kind, disallowed a balanced assessment of Jewish qualities and defects of the kind that could be made in other cases. There was now the additional consideration that Israel had become a nation armed to the teeth (*L* 429–30). The thoughts trail off inconclusively as other topics are broached. But not before Jewish identity is associated, if only haltingly, with a residual Oriental influence – "la mince gouttelette venue d'Orient" (*L* 430) – a statement that encapsulates what might well be construed half a century later as a set of completely offensive remarks. Merely to propose the existence of readily discernible ethnic features will seem to many inherently indicative of prejudice. And Yourcenar's biographers have pointed to such a latent attitude, seeing it as the legacy of an antisemitism present in the society of her childhood, members of her own family circle included.[86] That her father, the key figure in her early life, had always been innocent of such proclivity Yourcenar was adamant: the problem had never arisen for him; he had been for Dreyfus (*YO* 281–2). Nevertheless, there may well have been preconceptions when she was composing *Mémoires* of which she was scarcely herself aware, not least perhaps due to Renan's theories of Semitic inferiority.[87]

A definitive statement is beyond reach, and allowance should perhaps be made for refinements of attitude due to experience and the passage of time. Yourcenar was overcome for instance by visits made in the spring of 1964 to Auschwitz and Mauthausen (*L* 200, 202; *HZ* IV 103, 106).[88] There were thoughts also of how posterity was to remember her. Her early novel *Le Coup de grâce* (1939) is set in the Baltic shortly after World War I and tells a story of a complex love triangle. Its narrator is a young Prussian, Erick von Lhomond, who, as Elaine Marks has put it, draws on "many of the stereotypes and clichés that have developed since the Middle Ages to depict Jews" – "usurers, jewellers, furriers; omnivorous readers; obese and ugly; revolutionary and pusillanimous," a catalogue that, given the year of the novel's appearance, could well reveal an alarming authorial lack of sensibility.[89] It should not of course follow that the character speaks for his creator. Yet when *Le Coup de grâce* was republished in 1962 Yourcenar wrote a preface in which, rather defensively, as if a nerve had been struck by responses to the book's initial appearance, she took pains to separate the simplistic inferences of a naive reader from an understanding of how a novelist must keep her protagonists true to type: it would be wrong, she said, for such a reader "de prendre pour un antisémite professionnel cet homme chez qui le persiflage à l'égard des Juifs fait partie d'un conformisme de caste" (*CG* 81).[90] As Marks astutely observes, however, the "marchands juifs" who in an early passage of the story have arrived from New York to buy jewellery from Russian refugees, became in Frick's translation of 1957, made with Yourcenar's full involvement, simply "dealers from New York." A concern to protect her reputation was apparently at work.[91]

No one aware of Roman realities will be convinced that the Hadrian of *Mémoires* speaks directly for his creator on Jews and Judaism. Again, the historical consequences of the clash between Roman polytheism and Jewish monotheism are too obvious and uncontroversial for this to be the case; and to have presented the Bar Kokhba war as a religiously inspired nationalist uprising to which Hadrian had to respond was a historically defensible position.[92] Yet there is no denying that Hadrian's views, and the often uncompromising way in which he expresses them, are disturbing despite their historical setting. Hesitations inevitably persist. The letter to Jeanne Carayon belongs to a late period of Yourcenar's life, and the Jewish merchants of *Le Coup de grâce* are still there in the Pléiade (*CG* 92).[93]

VI

The scale of Rome's military response to the Bar Kokhba uprising was extraordinary. Werner Eck has calculated that twelve or thirteen legions participated in the war, if only sometimes in detachments. The force included the two legions ordinarily garrisoned in Judaea, troops from the north brought by the highly experienced Cn. Julius Severus, others from Syria brought by C. Publicius Marcellus, and others still from the legion stationed in neighbouring Arabia under T. Haterius Nepos. Marines from the Roman fleet at Misenum reinforced Legion X. Such allocations are obviously a measure of the seriousness of the rebellion and the dangers it represented to Roman rule. An unusual level of conscription in Italy during the war, in response perhaps to the annihilation of Legion XXII, Hadrian's acceptance when it ended of an imperatorial acclamation, for only the second time, and the exceptional award of the *ornamenta triumphalia* to the three generals just mentioned responsible for Rome's success are further indications of the war's gravity. That it had extended furthermore over a broad geographical area is symbolized by the later construction of a victory monument at Tel Shalem in the Galilee, some twelve kilometres south of Scythopolis.[94] The absolute number of Roman troops deployed cannot be known, nor the precise numbers of casualties on either side. But Fronto's allusion to Rome's great losses and the memory in Jewish lore of the deaths of "myriads" of insurgents consist with all that can be recovered of Rome's management of the war. Archaeological investigation of the caves used as hiding complexes likewise aligns with Cassius Dio's record of the devastation finally suffered by the Jewish rebels.[95] There is every reason, therefore, for Yourcenar to have conceived of the Bar Kokhba war as a turning point in Hadrian's life. She did not know all the details known now to historians. But she might well be considered almost prescient in estimating the war's impact upon Hadrian. It was not simply a setback to the ideological mission of promoting imperial peace, represented above all, recall, by the Panhellenion, but an episode from which an internal crisis could also be deduced and reimagined as she assessed his life's history.

The varying emotions experienced during the crisis are set in Hadrian's elaborate recollections of the physical contexts in which the events of the war unfolded. The night-time sights, sounds, and smells of the Roman camp at Bethar are vividly detailed for instance in a manner completely alien to academic life writing – salutes from sentries, the stench of hospital dysenteries, a wind blowing in from Egypt, a ghostly swirl of dust (*MH* 469–70, 474, 476) – while two contrasting passages evoke, in turn, the human misery of war that lingered long in Hadrian's consciousness, and the delights of his final sea passage that had brought relief at war's end. Again, they are far from typical of conventional imperial biography.

The former should be read not with Rome's traditional glorification of war in mind – triumphalism, military discipline, promotion of empire – but with the realities of war front and centre, perceptible as they are from such material representations as the Portonaccio and Ludovisi sarcophagi: Roman generals and troops viciously striking down barbarian enemies and prisoners not already in the throes of death bound in chains for sale into slavery, their faces filled with panic and desperation, their bodies writhing in pain. The moment is that of Bethar's capitulation and the horrors it brought:

Trois mois plus tard, par un froid matin de février, assis au haut d'une colline, adossé au tronc d'un figuier dégarni de ses feuilles, j'assistai à l'assaut qui précéda de quelques heures la capitulation de Béthar; je vis sortir un à un les derniers défenseurs de la forteresse, hâves, décharnés, hideux, beaux pourtant comme tout ce qui est indomptable. À la fin du même mois, je me fis transporter au lieu-dit du Puits-d'Abraham, où les rebelles pris les armes à la main dans les agglomérations urbaines furent rassemblés et vendus à l'encan; des enfants ricanants, déjà féroces, déformés par des convictions implacables, se vantant très haut d'avoir causé la mort de dizaines de légionnaires, des vieillards emmurés dans un rêve de somnambule, des matrons aux chairs molles, et d'autres, solennelles et sombres comme la Grande Mère des cultes d'Orient, défilèrent sous l'œil froid des marchands d'esclaves; cette multitude passa devant moi comme une poussière. (*MH* 479)

Three months later, from the top of a hill on a cold morning in February, I sat leaning against the trunk of a leafless fig-tree to watch the assault which preceded by only a few hours the capitulation of Bethar. I saw the last defenders of the fortress come out one by one, haggard, emaciated, hideous to view but nevertheless superb, like all that is indomitable. At the end of the same month I had myself borne to the place called Abraham's Well, where the rebels in the urban centers, taken with weapons in hand, had been assembled to be sold at auction: children sneering defiance, already turned fierce and deformed by implacable convictions, boasting loudly of having brought death to dozens of legionaries; old men immured in somnambulistic dreams; women with fat, heavy bodies and others stern and stately, like the Great Mother of the Oriental cults; all these filed by under the cool scrutiny of the slave merchants; that multitude passed before me like a haze of dust.

For Hadrian's description of the aftermath of the Dacian wars, Yourcenar had used scenes on Trajan's Column as source material (*OR* 547–8). I assume that in this case she knew of Josephus's record that in the Jewish War begun by Nero Rome took a total of 97,000 prisoners, some of whom were systematically slaughtered, while others were sold into slavery or else assigned to the arena and far distant construction projects. What she once unforgettably called "ce flot rouge qui détrempe l'histoire" – "the scarlet flood that soaks all history" – was not forgotten here (*AN* 1036).[96]

A different kind of vividness emerges in the second example, a lyrical passage brimming with sensory appeal that records Hadrian's departure by sea at war's end, in the company of his new companion Celer and the beautiful Greek boy Diotimus. The cultural complexities of Roman slave-owning practices are adumbrated, and authentic touches of the ritualistic, the philosophic, and the erotic passingly added. Above all, however, the atmospheric details are due, I suspect, to the memories of a traveller whose early adult years had been spent in the Mediterranean, leavened now in the New World by mid-life nostalgia. The combination is empathetically projected into the mind of the biographical subject:

Vers la fin du printemps, je m'embarquai pour l'Italie sur un vaisseau de haut bord de la flotte … La route du retour traversait l'Archipel; pour la dernière fois sans doute de ma vie, j'assistais aux bonds des dauphins dans l'eau bleue; j'observais, sans songer désormais à en tirer des présages, le long vol régulier des oiseaux migrateurs, qui parfois, pour se reposer, s'abattent amicalement sur le pont du navire; je goûtais cette odeur de sel et de soleil sur la peau humaine, ce parfum de lentisque et de térébinthe des îles où l'on voudrait vivre, et où l'on sait d'avance qu'on ne s'arrêtera pas. Diotime a reçu cette parfaite instruction littéraire qu'on donne souvent, pour accroître encore leur valeur, aux jeunes esclaves doués des grâces du corps; au crépuscule, couché à l'arrière, sous un tendelet de poupre, je l'écoutais me lire des poètes de son pays, jusqu'à ce que la nuit effaçât également les lignes qui décrivent l'incertitude tragique de la vie humaine et celles qui parlent de colombes, de couronnes de roses, et de bouches baisées. Une haleine humide s'exhalait de la mer; les étoiles montaient une à une à leur place assignée; le navire penché par le vent filait vers l'Occident où s'éraillait encore une dernière bande rouge; un sillage phosphorescent s'étirait derrière nous, bientôt recouvert par les masses noires des vagues. (*MH* 481)

Towards the end of spring I embarked for Italy on a large galley of the fleet … The route of return crossed the Archipelago; for the last time in my life, doubtless, I was watching the dolphins leap in that blue sea; with no thought henceforth of seeking for omens I followed the long straight flight of the migrating birds, which sometimes alighted in friendly fashion to rest on the deck of the ship; I drank in the odor of salt and sun on the human skin, the perfume of lentisk and terebinth from the isles where each voyager longs to dwell, but knows in advance that he will not pause. Diotimus read me the poets of his country; he has had that perfect instruction in letters which is often given to young slaves endowed with bodily graces in order to increase further their value; as night fell I would lie in the stern, protected by the purple canopy, listening till darkness came to efface both those lines which describe the tragic incertitude of our life, and those which speak of doves and kisses and garlands of roses. The sea was exhaling its moist, warm breath; the stars mounted one by one to their stations; the ship inclining before the wind made straight for the Occident, where showed the last shreds of red; phosphorescence glittered in the wake which stretched out behind us, soon covered over by the black masses of the waves.

From such items it is a small step into the deeper introspection that occupies much of Hadrian's account of the war. The military crisis is matched by an emotional turmoil that manifests itself first in a physical breakdown – the body is a constant preoccupation – that resolves itself in part as the fortunes of war gradually turn in Rome's favour. The toll is severe, however, leaving Hadrian with rather more than intimations of mortality. In retrospect he can feel no regret for having spent the last two years of his active life on campaign, since the military life, as he reminds Marcus, had always been important to him (*MH* 470). And despite the limitations wrought by age, he had at first found it almost enjoyable to be once more engaged in military preparations and to be sharing in the camaraderie of his troops. As the siege of Bethar dragged on, however, with the tactics of the rebels a constant frustration, food in short supply, and disease endemic in the heat of summer, he had begun to succumb (*MH* 471). In turn, resignation and self-reproach had taken over, and self-recrimination becomes something close to despair: more could have been done to forestall the rebellion; sixteen years of the peace policy had produced many good results in the affairs of the east, but he had been blind to the problems that Judaism provoked (*MH* 473). If indeed the war had been a war to save the peace, insomnia afforded an opportunity regardless for acknowledging Jewish intransigence, for wearily lamenting as he wandered through the camp at night the prospect of a world deprived of Roman leadership and the consequent decline of civilization. He had seen signs of enervation, illiberality, and corruption everywhere. And yet, if Rome were to collapse that was a problem for his successors. The peril of the moment had been his preoccupation (*MH* 476).

With these observations the first section of the war narrative closes. They are patently Yourcenar's inventions, but as so often they are inventions based on elements of the historical tradition. The description of Hadrian as exemplary general in the Latin life is evidently at work in the passage on physical decline (*HA Hadr.* 10).[97] The desperate logistical difficulties faced by the Roman army during the siege of Bethar recreate the circumstances that presumably had controlled Cassius Dio's report of Hadrian's inability to give the senate in Rome the conventional assurance that all was well with the army. (It follows the succinct statement that many Romans had died in the war.)

His self-recrimination for having failed to learn more of Jewish cultural particularity reminds of the essentially antagonistic character of his questions in the rabbinical texts to Jewish sages, as well as of his reputation in the Latin life for intellectual argumentativeness (*HA Hadr.* 15.11–13). And his fatalistic prediction of Rome's decline, leaving his own age to be remembered as an Age of Gold, draws on the familiar coin legend to which such great importance was attached (*MH* 475). Yourcenar confessed, in a letter of August 1968 to Lidia Storoni Mazzolani, that this prediction was the most hypothetical and audacious item to be found in *Mémoires* – there was no proof that Hadrian had ever entertained thoughts of this kind – but she believed that it was justified by what could be detected in the mindset ("l'esprit") of certain contemporary philosophers (*L* 291); and she continued to assure later interviewers that Hadrian had come to realize during the war that his earlier successes would not last, that all his earlier optimism had given way to discouragement.[98]

The episode's second section opens in the same self-absorbed, melancholic mode. Hadrian recalls his fear-inducing awareness of a string of physical symptoms – incipient chest pains, an insomnia now chronic, headaches, fatigue, trembling limbs – and then the culmination of his fears: first an unstoppable nosebleed resulting in a near-death experience (lengthily described), and soon afterwards an apparent heart attack, an agonizing, terror-laden event experienced one evening while riding:

L'espace d'une seconde, je sentis les battements de mon cœur se précipiter, puis se ralentir, s'interrompre, cesser; je crus tomber comme une pierre dans je ne sais quel puits noir qui est sans doute la mort. Si c'était bien elle, on se trompe quand on la prétend silencieuse: j'étais emporté par des cataractes, assourdi comme un plongeur par le grondement des eaux. Je n'atteignis pas le fond; je remontai à la surface; je suffoquais. Toute ma force, dans ce moment que j'avais cru le dernier, s'était concentrée dans ma main crispée sur le bras de Céler debout à mon côté: il me montra plus tard les marques de mes doigts sur son épaule. (*MH* 477–8)

For the space of a second I felt my heartbeats quicken, then slow down, falter, and cease; I seemed to fall like a stone into some black well which is doubtless death. If death it was, it is a mistake to call it silent: I was swept down by cataracts, and deafened like a diver by the roaring of waters. I did not reach bottom, but came to the surface again, choking for breath. All my strength in that moment, which I thought my last, had been concentrated into my hand as I clutched at Celer, who was standing beside me; he later showed me the marks of my fingers upon his shoulder.

In the sequel, during the long days of indisposition in his tent at Bethar, the weakness of his heart scarcely observable to others, fear had given way first to shame and then to resignation, as Hadrian's mind had become obsessed by indications of decline:

Un silence extraordinaire s'établit autour de ma tente; le camp de Béthar tout entier semblait devenu une chambre de malade. L'huile aromatique qui brûlait aux pieds de mon génie rendait plus lourd encore l'air renfermé sous cette cage de toile; le bruit de forge de mes artères me faisait vaguement penser à l'île des Titans au bord de la nuit. À d'autres moments, ce bruit insupportable devenait celui d'un galop piétinant la terre molle; cet esprit si soigneusement tenu en rênes pendant près de cinquante ans s'évadait; ce grand corps flottait à la dérive; j'acceptais d'être cet homme las qui compte distraitement les étoiles et les losanges de sa couverture. (*MH* 478)

An extraordinary silence reigned round my tent; the entire camp of Bethar seemed to have become a sick room. The aromatic oil which burned below my Genius rendered the close air of this canvas cage heavier still; the pounding of my arteries made me think vaguely of the island of the Titans on the edge of night. At other moments the insufferable noise changed to that of galloping horses thudding down on wet earth; the mind so carefully reined in for nearly fifty years was wandering; the tall body was floating adrift; I resigned myself to be that tired man who absently counted the star-and-diamond pattern of his blanket.

Three months later, however, the tide of war had turned – the siege of Bethar was broken and the rebuilding of Aelia Capitolina resumed – and the crisis of breakdown had resolved itself. A period of convalescence in Sidon restored Hadrian's health and prepared for his return to Italy. Even so, the voyage was undertaken with the pressing knowledge that restraint was now imperative, that a successor had to be chosen: if only to himself, death had become eminently foreseeable (*MH* 479–82).

The psychological profile continues imaginatively in this second instalment, but again the technique is clear. The nosebleed comes from Cassius Dio (69.17.1), although whether the incident belongs to the period of the war is uncertain, since according to the source tradition Hadrian's late years were years marked by illness, with reports emerging of oedema (dropsy) and life-threatening haemorrhage (*HA Hadr.* 23.1, 23.7, 24.1, 24.9, 25.4). Yourcenar embellished these details, assigning to Hadrian's doctor Hermogenes for example a diagnosis of Hadrian's heart condition in Bethar as "un commencement d'hydropisie du cœur" (*MH* 478).[99] She was confident, as she again affirmed to Storoni Mazzolani, that Hadrian first experienced symptoms of heart disease after Antinous's death, and believed on the authority of the art historian Jean Charbonneaux that many of his portraits showed a type of facial puffiness characteristic of those suffering from this problem (*L* 290).[100] What she did not know is that diagonal earlobe creases of the kind easily visible in his portraits are now medically regarded as a sign of coronary artery disease to which persons of a temperament perhaps resembling that of Hadrian are predisposed.[101] Instead Yourcenar relied on her own experience. A brief entry in the *Carnets* suggests that she was herself experiencing a heart problem when writing *Mémoires* that gave insight into, and allowed her to describe as fully as she did, the illness she believed to have afflicted Hadrian during the siege of Bethar (*CNMH* 529).[102] It closely follows the extended passage on the "rules of the game" and is interrupted only by the statement that she had several times consulted doctors for a diagnosis of Hadrian's illness (*CNMH* 529). How serious her problem then was it is difficult to tell. But "vascular weakness and impaired heart muscle function" are medically attested in 1965, and she remarked to Joseph Breitbach in February 1977 that for years she had suffered from a slight cardiac weakness which had allowed her to describe Hadrian's condition (*L* 535) – a self-evident illustration of her belief that it was natural for the novelist to use first-hand knowledge to lend substance to her characters. In 1985, at the age of eighty-two, she was to suffer a heart attack and undergo quintuple coronary bypass surgery.[103] Perhaps therefore the descriptions of Hadrian's physical symptoms, and of his emotional responses as well, do indeed owe something to her own circumstances, permitting on a generous estimate a special display of empathetic imagination. In any case, Hadrian's psychological profile is hardly irresponsibly contrived.

Altogether, the range of Hadrian's emotions evoked through the crisis of the Bar Kokhba war is vast: initial excitement and enthusiasm for a return to military life, resignation, self-torment, and shame when the campaign falters, despair for Rome's future, a morbid obsession with the deterioration of an aging body, fear of impending death, and no more than tempered relief and hope for whatever time may remain after a brutalizing victory. They are emotions comprehensible at any ordinary level of human understanding, derived in this case from Yourcenar's reconstruction from the historical tradition of the course of the war, and validated as inner responses to political and military events by the constancy of human nature her rules of the game require. The Jewish War was won, but at the cost of a failure in policy that, together with the loss of Antinous, had now to be endured uncompromisingly as preparation for life's inexorable end was made. The biographical portrait is both explicable and inherently consistent. It is also compatible with conclusions reached by historians that closely conjoin the public and the personal: "In truth Hadrian could not have been proud of his victory in Judaea. For him the Jewish struggle was a revolt without reason or sense.

It was an attack on his great dream, a personal affront to himself, since he was convinced that for their own sake the Jews in Judaea should be forced to become full members of his Graeco-Roman world."[104] Or again: "Setting himself in studied contrast to his predecessor, Hadrianus Augustus ... advertised peace and concord. Rebellion in Judaea and the measures needed to quell it came as a cruel and sudden disappointment to his aspirations. The effort and the cost was excessive: heavy casualties, and a whole legion, XXII Deiotariana, may now have ceased to exist. Add to that, the failure of the rigorous policy he adopted towards the Jews (Aelia Capitolina and the ban on circumcision) and the blow to the pride of the 'Olympius' who paraded as a philhellenic statesman and cosmopolitan citizen."[105] Consistency of judgment is clear.

Yourcenar's first-person mode of presentation differs of course from that of historians, and doubts concerning emotional equivalence might still remain. Comparison on the flank can be made with an autobiography from late antiquity on which Yourcenar might well have drawn when setting out her rules of the game. Augustine's *Confessions* is a work analogous in both form and psychological range to *Mémoires*, a work in which analysis of emotions is relentless. Allowance must be made for its Christian setting – Chabrias's anxieties about the bishop of Christ have been realized – most glaringly perhaps in its preoccupation with sexual guilt, a perennial Christian fixation as Yourcenar well knew (*YO* 77). But in this "manifesto of the inner world," there is a fascination with emotions that are far from foreign to readers of Hadrian's memoirs. Remorse attributable to a childhood indiscretion, tear-laden grief at the premature death of a close friend, turmoil induced by religious confusion – these are only the most obvious illustrations of the intense interior history Augustine's confessional narrative unfolds with which the modern reader might readily identify. The fascination makes itself especially apparent in the complex questions raised of how it was that the viewer of a tragedy in the theatre experienced pleasure in the depiction of pain, while not wanting directly to experience pain himself, of how sympathy the spectator felt for fictionally presented suffering could be genuine, and of why admiration for a tragic author was controlled by the extent to which, through illusion, the author elicited an emotional response from his audience. English or French equivalents of such Latin terms as *dolor*, *voluptas*, and *misericordia*, the terms that underlie these questions, can be approximations only; but the questions themselves are comprehensible and the emotions on which they depend easily recognizable as, in Yourcenarian terms, human absolutes. Any suspicion that Hadrian's emotions are too glibly or uncritically evoked is countered by the autobiography of a man who confessed himself capable, like an epic hero, of breaking down at any moment in a flood of tears.[106]

VII

For the third time, the chief difficulty with which Yourcenar was confronted in composing an account of the critical Bar Kokhba war was the meagre amount of information that remains in classical sources. Her response was not quite to privilege, but to pay special attention to, a wealth of material preserved in Jewish rabbinical literature from which various additional details could be gathered. Most of the material concerned is legendary, its chief value lying in its preservation of memories of deep division within the Jewish constituency of the Imperial age, and of a profound hatred long felt for Hadrian himself. It also reinforces the fundamental distinctiveness of a culture that flowed from a monotheistic "otherness" of isolation in a polytheistic Mediterranean world. To the biographical novelist, nonetheless, the material offered a rich palette from which to add colour to the classical outline of the war, and to enhance thereby the portrait of her biographical subject. As she proceeded, however, Yourcenar set aside Renan's view that Hadrian directed the war from Athens, and chose to have him actively engaged in its operations. The decision was an exercise of judgment of a sort that every historian has at times to make, but in doing so Yourcenar had to know that her reconstruction was contestable. A half-century and more on, this is truer than ever. Much of her narrative is now impossible to accept at all. Prosaic matters of chronology obtrude.

The item of the senatorial despatch apart, there is strong circumstantial evidence that Hadrian took part in the war. It comes from certain Latin inscriptions that refer to the war as an *expeditio*, a term used of a military action in which by general consensus the emperor is understood to have personally participated. This therefore was the *expeditio Iudaica*, as known for instance from a North African inscription recording that Q. Lollius Urbicus (*cos* c. 136) was a legate of Hadrian and was decorated for his service "in the Jewish expedition" (*in expedition[e] Iudaica*).[107] Even so, the amount of time Hadrian spent at the warfront can have been no more than minimal. Since 129, he had incorporated the title of proconsul in his formal titulature, which indicated that he was abroad in the provinces, given that the title could not be held when the emperor was resident in Italy. Hadrian spent the winter of 131/132 in Athens, and a document of 9 December 132 shows from its inclusion of the proconsular office that he was still abroad at that time. The

document concerned is a military diploma of a common type that awarded
Roman citizenship to veteran auxiliary troops. In a diploma of 8 April 133,
however, the title of proconsul is absent, which means that Hadrian had by
then returned to Italy.[108] By 10 December 132 he was indeed in Macedonia,
apparently en route to Illyricum and Italy, to judge from the document, seen
earlier, that records the edict Hadrian passed providing relief to the cities of
Maroneia and Abdera. It appears, therefore, that he had left the warfront by
whatever amount of time was needed to travel from Judaea to Maroneia.[109]
As seen at the beginning, estimates of when the Jewish revolt began vary
between mid- and late 132. If consequently Hadrian left Athens for Judaea as
soon as, or soon after, the Jewish emergency arose, his presence in the theatre
of operations can have lasted no more than a few weeks or months at most
before his departure for Italy in the winter of 132/133. There is no question that he was in Italy well before the war ended. In a document of 5 May
134 sent from Rome, he promised the Gymnastic Synod of Athletes, Sacred
Victors and Crown-Wearers Devoted to Heracles a site and building in the
capital to house the synod's records.[110] Some months later, in August and
September, he attended a celebration of the *Italica Romaea Sebasta Isolym-
pia*, the Greek games established long ago to honour Augustus in Naples.[111]
These details were not all known when Yourcenar wrote *Mémoires* because
the materials from which they result have mostly come to light since (and
recently). They mean, however, that her construction of a two-year stay in
Judaea until the conclusion of the war has to be discarded. (And any number
of historians' accounts have likewise to be set aside.)[112] She followed, I think,
and predictably, the chronology of Weber, who had placed Hadrian in the east
between 130 and 132, then returned him to Rome before having him depart
for Judaea in the summer of 134 as the military situation deteriorated, keeping him there into the following year.[113] Clearly this can no longer be right.
Hadrian cannot have witnessed the fall of Bethar or experienced there the
agonizing turmoil Yourcenar attributed to him. Nor can he have been presented with the decapitated head of Bar Kokhba.[114] To her literary followers
this may bring disappointment; but whether the crisis should altogether be
discarded is another matter.

During the festival of 134 at Naples, Hadrian dealt with a number of issues
raised by delegates from cities in the Greek east, representatives of the Gymnastic Synod of Athletes included. They concerned abusive habits on the part
of city officials in defrauding athletes of their prize moneys. He also set out
an elaborate schedule for the future holding of the major athletic and musical competitions across the empire in which athletes were to compete. The
business required a considerable amount of communication with provincial
governors and city populations, and the decisions reached were substantial

enough for Hadrian to suggest that they be publicly displayed. One example speaks to the maintenance of discipline among the athletes when games were being held and seems to convey his personal voice particularly well:

If it should be necessary to whip a contestant, let there be whip-bearers chosen by lot for the purpose, and let them approach in pairs in whatever order they may happen to have been allotted, first or second, and if necessary third. For there must be some deterrent hanging over the contestants and those who err must be corrected, but not so that they are beaten by many persons at once, and only on their legs, and so that no-one be crippled or incur any injury from which he will be worse at his profession itself.[115]

Hadrian's decisions are known from three letters written to the Synod of Athletes that are inscribed on a well-preserved inscription from Alexandria Troas discovered in 2003.[116] The marble plaque on which the letters are recorded was presumably erected in accordance with Hadrian's suggestion. In the titulature with which they open, there is notably no indication that Hadrian had as yet received his second imperatorial salutation. Evidence of that award first appears only a year and more later.[117] It follows that in the late summer of 134 the war in Judaea was still in progress, and that his presence in Naples notwithstanding, Hadrian cannot then have been altogether free from the concerns generated by an as yet unresolved military crisis. Wherever Hadrian found himself, the war was no less serious a problem, and the distress Yourcenar imagined it caused no less natural an emotional response. In saying which, my intent is not to make a straw-clutching attempt to redeem Yourcenar's text from complete rejection. As I have said, her account of Hadrian's full engagement in the events of the war cannot be taken at face value. Yet as far as can be told, she recreated as plausible an account as possible from the information available to her at the time of writing, and one that in her mind was historically valid. The ultimate tragedy of the Bar Kokhba war, as she explained to Matthieu Galey, was that the man of peace, that long peace once foreseen by the Sibyl, was compelled regardless to fight a war late in his reign that flowed from an eternal conflict between two irreconcilable cultures (YO 160).[118] The insight has an inherent authority, and to this extent Yourcenar's construction of the crisis Hadrian endured, in harmony with the psychologizing reflections from historians I quoted a moment ago, may stand as an authentic feature of the historical personality she sought in her poetic manner to bring to life at one juncture of his reign. Fictive, yes; fictional, no.

8

Rise and Fall

The past could not be changed ... Everyone had his own share of memory to live with.

Martha Gellhorn

I

The three episodes of crisis Yourcenar detected and recovered in Hadrian's life are prime examples of second-order authenticity in *Mémoires*. Since they combine the subject's inner responses to the record of external events they are also prime illustrations of how *Mémoires* meets the requirements of true biography. The importance Yourcenar attached to them was great. This is what she said of the *fléchissements* in an all-embracing statement made some twenty years after *Mémoires'* publication to Patrick de Rosbo:[1]

After the long ascent from the post of tribune to that of governor of Syria and of being "second man in Rome," the first crisis comes with the preparations for the Parthian campaign. Hadrian has no guarantee that Trajan will make him his heir; he feels threatened by the leaders of the military faction, and he knows that he risks being supplanted by them. This excellent officer, aware of the dangers this new war of conquest poses, and alert to the absurdity of plans that while carefully outlined cannot, by definition, foresee every eventuality, prefers peaceful solutions. (Such are the plans of generals and high commands in every age.) He knows the Orient better than Trajan, he is better informed on the real state of opinion and of finances, and he calculates that one of those great expeditions is being launched, like those of Napoleon and Hitler will later be launched into Russia, from which there is a risk of no return. Impotent, confined within his palace at Antioch, receiving news he knows in advance has been censored, not knowing if he will ever succeed to the emperorship and be able to impose his peace program, Hadrian suffers a period of true and utter dejection, from which he's rescued by the death of Trajan and the intervention of Plotina, who somehow installs him as successor. But at this time, and for the first time in his life, he felt his powers fail.

The second setback is due to despair of an intimate character. Once emperor Hadrian had a brilliant career ... In these years he met Antinous, who became not merely the sensual object of preference but the very image of what Hadrian calls his happiness, in the word's almost religious sense, his "Genius." In this adoration of a human being, he forgot the human being himself: a young man distressed by the prospect of a fading passion, of being one day relegated, soon perhaps, to the rank of discarded favourites, and who, trapped in the net of court intrigues, finally takes refuge in a mysticism not at all unusual in Hadrian's entourage and decides to sacrifice his life for the emperor's safety and future. When Hadrian finds himself face to face with this suicide, an act of despair and possession, he completely falls apart. For the first time he finds himself confronting the death of someone he loves, a death for which he is chiefly responsible; and to the horror of loss, the horror of the irreversible and irreparable, is added the horror of neither having foreseen, nor understood, nor known – his intellect notwithstanding – how to control a situation that has unfolded before his eyes. The breakdown is total. For several pages, we see Hadrian crossing what Zeno will later call "his abyss"; that is to say that life appears to him in its true colours, and it is worthless. He comes out of this crisis slowly, sustained by his imperial duties; he resumes work, somewhat battered by life, rather more abandoned to his whims, to his momentary irritations and, as he says himself, feeling that Antinous's sacrifice, if indeed it was a sacrifice, will in the end have "damaged more than saved" him.

The third crisis is entirely of a political character. Hadrian finds himself faced with the rebellion in Palestine as if before an impassable abyss. As friends he has rabbis who know Greek and are, like him, men of letters, and liberal Jews have invested much hope in his reign. But, on the other side, there are the Zealots, the implacable Jews, the terrorist group Hadrian does not understand. He is incapable of admitting (and here it must be said that he is to some extent naive and blind) that these people do not want the benefits of Greco-Roman civilization. When rebellion erupts, it becomes an atrocious guerrilla war that lasts three years, and for the first time Hadrian, in his camp in Palestine, facing the fortress of Bethar where his final opponents have taken refuge as they refuse to surrender, understands that to establish peace is unfortunately not so easy a task, that the world is constantly threatened by war and civilization by death.

At this point Yourcenar asked de Rosbo to read the passage where Hadrian at Bethar expatiates on the decline of Rome that in his state of total discouragement now seems unavoidable.[2] Reference followed to the subsequent onset of illness, Hadrian's resort in his last years to *patientia,* and the blend of moderate optimism and lucid despair with which he finally meets his fate (*ER* 109–11). Throughout the statement, Yourcenar drew no distinction between the Hadrian of her novel and the historical Hadrian. To her they were inarguably one and the same. It did not matter that her summary conjoined with the historical tradition knowledge of events from later history unknowable to the real Hadrian, that it introduced comparison with a fictional character non-existent when *Mémoires* was composed, or that it included personal intrusions from Yourcenar herself. At a remove of twenty years, the biographical truth as Yourcenar conceived it, including the emotional truth with its "fidelity to human experience," was securely established.[3] In this, a trajectory of a rise and fall is evident, a progression by no means exceptional in and of itself, but one that allowed Yourcenar to express the singularity and complexity of her subject's life through the framework of the three dominant crises. The consequence is a developmental portrait of Hadrian of a kind alien to academic imperial biography, the certitude Yourcenar's statement embodies compounding further the issue of "fidelity to facts."[4] I now discuss accordingly the criticisms made of *Mémoires* by Yourcenar's most eminent critic, and speculate, unreservedly, on what her reaction to them might have been. This in turn leads to consideration of Yourcenar's essay, *Les Visages de l'histoire dans l'«Histoire auguste»,* which she first published in June 1959 and later included in the collection *Sous bénéfice d'inventaire* of 1962. Well-known to Yourcenarian scholars but less so to Romanists, it is a document in which the theme of rise and fall is likewise prominent. The intent in both aspects is to contribute further to the aim of understanding the novel.

II

On Thursday, 22 January 1981, Marguerite Yourcenar was received into the Académie française. She succeeded to the chair of Roger Caillois that had earlier still been occupied by Jérôme Carcopino. In his address of welcome, Jean d'Ormesson spoke of the difficult gestation of *Mémoires* and paid tribute to the "longues recherches" that formed its underpinning. The scholarly resources he itemized as evidence could all have been, and perhaps were, taken from Yourcenar's *Note.* But he alluded also to a body of work that for obvious reasons the *Note* could not include, namely the studies Ronald Syme had devoted in the 1960s and early 1970s to consolidating Hermann Dessau's theory of the *Historia Augusta*'s date and authorship.[5] The allusion, I imagine, was due to d'Ormesson's long association with, and admiration of, Syme, since they had served together for many years as members of the Conseil international de la philosophie et des sciences humaines, an organization housed in Paris that was founded by the United Nations in 1949: d'Ormesson was a leading figure in its formation and Syme became its Secretary-General in 1952.[6] The reference is particularly striking, however, because Syme's name never appears in Yourcenar's writings, which is something of a surprise given Syme's academic eminence. His most celebrated book, *The Roman Revolution* (1939), describing and explaining the rise to power of Rome's first emperor Augustus, was not immediately relevant to *Mémoires* and this may be enough to account for his absence from Yourcenar's *Note*.[7] But much of his later scholarship, especially the landmark *Tacitus* of 1958, was relevant after the event, and in view of her many commentaries on *Mémoires*, her sustained interest in Hadrian himself, and her continued classical reading beyond 1951, some awareness of his work might have been expected. He seems to have remained unknown, however, and among the many references in Yourcenar's correspondence to her classical books and interactions with classical scholars, his name cannot be found. Her library at Petite Plaisance contains nothing from him.

More surprisingly still, Yourcenar never came to learn, as far as I can discover, of a lecture Syme gave in Oxford some years after her reception in which he catalogued what he regarded as a series of historical blunders in *Mémoires* and warned against its being read as historically trustworthy. The lecture, a James Bryce Memorial lecture delivered at Somerville College on 10 May 1984, was called "Fictional History: Old and New: Hadrian." It was published as a pamphlet in 1986 and is now reprinted in the sixth volume of his *Roman Papers*. Its effect was, and remains, to ridicule both the novel and its author.

As stated at the outset, Hadrian was a figure of abiding interest to Syme. He proposed at one stage that Tacitus's history of the Julio-Claudian emperors contains covert and critical allusions to political events from the early years of the reign, including the murder of the four consulars considered enemies of the new regime. He suggested also that the model for Tacitus's notoriously damning and subversive portrait of Augustus's first successor, the tyrannical Tiberius, was not the last Flavian emperor Domitian, as usually thought, but the new despot Hadrian.[8] In turn, his many topical studies concerned the dates and itineraries of Hadrian's provincial journeys, his relationships with individual cities, the personnel involved in government and administration, and the recruitment of new members of the Roman senate: Spaniards, like Hadrian himself, or Africans, like Suetonius. Often intricate and technical, marked by rigour and precision in matters of chronology and topography, they typify the prosopographical methodology with which Syme is most identified.[9] Interest in other aspects of Hadrian's life, however, was limited. Hadrian as sponsor of new buildings, the Villa included, was of no interest, nor was the relationship with Antinous, a subject Syme addressed only in language oblique and euphemistic, ascribing Hadrian's "infatuation" merely to the emperor's "proclivities" and "habits."[10] On Hadrian and religion likewise little was offered. Syme was, recall, keenly interested in Hadrian's personality, despite the grand pronouncement that "in the end, human personality is a mystery." Above all, however, it was "the power" that appealed to him, the absolute power of an autocrat.[11]

Its biographical character, consequently, was an immediate reason for Syme's suspicion of *Mémoires*; the faults of the genre were all too plain: "Birth to death, the order of events is laid down in advance, with few problems of arrangement or structure. Most of the hard work has been done already – and predecessors can be looted."[12] The novel's style was generously applauded – "[t]he book would stand by its own quality as an imaginative evocation: duly acclaimed and admired, not least for grace and power of style, fluent and vivid, yet severe and classic – and archaic. Never a word or expression to betray the middle years of the twentieth century" – but this was not enough to redeem *Mémoires*: the *politesse* of the stylistic compliment was no more than a screen to soften the harshness of the assault the lecture made as a whole, for at its core is a roster of errors and misconceptions in the work.[13] They are complemented by indications of misprision from earlier scholars that allowed Yourcenar's occasional historical superiority to be acknowledged, but this careful concession scarcely softened the blow. The scholars concerned were men for whom Syme had little sympathy: Henderson, Carcopino (Yourcenar's erstwhile predecessor in the Académie), and least of all Wilhelm Weber. The result was to condemn with faint praise.[14]

The catalogue is preceded by Syme's exposition of the "fictional history" of his lecture's title, a form of writing about the past distinct from historical fiction characterized by its author's intention to deceive. The prime example is the *Historia Augusta*, the contrivance of an impostor and a work of whose problematical nature Syme believed Yourcenar to be ignorant. Her *Note* provided the evidence. Unlike a writer of historical fiction, in which accuracy of detail was unnecessary, she claimed to be writing with "fidélité aux faits," but in a key passage on the literary sources for Hadrian's life she took the author of the biography of Hadrian (as that of Aelius Caesar) to be Spartianus and accepted its ostensible date of composition, unaware of the *Historia Augusta*'s assignment to the late fourth century and its authorship by a rogue biographer. Which meant that she had taken certain details from the life that an expert could show had no historical purchase. At the heart of the lecture, therefore, was Syme's fixation with the *Historia Augusta*, and his conclusion, severe and damning, was inevitable. *Mémoires* was a duplicitous work from an author who was herself an impostor.

What then were the problems? A representative list follows, given for the sake of clarity and convenience in summary form.

1. *Family Matters*.
   (a) Hadrian was born in Rome, not Italica (the *Historia Augusta* is credible on this point); Hadrian therefore was not raised in Spain.
   (b) The Marullinus portrayed as his grandfather was his great-grandfather (the Latin life again), and he is conflated on astrological matters with a paternal great-uncle.
   (c) The governorship of Africa allotted to Hadrian's senatorial father, Aelius Afer, is an example of excessive embellishment; likewise the unsubstantiated literary tastes of another great-uncle, Aelius (said to have been hostile to everything written after the age of Augustus), and the fanciful description of Hadrian's mother: a woman from Gades with tiny feet and the swaying hips of a dancing girl.
   (d) Since Julius Servianus was probably aged forty-two when he married Domitia Paulina, he cannot be called an old man; the alleged Spanish origin of Sabina is unattested.
   (e) Long-standing antipathy between Hadrian and Trajan can be accepted, but not the rate of progress of Hadrian's pre-imperial career, or Plotina's promotion of his marriage (a notion attributable to the unreliable Marius Maximus); Hadrian was twenty-four, not twenty-eight, when he married Sabina.
   (f) Hadrian's characterization of Plotina as "le plus sage de mes bons génies" is admissible; yet "nothing is known about the other 'bons génies.'"
   (g) Pestilence is a likelier cause of death for Pedanius Fuscus and his wife Julia than consumption.[15]
2. *Travel and Chronology*.
   (a) Two pre-imperial journeys are inventions: one to Greece when Hadrian was sixteen to study with the sophist Isaeus, the other a winter excursion on the upper Danube between two periods of military service; a third journey, to inspect his family's copper mines in Spain after his consulship, in 108, exaggerates his economic perceptiveness.
   (b) Yourcenar is "a little unsatisfactory" on the chronology of the major provincial journeys Hadrian made (and on geography throughout); to place him in London for the winter of 122/123 is offset by the evidence for Tarraco in Spain in the (again) reliable Latin life.
   (c) In contrast, the biography is unreliable for the nonetheless appealing distaste for the people of Antioch attributed to Hadrian.

(d) Suetonius's dismissal from Hadrian's service is set in Rome; but on the assumption that the secretary *ab epistulis* normally travelled with the emperor, the *Historia Augusta* seemingly situates the event in Britain; the inference that Suetonius subsequently became an opponent of Hadrian is false.

(e) To suppose that Hadrian exiled Juvenal to Egypt as a result of personal disinclination is to succumb to "the biographical fallacy": Hadrian may have found him "congenial company" when visiting Egypt.

(f) The first meeting between Hadrian and Antinous is placed towards the end of the first great journey; a date four or five years later during the second journey is preferable.[16]

3. *Other Issues.*

(a) How is Hadrian's surprising choice of L. Ceionius Commodus – Lucius Aelius Caesar as he became – as his successor to be explained? Yourcenar commendably avoided Carcopino's specious theory that the young man was Hadrian's illegitimate son; but she missed the value of the choice for reconciling the families involved: the stepson and son-in-law of C. Avidius Nigrinus, a former friend long since executed for treason, was brought to the forefront of imperial politics.

(b) She was equally unaware of the entry to the senate of Greeks from Asia Minor.

(c) She wisely avoided developing the tradition that Hadrian was an expert astrologer (traceable to Marius Maximus in the Latin life and the heavily fictional life of Aelius Caesar), but seriously underestimated Plotina's commitment to Epicureanism and the philosophical bond shared with Hadrian; she did not know the inscriptional evidence on Plotina's involvement in the choice of a new leader of the Epicurean school at Athens.[17]

Further objections were raised indirectly. But the final verdict on the book is crystal clear. "In view of the plethora of fabrications, it 'fails to satisfy or to silence our reason.'" It is "a masterpiece of fictional history," and because fictional history is a "perversion," its author must be deemed a successor to its ancient fraudulent practitioners.[18] In this, Yourcenar's name was crucially significant: "Not her real name, and the lady, Belgian by birth, was an American citizen, and is now a member of the French Academy."[19] Discovery of the pseudonym, together with a smattering of biographical details, provided proof of a spurious identity, and of imposture.

In 1984 Yourcenar and Syme were in their eighties and by 1991 both had died: Yourcenar in 1987, Syme in 1989. There was little time therefore for Yourcenar to have learned of the Bryce lecture. Had she done so, it can hardly be doubted that she would have offered a vigorous response, as on previous occasions. If so, I suspect that she would have begun by immediately admitting Syme to the company of Molière's buffoons, "Les Blazius et les Vadius," but perhaps allowing at the same time that some of his criticisms were defensible in view of the technical problems the *Historia Augusta* raised, and even agreeing that there was a certain risk in adding *Mémoires* to scholarly bibliographies.[20] Equally, however, she can be presumed to have carefully scrutinized the indictment and to have countered the various charges, motivated by her dictum of long standing: "Il faut toujours lutter." What might she have said in reply?

First, I imagine, a rejoinder concerning her name. Throughout her adult life, Yourcenar was unquestionably concerned to manage and marshal her public image, not least with an eye to posterity. Her principal biographer has described her indeed as "a singular fictional character" who "ceaselessly remade, relived, [and] reconstructed her past." Yet the basic facts are irrefutable: Marguerite de Crayencour was of French ancestry and took Yourcenar first as a nom de plume and then as her legal name when she became an American citizen in 1947. On occasion she referred to her adoption of a pseudonym. But the allegation that she purposely set out to write a false account of Hadrian's life because she did not write under her birth name stretches every limit of belief. Anyone familiar with the personal details given in the *Chronologie* of the Pléiade or in *Les Yeux ouverts* could see at once see the absurdity of the proposition. The Tacitean technique of arranging materials to consist with a preconceived conclusion is self-evident.[21]

Yourcenar would certainly have noticed right away that Syme's quotations from her book were taken from the Plon edition of 1951, not the Pléiade of 1982. Which means that Syme was unaware of her subsequent revisions of, and additions to, her text, and of her expansion over time of the *Note*. This he called "an appendix of nine pages," correctly for the edition of 1951. In the second Plon edition of 1958, however, the *Note* had grown to eighteen pages; in the English version of 1954 from Farrar, Straus and Young it took up fifteen pages; and in the Pléiade it occupies thirteen pages of very small print.[22] For the same reason Syme did not know the *Carnets*, first published independently in 1952 and then included with *Mémoires* in the limited Le Club edition of 1953, and from 1958 in editions more widely, the English translation included; consequently he took no account, and could not inform his audience, of the methods and procedures Yourcenar described there, especially the essential entry on "Les règles du jeu." Nor did he know the *Chronologie* and the details it gave of the history of Yourcenar's name – though why he had not disclosed those details from his reading of *Les Yeux ouverts*, noted in the published lecture as a biographical source, was an obvious question to pose.[23] He could not be expected to have had recourse to Yourcenar's *Notebook* and her correspondence, one result being that he knew nothing of the amendments to the novel made in her earlier response to Picard, whose caustic review he cited, or of such items as Yourcenar's lists of developed scenes and omitted facts. He recognized that Yourcenar had explained in the original *Note* where she had altered what she took to be the historical record for reasons of compositional expediency. But altogether, the assault was based on imperfect evidence and by default it seriously misled his audience. The printed text continues to mislead, with the caricature it creates leading to unwitting advertisement of Yourcenar's inadequacies.[24]

The treatment of Hadrian's forebear Marullinus serves to illustrate the unnoticed changes Yourcenar made to her text over time. In the *Notebook*'s list just mentioned, the relevant entry states that history gives us the name of Hadrian's grandfather, his position and rank, and informs us that he was involved with magic and had predicted empire for his grandson. The rest of his characterization, it continues, is deduced from these few facts, and from what we know in general of public and private life in Spain of the second century. For the *Note* of 1951, this was apparently boiled down as follows: "Le personnage de Marullinus est historique; les circonstances de sa mort sont imaginaires." ("The character of Marullinus is historical; the circumstances of his death are imaginary.") In the Pléiade, however, this has become: "Le personnage de Marullinus est historique, mais sa caractéristique principale, le don divinatoire, est empruntée à un oncle et non à un grand-père d'Hadrien; les circonstances de sa mort sont imaginaires." ("The character of Marullinus is historical, but his chief characteristic, the gift of divination, is based on an uncle of Hadrian and not on a grandfather; the circumstances of his death are imaginary.") In between, this is the entry in the English version: "The character Marullinus is built upon a name, that of an ancestor of Hadrian, and upon a tradition which says that an uncle (and not the grandfather) of the future emperor foretold the boy's fortune; the portrait of the old man and the circumstances of his death are imaginary."[25] This may well be a case where, I suspect, there was real confusion from the outset that was never fully overcome. But that is not the point. Revisions of this sort made to succeeding editions of the *Note*, like the many corrections periodically made to the main text, were meant to promote accuracy, not to misinform readers. And while embellishments such as Acilius Attianus's unattested sick wife and married daughters (with children), or a contrived episode between Hadrian and a former mistress might elicit a positivist's annoyance, they hardly justify equating Yourcenar with Syme's putative rogue biographer, a figure, recall, for whom no hard evidence exists.[26] Offsetting account needs to be taken of the remarks in the *Carnets* on the difficulty of seeing principal characters such as Plotina and Suetonius other than at an angle (*CNMH* 531), and of reliance on historians consulted in good faith. In 1934, Paul Graindor for instance had thought that a young Hadrian did indeed study with Isaeus in Athens, on the basis of epigraphical evidence of poems written by a descendant named Glaucus of Marathon. He was clearly Yourcenar's source.[27] Everything Syme said, however, depended on the assumption that his views of the *Historia Augusta* were unassailably correct. There could be no question, therefore, that Hadrian was born in Rome because the Latin life of Hadrian was beyond reproach on this point. If "inferior compilers in late antiquity" said otherwise, they were wrong.[28] It was of no concern that the source's reliability depended on an unverifiable hypothesis about its derivation. Nor did it seem worth mention that Yourcenar's picture of Hadrian's career under Trajan was, as it happens, consistent with the "long period as crown prince" Syme posited: Hadrian for Yourcenar advanced to the full possession of power slowly and deliberately.[29]

Yourcenar might also have remarked that the critique relies on other verities not quite as veracious as they initially seem. Syme attributed the dearth of reliable material about Hadrian in the *Historia Augusta* to "concealment" of the truth on the part of those in positions of power: "governments and their agents."[30] Yet how this reality was known, and who the agents were, he did not explain. Of Hadrian as "crown prince" he wrote: "The ambiguous role taught duplicity and hardened the character." As perhaps it did. And again it happens to consist with Yourcenar's view. But why it is true is unstated except for a daring supposition: "No autocrat smiles upon his successor – unless he happens to be a small boy."[31] Assurance extends to the emperor's personality: "By normal habit, Hadrian was serene and tolerant." To which an impartial reader might well react by asking how Hadrian's "normal habit" can ever be known when the historical record is so inadequate, and, similarly, why the confident sequel of the "fact" of his place of birth can be believed: "Hadrian became a 'Graeculus' in Rome under Domitian."[32] It is taken for granted, moreover, that an "official version" of events was a staple of Roman Imperial politics, as in the matter of Hadrian's adoption by the dying Trajan – Trajan was already in fact dead: the truth can be learned from Cassius Dio because Dio's father told Dio the facts – but on what foundation of evidence for officialdom is unclear.[33] In reality, much tends to the fictional: Pedanius Fuscus and his wife dying from pestilence, Juvenal joining Hadrian's entourage on a journey to Egypt, Lucius Aelius as heir remedying political mistakes of the past, and Hadrian meeting Antinous later than sooner; or, on a dispassionate estimate, the fictive.[34] Admittedly, such possibilities and others like them could be acknowledged as the soberly formed opinions of an authoritative and deeply experienced historian, with a distinction drawn between the historian's "rational conjecture" and a novelist's "constructive fiction," even if history at times has to rely on invention; and the conjectures of a great historian who had thought long and hard about the past, who commanded a masterful knowledge of literary and epigraphical evidence, and who was motivated to recreate the past accurately, must take precedence over those of an imaginative writer. So it has been urged.[35] Yet as I noted in an earlier chapter, "rational conjecture" is a far from secure means by which to reveal truth: what seems rational to one may seem quite irrational to another, with conjecture easily outrunning both truth and likelihood. In any case, given the inventiveness required historians and novelists could easily be equated, both becoming "fabricators and creators of illusion."[36]

Syme was relatively generous in noting that some of *Mémoires'* defects could be excused because of what he rightly called the book's "impressionistic" character.[37] He was not obliged to emphasize that the novel is conceptualized and constructed as a set of memories, with all the liabilities memory brings – its propensity as a vital force to discard some recollections altogether, to fuse others into a jumble, to distort them in the remembering, and with age, so that they never resemble a neatly preserved collection of documents (*QE* 1383–4; *AN* 1087) – nor did he have to observe that as an epistolary novel *Mémoires* is cast in the form most apposite for expressing, and exploiting, private thoughts and intimate feelings.[38] Yet Yourcenar could justifiably have pointed to his decision, when seizing on the crucial phrase, not to draw his audience's attention to the full content of the *Note*'s opening sentence, which even in the version of 1951 made clear that while the "valeur humaine" of her portrait was increased by its fidelity to facts, in the first instance it was a reconstitution that "touche par certains côtés au roman et par d'autres à la poésie" (*OR* 543). Despite an early pronouncement, "history, indeed, is a form of poetry," the poetic dimension of *Mémoires* was altogether overlooked and the sole impression conveyed that Yourcenar claimed to have written a factually accurate narrative throughout. Mischaracterization of the book was a necessary consequence, all the more so given the vitally important, but unknown, epigram on intent from the *Carnets*: "Refaire du dedans ce que les archéologues du XIXe siècle ont fait du dehors."[39] Recourse to the principal biography would have revealed a statement stressing the novel's concentration on Hadrian's inner life, and pointing to the licence the chosen medium permitted:

Fiction et réalité tendent, au moins en ce qui me concerne, à former dans le roman une combinaison si homogène qu'il devient rapidement impossible à l'auteur de les séparer l'une de l'autre, si solide qu'il n'est pas plus possible au romancier d'altérer un fait fictif qu'un fait réel sans le fausser ou sans en détruire l'authenticité. Il me serait assurément possible, dans les *Mémoires d'Hadrien*, de distinguer la part de fiction de la part de réalité, mais c'est qu'Hadrien n'est pas un roman proprement dit, mais une méditation ou un récit placé à la limite de l'histoire.

Fiction and reality tend, at least where I am concerned, to form in a novel a combination so homogeneous that it rapidly becomes impossible for the author to separate them one from the other, so solid that it is no more possible for the novelist to alter a fictional fact than a real fact without distorting it or without destroying its authenticity. It would certainly be possible for me, in *Memoirs of Hadrian*, to distinguish the part played by fiction from the part played by reality, but that's because Hadrian is not, strictly speaking, a novel, but a meditation or a narrative situated on the limit of history.[40]

Rather more, that is, was involved in the creation of *Mémoires* than Anglo-Saxon empiricism. In which connection, Syme's declaration on history and the novel with regard to the much admired Proust is striking: "les deux genres ont plusieurs points de contact, ils peuvent s'illuminer réciproquement, et même se faire fructifier."[41] And perhaps more quizzically still, contemporary readers who find themselves beguiled by a mesmerizing style might well be surprised to learn that Syme had much in common with Yourcenar. By which I mean that his views of human behaviour were both as presumptive as, and analogous to, those of Yourcenar. Although he gave no methodological summary of the rules of the game as she had done, the Gibbonesque seasoning of aphorisms that typify his writing is enough to prove a belief in the immanence of human nature more or less identical to that of Yourcenar. It is an element that betrays an essentially Tacitean posture, ironic and sceptical, and one of the compositional devices that made Syme a magnificent stylist and literary figure in his own right, with everything written in a distinctively majestic and imperious manner unique in modern ancient history. It is also a feature that allies him with "the illustrious lady."[42] Rhetorical flourishes of this kind leave no doubt: "In any age it is incumbent on an autocrat to hold a balance between rival groups and factions in his entourage"; "In any age advisers and ministers, sometimes peculiar or even sinister, lurk unobtrusive in the precincts of secret power"; "In any age immoral behaviour is suitably adduced to enhance, or to cover up, offences of another order."[43] Their connection to political history is obvious. But that in no way detracts from their underlying presumption that in all comparable conditions human behaviour is predictable due to the constancy of human nature over time and place, just as Yourcenar had maintained. Commonality extended, moreover, to historical interpretation. Syme intuited that Trajan's Parthian war was motivated by ambition and anger, his reluctance to designate a successor by his stubborn pride and arrogance: in "character and tastes," he declared, Trajan found Hadrian "far from congenial," and resorting once more to the universal he affirmed that "an autocrat is seldom at ease with a predictable heir." As for the critical transfer of power, "it does not pass belief that a resolute and sagacious woman, aided by the Prefect of the Guard, took the necessary measures entailed by the Emperor's decease."[44] The range of ordinary human emotions on display is self-evidently Yourcenarian. And the modern upshot, a verdict on General de Gaulle, is one with which she would readily have concurred: "an epitome of several Caesars: the decision of the Dictator (and also his pomp and arrogance), the patience and restraint of Augustus, the depth and duplicity of Tiberius." Why the assault should ever have been made is an unsettling question.[45]

For Yourcenarian scholars unfamiliar with the controversies surrounding the *Historia Augusta*, the Bryce lecture is an important, if idiosyncratic, corrective to the easy assumption to be made from her *Note* that Yourcenar's portrait of Hadrian is based on solid historical foundations. Yet strikingly to an outsider it is little known in critical circles. Well into the twenty-first century, critics hardly notice the enigmatic character of the *Historia Augusta* and continue to write of "Spartianus" and his five companions as authors whose existence in antiquity is as assured as that of Virgil or Tacitus.[46] Romanists in turn might find the lecture valuable for the insights it gives into Syme's views of history and for the way it confirms the difficulty of recovering Hadrian when the basic Latin narrative is beset by so many uncertainties. They might also now be alert to its tendentious character. Yet they seldom, if at all, ask what I surely think would have been the final question Yourcenar asked of Syme, which is why he had not introduced his audience to, or even acknowledged the existence of, *Les Visages de l'histoire dans l'«Histoire auguste»*. To have introduced the essay might not have saved Yourcenar from the charge that she was ignorant of the problems inherent in the *Historia Augusta*. But to have done so might have made a difference, raising the question, for instance, of whether the collection of imperial biographies is anything more than a perplexing puzzle of sources and dates. Like Syme, Yourcenar took a literary approach to her study of the late imperial lives. But her sense of the literary was very different from his, embracing something far more consequential than a pedestrian concentration on "structure, composition, and authorship."[47] To examine its origins and content is illuminating.

III

In 1930 Yourcenar wrote a poem called "Hospes comesque," a free adaptation of the "five exquisite lines" Hadrian is said to have composed on his death-bed (*HA Hadr.* 25.9). It was published the following year and later included in the collection *Les Charités d'Alcippe* (*CA* 20).[48] The poem must mean that Yourcenar was familiar with the text of the Latin life in her late twenties, but whether she knew anything then of the "problem" of the *Historia Augusta* it is impossible to tell. Given the evidence of the *Note*, the answer is probably no. And indeed, several items in her correspondence from late March 1953 to mid-January 1957 continue to refer or allude to "Spartianus" as the author of the life, as when she wondered whether Atanazio Mozzillo had placed too much confidence, in his essay in the journal *Labeo*, not in the details Spartianus provided in his biography of Hadrian – they were reliable enough apparently – but in the author's judgments, which, Yourcenar said, were coloured by the atmosphere of what was a culturally weak age in comparison with the second century (*HZ* II 42).[49] A little later, however, on 19 April 1957, she had occasion to mention to another correspondent that she had in her possession two editions of the *Historia Augusta*, one of which was Magie's three-volume set of Loebs (*HZ* II 100), its first volume being, recall, the "édition quelconque" mentioned in the *Carnets* on which she had drawn when composing *Mémoires* (*CNMH* 525). If at some point she had read its introduction with care, she will have noticed there a reference to Hermann Dessau and to the "charge," as Magie put it, "of utter spuriousness against the *Historia Augusta*" that Dessau had made in 1889, together with Dessau's assertion that the *Historia Augusta* is "the work of a forger."[50] And if at some further point she had read the introduction to the second volume, she will have found a lengthy discussion of the controversy surrounding the authorship and date of the work up until 1924 to which Dessau's proposal had led. Magie came to conclusions on the issues concerned that today are generally discountenanced. But the controversy itself could not be missed, and while Yourcenar would have had to follow up Magie's survey with other reading to know its extent it is not impossible, in theory, that she knew something of its main lines even when writing her novel. (The other edition she possessed in 1957 was Hohl's Teubner of 1927. Dessau was its dedicatee, which also might have been noticed.)[51]

However that may be, Yourcenar certainly knew the main lines when she wrote the letter of April 1957, and there can be little doubt of her source of knowledge. Magie had acknowledged that a single redactor was responsible for the full collection of imperial biographies but he inclined to plural authorship nonetheless and classified the lives into six groups labelled A to

F, adapting a theory that went far back to Theodor Mommsen's reaction to Dessau's original theory. Composition of four groups of lives was assigned to the era of Diocletian (A, B, E, F), and of the remaining two to the era of Constantine (C, D).[52] Yourcenar now wrote in her letter of "deux siècles d'argumentations embrouillées sur les auteurs et les dates respectives des groupes A, B, C, D, E, F," and in the absence of contrary evidence I suppose these to be the groups she found in Magie (*HZ* II 100).[53] Her letter implies that this was, if not completely new information, information that was being given more serious attention than in the past. It also implies a preponderant belief still in plural authorship ("auteurs").

The person Yourcenar addressed in April 1957 was the classical scholar Henry Bardon, whose book *Les Empereurs et les lettres latines* (1940) she had included as a resource in her *Note*. Having made his acquaintance after the publication of *Mémoires*, she brought Bardon into contact with her publisher at Plon, Charles Orengo, who invited Bardon to undertake a French translation of the *Historia Augusta* for the series *Éditions du Rocher*. Simultaneously, Orengo proposed to Yourcenar that she write its preface. The two agreed, and it was this prospective joint undertaking that prompted the April letter.[54] Yourcenar enquired of Bardon which of them should deal, in introducing the collection, with the controversial technical issues at hand, asking if it were to be she for assistance with scholarly bibliography and for Bardon's own opinions. She suggested, however, that the best plan was for her to write a preface of a dozen or so pages discussing "cet étrange recueil" in general terms, with Bardon in a matching foreword dealing with matters of date and authorship. She added in a postscript that the only French translation she knew belonged to the turn of the nineteenth century and asked for information on more recent versions (*HZ* II 99–100). All of which seems to prove that she became seriously aware of the compositional questions surrounding the *Historia Augusta* only in 1957. She may indeed never have fully accepted the theory of single authorship.[55]

There was no immediate progress on the new project. A letter of 24 June 1957 to Louis Evrard of the *Éditions du Rocher* discloses that Yourcenar had corresponded several times with Bardon since 19 April, and confirms that their respective contributions would not clash. It also indicates that her principal theme was to be the way in which the *Historia Augusta* reflected what she termed "la lente désagrégation politique et culturelle du monde antique," which could be found, she said, in the events the work recorded and in its tone (*HZ* II 122–3).[56] Evidently, however, she had not yet begun what was to be her essay, and this was still the case on 13 September when she again wrote to Evrard after he had informed her that he was expecting to receive Bardon's manuscript in November. She insisted that she would not begin her preface at all until she saw Bardon's contribution, because she wanted to cite his translation in her references and to be sure, given the technical issues concerned, which now included the manuscript tradition, of avoiding conflict with anything he said, as she had made clear to Orengo in April. She was also now aware that Bardon intended to translate only a selection of the biographies, not the full collection as originally thought. Nonetheless, she anticipated that she could write her essay in a month or so, but reiterated that she could not begin until she saw Bardon's manuscript towards the end of the year (*HZ* II 151–2). In late November, with no reference to anything received from him, she mentioned to a friend that she had a month or so in which to finish the project (*HZ* II 178).[57]

Almost a year passed before further developments are visible. By mid-October 1958, however, the essay was complete, and, as her correspondence surprisingly shows, Yourcenar made two successful efforts to publish it independently in magazines before the project with Bardon was concluded.[58] The publications concerned were *Le Figaro littéraire* in France and *Merkur* in Germany, journals respectively edited by Maurice Noël and Joachim Moras. Commitments with both already existed: for an article on an aspect of French history with the former, and with the latter for an appreciative essay on Cavafy that ultimately became the introduction to her translation of his poems. When, however, the two editors each expressed interest in receiving an alternative contribution, Yourcenar sought to replace these items with her essay on the *Historia Augusta*, which she apparently wanted to see in print as quickly as possible. To Moras, she offered to remove, if need be, three paragraphs on Roman art from her original version, and to Noël she said she was open to pruning, agreeing at one point with his recommendation to condense the essay's early pages because they dealt with matters too abstruse to engage the general reader (*HZ* II 299; 328).[59] She also suggested to Moras addition of an extra note explaining that of the two principal manuscripts of the *Historia Augusta*, from the ninth and tenth centuries, one, the Palatinus, written at Fulda and now in the Vatican, had once been housed in Heidelberg, while the other, the Bambergensis, was in Munich, or at least was there in 1954 when she visited the city: it was through the mediating assistance of Carolingian Germany therefore that the imperial biographies had reached the modern world (*HZ* II 421–2).[60] The upshot was that the essay was published in *Le Figaro littéraire* of 13 June 1959, and, in German translation, in *Merkur* of April 1960. In this latter case Fritz Jaffé, the German translator of *Mémoires*, played a role. Two years later the essay reappeared as the opening contribution to *Sous bénéfice d'inventaire*.[61]

In all of this this, Henry Bardon and the progress of his translation find no mention. Nor is there is evidence of any direct exchange with him other than the letter of April 1957. Three unpublished notes of 1956 and 1957 from Bardon to Yourcenar are on file in the Houghton Library, but they contain nothing of relevance to the joint project.[62] There can hardly be any doubt, therefore, that in 1958 Yourcenar completely changed her mind about waiting for his translation before writing her essay. Instead, she forged ahead by herself, disregarding the reasons previously given for delay, and chose to publish the finished essay for her own benefit, assuming all the same that it would appear in the joint volume sooner or later. Self-interest clearly prevailed over commitment to a common goal. In the event, however, the joint project fell apart. On 29 October 1959, Yourcenar wrote to Gérard Worms of the *Éditions du Rocher* in response to what appears to have been a complaint that waiting for her essay had caused the joint venture some delay; Worms also expressed disappointment at seeing her essay published, without his agreement and copyright authorization, in *Le Figaro littéraire*. Yourcenar was typically recalcitrant. She rehearsed in painstaking detail her past communications with Evrard and Orengo, absolving herself of any blame or indiscretion: a deadline for the essay had depended on receipt of Bardon's translation; Orengo in any case had been informed of, and did not object to, her wish to publish a pre-publication version; she would of course have wanted to take account of Bardon's work before writing the essay; but his translation had never arrived (*HZ* II 405–7). Much later, on 1 May 1961, she replied to a communication from Antoinette Fiori of the *Éditions du Rocher* to acknowledge receipt of a revised preface for the joint project and requested timely despatch of the proofs, which means that the original enterprise must still then have been viable (*HZ* III 86–7). But there is no evidence of any further progress. When in 1964 Bardon published *Le Crépuscule des Césars: scènes et visages de l'*Histoire Auguste, an illustrated collection of extracts in French translation with introduction and bibliography, it had no contribution from Yourcenar at all. Personal relations between the two, however, seem not to have suffered. In May 1959, Yourcenar notably referred a correspondent to Bardon's translation and discussion of Hadrian's deathbed poem in the second volume of *La Littérature latine inconnue*, giving the relevant page numbers of what she called a recent book; and when Bardon's *Crépuscule* appeared, she sent a gracious letter of thanks for the copy he sent to her, calling it a great success, complimenting its selection of texts and notes, regretting that their planned meeting years earlier had never eventuated, and observing that her essay would in any case have now been unnecessary. She was grateful that his book acknowledged both *Les Visages* and *Mémoires*.[63]

IV

Nothing is said in the correspondence on the genesis of *Les Visages* about academic technicalities and controversies, the passing remark on "argumentations embrouillées" apart. It is Yourcenar's not unexpected wilfulness that stands out. Yet no reader of her essay then or now can fail to see that it shows some familiarity with them. Yourcenar refers from the outset to the plural authorship of the *Historia Augusta*, using the traditional names throughout for the authors of the individual lives cited – Spartianus, Capitolinus, Lampridius, Pollio, Vopiscus – identifying them predominantly as biographers ("biographes"), but sometimes calling them, individually, a compiler, a historiographer, or a chronicler ("rédacteur," "historiographe," "chroniqueur"). Usage, however, can be qualified, as in "Spartien, ou le biographe qui assume ce nom," or "Spartien, ou l'anonyme auquel Spartien servit de prête-nom."[64] Equally, she is explicit that the names and even the existence of the authors are matters of debate, and that the dates of composition of the lives proposed by scholars range from the late third to the end of the fourth century: the terminal points of 284 and 395 are specified. She knows, too, that the biographies draw considerably on, or epitomize, works no longer extant, indicates that they have been abundantly interpolated, observes that they include forged documents, inept assertions, and confusion of names, dates and events, and appreciates that the work is full of "l'erreur et le mensonge."[65] She does not go so far as to say that they may all have been written by one person; she prefers instead to speak of a compilation ("rédaction"), which suggests that she thought the final version had gone through previous stages of composition. She makes clear, however, that distinguished scholars have reasonably suspected that the work is fraudulent: "une quasi totale imposture."[66]

The opinions conveyed are generally congruent with those of Bardon, who must be presumed through his correspondence with her in 1957 to have played a role in shaping Yourcenar's views. In the two relevant chapters of *Les Empereurs et les lettres latines*, Spartianus is always identified as the author of the life of Hadrian, which unambiguously connotes belief in plural authorship for the *Historia Augusta* as a whole; and in the second volume of *La Littérature latine inconnue* (1956), the names of all six authors are taken as authentic. In addition, the collection is said there to have been compiled in stages over many years, the theory of single fraudulent authorship in the late fourth century is rejected, and a date of composition about 350 is postulated.[67] So too in the introduction to *Le Crépuscule des Césars*, Bardon is resolute that the biographies were written by six authors, sets out what he takes to be their individual characteristics, and posits that there were originally two sets of lives, one written under Diocletian, the other under Constantine, and that both, unsystematically compiled, were frequently interpolated and finally brought together as a single entity some time after 360, a little later than earlier suggested. His title, incidentally, seems to echo the main theme of Yourcenar's essay, which although not included in his bibliography – he simply calls it the chapter devoted to the *Historia Augusta* in *Sous bénéfice d'inventaire* – is quoted on its back cover.[68]

To Yourcenar, however, academic exchanges on technicalities were far less consequential than what could be learned from the lives of the emperors in their entirety. This is how she described the essay to Noël: "L'essai, détaché du volume auquel il doit servir de préface, devrait s'appeler *Réflexions sur l'Histoire Auguste* ou, tout simplement, *L'Histoire Auguste*. Il est d'environ 5000 mots. Comme vous le verrez, le sujet en est emprunté à l'antiquité, mais n'est pas, parfois, sans un intérêt d'actualité, ou un intérêt de tous les temps" (*HZ* II 271).[69] To Jaffé, she spoke of it as a historical study of the biographies of the emperors between Hadrian and Diocletian that she had seasoned with remarks on current affairs (*HZ* II 276). To Moras, in turn, she said that while the essay was written to accompany a French translation of the Latin text, it aimed to introduce a difficult work to the general public and to discuss the concept of decadence in political culture (*HZ* II 296), the implication being that the work has historical value as a unity.[70] This was affirmed early in the essay itself: "Et cependant, il n'est pas possible aux historiens modernes de l'Antiquité d'ignorer l'*Histoire auguste*; ceux mêmes qui lui dénient toute valeur sont bon gré mal gré forcés de s'en servir" (*SBI* 6).[71] Accordingly, she did not approach the work as a quarry from which "factual" nuggets were to be mined piecemeal in the manner of classical source critics. Rather, she assumed as a point of departure that the collection, set in a broad literary context allowing comparison with the works of post-classical giants such as Shakespeare and Tolstoy, expresses something of genuine historical import in its totality for which precision on date and methods of composition was extraneous, and that historical meaning should include relevance to contemporary life with interplay between past and present both constant and essential. What she discovered in the document was an all-pervasive anxiety in the later Imperial age that was induced by the slow disintegration of Rome's empire from the Antonines onwards, and that brought into relief the dangers by which her own and her readers' world was currently threatened. It was from Hadrian's reign precisely that the long period of decline had begun.[72]

The essay opens with a pronouncement on Rome's special place in history, which as far as its early emperors are concerned is attributed to the achievements of the great Plutarch, Tacitus, and Suetonius. For emperors after Domitian, in contrast, no more than mediocre and often propagandistic reporters remain, and while their mediocrity gives what they report a certain veracity ("véracité"), this is a sign in itself of the waning of Greco-Roman culture that defines the later Imperial age. Yourcenar emphasizes the value of the *Historia Augusta* for third-century history as strongly as any ancient historian must do, but claims that the portrait it offers lacks any inherent consciousness of Rome's imminent decline. She begins, therefore, with knowledge that is knowledge of her own time and place, not that of whoever was responsible for creating the portrait, and it is knowledge dependent on a rigid view of historical change culminating in the finality, the decline, and, in the end, the indisputable fall of Roman civilization. Any alternative notion of historical transformation has no place in her thinking.[73]

The chief issue the *Historia Augusta* raises, she continues, is its reliability. Due to differences in compilation, variability in trustworthiness is to be expected and plausibility of content will be controlled by the truism that the circumstances under which a work is read are all-important. The atrocities of the recent totalitarian past make the long accounts of emperors' crimes in the biographies less preposterous than they might otherwise seem; and if more were known about the private lives of contemporaries, sexual extravagances of the sort associated for instance with Elagabalus would likewise be more credible, a remark that now seems decidedly prescient: the reference is to a female impersonator who enjoyed playing a seductive Venus to Paris in concert performance and encouraged at the mimes live rather than simulated sex (*HA Elag.* 5.4–5; 25.4). As with Hadrian, documentary evidence sometimes confirms the text's accuracy, so that altogether, "c'est moins dans l'énoncé des faits que dans l'interprétation donnée aux faits que fleurissent souvent dans l'*Histoire auguste* l'erreur et le mensonge" (*SBI* 8).[74] In this there is much that consists with current scholarship. Which is true also of the view that the distortion evident in the record is due to the partisan attitudes of authors who supported a plutocratic, conservative senate rather than to notions of deliberate deception. The factual record is taken to be more secure than many historians would now allow, but its inconsistency, the result of uncritical reliance on both gossip and official pronouncements, is properly recognized, as is the impediment of the vast chronological distance between the events recorded and the time at which the record was made. This is especially the case with the early biographical subjects. It was impossible therefore in the later Imperial age to comprehend the Antonine apogée: "le monde avait changé … au point de rendre le mode de vie et de pensée des grands Antonins à peu près impénétrables" (*SBI* 9), a statement that can refer, I think, only to what must be taken to be the ill effects of the Christian revolution on biographers who were reactionary pagans of the kind the putative sole author of modern scholarship is often thought to be.[75] Their mediocrity, moreover, means that the authors could never reveal the full complexity of their subjects' personalities and accomplishments. Spartianus appreciated Hadrian's success as a pragmatic administrator, but he failed to see the statesman because the superstitions of the later age, almost mediaeval in character, adversely affected his understanding of elements of the historical tradition such as the genuine interest Hadrian had for example in the science of astrology. The tendency is endemic. So of Gallienus: "cet homme cultivé, gagné à la cause de la tolérance religieuse, ami et protecteur du grand Plotin, gardant des raffinements d'une autre époque au cours des années d'anarchie, semble avoir été encore plus méconnu, s'il se peut, que calomnié par son médiocre peintre" (SBI 11).[76] The authors' inability to grasp the impact of the great historical forces around them, the rumbling tide of Christianity, economic deterioration, the pressure of barbarians on the frontier, blinded them to Rome's imminent death. As Yourcenar observed much later, these dry as dust chroniclers were not the great historians her classically educated grandfather Michel-Charles had read in his day (AN 1031).

Nonetheless, the Historia Augusta is an overwhelming document: "Une effroyable odeur d'humanité monte de ce livre." It shows life in the raw, and despite all its shortcomings it reflects opinions of the historical moment from ordinary Romans: "l'homme de la rue et de l'antichambre."[77] It reveals therefore pure, which is to say impure, thought, a notion that again suggests a correspondence with Bardon (SBI 12).[78] Its vignettes can be vivid – Caracalla killed by his guards as he dismounts from his horse to relieve himself at the roadside (HA Ant. Car. 7.1–2) – and sometimes the effects verge on the poetic. When for example Septimius Severus at Carlisle is followed to his door by ominous black animals mistakenly selected for sacrifice but now presaging his death (HA Sev. 22.6–7), the reader can easily imagine the cold or rainy February day on the Scottish border: "l'empereur en tenue militaire, son teint africain pâli par la maladie et le climat du Nord" (SBI 13).[79] Such effects are few and far between, however, and it is in the reader's imagination that they emerge from the morass of details the text contains and the realities of life they communicate.

A distinctive observation is then made. The best commentary on the Historia Augusta comes from works of art and monuments. Portraits offer a control on the biographies' representations of emperors, with Hadrian, the humane ruler always at the forefront of Yourcenar's mind, again offering an illustration: "le visage à la fois judicieux et songeur d'Hadrien, sa bouche nerveuse, ses traits vite gonflés par les progrès de l'hydropisie" (SBI 14).[80] The influence of, say, the Tel Shalem bronze or a less harried representation now in the British Museum may be imagined.[81] (Marcus, incidentally, is here the man of the Meditations, not the boy of Mémoires.) Again, to say that

Spartianus's reference to the death of Antinous in Egypt is corroborated by the obelisk at Rome on the Pincio does not solve the problem of how he actually died, but once the divine powers attributed to the new divinity and the grandiloquence with which the obelisk characterizes Hadrian are pursued, it opens up a vista on the event and its sequel that conventional investigations overlook (*SBI* 14–15): in one version, "the king," "the ruler of every country," who with his queen Sabina is "safe and healthy" and "lives for ever."[82] In turn, the quality of imperial portraiture on the coinage degenerates in the third century, an indication of the death throes of the economy at large. The enormous Baths of Caracalla and Diocletian confirm the extravagant devotion of emperors to prestige and pleasure the biographies describe. And above all, Aurelian's walls, majestic but ultimately of no avail, symbolize Rome's fatal sickness of insecurity, whose symptoms pervade the biographies and herald the appearance, a little more than a century away, of Alaric. Methodologically, Yourcenar is a reader who exploits the *Historia Augusta* for the sake of panoptic historical explication.

Through comparison with historical writing from Rome's "belle époque" (*SBI* 16), she next returns to the work's inadequacies. As with Suetonius, an appetite for the anecdotal is much in evidence, but Suetonius was a psychological portraitist the authors of the *Historia Augusta* never rival. The speeches found in Livy and Plutarch are certainly contrived, but the comparably fabricated documents of the biographies never illustrate character to the same degree. Excessive moralizing in ancient historiography might be considered a shortcoming, yet with Tacitus it was inspired by ideals of civic virtue which the present authors, intent only on recording the exotic, do not share. Their work permits a pattern of decline to be discerned, from the Antonine, Andalusian highpoint to an anarchy no more than temporarily relieved by the energies of the Illyrians, with which the ever-broadening geographical origins of rulers less and less "Roman" are associated; but it is chaotic, and its authors are indifferent to structural historical issues. They fail to see the dissolution in their midst of traditional institutions, to recognize that an emperor's adoption of a successor is a veil for a coup d'état, that the increasingly barbarized armies, fomentors of anarchy, are all that matter, that once conquered peoples now resist Roman rule, that mass migrations are in process, and that new forms of dogma – Yourcenar can again only mean, critically, Christian dogma – have become ascendant. Yet to judge them harshly serves no purpose. Every individual has the capacity to react, for good or ill, to the unfolding of events: "de pousser à la roue, de laisser faire, ou de lutter" (*SBI* 19).[83]

As the essay approaches its climax, its originality becomes ever more evident. The story the *Historia Augusta* tells is incomplete. At its close a century and a half of relative recovery is at hand, marked by the advent of Diocletian and Constantine. Yet Rome was never to return to what it had once been, and for a thousand years, as the same chaotic game of power seeking incessantly played out across the centuries, its ghost hovered over Byzantium in the east and the Holy Roman Empire in the west, leading ultimately to the autocrats of the modern age – the present day Caesars always in Yourcenar's mind, and not only such an obvious candidate as Hitler, but Juarès, Pétain, and de Gaulle as well (*SBI* 9). Such men recall the Romans of the essay's grand opening paragraph: Caesar, brutally assassinated, as Plutarch recounts; the misanthropic tyrant Tiberius and the pathetic *artifex manqué* Nero unforgettably portrayed by Tacitus; and now there is Mussolini, killed on the run and hung up by the feet in a garage in Milan, dying latterly the death of a third-century emperor. The fall – the "décadence" – continues, with the difficult problem of the fall of Rome persisting into the modern age. The final paragraph, transporting the reader across "la longue durée" to powerful effect, collapses all distinction between past and present, and makes of the *Historia Augusta* a tragic symbol of an unchanging human condition:

Mais nous avons appris à reconnaître ce gigantisme qui n'est que la contrefaçon malsaine d'une croissance, ce gaspillage qui fait croire à l'existence de richesses qu'on n'a déjà plus, cette pléthore si vite remplacée par la disette à la moindre crise, ces divertissements ménagés d'en haut, cette atmosphère d'inertie et de panique, d'autoritarisme et d'anarchie, ces réaffirmations pompeuses d'un grand passé au milieu de l'actuelle médiocrité et du présent désordre, ces réformes qui ne sont que des palliatifs et ces accès de vertu qui ne se manifestent que par des purges, ce goût du sensationnel qui finit par faire triompher la politique du pire, ces quelques hommes de génie mal secondés perdus dans la foule des grossiers habiles, des fous violents, des honnêtes gens maladroits et des faibles sages. Le lecteur moderne est chez lui dans l'*Histoire auguste*. (*SBI* 21)

But we have learned to recognize that gigantism which is merely the morbid mimetism of growth, that waste which makes a pretense of wealth in states already bankrupt, that plethora so quickly replaced by dearth at the first crisis, those entertainments for the people provided from the upper levels of the hierarchy, that atmosphere of inertia and panic, of authoritarianism and of anarchy, those pompous reaffirmations of a great past amid present mediocrity and immediate disorder, those reforms which are merely palliatives and those outbursts of virtue which are manifested only by purges, that craving for sensation which ends in the triumph of a politics of violence, those unacknowledged men of genius lost in the crowd of unscrupulous gangsters, of violent lunatics, of honest men who are inept and wise men who are helpless ... The modern reader is at home in the *Historia Augusta*.

IV

How might all this be assessed? An answer, I think, has to start with the question of what Yourcenar understood by the concept of "decline." The cardinal term, as intimated a moment ago, is the word "décadence," the meaning of which as Yourcenar used it can vary. It may refer simply to Rome's historical decline, as in the conventional phrase "the decline of the Roman Empire" and be a natural antecedent of "fall," which Yourcenar also used and which in one of her interviews from 1979 she identified as her essay's subject (*SBI* 19, 20: "la chute"; *PV* 232–3).[84] But the word may also carry broader moralistic connotations of luxuriant corruption, as apparently in an earlier passing description of the essay from 1962 as an "étude sur la décadence romaine" (*HZ* III 183).[85] The two meanings naturally coalesce. Conspicuously, however, in the Gallimard edition of *Sous bénéfice* from 1978 they seem to be distinguished by use of lower- and upper-case spellings ("decadence" / "Décadence"), an idiom not preserved in the Pléiade where the word is always printed in lower case.[86] This may be a matter of simple typographical inconsistency. Yet from the possible broader meaning some support might be claimed for Stephen Bann's view that Yourcenar was influenced when writing *Mémoires* by the Decadent movement of "art for art's sake" of the late nineteenth century, the premise of which, her extensive knowledge of "fin-de-siècle" culture, is irrefutable.[87] Yourcenar knew such key texts as J.-K. Huysmans's emblematic *À Rebours* and Walter Pater's *Marius the Epicurean*, and she was obviously devoted from an early age to the Decadently tinged poetry of Cavafy. Significantly also, as Bann observes, she displayed a special sympathy in an earlier essay for Oscar Wilde, the movement's peerless symbol, depicting him in her essay of 1929, *Wilde rue des Beaux-Arts*, during his last days in Naples, the city of the *Satyricon* as she tellingly called it, as a broken, impoverished exile, shunned and shamed and soon to die in Paris (*EM* 499–509).[88] In turn, since novel and essay are intimately connected, and especially with Elagabalus in mind, perhaps Decadent influence is similarly to be sought in *Les Visages*. I cannot see, however, that Decadent luxuriance does in fact characterize *Mémoires* at large. Yourcenar's classically restrained style forbids it. And the episode where impact might be most expected, the story of Hadrian and Antinous, is driven, as I have suggested, by socio-historical plausibility, not as might be anticipated by the promotion of a Decadently inspired homoeroticism, the debt to Symonds notwithstanding. Direct evidence from Yourcenar herself is conclusive. This is what she said in September 1963 when replying to a correspondent who intended to write an essay on her work:

Quant au mot *esthétisme*, je le rejette complètement. Depuis près d'un siècle, ce mal-heureux terme tend à signifier dans la littérature française l'idolâtrie de la «beauté» considérée comme une fin en soi, et complètement dissociée des valeurs morales ou pragmatiques. Rien, je puis vous l'assurer, n'est plus éloigné de ma pensée ou de mon tempérament. (*HZ* III 463–4)[89]

As for the word *aestheticism*, I reject it completely. For close on a century this unfor-tunate term has tended to signify in French literature the idolatrous worship of a "beauty" conceptualized as an end in itself that is utterly divorced from moral or practical values. Nothing, I can assure you, is more remote from my manner of thought or my temperament.

She added that beauty was important to Hadrian as an idea, but only to the extent that it formed an aspect of the human order he saw as an imperial ideal. He was not a cultist of beauty for its own sake. Her final words are definitive: "Évitons de faire d'Hadrien une sorte de fade Des Esseintes" (*HZ* III 464).[90] It is the notion of "fall" in the turning of a historical cycle that is most important in both *Mémoires* and *Les Visages*, with the Hadrianic moment representing the pinnacle of attainment before the onset of decline demanded by a notion of cyclical change, but which in due course necessarily leads to resurrection.

That moment, Hadrian's imperial Golden Age, coinciding with the upward swing of his parabolic life's journey, is elaborated in *Mémoires* in the third and by far the longest section of *Tellus stabilita*, where Yourcenar allows Hadrian to catalogue his greatest successes as he ruminates on any number of topics: law, slavery, the role of women in society, the unequal distribution of wealth, military discipline, governmental bureaucracy, the emperor's "métier" (relations with men of letters, building projects, the founding of cities) and, finally, art and sculpture. In every case, he combines his personal views with details on remedies he has introduced to improve society and fulfil the civilizing mission earlier announced, the promotion far and wide of the ideals of *humanitas*, *libertas*, and *felicitas*. His idealistic world view is epitomized in a credo of Spartan origin centring on "la Force, la Justice, les Muses":

La Force était à la base, rigueur sans laquelle il n'est pas de beauté, fermeté sans laquelle il n'est pas de justice. La Justice était l'équilibre des parties, l'ensemble des proportions harmonieuses que ne doit compromettre aucun excès. Force et Justice n'étaient qu'un instrument bien accordé entre les mains des Muses. Toute mis-ère, toute brutalité étaient à interdire comme autant d'insultes au beau corps de l'humanité. Toute iniquité était une fausse note à éviter dans l'harmonie des sphères. (*MH* 391)

Strength was the basis, discipline without which there is no beauty, and firmness without which there is no justice. Justice was the balance of the parts, that whole so harmoniously composed which no excess should be permitted to endanger. Strength and Justice together were but one instrument, well tuned, in the hands of the Muses. All forms of dire poverty and brutality were things to forbid as insults to the fair body of mankind, every injustice a false note to avoid in the harmony of the spheres.

Here the vexed question of how policy in the Imperial age was formed and implemented is of no consequence. The autobiographical form of *Mémoires*, as I have maintained, cuts through the historical impasse with the all-pervasive first person serving as the animating device that permits Hadrian to arrogate to himself all responsibility for every accomplishment of his reign and to bring the record of his achievements to life. More importantly still, Hadrian is conscious of the cycle that controls the course of history, a view essentially Stoic but one astronomically determinable as well, according to which civilizations rise, fall, and rise again, tied to which is the personal trajectory that first elevates him to supreme power and then reduces him to an old age of patient endurance (*MH* 401–2). He is able consequently to foresee with a certain credibility the distant fate of Rome known to his creator from her reading of authorities as great as Gibbon and Renan: "Les catastrophes et les ruines viendront; le désordre triomphera, mais de temps en temps l'ordre aussi" (*MH* 513).[91]

In strict terms this is completely unrealistic, as is the notion in *Les Visages* itself that Rome's decline was, or ought to have been, anticipated by the favoured Antonines, for how could Hadrian, Pius, or even Marcus possibly have known what was to become of their empire two hundred and more years into the future? As often, a passage from the *Carnets* is instructive:

Retrouvé dans un volume de la correspondance de Flaubert, fort lu et fort souligné par moi vers 1927, la phrase inoubliable: «Les dieux n'étant plus, et le Christ n'étant pas encore, il y a eu, de Cicéron à Marc Aurèle, un moment unique où l'homme seul a été.» Une grande partie de ma vie allait se passer à essayer de définir, puis à peindre, cet homme seul et d'ailleurs relié à tout. (*CNMH* 519)[92]

In turning the pages of a volume of Flaubert's correspondence much read and heavily underscored by me about the year 1927 I came again upon this admirable sentence: "Just when the gods had ceased to be, and the Christ had not yet come, there was a unique moment in history, between Cicero and Marcus Aurelius, when man stood alone." A great part of my life was going to be spent in trying to define, and then to portray, that man existing alone and yet closely bound with all being.

The sentence is an extract from a letter written most likely to Mme. Edma Roger des Genettes in 1861 when Gustave Flaubert was composing *Salammbô*, his grand story of the mercenaries' revolt against Carthage in the wake of the first Punic war. The book was published on 24 November 1862. The letter does not survive in its entirety, but it seems to have begun with discussion of how the subject of a novel is chosen before taking up a question Flaubert's correspondent had raised regarding the poet Lucretius. The sharp contrast between modern and ancient views of the afterlife, what Flaubert calls the "dark hole" of immortality ("trou noir"), becomes his concern:

Mais pour les Anciens, ce trou noir était l'infini même; leurs rêves se dessinent et passent sur un fond d'ébène immuable. Pas de cris, pas de convulsions, rien que la fixité d'un visage pensif. Les Dieux n'étant plus et le Christ n'étant pas encore, il y a eu, de Cicéron à Marc-Aurèle, un moment unique où l'*homme* seul a été. Je ne retrouve nulle part cette grandeur ...

But for the ancients that "black hole" was infinity itself; their dreams loom and vanish against a background of immutable ebony. No crying out, no convulsions – nothing but the fixity of a pensive gaze. With the gods gone, and Christ not yet come, there was a unique moment, from Cicero to Marcus Aurelius, when man stood alone. Nowhere else do I find that particular grandeur ...[93]

Criticism of Lucretius follows for the unwavering assurance of his materialistic theories – his preoccupation with explanations and conclusions was a sign of weakness; had he kept to the spirit of Epicurus, his work would have become immortal and radical; yet modern poets were far inferior in comparison – and evidently enough it was Lucretius's denial of a conventional afterlife, a consequence of his "atheism," that underlay these allusive remarks. It was a denial that Flaubert assumed to have been widespread at Rome in the era from Cicero to Marcus, an era free as he saw it from superstition and religious dogma, and, because the gods were dead free from fears of a terrible sequel to the end of life. Soon after *Mémoires'* first appearance, Yourcenar duly spoke of Flaubert's key sentence as one of its original impulses that permitted Hadrian to contemplate himself "dans le pur miroir de l'humanisme" (*PV* 28–9).[94]

It was long an axiom of scholarship, to summarize baldly, that during the final decades of Republican history traditional Roman beliefs in and about the gods lost their meaning and popular appeal, and gave way in the early Imperial age to the so-called mystery religions, the cults of divinities such as Isis and Mithras, until at a further remove "paganism" was altogether obliterated by the conversion of Constantine and the "triumph" of Christianity. Only in the last quarter of the twentieth century did challenges to this orthodoxy emerge, as its Christianizing assumptions were gradually exposed, notions of religious sterility were replaced by concepts of vitality and relevance, and the dynamic adaptability of Rome's religious conventions was brought to the fore. The culmination was a new, vivid recognition of a Roman world that was always and uninterruptedly a "world full of gods."[95] This advance came much too late for Yourcenar, however, who must be presumed to have been influenced throughout the period of *Mémoires'* composition and beyond by then current views of Rome's religious history. The inclusion of Flaubert's sentence in the *Carnets* is otherwise inexplicable. She understood the Antonine era, and Hadrian's reign in particular, to be an age free in a Lucretian sense from the shackles of religious constraint, and so an age representing a high point of humane enlightenment in the grand course of history. The religious and philosophical explorations that the source tradition attributed to Hadrian could be, and were, in *Mémoires* described with some accuracy, but without any impediment to the essentially humanistic and liberal disposition Yourcenar believed to have been at the heart of her character. From a modern perspective the perception was misguided, but in context it is comprehensible and helps to explain why Hadrian, with a clarity of vision endowed by humane enlightenment, is able to foresee *décadence* as he does.[96]

For Yourcenar herself, however, decline was presently, immediately at hand. Of this there is no doubt. The *Historia Augusta* gave evidence of a society's inability to recognize the signs of its own decomposition, and such signs, comparable to the structural defects – the "evils" ("maux") – that had led to Rome's decline, were everywhere now apparent. Their ubiquitous trappings of grandeur made them invisible to the majority, as had been the case in antiquity. Decline nonetheless was an inalterable feature of the human condition, sustained moral progress was impossible, and the present very much imperilled (*SBI* 21).[97] This deeply pessimistic view was shaped primarily by memories of the totalitarianism of the 1930s and 1940s, which Yourcenar was intent on keeping before her public not only in her essay, but also in the novel *Denier du rêve*, the story, recall, rewritten in 1959, of an unsuccessful attempt on the life of an unnamed Italian dictator who is clearly a stand-in for Mussolini.[98] The work was meant to evoke the troubled atmosphere of 1934, the year in which the novel was first published, and of the unfulfilled aspirations to effect change doomed by the isolation of its protagonists. Essay and novel combine accordingly to express that sense of disillusion so strongly in contrast with the hopeful frame of mind in which *Mémoires* had been written a decade earlier. The attitude is surprising at

first sight. From her arrival in 1939 until the completion of *Mémoires*, Yourcenar's life in the United States had been filled with professional obscurity and general instability. But the success of *Mémoires* brought an end to
the darkness: fame, financial independence, the resumption of travel, and
a major new work in gestation, eventually to reveal itself as *L'Œuvre au
Noir*.[99] Nevertheless, as seen earlier, the mid- and late 1950s brought a low
ebb. 1956 was not only the year of Suez, but also of the Soviet suppression
of dissent in Hungary. A visit to Western Europe and the Near East had to
be abandoned, with a letter from February 1957 lamenting the disappear-
ance from the itinerary of Damascus, Aleppo, Alexandria, and, it might have
been, Israel. The consequent mood was sombre: "Je vous avoue … que l'état
du monde m'a jetée dans une crise de désespoir dont je ne suis pas encore
sortie" (*L*130).[100] In November, she described the time as "une époque où
toutes les idéologies et tous les systèmes se sont déshonorés" (*HZ* II 180).[101]
The following year, despite a winter spent in Europe, pessimism deepened
with the eruption in June of the Algerian crisis and the appearance in France,
as Yourcenar saw it, of a form of quasi-dictatorship: General de Gaulle, seizing power through a coup, was a figure like a third-century Roman emperor
lacking in Antonine wisdom. Hope, she wrote to her friend Natalie Clifford
Barney, was in short supply: "La situation est partout (et surtout peut-être
en France) si grave qu'on ne peut que prier, de quelque opinion ou confession
qu'on soit, pour que ceux qui gouvernent soient «inspirés» dans le sens de la
justice, de la sagesse, et simplement du sens commun. C'est de cette façon-là,
et de cette façon seulement, que je prie pour le gouvernement de de Gaulle"
(*HZ* II 251).[102]

Still, if the bleakness of *Les Visages* is overpowering, a positive element redeems it from utter nihilism. The documentary record is clear on
what it was meant to achieve. To Maurice Noël in April 1959 Yourcenar
wrote: "mon but était de montrer que les maux dont meurt une civilisation ne sont pas les scandales ou les crimes romanesques dont s'empare
l'histoire populaire, mais une certaine bassesse, une certaine inertie, un
certain abaissement insensible de l'esprit public et de la culture" (*HZ* II
323).[103] Similar statements followed both to Noël and Hans Paeschke: the
essay was intended as a set of reflections on a particular historical document, not on history at large, and although connected to the world of
scholarship its chief concern was engagement between past and present,
bringing together their several enormities for mutual illumination: the
mistakes and misfortunes of time past portended and prepared for those
of the present, while today's experience clarified that of yesterday (*HZ* III
109; 142; 274–5).[104] The decorous letter to Henry Bardon of August 1964
had already referred to Rome as an example of where the signs of a world

in decline, their present world, were evident (*HZ* IV 133). Later still, to the Canadian student Jean-Louis Côté, she defined *Les Visages* first as an essay "sur la véracité des historiens de l'*Histoire Auguste*, et ce qu'ils nous apprennent, quasi malgré eux, sur la civilisation de leur temps," and secondly as a case study from late antiquity "sur l'éternelle tragédie de l'histoire, qui consiste en ce que nous ne sommes pas capables de lutter contre les maux dont nous mourons, ou même de les voir avec quelque clarté" (*HZ* IV 46).[105] The evils of the late fifties were clearly meant. In turn, to Simon Sautier, the student who had asked for a reaction to the thesis he had drafted on her work, she distinguished the historical essay from a work of the imagination, given the particular kind of authorial discipline the essay required in the pursuit of truth, emphasizing that what was of supreme importance in *Les Visages* was the unremitting assault on modern man's megalomania (*L* 361).[106]

There is no ambiguity here: the unchanging nature of the human condition overrides and collapses rigid distinctions between one age and another. And in the last analysis therefore the *Historia Augusta* is to be seen not only as a record of the death of Rome but also, constructively, as a warning of the impending death of the present. If Yourcenar was committed to disclosing the historical truth the work contains, she was equally intent on revealing its admonitory significance. Which means that in the expansive interplay between past and present there lies in the essay the saving grace of a didactic potential, detectable once the complexity of the curve of decadence is recognized and the saviour-emperors kept in mind, who, for centuries, were able to postpone Rome's fall: Diocletian, Constantine, Theodosius (*SBI* 19).[107] The point was made in *Ton et langage*, where Yourcenar passingly but rightly referred to the life of Commodus as a very mediocre work, but from which something meaningful could be extracted. This is her comment on the passage listing the senate's torrent of vengeful acclamations in the wake of Commodus's murder (*HA Comm.*18–19). It combines high emotion with sober perception, and illustrates unmistakably her belief that the lives have historical value:

le décret vouant Commode aux gémonies bouleverse, parce qu'il nous fait sentir l'énorme sursaut de haine des sénateurs devant l'empereur mort. C'est un des rares cas où passe jusqu'à nous le grondement d'une foule. (*TGS* 292)

the decree condemning Commodus to the Scalae Gemoniae stuns us, because it makes us feel palpably the enormous surge of hatred that swept over the senators as they looked on the dead emperor. It is one of the rare cases where the rumbling of a mob can be heard across the centuries.

The ills of the present, it follows, might even yet be averted, if only temporarily. Conveying as it does therefore the *Historia Augusta*'s enduring capacity to instruct, Yourcenar's synoptic, philosophizing study was in 1959 an exceptional contribution, as it remains today, its insight of a far different order from anything propounded by the successors of Hermann Dessau. This in the end is the difference, a redemptive difference, I think, that *Les Visages* makes. And it is impossible consequently to accept that the author of Hadrian's rise and fall was in any sense an impostor, or that she harboured any intent to deceive in her reconstruction of Hadrian's life. She could acknowledge that she had intruded into the jealously guarded territory of obsessive scholars, and seeing herself as a "franc-tireur" could sympathize with their resentments. To which there was a characteristically forceful retort: academics who took scholarship as a point of departure were hardly the best qualified judges of a book that ultimately belonged to the domain of creative literature (*HZ* III 424).[108]

V

Petite âme, âme tendre et flottante, compagne de mon corps, qui fut ton hôte, tu vas descendre dans ces lieux pâles, durs et nus, où tu devras renoncer aux jeux d'autrefois. (*MH* 515)

Little soul, gentle and drifting, guest and companion of my body, now you will dwell below in pallid places, stark and bare; there you will abandon your play of yore.

Hadrian's final, or almost final words in *Mémoires* are those of Hadrian's deathbed poem. In the Pléiade it appears, in Latin, on the title page:

> *Animula vagula, blandula,*
> *Hospes comesque corporis,*
> *Quæ nunc abibis in loca*
> *Pallidula, rigida, nudula,*
> *Nec, ut soles, dabis iocos ...*

The text is identical with that of the Plon edition of 1951, there printed on the page following, and nowhere is there any indication of textual uncertainty. Various items from her correspondence show that Yourcenar was in fact thoroughly familiar with the difficulties the text presents.[109] Much more noteworthy, however, is the poem's importance to Yourcenar over time, an importance far greater than her novel's casual reader might suppose. Its appearance on the amber shade of a living room table lamp at Petite Plaisance, inscribed by Yourcenar herself on a bold red panel in a clear white script, is a simple, literal illustration of Hadrian's continuing presence in her everyday world long after 1951.[110] And its prehistory of course is the poem of 1930, which opens in derivative apostrophe and ends with unmissable reminiscence:

> Corps, portefaix de l'âme, en qui peut-être croire
> Serait plus vain, cher corps, que de ne t'aimer pas;
> Cœur sans fin transmuté dans ce vivant ciboire;
> Bouche toujours tendue aux plus récents appâts.
>
> Mers où l'on peut voguer, sources où l'on peut boire;
> Froment et vin mêlés au ritual repas;
> Alibi du sommeil, douce cavité noire;
> Inséparable terre offerte à tous nos pas.
>
> Air qui m'emplis d'espace et m'emplis d'équilibre;
> Frissons au long des nerfs; spasmes de fibre en fibre;
> Yeux sur l'immense vide un peu de temps ouverts.
>
> Corps, mon vieux compagnon, nous périrons ensemble,
> Comment ne pas t'aimer, forme à qui je ressemble,
> Puisque c'est dans tes bras que j'étreins l'univers?

Here, however, "body" has superseded "soul" as the object of address, anticipating a similar inversion on the first page of *Mémoires* as Hadrian recollects the morning's medical inspection: "mon corps, ce fidèle compagnon, cet ami plus sûr, mieux connu de moi que mon âme" (*MH* 287). The body is already a fixation as the emperor, wretchedly sick, senses the approach of death, the thought of which is present in the poem in sleep's alibi, the "douce cavité noire," a phrase that recalls Flaubert's "trou noir" and suggests a view of the poem as a remnant of Yourcenar's early thinking about the project that was finally to become her novel.[111] Its title acquired a special significance, appearing at the end of the moving tribute to Grace Frick included in the *Carnets* (*CNMH* 537–8) and, more poignantly still, on the small, unassuming stone in the cemetery at Somesville close to Petite Plaisance that marks Frick's final resting place. The deathbed poem, as the Latin life of Hadrian as a whole, was for Yourcenar a lifelong companion.[112]

Endnote

ER 103–6

Le premier fléchissement, après la longue montée qui va du poste de tribun à celui de gouverneur de Syrie et de «second dans Rome», c'est l'époque de la préparation de la campagne parthe. Hadrien n'a aucune assurance que Trajan fera de lui son héritier; il se sent guetté par les chefs du parti militaire, et sait qu'il risque d'être supprimé par eux. Conscient des dangers de cette nouvelle guerre de conquête, sentant l'absurdité de ces plans si soigneusement tracés, mais qui par définition ne prévoient jamais tout, qui sont ceux des stratégistes et des états-majors de tous les temps, cet excellent officier préfère les solutions de paix. Connaissant mieux que Trajan l'Orient, plus instruit de l'état véritable des esprits et des finances, il se rend compte qu'on se lance dans une de ces grandes expéditions dont on risque de ne pas sortir, comme le seront plus tard celles de Napoléon et de Hitler en Russie. Impuissant, enfermé dans son palais d'Antioche, recevant des nouvelles qu'il sait d'avance être censurées, ignorant s'il accédera jamais à l'empire et pourra imposer son programme de paix, Hadrien traverse une période de véritable effondrement. Il en est tiré par la mort de Trajan et par l'intervention de Plotine qui l'impose, en quelque sorte, comme successeur. Mais à cette époque, et pour la prémière fois de sa vie, il a senti ses forces fléchir.

Le second fléchissement est dû à un désespoir d'ordre intime. Hadrien devenu empereur a fait une carrière éclatante. Il a, comme le disent ses monnaies, «stabilisé la terre»; il a rétabli l'économie de l'empire, développé ses resssources, et assuré la paix romaine, peut-être pour un demi-siècle. Il a fait ces immenses voyages qui ont été pour lui des voyages d'études, d'administration et de plaisir. Il s'est livré à tous les élans d'une nature avide d'action, de culture et de vie. Antinoüs, rencontré durant ces années-là, est devenu, non seulement l'objet sensuel préféré, mais l'image même de ce qu'il appelle son bonheur, au sens presque religieux du mot, son «Génie». Dans cette adoration pour un être humain, il a oublié l'être humain lui-même: le jeune homme inquiet de voir s'éteindre cette passion, d'être relégué un jour, bientôt peut-être, au rang des favoris déchus, pris dans le filet des intrigues de cour, et finalement prenant refuge dans un mysticisme point rare d'ailleurs dans l'entourage immédiat d'Hadrien, et décidant de sacrifier sa vie pour le salut et l'avenir de l'empereur. Le jour où Hadrien se trouve confronté à ce suicide de désespoir et d'enthousiasme, il perd pied complètement. Il se trouve pour la première fois devant la mort d'un être qu'il aime, devant une mort dont en somme il est cause, et à l'horreur de la perte, à l'horreur de l'irréversible et de l'irréparable, s'ajoute, pour cet homme intelligent, l'horreur de n'avoir ni prévu, ni compris, ni su contrôler cette situation qui s'est créée sous ses yeux, et l'effondrement est total. Pendant quelques pages, Hadrien nous est montré traversant ce que Zénon appellera plus tard «son œuvre au noir», c'est-à-dire que la vie lui apparaît sous son vrai jour, et ce n'est pas grand-chose. Il sort lentement de cette crise, soutenu par ses obligations d'empereur; il se remet au travail, un peu abîmé par la vie, un peu plus abandonné à ses caprices, à ses irritations du moment et, comme il le dit lui-même, ayant le sentiment que le sacrifice d'Antinoüs (si c'était bien un sacrifice) l'aura finalement «plus détérioré que sauvé».

La troisième crise est entièrement d'ordre politique. Hadrien se trouve en présence de la révolte en Palestine comme devant une sorte d'abîme infranchissable. Il a pour amis des rabbins sachant le grec et lettrés comme lui, et les juifs libéraux ont fondé beaucoup d'espoir sur son règne. Mais, d'autre part, il y a les Zélotes, il y a les juifs irréductibles, le groupe terroriste qu'Hadrien ne comprend pas. Il est incapable d'admettre (et il y a là, il faut bien le dire, une part chez lui de naïveté et d'aveuglement) que ces gens ne veulent pas des bienfaits de la civilisation gréco-romaine. Quand la révolte éclate, elle devient une affreuse guerre de guérillas qui dure trois ans, et pour la première fois Hadrien, dans son camp de Palestine, en face de la forteresse de Béthar où se sont réfugiés ses derniers adversaires qui refusent de se rendre, s'aperçoit qu'établir la paix n'est malheureusement pas une tâche si facile, que le monde est perpétuellement menacé de guerre et la civilisation menacée de mort.

9

The Isle of Achilles

... the union of the prince and the sage, of the active and speculative virtues,
would indeed constitute the perfection of human nature.

Edward Gibbon

I

Late in Hadrian's reign the governor of the Roman province of Cappadocia, L. Flavius Arrianus, undertook a voyage to survey the coastlines of the Black Sea. He recorded his findings in a letter addressed directly, and familiarly, to Hadrian that can still be read. The *Periplus of the Black Sea* is not the most riveting of Arrian's compositions to have survived from antiquity. Much is given to prosaic records of travelling distances from one location to another. But it contains some details of topographical interest nonetheless. Especially striking is a description of the island of Leuce, which Arrian based not on autopsy but on reports he found credible from people who had been there. It was a deserted place, he said, except for a few goats, but a place sacred to Thetis's son Achilles, an ancient wooden statue of whom was housed in a temple where passing sailors and voyagers paused in order to render worship. The temple, miraculously, was cleansed every day by a profusion of seabirds that watered and brushed its flagstones with their wings, and its treasury prospered from the prices an oracle demanded for the animals offered in abundant sacrifice. Many travellers claimed to have seen Achilles himself there, both in dreams and while awake, and sometimes his companion Patroclus as well, a report that drew from Arrian an expansive comment: "For I myself believe that Achilles was a hero second-to-none, for his nobility, beauty, and strength of soul; for his early departure from mankind, and for Homer's poem to him; and for the love and friendship because of which he wanted to die after his beloved." The comment is commonly taken to be a discreet allusion to the relationship between Hadrian and Antinous, perhaps expressing to the emperor Arrian's sympathetic understanding of the continuing effects upon him of the loss, now some eight or nine years earlier, of the young Bithynian.[1]

Marguerite Yourcenar drew on the *Periplus* liberally at the beginning of *Patientia*, the final segment of *Mémoires*, where Hadrian quotes a comparable letter from Arrian sent from the Black Sea, the *tutoiement* used signifying the implicit bond between imperial legate and emperor the Greek text communicates. The letter refers to the building projects Hadrian has initiated in the region, to Arrian's inspection of military garrisons and his geographical investigations, and at an appropriate juncture to the story of Jason and the Argonauts, items that all appear in the *Periplus*. Then comes this passage:

Sur la rive septentrionale de cette mer inhospitalière, nous avons touché une petite île bien grande dans la fable: l'île d'Achille. Tu le sais: Thétis passe pour avoir fait élever son fils sur cet îlot perdu dans les brumes; elle montait du fond de la mer et venait chaque soir converser sur la plage avec son enfant. L'île, inhabitée aujourd'hui, ne nourrit que des chèvres. Elle contient un temple d'Achille. Les mouettes, les goélands, les longs-courriers, tous les oiseaux de mer la fréquentent, et le battement de leurs ailes tout imprégnées d'humidité marine rafraîchit continuellement le parvis du sanctuaire. Mais cette île d'Achille, comme il convient, est aussi l'île de Patrocle, et les innombrables ex-voto qui décorent les parois du temple sont dédiés tantôt à Achille, tantôt à son ami car, bien entendu, ceux qui aiment Achille chérissent et vénèrent la mémoire de Patrocle. Achille lui-même apparaît en songe aux navigateurs qui visitent ces parages: il les protège et les avertit des dangers de la mer, comme le font ailleurs les Dioscures. Et l'ombre de Patrocle apparaît aux côtés d'Achille. (MH 499–500)

On the northern shore of that inhospitable sea we touched upon a small island of great import in legend, the isle of Achilles. As you know, Thetis is supposed to have brought her son to be reared on this islet shrouded in mist; each evening she would rise from the depths of the sea and would come to talk with her child on the strand. Nowadays the place is uninhabited; only a few goats graze there. It has a temple to Achilles. Terns, gulls, and petrels, all kinds of sea birds frequent this sanctuary, and its porch is cooled by the continual fanning of their wings still moist from the sea. But this isle of Achilles is also, as it should be, the isle of Patroclus, and the innumerable votive offerings which decorate the temple walls are dedicated sometimes to Achilles and sometimes to his friend, for of course whoever loves Achilles cherishes and venerates Patroclus' memory. Achilles himself appears in dream to the navigators who visit these parts: he protects them and warns them of the sea's dangers, as Castor and Pollux do elsewhere. And the shade of Patroclus appears at Achilles' side.

The dependence of the passage on Arrian's original is self-evident. The brief mention of Thetis in the Greek has been expanded, but otherwise Your-cenar's text is a close adaptation of Arrian's words, or as she once implied, a virtual translation.[2] The letter continues with Arrian vouching for the cred-ibility of what he has recorded. It concludes:

Achille me semble parfois le plus grand des hommes par le courage, la force d'âme, les connaissances de l'esprit unies à l'agilité du corps, et son ardent amour pour son jeune compagnon. Et rien en lui ne me paraît plus grand que le désespoir qui lui fit mépriser la vie et désirer la mort quand il eut perdu le bien-aimé. (MH 500)

Achilles sometimes seems to me the greatest of men in his courage, his fortitude, his learning and intelligence coupled with bodily skill, and his ardent love for his young companion. And nothing in him seems to me nobler than the despair which made him despise life and long for death when he had lost his beloved.

It should not cause surprise that Hadrian responds by acknowledging, self-pityingly, a friend's understanding of his tragic loss, and in the heat of May at Tivoli, as he succumbs further to decline and approaches life's end, by fantasizing about the Isle of Achilles – listening for the waves' lament, breathing in the cool sea air, wandering through the temple, and, like the sailors at Leuce even glimpsing Patroclus (*MH* 500–1). Arrian's description of the island has been thought to convey a sense of the time-less and the paradisal, perhaps in association with the motif of the Golden Age promulgated in Hadrian's reign. At this point of the novel, however, Hadrian's personal age of gold has long since ended. The allusion was clearly understood.[3]

Friendship is the theme of this last sounding, its impetus arising from the attention the subject normatively receives as a vital means of biographical illumination in pre-eminent examples of true life writing. Hermione Lee's biography of Virginia Woolf is the paradigmatic example. Its histories of Woolf's relationships with members of the Bloomsbury set, Lytton Strachey included, with her intimate female friends Vita Sackville-West and Ethel Smyth, and with many members of her family, show friendships variously emerging, perduring, faltering and resuming at every stage of Woolf's life, the result being that her emotional and psychological evolution over time is brilliantly brought before the reader's eye. What makes this possible is the survival of a mountain of correspondence the friendships generated, a mass of evidence revealing the confidences, moods, feelings, and thoughts the correspondents shared from day to day, in all their shifting varieties and complications, even, sometimes, from moment to moment. The achievement, however, if stunning in detail and execution is far from unique, and devotees of modern biography might easily summon up any number of comparable examples of memorable relationships made recoverable by the availability of similar documentary resources. Together they point once more to the dimness of prospect with which a biographer of a Roman emperor is faced.[4]

There is also a historically pertinent impulse. In the early Antonine age commentators were sensitive to the subject of imperial friendship. Tacitus made clear that an emperor could have no better instrument of good governance than good friends (*Hist.* 4.7), and Pliny that his chief responsibility was to secure such men (*Pan.* 85). Their contemporary Dio Chrysostom was profuse on the subject in his orations on kingship, with Trajan of course the "king" he had in mind: a king's friends were virtually god-given in view of the support, protection, and counsel they provided, indispensable as the recipients of delegated duties, men to be judiciously chosen to communicate his will and assist in accomplishing his ambitions, a source of personal happiness and greater in value than even members of his family. Imperial friendship bore within it an element of the sacred (*Or.* 1.31–2; 3.86–90; 3.94–115). It is understandable therefore that friendship was a matter of ancient as it is of modern biographical concern; and for Hadrian the Latin life is relatively fulsome on the topic, preserving a generic feature sporadically visible in Suetonius's *Caesares*. A contrast with modern resources nonetheless remains: details are minimal.[5]

In *Mémoires*, Arrian figures prominently as Hadrian's special friend. I begin this chapter by examining the treatment of his relationship with Hadrian in Yourcenar's educated imagination as a final case study of technique, asking how authentic, credible, justifiable the treatment is. Then, in contrast, I explore the meaning of a statement Yourcenar made in the letter to Hortense Flexner of 1953, the letter in which she responded to questions raised by Martha Gellhorn where, startlingly, she identifies herself as one of Hadrian's friends: "J'appartiens, bien sûr, aux amis; je ressens en effet pour lui cette extraordinaire amitié née de la compréhension qui résulte de la tentative de suivre un homme dans tous les incidents de sa vie et d'être à l'écoute de ses pensées; qui résulte aussi du fait que je n'aurais jamais pris Hadrien comme modèle de ce portrait s'il n'avait pas appartenu à l'espèce d'hommes que j'admire le plus" (*HZ* 237).[6] It is the source of her admiration that will be of interest, especially for clarifying how in Yourcenar's conception Hadrian is finally to be remembered.

II

Two categories of Hadrian's friends are named in the Latin life, men from the senatorial and equestrian orders. One gives the names of six friends at the time of Trajan's war against Parthia; the other, in a rubric specifically addressing friendship, discloses a dozen figures, including three from the first list, against whom Hadrian turned and came to regard as his enemies.[7] Of these, however, not all can be taken as true friends: the second passage glides ambiguously from the topic of friendship to that of persecution of enemies, and at least four names should perhaps be excluded. Something of their public careers and personal connections is on record for most – figures such as Platorius Nepos, Acilius Attianus, and Marcius Turbo – but of their personal engagement with the emperor little information is preserved. It is impossible consequently to trace Hadrian's relationships with them either over time or in any depth. All that is possible is to posit interactions at various moments from the record of external events, as Anthony Birley's procedure in the standard biography well illustrates. His reconstruction of the occasions when engagement between Hadrian and Platorius Nepos could be reasonably expected provides a model example – this is the man who as governor of Britain supervised the early construction of the Wall – a particularly useful example because the Latin life records a memorable detail: the emperor was at one point very fond of Nepos, taking no offence after once visiting him when ill and being refused admission, but later (no reason is stated) Hadrian came to detest him (*HA Hadr.* 23.4).

Accordingly, from the date of his consulship in the spring of 119, Nepos can be deduced close in age to Hadrian; and since he belonged to the same voting tribe (the *Sergia*), he could well have had a similar southern Spanish origin. Friendship with Hadrian can be posited therefore as early as the year 90 either in Italica, or at Rome or Tibur, where Nepos's family may have held property. Both men were involved in Trajan's war against Parthia, and since Nepos was governor of Thrace soon afterwards, Hadrian will have been pleased to see him when journeying there shortly after his accession. In 119, indeed, although a suffect consul, Nepos enjoyed the distinction of being Hadrian's consular colleague, a sign of rapid promotion directly attributable to his connection to the emperor. He might have remained in Thrace until assuming the governorship of Lower Germany soon afterwards, and when Hadrian visited that province in 121–2, there could be "a reunion with an old friend." In fact, "Hadrian will have stayed with Nepos in the governor's palace at Colonia Agrippinensis." Subsequently, they will have travelled together to Britain in 122 as Nepos advanced to his next, and senior, post as governor, where he will have heard the speech concerning the building of the Wall Hadrian is thought to have made on the banks of the Tyne, and will have accompanied the emperor westwards to the Solway along what was to be its line. After Hadrian's departure, he could be expected to have kept the emperor informed of the difficulties arising from the Wall's construction at least until 124, when he is last attested in office; and having returned to Rome he will have reported on its latest progress. How long afterwards he survived is unknown, but the problems the Wall's construction brought provide a satisfactory reason for the friendship's rupture.[8]

These suggestions clearly depend on taking the testimony of friendship in the *Historia Augusta* at face value and concern *histoire événementielle* alone. In themselves they are altogether unobjectionable, the Tyneside speech apart, but they hardly reveal whatever personal relations the friendship may have involved across the generation it is thought to have lasted.[9] Cicero once defined friendship's ideal constituents as consensus in all matters human and divine, goodwill and affection born of nature not expediency, and a union of souls in mutual love (*Amic.* 20, 27). Plutarch later advocated having just a small number of friends with whom genuine intimacy was possible, and even allowed for a single special friend, stressing the elements of constant companionship, displays of mutual kindness, shared interests and feelings, and a comparability of character (*Mor.* 93a–97b). The role, however, such features played, or may have played, in the relationship between Hadrian and Nepos is irrecoverable, and while the occasions of interaction proposed are entirely reasonable, they are also entirely fictive. To all intents and purposes, the friendship concerned, in Yourcenar's idiom, is lost to history. This is true of other similar reconstructions. How then does Yourcenar compare in her presentation of Hadrian's friendship with Arrian?[10]

Arrian first appears in *Mémoires*, in purely passing terms, when Hadrian is explaining to Marcus in *Tellus stabilita* the ideal of imperial peace and harmony that had motivated his acts of policy: "Arrien de Nicomédie, un des meilleurs esprits de ce temps, aime à me rappeler les beaux vers où le vieux Terpandre a défini en trois mots l'idéal spartiate, le mode de vie parfait dont Lacédémone a rêvé sans jamais l'atteindre: la Force, la Justice, les Muses" (*MH* 391).[11] No indication is given of when an association began. The passage merely assumes a late-in-life connection and an earlier recollection that cannot be verified. Whether Arrian ever spoke the words to

Hadrian Yourcenar attributes to him, or if so whether Hadrian ever recalled them as expressed here, it is impossible to say. But the thought that Hadrian communicates is not pure invention: the definition of the Spartan ideal does indeed come from Terpander, and is quoted by Arrian at the end of the treatise on military techniques, the *Tactica*, that he composed towards the end of Hadrian's reign. It was introduced to substantiate the encomiastic claim that Hadrian's Rome, flourishing in its military excellence, its culture and its law, was far more deserving of Terpander's praise than the Sparta for which the words had originally been written: "There the spear of the young men flourishes and the clear-voiced Muse and Justice who walks in the wide streets, that helper in fine deeds" (*Tact.* 44.3). Yourcenar knew the lines and imaginatively made them the basis of her text, with a qualitative judgment she presumably shared.[12]

Arrian assumes a much more prominent place in Hadrian's memory when the emperor recalls in *Sæculum aureum* a winter spent in Athens among a cluster of stimulating companions, in modern terms the period of the mid-120s. A passage that intersperses objective facts about his life with subjective impressions of his personality offers an impressive portrait:

Mais la recontre la plus précieuse de toutes fut celle d'Arrien de Nicomédie, mon meilleur ami. Plus jeune que moi d'environ douze ans, il avait déjà commencé cette belle carrière politique et militaire dans laquelle il continue de s'honorer et de servir. Son expérience des grandes affaires, sa connaissance des chevaux, des chiens, de tous les exercises du corps, le mettaient infiniment au-dessus des simples faiseurs de phrases. Dans sa jeunesse, il avait été la proie d'une de ces étranges passions de l'esprit, sans lesquelles il n'est peut-être pas de vraie sagesse, ni de vraie grandeur: deux ans de sa vie s'étaient écoulés à Nicopolis en Épire, dans la petite chambre froide et nue où agonisait Épictète; il s'était donné pour tâche de recueillir et de transcrire mot pour mot les derniers propos du vieux philosophe malade. Cette période d'enthousiasme l'avait marqué: il en gardait d'admirables disciplines morales, une espèce de candeur grave. Il pratiquait en secret des austérités dont ne se doutait personne. Mais le long apprentissage du devoir stoïque ne l'avait pas raidi dans une attitude de faux sage: il était trop fin pour ne pas s'être aperçu qu'il en est des extrémités de la vertu comme de celles de l'amour, que leur mérite tient précisément à leur rareté, à leur caractère de chef-d'œuvre unique, de bel excès. L'intelligence sereine, l'honnêteté parfaite de Xénophon lui servaient désormais de modèle. Il écrivait l'histoire de son pays, la Bithynie. J'avais placé cette province, longtemps fort mal administrée par des proconsuls, sous ma juridiction personnelle: il me conseilla dans mes plans de réforme. Ce lecteur assidu des dialogues socratiques n'ignorait rien des réserves d'héroïsme, de dévouement, et parfois de sagesse, dont la Grèce a su ennoblir la passion pour l'ami; il traitait mon jeune favori avec une déférence tendre. Les deux Bithyniens parlaient ce doux dialecte de l'Ionie, aux désinences presque homériques, que j'ai plus tard décidé Arrien à employer dans ses œuvres. (*MH* 410–11)

But the most precious of all these encounters was that with Arrian of Nicomedia, the best of my friends. Younger than I by some twelve years, he had already begun that outstanding political and military career in which he continues to distinguish himself and to serve the State. His experience in government, his knowledge of hunting, horses, and dogs, and of all bodily exercise, raised him infinitely above the mere word-mongers of the time. In his youth he had been prey to one of those strange passions of the soul without which, perhaps, there can be no true wisdom, nor true greatness: two years of his life had been passed at Nicopolis in Epirus in the cold, bare room where Epictetus lay dying; he had set himself the task of gathering and transcribing, word for word, the last sayings of that aged and ailing philosopher. That period of enthusiasm had left its mark upon him; from it he retained certain admirable moral disciplines, and a kind of grave simplicity. In secret he practiced austerities which no one even suspected. But his long apprenticeship to Stoic duty had not hardened him into self-righteousness; he was too intelligent not to realize that the heights of virtue, like those of love, owe their special value to their very rarity, to their quality of unique achievement and sublime excess. Now he was striving to model himself upon the calm good sense and perfect honesty of Xenophon. He was writing the history of his country, Bithynia; I had placed this province, so long ill governed by proconsuls, under my personal jurisdiction; Arrian advised me in my plans for reform. This assiduous reader of Socratic dialogue treated my young favorite with tender deference, for he knew full well the rich stores of heroism, devotion, and even wisdom, on which Greece has drawn to ennoble love between friends. These two Bithynians spoke the soft speech of Ionia, where word endings are almost Homeric in form. I later persuaded Arrian to employ this dialect in his writings.

First the objective details. Much is known of Arrian's public life and literary career. He was born in Nicomedia, in the period 85–92. He became a Roman senator, rose to hold the consulship under Hadrian, in 129 or 130, and for an unusually long period governed the province of Cappadocia from 130/1 to 137/8. (His tenure ended before Hadrian's death in July of 138.) He may have held earlier magistracies, or been adlected to the senate at praetorian rank. About the year 110, he is attested at Delphi as a member of the *consilium* of C. Avidius Nigrinus, and a governorship of Baetica, unknown in Yourcenar's day, is now on record before the consulship. Basic information could have been learned from a handbook of Greek literature such as that of the Croisets, including the possibility that Arrian took part in Trajan's Parthian war; to have made him twelve years younger than Hadrian, notionally born in 88, does no injury to history; and there can be no quarrel with Hadrian's attribution to him here, during the winter stay in Athens, of a military and political career in progress or of its continuation late into the reign as Hadrian writes his memoirs.[13] The references to hunting, horses, and dogs follow from Yourcenar's deployment of Arrian's *Cynegeticus,* while the reference to physical exercise is due especially to the *Tactica.* On one estimate the *Cynegeticus* belongs to the 140s, which means that chronological confusion would ensue if the present passage were taken to imply that Hadrian, at the moment of writing, knew Arrian's entire literary corpus. Yet his interests in hunting and military exercises cannot be confined to the several moments of the treatises' composition, and in any case Arrian remarks in his treatise that warfare and hunting (and philosophy) were interests of his from an early stage of life (*Cyn.* 7.4). There is nothing therefore to counter Hadrian's image of him given here, and historians today might well agree to assign him a greater stature than the "wordmongers" with whom he is compared, which I take to mean contemporary sophists such as Favorinus – windbags all.[14]

Nor of course is Arrian's association with Epictetus in doubt. The letter prefacing the first book of his *Discourses* explains how his record of Epictetus's teachings came into being from notes taken at the philosopher's lectures that eventually entered the public domain (*Epict. diss.* 1 *praef.* 1–4). His years of study with the philosopher began when Arrian was about eighteen, and are usually assigned to the latter portion of Trajan's reign, after Epictetus had taken up residence in Nicopolis following Domitian's expulsion of philosophers from Rome in the year 95. His reputation as a teacher attracted a wide range of pupils and visitors from the ranks of the prosperous, including perhaps the young Hadrian, who is said to have had a high regard for him (*HA Hadr.* 16.10).[15] Yourcenar situates a consultation in Rome, in an appealing vignette, before the exile (*MH* 398). As for Arrian following the example of Xenophon, this too Yourcenar will have known from passages in his writings where he adopts Xenophon's name as his own, from their common interests in military affairs and hunting, and from Arrian's avowal of Xenophon as his literary and philosophical exemplar. She cannot have known that he may have taken "Xenophon" as a formal element of his Roman nomenclature to become L. Flavianus Arrianus Xenophon because the relevant evidence was unavailable to her; but that he was celebrated at Athens in later life as the New Xenophon was a handbook detail again readily accessible. So, too, information on Arrian's *Bithyniaca,* a history of his homeland from earliest times until its bequest to Rome thought to have been an early literary product, whose eight books survive now only in fragments. The first identifies him as born and educated in Nicomedia and the holder of a local priesthood of Demeter and Persephone. The reference here is reasonably situated.[16]

The one oddity in the passage is Hadrian's statement of the change made in the administration of Bithynia. For a century and more senatorially appointed proconsuls had governed the province until Trajan took the decisive step of directly appointing an imperial legate with consular authority. His choice famously fell on the younger Pliny, whose *Letters* expose firm evidence of his predecessors' administrative mismanagement, the reason for the change, and perhaps the source of Hadrian's remark here on poor government. Pliny is usually thought to have died in office in 111 or 112, some eighteen months or so after his arrival, given that his communications with Trajan collected in the final book of the *Letters* seem suddenly to break off in midstream. (Hadrian was well aware of this [*MH* 349].) His successor, C. Julius Cornutus Tertullus, also an imperial legate, was a close associate. The implication therefore that Hadrian made a radical administrative change might be thought misleading. Cassius Dio's epitomator, however, speaks of Pamphylia, perhaps in the mid-130s, being given to the senate in return for Hadrian's direct appointment to Bithynia of a man named Severus, which may mean that Bithynia had reverted to proconsular control at some stage after Cornutus Tertullus's brief tenure (69.14.4). Certainty is impossible, because the record of Bithynian governors is incomplete, and this Severus is the sole Hadrianic governor who can be identified: C. Julius Severus (*cos.* 138?), a Cappadocian descendant of eastern kings and potentates, who was sent to effect reforms in the province with the right to use the five *fasces* customarily allowed to imperial legates. Greek inscriptions discovered in Ankara early in the twentieth century supply the evidence. Whether Yourcenar knew them, or relied on Dio's notice alone, the detail she includes on Bithynia is apparently misdated but not unfounded.[17]

In sum, the essential veracity of the extract is clear. What cannot be validated, however, is Hadrian's assessment of Arrian's personality. The long-term impact exposure to Epictetus is said to have made upon him and the sympathetic attitude attributed to him concerning Hadrian's relationship with Antinous are novelistic inventions. They are not inventions that stretch the limits of belief, however, and are no less unreasonable than conventional speculations of the sort just seen. At a minimum, and I think both importantly and distinctively, they show that Yourcenar had thought about the effect of Epictetus's teachings on Arrian as his life unfolded, and about the kind of response he could be expected to have formed to Hadrian's relationship with Antinous. In this they provide substance to a figure who, as so often in Roman history, can be seen no more than one-dimensionally. I regard them as further examples of appropriate biographical colouring. That Hadrian promoted the adoption of Ionic Greek in Arrian's compositions is an exaggeration, but as Rémy Poignault has commented, the reason behind the claim is determinable: "il s'agit d'une allusion à *L'Inde*, qui est rédigé dans le dialecte ionien."[18] As for Arrian at some point acting as an adviser on Bithynia, an undated item from the *Digest* may be noted: a rescript from Hadrian to the provincial governor Flavius Arrianus giving an opinion on legal cases concerning the imperial treasury (*fiscus*) in which relevant documents had been withheld (49.14.2.1). Arrian's crucial designation as Hadrian's "best friend" has much to commend it.

His next appearance, still in *Sæculum aureum*, is purely incidental and similarly inventive. Hadrian refers to the military manoeuvres carried out under his supervision when at Lambaesis in the heat of July, concluding with what seems like an indiscriminate afterthought: he thought of having Arrian write a treatise on military tactics and discipline as perfect as a well-formed body (*MH* 422). This seems to reflect little more than a loose connection between the military exercises and Arrian's composition of the *Tactica*. But a detail elsewhere that has nothing directly to do with Arrian confirms the thought. Speaking in *Tellus stabilita* of his measures for promoting military preparedness during peacetime, Hadrian reminds Marcus that Rome's armies include auxiliary troops drawn from a wide variety of peoples, each contributing its distinctive traditions and methods of engagement; their diversity in a unified army has symbolized the imperial unity sought as an objective of Hadrianic policy, but it is a military diversity that the emperor has encouraged: "J'ai permis aux soldats l'emploi de leurs cris de guerre nationaux et de commandements donnés dans leurs langues" (*MH* 379).[19] In the final chapter of the *Tactica*, a passage Yourcenar evidently knew, Arrian was to commend Hadrian precisely for adopting the military exercises of foreign peoples – Parthians, Armenians, Sarmatians, and Celts – and for urging contingents of barbarian cavalrymen to use their native war cries.[20] Nothing can prove the factual truth of Hadrian's passing thought at Lambaesis, and Yourcenar does not go as far as to place Arrian in Africa with him. But the thought once more makes biographical sense, and her reader could be forgiven for thinking that Arrian's presence accounts for why Hadrian had the thought he did. The close resemblance, it happens, between the inscriptional descriptions of the military exercises Hadrian supervised at Lambaesis and the lively details of contemporary Roman cavalry manoeuvres in the *Tactica*, has been judged far from coincidental.[21]

Inventive, not to say fictional, details obtrude, however, when in *Disciplina Augusta* Yourcenar allows Hadrian a fulsome record of time spent in Athens before the outbreak of the Jewish War, the winter of 131/132 in modern dating.[22] In this final visit to his favoured city, literary and intellectual matters occupy him greatly, and Arrian figures prominently as his companion.

Like Hadrian, he is an Eleusinian initiate. He has an Athenian wife who belongs to the priestly family of the Kerykes, and Hadrian lodges in their house, a stone's throw from his new library, where at night he reflects on the words carved on Antinous's tomb and one evening discusses with his host the philosophical inadequacy of the Christians' Golden Rule. (They agree that dogmatic sectarianism poses a threat to traditional Roman polytheism and the formulation of a moral code free from constraint and hypocrisy.) On topics of every kind, Hadrian remembers Arrian as a superior conversationalist, whose sympathy for the heroic love felt for Antinous is specified as a special reason for his gratitude (*MH* 453, 456, 457–8, 458–9). This can all be dismissed out of hand: "The evocative picture of Hadrian being entertained at Athens by Arrian and his wife … is purely imaginary." And indeed Arrian will have been in Cappadocia at this time. But the picture is not entirely fanciful. That Arrian was an Eleusinian initiate has been inferred from a remark made when speaking of Athens in his most celebrated work, the *Anabasis*; he is known also to have had descendants who held office in Athens in the next generation, which validates well enough the postulate of a wife; and while Yourcenar acknowledged in the *Note* that for Hadrian to call this woman "fine et fière" was excessive (*OR* 545), the family identity was seemingly derived from Graindor's deduction that Arrian was adopted into the Kerykes after his Eleusinian initiation.[23] No further administrative or official positions after the governorship of Cappadocia are attested for him, and after Hadrian's death Arrian is thought rather to have spent many years in Athens engaged in literary activity, becoming an Athenian citizen and finding fame as the New Xenophon. Yourcenar redisposed such broad information to a point convenient for her narrative, untroubled by precise chronological considerations.[24]

Finally, there is among Hadrian's recollections of imperial business after his return to Italy receipt of a report from Arrian shortly after his appointment to Cappadocia. It warns of a threat represented by the independent Caspian king Pharasmenes, who was continuing a duplicitous policy of on-and-off support for Rome that had caused problems as long ago as the time of Trajan's Parthian war:

Ce roitelet poussait sournoisement vers nos frontières des hordes d'Alains barbares; ses querelles avec l'Arménie compromettaient la paix en Orient. Convoqué à Rome, il refusa de s'y rendre, comme il avait déjà refusé d'assister à la conférence de Samosate quatre ans plus tôt. En guise d'excuses, il m'envoya un présent de trois cents robes d'or, vêtements royaux que je fis porter dans l'arène à des criminels livrés aux bêtes. Cet acte peu pondéré me satisfit comme le geste d'un homme qui se gratte jusqu'au sang. (*MH* 465–6)

This petty prince was slyly pushing hordes of barbarian Alani toward our frontiers; his quarrels with Armenia endangered peace in the Orient. When summoned to Rome he refused to come, just as he had already refused to attend the conference at Samosata four years before. By way of excuse he sent me a present of three hundred robes of gold, royal garments which I ordered worn in the arena by criminals loosed to wild beasts. That rash gesture solaced me like the action of one who scratches himself nearly raw.

The passage is founded on material from the Latin life (*HA Hadr.* 13.9; 17.11–12; 21.13) and Cassius Dio (69.15.1). The former records that Pharasmenes of Iberia contemptuously declined an invitation to attend a council of eastern monarchs, an event that can be dated to 129; that Hadrian gave him magnificent gifts, together with an elephant and a cohort of fifty troops, in return for gifts he had received from the king (they included gold-embroidered cloaks worn by 300 criminals Hadrian later sent to the arena to show his scorn for the man); and that despite the insulting refusal to meet him, he secured the king's friendship.[25] In turn, Dio's epitomator claims that Pharasmanes provoked the Alans to invade Albania and Media, a venture affecting Armenia and Cappadocia, but that in the event the invaders were bought off with gifts from the Parthian king Vologaeses, who was deterred by the Roman governor of Cappadocia, Flavius Arrianus.[26]

These are pitiful scraps of information. They signify problems and activity on Rome's northeast frontier that cannot be assessed fully or incontestably. Experts nonetheless surmise two relatively secure developments. First, that when in Cappadocia in 129, Hadrian invited to a peace congress, held perhaps at Satala, an assemblage of foreign petty kings and dynasts, one being Pharasmenes II of Iberia, who refused to attend. Second, that in the mid-130s the Transcaucasian Alans embarked on dangerous migrations, possibly at the instigation of Pharasmenes, that threatened both Parthian and Roman interests. As governor of Cappadocia, Arrian successfully repulsed the threat to Rome by organizing a military response. Direct engagement proved unnecessary, but in a work called *Ectaxis*, he subsequently gave an account of the steps he had taken.[27] The basis, therefore, of Hadrian's recollection here is clear. There is no evidence that Hadrian summoned Pharasmenes to Rome as well as to an eastern congress, as some scholars have argued, and I assume that Yourcenar, as so often, embellished a confused tradition. I assume further that she knew of the *Ectaxis*, and also of the *Alanike*, a work Arrian wrote on the Alans that has not survived.[28] At any rate, this same complex of material underlies Hadrian's appended memory that at Bethar he had felt confident of Arrian's ability to safeguard Armenia from the advance of the Alans, knowing full well that other invasions would bring an eventual end to Rome's empire. Intellectual enervation is diagnosed as another intimation of imminent imperial decline, with literature close to exhaustion and even Arrian, their friendship notwithstanding, in reality no new Xenophon, but rather a symbol of decadence (*MH* 474, 475). Once more such thoughts cannot be verified. But nor can they be altogether denied.

The summary I have given suffices, I think, to account for Arrian's designation and role in *Mémoires* as Hadrian's best friend. The evidence discussed is tenuous, and it is notable that Arrian does not appear among the friends of Hadrian named in the Latin life. But his writings suggest a disposition much like that the tradition ascribes to the philhellene Hadrian, a Greek of soldierly and intellectual interests devoted to the hunt, so that personal compatibility is a natural inference. Yourcenar took an imaginative leap in her presentation of him, influenced if not by classical pronouncements then certainly by the understanding of friendship she gave to Matthieu Galey, in which she placed considerable weight on the defining qualities of sympathy and mutual support (*YO* 244–5).[29] It is from this position, however, that her achievement is best appreciated, because the result is to create a sense of a real intimacy between emperor and like-minded companion that resembles as far as is possible the histories of friendship that are a staple of modern biography. Judged as a whole, the passages in which Arrian enters Hadrian's memory are not lists of possible encounters between the two inferred from a lacunose tradition of public activities, but substantive attempts to portray the essence of a genuine and mutually meaningful relationship. In this, methodologically, Arrian's report from the Black Sea was of inordinate importance, its delicate allusion allowing Hadrian on its receipt to speak rhapsodically of Arrian's percipience (*MH* 500–1). An entry in the *Carnets* leaves no doubt of its value for the recovery of both Hadrian and his friend:

Dans l'absence de tout autre document, la lettre d'Arrien à l'empereur Hadrien au sujet du périple de la mer Noire suffirait à recréer dans ses grandes lignes cette figure impériale: minutieuse exactitude du chef qui veut tout savoir; intérêt pour les travaux de la paix et de la guerre; goût des statues ressemblantes et bien faites; passion pour les poèmes et les légendes d'autrefois. Et ce monde, rare de tout temps, et qui disparaîtra complètement après Marc Aurèle, dans lequel, si subtiles que soient les nuances de la déférence et du respect, le lettré et l'administrateur s'adresse encore au prince *comme à un ami*. Mais tout est là: mélancolique retour à l'idéal de la Grèce ancienne; discrète allusion aux amours perdues et aux consolations mystiques cherchées par le survivant; hantise des pays inconnus et des climats barbares. L'évocation

si profondément préromantique des régions désertes peuplées d'oiseaux de mer fait
songer à l'admirable vase, retrouvé à la Villa Adriana et placé aujourd'hui au Musée
des Thermes, où, dans la neige du marbre, s'éploie et s'envole en pleine solitude une
bande de hérons sauvages. (*CNMH* 534–5 [my emphasis]; cf. 531)

If all other documents were lacking, the *Letter of Arrian to the Emperor Hadrian on
the Circumnavigation of the Black Sea* would suffice to recreate in broad outline that
great imperial figure: the scrupulous exactitude of the chief-of-state who would know all
details; his interest in the work both of war and of peace; his concern for good likenesses
in statues, and that these should be finely wrought; his passion for the poetry and legend
of an earlier day. And that society, rare in any period, but destined to vanish completely
after the time of Marcus Aurelius, wherein the scholarly administrator can still address
his prince *as a friend*, however subtly shaded his deference and respect. Everything is
there: the nostalgia for ancient Greece and its ideals, discreet allusion to a lost love and to
mystical consolation sought by the bereaved survivor, the haunting appeal of unknown
lands and barbarous climes. The evocation of desert wastes peopled only by sea-birds, so
profoundly romantic in spirit, calls to mind the exquisite vase found in Villa Hadriana,
to be seen today in the Museum of the Terme in Rome; there on a field of marble snow a
flock of wild heron are spreading their wings to fly away, in utter solitude.

This entry is in fact a revised and polished version of a page in Yourcenar's
Notebook, a single, typed, and intriguingly undated page but one that must be
taken, I think, to signify an engagement with the *Periplus* of long standing. It
concludes with a key sentence for present purposes that did not find its way
into the final version: "Il faut attendre la Renaissance pour retrouver ce ton
dans une correspondance entre érudit et prince."[30] Yourcenar found so many
features of the *Periplus* consistent with elements of her overall conception of
Hadrian, and its tone so personal, that a close friendship was the conclusion
logically drawn. It convinces far more than any rival supposition.[31] And this
was not a simple matter of wishful sentimental thinking. Her preparation had
been academically thorough. One early reader alleged that she had somehow
made a mistake with her location of the Isle of Achilles, and questioned where,
as her version of Arrian's letter reported, Xenophon had once looked out on
the Black Sea. In response she cited M.I. Rostovtzeff's *Iranians and Greeks
in South Russia* of 1922 as her source for the island's identification, though
her memory was limited, she said, because she no longer had the book with her
or the notes taken from it. She referred also to K. Müller's *Geographi Graeci
Minores* of 1855 as the volume in which she had read the *Periplus* – colloquially
the "*Géographes Grecs* de Didot" – a rare work that she did not own herself
and had used only in public libraries. Unable therefore to say more about the
spot from which Xenophon had looked out, she remembered all the same that

the reference came in the first paragraph of the *Periplus*. Moreover, acknowledging the possibility of error, or of an interpolated Greek text or a defective edition, she was fairly sure that she had "translated" ("traduite") Arrian as accurately as possible (*HZ* 474–6).[32] A second communication the following year explained the confusion between her Sinope in the earliest lines of her version of Arrian's letter to Hadrian (*MH* 499) and the Trapezus of Arrian's text: it was due to her initial "inadvertance," hasty note taking or the like. She had not made a correction in later printings, however, because a French reader would find Sinope more classically suitable than Trebizond, a mediaeval Asiatic name that evoked the Crusades. Her policy was to make light changes with names to avoid complications and to promote readability. But she was open to making the correction in the interests of "exactitude passionnée" (*HZ* 522–3). In the event this never happened.[33]

Almost at the end of the *Carnets*, a final, brief statement of relevance appears, again with an antecedent draft in the *Notebook* (written this time in Yourcenar's sprawling hand):

Lieux où l'on a choisi de vivre, résidences invisibles qu'on s'est construites à l'écart du temps. J'ai habité Tibur, j'y mourrai peut-être, comme Hadrien dans l'île d'Achille. (*CNMH* 540)

There are places where one has chosen to live, invisible abodes which one makes for oneself quite outside the current of time. I have lived in Tibur, and shall die there, perhaps, as Hadrian did on Achilles' Isle.[34]

The reader knows of course that Hadrian died at Baiae. To understand what is meant depends on recalling the emperor's response to his reading of Arrian's report. This occurs at the Villa in a secret chamber that lay in the centre of a pool (*MH* 500). Yourcenar was presumably thinking here of the feature commonly known as the Maritime Theatre that is often taken to have been Hadrian's private retreat.[35] As he ponders the report, memories of the many places once visited flood his mind, all to be superseded by the vision of the Isle of Achilles Arrian brings before him: a place, ironically, that the great traveller has not seen for himself and never will see, but where because of its special associations he would feel himself to be at the very moment of life's end:

À Tibur, du sein d'un mois de mai brûlant, j'écoute sur les plages de l'île d'Achille la longue plainte des vagues; j'aspire son air pur et froid; j'erre sans effort sur le parvis du temple baigné d'humidité marine; j'aperçois Patrocle ... Ce lieu que je ne verrai jamais devient ma secrète résidence, mon suprême asile. J'y serai sans doute au moment de ma mort. (*MH* 501)

Here in Tibur, in the full heat of May, I listen for the waves' slow complaint on the beach of the isle of Achilles; I breathe there in cool, pure air; I wander effortlessly over the temple terrace bathed in the fresh sea spray; I catch sight of Patroclus ... That place which I shall never see is becoming my secret abode, my innermost haven. I shall doubtless be there at the moment of my death.

As that moment approaches, with thoughts concentrated on Antinous, there is the sense, repeatedly, of a visitation: "*Et l'ombre de Patrocle apparaît aux côtés d'Achille*" (*MH* 510).[36] The authenticating influence of Arrian's paradisal island is felt almost to the last.

III

There is something else here, however, of which to take account, something authorially suggestive about this late item in the *Carnets*. It implies that Yourcenar, no more than in her late forties, was already thinking when she wrote them of her own death in terms similar to those imputed to Hadrian, under the influence of the *Periplus*, with Tivoli becoming a simple replacement of the Isle of Achilles as her ultimate resting place. It is impossible to be sure. But there is, I think, a sense of finality in the extract's melancholy words. It reads almost as a *sphragis*, as if with the labour of *Mémoires* completed, author and authored are sealed together, as friends, in the same thought process. And while the very last entry in the *Carnets* looks forward to new projects, this sense of an ending still persists: Yourcenar has returned to Tivoli, to the Pantheon, to the Castel, and, although not forgotten, the immediacy of Hadrian's final days and the presence of his deathbed attendants have begun to fade, becoming no more than memories. The portrait of Hadrian has been painted. The project is finished. There is no going back:

Notre commerce avec autrui n'a qu'un temps; il cesse une fois la satisfaction obtenue, la leçon sue, le service rendu, l'œuvre accomplie. Ce que j'étais capable de dire a été dit; ce que je pouvais apprendre a été appris. Occupons-nous pour un temps d'autres travaux. (*CNMH* 541)[37]

Our commerce with others does not long endure; it ceases once satisfaction is obtained, the lesson learned, the service rendered, the book complete. What I could say has been said; what I could learn has been learned. Let us turn, for the time that is left to us, to other work.

It was not of course to be this way. Yourcenar's dedication to recreating Hadrian's life story by no means came to an end in 1951. For thirty years and more after the novel's publication Hadrian remained a preoccupation, as is surely more than evident from the many passages from the letters and interviews to which I have drawn attention in preceding chapters. Yourcenar continued always to speak and to write of him as a vital presence in her life and, it might well be said, as a friend with whom she remained in constant contact and dialogue, no matter that there was undoubtedly much other work that occupied her.

The preoccupation can be understood at one level from Petite Plaisance, which is maintained today as it was when Yourcenar lived there. It is a modest house by North American standards, its rooms comfortable but compact, its walls lined throughout with thousands of books, to contemplate which is to reinforce awareness of the astonishing vastness of Yourcenar's intellectual interests. The classical books are located mostly in the study where she and Grace Frick worked together, opposite one another at a surprisingly small desk, and give some sense of the research undertaken for writing *Mémoires*. They also show how interest in Hadrian continued long after the novel's appearance, with new items constantly accruing: Anthony Birley on Roman Britain in 1964, or Brian Dobson and David Breeze on the Wall in 1973. Marginalia and underscorings evince serious use in some cases, as with the tenth edition of Collingwood Bruce's *Handbook to the Roman Wall*, edited now in 1951 by I.A. Richmond, or with Jacquetta Hawkes's *A Guide to the Prehistoric and Roman Monuments in England and Wales* from 1952.[38] Some books were gifts from authors, a case in point being Henry Bardon's *Le Crépuscule des Césars* with its enigmatic inscription, "À Mme. Yourcenar … en souvenir d'un rendez-vous manqué." Bardon also sent a personally inscribed copy of the second volume of *La Littérature latine inconnue* (Yourcenar mentioned, recall, how much she was enjoying it in July 1956 [*HZ* 562]).[39] In September 1968, as earlier noted, she thanked another correspondent for sending an exhibition catalogue in which objects associated with the Bar Kokhba rebellion were illustrated, pleased that they seemed to corroborate what she had tried to bring to life in her account of the rebellion (*L* 297). Of special note is a manila folder marked "Archeologia" kept in the index volume of Daremberg and Saglio's encyclopaedia. It contains annotated clippings from French and Belgian newspapers and journals of the 1970s that preserve information on the Wall, the clothing of Roman soldiers (with reference to Robin Birley's early discoveries of the Vindolanda writing tablets), the restoration of Roman Cologne, and the unearthing of Roman baths at Cephisia close to Athens. If the annotations are perhaps in the hand of Grace Frick, the materials and their contents clearly mattered to Yourcenar. Her Roman reading, if professionally unsystematic, was a lifelong pursuit.[40]

If further domestic evidence were needed of Hadrian's pervasive influence, it comes from decorations no visitor to Petite Plaisance can miss: the Piranesi drawings of Rome and Tivoli that had long cast a spell, the ubiquitous images of Hadrian and Antinous – "c'est presque un recueil de souvenirs" (*PV* 217) – and the living-room lampshade on which Yourcenar had traced not only Hadrian's deathbed poem, but also coin legends and other associated phrases: SOTER, AUDIVI VOCES DIVINAS, ITALIA FELIX, PATER PATRIAE, EUSEBES.[41] Yourcenar may have assumed too readily that TRANQUILLITAS was a leading Hadrianic concept, but it is an attractive thought that she chose to live on an island that naturally fostered peacefulness, a region dominated by the delights of Acadia National Park, with huge vistas of undulating terrain and ocean waters calm in summertime offset in winter by deep snows and barren landscapes that, as photographs show, allowed for horseback riding once the harshness of the season had given way to spring. This was the setting in which the extraordinary friendship was experienced. Mount Desert could easily and favourably be compared with the Isle of Achilles, and perhaps remind of adventures from an early time in life when Yourcenar had herself sailed on the Black Sea.[42]

Continuation of the friendship was due not least to *Mémoires'* continuing success. Corrections had to be made for successive impressions, translations, and new editions, and once illustrated versions were a concern photographs had to be acquired from museums and institutions all over the world. The number of requests in the correspondence for illustrations and permissions to print is enormous. A compulsive desire for accuracy and the business of selling books combined therefore to keep Hadrian always in Yourcenar's mind. And yet there was more to the relationship than the practical. Her reading apart, Yourcenar's knowledge of Hadrian and his world constantly refined itself as she travelled. She wrote with excitement in May 1952 of having recently seen new finds and a distinctive statue of Trajan in the Archaeological Museum of Seville, while ten years later she could say of another visit to Spain that she had been more impressed with Carmona than Italica.[43] In England in 1953, she was able at last to study the frontier area of the Wall, taking part in the discovery of a small Mithraic temple and visiting the Carlisle museum, where for the first time she noted a particular Hadrianic inscription from Wroxeter, shown on a postcard she soon afterwards found at Shrewsbury. In Cheshire she saw the portrait known as the Hope Antinous, but whether at Ainwick she saw the Rudge Cup, the bowl perhaps inscribed with names of some of the forts along the western Wall, is not quite so certain. Later, in a letter of early May 1969 to Lidia Storoni Mazzolani, she wrote of a recent stay in the southwest of France, a region previously unknown but to which there was a predictable response: this was Narbonese Gaul, and it was impossible for her not to think of Hadrian travelling there on his way to Spain: he had known that Arles differed in beauty from Nîmes (*MH* 386).[44]

There were replies also to letters from admirers of *Mémoires* and, as her celebrity grew, answers to questions from interviewers, in the totality of which an important development becomes discernible. The responses not only evince an uninterrupted fascination with, and an increase in factual knowledge about, Hadrian; they also reveal a growing and ultimately characteristic "slippage" – a blurring of the line between the Hadrian as Yourcenar had recreated him in her novel and the Hadrian of history as he can realistically be known.[45] As various passages earlier quoted imply, the two increasingly became for Yourcenar indistinguishable, so that present-day readers of her correspondence and interviews, like her original correspondents and interlocutors, are left in no doubt that the fictive Hadrian she had created is indisputably the historical, the real Hadrian. The evidence is abundant and I specify here a few examples only.

First, Yourcenar's letter from March 1952 to Christian Murciaux, in which she responds to the comparison Murciaux drew, seen earlier, between Yourcenar's Hadrian and the Alexis of *Alexis ou le Traité du vain combat*, a contemporary story of a young musician compelled by the demands of an undeniable and, as he hopes, liberating homosexuality to leave the wife he loves and their newborn child.[46] Murciaux had found a number of resemblances between the two figures. Yourcenar took pains, however, to emphasize the dissimilarities involved, to differentiate one from the other. She would not have considered writing Hadrian's history, his "histoire" she significantly said, had he not dreamed of the gods, loved Greece, and wept for Antinous, a statement that reflects basics of the source tradition that anyone could recognize as depicting the historical Hadrian. And yet, she continued, he would have interested her far less had there been nothing more to him: emperor and man completed and supported each other, a position that moves away from identifiable aspects of the tradition to a far more subjective view of Hadrian. What gave her pleasure ("voilà ce qui me plaît"), which I take to mean what especially attracted her to Hadrian's history, was that a voluptuary discovered how to become a great statesman, that an artist forced himself to think sensibly and lucidly on all manner of matters, and that in the domain of the senses and the mind, of practical deeds and great dreams, Hadrian the man was never guilty of negligence or tempted to make sacrifices. The poet, the lover, and the invalid, weighed down by sixty years of life, could not be separated from the simple, even simplistic, figure of "the emperor" (*HZ* 137–8). In which of course the skeletal tradition has been expanded and elaborated to reveal a personality far more complex than the individual known merely as once a ruler of Rome's empire. His history is conceptualized as diachronic and his character as having evolved over time in a way that contrasts sharply with the static, fixed descriptions of emperors given by writers both ancient and modern.[47] A link with the tradition is retained, but the interpretative development shown in the novel is now strongly consolidated as a historical truth. For Yourcenar, her reconstitution of Hadrian was historically valid because in creating a "temps perdu" she had worked, she assured Murciaux, from facts to be found in Cassius Dio's anecdotes and other sources, poring over them interminably and concentratedly, so that through a magical operation Hadrian's voice could be heard in one situation after another. She invokes, that is, that experience of mediumistic revelation that enabled her to dispense with any formal distinction between the figure of her novel and the figure of history. To her, they were in all respects one and the same. None of this applied in the case of the fictional Alexis.

A decade and more later, in August 1968, Yourcenar drew a similar contrast between Hadrian and the later Zeno. It came in the letter to Lidia Storoni Mazzolani confessing that Hadrian's meditation during the Jewish War on the possible end of the world was the boldest item in her novel.[48] Now, she wrote, Zeno was "le philosophe imaginaire," whereas Hadrian was "l'empereur reconstruit," a phrase that presupposes a portrait of a real figure from the past who could indeed be recovered and who in *Mémoires* had in fact been brought back to life (*L* 290). The form in which the reconstruction took place was the choice of a creative artist, but the result was a historical account whose overall veracity was beyond challenge, as solid as an ancient marble sculpture. While susceptible here and there to refinement from the glancing blow of a chisel, the sculptural representation unambiguously captured and conveyed on inner and outer planes alike the essence of the real man. And as the reference to the philosopher makes plain, the fixation with accuracy was abiding.

On the inner plane, again comparing Hadrian with Zeno, whose life ends in suicide, Yourcenar remarked in an interview of 1971 that Hadrian had often thought of dying in the same way (*PV* 111: "souvent"). The assertion is not a complete invention, because both main sources refer to Hadrian's attempts to procure his own death during his late illness, either by poison or the sword.[49] Appropriate thoughts and emotions, if formally unattested, could therefore reasonably be deduced. Yourcenar knew that the attempts on record had a precise setting, and her procedure of having Hadrian contemplate and seek death in *Patientia* is comprehensible enough, and could even justify his much earlier declaration in *Varius multiplex multiformis* which Yourcenar quoted in her interview (not quite accurately): "Si j'ai jamais à subir la torture, et la maladie va sans doute se charger de m'y soumettre, je ne suis par sûr d'obtenir longtemps de moi l'impassibilité d'un Thraséas, mais j'aurai du moins la ressource de me résigner à mes cris" (*MH* 319).[50] Despite the pre-accession context, Hadrian's mind in this passage is clearly on the narrative present, the final period of ill health and decline, and it is not impossible (again) that thoughts entered his mind of the noble suicide of the Stoic martyr from the reign of Nero heroized by Tacitus (*Ann.* 16.34–5). In *Sæculum aureum*, however, in connection with the much earlier death of the philosopher Euphrates, Hadrian states that he had never been opposed to suicide and had even considered taking his own life during the crisis of his accession, many years, that is, before the narrative moment. The issue had been an obsession ever since: "Je n'ai jamais été l'ennemi de la sortie volontaire; j'y avais pensé comme à une fin possible au moment de la crise qui précéda la mort de Trajan. Ce problème du suicide, qui m'a obsédé depuis, me semblait alors de solution facile" (*MH* 411).[51] Perhaps again this was true. But it cannot be shown to be true, and the "often" of Yourcenar's original remark is impossible to verify. The Hadrian of whom she spoke in this way is her fictive Hadrian, but the interview leaves the indelible impression that he is also the Hadrian of history. The fictive and the factual were increasingly elided, with Yourcenar unconcerned to draw any boundary between the two.

There are many similar illustrations. In September 1963, now comparing Hadrian not only with Alexis but also with Éric von Lhomond of *Le Coup de grâce*, Yourcenar wrote that a certain solitude surrounded Hadrian, as all men of high intellect in positions of supreme power, but that he enjoyed society all the same; there was nothing of the Romantic about it (*HZ* III 463). The verdict was unambiguously historical, as if Yourcenar's Hadrian were not at all a *re*-creation. Speaking in 1977 of cultural differences between Greece and Italy, she stated that for Hadrian Greece represented the exercise of intelligence, her point being to contrast Greek idealism with Roman practicality. She then quoted the Hadrian of *Disciplina Augusta*, again not quite verbatim, to show that while Plato invented the idea of justice, Hadrian and his legal advisers had taken concrete steps to achieve justice by passing laws that gradually improved the lives of slaves (*PV* 193). Whether there was a distinction between the fictive Hadrian shortly to be quoted or the historical Hadrian was irrelevant, and the present-day reader of the interview might easily assume that Yourcenar has the authority of a historian able to make an unassailable judgment, as must have been the supposition of those who heard the interview when it was broadcast for the first time. The statement may be historically true, or now find support among historians, but once more it cannot be shown to be true. And if Hadrian was in some way remembered as a *Graeculus*, this is scarcely enough to corroborate Yourcenar's introductory comment which, once more by a sort of intellectual sleight of hand, fuses fictive and factual in a manner that lasted until very late in life. Imagining her grandfather's experience in Sicily, she recalled that when Hadrian climbed Mt. Etna with Antinous, he was as yet on the upward slope of his destiny, powerful, loved, full of plans and dreams, showing hardly any signs of age (*AN* 1038).[52]

On the outer plane, perhaps more controversially still, slippage of this kind could become absolute. Yourcenar's Hadrian as a young man spends two days at Chaeronea as the guest of Plutarch. The item is mentioned during the holiday visit to Greece when Hadrian held the archonship at Athens (*MH* 343).[53] There is nothing, however, to prove that such a meeting with Plutarch ever took place. A tenth-century Byzantine historian reports that Hadrian appointed Plutarch procurator of Achaea very late in life, but the notice is inherently unreliable and while an allusion to Hadrian has been detected in one of Plutarch's treatises (*Mor.* 409B-C), certainty is beyond reach. In any case, neither item is germane to an encounter at Chaeronea.[54] Hadrian can be associated with Romans known to Plutarch – the Q. Sosius Senecio to whom Plutarch dedicated the *Table-Talk* and *Parallel Lives* is a clear case – and a meeting with the elderly figure has been duly hypothesized at a date later than that given in *Mémoires*.[55] But it remains a purely circumstantial possibility. In reply, however, to a question during an interview in 1952 whether Hadrian ever met Plutarch, Yourcenar was categorical: "Oui, mais très jeune, à trente ans, quand Plutarque en avait quatre-vingts. On ne pense pas sans émotion à cette rencontre qui exerça une grande influence sur l'empereur" (*PV* 29).[56] Here, as in her letters to Murciaux, Storoni Mazzolani and others, there is no trace of separation between the literary creation and the Hadrian of history. The meeting is an unquestionable fact, with a consequence added to the biographical record impossible to authenticate or even to be regarded as likely. It is far from an isolated example. Despite an academic-like qualification, a firm opinion about the personality of Antinous was given in a letter of 1952 – "Antinoüs lui-même était d'ailleurs sans doute assez peu compliqué" (*HZ* 158) – a historical assessment for which there can be no justification at all.[57] And various other similarly indeterminate "facts" were constantly reported: that at Tivoli Hadrian dedicated the Canopus to Antinous, that he went to Scotland during the visit to Britain, that he must often have contemplated the well-known mosaic of the doves from Tivoli used to illustrate the Folio edition of *Mémoires* (1977), that once in power he virtually forgot the earlier stage of his career under Trajan.[58] Yourcenar claimed again and again that Hadrian himself had said that he had "stabilized the world," pronouncing him the last representative of antiquity's grand intellectualism – "la grande pensée antique" – and the author, through his policies and the arrangements he made for the succession, of a half-century of peace in the Mediterranean world. As for his friends, they included, as did hers, many who were Jews.[59]

The major interviews with Patrick de Rosbo and Matthieu Galey show just how ingrained this habit of assimilation became. Discussing once more with de Rosbo her novels' homosexual characters, Yourcenar again distinguished Hadrian from Zeno and others due to antiquity's cultural openness to same-sex relationships, and speaking of him in the present tense said that the Roman Hadrian considers sensuousness, even debauchery, a normative aspect of human existence, and that as a passionate admirer of classical Greek culture he turns back to what, for better or worse, can be called Greek love. She could be understood in this mode to be speaking uncontroversially of the Hadrian of the novel. She continued, however, that her view has scholarly support, and that it is evident from the manner in which Hadrian tried to exalt Antinous that there is a conscious need in him to return to the erotic and heroic values of the Greek past. The tenses now are blended, which means, the allusion to scholars regardless, that it is far from clear to which Hadrian she is referring: the Hadrian of her overloaded imagination or the historical Hadrian. Stressing next his multifaceted personality, with appropriate reference to *varius, multiplex, multiformis*, she introduced both his heterosexual and homosexual affairs, obviously with the relevant passage from the Latin life in mind for the first, and for the second, in reference to the young men to whom Hadrian was attached – the tense is again significant ("il fut attaché") – specifying first Antinous, as if no validation were required, and then Lucius Aelius, with appeal to the innuendo of the historical tradition (*ER* 81).[60] At this stage, there seems to be no doubt at all that it is the Hadrian of history who is meant. But the conclusion that Hadrian in matters sexual is – in the present tense – a man free from constraints, leaves the issue unresolved. Does she mean her Hadrian or the Hadrian of history, or are her Hadrian and the Hadrian of history one and the same? The interviewer and his audience could again only presume the latter, which from the beginning, I suspect, was the case with Yourcenar herself.[61]

In a comparable exchange with Galey, the topic now being the difference between pleasure and love, Yourcenar was evidently speaking of her literary character when she summarized Hadrian's erotic history as given in the novel. Yet the passing remark that during his early military service the young man "a sûrement aimé," again fudges the line between literary creation and historical figure, while a comment on his relationship with Antinous similarly slides from the world of the novel to the world of history: "elle a dû également compter pour beaucoup dans la vie d'Hadrien" (*YO* 74, 99–100).[62] Few historians would disagree that Antinous was in some way important to Hadrian, but for obvious reasons the extent of that importance is immeasurable. The pattern continued as Yourcenar addressed questions about the genesis and success of *Mémoires*: Hadrian enjoyed divine status during his lifetime; historians concur with her judgment that his reforms and legislation prove him to have been a genius; the survival of Greek art today is due in part to his aesthetic commitment (*YO* 159, 160–1). These factual assertions followed questions Galey posed that inherently assumed identification of Yourcenar's Hadrian with the historical Hadrian, and they are combined with defensible but in the last analysis subjective conclusions: "Il fut très intelligent, en tout … Bien plus près de nous que le typique empereur romain de Suétone, ou des films et des romans à grand spectacle; en un sens, c'est un homme de la Renaissance" (*YO* 161).[63] The psychological thread of the novel is then resumed, with Antinous as positively "le grand moment" of Hadrian's life and the demands made by advancing years perfectly perceptible: lucidity developed over time into mistrust, which according to some sources was accompanied by bouts of delirium due to bitterness over the Jewish War and desperation in the face of illness; but each time Hadrian recovered his courage, or at least his self-discipline (*YO* 164–5).[64] The novel's account of Hadrian's emotional history is both affirmed and confirmed as history itself.

The post-publication commentary on the novel of Yourcenar's correspondence and interviews, extending over many years, reveals then how impervious to amendment her portrait of Hadrian as an individual became, no matter what refinements of detail might be required for historical accuracy. In the first instance, such self-assurance was the residue of Yourcenar's belief that she had full command of the sources of information about Hadrian and of practically everything that had been written about him. Martha Gellhorn's allegation, transmitted by Hortense Flexner, that despite her "érudition" there was insufficient documentation from which to paint such an all-embracing portrait, drew a characteristically indignant retort: Gellhorn should have read the *Note*: there was more available than even many scholars realized let alone the general public; the chronicles were not the usual grand classical works of literature scholars read, and new material discoveries had to be found through recourse to specialist publications; the printed version of the *Note*, moreover, was much shorter than the original (*HZ* 238). In an interview in 1986 at Petite Plaisance with Francesca Sanvitale, aired in Italy the following year, Yourcenar reiterated these points in reply to a question about how she had organized her research:

J'ai beaucoup lu, évidemment, en ce qui concerne Hadrien. Il y a beaucoup de documents. Seulement, ils sont dispersés et ce ne sont pas des documents de grands écrivains. Quand on s'occupe de Néron ou de Tibère – ou qu'est-ce que je sais – , on a de très grands écrivains, comme Tacite, ou de très grands portraitistes, comme Suétone, pour nous aider: ils ont déjà fait une image sur le moment – presque sur le moment. Tandis que [*pour*] Hadrien, tout est dispersé chez des écrivains obscurs, dans ses propres recherches légales, dans les traités de droit romain, dans des inscriptions, dans des lettres authentiques ou non, en partie authentiques: il faut utiliser un fond excessivement varié pour écrire Hadrien. (*PV* 368–9)[65]

Obviously I read a lot about Hadrian. There are many documents. Except that they are widely scattered, and not documents from great writers. When the subject is Nero or Tiberius, or whoever, there are very great writers, like Tacitus, or very great portraitists, like Suetonius, to help us: they have already created a contemporary, or near contemporary, image. But for Hadrian, everything is scattered among obscure authors, in their own legal researches, in treatises on Roman law, in inscriptions, in letters, whether authentic or not or partly so: to write about Hadrian an extremely diverse repository of materials has to be used.

This may well have become in time an almost formulaic reply. But in her continuing willingness to explain to non-specialist audiences the issues that confront any historian or biographer of Hadrian, Yourcenar's conviction that she knew the emperor better than anyone else, and that her presentation of him was historically complete, consolidated itself with each successive description she gave of the Hadrian she had created. The emperor presented to the world in 1951 was the real Hadrian, and the parabolic trajectory of his life Yourcenar had deployed as her chief organizational principle, a product of thorough historical research, was factually accurate. Her letters and interviews leave no question but that over time her Hadrian assumed a life of its own as the portrait painted in the novel hardened into an unchallengeable biographical truth. When necessary, a rival enterprise could be savagely excoriated.[66]

IV

As I have tried to show, Yourcenar's account of Hadrian's life history is rationally based and in many respects is no more divinatory than the accounts of professional historians. Whether Hadrian's achievements in governance and cultural development were the result of his own ideas and decisions remains to my mind a perennially unanswerable question, but for Yourcenar, as for many historians, the question scarcely arose. Her life history, however, differs from theirs not simply because the nature of the evidence allows for and sometimes demands speculation in matters of fact and interpretation, but because so much of her narrative recreates Hadrian's inner life in a manner professionals normally avoid. Historians at times identify elements of Hadrian's personality – I have given some examples – and often, it happens, they match Yourcenar's views. Royston Lambert's book apart, however, Yourcenar's concentration on the evolution of Hadrian's character has no parallel in conventional scholarship. Yourcenar claimed that revelation of this development had always been her object, saying at an early date that to capture the uniqueness of Hadrian's personality had been what had appealed to her in writing her novel – its extraordinary mixture of will and temperament, of chance and destiny – and long afterwards, she reiterated that despite the rashness of attributing to him thoughts that could only be imagined, she had aimed to show Hadrian's mind at work, no matter that it could only be half seen or that there were periods of shadow in his life.[67] The model of the wrinkled Roman bust encouraged creation of a singular portrait, with the novel accepted as the best medium in which to explore a character's psychology and to establish a relationship with her reader. While acknowledging an interviewer's distinction between the objectively knowable Hadrian and her reconstructed figure, she insisted regardless that although Hadrian's emotional world was not the concern of the historical sources, his inner life was accessible and his personality, in all its variety, was recoverable as it must actually have been from the details the source tradition preserved. Not only could his voice be heard, but through concentrated contemplation his presence could also be felt. In both dimensions, therefore, the inner and the outer, the results were historically secure.[68]

The many passages in the long meditation in which Hadrian expresses his thoughts and feelings, if often beguiling in effect, have no purchase of course on historical truth in any ordinary sense. They are the inferential product of Yourcenar's imagination and introduce the reader to what gradually emerges as an existential question of how Hadrian comes to terms with the world, finds his place within it, deals with adversity and finally resigns himself to the inevitable. The answer comes in what Yourcenar presents as his gradual discovery of a "method of living," a way of confronting and responding to life's vicissitudes fundamental in her thinking, a method that by melding several philosophical strands together leads Hadrian to an increasing self-knowledge that culminates in the notion of wisdom: "sagesse." It is this, from the very beginning, that allows him to recount his life's story to Marcus with candour and confidence. Yourcenar explained its nature, almost clinically, to Patrick de Rosbo:

En ce qui concerne Hadrien, sa sagesse est essentiellement humaniste. Je veux dire par là qu'elle est une sagesse basée sur la confiance en la raison humaine, en la capacité de l'homme de concilier les contraires, sur l'action, sur un équilibre intel-ligemment maintenu entre deux tensions contraires. Cette sagessse humaniste est aussi éminemment pragmatique, une façon d'accepter les faits et de partir d'eux pour construire, l'un de ces faits étant soi-même ... En un sens, cette sagesse d'Hadrien est une sagesse religieuse, puisqu'elle inclut le sentiment de ce qu'a de sacré l'exercice même du pouvoir et la condition humaine tout entière. (*ER* 100–1)

As far as Hadrian is concerned, his wisdom is essentially humanistic. By that I mean that it is a wisdom founded on confidence in human reason, in man's capacity to reconcile opposites, on action, on an equilibrium that is intelligently maintained between two opposing tensions. This humanistic wisdom is also eminently prag-matic, a way of accepting facts and of taking them as a point of departure in order to build, one of these facts being oneself ... In a sense, this wisdom of Hadrian's is a religious wisdom, since it includes the sensation of the sacred contained in the very exercise of power and the human condition as a whole.[69]

This metaphysical aspect of *Mémoires* separates it appreciably, and arrest-ingly, from any commonplace biography of Hadrian. If the sources give hints of Hadrian's intellectual interests, philosophy included, the "method of liv-ing" is in the end Yourcenar's most daring invention in her shaping out of Hadrian, but something historically real, its sapiential goal a corollary of her belief in the continuity of human experience over time and place, and the logical climax to the parabolic structure of Hadrian's life as she con-ceived it. In *Animula vagula blandula*, the novel's overture to the unfold-ing documentation of self-discovery to come, the outcome of the method is adumbrated in Hadrian's reflections on corporeal experiences that will lead eventually through an eclectic combination of philosophical, even spiritual, influences – Epicurean pleasure, Stoic self-mastery, Buddhist mysticism – to a state of equilibrium that Yourcenar took to mean not "happiness," as popularly conceived, but a condition in which everything has been drawn from life that life can give of wisdom, and in which everything has been demanded from life that life can bring of perfection. In this process, one of learning and selecting, every realistic possibility is to be pursued, the futil-ity of impossible demands to be avoided, and the pitfall of self-absorption in one's choices to be evaded; and it is a process to be pursued with open eyes, just as Hadrian brings his life to an end with open eyes, fearlessly and calmly. In a time-free world, Yourcenar's "wisdomed" Hadrian becomes finally a symbol of what she asks her readers permanently to take from her book: recognition of the means by which they themselves might achieve their own "équilibre humain," a concept traceable not least to the *équilibre* of the far-distant "Hospes comesque."[70]

There is every reason consequently to agree that Yourcenar's Hadrian becomes in the end something of a mythical figure.[71] But a further step is possible too. For inherent in the mythical there is a notion of the exemplary, and *Mémoires* might well in the very end be defined, and best be appraised, as a study in an implicit exemplarity that its author's commentary on the authenticity of her novel comes, over time, to render explicit and overt. Crucially, that is to say, Hadrian's method of self-examining contemplation is made available to all, at any time and in any place, no matter that in absolute terms the goal of achieving wisdom might remain unrealizable – for even Hadrian, humanly frail, could become no more than "almost wise" (*CNMH* 525: "presque sage"). Significantly, replying to an appreciative letter from the academician Henri Godard, Yourcenar said in January 1957 that it had always been her purpose not simply to write a historically valid account of Hadrian's remarkable life, but also, if more secretly, to reveal in the novel a method of living and a way of being. It was a purpose to be communicated discreetly in order to reduce the risk of seeming didactic or almost propagandistic, and it was one in which she thought she had succeeded (*HZ* II 36–7).[72] Allowing both the symbolic and the exemplary quality of her creation, "en partie symbole ... un exemple ou un modèle," she expatiated on the difficulty of the decision Godard had apparently made to commit himself to a Hadrianic regimen of self-examination, writing almost as a counsellor to a disciple but in a manner that makes her intentions plain:

Mais cette sagesse hadrianique (qui n'est d'ailleurs qu'une sorte de précipité de la sagesse antique, où j'ai essayé de retenir ce qu'elle a encore pour nous de plus valable et de plus vivant) demande une attention perpétuellement en éveil, une volonté sans fléchissement et sans raidissement dont bien peu de nous sont capables, surtout au milieu des vaines violences, des bruyants lieux communs, et des écrasantes routines de notre temps. (*HZ* II 37)

But this wisdom of Hadrian's (which to be sure is only a sort of offshoot of ancient wisdom, from which I have tried to keep what still remains that is most valuable and alive for us) demands an attention for ever alert, an unbending yet supple will very few of us have the capacity for, especially amid the meaningless violence, deafening platitudes, and crushing routines of our age.

This is by no means an isolated item of evidence. Already in the *Carnets*, aware of the threat to objectivity represented by personal disposition, Yourcenar had pointed to the inherent exemplarity of all biographical writing: "En un sens, toute vie racontée est exemplaire; on écrit pour attaquer ou pour défendre un système du monde, pour définir une méthode qui nous est propre" (*CNMH* 536).[73] To Matthieu Galey she was frank about the writer's potentially utilitarian function – "Il est utile s'il ajoute à la lucidité du lecteur, le débarrasse de timidités ou de préjugés, lui fait voir et sentir ce que ce lecteur n'aurait ni vu ni senti sans lui" (*YO* 248–9) – and to Jacques Chancel's question of whether she took refuge in history to look for the most exemplary "spécimens d'humanité," she denied taking refuge in history at all but did not deny the sequel: "Je trouve simplement intéressant de voir ce que les autres ont fait, s'ils se sont trompés autant que nous, ou autrement" (*RC* 70).[74] Consciousness of the exemplary remained until the end, when in reconstructing her own ancestral history as the historian-poet and novelist she said she had always tried to be, she acknowledged its value especially in times of duress (*SP* 877).

In all of this, there is a connection, and consistency, with the traditionally pragmatic character of French biographical writing that the critic Ann Jefferson has observed.[75] But with Yourcenar's explication of *Les Visages de l'Histoire dans l'«Histoire Auguste»* in mind, the more important connection to be made, I think, is with the tradition of didactic historiography of Hadrian's own Roman antiquity. The didactic was an intrinsic, indeed paramount, ingredient of Latin historical writing, its classic formulation appearing in the sombre preface to the first book of Livy's epic history of Rome, where the author pleads with his readers at a desperately critical juncture in their fortunes to remedy the ills of the present by avoiding the vices and emulating the virtues of their forebears. It is present in the age of Trajan and Hadrian in the works of Tacitus, as also in the biographies of Plutarch, and something to the same effect appears even in Pliny's letters. Those compositions were *paulo curatius scriptae*, and so too were those of Yourcenar, not missives of momentary import, but documents immediately copied, preserved, and destined for eventual entry into the public domain, as were also the transcripts of her interviews.[76] In everything written and said there was a seeming degree of calculation, in keeping perhaps with Yourcenar's persistent concern Josyane Savigneau and others have shown to control her public image and reputation as a literary celebrity.[77] Eager to spread the gospel of Hadrianic *sagesse*, she was certainly unceasing in her efforts to manage the reception of her novel and to define its significance; and in writing of the value of the past at large, she could identify an urgent need to learn and to reflect seriously on its virtues and vices before it became too late to cure the crimes and follies of the present, using language that is quintessentially, strikingly, Livian: "À notre époque surtout, où nous avons si grandement et si gravement besoin des leçons du passé, de réfléchir *sérieusement* sur ses vertus, et peut-être surtout sur ses erreurs et ses crimes, avant qu'il ne soit trop tard pour réparer les nôtres ..." (*HZ* III 122).[78] I conclude accordingly

that *Mémoires* in effect extends the Latin legacy by adding, in the reconstructed figure of Hadrian, a new member to the repertory of characters
from whom readers in Roman antiquity were expected to learn life lessons
of moralistic instruction, and that Yourcenar took every opportunity to make
this meaning understood.

As she did so, Hadrian came in Yourcenar's always intimate engagement
with him to acquire a powerful reality that far exceeds what can ever properly be known of the historical figure. From one year to the next, the portrait of the novel gradually hardened into an unimpeachably true likeness,
rendering its creator, I think, more and more the victim of her own creative
imagination. The exemplar reconstructed for readers of *Mémoires* to follow
became, as she later wrote and spoke of him, a suprahistorical figure, a development that intensifies appreciably and even supersedes, or displaces, the
many issues of authenticity that *Mémoires* raises. And at times Yourcenar
could well acknowledge the impact of her own subjectivity on her novel's
formation, despite all the claims made to factual fidelity. To write of Hadrian
as she had, a certain maturity and the experience maturity brought had been
vital; knowing the historical evidence alone was not enough; reflection on
the order, or chaos, of life's vicissitudes had also been needed (*YO* 157); and
sometimes an almost trivial detail had had an effect – a childhood memory
of a book on ancient Egypt intruding into Hadrian's vivid recollection of
his sunsetting arrival at the banquet prior to Antinous's death (*YO* 45; *MH*
439). There were more substantive influences as well. Her lifelong passion
for travel forged a link with the peripatetic emperor whose love for what he
termed barbarian lands and whose preference for life in remote locations
were tastes she shared, as if both creator and created belonged simultaneously everywhere and nowhere.[79] And like any artist, she had found in her
own experiences ways of vouchsafing the veracity of her reconstruction,
as when she described Hadrian's cardiac problems, episodes of fatigue, or
moments of decision making: a touch could always be added and the historical character be made more convincing, given human substance, better
interpreted. No matter how self-effacing the writer tried to be, connections
were unavoidable and perhaps essential, in the choice of subject. When critics and correspondents asked whether author and authored were not one
and the same, the denials, no matter if confined to public rather than private
matters, must be judged at some level specious. The result nonetheless was
enrichment rather than misrepresentation.[80]

With the passage of time confidence in the portrait's faithful execution
transformed itself into absolute certitude. Hence the wilfulness of the factual
statements made about Hadrian, and Yourcenar's insistence on the independence of her representation throughout. The narrating "Je" of *Mémoires*

was the "real man." His thoughts, views, and achievements might be the product of her intelligence and her emotions (affection included), but they could be successfully recovered through the experience of "visitation," when voice and presence made the emperor accessible to her even to the point of knowing when he lied (*HZ* II 44; *YO* 238–9). It was no impediment consequently that her thoughts and his might correspond when the voice heard in the silence had a distinctive tone she could register. Engagement was then at most unconscious. A mutuality of sentiment ensued, as most clearly revealed perhaps in the novel's opening pages, where thoughts on life's shapelessness and the indeterminacy of selfhood are expressed; where her ecological concerns and abhorrence of animal suffering lie beneath the horror Hadrian feels for living creatures sacrificed at religious ceremonies; where her notion of sympathetic love, allowing for nothing of the conventionally romantic, controls his understanding of love as a form of pleasure that combines rapture with agony; and where her opinions of their inadequacies explain his dismissal of historians' systematic methods of recording the past as far too simplistic to capture history's complexities. The intrusive author cannot be missed.[81] Even so, through concentrated contemplation the pattern of Hadrian's life and the evolution of his character were satisfactorily indited, and for a generation afterwards Yourcenar laboured to entrench her biography as a portrait to endure for all time, and, to the percipient, as a source of inspiration for the acquisition of self-knowledge.

It was labour indeed that never ended. On 26 October 1982 Yourcenar gave a lecture at the Institut français de Tôkyô entitled *Voyages dans l'espace et voyages dans le temps*, the text of which is now included in the Pléiade's edition of *Le Tour de la prison*, a collection of travel essays left incomplete at her death. Its theme is the benefits travel naturally conveys, and unsurprisingly it includes a disquisition on her great novelistic traveller Hadrian. The factual reality is stated: his journeys across the great circle of lands that comprised Rome's vast empire, journeys to the very edges of its barbarian limits, were undertaken for reasons of state, but equally to satisfy his personal tastes and passions. They were also, as even now with every intelligently undertaken journey, lessons in endurance, discovery, and self-discipline, a means of shedding presumptions in the face of the Other. Hadrian was able to detach himself from Roman conventions, or rather to draw on his cultured personality in order to integrate new elements into them; and so the grand experience of climbing a mountain in Syria or Sicily combined sensations of religious awe with the aesthetic and scientific pleasures of contemplating the sunrise from on high, allowing this organizer and pilgrim to be simultaneously a lover and observer of all that was wonderful and beautiful in the world (*TP* 692). The truth is plain. Hadrian embodied all the advantages that travel confers, with Yourcenar remarkably transferring the experience of the historical figure as she had created it to a contemporary like-minded Everyman. The genuine journeys of his reign that no historian will dispute were for the artist a means, once more, of promoting Hadrian, imperially, as both model ruler and model for life.[82]

V

On occasion Yourcenar said that she would have given a year of her life to spend an hour with Hadrian, or else that he was a figure she had spent her whole life trying to hear, as if, like Antinous, he was the friend forever mourned.[83] An irony nonetheless persists. The model ruler and guide to self-knowledge advanced especially in *Mémoires'* afterlife was historically as supreme a ruler as the dictators of Yourcenar's early adulthood for whom, when writing her novel, she still felt such repugnance. She understood the diverse character of Hadrian's empire and could distinguish it from modern regimes, but she was under no illusions about the autocratic nature of Rome's emperorship as an institution. If Hadrian could qualify his power as "puissance presque absolue" (*MH* 297), the caprice with which he could exercise it she readily admitted, with the disturbing result that the political executions for which Hadrian was thought to have been responsible – those of the four consulars at the beginning of the reign and those of Servianus and Pedanius Fuscus at its end – she could rationalize and justify: they were relatively trivial affairs compared with the great crimes of modern dictators indifferent to their criminality. Hadrian crossed a line, but pragmatism demanded it.[84] It is a view that gives pause, and almost brings shock, coming from an author who so frequently associated herself with liberal humanistic sentiment. Yet it is explicable from the continuing engagement and identification with the biographical subject that the decades-long commentary on *Mémoires* reveals. Other literary projects and triumphs intervened to occupy Yourcenar and to further her reputation. But the voice of Hadrian continued to be heard, and complementarity of thought and opinion to be both maintained and sustained. Engagement and identification were, I believe, manifestations of that "extraordinaire amitié" of which Yourcenar wrote to Hortense Flexner, a friendship that is more securely, and more richly, recoverable than any of Hadrian's putative historical friendships ever can or ever will be. Which means in the last analysis that it is not a figure from antiquity, whether Arrian or any other candidate, who has the strongest claim to have been Hadrian's special friend. That privilege belongs to the artist who once brought him faithfully to life, and whose history she long promoted for the fullness of its exemplary potential. In the seclusion of her own Isle of Achilles, "mon île américaine des Monts-Déserts," where on the summit of a local hill the dawn's spectacular unfolding over the surrounding seascape could be witnessed, and a prayer for the peace of the world be offered, conviction was all (*TP* 692).

Endnote

LETTRE D'ARRIEN

Immense envergure de cette lettre – elle touche à presque tous les sujets qui ont intéressé ou occupé l'empereur. Travaux publics, tactique et discipline militaire, navigation, sentiments de loyalisme des populations de l'empire; mais aussi art (jugement porté sur la statue, qui est médiocre), littérature et légendes anciennes (Xénophon, histoire de Médée, légendes de Thétis et d'Achille) sens presque romantique des paysages sauvages de l'ile [*sic*] abandonée, occultisme et magie, allusions aux amours, à la douleur après la mort d'Antinoüs, à la réalité des rapports d'outre-tombe entre l'amant et l'ami; et en même temps que s'y révèle discrètement l'intimité entre l'auteur de ces pages et l'empereur, on y discerne partout le grand style de cette civilisation encore dans toute sa force, son sens critique appliquée [*sic*] à ses propres traditions, son humanisme. Il faut attendre la Renaissance pour retrouver ce ton dans une correspondence entre érudit et prince. [Edited lightly.]

ARRIAN'S LETTER

Immense scope of this letter – it touches almost every subject that interested or occupied the emperor. Public works, military tactics and discipline, navigation, loyalist sentiments on the part of the imperial populations; but also art (judgment rendered on the statue, which is mediocre), literature and ancient legends (Xenophon, the story of Medea, legends of Thetis and Achilles), an almost romantic feeing for the wild landscapes of the abandoned island, the occult and magic, allusions to love affairs, to the grief felt after Antinous' death, to the reality of relations between the lover and his friend beyond the tomb; and at the same time that an intimacy between the author of these pages and the emperor is discreetly revealed, one perceives everywhere the grand style of this civilization still at its full strength, its critical sense applied to its own traditions, its humanism. To find this tone again in correspondence between a man of education and a prince one has to await the Renaissance.

10

Residue

I

At an exhibition in the British Museum I once found myself able to look for a few moments at the portrait known as the Mondragone Antinous alone and in silence. Inevitably two other visitors soon appeared, a woman and her daughter, a little girl of perhaps nine or ten. For a while they too quietly contemplated the portrait, until the little girl looked up and in all innocence said to her mother, "Is it a girl or a boy?" The woman hesitated, then replied, quizzically, "I don't know." It was not my place to intervene. I said nothing. Mother and child soon moved on. I was struck by the moment, however, and have often recalled it since. I can still almost hear the child's voice asking her entirely forgivable question, one far more consequential than it superficially seems. What do we, present-day scholars, really know about Antinous? What do we really know about Hadrian? How will we ever know?

Marguerite Yourcenar thought of the Mondragone Antinous as a living remnant of a time long since dead (*CNMH* 520). But in *Mémoires d'Hadrien*, restoring to life a Hadrian on the brink of life's end she came, I think, as close as anyone ever has done to answering those questions. Her book is a life story. And while the multitude of terms by which she spoke of it in its afterlife is an indication of its exceptionality in form, its fundamental biographical character is indisputable. It is cast as a letter in which Hadrian tells his story in his own voice and conjures up for his youthful

Figure 3. Marble bust of Antinous. Louvre, Paris.
Wikimedia Commons (Mondragone Antinous).

addressee an array of memories and thoughts from infancy almost to his last mortal moment. It is also a carefully contrived narrative that in theory allows its author to suppress her individuality for the sake of revealing that of her biographical subject. And it is written in an ultra-refined, timelessly classic style that betrays little of its mid-twentieth-century date of composition. As such, *Mémoires* is an as yet unmatched account of a Roman emperor's life.

The book belongs to a genre whose origins lie in antiquity itself, since from the inception of the Principate the lives of their emperors were a source of continual fascination to those the emperors ruled. Suetonius's archetypal *Caesares* and the works of his biographical successors leave no doubt of this, and it is a fascination easily explained: the men who ruled Rome's empire were figures of curiosity precisely because they were the men who ruled Rome's empire. The appetite for knowledge of figures who exercised unlimited power over a vast population was natural and unrelenting, and it is an appetite that has endured to the present day, with both academic and popular practitioners toiling incessantly in an imperial life-writing industry. Whether the products customarily manufactured meet the standards of true biography is the crucial question.

Since the emergence of "new biography" in the early twentieth century, it has become axiomatic that life writing should comprehend both the outer and the inner life of its subject, and thereby not only provide a contextualized record of significant life events but also examine the subject's emotional or psychological responses to them. Its raison d'être is to create an accurate, credible, vivid, and dynamic portrait of an individual's individuality in an identifiable and identified setting. Some specimens of Roman imperial biography come closer than others to meeting these requirements, but comparison with the rich examples of true biography to which I have referred in the preceding pages suggests success that is relatively limited. The chief reason for this hardly now needs to be restated. To achieve the desired result contemporary evidence is required from the biographical subject and those close to him of a kind and quantity that is largely non-existent. Without correspondence, journals, diaries, and family records, the degree of depth to which the life of any Roman emperor can be securely recovered is minimal, and whether a true imperial biography might ever be written is a question more pressing still. Many contemporary documents remain of course that attest decisions of governance Roman emperors made, but as I have maintained with regard to Hadrian, what they reveal personally about the individuals concerned is far from clear; and once allowance is made for what I have called the Crick factor a virtually insuperable complication sets in. In saying which I am not accusing the deficiency of the materials that remain but simply stating a fact.

It is true in some instances that guiding narratives have survived from antiquity that make possible outlines of emperors' public lives and point to some of their personal idiosyncracies. The Julio-Claudian and Flavian emperors especially seem accessible from the works of Suetonius and Tacitus. Even here, however, the narratives concerned are neither contemporary nor independent, but depend upon earlier accounts no longer extant and are further constrained by generic demands and authorial prejudice.[1] Their essentially identical views, later repeated by Cassius Dio, prove only that by the early second century what are more or less stereotyped images of the first twelve Caesars had firmly established themselves from which it was impossible to deviate. The resultant reality was summed up as long ago as 1863, when in an essay in the *Cornhill Magazine*, George Henry Lewes tried to absolve Nero of responsibility for several of the flagrant crimes traditionally attributed to him by stressing the shortcomings of the guiding accounts:

Suetonius, Tacitus, and the Greek Dion Cassius, are the three historians cited as witnesses against Nero. What credit can they claim? Suetonius, from whom the worst stories proceed, was not born till many years after Nero's death, and did not write until some forty years after the events. Tacitus was six years old when Nero died, and wrote many years after the events. Dion Cassius lived some hundred and fifty years later. Let us ask what would be the credibility of historians writing about Cromwell long after the Protectorate had been destroyed, and with nothing but the rumours current in royalist circles to furnish the facts; in such narratives what sort of figure would that heroic man present?[2]

The selective traditions of the few extant narratives have far less value for biography therefore than is commonly assumed, and any prospect of liberating Rome's early emperors from the images they create is minimal.[3] Ultimately, the narratives that remain leave untouchable what are in effect mythical images of the early emperors – Tiberius the tyrant, Caligula the madman, Claudius the fool, and so on – and render imperial biography an altogether perplexing enterprise. It has to be allowed that in practice much imperial life writing is either informed speculation, if not what Lewes went on to call "immense amounts of fiction."[4]

This is especially so in Hadrian's case, because the evidentiary problems are here more intractable than ever. There is no guiding narrative at all for Hadrian comparable in quality and authority to the narratives of Tacitus and Suetonius for earlier rulers, one ironic result being that a "mythical" Hadrian analogous to his mythical Julio-Claudian and Flavian predecessors never came into being. Rational or legitimate conjecture will be invoked in order to redress the balance, with appeal to the criteria of the probable and the possible; yet as I have stressed these are intrinsically vulnerable notions that are always open to dispute. Relatedly, there is also the matter of ensuring that the currently normative is not taken to be historically normative, and the temptation avoided of forcing fragments of evidence into fleetingly fashionable theories. Much can be gleaned of what took place in Hadrian's reign, and his associations with what took place are uncontroversial: recall once more the Pantheon, the Wall, the Villa, the Castel, and of course Antinous. But as an unabating flood of scholarship proves, the precise role Hadrian himself played in initiating what took place, the degree to which he himself was responsible for what took place, is irresoluble, and with new evidence constantly accruing the creation of an impeccable narrative of events is an objective still in progress. I do not doubt the likelihood that Hadrian held views of how his empire was to be governed and the lives of its peoples regulated, nor do I doubt the likelihood that a mind lay behind the projects and undertakings with which he is associated. (Which is a subjective statement of possibility that seems legitimate to me.) It is the collocation of one with the other that gives pause, the presumption that every accomplishment or outcome must be attributed to the emperor directly; because without irrefutable contemporary evidence of the motivations that underlay the initiatives the historical tradition has preserved, Hadrian as an individual remains inscrutable. Yes, there may be indications of temperament in the sources. But the impact temperament made on the minutiae of imperial governance recorded is far from clear and will always be a matter of dispute.[5] Establishment of Hadrianic "policy" consequently is a chimerical project, and the broader implication more disquieting still: much of what passes for history in ancient history is fiction. All that can safely be said, to repeat, is that much is known about Hadrian but little of him, and that the source tradition encapsulates a cluster of memories from many disparate points of view in place and time of varying reliability. Strictly speaking, Hadrian is unbiographable. Which means that in reconstituting his life story Marguerite Yourcenar attempted the impossible.

II

My purpose in this study, modest at most, has been to investigate how Yourcenar made that attempt and to promote appreciation of what she achieved in so doing. Given the hazards involved, it might be thought that *Mémoires* should be dismissed as an aberrant imaginative oddity. And perhaps it should. But in view of the claims to historical authenticity its author made on its behalf, not to mention its reputation as a classic work of art, it can hardly be ignored. It is not in my view a work of fiction or a novel in any accepted sense, but as I have suggested a work best approached and defined in terms of true biography. This follows from its reconstruction of both Hadrian's outer and his inner life, as true biography demands, and the reconstruction's foundation on its author's command of the relevant historical sources and accompanying scholarship at the time of composition. It has a creative, or poetic, quality that ultimately renders the result sui generis, but that quality is by no means antithetical to its overriding biographical character. The methods adopted for the reconstruction and the conditions under which it was made are ascertainable, and assessment of the finished product is possible. It would be foolish to argue, and I do not do so, that the impossible was fully accomplished. To insist nevertheless that *Mémoires* is best understood in the context of twentieth-century biography is, I believe, a defensible proposition.

For the Yourcenarian scholars I have had in mind in making this case it cannot be stated too many times that *Mémoires* is not a fully accurate record of Hadrian's life. The complexities of the historical tradition are too numerous for such a record to be made, and they are greater in fact than Yourcenar herself realized. A given passage may well be based on a text or document from antiquity, but the existence of the text or document alone does not automatically lead to positivist truth when the validity and significance of many texts and documents continue to baffle; and due to advances in knowledge made since the novel was written, some sections, if comprehensible in compositional context, are now clearly erroneous. Conversely, the Romanists I have also wanted to address must recognize that Yourcenar's recovery of Hadrian's life is founded on a knowledge of antiquity that might well cause surprise (and allay many misgivings about her achievement), which means that her depiction of Hadrian's life cannot be simply rejected out of hand unless the original sources on which the depiction is based are known as well as Yourcenar herself knew them. Contemporaries might also concede that to draw inferences from individual items of evidence is a fundamental practice in all historical and biographical writing, and that the character of a given work is necessarily influenced by the circumstances under which it is produced. Familiarity with the context in which *Mémoires* came into being is vital.[6]

If Yourcenar is to be believed, the inspiration for *Mémoires* is to be traced to her childhood stay in England and her travels in Italy as a young adult. Composition took place, however, in the United States where, in the relative safety, prosperity, and even tranquillity of the postwar period, she came to conceive of Hadrian as a symbol of a prospective enlightened political leadership the course and outcome of World War II had fostered, a form of leadership radically different from the pre-war dictatorships she had witnessed in Europe. The tendency to control her public persona notwithstanding, it would be unforgivably cynical to doubt the essence of her frequently made claim that the Hadrian of *Mémoires* embodied hopes in the immediate aftermath of war for a new world order marked by peace and security. These were sentiments, surely, widely shared, and they account in my view for what seem today certain anachronisms in the novel, notably its conception of Hadrian's pacifism and of the degree to which he brought stability to Rome's empire. Yourcenar's equally frequent admissions that her hopes for enlightened political leadership quickly evaporated are likewise not to be impugned.

If critical, however, the influence of the present cannot be taken too far. The many successes Hadrian's autobiography describes are tempered by a tragic overlay, both in the overwhelming personal setbacks he experiences and the anxieties about Rome's future he expresses. The sense *Mémoires* conveys of a turning point in Rome's historical fortunes from incline to decline is unmistakable, and there is something curious, perhaps even disturbing, in Yourcenar's promotion of an absolutist Roman emperor as a model for contemporary political leadership.[7] Whatever Hadrian was, he was no Churchill. Yourcenar could identify as a significant moment in her political awakening the year 1922 when in Italy, and assert that she had witnessed that year the march that brought Mussolini to power in Rome. But hostility to European despotism aside, there are indications in a document of "Self-Commentary" of her fruitless efforts when war broke out to return to Greece that well divulge her indecision about how to react in, or to, the moment, and I know of no evidence that she seriously considered remaining in Europe at that time. An arrangement to join Grace Frick in the United States had been made before France's declaration of war against Germany, and whether the personal decision and all that it involved will sufficiently explain why there are shadows dimming the brightness of *Mémoires'* portrait of Hadrian, I know no way of telling.[8] Flee Europe Yourcenar did, however, and there is something disingenuous about her much later passing statements that this had made her an exile, that she had lived on the fringe of history.[9] I share indeed the suspicion, put forward by their editors, that her letters of the mid-1940s to Emmanuel Boudot-Lamottte betray an attempt at self-justification for having escaped at such a dark moment when her compatriots found themselves compelled to make any number of harrowing decisions.[10] In March 1947, she wrote with a certain irony that it was difficult at a distance to imagine the atmosphere in France during the years of the occupation, and to know how she would have comported herself had she been there amid such confusion.[11] And when later writing of the poet's function to bear witness to the sacrifice made by martyrs in any age, she could refer to the dead of the Resistance becoming legendary, or forgotten, to comparable effect.[12] Whatever therefore the postwar mood to which she said she responded, the impact of the compositional moment is not free from ambiguity, and the optimism perhaps to be found in the novel is not unbridled. At the same time, a critic or commentator fortunate enough not to have known what Ian Watt called for his and Yourcenar's generation the "bleak perspectives of recent history" is hardly qualified to pass judgment.[13] If Marguerite Yourcenar was no Simone Weil, it remains the case that as late as 1977 memories of pre-war fascism still haunted her – Mussolini and his mistress hanging by their feet in the garage in Milan, Hitler ranting in Naples ("je l'entends encore") – and Hadrian could still be described, in contrast, as the most modern, and most complicated, man among those who had been summoned to rule. A period of dislocation and transition may well be allowed (*AN* 1035–6; *PE* 545).

For composition itself there was no alternative to reliance on the classical source tradition. But the strategy Yourcenar employed in her response to it was innovative and is perhaps best described as experimental, in at least two dimensions.

The autobiographical memoir, first, was a bold choice as the form in which to present Hadrian's biography. By having her subject reconsider his life, as she put it, from the perspective of memory – "La vie reconsidérée ... dans les perspectives de la mémoire" (*TGS* 298) – Yourcenar avoided the positivist problems of chronological precision and situational detail that strict historical biography expects, and without any sacrifice of credibility could justifiably offer an impressionistic narrative consistent with the historical record and the credible distortions of memory that later life brings. History as Yourcenar defined it was in fact memory, which meant that every item in the tradition could be thought of as containing a historical recollection Hadrian had of some sort, and material consequently for inclusion in the operation of biographical reconstitution. From a purist's standpoint many of the recollections the tradition preserves are unreliable at worst and contestable at best: their mere existence, again, is no guarantee of truth. But for Yourcenar this was irrelevant. She understood the inconsistencies of the tradition, its factual conflicts included, but her procedure was to regard its several elements as multifarious aspects of a fundamental, underlying reality, a grand body of memories that she could deploy and exploit as the memories of the emperor himself. The inadequacies of the sources could be accommodated thereby and Hadrian's reputation for the excellence of his memory be preserved, even as sensitivity to the frailty of remembrance was maintained; for memory was, and indeed is, vulnerable, losing precision and sharpness over time, resembling as Yourcenar herself put it a weary traveller who discards an item of increasingly burdensome luggage at every stop on his journey. The effect was to render the portrait painted no more than a sketch (*TGS* 281, 416).[14] The autobiographical memoir also permitted solution of the problem historians must always confront of determining exactly how decisions of Hadrianic governance were made. Figures who reputedly made substantive contributions to administrative efficiency could be introduced, but the futility of guessing who otherwise might have served as agents and allies in government was avoided. In Suetonian fashion, Yourcenar severed the administrative Gordian knot by attributing to the emperor directly all the measures the historical tradition records of him in a kind of Hadrianic *res gestae*. Meaning was then extracted from them in a manner comparable to the deductions and divinations of trained historical minds, with results placed in a setting textured by a compendious knowledge of classical culture, and enlivened by the benefits of extensive travel in the Mediterranean world.

Secondly, Yourcenar asked what human emotions lay beneath the substrate of factual events she believed the tradition to contain in order to determine the course of Hadrian's self-understanding over time as he reacted to them. These she elaborated inventively, as a novelist, from the evidence of the "grandes vérités sur la nature humaine" (*PE* 535–6), a human nature categorically taken to be unchanging and predictable in all times and places, subject only to the varying pressures of the culturally contingent. It was hardly a new way of thinking, although the ease with which she collapsed the centuries between time past and time present will strike many as a more than taxing leap of faith: "Il n'y a ni passé, ni futur, mais seulement une série de présents successifs, un chemin, perpétuellement détruit et continué, où nous avançons tous" (*TGS* 283).[15] Nonetheless, as prevalent developments in biographical writing demanded, her object was to create a rounded portrait that conjoined a record of external events and accomplishments with the inner personal reactions to them that the immanence of human nature as she conceived it made feasible. Three critical episodes were duly identified from the public record that allowed the display, in all their richness and volatility, of a range of easily recognizable emotions as Hadrian confronted, endured, and recovered from the challenges the episodes brought, with a framework for the biography suitably delineated and the defective sources imaginatively supplemented. These were the "transformative moments" from the outer life that, on the biographical principle of selectivity established by Lytton Strachey and still currently advocated in literary biography, could be seen to "shape the inner life in significant ways."[16] Mere chronography was avoided.

In both dimensions, once represented as a sensate, thinking individual, Yourcenar's Hadrian became a true biographical character, mosaically pieced together from the tesserae left by the dry-as-dust late Roman chronicles (*AN* 1031). At the same time, however, Yourcenar did not attempt in her reconstitution the absolutely impossible. True biography often attaches importance in the reconstruction of its subjects' adult lives to the formative experiences of childhood. Yet for this stage of Hadrian's history the record is virtually blank. His parents are almost invisible, and the conflicting evidence on his place of birth means that there can be no assurance of where he spent his early years or of what his childhood experiences were. In *Mémoires*, Hadrian is just twelve years old when his father dies, and after leaving Spain in his early teens he never sees his mother again, if aware until the end that she enjoyed a long life. A brief notice in the Latin life of two dreams presaging his imminent demise, in one of which Hadrian requested of his father a sleeping draft, became the basis of a paragraph where, contemplating life after death, the emperor considers the meaning of dreams at large, amplifying the lapidary source on the far from extravagant principle that dreams in antiquity were much like ours today (*MH* 512).[17] But parental intrusion generally remains negligible. Yourcenar avoided altogether the trap of postulating psychological effects childhood eventualities might have had on the mature figure, the obvious reason being that they could never be known. In an erotic context, she altogether dismissed the notion of Freudian narcissism (*L* 369).

In sum, the form of biographical reconstitution that Yourcenar conceptualized as poetic history demanded fidelity to the facts of the tradition – accuracy was a compulsion – but as with Hadrian's dream it also allowed a certain licence. Aspects of the tradition could be fleshed out in developed scenes, names could be changed for the sake of communicative convenience, and suitable if historically unattested characters could be added to fill in pieces of the picture the tradition left in darkness. The opportunities for invention depended on the extent of the factual record and are self-evidently greatest in the story of Antinous. None of this, however, transgressed the guidance of the tradition or the limits of the plausibilities of human nature as Yourcenar construed them. In a free-flowing memoir, Hadrian documented his perceptions of his most successful achievements, his most painful failings, and the most meaningful aspects of his progress through life – a narrative of memories not randomly dictated but one written down for Marcus to read, and so one over which sufficient control was exercised to allow the biographical vacuum of the historical tradition to be filled, and to compensate for the lack of any authoritative biography of Hadrian to which in 1951 Yourcenar could refer her readers. Those elements alone remained obscure that the tradition, if not Hadrian himself as Yourcenar believed, had purposefully concealed.

These considerations combine to offer not an apologia for *Mémoires*, but an explanation of what the novel is and how it came to be: a fictive biography designed through an imaginative conceit to bring to life the life of Hadrian, its plausibilities both contending with and surpassing the probablies and possibles of conventional academic discourse given their basis in aspects of human behaviour universally documented. Once that is understood, the idea that *Mémoires* can be misread lapses, and the quixotic notion that its author was motivated by deceit be once and for all abandoned. The biography gives a panoramic sense of what it was like to be in the world of Rome in all its regional and cultural diversity at a moment in the early Antonine age when intimations of structural mortality could be perceived beneath its surface brilliance; and against that background the biography gives a sense of what it was like to be Hadrian himself as he passed through life, rising from a relatively pedestrian public beginning to become the most powerful man on earth, and, through the achievements to which the power at his disposal led, a living god as well. A god, however, who came to know the perils of political ambition, the oppressive weight of lost love, and the despair of an unrealized ideological goal; yet who also resolved the turmoil of successive crises and

survived, through unremitting self-examination and phlegmatic resignation, to fulfil an inexorable destiny and finally emerge as "the pattern of all
patience." That is to say, it leaves an unforgettable "impression" of the kind
Yourcenar thought every writer wished to achieve (*AN* 1037).[18] Scored in a
minor key, it is periodically brightened as the pulse of Hadrian's Hellenism
makes itself felt; but in the face of fears for the future a disquieting melancholy prevails. As a result, in place of a conventionally mythical image, Yourcenar discerned and brought to life an authentic personality comprehensible
in time and place in a "long récit" that the memories of a solitary individual
placed at the summit of the world had to be, an "imaginative evocation" to
be sure, but one best defined by Yourcenar herself with words that distance
Mémoires from any popular conception of the historical novel: "une méditation sur une vie d'homme d'un autre temps, conditionnée en grande partie
par d'autres idées et d'autres usages que les nôtres, mais rejoignant sur bien
des points notre vie à nous" (*HZ* IV 313–14).[19]

The objections to such an appraisal are obvious. The technical problems of the
source tradition were underestimated and the reliability of its factual substrate
overvalued. The personality of the author overly determined the personality of
the character she created, and documents newly available now undermine the
accuracy of the narrative in important respects. The author's purported ability
to enter into virtual communion with her subject stretches to breaking point all
limits of biographical enquiry, and reliance especially on "sympathetic magic"
cannot be countenanced as a normal method of impartial historical investigation.

Such objections cannot be explained away, and I make no attempt to do so.
I reiterate only what I have maintained throughout, that Yourcenar was no
more culpable in her procedures than historians who rely on intuition and
divination to establish facts and draw conclusions from them about Hadrian's personality; and that while requiring revision in matters of strict chronology, the documents that have come to light since *Mémoires* first appeared
have no seriously adverse bearing on the personality portrayed. Hadrian at
life's end is shown in *Mémoires* assiduously attentive still to imperial business, which, as it happens, the documents concerned prove to be factually
true. His opinions are, of course, in many respects those of his creator and
this presents a genuine problem of verifiability, to which all that can be said
is that any work of history carries signs of the historian's disposition in time
and place – personal proclivities can scarcely be concealed – and that authorial transference is an occupational hazard of all biographical writing. Those
signs and proclivities, however, including the moments of entrancement permissible to poets, can be identified and taken into account.

My assessment is not intended to mean, or even to imply, that *Mémoires*
is somehow "better" than the works of Hadrian's historians with which

I have engaged in making it, and on which I have constantly relied in so doing. It is intended only to explain how and why the novel is the historical biography I take it to be, and to show that its fictive nature is little different from the fictive character of much formal historical writing. Indeed, the inventions found in *Mémoires* are often comparable to what are self-evidently fictions in historical works often unacknowledged or conceded. I might well be accused in making the assessment of having deployed methods decried when conventionally employed – the "fearsome sciences of *Quellenkritik* and *Quellenforschung*."[20] But to this there is a rejoinder. The point of the critique has been to emphasize the disparity between the minimal gains for historical knowledge and the amount of labour expended on hypothesizing how late Roman writers produced their chronicles when so much depends on materials no longer extant; whereas, in cogent contrast, Yourcenar left records of what she had read and used to create her Hadrian, so that the resources on which she drew remain accessible for direct investigation. I have concentrated accordingly on bringing certain of these sources to the fore, my object being to show how claims to authenticity in *Mémoires* can be advanced within the orbit of knowledge and authority on display. Conclusions must always be provisional and subject to correction. But extravagances of the sort that typify modern analyses of the *Historia Augusta* can be evaded.

III

When in the *Carnets* Yourcenar contemplated writing her own life story, she admitted the perils of the enterprise. Memories, she said, were like crumbling walls or patches of shadow, no more than partial, and to substantiate them correspondence had to be consulted and information secured from third parties. Elements of truth were recoverable, but totality was another matter: "on se trompe *plus ou moins*" (*CNMH* 527–8).[21] The passionate seeker after truth, if aiming only for accuracy, was often best placed to know that truth is not absolute (as Pilate was aware): firm assertions could be advanced, but hesitations, misgivings, and deceptions of a sort that would never occur to ordinary minds everywhere injected themselves. So it was, she thought, that from time to time the voice of Hadrian Yourcenar heard had lied to her (*CNMH* 535–6). There was always therefore a certain leeway of which to take account: "La substance, la structure humaine ne changent guère. Rien de plus stable que la courbe d'une cheville, la place d'un tendon, ou la forme d'un orteil. Mais il y a des époques où la chaussure déforme moins. Au siècle dont je parle, nous sommes encore près de la libre vérité du pied nu" (*CNMH* 529).[22]

Such remarks could be taken, I think, to imply that for all the erudition, for all the reading of everything that Hadrian had read, for all the confidence in the reliability of human nature as a guide to behaviour, at times in the 1950s Yourcenar harboured lingering doubts about her portrait's authenticity. If so they did not mature into lasting hesitations or misgivings. Far from it. Instead, with the passage of time they completely disappeared, as certitude in the veracity of the portrait she had painted increasingly consolidated itself. Today, her reader will be unable to shed those doubts to the same degree. For the inescapable fact remains that the frailty of its evidentiary base renders any life of Hadrian suspect: evocations and impressions, yes, but absolute authority, no, unless and until a latter-day Poggio Bracciolini should retrieve a cache of lost revelatory documents. If *Mémoires* is explicable in terms of design and execution, Hadrian's life history in all its true totality will always remain unattainable.

Even so, Marguerite Yourcenar's novel stands alone as a work of biographical literature, distinguished by its symmetry of structure, marble-like richness of style, and imaginative depth. One modern expectation of biography is that it should mould the individual life into a meaningful whole; in antiquity Plutarch had already judged it a vehicle for revealing "signs of the soul."[23] Meeting both tests, *Mémoires* discloses a real human being, reveals through its gentle didacticism the timeless value of self-reflection, and provides as viable a life of Hadrian as was possible some seventy years and more ago. So it might be proposed from the soundings of these pages, limited investigations admittedly that leave much more still to be explored, but with challenges also presented to new and continuing readers. Yourcenarians on the one hand must wonder whether the problems of historicity the novel raises and the traditions of imperial biography with which it associates itself can ever again be disregarded in the elucidation of its artistry; Romanists on the other hand must ask whether a life of Hadrian, or of any Roman emperor, can ever be attempted without attention to the conventions of modern life writing. *Mémoires* endures meantime as a unique experiment in Roman imperial biography, a work that meets its author's own requirements of success in making her readers think more deeply than they might otherwise do, and in offering something from which they might learn (*HZ* IV 605). It is the creation of an author who in writing the lives of her own ancestors could blur, if not altogether erase, the distinctions between biographer, historian, and novelist, and illustrate thereby how impossible it is to try to categorize her as an artist (*SP* 949). The gifts of all three coalesce in the concept of the historical poet, and it is to that abiding identity that Yourcenar's Hadrian is ultimately owed.

NOTES

Preface

1 Bradley 2008a, 2011, 2012a, 2012b, 2016a, 2016b, 2017a.

1. Imperial Biography

1 *Mémoires* went on sale on 5 December 1951: Savigneau 1993: 216; J.E. Howard 2018: 186. Extracts appeared earlier in the year, in August, July, and September, in issues of the journal *La Table ronde* (Blanchet-Douspis 2008: 446).

2 For the rhapsodic early reviews, see *Réception critique*.

3 Grant 1956: 292.

4 MacDonald and Pinto 1995: 10, 11. *Mémoires* was cited positively in the entry on Hadrian in the second edition of the *Oxford Classical Dictionary* (1970), and Perowne 1996 [1960]: 8 stated: "It is one of the most scholarly and beautiful psychological romances of our age." In turn Turcan 2008: 8, 179 still refers to its "charme impériaux," and Opper 2008: 29 refers to its "lasting impact." (Opper's monograph accompanied the exhibition of 2008 at the British Museum, "Hadrian: Empire and Conflict," where the first item visitors saw was a display honouring Yourcenar that included her portrait and handwritten entries from her notebooks.) On the other hand, Everitt 2009: xii–xiii pronounces: "The *Memoirs* are a masterpiece, but (just as a fake antique, completely convincing when it first appears on the market, loses its authenticity with the passage of time) they now reveal as much about mid-twentieth-century French literary attitudes as they do of second-century Rome. Yourcenar's Hadrian is a romantic rationalist with a taste for the exotic, a classical André Gide." Cf. similarly Danziger and Purcell 2005: 295: "Margeurite [*sic*] Yourcenar's anguished Hadrian makes an admirable subject for a great historical novel, but hers is

not our view of the emperor." Brennan 2018: 205 is more sympathetic: an "exceptionally well-researched and stunningly perceptive work." Poignault 2010 notably has no entry on the book's reception in the United Kingdom or elsewhere in the English-speaking world.

5 I realize that in combining critical studies of Yourcenar with Roman historical studies I risk falling between two stools and may consequently add nothing positive to knowledge. I recognize also the prospect of seeming at times either apologetic or polemical. The former is unintended, while for the latter I follow Rudd 1976: vii: "when other writers are referred to, it means that I value their work, have learned much from it, and wish to put forward a different view only on the particular point at issue." The historiographical bias forecloses any concern with the field of reception studies.

6 The *Carnets* were first published in *Mercure de France* 316 (1 November 1952): 415–32, preceded by "Comment j'ai écrit *Mémoires d'Hadrien*" (*Combat*, 7 March 1952). Publication with *Mémoires* followed in the Club du meilleur livre edition of 1953 and in the illustrated Plon edition of 1958. On both *Note* and *Carnets*, see esp. Poignault 2007a; 2007b.

7 *ACB* contains also a few letters to Boudot-Lamotte's sister.

8 Opinion: Auden 1989: 302–3 (from "An Improbable Life," first published in 1963; an exception was made for Oscar Wilde). Wide range: Castellani 2015, with special reference to *HZ* III.

9 Houghton modbm_ms_fr_372_2_266; modbm_ms_fr_372_2_268, on which see Sarde 1995a: 306–10; Goslar 1998: 171–8, 184. The *Notebook* includes a *Journal* that is in effect an early version of the *Carnets*. Yourcenar's investment of time and energy in maintaining a prolific correspondence is remarkable judged in an age of electronic correspondence and social media. The self-discipline involved places her firmly in a different and perhaps lost world of intellectualism. Copies of her letters were scrupulously made and carefully maintained by her companion Grace Frick. Having discarded certain items, Yourcenar towards the end of her life arranged for the copies to be donated to the Houghton Library at Harvard University together with many other documents, specifying particularly that her correspondence with Frick be sealed for fifty years after her death. Many letters remain unpublished, with further volumes expected as editors work through the Harvard materials. Anything concluded here must therefore be provisional. Hence the designation of my chapters as "soundings."

10 Yourcenar's biography is outlined in the *Chronologie* of the first volume of the Pléiade edition of her works (*OR* XIII–XXXVIII), which I take to have been compiled by Yourcenar herself, other than the details of her final illness and demise supplied by an editor in the edition of 2011. For full accounts, see Savigneau 1993; Sarde 1995a; Goslar 1998; and, for Grace Frick, J.E. Howard 2018. Exile: Castellani 2011: 41–2; 2015, clearly Eurocentric; *ACB* 15; cf. 22, 24

(editorial remarks); for balanced views, see Blanchet-Douspis 2008: 20; Deprez 2012. Anticipated: on the complex decision to remain in the United States once war ended, see Savigneau 1993: 156–60.

11 Yourcenar's Certificate of Naturalization, dated 12 December 1947, is kept in the Houghton Library. It is reproduced by Deprez 2012: 36. Its two signatures, one on its accompanying photograph, the other on the document itself, are clear statements of Yourcenar's legal name and identity at the time. The application for US citizenship began in 1942. Difficulties over passport renewal due to McCarthyist hostility to homosexuality arose in 1954 (J.E. Howard 2018: 155, 204–6).

12 Savigneau 1993: 170; J.E. Howard 2018: 334; Brémond 2019: 19. Fraught: the campaign to elect Yourcenar to the Académie was marked by sexism and other reactionary issues, politics and prejudice making immortality seem a dubious honour; see Savigneau 1993: 382–90; Brémond 2019: 11–40; "Marguerite Yourcenar par TD Allman" in Deprez 2012: 145–63, esp. 151–5. The only occasion on which Yourcenar identified herself as Belgian was during her voyage in 1939 to the United States on the *Manhattan* (J.E. Howard 2018: 86; cf. *HZ* IV 218: "à demi belge" [1965]). Sarde 1995a: 294 quotes this extract of an unpublished letter of 5 September 1977 to Jean-Marie Debasse: "Je n'appartiens pas à la belge, ayant été française avant d'être américaine, et c'est à titre étranger que l'Académie Royale belge a bien voulu m'accueillir. Mais le pays de ma mère et de ma naissance à Bruxelles … m'est cher" ("I am not Belgian, having been French before American, and it was as a foreigner that the Royal Academy of Belgium wanted to receive me. But the country of my mother and of my birth … is dear to me"). She described her family on one occasion as "cette vieille famille patricienne franco-flamande" (*HZ* IV 405). It amused her as a French speaker to be thought Canadian (*HZ* 394).

13 French: Savigneau 1993: 171: "invincibly French by way of her language." Travels (interrupted by straitened circumstances in the decade following emigration, and in the 1960s by Frick's ill health): Goslar 1996; cf. Castellani 2011: 27–8.

14 Evers 1994: no. 55: still in the British Museum.

15 See esp. *YO* 146–66. Yourcenar told interviewers of the trunk soon after initial publication (*Réception critique* 57, 92–3, 123, 129). Present form: the precise dates of composition are ambiguous: writing seems to have begun in December 1948 according to the *Chronologie*, but other records show February 1949 as the true starting-point, following arrival of the trunk in January (Savigneau 1993: 10; J.E. Howard 2018: 159–61, 166–7, esp. on Frick's assistance, as recorded in Frick's journals.). The *Chronologie* gives December 1950 as the month of completion, and independent evidence shows that the final instalment was mailed to the publisher (Plon) on 2 January 1951 (Savigneau 1993: 175–91,

pointing to inconsistencies in the tradition, 206–7; Goslar 1998: 172–7). Two full years were involved, 1949 and 1950, but *CNMH* 526 gives three years of research.

16 Cf. *CNMH* 537 and Gaudin 1994: 53, quoting from the *Journal* on *Mémoires'* composition contained in the *Notebook*: "Le travail recommencé le 10 février 1949 s'achève. J'éprouve la sensation d'un coureur de marathon arrivant au but épuisé, ou de Lorenzaccio après son crime" ("The work re-begun on 10 February 1949 is coming to an end. I feel like a marathoner reaching the finish line exhausted, or like Lorenzaccio after his crime").

17 See Savigneau 1993: 57–8.

18 "ceci ne répond pas à grand-chose pour Hadrien, qui connaissait très mal les chrétiens, qui n'a eu des rapports très vagues avec eux que tout à fait vers la fin et qui se sentait vivre au VIIIe siècle de l'ère romaine" (from 1971).

19 Few days: *CNON* 866. Baiae: ironically termed the Bar Harbor of the time by E. Clark 2015 [1952]: 201. Tel Shalem: Opper 2008: 63 fig. 46; 88 fig. 73; 230 no. 64 (with esp. Evers 1994: 119–20 and Gergel 1991 for technical details). *Sibylline Oracles*: note Yourcenar's translation at *CL* 423–4. Museo Capitolino: Kleiner 1992: 270 fig. 234 and 314.

20 Latin poem: *HA Hadr.* 25.9. Latin source: *Epit. de Caes.*14.6: "inconsistent, complicated, many-sided." Legends: *BMC* III cxxxi; cxl–cxli; cxliv–cxlvi; cxlviii; clxix; clxxxi; clxxxxii ("The World Stabilised," "Age of Gold," "Imperial Discipline," "Endurance"). *Tellus stabilita*, a distinctively Hadrianic coin legend – "an epitome of the story of Hadrian's work for the Roman world" (Toynbee 1934: 137) – was an inspired choice.

21 Castellani 2011: 211–21. See ch. 8.

22 "Let us try, if we can, to enter into death with open eyes."

23 Guppy 1988 = *PV* 378–99: French version of the original English.

24 Gallimard: *HZ* 185: but allowing the term for her early works of fiction. Savigneau: *PV* 319. Uncompromising: Guppy 1988: 234 = *PV* 382. On Yourcenar's illness and death, see Savigneau 1993: 431–9.

25 Cf. *L* 221; 333; *ER* 41; *L* 149; *HZ* 137–8; *HZ* III 279.

26 *HZ* II 36–7: 8 January 1957; *L* 333: 3 July 1969; *L* 346: 5 February 1970; *L* 409–10: 13 October 1973.

27 From 1954; cf. *HZ* 388: 11 September 1954.

28 Cf. *YO* 60: the novelist as the modern-day successor of the tragedian and epic poet.

29 *PV* 71–2 (from 1969); *PV* 300–1 (from 1981); *L* 221: 17 February 1965; *ER* 39.

30 7 March 1952.

31 28 June 1960.

32 *HZ* 197: 21 November 1952; *PV* 34; 37–9 (from 1954); *YO* 47; *PV* 319 (from 1984); *PV* 121–2 (from 1971); Guppy 1988: 234 = *PV* 382; *YO* 149; cf. *HZ* II 71:

13 February 1957: a "historical reconstitution" of Hadrian's life in monologue form.

33 Sometimes: *HZ* 363: "biographe historique" (June/July 1954); *ER* 23: "roman-biographie … du berceau à la tombe," "des romans de type biographique." Grant: *HZ* II 57 (quoted in ch. 3). Yourcenar's understanding of "poetry" here aligns with its meaning of "the interior, the personal, the spiritual or psychological," that in the history of the English novel had occurred by the middle of the nineteenth century (Eagleton 2005: 12); see ch. 4. Hesitation: *L* 248: 12 May 1966; *HZ* IV 328–9: 25 November 1965.

34 Intent: *L* 83: 7 April 1951. Another definition: *HZ* 78: 7 October 1951: before publication; *HZ* II 36–37: 8 January 1957; *HZ* III 279: 14 January 1963. Yourcenar's views on the singularity of the individual's life consist with those of Watt 2001 [1957]: 18–34, on the particularization of character and context as essential elements of the novel as a literary form. It may be true that biography is determined by biology, but it does not follow as far as I can tell that "no life is actually unique" (Eagleton 2005: 81). Assert: *HZ* 37: 21 August 1951: before publication.

35 The "caractère anomique" of *Mémoires* has been taken as a sign of Yourcenar's modernism: Wagner 2014: 44; cf. Blanckeman 2014a: 13.

36 Hörmann 1996; cf. Brochard and Pinon 2014: 58; Cordonnier 2019: 64.

37 Lejeune 1975: 14: "A retrospective prose narrative produced by a real person concerning his own existence, focusing on his individual life, in particular on the development of his personality."

38 Adler 2014; Šubert 2015; Ness 1994; Houssais 2014.

39 Whatley 1980–1; Kiebuzinski 2004. On the difficulty of describing *Mémoires* as a historical novel, observe Portmann 2001: 104: "Plus exactement, il ne s'agirait pas du "roman historique", mais d'un courant plus vaste en littérature où l'adjectif historique n'est qu'une marque extérieure renvoyant à la thématique de l'ouvrage." On a definition from Graham Greene, *Mémoires* can hardly be called a novel at all: "A novel is a work in which characters interrelate. It doesn't need a plot. The novelist's own intervention must be very limited. What happens to the author of a novel is rather like the pilot of a plane. The pilot needs to get the plane off the ground. It takes off with the help of the pilot. Once it is in the air, the pilot does virtually nothing. Once everything has started working, the characters begin to impose themselves on the author, who no longer controls them. They have a life of their own. The author has to go on writing. Sometimes he writes things which appear to have no raison d'être. Only at the end is the reason apparent. The author intervenes to allow the plane to land. It is time for the novel to end" (Greene 2020: 434).

40 "True biography": the phrase of Syme *RP* VI 122; 126, notably including the criterion of "inner, and personal biography." Wilde: Ellmann 1987, generally

regarded as a lesser achievement than his biography of James Joyce (Kermode 2019: 15–25), but relevant regardless. Interest: see ch. 8. Darwin: Wilson 2017.

41 Lowell: Jamison 2017: despite a non-biographical disclaimer (5). Clare: Bate 2003. Correspondence: note Watt 2001 [1957]: 176: "letters are the most direct material evidence for the inner life of their writers that exist." Disposal: a few examples of emperors' private letters are preserved in classical sources, but most have been lost to history; so too with the memoirs emperors and those close to them are reputed to have composed, those for instance of Nero's mother Agrippina.

42 Balsdon 1934; Ferrill 1991; Winterling 2011; Barrett 2015.

43 Barrett 2015: 99: all of which may be true but cannot be shown to be true. The assumption that the survival of Tacitus's account of Caligula's reign could have made a real biography possible is dubious.

44 See esp. Winterling 2011: 103; 114; 127–31. Signs of aberration: Sen. *Ira* 1.20.8–9; 3.21.5; *Clem.* 1.25.2; *Tranq.* 14.5; *Consol. ad Polyb.* 13.1; 17.5; *Ben.* 7.11.1–2; *Constant.* 18.1; Philo *Leg.* 93; Joseph. *AJ* 19.1, 5; 11; 39; 50; 69; 130; 193; 284; 285; Tac. *Agr.* 13.2; *Ann.* 6.45; 11.3; 13.3; *Hist.* 4.48; Suet. *Calig.* 50.2. Many attempts at diagnosis have been made, but all fail from the insufficiency of information available and the assumption that a solution must be found in modern Western medical terms. (Ferrill 1991 gives a good overview of biographical approaches.)

45 Senate: Talbert 1984: 131–4; Syme *RP* II 565: "The bottom 200 at any time evade record and defy recognition." Any sentence beginning "Most senators … " is obviously questionable. Elusive: Marañón 1956 is an exception. "Biographical turn": Caine 2010: 1–2; cf. 23; 39–40: much in evidence by the 1970s. Theorists: see Kendall 1965; Edel 1957; 1984; Backscheider 1999; Lee 2009; Caine 2010; cf. Gibson 2020: ch. 2, reverting with good reason to Highet 1957. Constantine: Barnes 2011: 2; 80; cf. 175.

46 D.R. Howard 1987: 171–6: quotations: 172; 173; 175–6.

47 Levick 2015: 167–8.

48 Osgood 2011: 24 sensibly considers a biography of Claudius impossible. Note Levick 1976: 201 on the fall of Sejanus in Tiberius's reign: the events are ascertainable, but "It is more difficult to imagine the state of mind of Tiberius himself."

49 Bate 2009.

50 Quotation: Yavetz 1996: 106. He continued: "His experience as a baby in a mutinous army camp; the shock that the early death of his father must have caused him; the stress he must have gone through, while living under the tutelage of two formidable grandmothers, especially Livia, whom he called 'a Ulysses in petticoats'; the banishment of his ambitious mother and the murder of his older brothers Nero and Drusus; and last but not least, his undying efforts to survive the whims and atrocities of an ageing and vengeful Tiberius

on Capri. All those could have caused his development into a man of whom it was said that 'no one had ever been a better slave or a worse master.'" Dickens: Wilson 2020: a daring proposition.

51 Madness: see P.A. Clark 1993; Thumiger 2013; Jouanna 2013. Evidence from Celsus is esp. important: *Med.* 2.1.6; 2.1.15; 2.1.21; 2.4.8; 2.7.17–18; 2.7.24–7; 3.18, with P.A. Clark and Rose (unpublished); W.V. Harris 2013: 8, 22; see also *Dig.* 21.1.4.3; 21.1.65 pr., with Toohey 2013. The tradition of Caligula's insanity, as with other emperors, may have been due to the upheavals the emperorship is thought to have brought to Roman society (Toner 2009: 84).

52 Nero: Drinkwater 2019: 276–86 (cf. Bradley 2020); Champlin 2003: the strategy can lead to riveting effects, as in a description of Nero's coronation in the Roman Forum in 66 of the Parthian king Tiridates, the pageant permitting "a splendid theatrical affirmation of [Nero's] role as the new god of the Sun" (228–9).

53 A statement presumably appeared before the lost portion of the life of Julius Caesar. Stylistically the *Caesares* are not in the first rank of Latin literature. But what Suetonius wrote is important especially because of his success in public life. He belonged to Rome's upper classes, enjoying in early life the patronage of the younger Pliny, and he undertook a public career that culminated with positions as a high-level functionary in the courts of Trajan and Hadrian, at one stage holding a position in charge of Hadrian's official correspondence. He can be assumed therefore to have been privy to confidential imperial business of all kinds. An association, however, with Hadrian's first praetorian prefect, C. Septicius Clarus, seems to have brought a fall from favour in the year 122, with dismissal from office perhaps occurring in the summer of that year when with Hadrian in Britain (Syme *RP* III 1251–75; 1337–49: now followed by most scholars; cf. *HA Hadr.* 11.2–3, with Fündling 2006: 577, 581–2). The office is known from a career inscription discovered at Hippo Regius in North Africa in 1951, first published in 1952 (*CRAI* 1952: 76–85 = Smallwood 1966: no. 281).

54 Bradley 1991a; 1998; cf. Wardle 1998: 446–7. Wallace-Hadrill 1983: 5–28, followed by Pelling 2009, suggests that Suetonius wrote generic "not-history," which cannot mean that the sequence of lives is not a form of history tout court. See further Bowersock 1998; Hägg 2012: 214–38; Power and Gibson 2014. I am unconvinced that Suetonius was dismissed because he addressed to Hadrian an "avertissement sévère sur la concentration du pouvoir," influenced by the younger Pliny and a group identifying Trajan as an ideal prince (Roman 2008: 16–18, 119); or that the *Caesares* were intended as a vengeful response to his dismissal, warning Hadrian that absolute power leads to insanity (Husquin 2018); or that the lives of Nero and Domitian are deconstructing responses to (non-extant) accounts from a previous generation (Schulz 2019); or that the equestrian Suetonius was a conveyer of "senatorial tradition" (Husquin 2020: 141–4).

55 Admired: see Bradley 2016a. Suetonius is one of antiquity's two great extant biographers, the other being his near coeval Plutarch, whom Yourcenar also held in high esteem (*SBI* 5). He composed biographies of the early emperors at roughly the same time as Suetonius, but only those of Galba and Otho survive. For his concern with the ethical import of his subjects' lives, see esp. Duff 1999. Minor character: Yourcenar identifies him as Hadrian's "curateur d'archives" (*MH* 383), following *HA Hadr.* 11.3. She situates him in Rome at the time of dismissal, a member of a small circle of "conservateurs mécontents" allied to Trajan's widow Plotina while Hadrian is travelling in the provinces (cf. Fündling 2006: 583–6). When writing *Mémoires* she can hardly have known the career inscription (above n.53), and as far as I know did not refer to it subsequently; see, however, Poignault 1995: 543.

56 Strachey 1918; 1921. "New biography": Hoberman 1987: 35–57; Marcus 2002; Lee 2009: 72–82; Caine 2010: 39–40. For public figures such as Roman emperors, biographers "must set the central performance of their subjects in the context of the political conditions that produce them, the society in and on which they operate, their race, class, nationality, and gender, and the many other figures who surround them" (Lee 2009: 104: observing that the metaphor of the portrait does not imply a static account).

57 Yourcenar owned a 1934 edition of *Eminent Victorians* and a 1935 edition of *Queen Victoria* (Bernier 2004: nos. 6641; 6616); cf. *YO* 291: allusion to the former.

58 Ov. *Tr.* 1.1.29; 1.5.61; 2.1.124 (*ira Caesaris*); cf. 1.2.13; 1.5.44, 83; 2.1.28; 3.8.13–14. See Syme 1978: 214.

59 Nero: see M.T. Griffin 1984: a biographical study attributing the collapse of the Julio-Claudian dynasty to the reign of an immature and irresponsible monarch (cf. Bradley 1986).

60 Millar 1977 (fundamental); Ste Croix 1981: 372–408; Roller 2001; Veyne 2005: 13–91; cf. Syme 1986: 451: "absolute rule based on delegated authority."

61 *ILS* 244.17–19: *utique quaecunque ex usu reipublicae maiestate divinarum hum[an]arum, publicarum privatarumque rerum esse censebit, ei agere facere ius potestasque sit.* ("And that he shall have the right and power to transact and do whatever things divine, human, public, and private he deems to serve the advantage and the overriding interest of the state"). See Brunt 1977.

62 *Basileus*: e.g. App. *BC* 1 pref. 6 (Caesar as the initiator of autocracy). Decree: Jones 1999 (trans.). Recourse: cf. Brown 2012: 487: "the constitution of the Roman empire … was an autocracy tempered by assassination."

63 "It is difficult for us today to imagine the omnipotence of a man who spoke as master in Alexandria as in England, at Athens as at Rome. No monarch, no dictator in our time has ruled over so many peoples, has had the opportunity to compare such diverse ways of life" (from 1952). See *MH* 348, with Suet. *Iul.* 29.1.

64 Note the defeatist remark: "It is only in rare episodes that it is possible to come near to Hadrian himself" (Henderson 1968 [1923]: 80).

65 He was remembered as "the most dogmatic man in Oxford" (Rowse 1944: 237).

66 Millar 1996: 444; cf. Bowersock 2009: 6: "the greatest historian of Rome in the twentieth century."

67 Quotation: *RP* V 552. Prosopography, ironically, is sometimes called collective biography. The most relevant of Syme's studies of Hadrian are the following, cited chiefly from *RP*: "Hadrian and Italica" (*RP* II 617–28); "Les Proconsuls d'Afrique sous Hadrien" (*RP* II 629–37); "Ummidius Quadratus, *capax imperii*" (*RP* III 1158–78); "Guard Prefects of Trajan and Hadrian" (*RP* III 1276–1302); "Hadrianic Proconsuls of Asia" (*RP* III 1303–15); "The Travels of Suetonius Tranquillus" (*RP* III 1337–49); "Hadrian and the Vassal Princes" (*RP* III 1436–46); "Hadrianic Governors of Syria" (*RP* IV 50–61); "Hadrian and the Senate" (*RP* IV 295–324); "Hadrian as Philhellene. Neglected Aspects (*RP* V 546–62); "Praesens the Friend of Hadrian" (*RP* V 563–78); "Hadrian the Intellectual" (*RP* VI 103–14); "Journeys of Hadrian" (*RP* VI 346–57); "Hadrian's Autobiography: Servianus and Sura" (*RP* VI 398–408); "Hadrian and Antioch" (Syme 1983: 180–8).

68 Disdained: *RP* III 937; V 703; VI 247, 329, 332; cf. 1939: 7. Contemporary: Syme died in 1989; on his career, see Bowersock 1994a; Edmond 2017: 104–79. Interest: see esp. ch. 8.

69 Influence: Everitt 2009 is heavily indebted to Birley but lacks his authority; Speller 2003 draws on him to achieve highly evocative effects; Morwood 2013, a "shilling life," takes as a starting point this "shrewdly insightful book" (ix). Refinements are now necessary as a result of new discoveries but this scarcely detracts from the book's status.

70 Auden 1989: 89. The positivist approach and methodology owe much in fact to Syme, Birley's mentor.

71 Birley 1997a: 9.

72 Mortensen 2004, cataloguing scholarly views of Hadrian through the course of the nineteenth and twentieth centuries, rightly concludes that Birley is Hadrian's most comprehensive positivist biographer, but notes his avoidance of investigating the "real man" (19, 363); *Mémoires* in turn is given credit for its scholarly foundation and aesthetic merits, but is dismissed as unhistorical because so much attention is given to Hadrian's personality, all of which is dismissed as fiction (20, 285, 362). J. Griffin immediately observed that Birley's "interests are more British" than Yourcenar's, and that he avoided writing in her "Gallic mode" (*The Spectator*, 8 November 1997). Roman 2008 is a study of policy as a guide to personality influenced by the tradition that Hadrian was a devotee of astrology; written in Yourcenar's shadow, it engages with Birley only on the meaning of the word "restless" (363).

73 Elton 1992: 147: the impossibility of writing a biography of Thomas Cromwell; valid still, perhaps, despite MacCulloch 2019.

74 23 June 1951 (cf. 139): "The object is a reconstruction from within of the motives and thoughts of the great second-century emperor, a liberal man of letters"; cf. *Chronologie* XXIV: "«recréer du dedans»."

2. Authenticity Pursued

1 Lambert 1988 [1984]: xviii.

2 Hetland 2015; Wilson Jones 2015.

3 Wilson 2014: 607–19.

4 MacCulloch 2019: 1.

5 "One was Dio Cassius in Henri Estienne's beautiful printing, and the other a volume of an ordinary edition of *Historia Augusta* … purchased at the time that I was intending to write this book."

6 Bernier 2004: no. 3898 reads: "Ex Dione Nicaeo excerptae & in epitomes forma redactae vitae Pompeii Magni et Ceasarum [*sic*], usque ad Alexandrum Mamaeae filium, per Ioannem Xiphilinum. Texte grec-latin dont il est impossible de donner la référence exacte du fait d'une page manquante, p.1–714 et p.1–491." I take this to be the Cassius Dio concerned. Henricus Stephanus was the son of the Robertus Stephanus (Robert Estienne, d. 1559 aged c. 56), who published the first Dio in 1548 and the first Xiphilinus in 1551 (Armstrong 1954: 29, 136). The third volume of the standard edition of Cassius Dio from 1895 by U.P. Boissevain, which contains the relevant material on Hadrian, gives the notation (xi): "nam a. 1592 postremus edidit Henricus Stephanus." Bernier 2004: nos. 3105–7 records the three volumes of Yourcenar's Loeb *Historia Augusta*, with dates of 1922, 1924, and 1954. The first volume was originally published in 1921, the third in 1932. I take the last as a replacement copy, on the assumption that Yourcenar owned a complete set before 1951, or else a volume later acquired for other purposes (see ch. 8).

7 Ernestus Hohl, *Scriptores Historiae Augustae* (2 vols. EDITIO STEREOTYPA CORRECTIOR ADDENDA ET CORRIGENDA ADIECERUNT CH. SAMBERGER ET W. SEYFARTH [Leipzig 1965]). Hohl's Preface is dated 1927, the year of first publication. The collection has a lacuna for the years 244–59.

8 Dessau 1889; Syme 1968; 1971a; 1971b; 1983. For the history of scholarship on the *Historia Augusta*, see Chastagnol 1994: "Introduction générale" (esp. IX–XXXIV); cf. Cornell 2013. Not universally: see Den Hengst 2002. White 1967 is important on stylistic questions.

9 Technical grounds: Cameron 2011a: 743: "a passage in the *Life of Severus* derives from the *Caesares* of Aurelius Victor, published in 361." Posit: Cameron 2011a: 772: "between 361 and 386"; Rohrbacher 2016: 158–68: between 408 and 410; Paschoud 2012: 400 or later; Savino 2017: the decade after 408; Danziger and

Purcell 2005: xv: "at the end of the fifth century." New discoveries now reopen the accepted manuscript tradition of the work (Stover 2020).

10 Renaissance: Syme: 1971b: 112 (cf. Brown 2012: 131–4: Golden Age). Models: Q. Aurelius Symmachus allegedly wrote literary letters emulating those of Pliny, Ammianus Marcellinus continued the histories of Tacitus, and Claudian followed the epics of Lucan and Statius. Dismissed: Cameron 2011a: 399–420; 743.

11 Ratti 2007 = 2010: 217–23; cf. 2012: 105–27; 2016a: 191–225; 2016b.

12 Counter view: Cameron 2011b (cf. 2011a: 636); 2016 (quotations: Cameron 2014: 163, 164). Third contender: Savino 2017.

13 Rohrbacher 2016: a difficulty here is that evidence for a coterie of devoted biographical enthusiasts is non-existent, and understanding of the literarily allusive too tendentious to make the case convincing; cf. similarly Burgersdijk 2013, with subsequent narratological analysis (2016): the author was concerned with the question of how a good emperor could find a good successor.

14 Momigliano 1969a [1954]; see also 1969b; 1973; 1984: responding to criticism from Syme. In my view the *Historia Augusta*'s seemingly interminable, enervating catalogue of gory crimes and violent follies makes any explanatory theory dependent on humour utterly bizarre.

15 Seriously: Rizzi 2010: 14. Deprived: Syme 1971a: 155.

16 See Syme 1971a: ch. III (widely followed): the life is one of the nine relatively good lives in the early sequence from Hadrian to Caracalla (i.e. excluding the lives of Aelius, Avidius Cassius, and Pescennius Niger). Signs of a scissors-and-paste-like method of compilation were detected by Crook 1956–7: 20–1.

17 Birley 1997a: 97; cf. Birley 1997b; 2006a: 20: the *Historia Augusta* is enthusiastic towards Diocletian and hostile to Constantine, and makes a plea despite its humour for a new Diocletian to restore traditional Roman religion and Roman values against the rise of Christianity.

18 Syme 1971a: ch. VII (Marius Maximus); ch. III ("Ignotus"): with a date after 217. For anyone interested in the relationship between history and fiction this is a startling theory: note Sidebottom 2007: 58: "the reality of Ignotus should be thought extremely problematic."

19 See Cornell ed. 2013: Vol. 2: 1106–27 for *testimonia* and fragments; Vol. 3: 635–47 for commentary. I follow the common view that Marius Maximus is identifiable with the consular L. Marius Maximus, but observe that this is an assumption only. For a rightly cautious approach, see Cornell ed. 2013: Vol. 1: 602–11.

20 Four sources: Syme *RP* VI 162–3; cf. Barnes 1978 (relentlessly positivist): firm belief in "Ignotus" as a sober source and in Marius Maximus as provider of enlivening effect. Solution: Lapini 2020.

21 Bardon 1952 I: 13 (see Bradley 2008b); cf. Syme 1958: 200; *RP* II 731; VII 657. The factor is often unnoticed in Yourcenarian scholarship (Demanze 2014; Brochard and Pinon 2014: 132; Chabot 2015: 107).

22 Millar 1964: 34. Fündling 2006 provides a massive commentary on the Latin life much indebted to source criticism; its often inconclusive results are symbolized by the generous use of question marks and the contentious designation of many passages as "fiktiv." Cornell ed. 2013 (n.19) brings out how little is really known about Hadrian from the *Historia Augusta*.

23 Temptation: Roman 2008: 20–3 takes the life at face value as an evidently pro-senatorial work; cf. 85; 330: discussion of Marius Maximus omitted. Disturbing: underestimation of Yourcenar's historical preparation may be suspected; see J.E. Howard 1992: 4; Sarde 1995a: 305; Hörmann 1996: 45; Goslar 1998: 171 n.217; Hébert 2012: 244–71; Brochard and Pinon 2014: 58; Houssais 2014: 127; Jouanny 2014: 217.

24 For descriptions of the Wall's features and date, see Breeze 2006: ch. 2; Hingley 2012: ch. 2 (construction took up to ten years); for the epigraphical evidence, see Tomlin 2018: 86–118; cf. Fündling 2006: 577–80. It is unknown whether work began after or before Hadrian's arrival in Britain, but Birley 1997a: 128 (cf. 2005a: 121) believed the decision to build had been taken before Hadrian crossed from Germany. So Toynbee 1934: 54, assigning the decision to 119 and Hadrian personally inspecting progress in 122. Hadrian never saw the finished product.

25 Belief: Birley 2014, with Jarrett 1976. Measures: see Fündling 2006: 577 for possibilities: "Die moderne Literatur zum Hadrianswall ist schier uferlos, der persönliche Anteil des Kaisers weit schwerer zu bestimmen." Agreement on the issues raised is non-existent: on the Wall's purpose, see Breeze 2006: 107–11 but with Hingley 2012: 298: "The function of the Wall remains a contested issue"; see also Breeze 2006: 28: "We cannot be certain that the emperor visited the site of the Wall. Its very size and impressiveness have been taken as an indication of the involvement of the emperor, who, we may note, fancied his architectural skills, while the rigidity of its planning points to some decisions being taken without local knowledge." Birley 2003: 435–6 is certain that Hadrian emulated Augustus in firmly demarcating Rome's frontiers (cf. W.V. Harris 2016: 118–19: confident that frontier retrenchment was "a new policy" inaugurated by Hadrian); and believes (2005a: 121–2; cf. 1997a: 123) that the individual appealing to someone addressed as "majesty" in *Tab. Vind.* II 344 was anticipating Hadrian's arrival in the north. The editors of the text disagree. Hingley 2012: ch. 14 shows that many uncertainties still abound. Bidwell writes that Hadrian "*almost certainly* inspected the building of his great wall" (2022a: 3; my emphasis), but after discussing its "structural sequences" in construction, is "agnostic" on whether "Hadrian ordered the building of the Wall when he visited Britain in AD 122 … or had inspected work already in hand" (2022b: 121).

26 See ch. 8.

27 *OR* 549 refers to Collingwood's 1933 revised ninth edition of J. Collingwood
Bruce's *Handbook to the Roman Wall*, and to Collingwood and Myres 1968
[1937]. The latter states unambiguously that Hadrian "surveyed the whole
line afresh" (130). The suggestion that some of the building carried out by
British tribes took place when the Wall was rebuilt under Septimius Severus
(Collingwood and Myres 1968 [1937]: 136) seems to lie behind Yourcenar's
sentence: "Les terrassiers de la légion étaient secondés dans leur tâche par des
équipes indigènes" (*MH* 393: "The trench-diggers of the legion were aided
in their task by native crews"); cf. Poignault 1995: 797–9. On Yourcenar's
adaptation of material in the Augustan life as a whole, see Poignault 1991.
Yourcenar spent six weeks in 1953, 31 July–2 September, exploring the Wall
(Goslar 1996: 27–8, with *HZ* 296–7).

28 Dio: see Millar 1964 (fundamental): 1–3 (excerptors), 60–72 (the Hadrianic
material), with Molin 2016: summary of new evidence on Dio's identity: L.
Claudius Cassius Dio. Recollections: breathtakingly trusted by Roman 2008.

29 Goals: Mallan 2013: interests in biography, the mechanics of monarchy, and
displays of erudition; contrast Brunt 1980: 491: the account "largely a string
of isolated episodes." Administration: Brunt 1980: 490–4. See further Pelling
1997; Kemezis 2014: 139–41; Berbessou-Broustet 2016: prudent assessment of
the excerpts required; cf. Bellissime and Berbessou-Broustet 2016: distinction
of Xiphilinus from Dio's other principal epitomator, the twelfth-century
Zonaras (of no concern for Hadrian); Migliorati 2003: 203–368: examination
of Dio's text through comparison with documentary evidence and recourse to
Spartianus [*sic*].

30 Since full membership of Rome's senate is never on record and unanimity of
opinion among its members undemonstrable (ch. 1), the notion of a senatorial
tradition seems to me unrealistic, especially when the writings of those who
supposedly created it are non-existent. Belief nonetheless is widespread: see
Galimberti 2017: senatorial tradition as the basis of Dio's account of Antinous's
death; assertion that the senate "never forgave Hadrian for the heroisation and
deification of Antinous" despite the discovery of an Antinous statue "in the
house of the senator … Herodes Atticus" (107–8); cf. Lapini 2020.

31 Millar 1964: 71–2. I generally cite Xiphilinus's excerpts as Dio's work (with
translations when given adapted from the version of E. Cary), but insist here
on the need throughout for chronological caution and perspective: Book 69 can
hardly be taken to illustrate Dio's portrait of Hadrian as a whole (Madsen 2016:
151–2) when its epitomated form is unremarked (Roman 2008: 18–20; cf. 52:
the phrase "abrégé par Xiphilin" unexplained).

32 See Spawforth and Walker 1985; 1986; Willers 1990, with Boatwright 1994;
Jones 1996; Swain 1996: 75–6; Birley 1997a: 264–6; 1997c: 221–2; Boatwright
2000: 147–53; Spawforth 1999; Romeo 2002; Spawforth 2012: 249–52; Karivieri

2019. Migliorati 2003: 328–32 resumes the possible meanings of Dio's text; cf. Syme *RP* V 555: certain of "coherent policy."

33 Polemo: Philostr. *VS* 533. The speech attributed to Hadrian in his last days explaining his choice of Antoninus Pius as his successor (Dio 69.20.2–5) is a glaring example of a passage of little historical value. Rhetorical conventionality aside, the claim that it reflects Dio's personal ideological interests (Davenport and Mallan 2014) will hold only on the assumption that Xiphilinus copied Dio's original text with scrupulous accuracy.

34 See Chastagnol 1994: LXVI–LXXII. Yourcenar owned an antiquarian copy of Victor's *Liber de Caesaribus* (Bernier 2004: no. 3109).

35 Brennan 2018: 30 rightly associates the *Epitome*'s remark with what would have been remembered as a childless marriage.

36 Note Birley 1997a: 306: *Epit. de Caes.* 14.6 "must" derive from Marius Maximus.

37 *idem severus laetus, comis gravis, lascivus cunctator, tenax liberalis, simulator dissimulator, saevus clemens et semper in omnibus varius.* ("He was in one and the same person both stern and cheerful, affable and harsh, impetuous and hesitant, mean and generous, hypocritical and straightforward, cruel and merciful, and always in all things changeable" (trans. Birley).

38 Bird 1994: 88. They are often used regardless in the Augustan-styled biographies of Nerva and Trajan compiled in Birley 1976. The Athenaeum attributed to Hadrian by Aurelius Victor (*Caes.* 14.3) may now have been located in the centre of Rome close to Trajan's Column; see Villetard 2020.

39 By that time a peculiarly Jewish variant had also developed; see ch. 7.

40 Absurd: see Gibbon *Decline and Fall* II: 176–7: "We are required to believe … that the memory of this extraordinary transaction was preserved in the most public and authentic records, which escaped the knowledge of the historians of Greece and Rome, and were only visible to the eyes of an African Christian, who composed his Apology one hundred and sixty years after the death of the emperor Tiberius."

41 But cf. Jerome's *Chronicle s.a.*117 (Helm).

42 See Bradley 2012b: 613. One hypothesis is that Antigonus wrote the horoscope perhaps at Alexandria shortly after Hadrian's death, and that its favourable presentation of Hadrian is explicable by identifying its sole source as a Greek translation of Hadrian's Latin apologetic autobiography supposedly written by the freedman Phlegon (Heilen 2005, inclining to Rome as the birthplace; see below). This depends in part on the notion I consider unacceptable, that by the time of Cassius Dio and Marius Maximus senatorial attitudes to Hadrian were uniformly hostile. For the autobiography, see ch. 3. The fabricated nature of the horoscope, which may have included a now-lost genuine horoscope from Hadrian's lifetime, was already clear from the description of its origins given by

Cramer 1954: 164–5; 168–9, who (163 nn.121b; 122) was certain that Hadrian was born in southern Spain.

43 Cf. *YO* 104: "Il faut bien songer qu'Hadrien était Andalou" ("Remember that Hadrian was Andalusian").

44 Claim: "Les documents sur la vie de l'empereur Hadrien ne sont pas inédits, mais ils avaient été rarement rassemblés. Je crois avoir été une des premières à en entreprendre le recensement complet" ("The items documenting the emperor Hadrian's life are not unpublished but have rarely been fully assembled. I consider myself to have been one of the first to undertake a complete inventory of them" [*PV* 35: from 1954]). *Thèse*: Poignault 1995: a remarkable work of scholarship.

45 Process: Woytek 2012: 100–17. Slaves: of the almost one hundred slave and ex-slave mint workers epigraphically, and fortuitously, attested late in Trajan's reign (*CIL* VI 42–4), some may well have been the very men manufacturing Hadrian's coins at the Roman mint once his accession was secure. Reality: Ste Croix 1981: 392; 394; Peachin 1986; Duncan-Jones 2005: 463; Beckmann 2007: 415–17. For classic rationalization of the unknowable, see Levick 1976: 84 on Tiberius's coin types: "Nor is it clear how far the Princeps himself was involved in choosing them, even if it were universally accepted that they represent an attempt to bring round a populace (or a section of it) to one or the other view of its ruler and his policies. There is a safer hypothesis: the coins show the Princeps as he wished, or those close to him thought he wished, to be seen; possibly as he wished to be." The communicative impact of coins is difficult to judge, but illiteracy and weak eyesight among the elderly were unavoidable impediments (Syme 1986: 440: relevant to the assertion that "Imperial coins were the perfect visual and symbolic expressions of *le style monarchique*" [Noreña 2011: 108]).

46 Exceptions: Suet. *Aug.* 94.12; *Ner.* 25.2; Euseb. *Vit. Const.* 4.15.1; cf. *HA Duo Gallieni* 12.1: Gallienus said to have ordered coins to be struck commemorating victory against the Persians with captives displayed; *Tyranni Triginta* 26.2: Trebellianus said to have ordered the striking of coins as an imperial prerogative. They resemble the one-time introduction of new coins in 1802 by the revolutionary slave leader Toussaint L'Ouverture, following the unification of Saint Domingue and Santo Domingo, that bore the legends *République Française* and *Colonie de Saint-Domingue* (Hazareesingh 2020: 236.) That Nero regularly dictated choices to the central mint (Hekster, Claes, Manders, Sootjes, Klaassen de Haan 2014) I find unconvincing. Turcan 2008: 68 ascribes a change in portraiture from head and chest to head alone on coins from 124 onwards directly to Hadrian. Officials: Woytek 2012: 100–17, with Stat. *Silv.* 3.3.104–5 for the *a rationibus*, who may not have worked closely with the emperor (Millar 1977: 106). Queen Victoria: Wilson 2014: 478–9; cf. Carson 1990:

244: "not improbable" that Roman emperors behaved like British monarchs, responding to submitted designs.

47 See e.g. *PV* 275; 367, with *BMC* III cxlviii (quotation).

48 Duncan-Jones 2005: 463, with *BMC* III cxliii: "a new impulse of originality reveals the hand of Hadrian himself."

49 Yourcenar was clearly familiar with Toynbee 1934: ch. III, the fundamental discussion of what is conventionally called the "province series" of coins (*OR* 552–3). Note esp. the following: "The rocks on which Britannia's right foot is placed are, perhaps, intended to suggest the bleak and rugged character of the scenery of northern Britain"; "The curved sword, or scimitar, the characteristic of the Thraco-Phrygian peoples of north-western Asia Minor and north-eastern Europe, is already familiar to us as an attribute of Dacia from the Column and the Trajanic coin-types; and we can trace it back in art to the end of the fifth century B.C." (Toynbee 1934: 56, 79).

50 "I have chosen for it this legend, which will be my last watchword." Domitius Rogatus: Demougin 1997: 43 dates him as *procurator monetae* c.142; he was *ab epistulis* to L. Aelius Caesar in 137 (*PIR*² D 160), which would make it just conceivable that he was in office in the mint in Hadrian's last year (cf. Poignault 1995: 642 n.5); his predecessor M. Petronius Honoratus is dated in office c.130. However, Peachin 1986: 96–7 posits c.142–5 for Rogatus, with Petronius Honoratus assigned possibly to the early years of Hadrian and L. Sempronius Senecio to the late years (c.130–45). There is no assurance on the order or precise dates of these officials. Rogatus's career is known from *ILS* 1450 = Smallwood 1966: no. 258, which Yourcenar evidently knew. Her Hadrian earlier makes him a secretarial chaperon of Aelius Caesar (*MH* 492).

51 Years before: *BMC* III cxl–cxli; cf. Poignault 1995: 642. Endurance: *BMC* III cxl–cxli: on issues of 131–2. Defined: *RIC* II 328.

52 Duncan-Jones 2005 makes a strong case against emperors' use of coins as instruments by which to communicate items of policy in general, but, the "province series" apart, allows (464) that Hadrian may have been unusual in sponsoring some observable changes in numismatic design and practice; cf. Price 1987: 68, suspecting "some degree of central organization" behind local coinages portraying Antinous; and contrast Fuduli and Salamone 2015, arguing in the case of Sicily that archaeology does not support suggestions of Hadrianic liberality theoretically inferable from the legend RESTITUTOR SICILIAE.

53 Brennan 2018: 156–74, 212–13.

54 "I rather liked to have the profile of an empress on the Roman coins, with an inscription on the reverse, sometimes to Matronly Virtue, sometimes to Tranquillity." The former attribute, as an allegorized figure of *Pudicitia*, became a special mark of Imperial women in the Antonine age; it was of interest to the trenchant Tertullian (Bradley 2012c: 242; 246).

55 *CIL* XIV 3579 = Smallwood 1966: no. 114 = Jones 2004.

56 "My mother-in-law Matidia had come back from the Orient already revealing the first symptoms of a mortal disease; to distract her from her suffering I devised simple dinners, and contrived to inebriate this modest and naïve matron with a harmless drop of wine." See Poignault 1995: 580–1.

57 Coarelli 2007: 291–2, with the delicious remark: "Hadrian is perhaps the only man in the world to proclaim his mother-in-law a goddess." December: *CIL* VI 2080 = Smallwood 1966: no. 7 (*Acts of the Arval Brethren* for 119: the Arvals provided a gift of perfume and incense on 23 December for the consecration; but cf. Scheid 1998: no. 69: 12 December).

58 André 1993: 594–6; Birley 1997a: 107; Jones 2004: 272; Brennan 2018: 50–1.

59 See Temporini 1979: 170–3; Syme 1958: 246: *HA Hadr.* 9.9, 19.5, *CIL* VI 2080 and XIV 3579 show the speech as Hadrian's "own composition" (cf. Migliorati 2003: 234; I cannot see this); Jones 2004: 270: Vell. Pat. 2.130.5 and the *Senatus Consultum de Pisone* (lines 115–17) support the conventional content of lines 21–2.

60 "Whether sincere or not, the official eulogies and epitaphs continue to attribute to our matrons those same virtues of industry, chastity, and sobriety which were demanded of them under the Republic."

61 Famous records: Speidel 2006 (Yourcenar well understood the speeches' insistence on military discipline). Letter: *IGRR* 1.146 = Oliver 1989: no. 86 (trans. slightly adapted).

62 Model: Millar 1977. Discoveries: Hauken and Malay 2009; Jones 2011; *SEG* 51 (2001) no. 641 with Jones 2006 (trans.), illustrated in Giroire and Roger 2007: 96; see also Jones 2009.

63 Crook 1955.

64 Millar 1977: 228–40; cf. J.M. Reynolds 2000: 8.

65 Style: Bardon 1968: ch. XIV: a certain preciosity, due to the source tradition's record of Hadrian's archaizing literary taste. A distinction, however, between administrative documents and literary compositions is needed. Quotation: Burton 2002: 252.

66 See ch. 7.

67 Jones 2006: 162 (quotation); *SEG* 64 (2014) no. 482 (Dominguez Monedero); cf. *SEG* 60 (2010) no. 542 (Chaniotis).

68 Jones 1998.

69 Model: Hannestad 1988: strong challenge; Cortés Copete 2017a: full-scale rejection; for summary and discussion, see Spawforth 2012: ch. 1. Initiative: Cortés Copete 2017b: agonistic associations at Rome; Gordillo Hervás 2017: promotion of Hellenism; Galimberti 2007: conviction on Hadrianic policies; cf. Rizzi 2010 (all to my mind unverifiable).

70 Story: Crook 1955: 50–2. Limitations: institutional mechanisms of Roman rule can be identified: laws which stipulated obligations Rome imposed on its

provinces (*leges provinciarum*), instructions given to governors for provincial administration (*mandata*), edicts governors issued within their jurisdictions (Burton 2002). But there is remarkably little first-hand evidence to show emperors, with or without advisers, actively engaged in the formulation of policy. If the identities of individuals who wielded power under given regimes are sometimes known (as in Tacitus's account of relations between Nero and Seneca and others [Drinkwater 2019]), the deliberations between Hadrian and courtiers close to him that led to decisions of the kind that documents finally preserve, as in the case of the fragmentary record of a petition presented to Hadrian in 129 found near Phrygian Eumeneia (Jones 2009), remain completely obscure.

71 Hazareesingh 2020.

72 Gualandi 1963: I 24–57.

73 "There was a great outcry when I banished from Rome a rich and highly esteemed patrician woman who maltreated her aged slaves." See *Dig.* 1.6.2: female, not old, slaves; cf. Poignault 1995: 825–7.

74 Argument: W. Williams 1976: 69–74 (quotations: 69; 70). Example: trans. Watson ed. 1985.

75 Contentious: Honoré 1981; Tuori 2016: ch. 4. Described: Humfress 2005: 168.

76 *P.Mich.* XXI 827, with Claytor and Verhoogt eds. 2018: 31–83 (c. 120–4). Predecessors: strikingly including the undeified Tiberius.

77 *P. Fayum* 19 = Smallwood 1966: no. 123 (trans. Alexander 1938: 170) = Cornell ed. 2013: Vol. 2: F7. For illustration, see Opper 2008: 218 fig. 209.

78 Autobiography: Cornell ed. 2013: Vol. 2: 1084–9; see further ch. 3. Phlegon: *HA Hadr.* 16.1. Theory: Bollansée 1994; cf. Birley 1997a: 299; 2005b: 230–1; Cornell ed. 2013: Vol. 3: 627–8: cautious; cf. Millar 1964: 37; 70. Tradition: Momigliano 1971: 93–5; cf. Pelling 2009: 41–7: a fixed form unlikely. Controversial: Harker 2008: 54. Note Brochard and Pinon 2014: 38: "Si la biographie est donc bien un genre antique, l'œuvre de Marguerite Yourcenar relève davantage de la tradition des mémorialistes de l'Ancien Régime"; this seems to me to underestimate the classical convention.

79 "If my calculations are exact, my mother died at about the age which I am today; my life has already been half again as long as that of my father, who died at forty." See *OR* 546–7; cf. *HZ* 215 (December 1952); *TGS* 295: allowing the possibility of authenticity. Alexander 1938: 170–2, known to Yourcenar (*OR* 549), inclined to believe the papyrus genuine. It helps to explain her decision to cast her novel, on whose final pages see esp. Poignault 1995: 577–9, in the form that she did.

80 Study: Goslar 2007; cf. Poignault 1995: 643–8. List: *HZ* 211–17. Care: Terneuil 2020.

81 Fittschen 2010: 234.

82 Vout 2003; 2010.

83 See Poignault 1995: 722–35, esp. 723 n.142.

84 Speller 2003: 242–3.

85 MacDonald and Pinto 1995: 194–5: my emphasis; cf. Opper 2008: 132; Calandra 2010: a gradually evolving self-conscious statement of personal power that in its final stage, through association with Antinous, included salvific cult.

86 "jasper as green as the depths of the sea, porphyry dense as flesh, basalt and somber obsidian. The crimson of the hangings was adorned with more and more intricate embroideries; the mosaics of the walls or pavements were never too golden, too white, or too dark." Eleanor Clark had earlier tried desperately to find Hadrian within the Villa's remains: "Who was this man? What on earth was he thinking about all that time? The questions become obsessive, the drama is so unlike any other; and most of all you wonder as you snoop and pry in the desolation how much, being both agent and victim on such a scale, he knew of what he represented" (E. Clark 2015 [1952]: 170). For Clark, the Villa was a direct expression of Hadrian's complex personality, with every aspect of its construction and decoration due to him alone. For Yourcenar's snippy reaction, note *HZ* 240 (March 1953): "elle essaie de titiller le lecteur avec ce qui est (pour elle) la débauche d'Hadrien" ("she tries to titillate the reader with what is [for her] Hadrian's debauchery").

87 Quotation: "fragments of reality." Statue: Gergel 1991.

88 Henderson 1968 [1923]: 57; André 1993: 596; Birley 1997a: 147 (cf. 2003: 436–7); Hannestad 1988: 197; Opper 2008: 100; Morwood 2013: 7.

89 Conjecture: see further ch. 8. As one more striking example of a definitive but in fact problematic (and proleptic) statement on Hadrian's mind, here at his accession, observe Roman 2008: 123–4: "Les préoccupations d'Hadrien étaient alors simples: se présenter comme l'héritier incontesté de Trajan, voire Auguste, pour être enfin lui-même, c'est-à-dire un homme ayant son propre programme politique, appuyé sur la maîtrise du temps et de l'espace, et cela pour l'éternité de Rome."

90 *Epig. Gr.* 728, with Bowie 2002: 183–4 (cf. *SEG* 52 [2002] no. 986). Verses: Yourcenar included four short items from Hadrian in her anthology of ancient Greek poetry (*CL* 402–4). Campaign: see ch. 5.

91 Birley 1997a: 128; 206.

92 Observe esp. Birley 1997a: 152, on Hadrian in North Africa in the year 123: "The identity of the proconsul, who *would have* received Hadrian at Carthage, is not known. It *might well have been* Atilius Bradua, who had been consul the same year as Hadrian, and had been governor of Britain under Trajan. Bradua *seems to have accompanied* Hadrian on his travels, to judge from his career inscription. It *might be* that he first joined the imperial party at this stage. But he *could have been* with Hadrian for the past two years, and have stayed at Carthage to take up his proconsulship" (my emphasis). The career inscription concerned is fragmentary, and Bradua's presence in Africa as governor and his

accompaniment of the travelling Hadrian depend on textual restorations (cf. Birley 2005a: 112–14 on *ILS* 8824a.). Despite the reasonable nature of all that is said and the expertise on display, no hard information results.

93 The historian's remit: Syme 1968: v (or, more ominously, "from fraud" [1983: 214]).

94 Syme 1958: 248; 249; 251; *RP* III 1443; IV 306. Note also: *RP* II 492: Hadrian in his early years was "menaced and insecure"; *RP* II 493: "The ruler was subject to moods and caprice" and had a "passionate addiction to polite letters"; *RP* III 1346: he had "a strong and violent propensity to omniscience"; *RP* III 1178: he was "conscious of instability in his own character"; *RP* IV 306: he had "catholic curiosities and taste for the exotic"; *RP* IV 315: he was "unresponsive to pomp and pedigree"; *RP* V 551: he "formed his character and tastes in deliberate opposition to his formidable predecessor." Cf. *MH* 332: "j'étais multiple par calcul."

95 *RP* VI 103. The study, "Hadrian the Intellectual," originated as a paper presented in the spring of 1964 to a conference held in Italica on the Roman emperors from Spain. For analysis, see Bradley 2012a.

96 *RP* VI 103.

97 Syme 1971b: written to justify his theories about the *Historia Augusta* against the criticisms of Momigliano (see n.14), and modelled on Gibbon's *Vindication of Some Passages in the Fifteenth and Sixteenth Chapters of the Decline and Fall of the Roman Empire* (1779).

98 Syme 1971b: 5; 26; 29; 33; 48; 59; 77; 79.

99 Syme 1971b: 6; 31; 48; 41; 67; 51; 77; 10; 89 (quotations; literary allusions also appear: see Bradley 2017a). Rank: elsewhere "a professor on the loose, a librarian seeking recreation, a civil servant repelled by pedestrian routine" (Syme 1983: 221).

100 *PV* 382: to Shusha Guppy; cf. *PV* 223; *HZ* III 463: 4 September 1963; *YO* 154; *L* 367: 8 October 1970: "«intellectuel»".

101 See esp. Kiebunski 2004: 150–1; Blanchet-Douspis 2008: 202 (cf. 197; 379): "Au travers des *Mémoires d'Hadrien*, Marguerite Yourcenar trace un tableau très complète et juste du règne de cet empereur du IIe siècle"; Vásquez de Parga 1995: 441: "Antinoüs est un être historique, les documents et l'art nous le montrent. Ses rapports amoureux avec Hadrien sont constatés dans les écrits de l'époque."

102 Quotations: Pocock 2003: 427; Birley 1997a: 19. Truly: cf. Lee 2009: 7; in which "the discipline of doubt" must be paramount (Brown 1988: 420, in reference to Momigliano).

3. Authenticity Filtered

1 Note Bate 2009: xviii: "the deadening march of chronological sequence that is biography's besetting vice" (cf. 2015: 19), with Levick 2017: 126: Roman troop movements.

2 14 June 1952: "such as the tradition presents him to us"; *HZ* 495: 22 September 1955.

3 Memory: see Maurois 1928: ch. V. Insight: perhaps influenced by Maurois 1928: 174: "Quand il s'agit d'un être mort, dont les os reposent dans quelque boîte de bois ou les cendres dans une urne, images et pensées ont disparu à tout jamais et les plus patientes recherches ne nous révéleront plus que poussière." See ch. 4.

4 Cf. Chabot 2015: 112.

5 Reminders: *MH* 296; 301; 369; 412. Quotations: "curls of smoke"; "the iridescent bubbles of a child's game." For "confessional autobiography" and introspection, see Watt 2001 [1957]: 75–6.

6 Memory palace: note the faint allusion at *MH* 289. Quintilian: cf. August. *Conf.* 10.8–25: aware in midlife of memory decline; see Lane Fox 2015: 39–40. Reputed: *HA Hadr.* 20.7; *Epit. de Caes.* 14.3.

7 In her essay on the *Historia Augusta*, Yourcenar distinguished authenticity from veracity – "Authenticity is one thing, veracity another" (the epigraph of this chapter) – terms that are almost but not quite synonymous (*SBI* 6). I take authenticity here to mean socioculturally realistic, as opposed to the positivist connotations of veracity. See ch. 8.

8 Wyss 1995.

9 *HA Hadr.* 1.1; 3.3; 3.5; 7.2; Cass. Dio 66.17.1 (cf. Cornell ed. 2013: Vol. 2: 1084–9). Cass. Dio 69.11.2 may suggest a *terminus post quem* of 130.

10 See Bardon 1968: 411–13 (known to Yourcenar in the edition of 1940); 1956: 211; Syme *RP* VI 398–9: from "the last biennium of his life"; Lewis 1993: 699–700; Birley 1997a: 356 n.38; Birley 2005b; Turcan 2008: 144; Opper 2008: 26: "probably in the form of a series of letters"; Westfall and Brenk 2011: 372–89.

11 Style: *TGS* 294: "half narrative, half meditative"; cf. *ER* 52–3. Voice: Poignault 2000. Remains: Bardon 1968: ch. XIV. Obtruded: the opening words, "Mon cher Marc," are, to me, an obvious, grating example. On the importance of opening sentences in novels and biographies, see Lodge 2011: ch. 1; Lee 2009: 124–6.

12 "Obviously, it was not a question here of imitating Caesar or Seneca, or even Marcus Aurelius, but of deriving from them a pattern, a rhythm, the equivalent of a piece of fabric which one subsequently drapes as one will over the nude model."

13 Furbank 2004; cf. A. Bennett 2015.

14 14 January 1963; cf. *HZ* III 463: 4 September 1963: Romantic solitude anachronistically inappropriate for Hadrian. See *TGS* 290–1: on comedy and the Latin novels.

15 "If I have chosen to write these *Memoirs of Hadrian* in the first person it is in order to dispense with any intermediary, in so far as possible, even were that intermediary myself. Surely Hadrian could speak more forcibly and more subtly of his life than could I."

16 Truth: Syme *RP* VI 398, with Suet. *Tib.* 61.1; cf. IV 297. Details: *RP* VI 399–400, with *HA Hadr.* 2.4; 5.5–6; 2.6; 2.10; cf. *RP* II 494; IV 25, with *HA Hadr.* 7.1; IV 301; V 568, with *HA Hadr.* 3.10. Mental state: *RP* VI 400. Reference: *RP* VI 398, with n.2. Breathtaking: not least because of a curious opening reference to the "many inventions" in "the *Mémoires d'Hadrien* composed by Mme Yourcenar." As Hadrian's words to Marcus quoted at the head of this section show, Syme's view of Hadrian's autobiography was not altogether different from that of Yourcenar.

17 Birley 2005b, with *HA Hadr.* 1.1; 3.5; 7.1–2. The first proposition overlooks the obvious point that family history is a staple of biography in any form and age. For other speculations, see Migliorati 2003: 360–4.

18 Fronto: cf. *HA Hadr.* 16.5. Effort: *HZ* 546: 24 May 1956. Close examination: *PV* 29 (from 1952). Compliments: *HZ* III 112: 28 August 1961.

19 Trans. Behr; see Behr 1968: 164–5; Israelowich 2012: 105; Swain 1996: ch. 8.

20 Dodds 1970 [1965]; cf. Whitmarsh 2004: 154–5: psychologically anachronistic and governed by a "Christianocentric teleology" (cf. Swain 1996: 105–9), despite Dodds 1970 [1965]: 5; Perkins 1995: 173–89, following Michel Foucault, *History of Sexuality Vols. 2 and 3* (New York 1978–86), for the historical inadequacy of which, however, see Cohen and Saller 1994; Bowersock 1969: ch. 5; cf. Gleason 1995: 3–8 (Favorinus).

21 Mattern 2013: ch. 6; cf. Sallares 1991: 221–93.

22 Sabina predeceased Hadrian, at not much more than fifty years of age, by less than a year, but the cause of her death is unknowable (Brennan 2018: 182–7); Yourcenar drew on the tradition that Hadrian poisoned her.

23 Lucius was adopted in late 136 and died on 1 January 138.

24 Plin. *Ep.* 1.12; 3.7; 6.4; 6.24; 7.1; 7.19; 7.21; 7.26; 7.30; 8.1; 8.10; 8.11; 8.16; 8.19; 10.3; 10.5; 10.8; 10.11.

25 See Holford-Strevens 1988: 224–6. Calvenus Taurus: see Dillon 1996: 237–47. For cultural visits to Athens by elite Romans, see Hutchinson 2013: 81–97.

26 Trans. Hilton; see Harrison 2000: 118: sophistic influence.

27 Friendship: Birley 1987: 69–88; Richlin 2006: an erotic bond; Griffin 2014 (= 2018: ch. 49); cf. Champlin 1980: 94–117; Freisenbruch 2007: Fronto's letters as pedagogical; Whitehorne 1977: Marcus not a hypochondriac.

28 Fronto 1. 32; 34; 38; 52; 54; 172; 180; 184; 186; 188; 192; 194; 196; 198; 202; 212; 218; 224; 226; 240; 242; 246; 248; 250; 252; 2.18; 30; 32; 42; 44; 84; 156; 174; 252. Gellius knew of Fronto's periodic podiatric problems (*NA* 2.26; 19.10).

29 Christian writer: Epiph. *De mens. et pond.* 14, with Baker 2012 on chronology; cf. Poignault 1995: 540: Hadrian has an abiding respect for his doctors. Mortality: see Parkin 1992: 92–111; Saller 1994: chs. 2, 3 (fundamental).

30 Conditions: see *OR* 547: Pliny, Fronto, Gellius, Aristides; Frick 302: Apuleius.

31 *HA Hadr.* 26.1–3; 10.4; Cass. Dio 69.9.3–4.

32 "But my greatest asset of all was perfect health: a forced march of twenty leagues was nothing; a night without sleep was no more than a chance to think in peace."

33 Aymard 1951: 483–502; Anderson 1985: chs. 3–6; Lane Fox 1990: the Greek tradition of hunting's erotic associations. Arrian: Stadter 1980: 52–9; see ch. 9.

34 Trans. Cohoon.

35 Polyb. 31.29.5–12.

36 Pliny and Tacitus: Aymard 1951: 159–62; Syme 2013: 132: the detail on Tacitus a surprise; Jones 1978: 120, 130: the hunting of Trajan and Hadrian a new aspect of imperial comportment reflecting Spanish influence; offset by comparison of Arrian's *Cynegeticus* with Xenophon's treatise (Stadter 1976, despite Jones 1978: 194 n.43). Scenes: Dunbabin 1978: ch. IV; Blanchard-Lemée, Ennaïffer, Slim, and Slim 1996: 170–87 (cf. Bradley 2012c: 251). Image: Stadter 1980: 51.

37 *HA Hadr.* 2.1–2; 20.13; 26.3, with Fündling 2006: 270–1; 1132–5: conservative on Roman practices; Cass. Dio 69.2.5; 69.7.3; 69.10.2; 69.10.3[3]. For Mysia see also Polemo, *Physiog.* 1.1.138–42; 148: in Arabic: Gleason 1995: 44–6, with Hadrian a "Spaniard"; Birley 1997a: 164–6.

38 Athenaeus: cf. *P. Oxy.* 1085. Tondi: originally made for a Hadrianic monument, with the emperor's image recut to show that of the later ruler: "On the first tondo, a group of hunters with a horse and a large dog moves forward from an arched gateway, evidently setting out for a day of sport; this is followed by three scenes of the chase, each paired with a scene of sacrifice, and a concluding tondo shows a sacrifice to Apollo at the return from the hunt. In each of the three pairs we see first the hunt of a wild animal – a bear, a boar, and a lion – and then, presumably after the successful kill, sacrifices to Silvanus, Diana, and Hercules respectively" (Boatwright 1987: 191–2, with illustrations 45–52). Medallions: Boatwright 1987: 198, with illustrations 53a and 53b. Inscriptions: *CIL* XII 1122 = Smallwood 1966: no. 520; cf. Cass. Dio 69.10.2; *IG* VII 1828 = *Epig. Gr.* 811. See in general Aymard 1951: 173–82, attributing Hadrian's enthusiasm to his Spanish heritage, a view with which Yourcenar would sympathize.

39 Quotation: Stadter 1980: 50–1; cf. Bowie 2002: 180–3. Samis: *AE* 2000: 380.

40 Folded: *MH* 343; 362; 386–7; 431–2; 512; 463. Hint: Cass. Dio 69.22.2, with *MH* 503, 515.

41   Archer, fils de Cypris, Hadrien te rend grâce.
      Sur les coteaux de l'Hélicon, près de la source
      De Narcisse, lançant son cheval sur la trace
      Des fauves de ces bois, il abattit une ourse.
      Il suspend sa dépouille au mur du sanctuaire.
      Amour, ô sage dieu! exauce sa prière,
      Et répands sur ses jours le charme et l'harmonie
      Que dispense d'en haut Aphrodite Ouranie.
    Adapted: see esp. Halley 2005: 485–502.

42 Cf. Bradley 2012c: 250; note similarly Ach. Tat. 2.34. That the plot against Hadrian involved Lusius Quietus cannot be confirmed. See Poignault 1995: 885–8 for the contamination of sources at *MH* 362 (*HA Hadr.* 7.1 is relevant), with reference to A. von Premerstein, *Das Attentat der Konsulare auf Hadrian im Jahre 118 n. Chr.* (*Klio Beiheft* 8 [1908]), cited by Yourcenar in the *Note* (*OR* 550) but now discredited; Bowersock 1969: 120–3; Birley 1997a: 87, 165.

43 Birley 1997a: 137; 145; see also 38; 181; 262. Arrian: cf. Stadter 1980: 50.

44 Deprez 2012: 133–7.

45 Ride: J.E. Howard 2018: 258–9. Opposition: J.E. Howard 2018: 277–9. Description: *SP* 842–3. Essays: *TGS* 331–3: *Bêtes à fourrure* (1976); 370–6: *Qui sait si l'âme des bêtes va en bas?* (1981).

46 24 October 1958. See J.E. Howard 2018: 248.

47 Correctly: *CL* 427. Alexander: Aymard 1951: 45–7; 416–19; 522–37; Lane Fox 1990: 142; Roman 2008: 84; cf. 188–92: monarchical associations.

48 See Cordonnier 2019: 118–26: hunting as a means of acquiring self-knowledge; and note E. Clark 2015 [1950]: a way to offset conflicts. See ch. 9.

49 Cicero: *Off.* 1.1–7; 1.15; 1.78; 2.1; 2.44; 3.1; 3.5–6; 3.33. Cato: Plut. *Cato Maior* 20.3–5. Augustus: Suet. *Aug.* 64.1; 64.3. Artisans: Bradley 1991b: ch. 5; Hawkins 2016: ch. 4. Horace: *Sat.* 1.6.71–8; Augustine: *Conf.* 2.3. Expected: symbolized by Aeneas's instruction to Ascanius to learn *virtus* (Virg. *Aen.* 12.435); see Bradley 2012c: 194–8; 2017b: 326.

50 Father died: see Hübner and Ratzan 2009: not unusual. Succession: Birley 1987: 33; 42–9; 294–6. (The adoption of Antoninus Pius belongs to 25 February 138.) *Tutoiement*: cf. Chabot 2015: 96–7: an affinity between Hadrian and his reader as well.

51 See Poignault 1988a: 94–6; 1995: 867–73; 2003: 76; 2014: 93: the letter as a lesson in philosophical rigour. Imperial box: cf. Suet. *Iul.* 45.1, with Millar 1977: 370–1. Miracles: cf. Suet. *Vesp.* 7.2; Tac. *Hist.* 4.81–2; Cass. Dio 65.81–2 (Vespasian). Quotation: "the essential is that the man invested with power should have proved thereafter that he deserved to wield it." For Marcus's continual presence as addressee, see also *MH* 288; 403; 497.

52 Cf. Poignault 2003: 76: "la vie d'Hadrien aidera à sa formation même si Hadrien est conscient de la distance qui les sépare." Arval priesthood: the detail is inaccurate; see Poignault 1995: 868–9.

53 See esp. Rutherford 1989; Brunt 2013: 360–93.

54 Cf. Rutherford 1989: 108: possibly critical of Hadrian.

55 Birley 1987: 28–52; 2012; to be supplemented with at least B.M. Rawson 2003.

56 System: see Bonner 1969 [1949]; 1977: chs. XIII-XXI; Morgan 1998: chs. 5–7; Cribiore 2001: 231–8; Gunderson 2003; Penella 2014: 107–27. Replicated:

Bradley 2019: 74–83. Habits: remarkably captured in the *Colloquia* of the *Hermeneumata Pseudodositheana* (Dickey 2012; 2015).

57 The dream is modelled on *HA Hadr.* 26.10; cf. Poignault 2003.

58 *CIL* XIV 3721; see Opper 2008: 34; 36 fig. 19; cf. Quint. *Inst.* 1.10.9–33; 1.10.34–49; 1.11.1–18. To judge from the *Note* and her *Notebook*, Yourcenar never came across Germana.

59 Cf. Plin. *Ep.* 5.12.

60 *Notebook*: in the list of historical facts modified or facts imagined (see ch. 4). Record: Zetzel 2018: 92–3; 131; 174; 318–19; cf. Poignault 1995: 521–2; 611. Disputes: *HA Verus* 2.5; Charisius 2.209; 219. Suetonius's attention to eminent imperial teachers is relevant: *Aug.* 89.1; *Tib.* 57; *Claud.* 41.1; *Ner.* 7.1; 52.

61 Sen. *Suas.* 1, 3, 6, 7; Xerxes and Themistocles have no set speeches in the *Suasoriae* but, as Antony and Octavian, are prominent throughout.

62 Lucian, *Rhet. didask.* 18; Lib. *Decl.* 9, 10; cf. Poignault 1995: 522. The major study of classical education when Yourcenar was writing *Mémoires* was Henri Irène Marrou's *Histoire de l'éducation dans l'Antiquité* (Paris 1948). Marrou found it difficult, however, to understand the degree of attention given in Hellenistic and Roman culture to the study of declamation, regarding its hackneyed themes as a symptom of decadence. Yourcenar does not cite the book in her *Note* and had no copy at Petite Plaisance. It seems to have had no influence.

63 Cf. Holford-Strevens 1988: 64–6.

64 Cf. Van der Starre 1995: 421–2: perhaps influenced by R.G. Collingwood's "reenactment of the past" in *The Idea of History* (1946).

65 Tutelage: Sarde 1995a: 27–109: Yourcenar's father a Pygmalion-like figure in her educational formation. Age: *YO* 30; cf. *PV* 134. Access: Waquet 2015. But note Savigneau 1993: 50–1: no formal schooling, but the secondary school examination independently taken in 1919. Lee 1999 [1996] provides a contrasting parallel: Virginia Woolf also educated by her father and subsequently resentful of no opportunity to attend public school or university.

66 Bernier 2004: nos. 3369–78.

67 Preface: Halley 2005: 496. Note Lebel 1979: 781: "Elle fait penser à l'admirable traducteur que fut Jean Racine. C'est tout dire."

68 *CNMH* 521; *Chronologie* XX.

69 Savigneau 1993: 175–85.

70 "one is working with a real world" (from 1968: of all her novels). Standard: cf. Massimilla 2016a; 2016b: the classical influences permeating *DR*.

71 Cf. Rutherford 1989: 119; Poignault 1995: 440–1.

72 16 December 1951.

73 Letters: *MH* 460–1: 5 March 1955 to Durry; 461–2: 5 March 1955 to Vermeule; 460 n.1: to Gross. Reply: 10 March 1955 to Maria Luisa Cisneros, preceded by *HZ* 459–60: 5 March.

74 *HZ* 267–70: 23 May 1953 (with editorial details on amended phrases).

75 "No one knows better than I that you never achieve more than an approximation, but I did what I could to remain faithful to the letter and the spirit of history, while trying to recover from behind texts that are always more or less frozen, the obscure and changing reality that is the reality of life itself."

76 Julien 2002: 163–73.

77 Travels: Savigneau 1993: 92–3; 100, with esp. *L* 114–15 for Greece; *PV* 35 for Asia Minor; *HZ* III 113 for Byzantium. For Yourcenar's Hellenism, see Grodent 1988 and ch. 4.

78 Backscheider 1999: ch. 2; Caine 2010: 71–2.

79 See *HA Hadr.* 12.5: a mining slave substituted for a local domestic.

80 Record: Gualandi 1963: I 24–57.

81 *Dig.* 29.5.1; 29.5.1.28. Consiliar practice: attested at *HA Hadr.* 18.1; *HA Hadr.* 18.11 generalizes the case.

82 See Poignault 1995: 825–7 (perhaps underestimating the character of Hadrian's legislation on slavery).

83 Cf. Sarde and Dezon-Jones 2019: 75–80: immigration and Yourcenar's emergent interests in new literary forms.

84 "raids carried out by Mauretanian merchants procured for the Romans the luxury goods that bronze- or ebony-skinned slaves were for them – their litter-bearers, majordomos, or gladiators."

85 A note added to the essay in 1974 for republication of *FP*, alluding inter alia to Martin Luther King Jr.'s assassination, was sombre regarding prospects for racial reconciliation in the United States. It has a currently uncanny prescience.

86 Definition: "the horrible condition which puts one man at the mercy of another." See Deprez 2012: 123: correspondence with *FP* 14: "Ce qu'on peut dire de plus amer au sujet de l'institution de l'esclavage, c'est qu'elle met légalement l'être humain à la merci de ce monstre d'insensibilité, de folie ou d'avarice, qu'est trop souvent un autre homme" ("The bitterest observation to be made of the institution is that it puts one human being legally at the mercy of another who is a monster all too often of insensitivity, madness, and greed"). See Blanchet-Douspis 2008: 104–14: the political background to which publication of *FP* belongs; cf. Blanchet-Douspis 2014: 40 for doubts of any notion of social equality. Human rights: Bradley 2010a.

87 "I'm not sure that Hadrian could have spoken like that. There wasn't yet the sort of problem that would have allowed him to think that way and in that regard I allowed myself certain liberties."

88 Fixation: epitomized by Horace's declaration (*Odes* 3.30.1): *non omnis moriar.*
   Commemoration: Carroll 2006; see further ch. 6.
89 Oppian: *TGS* 393–4. Feature: *HZ* 115: 6 January 1952.
90 *HZ* IV 327–9: 25 November 1965, with editorial citation of Origen, *C. Cels.*
   2.14; 2.33; 2.59; Gell. *NA* 16.17; *HA Hadr.* 25.1–4; *Sibylline Oracles* 8.52–8.
91 *HZ* II 37: 8 January 1957; cf. *CNMH* 536; *HZ* II 37; *PV* 182; *ER* 64; *L* 83; *HZ* II 44.
92 See *MH* 425: deeper understanding still with knowledge of the mysteries of the
   Cabiri.
93 Eleusinian mysteries: *HA Hadr.* 13.1; Cass. Dio 69.11.1; see Poignault 1995:
   921–3. Cybele: Turcan 1996: 195–247. Prudentius: cf. Firm. Mat. *Err. prof. rel.*
   27.8; see McLynn 1996; Cameron 2011a: 160: extreme; cf. Poignault 1995:
   481–4. Yourcenar gave a careful statement on the limits of knowledge of the
   Mithraic cult in an interview of 1971, but regarded it as salvationist (*PV* 105–6).

4. Authenticity Invented

1 Legal action: Savigneau 1993: 213–16; 284–7; 294–7. Aphorism: "We must
   always fight." Preface: *HZ* 9; cf. *HZ* II 24: Yourcenar's "persistante combativité"
   (editorial comment); Ughetto 2009: 245: "pugnacité"; Brémond 2012: 211–12:
   her desire to exercise complete control over her work.
2 Characters: *HZ* 365 (August 1954): "on se croirait chez Molière" ("you would
   think yourself in the world of Molière"); *HZ* 481–2 (August 1955): "à la Basile … et
   à la Trissotin"; "le style Basile-Trissotin." Review: Picard 1954.
3 Quotations: Plon 34; 134. Robert Kemp, an early reviewer of *Mémoires*, had
   written, "Que les historiens y opposent des chicanes, c'est possible." Picard
   obliged, presumably without having seen Kemp's following remark: "Tout
   homme pensant la remerciera" (*Réception critique*: 54). L. Mummius: the proof
   depends on linking a statement in Livy, *Per.* 53 with Mommsen's speculatively
   restored *CIL* II 1119 (Italica). D. Cossutius: see Vitr. *De arch.* 7. pref. 15, with E.
   Rawson 1991: 190–3; Boatwright 2000: 152.
4 Letters: *HZ* 365–6: 10 August 1954 to the princess Hélène Schakhovskoy and
   Anne Quellenec; *HZ* 368–70: 14 August 1954 to Alexis Curvers; *HZ* 386–7: 11
   September 1954 to Jean Mirat. The first two were written from Munich, the third
   apparently from Paris (cf. J.E. Howard 2018: 213; Goslar 1996: 33–4: Yourcenar
   in Munich from 6 July to 5 September). For the affair, see Savigneau 1993:
   220–1; Poignault 2007a: 146–7; cf. Deprez 2009: 39–42: Yourcenar's responses to
   academic criticisms in general ("En fait, il n'y avait pas débat mais combat, une
   guerre de tranchée où chaque position est défendue pied à pied" [39]).
5 modbm_ms_fr_372_2_268–269. Yourcenar mistakenly gave the title of Picard's
   review, "L'Empereur Hadrien vous parle," as "Hadrien vous écrit" in her main
   draft.

6 Cf. Goslar 1998: 187.

7 "the mosaics of the walls or pavements were never too golden" (cited in ch. 1); "a single good Greek statue"; "From a reputable sculptor I purchased an entire lot of Venuses, Dianas, and Hermes for Italica, my native city, which I had in mind to modernize and adorn."

8 Article: cited as *Regard sur les Hespérides, Cahiers du Sud*, 2e Tr. 1953 (the correct date is 1952). It became *L'Andalousie ou les Hespérides* (*TGS* 379–90, dated 1952). Relevant authority: Antonio Garcia y Bellido, *Esculturas romanas* (1949), as recommended by Picard. Traces of the affair appear in modifications made to the *Note* (*OR* 553 [statues], 554 [mosaics]).

9 Cf. Deprez 2009: 41: the letter as the possible source of the entry in the *Carnets*.

10 See Savigneau 1993: 241–3: lecturing in Europe in the autumn; return to the United States in November.

11 Paul Minear: Savigneau 1993: 145; *HZ* II 202 n.7; J.E. Howard 2018: passim.

12 "I care about the question of historical truth too much to allow the matter to go without reply for ever and I feel morally obligated to do something to correct your implicit assault if you do not undertake to do so yourself." I take this to mean an intention to write a rejoinder for the *Anglican Theological Review*.

13 Drafts: cf. Blanckeman 2014b: 265–7 (overlooking their status). Quotation: Grant 1956: 298. I doubt that Grant knew the nature of Yourcenar's relationship with Frick.

14 Enquiries: Grant 1956: 293, 294.

15 Edenic: not Saturnian.

16 Letters: 25 March 1956; 14 January 1957. Essay: Mozzillo 1955.

17 *Dig.* 47.14.1. pr.; *Coll.* 11.7. 1–3; 5.

18 "I have tackled subjects that impinge on the realm of scholarship, or that indeed completely involve it, a realm that most of our contemporaries scarcely ever enter except for scholars; yet these scholars, such as they are, are not always in a position to judge a work which belongs above all to the realm of creative literature, and takes scholarship only as a starting point" (19 June 1963).

19 "the poetic interpretation of history and history plain and simple."

20 Characters: *OR* 303 (and often), 331; 336; 313; 322; 369; 423; 488; 437; 496 (originally Benedicta and Theodotus: M.Aur. *Med.* 1.17.6).

21 *OR* 307–8; 404; 325; 308; 425. So also with personal details on Acilius Attianus, the Alexandrian origin of the doctor Iollas, the duties of Onesimus and Arete, the betrayal of the evil Servianus by his secretary Crescens, the merchant Opromoas's journey with Hadrian to the Euphrates.

22 *OR* 544–55; 552. Gymnosophist: the *Notebook* shows Lucian's *Peregrinus* as the source. Mistresses: see *HA Hadr.* 11.7. Lucius: see *HA Quad. Tyr.* 8.8, which Yourcenar knew to be problematical, with details from *HA Ael.* Canopus: see ch. 6. Accident: *P. Oxy.* 475; cf. Poignault 1995: 484–5.

23 Impressions: cf. Lee 2021: 694: Tom Stoppard's paradox of "a relative instability of truth in history as opposed to the unchallengeable truth of fiction."

24 More numerous: see for proof Blanckeman 2014b: 266; cf. Brochard and Pinon 2014: 59: the *Note* permits the reader to distinguish the novel's fabricated content easily; I disagree.

25 The *Note*'s references to which sources underlie which episodes are of real importance. Its final form in the Pléiade is almost twice as long as that of the Plon edition of 1951: some 6,200 words to 3,200, due largely to additional bibliography and discussion of technical matters.

26 "Historical facts modified or facts imagined (i.e., without a direct source)." Fifteen pages in total, some of which change "source" to "base."

27 "The episode of Mithraic initiation is invented; that cult was already in vogue in the army at the time, and it is possible, but not proved, that Hadrian desired to be initiated into it while he was still a young officer." "The whole episode of Hadrian's initiation into the cult of Mithras during the Dacian wars is without historical foundation; the supposition relies only on the fact that this cult had spread rapidly in military circles, without all the same having the importance it was to have in the third century. It is not fanciful to suppose that Hadrian at age twenty allowed himself to take the bait of this foreign cult, and during a campaign." "'[C]ontamination' between the Mithraic cult and that of the Magna Mater (sacrifice and baptism), more than debatable, but on the edge of the possible."

28 "At this time when salvationist cults were contaminating one another." This was added to the original edition by 1958.

29 These items duly appear in the *Note*: *OR* 547–8.

30 Other sections of the *Notebook*, listing the various appearances of the novel's characters in the text, clearly identify the fictional characters, but with remarks that they are consistent with historical circumstances.

31 See Plett 2012: 7–14, with esp. Quint. *Inst.* 6.2.31–2; 8.6.67–70; 10.1.16; cf. *Rhet. Her.* 4.54.68.

32 "Do, from within, the same work of reconstruction which the nineteenth-century archaeologists have done from without"; "it was a matter of doing from within what the archaeologists before me had done from without" (cf. *HZ* 27, quoted in ch. 1.) I take "les archéologues" to mean not only authors of archaeological reports, but seemingly objective academics in general; cf. Brochard and Pinon 2014: 91 (more broadly still): "rebâtir un lieu, un monde, qu'elle (sc. Yourcenar) habite d'ailleurs par son écriture même."

33 Crick 2019 [1980]: xxxi; cf. Caine 2010: 41–2; W.V. Harris 2010: 9; Gellhorn 2018 [1959]: 83: "People may correctly remember the events of twenty years ago (a remarkable feat), but who remembers his fears, his disgusts, his tone of voice? It is like trying to bring back the weather of that time."

34 Momigliano 1985: 88; cf. Crick 2019 [1980]: xxxi: "We can only know an actual person by observing their [*sic*] behaviour in a variety of different situations and through different perspectives." On Momigliano and biography, see Bowersock 1991; Murray 1991.

35 "But no life can be judged from the outside."

36 "absorption in that *sympathetic magic* which operates when one transports oneself, in thought, into another's body and soul."

37 Cf. Benoit 1994: 65.

38 From 1968; cf. Halley 2005: 499: an unpublished letter from 1979 expressing interest in the point at which the same problems of today are confronted in the past when or if presenting differently.

39 From 1971; cf. *PV* 405: suicide as a noble art to classical Greeks.

40 History: from 1965. Fundamentals: from 1976; cf. *CNMH* 528; *YO* 93: the "durable" in human nature could be elevated to the "éternel"; *PV* 291 (from 1981): "Je crois à un éternel fonds de malveillance!" ("I believe in an eternal supply of ill will!").

41 "Time itself has nothing to do with the matter. It is always surprising to me that my contemporaries, masters as they consider themselves to be over space, apparently remain unaware that one can contract the distance between centuries at will"; cf. *PV* 220, 359.

42 Perspective: cf. *PV* 257. Quotation: Wilson Knight 2002 [1930]: 74.

43 School: King 2020. Benedict: 1989 [1934]: 46–7; 1946: 166–8; 199–201; 204–5; 289.

44 Concern: Benedict 1989 [1934]: e.g. 61; 75; 83; 86; 103; 106–8; 120; 151; 153; 161; 168; 189; 193; 215; 220; 233; 241; 250; 257; 278; 1946: 166–8 (suicide and Japanese culture). Instincts: note *SP* 717: doubts on the maternal instinct from observation of infant care practices among the socially advantaged. Summary: King 2020: 239: Ella Cara Deloria. Contrast the implications for contemporary ancient history represented by a statement attributed to H.M. Last, "the most commanding figure in his generation among Roman historians" in the United Kingdom (Brunt 2012: 435): "an acquaintance with the habits of savages is not an education" (Brown 1988: 431).

45 Memoir: "Traversée sur le Bathory" (unpublished: see Peyroux 2019); cf. *Chronologie* XXI; *YO* 129.

46 J.E. Howard 2018: 112. Malinowski had lectured at the college once before, initiating a friendship with Frick as his wife Valetta had earlier befriended Yourcenar. The 1941 lecture, given on 25 November and arranged by Frick, was entitled, "The Democratic Principle in Human Evolution." Frick subsequently wrote to Valetta: "What struck both Marguerite and me was that he could address an audience of dubious level of comprehension with just the right degree of authority, not once stooping to the more obvious and time-consuming methods of approach" (M. Young 2011: 19).

47 Malinowski had died in 1942.

48 Petite Plaisance: Bernier 2004: nos. 5141, 5153. Quotation: Malinowski 1944: 75.

49 Gibbon: *Decline and Fall* I 221 (quotation); III 75 (Julian); cf. IV 321: Gothic kings and bishops; see Womersley 1988; cf. Lee 2021: 713: a reflective modern playwright on competing moral absolutes: goodness, altruism, empathy, generosity; injustice, cruelty, self-interest, conflict; already in antiquity Augustine described emotions as the essence of the human condition (*Conf.* 9.12).

50 Furbank 2004: 104.

51 MacMullen 2003: chs. 1 and 3; cf. W.V. Harris 2010: confident on "normal" human behaviour. I assume that Yourcenar would endorse the definition of emotions as "innate responses acquired as genetically favored forms of adaptation" rather than "measurable elements of stimulus and response" dependent on "education and socialization" (Kaster 2005: 8–9, in a lexical study of Latin terms that underestimates the antecedent absolutes from which variations are said to be visible).

52 Cf. Chabot 2015.

53 Hopkins 1999: 2; 156; cf. 1983: 203–5.

54 G.M. Young 1948: 112; 1.

55 Hopkins 1999: 2. Dilthey: see Harrington 2001; Caine 2010: 96, with Rickman ed. 1976; cf. Basch 1983; Adler 2014: 48.

56 "la sympathie, ou l'empathie, capable de nous faire pénétrer à l'intérieur de ces milieux ou de ces êtres"; cf. Vago 2019: 390–1; W.V. Harris 2010: empathy in a strict sense impossible. Note also *PV* 36: the distinctive thought of a particular epoch and the eternity of human sentiments (from 1954).

57 Caine 2010: 114: historians' "use of imagination is contained within the documents and sources available and … depends on their detailed knowledge of the period and place under consideration" (rightly); contra Furbank 2004: 97: historians cannot combine the imaginative and the empirical. For what might be read as an unwitting de facto parody of *Mémoires*, see Hopkins 2018 [2005].

58 "the height of wisdom."

59 4 April 1959.

60 I draw here on an entry in the *Notebook's Journal* dated 26 December 1951 (but presumably 1950?: cf. *CNMH* 537). Quotation: "I tried to go as far as the last sip of water, the last feeling of pain, the last glance. The emperor now had only to die"; cf. *CNMH* 537, substituting "la dernière image" for "le dernier regard." The *Notebook's* handwritten pages are difficult to read and inaccurate in places. I give only what I think is the sense of the record, influenced not least by the much later phrase, "Cette capacité de souffrir d'autrui" (*SP* 857: "This capacity to suffer for others").

61 Savigneau 1990: 392: "On ne va pas loin dans la connaissance intérieure d'un personnage sans sympathie, au sens propre du mot, et il n'y a pas de sympathie sans exercice de l'imagination."

62 Term: Lejeune: 1986: 332–3. Theory: Ness 1994. The case depends in part on changes in Yourcenar's handwriting in the manuscript of *Mémoires* contained in the Houghton Library and in the *Notebook*'s *Journal*, from reasonably legible to more chaotic, evidence allegedly of Yourcenar's entry into delirium. Yet even at its best, Yourcenar's handwriting is idiosyncratic, and fatigue or haste could easily account for the variations concerned. Homosexuality: the *Notebook* contains two typewritten pages of notes from the so-called Kinsey report of 1948 (A.C. Kinsey, W.B. Pomeroy, C.E. Martin, *Sexual Behavior in the Human Male* [Philadelphia & London 1948]), and a page evaluating eleven male characters in *Mémoires*, Trajan, Hadrian, and Antinous included, according to Kinsey's sexual criteria. The report's conclusion that homosexuality "is an experience or capacity that is basic to the human animal" was evidently meaningful to Yourcenar as a partner in a same-sex relationship who had already written creatively on the subject elsewhere. But her interest in Kinsey can be regarded equally as an aspect of her preparations for writing *Mémoires*. The second page of her notes ends with a reference to the pseudonymous Hans Licht's *Sexual Life in Ancient Greece* (London 1956 [1932]), which Ness (1994: 115) believes the *Notebook* cites as a "source majeure" for *Mémoires*. I am unconvinced; the page gives the book's title only, the book offers nothing on Hadrian, and it is not listed as a source in the *Note*.

63 "J'ai goûté pour la première fois avec *Anna, soror ...* le suprême privilège du romancier, celui de se perdre tout entier dans ses personnages, ou de se laisser posséder par eux" ("With 'Anna soror ... ' I tasted for the first time the ultimate privilege of the novelist, that of losing himself completely in his characters, or of letting himself be possessed by them"); see also *CNON* 862; and cf. MacMullen 2003: 132–3: Flaubert, Dickens, and Tolstoy all reduced to tears as they wrote.

64 Intuitive: Brochard and Pinon 2014: 184; cf. *YO* 241: sympathy as a means to make contact with reality. I emphasize that much of the *Notebook* contains patiently methodical material, including the pages that form the basis of the *Carnets*. Yourcenar wrote for instance in one entry of the influence while writing *Mémoires* of the recently published *Memoirs* of Winston Churchill.

65 MacMullen 2003: 80.

66 See in contrast Michael Holroyd's major biography of Strachey himself (Holroyd 2005 [1995]), which conveniently illustrates what some historians consider the genre's limitations. An encyclopaedic cradle-to-grave narrative, it illustrates brilliantly the subject's eccentricities – his paranoia, hypochondria, unconventionality – and the privileged style of life people of his social rank enjoyed in Britain at the turn of the twentieth century, especially in all their *bizarrerie* the members of the Bloomsbury circle to which Strachey belonged. It does relatively little, however, to show how the major events of the age shaped Strachey. The lower classes he despised are altogether invisible: "For

a few moments I realized what it was like to *be* one of the lower classes – the appalling indignity of it!" he wrote when medically examined for military service (349); and while his activities as pacifist and conscientious objector during World War I are described (cf. Lee 1999 [1996]: 341–2), little is conveyed of the cataclysm that the war itself represented. Yet the book is another reminder that there is nothing like the extant correspondence Strachey had with family members, friends, and lovers from which to reconstruct the life of a Roman emperor.

67 "Historians propose to us systems too perfect for explaining the past, with sequence of cause and effect much too exact and clear to have been ever entirely true; they rearrange what is dead, unresisting material, and I know that even Plutarch will never recapture Alexander"; cf. *AN* 960: "L'histoire s'écrit toujours à partir du présent" ("History is always written from the starting point of today").

68 Lecture: subsequently published by the Centre National de Documentation Pédagogique; an amended text became available in 2015 with a second version containing changes Yourcenar made to the original some twenty years after 1954 when anticipating republication; see Poignault 2015; in the event it was not republished.

69 Memory and history: cf. *HZ* 138: 7 March 1952 to Christian Murciaux; *PV* 300–1 (from 1981). Yourcenar did not deal with the Greek invention of history, but certain points of convergence can be sensed with Finley 1975: 11–33 (esp. 27–8). For history as memory in Roman thought, see Gowing 2005: 7–15.

70 A new dimension of understanding was opened: to descend the subterranean staircases of Mycenae was to plunge into the well of centuries past (*PE* 531–2, a moving passage).

71 "We are in a domain there where for good reasons we will never know the truth because too many people have an interest in concealing it"; cf. *EH* 159.

72 Cf. *PV* 93–4 (from 1971): Hadrian's was not a Christian world; she did not consider "the Bardon factor."

73 "a world in which man enjoys the benefits of a long culture, has a past behind him and believes he has a future, believes in the possibility of reforming certain things, of preserving others, is able to travel from country to country, can create for himself a global concept of humanity."

74 "the eternal fluctuation of human affairs."

75 Cf. *YO* 269: Febvre on cultural change in French history; Poignault 2015: 142: her method dependent in part on the recovery of *mentalité*.

76 "You end up putting yourself in the place of the person evoked. You find yourself in a particular situation, that of this particular individual, at this particular time, in this particular place. This roundabout course is the best way to capture both the human and the universal."

77 See ch. 5.

78 Syme 1956: v.

79 Cf. *QE* 1350: the outcome of an aesthetic sensibility traceable to childhood visits to the Louvre.

80 "There is the bas-relief where the Carian Antonianos has transposed to a divine and melancholy shade the vintager clothed in a tunic of raw silk, his friendly dog nuzzling against his bare leg. And that almost intolerable mask, the work of a sculptor of Cyrene, where pleasure and pain meet on the same face, and seem to break against each other like two waves on the same rock."

81 *HZ* II 238: 17 April 1958.

82 "the essence of reality"; cf. *PV* 313.

83 5 February 1970; 29 March 1974: "Toute réalité décrite en termes non conventionnels est poésie."

84 See also *ER* 66; cf. (again) Eagleton 2005: 12: "By the mid-nineteenth century, the word 'poetry' has become more or less synonymous with the interior, the personal, the spiritual or psychological."

85 See Savigneau 1993: 106–9; Halley 2005: 472–85. A second edition appeared in 1978 with minimal, mostly bibliographical, changes.

86 Dimaras: quoted in Savigneau 1993: 108; cf. 364 on Dimaras's verdict on the wilfulness of her versions: "It's better this way." Co-author: Halley 2005: 484–5. E.M. Forster, an early promoter of Cavafy, was unenthusiastic about Yourcenar's translations and lukewarm towards the critical introduction; "But she says many good things … One of them is her discovery that Cavafy is, and always potentially was, an *old* poet, another her suggestion that his own erotic life may never have been continuous or strong" (Letter of 25 July 1958 to George Savidis: Jeffreys 2009: 119–20 [no. 86]).

87 See Auden 1989: 333–44: indebted to her.

88 Mackridge 2009: xxv.

89 Categories: Robinson 1988: 1: possibly attributable to Cavafy himself. Memory: cf. Beaton 1983.

90 Cavafy lived for the most part in Alexandria and visits to the homeland were no more than sporadic (Liddell 1974). For appreciation of his achievement, see esp. Bowersock 2009: chs. 12–14 ("undoubtedly one of the most historically minded poets of modern times" [162]); cf. on technique Keeley 1976: 95: "he slants, or extends, or re-creates selective aspects of his historical sources so as to permit his own interpretation of the material"; Forster 1972 [1951]: 236: "The warmth of the past enthralls him even more than its blunders, and he can give a sense of human flesh and blood continuing through centuries that are supposed to be unsatisfactory."

91 Period: *AS* 938. Poetic elements: Fort 2014: animal imagery in relation to Antinous; Julien 2014a: 239: lyrical description; cf. Grodent 1988; Weitzman 1998; Fréris 2000; Halley 2005: 470–85.

92 Despised: cf. Yourcenar's "étudiant orageux" (*SP* 820). Procession: "A Great Procession of Priests and Laymen." Caesar: "Ides of March." Actium: "The Year 31 B.C. in Alexandria." (Titles and quotations below from Mendelsohn 2012.) Limits: Beaton 1983. Many characters apparently historical are inventions.

93 "The Steps" begins: "On an ebony bed that is adorned / with eagles made of coral, Nero sleeps / deeply – heedless, calm, and happy; / flush in the prime of the flesh, / and in the beautiful vigor of youth." "Nero's Deadline" gives this self-contented reflection on the recent tour of Greece: "Now to Rome he'll be returning a little wearied, / but exquisitely wearied by this trip / which had been endless days of diversion – / in the theatres, in the gardens, the gymnasia ... / Evenings of the cities of Achaea ... / Ah, the pleasure of naked bodies above all." Both poems take up portents at Suet. *Ner.* 46.2; 40. The context of the first is clear, but not that of the second. Cavafy reasonably associates it with Nero's tour of Greece in the late stage of his reign. His opinion of Suetonius, "not of great value," appears in a letter quoted by Liddell 1974: 172.

94 Aristotelian: Arist. *Poet.* 9, with Mackridge 2009: xxv. Her mind: Fréris 2000: 65–6.

95 Not simple "poetic licence," but a controlled imagination, inventive as Aristotle allowed; see Else 1957: 301–2, 305; Ste Croix 1975; Halliwell 1987: 105–10; cf. Wilson 2015: 118 on the "absolute centrality of the imagination as a key to perception" (relevant to the literary biographer's recovery of personality).

96 Woolf 1994 [1927]; 2011 [1939]. Quotations: Woolf 1994 [1927: 473].

97 Strachey's biographies: Bernier 2004: nos. 6616, 6641. Woolf: Yourcenar met with her briefly on 23 February 1937, afterwards writing a memoir entitled *Une femme étincelante et timide* (*EM* 490–6); cf. *L* 464: 25 July 1975: "écrivain que j'admire, certes, mais qui au fond ne m'est pas très cher" ("a writer I admire, to be sure, but of whom I am not especially fond"). For Woolf's sanctimonious record of the meeting, see *The Diary of Virginia Woolf: Volume 5 (1936–41)* (London 1985): 61: "a woman I suppose with a past; amorous; intellectual"; "lives half the year in Athens"; "red lipped, strenuous; a working Fchwoman"; "matter of fact." Yourcenar's recollections are embedded in *PE* 490–8; see Cliche 2000: 323–5.

98 Maurois 1928, with quotation (85–6) from Forster 1927: 45 (cf. 173: axiomatic that "human nature is unchangeable" [173]); see Lemaitre 1968: 79–114; Jefferson 2007: 221–9; Hammett 2011: 1–13: the competing interests of realism and imagination that affect any historical novel. The superiority of knowledge Forster claimed for the novelist is inherently controversial given the element of subjectivity it involves (cf. Kermode 2009: 3–27), and the results of a historian's deduction of character from action are not necessarily as objective as Forster asserted.

99 Substance: cf. *SP* 745: "personnages imaginaires ou réels que j'alimente de ma substance pour tenter de les faire vivre ou revivre" ("characters, imaginary or real, that I nourish with my own substance to try to make them live, or live once again").

100 Yourcenar clearly knew *Aspects* (Bernier 2004: no. 6241) and thought highly
of his biographies (*YO* 64). A connection was made in 1938 through the
expatriate writer and critic Charles du Bos (*L* 59), then an associate professor
in the Department of English at the University of Notre Dame, a situation
Yourcenar reasonably judged a "dépaysement absolu" (*L* 52); he died in 1939.
See Savigneau 1993: 92, 119–22 on their correspondence. Maurois was to write
a preface to Yourcenar's translation of Henry James's *What Maisie Knew* (*L*
213 n.6).

101 "The historian-poet and novelist that I have tried to become"; cf. *YO* 246 n.1;
ER 55.

102 The arrangement of the *Note* in the English translation differs considerably
from the French. This passage (Frick 312) precedes the list of names and events
discussed earlier.

103 *L* 292: 22 August 1968 to Lidia Storoni Mazzolani; *PV* 111 (from 1971); 196–7
(from 1977): a tragic trajectory; 223 (from 1977–8); 240–1 (from 1977–8); *YO*
100–1: the pyramidal shape of the novel; cf. *ER* 102–111 and see ch. 8.

104 Cf. Backscheider 1999: xviii; Kohut 2003.

5. The Accession

1 Coins: *BMC Emp*. III cxxxv; 237 nos. 5–8 with plates 46.3, 46.4 (cf. Smallwood
1966: no. 110 (b)). There may have been a similar silver issue at Antioch: *BMC
Emp*. III 372 no. 1021 with plate 68.1. Other coins from 117 contained images of
Trajan handing a globe to Hadrian, the theme of a peaceful transference of power
equally evident: *BMC Emp*. III cxxv–cxxvi; 236–237 nos. 1–4. Practice: Lindsay
2009: ch. 16. Source tradition: Cass. Dio 69.1.1–4; *HA Hadr*. 4.6–10 (cf. Fündling
2006: 270–1; 1132–5: possible scenarios); Eutr. 8.6.1; Aur. Vict. *Caes*. 13.11; 13.13.

2 Section: on disposition, see Castellani 2011: 218. Imperfectly known: see already
Gibbon *Decline and Fall* I 90. Historians: Syme *RP* III 1437: "When Trajan died …
he was escaping in order to celebrate a Parthian triumph. For his successor
the first task was to repair the damage and move towards a lasting settlement
beyond the Euphrates … Hadrian also had to cover up a disaster, himself
thereby open to incrimination and disrepute because he surrendered what
Trajan had won for the Empire … Hence a double and equivocal role"; cf. Birley
1997a: ch. 8.

3 Double remove: cf. Eagleton 2005: 17–18: interlocked time. Strategy: cf.
Poignault 1988a: 19–21; 30–1; Houssais 2014: 138: "Paradoxalement, c'est donc
la perspective d'écriture la plus éloignée de l'Histoire qui paraît le plus juste
historiquement."

4 Cassius Dio: see Migliorati 2003: 127–200: the impact of documentary evidence.
Arrian: see Bosworth 1983; 1988: 20: his evidence unlikely to reflect Arrian's

participation in the war; Stadter 1980: 135–44: supporting participation. *HA Hadr.* 4.1–5.4 refers to the adoption but has few details on the war (cf. Fündling 2006: 358–60). Yourcenar knew the basic sources, but obviously not inscriptions discovered since 1951 that have led to refinements of logistical detail. For Hadrian's rebuilding of cities punished by Lusius Quietus (*MH* 352), see Fuks 1961; Schürer 1973: 529–34; Smallwood 1976: 396–9. For the supposition that Trajan's eastern ambitions were long held, see Mitchell 1993: I 252: two years of preparations necessary for the campaign. Syme attributed the expedition's collapse to personal failings, "Arrogance or a sequence of miscalculations," believing Trajan to have retreated in a state of "frustration and dejection" (*RP* III 1437; 1392); he had left Rome motivated by *dignitas imperii* (Plin. *Pan.* 17.4), "in majesty, and in anger" (Syme 1958: 235); cf. Hannestad 1988: 184: Hadrian's accession a coup d'état.

5 Experts: principal discussions: Longden 1931; 1954 [1936]; Lepper 1948; Lightfoot 1990; Millar 1993: 99–105; Birley 1997a: ch. 7; J. Bennett 1997: ch. 13 (a superior contribution treating the war as more than a chronological puzzle, but assuming a "senatorial tradition" to underlie the extant sources); Beckmann 2007; Horbury 2014: 164–6; Mitford 2018: 60–8. Attested: Cass. Dio 68.24.1–6. Adiabene: Lightfoot 1990: 120; Millar 1993: 101; J. Bennett 1997: 201. Ctesiphon: Longden 1931: 14; Lightfoot 1990: 120. Assyria: Lightfoot 1990: 121–5 (discussing Eutr. 8.6.2 and Festus, *Brev.* 14, 20); Potter 1991: 282–3. From numismatic arguments Beckmann 2007 maintains that Trajan fell ill in the winter of 114/115, earlier than usually assumed. For Yourcenar's de facto short chronology, implicitly beginning in the autumn of 114, cf. Longden 1931: 2; Lepper 1948: 24; 114–15. Roman 2008: 53–4, 88–9 underestimates the issues involved. Note esp. Campbell 1993: 234–6: Trajan's diplomatic crudity and the expedition's absurdity.

6 Earthquake: January: Longden 1931: 7; Birley 1997a: 71 (cf. Migliorati 2003: 153: January–February); December: Lepper 1948: 95–6; Lightfoot 1990: 120 (implicitly); Millar 1993: 101.

7 Malalas: Sherk 1988: no. 130. The allusion at Juv. 6.411 has no technical value. Malalas's date is sometimes said to be confirmed by an entry in the *Fasti Ostienses* for the year 115: [*Id. Dec. terrae m*]*otus fuit* (Vidman 1982: 48, 110–11). But the textual restoration is apparently based on Malalas, and any postulate of vindication therefore dubious (cf. Barnes 1989: 152 on Lepper 1948: 54–7).

8 Cf. Paribeni 1927: 284.

9 Rebuilding: Mitchell 2013: 232; Traiana 2017–18: 425; 427. Analysis: Treadgold 2007. Apparent: Galimberti, Rizzi 2020: 212–14.

10 Statement: Malalas 11.10; cf. 11.2, despite 11.5. Ignatius: Euseb. *Hist. eccl.* 3.36, with Frend 1984: 21, 129; Treadgold 2007: 721; cf. Poignault 1995: 831 n.33.

11 Illusory: for representative statements raising unanswerable questions, see M.T. Griffin 2000: 127; Claridge 2013: 5.

12 Glory: Cass. Dio 68.17.1; cf. Fronto 2.212: *gloria*; but there is a hint also (2.206) of a goal of strategic expansionism. Alexander: Cass. Dio 68.29.1; 68.30.1; cf. Paribeni 1927: 281; Syme 1958: 770: sceptical; Migliorati 2003: 127–31; 172–5: emulation of Alexander as Trajanic propaganda.

13 *BMC Emp*. III lxxxi–lxxxvi with 102–6 nos. 511–24, 108–24 nos. 532–646; civ–cvi with 215–25 nos. 1014–55; cf. Smallwood 1966: nos. 47, 48, 49, 50, 51; Sherk 1988: nos. 135A, B, C.

14 Arval Brethren: Smallwood 1966: no. 4. Laurelled despatches: Smallwood 1966: no. 23; Sherk 1988: no. 133.

15 Speller 2003: 23.

16 Anticipation: see Plin. *Pan*. 17.1–2. Attempt: Mitford 2018: 61.

17 Durry 1932 (paragraph: 323); as often the citation is slightly inaccurate.

18 "a whole series of new titles conferred upon him by the Senate"; "This time the Senate voted the emperor the right to celebrate not one triumph but a succession of triumphs which would last as long as he lived."

19 Paribeni 1927: chs. 21, 22, where again the Trajanic coin legends could not be missed; cf. Debevoise 1938 (Bernier 2004: no. 3113): ch. X. Whether Yourcenar knew the *Essai sur la guerre parthique de Trajan* (Paris 1937) of her sometime correspondent Julien Guey is unclear; it is uncited and no copy is listed in her library. Lepper 1948 is a surprising omission: unless unknown or inaccessible, the reason may be that she found its deadening source criticism of no avail for recovering the drama her narrative required. Its basic proposition, that an original account of the war can be detected that was both accurate and above reproach, with the "desire for glory" ascribed to Trajan by Cassius Dio copied from the *Parthica* of Arrian, who transmitted a charge invented by Hadrian against Trajan as an "official version" to justify his abandonment of Trajan's eastern conquests (191–204), is entirely fanciful, the common assumption that Dio drew on Arrian notwithstanding (Stadter 1980: 140; Migliorati 2003: 127; 134); see esp. Momigliano 1949.

20 Longden 1954 [1936]: 246: "With this extension of the Roman authority … the whole of the Mesopotamian trade route to the Far East, which had perhaps been closed to Rome for some years, fell into her hands. To secure it may have been a powerful incentive towards the annexation of Mesopotamia, though that it was the original cause of the war is much more doubtful"; cf. similarly Paribeni 1927: 279–80; 289.

21 "the problem was not only to conquer but to conquer again and again, perpetually; our forces would be drained off in the attempt."

22 Rostovtzeff 1957: I 362–3 (revised edition); cf. Gibbon *Decline and Fall* IV 335: "An experience of seven hundred years might convince the rival nations of the impossibility of maintaining their conquests beyond the fatal limits of the

Tigris and Euphrates"; Syme *RP* III 1437. Hadrian was perhaps historically aware that the expedition was doomed to failure: Macrob. *Sat.* 1.23.14–16.

23 New arguments: D. Graf 2018; cf. Millar 2006: 275–99: caravan cities; contra Mitford 2018: 61: economic argument dismissed because annexation of Armenia did not affect control of the principal trade routes.

24 "I sought allies where I could; for a price, in gold, I corrupted former slaves whom otherwise I would willingly have sent to the galleys; I caressed more than one curly-headed darling."

25 Fronto 2.8; Cass. Dio 68.7.4; *HA Hadr.* 3.3; *Sev. Alex.* 39.1; Aur. Vict. *Caes.* 13.10; *Epit. de Caes.*13.4.

26 See *PIR*² L 439, with Syme *RP* I 391; IV 297; Migliorati 2003: 136–9; 191–5 (note 138: a natural enemy of Hadrian). Themistius: Smallwood 1966: no. 221. Sequel: "Le boucher de Cyrène" (*MH* 362). Monuments: Lepper and Frere 1988: 104–5 plates XLIV–XLV; Mitford 2018: 66 n.56. (That Hadrian was responsible for the Beneventum panel [Ansel 2020: 51] assumes an inexplicable willingness to portray a murdered enemy.) Polemo: the Arabic phrase could indicate either Quietus's place of origin or a site associated with his military notoriety: it has been taken to mean Cyrene, but Carcopino 1934, known to Yourcenar, suggested identification with Cerne in the deep south of Mauretania (*OR* 550; see Poignault 1995: 885–8). Most scholars follow Cassius Dio in regarding him as Mauretanian (e.g. Vanacker 2013: a chieftain of the Baquates). Cf. Célo 2014: 99–104: a literary contrast between the evil Quietus and Hadrian's supporter, Marcius Turbo, perhaps exaggerated.

27 Palma: *PIR*² C 1412, with Syme *RP* III 1117; 1391; IV 298. Celsus: *PIR*² P 1049, with Syme *RP* III 1391; IV 298 (quotation); V 490–1.

28 *PIR*² A 1408, with Syme *RP* I 328; II 681; 782; III 1172; IV 298; 299, believing Nigrinus to be "a close friend" of Hadrian. Influence: Cass. Dio 69.2.5. Succession: *HA Hadr.* 7.1 (attributed to Hadrian's autobiography by Syme as evidence of intimacy).

29 "My friend Latinius Alexander, who was descended from one of the ancient royal families of Asia Minor, and whose name and wealth had great weight, was heeded no more than I."

30 *IGRR* 3.208 = Smallwood 1966: no. 498 = French 2003: no. 18: "twice chief-priest, *sebastophant*, (who) provided oil (for the gymnasium) at his own expense most brilliantly of his predecessors, (and who) gave distributions to the city at the time of the transit of the Emperor Caesar Traianus Hadrianus Augustus and his sacred armies, (and who) served as *archon* (chief officer) and *eirenarch* (magistrate), both together, with integrity and distinction, enriching the metropolis with his education and eloquence" (trans. French).

31 Experts: Birley 1997a: 83; cf. Syme *RP* VI 347; Mitchell 1993: I 132; French 2003: no. 18; Mitford 2018: 67; contra *PIR*² L 123. Quotation: Rostovtzeff 1957 (revised edn): 696 n.6: Weber 1973 [1907].

32 She miscounted there the number of references to him in her text: not three but five.

33 Notices: see *BNJ* s.v. 'Kriton' (T. Banchich); cf. Savo 2009: 501–4. Inscriptions: see Savo 2009: 504–6; 516–18 for summary and texts. Calculation of the dates depends upon the absence in Trajan's nomenclature in the inscriptions concerned of the elements *Optimus* (esp.) and *Parthicus*, awarded in 114 and 116 respectively; cf. *PIR*[2] S 823 (no date of death discussed).

34 Ambiguous entry: *BNJ* 200 F8: "'Caesar entered Asia, having settled at the same time the affairs of the subject peoples and the Parthians', and again 'having accompanied him when he was at war and settling affairs throughout his realm', says Kriton in *Getika*." This is accepted by Migliorati 2003: 198 to mean that Crito was present on the Parthian expedition and witnessed Trajan's death, which he recorded in an unattested work that became a source for Cassius Dio. *I.Ephesos* 719 = *SEG* 4.521 = Smallwood 1966: no. 175 does not support this. Balance: see the Biographical Essay of *BNJ* s.v. 'Kriton' (T. Banchich); cf. Savo 2009: 506.

35 Scarborough 1985: 394–7.

36 *PV* 183–4 (from July 1976); *ER* 87–9; *YO* 289; *RC* 47–8.

37 Misogyny: Sarde 1995a: 92, 181–2. (The Marcella of *DR* is an obvious objection to the view of absence.) Fraigneau: taken to be the inspiration for *Feux*; cf. Savigneau 1993, 97, 105. Patriarchal: Kiebusinski 2004: 157–9; cf. Julien 2014a: 234. It follows that a true biography of a Roman emperor's consort is an even more unattainable goal than that of an emperor. Quotation: "the austere, patriarchal sense of family."

38 "Hadrien ne pouvait les voir que de biais" ("Hadrian could know them only in part, from the point of view where he was standing"); cf. Watt 2001 [1957]: 112; Hörmann 1996: 13.

39 Late source: *Epit. de Caes.* 42.21. L. Pompeius: Syme 1958: 794; Temporini 1979: 10–11; Syme *RP* VI 223: "to be presumed a senator"; VII 565; cf. Temporini 1979: 18; Burnand 1975: 744–8: his status indeterminable.

40 Commonly: Syme 1958: 604; *RP* II 773; V 526; VI 23; 343; Burnand 1975: 744–8; Raepsaet-Charlier 1987: 631; Rivet 1988: 163. Yourcenar incorporates the detail of the temple's foundation at Nemausus into *Tellus stabilita* before Plotina's death, with reference to family associations (*MH* 394; cf. Poignault 1995: 680–1, with a change of date now necessary for Hadrian's visit). The *Historia Augusta* does not indicate that Hadrian's act followed her death. Whether the temple recorded by Dio 69.10.3[1] is to be identified with the basilica is uncertain.

41 *TGS* 382–3: "cette infiltration du clan espagnol à Rome."

42 Temporini 1979: 19; Syme 1958: 249 n.1; *RP* VI 223: suggesting she was not Trajan's first wife. For the full record, see *PIR*[2] P 679, with Temporini 1979: 10–183; cf. Temporini-Gräfin Vitzthum 2002: 188–213.

43 Tradition: Plin. *Pan.* 83.4; *Epit. de Caes.* 42.21; Dio Chrys. *Or.* 3.122. Contrast Syme *RP* III 1262: "it is far from certain that Trajan and Plotina formed a well-matched and harmonious couple. High society imposes constraints, and it demands respect for appearances."

44 Coinage: *BMC Emp.* III lxxxii, lxxxiii, 106–7 nos. 525–9 (cf. Smallwood 1966: no. 107). Documentary evidence: the so-called *Acta Hermaisci*: *P. Oxy.* 1242 = Musurillo 1954: no. VIII = Smallwood 1966: 516, with Temporini 1979: 90–100; Harker 2008: 91–2: inclining to fiction; Horbury 2014: 213–15; Capponi 2020: 195–6: propagandistic and countered by Jewish tradition; cf. Julien 2014a: 234: indirect political influence only.

45 In the list sent to her publisher in 1952 of illustrations possibly to be included in the Club du meilleur livre edition, Yourcenar included a photograph of a marble bust of Plotina in the Capitoline Museum, an image she knew well as the *Note* reveals. It is the basis for Hadrian's subsequent reference to Plotina's fashionable "lourdes tresses" and the "front lisse" that gave her the look of a judge (*MH* 350, quoted below); cf. Poignault 1995: 649 (note also Syme 1958 n.1: "a little weary but amused around the eyes"), and for Plotina's portraits as evidence of lucidity, Poignault 1995: 633.

46 Usage: Julien 2014a: 235. Rumours: Migliorati 2003: 209. Rejected: cf. Poignault 1991: 211; 1997: 184–90; 2005: 319: the relationship completely asexual and consistent with the ideals of Cicero's *De amicitia*.

47 Inscriptions: *ILS* 7784 = *SIG*³ 834 = Smallwood 1966: 442 (from 121). Items of scholarship: Graindor 1934: 203–7; Alexander 1938: 160–2; cf. Temporini 1979: 162–7. The letter to Hadrian is in Latin, that to the Athenians in Greek. A second confirmatory letter to the Athenians in Greek, unknown in Yourcenar's day, has also been attributed to Plotina: see van Bremen 2005 against S. Follet's ascription to Hadrian (an exemplary illustration of source problems). Underlie: cf. Poignault 1995: 579, 780–1.

48 Friend: Voconius Romanus, sometimes identified with Hadrian's friend Voconius (Apul. *Apol.* 11.3–4) and the Victor Voconius of Mart. 7.29; see Bradley 2016b: 5–6; cf. C.P. Jones ed. *Apuleius Apologia Florida De Deo Socratis* (Cambridge MA 2017): 36 n.28. Yourcenar does not credit Plotina with securing Hadrian's appointment as governor of Syria, aware perhaps of the uncertainties of the tradition. *HA Hadr.* 4.1 records that at the start of the Parthian War, Plotina gained for Hadrian a position as *legatus*, an appointment on Trajan's staff: "*legatus Augusti pro praetore* and *comes* of the Emperor" (Birley 1997a: 68). Cass. Dio 68.33.1 is commonly taken to mean that Hadrian was made governor of Syria only when Trajan began his fatal journey to Rome and left Hadrian in charge of Rome's troops, succeeding C. Julius Quadratus Bassus (*PIR*² J 508), governor in the years 115–17 (Sherk 1980: 1020–3; Birley 1997a: 75), known only since 1932 from the discovery of an inscription at Pergamum

(*AE* 1934 no. 176 = Smallwood 1966: no. 214 = Sherk 1988: no. 138; cf. Syme
1958: 646; 1971c: 163–4; 165–6; *RP* VII 635 n.2: critical of Weber's initial
publication). In the *Note* (*OR* 550), Yourcenar cites an early publication by
A. von Premerstein (1934) as a source on Hadrian's Greek entourage, and she
has Hadrian speak of the special funeral the inscription discloses which Bassus
received after his death in Dacia, and which was indeed given on Hadrian's
initiative (*MH* 361, quoted below). She could be expected therefore to have
known of his earlier governorship of Syria, making Hadrian wrong to say that
he was the first governor of that province. However, *HA Hadr*. 4.1 is ambiguous
(cf. Lepper 1948: 171–2) and could mean that Hadrian became governor of
Syria at the outset of the war, as by Magie in the Loeb edition of the *Historia
Augusta*: "The appointment as legate refers to his governorship of Syria; see §
6." Yourcenar's text emerges as an example of her belief that conflicting items
in the tradition could be reconciled. Hadrian's governorship, inferred from the
Historia Augusta, is conjoined with his subsequent charge of the Roman armies
known from Cassius Dio through Xiphilinus.

49 *HA Hadr*. 3.11 (speech assignment): placed following Hadrian's first consulship;
2.10 (marriage): attributed to Marius Maximus with no reason for Trajan's
disapproval. Poignault 1995: 531–2 detects critical allusions to Plotina's
manoeuvring on Hadrian's behalf at Plin. *Pan*. 7.4 and Tac. *Hist*. 1.16, perhaps
extremely; see Temporini 1979: 78–86. Syme *RP* V 549–50 doubted Plotina's
influence in the speech-writing appointment. Yourcenar will have known *HA
Hadr*. 4.1: *usus Plotinae quoque favore* (cf. Poignault 1995: 766).

50 *RC* 47; *PV* 197–8 (from November 1977); *AS* 935. On Yourcenar's ideal female
characters, see Hynynen 2005 (though I am not convinced that Hadrian thinks
of Plotina in maternal terms). Weakness: Boatwright 1991: 530–2. Paribeni
1927: 304–6 notably characterized Plotina as wise, with the following features:
"ma sopra tutto la viva simpatia e la protezione indulgente e affetuosa da lei
avuta per Adriano." Cf. Syme 1958: 249; *RP* V 549: a colourless "affinity" with a
"subtle and cultivated woman."

51 Law: Townend 1967: 84. Inevitability: it is impossible in modern biography
for doubt about Hadrian's accession to be expressed; Speller 2003: ch. 1 ("The
waiting game") is a rare exception.

52 "I desired the supreme power. I desired it that I might put my own plans into
effect, try my remedies, and restore peace. I wanted it above all in order to
become my full self before I died." Hatra: cf. Paribeni 1927: 310. *Libido*: Sall.
Cat. 2.2; Tac. *Ann*. 1.10; August. *De civ. D*. 1 praef.

53 There is an oddity here: Attianus is known to have been praetorian prefect and
present at Selinus when Trajan died; but when he began his tenure is unknown
(Syme *RP* III 1281–2). Yourcenar has given no reason previously for his
presence in the east. But if tenure began several years earlier (cf. Birley 1997a:

58) a likely reason would emerge. This cannot be reliable, however, and the influence of Plotina here can only be a guess.

54 "I pitied him; we were too different for him to find in me what most people who have wielded total authority seek desperately on their deathbeds, a docile successor pledged in advance to the same methods, and even to the same errors."

55 "Everything that for ten years' time had been feverishly dreamed of, schemed, discussed or kept silent, was here reduced to a message of two lines, traced in Greek in a small, firm, feminine hand."

56 "An extraordinary calm had come over me: ambition and fear alike seemed a nightmare of the past … My own life no longer preoccupied me; I could once more think of the rest of mankind."

57 Dio: the contexts differ. Ammianus: ch. 2.

58 Situated: see E. R. Bevan, *The House of Seleucus Volume 1* (1902): 212–13, a work Yourcenar called a "très beau livre" at *PCC* 137 (and to which Cavafy was much indebted). For the palace of Diocletian, perhaps an element in the decorative border of the so-called Yakto mosaic from the fifth century (Lassus 1969), see Downey 1961: 640–7, with esp. Lib. 11. 203–7.

59 Cf. Paribeni 1927: 307–9; Syme *RP* IV 296: "idle fancies current in a later age."

60 See Migliorati 2003: 211–14 (highly speculative); cf. Aur. Vict. *Caes.* 13.13; *Epit. de Caes.*13.11: Trajan adopted Hadrian while still alive; Eutr. 8.6.1: Plotina responsible for the succession with Trajan unwilling to adopt while alive.

61 Cf. Millar 1964: 63; Poignault 1995: 782 n.112 (rightly).

62 *ILS* 1792 = Smallwood 1966: no. 176: Phaedimus dead at age twenty-eight: murdered to prevent dangerous information becoming public, as some suggest, or from natural causes?

63 See Temporini 1979: 120–59, esp. 150–1. Ignorance leads to fantasy: see Roman 2008: ch. 3: a circle of Stoically minded and other senators lobbied for a successor to Trajan unrelated to him; they were opposed by Plotina and other senators such as Pliny; Trajan himself (150) supported the choice of Hadrian given the anecdote of the gift of Nerva's diamond (*HA Hadr.* 3.7: fiction according to Fündling 2006: 325; cf. *MH* 329).

64 *MH* 357: quoted in ch. 3.

65 Quoted by Kolbert 1985: 106, 112.

66 Commonplace: see Finley 1975: 76 for one formulation. Paribeni: 1927: 279. Henderson: 1968 [1923]: 137 (cf. 57; 76). Wall: Morwood 2013: 28.

67 *Chronologie*: ch. 4 n.45 (cf. ch.1 n.10). Lindbergh 1940: a forty-four page pamphlet rather than a book. In the *Carnets de notes, 1942–1948*, the entry preceding the one just cited has the heading, "*1944. Wave of the Future.*" It gives a précis of Yourcenar's article (*PE* 531).

68 Unanswerable: see Deprez 2012: 77–8: unable to trace the original version of the article; J.E. Howard 2018: 382 n.15: no copy of the French consulate's journal has ever emerged.

69 Lindbergh 1940: 18.
70 Cavafy's *Waiting for the Barbarians* is an obvious comparandum.
71 Deprez 2012: 76. Yourcenar thought that Lindbergh was supporting the
    European totalitarian regimes identified as the Forces of the Future but the
    argument is forced (J.E. Howard 2018: 109 perhaps exaggerates Lindbergh's
    position); see Blanchet-Douspis 2008: 33–4 (cf. 142): "une grande clairvoyance"
    in Yourcenar's essay; cf. Savigneau 1993: 142: dismissed as mediocre.
72 Yourcenar's essay was translated by Grace Frick, whose version of this
    paragraph is given by J.E. Howard 2018: 109 (cf. 382 n.17). I have made slight
    alterations.
73 *HZ* II 403: 27 October 1959 to Mary Elizabeth Storer. See variously *HZ* 530:
    5 April 1956; *HZ* II 180: 29 November 1957; *HZ* II 207: 3 January 1958; *HZ* II
    251: 26 June 1958; *L* 422: 29 March 1974; *PV* 34 (from 1954); 76–7 (from 1969);
    178 (from 1976); 222 (from 1978–9); 275–6 (from 1980); 324 (from 1984); 332
    (from 1985); 367 (from 1986–7); *YO* 98; 138. I do not doubt the essence of these
    later recollections of the postwar period, but they became almost formulaic, part
    of the mythology as it were Yourcenar created concerning the composition of
    Mémoires; they must be recognized as such.
74 *DR*: on the original version and its distinction from *Mémoires*, see Poignault
    2006. See further ch. 8.
75 *PV* 77 (from 1969); *RC* 75; *PV* 332 (from 1985); cf. 338; *PV* 275 (from 1980).
76 22 August 1968 to Lidia Storoni Mazzolani.
77 Suggested: Poignault 1991: 218.
78 Record: Fronto 2.209; Paus. 1.5.5; Cass. Dio 69.5.1; *HA Hadr.* 5.1; 10.2; 17.10;
    Eutr. 7.1; *Epit. de Caes.* 14.10; Malalas 11.13. Coinage: *BMC Emp.* III cxxv, cxxxi,
    cxxxii, clxvi.
79 "My predecessors, up to this time, had absented themselves chiefly for war;
    for me the great undertakings, the activities of peace, and my life itself began
    outside Rome's bounds."
80 "Peace will again establish itself between two periods of war; the words
    humanity, liberty, and *justice* will here and there regain the meaning which we
    have tried to give them."
81 Lukács 1983 [1962]: 300–1.
82 Romanists will appreciate the date of 10 December.
83 See ch. 2.
84 Toynbee 1934: 1; cf. Turcan 2008: 68.
85 Toynbee 1934: 24–5; cf. Syme 1958: 488; *RP* III 1194; VI 332–3: a clear "foreign
    policy" to defend; Hadrian parading as a "prince of peace" and advertising a
    Greco-Roman empire in the manner of modern premiers and presidents.
86 Peace: Weinstock 1971: 267–9; Woolf 1993. Wasteland: Tac. *Agr.* 30.5; cf.
    Sibylline Oracles 4.102–4; 8.50–1; 8.126–7 for subject peoples enslaved to

Rome. Title: *BMC Emp.* III cxxxiv; clxvii (cf. Smallwood 1966: no. 115), with Syme 1958: 247–8. Story: Macrob. *Sat.* 2.4.29. Revolts: see M. Goodman in Garnsey and Saller 2015: ch. 4: almost certainly a minimal record.

87 Cultural disposition: Syme *RP* VI 185: "Rome stands for war and conquest, power and authority, hierarchy if not regimentation" (see inevitably Virg. *Aen.* 1.278–9; 6.851–3; 7.98–101); Cornell 1993.

88 Trappings: Millar 1977: 61–6; Campbell 1984: 109–48. Enemies reduced: Bradley 2004.

89 Coins: *BMC Imp.* III: cxxiv with 236–7 nos. 1–5 (cf. Smallwood 1966: no. 110 (b)). Document: *P. Oxy.* 3781 (trans. Rea). Local celebrations of merriment followed: *P. Giss. Lit.* 4.4, with Harker 2008: 52; cf. 119.

90 Birley 1997a: 231, 276.

91 Prominently displayed: Kleiner 1992: 241. Statue: Kleiner 1992: fig. 205; Hallett 2005: 119; Haley 2005: 974. Quotation: Kleiner 1992: 241. (A statuette now in Liverpool [Birley 1997a: 277, pl. 29)] is equally notable.) Mars: Opper 2008: 71 fig. 54; Hallett 2005: 245 (with pl. 141). For a valuable passage on the portrayal of the defeated in Roman art, see Storoni Mazzolani 1972: 184, with some misprision, however, on Hadrian.

92 Frontiers: Britain, Cappadocia, Dacia, Germany, Spain, Mauretania, Moesia, Noricum, Rhaetia, and Syria. Circumstance: note *RIB* 1051 a-b = Sherk 1988: no. 141: "Son of all the [deified (emperors), Imperator Caesar] *Traianus* Hadr[ianus Augustus,] when the necessity of *keeping intact* the empire [within its borders] had been *imposed* upon him by divine *instruction* … having routed [the barbarians and recovered] the province of Britain, he *added* [a fortified boundary line between] each *ocean's* [shore for 80 miles.]" This may record military successes in Britain, but is obviously too heavily restored for certainty. But activity in Britain, and North Africa, apparently made an impact (Juv. 14.196). I think it unlikely that the coins reflect the views of the millions of provincial subjects the coins' symbolic figures represent.

93 Fronto 2.206–8, with Champlin 1980: 94–6; Campbell 1984: 399. W.V. Harris 2016: 125 is confident that Hadrian abandoned an ideology of conquest. Cf. Gibbon *Decline and Fall* IV 215: "It was the opinion of Marcian, that war should be avoided as long as possible to preserve a secure and honourable peace; but it was likewise his opinion that peace cannot be honourable or secure, if the sovereign betrays a pusillanimous aversion to war."

94 14 January 1963: "it would be a mistake to reduce Hadrian's complex policies to a conventional form of 'liberalism' or 'pacificism.'"

95 Use: *MH* 342, 350, 353; cf. Syme 1939: vii; 1999: 3, 4, 6, 15, 17, 22, 23, 24, etc. (esp. significant for the 1930s); and ubiquitous elsewhere.

96 Political opinions: Blanchet-Douspis 2008: 287; cf. Kiebunski 2004: 156: "Rather than an autobiography of a Roman emperor, the work presents itself as a sort

of treatise written from a post-Hitlerian and late French colonial perspective."
I think this underestimates Yourcenar's insistence on historical accuracy, but
recognizes a certain political stance.
97 Quotations: Marañón 1956: 83.

6. Antinous

1 For Hadrian's itinerary in Egypt, see Birley 1997a: ch. 19. Hunting expedition:
   MH 431–2; (ch. 3). Late October: Lambert 1988 [1984]: 129, with Plut. *Mor.*
   356c. Story: see fundamentally Poignault 1995: 448–9; 474–81; 492–4; 504–5;
   651–67; 710–16; 918–23; cf. Vier 1979: 34: "Marguerite Yourcenar se sert
   d'Antinoüs pour élever jusqu'à la dignité de Pygmalion un monarque de haute
   civilisation et pour faire cohabiter en lui un cœur ravagé et un esprit subtil."
2 Source tradition: Migliorati 2003: 293–301; Fündling 2006: 687–701 (noting
   Yourcenar's choice of the suicide option [692]).
3 Portraits: Meyer 1991: standard repertory. Details: *RE* I, 2 cols. 2439–40; *PIR*²
   A 737; *Brill's New Pauly* I s.v. 'Antinous' (2). Note esp. *SIG*³ 841 = Smallwood
   1966: no. 164 (cf. Paus. 8.9.7): the gift of a stoa with seats to the city of
   Mantinea and to their countryman, the god Antinous, from C. Julius Eurykles;
   see Jones 2010: 82: fragility of the source tradition; Vásquez de Parga 1995:
   the tradition unquestionably valid; Burns 2015: 286: Dio's evidence "a typical
   account"; Galimberti 2013: 91–2; 2017: 98: allusion to Antinous's disposal
   in Juv. 15.126–128; Hadrian's relationship with Antinous criticized "by his
   contemporaries during his lifetime" (both unconvincing). Cult: Jones 2010: 81;
   cf. Šašel Kos 2009: its possible promotion in Moesia by L. Aelius; Bruun 2016:
   Antinous's celebrity at Ostia in the 170s. Antinoopolis: Zahrnt 1988. Poignault
   1988a: 204 associates Antinous's suicide with a childhood nightmare Yourcenar
   describes at *EM* 1548.
4 21 March 1953 to Paul Dresse in reference to Peyrefitte's *L'Oracle* (1948).
   Glorified: cf. *HZ* 158: reference from June 1952 also to a tradition of Antinous
   as the personification of total personal loyalty ("dévouement"). Fiat: the
   deification was not sanctioned by the Roman senate, as usually in the creation
   of imperial *divi*, but it is doubtful whether this mattered to the mass of Rome's
   subjects who accepted Antinous as a new superhuman being (cf. Jones 2010:
   81): the word of the emperor, "the state" to all intents and purposes, was surely
   sufficient.
5 See Plon 1951: 315–16; 318–19; *OR* 550–5; 548; 546.
6 Goslar 2007: 31–2; 44; 64; cf. Jacquiot 1990; Chevallier 1990; Poignault 1990.
7 Experts agree, however, that the portraits derive from a "common type" created
   only after Antinous's death: Evers 1995: 448; 2013: 91–2; Fittschen 2010: 244;
   Smith 2018; cf. Vout 2005; 2007: ch. 2.

8 Brief details: *MH* 403–4 with *OR* 545. Aristeas: *MH* 390 with *OR* 553. Palmyra:
MH 425 with *OR* 544. Grief: "La description de la douleur d'Hadrien à la mort
d'Antinoüs s'inspire des historiens du règne, mais aussi de certains passages
des Pères de l'Église, réprobateurs à coup sûr, mais parfois sur ce point plus
humains, et surtout d'opinions plus variées qu'on n'aurait cru" (*OR* 547: "The
description of Hadrian's grief at the death of Antinous is drawn from the
historians of the reign, but also from certain passages in the Church Fathers,
who though indeed disapproving are sometimes more understanding on the
subject, and above all more varied in their approach to it, than the usual blanket
references to their opinions would reveal").

9 Interest: in 1926 Yourcenar submitted a work called *Antinoos* to the publisher
Fasquelle, apparently without success (Savigneau 1993: 177). Later, in 1945,
she featured Antinous in an essay that was never published called *Cantique de
l'âme libre* (*CNMH* 523). Later still, in 1958 and 1959, developing the research
undertaken for *Mémoires*, she turned to a historical and iconographical study of
Antinous, using the material for lectures in Europe but not completing it (*HZ*
II 234; 310–11). An unpublished (short) poem from the very early date of 1920,
Album italien: Tibur, ends with the line, "Le jeune Antinoüs pense à son destin"
(Sarde 1995a: 51). Love story: cf. Opper 2008: 174: a valid assumption.

10 Sections: on the disposition of material, see Castellani 2011: 218. Bithynia: not
provable as the place of first meeting (Burns 2015: 286). Proleptic thought: cf.
Suet. *Iul.* 2; 49.1.

11 Sacrifice: see J.E. Howard 1992: sacrifice as the novel's key literary theme, with
Antinous's death its "pivotal episode" (6; cf. e.g. 186; 188; 192; 199; 200).

12 Symbols: *EM* 1652–3 (from *Diagnostic de l'Europe* [1929]). Herodes Atticus:
Philostr. *VS* 545–6, with Birley 1997a: 63 (his wealth); Birley 1997a: 177,
217 suggests that father and son were likely Hadrian's hosts both in 124 and
128/129; cf. Poignault 1995: 533–4. Athens: Boatwright 2000: 144–57; Karivieri
2002; cf. Bradley 2012c: 154–5. The passage draws on the inscription from
Hadrian's Arch: *IG* II² 5185 = Smallwood 1966: no. 485. Reminiscences: Gell.
NA 1.26; 2.2; 7.18; 10.19; 17.8; 17.20; 18.2; 19.12, with Holford-Strevens 1988:
ch. 5; Howley 2014 (stressing preservation of Roman cultural identity). Taurus:
ch. 3. Alexandria: Dio Chrys. *Or.* 32, with Fraser 1972 I 708–800. Unaware of
such details, Furbank 2004 dismisses the Antinous episode as "modernist" and
not historically credible, claiming, surely absurdly, that Yourcenar "despised"
Cassius Dio and the Latin life. Instruments: Poignault 1988b: 197.

13 Hazily: e.g. *MH* 412: "Les dates se mélangent: ma mémoire se compose une seule
fresque où s'entassent les incidents et les voyages de plusieurs saisons" ("The
years merge: my memory forms but a single fresco whereon are crowded the
events and travels of several seasons"). On the issues raised by the chronology of
Hadrian's journeys, see Poignault 1988a; 1995: 477–81. Twenty: cf. *MH* 589.

14 Festugière 1932: 299–301 ("La Valeur religieuse des papyrus magiques"), citing *PGM* III 1; IV 2455–7; VII 628–9; I 4–10, 20–5; see Betz 1992: 334; F. Graf 1997: 113; Montserrat 1996: 184: normative magic in Egypt.

15 29 November 1965; cf. *HZ* 546.

16 Rare: see Mynott 2018: ch. 9 (cf. Gibbon *Decline and Fall* IV 324–5). Pachrates, the second of Festugière's examples: *PGM* IV 2450 = Betz 1992: 83; cf. Poignault 1995: 474–5; Birley 1997a: 244; Bradley 2012c: 11.

17 See Betz 1992: 3; 4; 26; 34; 37; 41; 68; 75; 99; 105; 152–3; 211; 313; cf. F. Graf 1997: 109–16. (In contrast, note Roman 2008: 131–4: astrological explanation of the suicide.) Sacrifice: note Cramer 1954: 172: "The belief that a man's life could be saved from fated death by the voluntary sacrifice of another's was an old one. The story of Alcestis and her devotion has become immortal."

18 Cf. Deprez 2003: 167. On pet-like terminology, see Deprez 2003: 45–7; Fort 2014: 204–5; Filaire 2012; Filaire-Ramos 2014; note also Cliche 2000: traces of Yourcenar's engagement with Virginia Woolf in reference to *MH* 406: "Ce tendre corps s'est modifié sans cesse, à la façon d'une plante." Lyre: on Greek music, see Yourcenar's remarks in her study of Pindar (*P* 1446–7). Plato: the works are discreetly unnamed. Prince: for the influence of the Lanuvium relief showing Antinous as Silvanus, see Goslar 2007: 94–8.

19 The sole passage with a hint of the salacious; Yourcenar showed no interest in the mechanics of male same-sex intimacy; contrast Osborne 2018.

20 15 March 1953. Gellhorn's opinion of *Mémoires* was otherwise admiring: an undated letter of the 1950s to the art historian Bernard Berenson calls it "wonderful" (McLoughlin 2007: 7). Hortense Flexner was Gellhorn's tutor at Bryn Mawr College and a friend of long standing (McLoughlin 2007: 3). Clark: E. Clark 2015 [1952]: 186: "But what his statues announce and glorify is sex, and less a fulfilment than a long languorous exacerbation, a voluptuous delay such as Tivoli had never heard of before. A new kind of experience has come in: the romantic obsession, and wrapped in a sensuality the very opposite of Roman; this sultry shepherd could only have come from the East."

21 Perhaps influenced by her father, who in the late 1920s encouraged Yourcenar to publish under her name the fragment of a novel he had composed many years before, the subject of which was the wedding night of a couple married at the turn of the century. The fragment duly appeared in a magazine under the title *Le Premier Soir* soon after Michel de Crayencour's death (*SP* 931–3). She commented: "Aux yeux de cet homme qui répétait sans cesse que rien d'humain ne devrait nous être étranger, l'âge et le sexe n'étaient en matière de création littéraire que des contingences secondaires. Des problèmes qui plus tard allaient laisser mes critiques perplexes ne se posaient pas pour lui" (*SP* 932: "This man, who continually repeated that nothing human should be alien to us,

viewed age and sex as merely secondary contingencies in the matter of literary creation. Problems that at a later date would leave my critics perplexed were not problems for him"). In 1954 Yourcenar arranged to have the line from Terence inscribed on her father's tombstone (*HZ* 349–51).

22 Cf. also *P* 1447: "les vives amitiés qui faisaient placer dans les palestres une icône de l'Amour"; *CL* 160; 173; 200; 208; 223. For the historical accuracy of Yourcenar's views, see Ughetto 2009: 246–50.

23 Cf. *CNMH* 531.

24 The sources on Alcibiades's death are hopelessly confused; for the courtesan, see Plut. *Alcibiades* 39.

25 Cf. *CNON* 868: Antinous as "*éromène.*"

26 MacMullen 1990: ch. 17 (from 1982).

27 8 October 1970.

28 Cf. *L* 369: "malheureux." "Gay": cf. Opper 2008: 168 (anachronistic?).

29 Interest: Foucault 1976; Dover 1978; cf. J. Griffin 1985: 24–6; Lambert 1988 [1984]: ch. VI; Montserrat 1996: 144–58; C.A. Williams 1999; Davidson 2001; Lear and Cantarella 2008 (stressing from art-historical sources the metaphor of hunting implicit in courtship); Lear 2014. The passage quoted from *YO* 182 anticipates the opening and closing paragraphs of Dover 1978.

30 "Le long essai consacré à Antinoüs par J.A Symonds dans ses *Sketches in Italy and Greece*, Londres, 1900, bien que de ton et d'informations parfois surannés, reste d'un grand intérêt, ainsi qu'une note du même auteur sur le même sujet, dans son remarquable et rarissime essai sur l'inversion antique, *A Problem in Greek Ethics.*" The first half of the sentence reads a little differently in the original edition of 1951, where Yourcenar called the essay "singulièrement pénétrant" (Plon 1951: 318). This is reflected in the English version: "The essay on Antinous by J. Addington Symonds in his *Sketches in Italy and Greece*, 1900, is singularly penetrating, although the tone is now outmoded and the information on some points is outdated by recent research … he tries with the help of literary and artistic documentation to approach the young Bithynian as a living reality. Symonds is one of the first critics to note the conscious revival by Hadrian of Greek erotic tradition (Note 4, p. 21, *A Problem in Greek Ethics* …)." I take the reference to recent research to refer to the Kinsey report, on which as seen earlier material is preserved in Yourcenar's *Notebook*. Her intent evidently was to validate her portrayal with reliable scientific data. Publication dates of the relevant items from Symonds are complex due to the number of reissues, publication on both sides of the Atlantic, and Symonds's composition of *Sketches and Studies in Italy and Greece* in two series. I refer in the following to the essay on Antinous from *Sketches and Studies in Italy* (London 1879): 47–90; cf. *Sketches and Studies in Italy and Greece* (London 1898): 184–229. Petite Plaisance contains *Sketches and Studies in Italy and*

Greece. Vols. I–III (London 1898, 1907, 1910) and the 1908 reprint of *A Problem in Greek Ethics: Being an Inquiry into the Phenomenon of Sexual Inversion Addressed Especially to Medical Psychologists and Jurists* (1973) (Bernier 2004: nos. 1695–7, 3707).

31 Protestant Cemetery: Zona vecchia File 15 Area 8. Epitaph: see Grosskurth 1965: 316–17: the words *cujus animus infirmo licet in corpore literarum et historiae studio ardebat* are memorable; the Latin text is followed by Symonds's translation of a hymn by Cleanthes. Jowett and Symonds: see Dowling 1994: 28–34, 59–60, 64–80, 130–1; cf. Evangelista 2007: 209–11, 218. Value: Holliday 2000; Nisbet 2013: Symonds's impact on contemporary gay culture.

32 Composed: Grosskurth 1984: 233. Letter: Schueller and Peters 1968: no. 1091. The poem was originally privately printed in Bristol (Babington 1925: 15, 21–3) and eventually appeared in Symonds's *Many Moods*.

33 Pancrates: poet and holy man (Lucian, *Philops.* 33–4), identified with the prophet Pachrates of the *Greek Magical Papyri* (Athenaeus knew him); see Birley 1997a: 240–1; 244–5; Dickie 2001: 204–5; 212–13; his poem is independently attested by *P. Oxy.* 1085 (fragmentary), which Symonds cannot have known; the flower was mentioned in other works written probably for honorific festivals after Antinous's deification; see *P. Oxy.* 4352 with J.R. Rea's commentary. Yourcenar knew *P. Oxy.* 1085, and Athenaeus's anecdote (*OR* 547).

34 Symbolize: on Symonds's poem and Antinous's emergence in the late Victorian era as a veiled icon of same-sex engagement, see Waters 1995.

35 28 July and 5 August.

36 On "The Garland Seller," see esp. Nisbet 2013: 199–200. Petite Plaisance has a five-volume set of Croiset and Croiset, with imprint dates of 1896, 1890, 1891, 1895, 1899, and the three volumes of Edmonds, with publication dates of 1934, 1931, and 1945 (Bernier 2004: nos. 3692–6, 3632–4). Yourcenar included a version of Strato's original, also a paraphrase, in *CL* 409. At the time: see now D.A. Campbell, *Greek Lyric Volumes 1–5* (Cambridge MA 1982, 1988, 1991, 1992, 1993).

37 Yourcenar owned copies of the American impression of both series (Bernier 2004: nos. 3704, 3705). Together, "by far the most important book on classical literature of which most professional classicists today have never heard" (Nisbet 2013: 11; see esp. his ch. 3).

38 Quotations: from the edition of 1880: 320, 321.

39 "This same Strato, who had preferred obscurity in the freedom of Asia's taverns to life in my court, was a man of exquisite sensibility, a mocking wit quick to assert the vanity of all that is not pleasure itself, in order perhaps to excuse himself for having sacrificed to it everything else."

40 Fantasy: as much else: Antinous's long speech when preparing to end his life
that folds in a servile background and a lost family of parents and siblings; a
claim of once having been captured by pirates.

41 Cf. *MH* 439: "Il s'était accoutré d'une longue robe syrienne, mince comme une
pelure de fruit, toute semée de fleurs et de Chimères. Pour ramer plus à l'aise,
il avait mis bas sa manche droite: la sueur tremblait sur cette poitrine lisse"
("He had arrayed himself in a long Syrian robe, sheer as the skin of a fruit and
strewn over with flowers and chimeras. In order to row more easily he had
freed his right arm from its sleeve; sweat was trembling on the smooth chest").

42 Postulate: see esp. Waters 1995: 209–10.

43 Correspondence: Schueller and Peters 1968: no. 1098, 2 February 1878 to
Eleanor Frances Poynter; no. 1105, 27 March 1878 to Gosse.

44 Waters 1995: 206; cf. Burns 2015: 292; Evangelista 2015: 656 (both less
appreciative).

45 Schueller and Peters 1968: no. 1091 to Gosse (1 February): request for details of
a work by the Swedish author A.V. Rydberg; no. 1093 to Gosse (13 February):
attempts to find a copy of Rydberg from a London bookseller; no. 1094 to
Henry Graham Dakyns (15 February): orders for Rydberg and another German
monograph; request for details from W.S. Smith's *Dictionary of Greek and
Roman Biography* of 1849 and Spartianus; no. 1098 to Poynter (23 February):
thanks for photographs from Rome; no. 1099 to Dakyns (1 March): request
for information on *devotio* and sacrifice; no. 1100 to Gosse (8 March): efforts
to have Rydberg translated; overture to the British Museum for numismatic
information disdained by the keeper R.S. Poole; no. 1102 to Gosse (20 March):
research in Florence by H.F. Brown; retort to Poole; no. 1104 to Dakyns (27
March): request for answers to questions from Smith's dictionaries (i.e. the
Dictionary of Greek and Roman Antiquities [1842], *Dictionary of Greek and
Roman Geography* [1857], and the biographical volume); request for books and
photographs from his library in England; no. 1105 to Gosse (27 March): receipt
of translation of Rydberg by Mlle. Sophie Girard; no. 1109 to Dakyns (15 April):
acknowledgment of replies to enquiries.

46 Symonds 1879: 62; 48. Oriental: used, as by Yourcenar, obviously well before
Said 1994 [1978].

47 But see more percipiently Evangelista 2015: 659: Symonds "clearly meant to
stimulate the homoerotic fantasy of his male readers"; cf. Bann 2000: 147: the
essay brings Antinous "to the cusp of modernity."

48 Quotations: Symonds 1879: 63; 81; 64; 82; 90. Prado: Symonds used an
illustration of the statuary as his frontispiece, although he knew it only from
photographs. It has long since been disqualified as pertinent. Yourcenar saw the
work, and knew of the interpretative difficulties it raised due to the substitution
of the head of Antinous for an original portrait, either during the Renaissance

or in antiquity; in the latter case, it might have been intended to allude to the legend of Antinous's sacrificial death (*HZ* 382–3, 25 August 1954).

49 Symonds 1879: 49.

50 "All that can be said of the temperament of Antinous is inscribed in any one of his likenesses. 'Eager and impassionated tenderness, sullen effeminacy': Shelley, with a poet's admirable candor, says the essential in six words, while most of the nineteenth-century art critics and historians could only expatiate upon the subject with righteous declamation, or else idealize about it, vaguely and hypocritically."

51 Cf. Julien 2014b: 243: "effiminate [*sic*] sullenness."

52 Bann 2000. In its American printings, however, *Sketches and Studies in Italy* was widely accessible (Babington 1925). In the *Note*, Yourcenar cited her source as *Sketches in Italy and Greece* (London 1900), both in Plon 1951 (318) and the Pléiade (*OR* 550). The three volumes of *Sketches and Studies in Italy and Greece* that she owned include the contents of the earlier *Sketches and Studies in Italy* (Babington 1925: 208). It is to this later work, I think, that Yourcenar refers in the *Note*, garbling the title and date of publication. Bann did not separate her references to Symonds in the *Note*, included in Plon 1951, from the passage on Shelley in the *Carnets*, not included in Plon 1951, assuming *Note* and *Carnets* always appeared contemporaneously, and working from Frick's translation alone (where both items appear). Yourcenar's *Journal*, from which much of the original *Carnets* derives, does not contain the Shelley passage; but it appears in the original *Carnets* in the *Mercure de France* of November 1952. I think it possible, though this is only a guess, that the mistitled *Sketches and Studies in Italy and Greece* was consulted in the interim. Inadvertence: cf. "Edmunds" above.

53 Symonds 1879: 63–4.

54 Assumption: cf. Birley 1997b: 2729.

55 Cogent: Holliday 2000: 94–6; Nisbet 2013: 124–7: "the first serious study in English of male same-sex attraction in antiquity," theorizing "a non-pathological, culturally situated homosexuality." Cf. Evangelista 2015: 660. Its Preface is dated 1873. Symonds tried to control circulation of the original ten copies (Nisbet 2013: 20, 127). Petite Plaisance: Bernier 2004: no. 3707 (and so not as rare as Bann 2000 claims). The 1908 reprint is the text quoted here.

56 Quotations: Symonds 1908: 8; 30; 44; 58 (Henderson's views on Oxford education will be recalled). On the tendency of his views, cf. Funke and Langlands 2015.

57 Musurillo 1954: 33–43 (trans). Vibius Maximus: perhaps identifiable with the addressee of Plin. *Ep.* 3.2: Syme *RP* I 353–60; Sherwin-White 1966: 210; Brunt 1975: 144; Birley 2000: 100. *Stuprum*: C.A. Williams 1999: ch.3. Trial: Lambert: 1988 [1984]: 87; Montserrat 1996: 151–3.

58 Symonds 1908: 21, with n.4: "Hadrian in Rome, at a later period, revived the Greek tradition with even more of caricature. His military ardour, patronage of art, and love for Antinous seem to hang together." Bann 2000: 150 detects here an ambiguity concerning Antinous's motivation in taking his own life – the sacrificial suicide of Symonds's poem and essay is no longer evident – and an indication that "Antinous is now a mere 'caricature.'" This completes his theory of a development in Symonds's thinking about Antinous, "from the poetic through the essayistic to the designedly scientific" (139). Yet Symonds says nothing here about Antinous's death; it is Hadrian to whom he attributes caricature (the two are reduced, literally, simply to a footnote). In any case, *A Problem in Greek Ethics* was composed before the essay.

59 Quotation: "the noblest statement of Hellenic eroticism." Relationship: cf. DeJean 1989: 297–8: the presentation is idealized.

60 "I think that J.A. Symonds was correct in supposing that the emphasis Hadrian put on his deep attachment (at least *after* the young man's death) was probably a conscious return to the erotic ideals of the past."

61 See Ness 1994: 111–17 (with appeal to the *Notebook*); Filaire-Ramos 2014: an infantilized Antinous is *Mémoires'* organizing principle; cf. Poignault 1995: 493–4.

62 "l'amour total … étant de tout temps un fait d'expérience" (with properties of disease and vocation affecting its victim).

63 "Dans la passion, il y a le désir de se satisfaire, de s'assouvir, quelquefois de diriger, de dominer un autre être. Dans l'amour, au contraire, il y a abnégation" (*YO* 98); cf. *PV* 126 (from 1971) on passion: "une attention passionnée pour un être humain me semble constituer une attitude tout à fait essentielle" ("an impassioned regard for a human being seems to me to constitute a completely essential standpoint").

64 "a deep feeling of tenderness toward another creature … who … shares our condition, with all its risks and vicissitudes"; "a bond – which may or may not be carnal but … is always sensual – in which sympathy takes precedence over passion."

65 "Ils sont sacrés, ces rapports sensuels, parce qu'ils sont l'un des grands phénomènes de la vie universelle;" "Le sacré semble assez absent, remplacé par la pruderie ou la gaillardise"; cf. *PV* 390 (from 1986–7).

66 Cf. *PV* 292–4 (from 1981).

67 Sarde 1995a. Note the rare comment in Yourcenar's late interview with Shusha Guppy on her relationship with Grace Frick. It had first been a passionate friendship, then the common story of two people with shared literary interests living and working together as a matter of convenience; Yourcenar had remained with her friend during Frick's long and ultimately fatal illness, but Frick was then no longer the centre of her existence, and perhaps never had

been. At this late stage, Yourcenar questioned the importance of the ardent desire that drives one being inexorably to another and, recognizing that falling in love was largely a matter of chance, subordinated sexual attraction to the more erotically consequential foundation of emotions and relationships (*PV* 386). More will be presumably revealed when Yourcenar's correspondence with Frick is unsealed; see meantime J.E. Howard 2018: 169; 193; 313; 330–1.

68 14 June 1952 to Nina Ruffini.

69 "But when at the age of forty-seven he meets Antinous, the older Hadrian almost immediately feels that this is a unique encounter, even though he soon notices that his passion occasionally lapses or wanes. Finally, death places its seal on Hadrian's sense that, of all his loves, this one was unique."

70 J. Griffin 1985 (quotation: 54); cf. Lyne 1980: viii–ix: brief typology of love, passionate, whole, romantic, with universalizing assumptions; Veyne 2001 [1991]: ch. 3 (from 1978): implicit and unresolved complexities; Bradley 2012c: ch. 12: forms of love in Apuleius's *Metamorphoses*.

71 Treggiari 1991: esp. ch. 8; cf. Hopkins 1983: 85–8; Bettini 1999: anthropological examination of multiple literary sources and material evidence.

72 Greek romances: see Doody 1997: 33–61: love stories.

73 Mesomedes (*MH* 442): known from the Byzantine *Suda* (s.v.); on his thirteen extant poems, including *The Sphinx*, to which Hadrian earlier refers (*MH* 432), see Whitmarsh 2004; cf. Poignault 1995: 526. Inscription: *IKourion* no. 104 with Pöhlmann 2019: Antinous is identified with Adonis and praised, if the text is correctly restored, as follows: "You blessed with curls of violet, with the beautiful hair, coming from Bithynia, with the face of a virgin, son of a mother with golden wings." All bereft: Virg. *Aen*.10. 464–5; Arr. *Anab*. 7.14.3; Pl. *Phd*. 117c; cf. Hom. *Il*. 18.272: Achilles weeps for Patroclus. Star (*MH* 446): an astral phenomenon was perhaps involved: Chinese records suggest the appearance on 29 January 131, three months after 30 October 130, of a comet or nova which could be associated with the star cluster called Antinous in the constellation Aquila known to the Greek astronomical writer Ptolemy (7.5); see J.R. Rea's commentary to *P. Oxy*. 4352, which gives fragments of verses that speak of Antinous's transformation into a star. Toomer 1984: 357 n.160 suggests that Ptolemy, active in Alexandria between 127 and 141, made the connection between Antinous and the astral event, though his work was not made public before 150. Yourcenar evidently knew the reference from Ptolemy. Cf. Poignault 1993: 193: the role of the star in preserving Antinous's soul. Embalmed: details from Hdts. 2.86–9 are perceptible (*MH* 441).

74 "I could feel that those around me began to take offence at a grief of such duration; furthermore, the violence of my sorrow scandalized them more than its cause. If I had given way to the same tears for the death of a brother or a son I should have been equally reproached for crying like a woman."

75 Quintilian: *Inst.* 6. pr. Cicero: Treggiari 1998, 2007: 136–7.

76 Tombstones: Carroll 2006. Manifestations: Dolansky 2011a; 2019. On Roman burial practices, see esp. Toynbee 1971: 43–64. Antinous's eventual resting place may have been at Rome in a tomb in the Gardens of Adonis on the Palatine (Grenier and Coarelli 1986; cf. *LTUR* s.v. "Obeliscus Antinoi").

77 Hopkins 1983: 217–26. Contrast Carroll 2006: 196–202.

78 Pomeroy 1999: 77–8.

79 *Suda* s.v.; cf. Poignault 1995: 552–3.

80 Menander II 413–14 [IX] (Russell and Wilson 1981: 160–5; 325–7).

81 Brief comment: Henderson 1968 [1923]: 133; Birley 1997a: 2, 9, 249 (the "personal trauma" Antinous's death caused and the relationship at large knowable only to "an historical novelist"); Opper 2008: 173; Turcan 2008: 168–72: valuable description of the sources' Egyptianizing associations; cf. Rodrigues 2014: Hadrian murdered Antinous to create a unifying imperial divinity (surely far-fetched). Antinous cult: Smith 2018 holds that Antinous's sculptured portraits derive from an exemplar made by a master court artist after Antinous's death that others copied to satisfy consumer demand. He identifies a marble bust from Thasos believed to have been exported to a buyer in Syria, on which the names of Antinous and the buyer appear in different hands, one supposedly inscribed in Thasos, the other in Syria. The cult grew therefore not from promotion by Hadrian but from the initiative of enthusiastic individuals and cities, some calling him a god, others a hero (cf. Jones 2010: 78). His full body portraits, lacking pubic hair, show a prepubescent boy of thirteen or fourteen known to Hadrian only briefly, with homoerotic interest doubtful. Pausanias (8.9.7–8) is reliable on his origins (13), and a Dio-dependent debate over his death arose "immediately" (11). But Dio on Hadrian's instruction for dissemination of image and cult is dismissed (14), and the suggestion that Hadrian ordered the sculptural prototype quickly becomes fact (68, 69). Cf. Belayche 2019: Greek terms signifying deification used by local communities.

82 Information from an obituary notice in *King's College, Cambridge: Annual Report of the Council Under Statute, D., III, 10 on the General and Educational Condition of the College*, October 1983: 29–32. The book's notes were added by an eminent colleague. Lambert died in 1982, shortly before his fiftieth birthday.

83 See Birley 1997a: 8: "a remarkable attempt at a biography of the imperial favourite, which must not be underrated." Symonds had a lingering impact: Lambert 1988 [1984]: 9–10, 83.

84 Lambert 1988 [1984]: 146.

85 Epigraph: Lambert 1988 [1984]: 12. In January 1965, Yourcenar remarked to a correspondent that a good book on Antinous was still to be written (*HZ* IV 213). Her library contains a copy of Lambert (Bernier 2004: no. 3427), but I know of no record of her reaction to it.

86 Legend: *BMC Imp.* III cxxxi; see Poignault 1995: 640–1; Birley 1997a: 111–12.
    Phoenix: for *aurei* issued in 117, see *BMC Imp.* III no. 49 = Smallwood 1966: no.
    138, deliberately overlooked by Yourcenar according to Lecocq 2020, with the
    design attributable to Hadrian himself; I am unconvinced.

87 Custom: Numenius fr. 31 Boys-Stones. Golden Age: already promoted in earlier
    Imperial history by Augustus and Nero; see Gatz 1967; Zanker 1988: ch. 5
    (illusory in some aspects); Davis 2006: 29–30; Feeney 2007: ch. 4; Drinkwater
    2019: 267–70. Saturn's festival: Dolansky 2011b; cf. R. Williams 1973: 35–45:
    the complexity involved.

88 Recorded: in a handwritten entry in the *Notebook*'s *Journal* that has no
    counterpart in the *Carnets*: "Pleuré, plusieurs nuits de suite, dans cette cave
    où j'habitais à Bronxville, aux murs seulement décorés des images de la
    villa des Misteri. Pleuré, non véritablement sur l'ami d'Hadrien, mais sur
    l'incommunicable douleur humaine. Un homme a soufert ceci, s'est débattu
    seul contre telle souffrance, et puis l'a oublié, et mort." (Cf. Brochard and
    Pinon 2014: 118.) See ch. 4 for the further tears when the end of the novel was
    reached.

89 Verisimilar: Manzoni 1984: 70–1: "for the verisimilar (the raw material of art)
    once offered and accepted as such, becomes a truth that is altogether different
    from the real, but one that the mind perceives forever, one whose presence is
    irrevocable." I do not know whether Yourcenar had read Manzoni on poetry
    and history, but the introductory discussion of S. Bermann to her translation of
    On the Historical Novel is of great interest (Manzoni 1984: 21–9). Techniques:
    "Les techniques du roman sont les seuls moyens d'atteindre une vérité de la
    biographie, seuls les liens tissés imaginairement entre les faits rendent ceux-
    ci plausibles et légitimes, notre vie est temporelle mais aussi hypothétique
    et affective" ("The novel's techniques are the sole means of attaining a
    biographical truth, the bonds imaginatively forged between facts alone make
    them plausible and legitimate, our life is of the world but also subject to
    speculation and emotion"); from a letter of 10 August 1974, quoted by Sarde
    1995a: 274–5. Contrast E. Clark 2015 [1952]: 186–93: engaging but fanciful.

90 Smith 2018: 6.

91 "On pourrait imaginer les *Mémoires d'Hadrien* sans l'amour; ce serait une vie
    incomplète, ce serait tout de même une grande vie."

92 Modern examples: it hardly needs to be said that biographies of such figures as
    Victoria, Wilde, and Strachey would also be incomplete if the same theme were
    omitted. Bate 2015: 566 on Hughes is a supreme example: "Sylvia Plath's death
    was the central fact of Ted Hughes's life. However he tried to get away from
    it, he could not; however the biographer broadens the picture, it is her image
    that returns." Hence the final evocation of her presence as Hughes writes to a
    translator: "Her ghost has returned in recognition of the knowledge that he loved

her until the day he died. Before him stands yesterday." Portraiture: cf. Melzi d'Eril 2009: 208: Hadrian shared his creator's constitutive capacity (*MH* 389).

7. The Jewish War

1 Revolt: modern accounts include Schürer 1973: 514–57; Smallwood 1976: ch. XVI; Birley 1997a: ch. 20; Schäfer ed. 2003; Eshel 2006; Hadas-Lebel 2006: 167–93; Horbury 2014: ch. 5. Occupies: see Castellani 2011: 218. Quotation: "There is no denying it; that war in Judaea was one of my defeats." Treatment: cf. Poignault 1995: 812–23.

2 Bar Kokhba is the spelling generally used in scholarship rather than Yourcenar's Bar-Kochba. For the Aramaic name's meaning, see Horbury 2014: 1.

3 "its religious frenzies, its strange rites, and the intransigence of its god"; "the fortress of a race and of a god isolated from human kind."

4 Accounts: see in full Horbury 2014: 287–94; cf. Geiger 2016: indeterminate on Greek sources.

5 See Migliorati 2003: 249–50; 303–13.

6 See Fündling 2006: 669–75: indeterminate on date.

7 See Mildenberg 1980; 1984; cf. Zissu, Porat, Langfort, Frumkin 2011: recent finds.

8 Objects: Yadin 1971; Cotton 2003; Kloner and Zissu 2003; Shahar 2003; cf. Opper 2008: 89–97. Letters: Millar 1993: 545–52; cf. Schäfer 2003: 9: "threatening coarse tone."

9 Frick 306.

10 "The archaeological discoveries made in Israel in recent years concerning the revolt of Bar Kochba have enriched our knowledge of the war in Palestine on certain points of detail; the majority, having appeared after 1951, could not be used in the course of the present work"; cf. *HZ* 301: 26 January 1954 to the Abbé Vincent.

11 Inscriptions: *IGLS* VIII.3, with *AE* 2002: 1524–5; *AE* 2006: 1572–7; *AE* 2009: 1559–62. See E. Renan, *Mission de Phénice* (Paris 1864) Vol. 1: 258–81, with Mikesell 1969; Meiggs 1982: 85–7. Influence: Petite Plaisance has a copy of Renan's *L'Église chrétienne* (Bernier 2004: no. 3008).

12 "Quelques détails historiques mêlés dans le *Talmud* à un immense matériel légendaire viennent s'ajouter pour la guerre de Palestine au récit de l'*Histoire ecclésiastique* d'Eusèbe" ("For the war in Palestine, certain details known to be authentic have been extracted from the *Talmud*, where they lie imbedded in an immense amount of legendary material; they serve to supplement the principal account of that war as given in Eusebius' *Ecclesiastical History*").

13 Plon 1951: 318 = *OR* 550: "W.D. Gray, *The Founding of Ælia Capitolina and the Chronology of the Jewish War under Hadrian, American Journal*

of Semitic Language and Literature, 1923; A.L. Sachar, *A History of the Jews,* 1950; et Lieberman, *Greek in Jewish Palestine,* 1942." (There are minor inaccuracies in the Plon references; later printings give "S. Lieberman".) Frick 306: "[W.D. Gray] *New Light from Egypt on the Early Reign of Hadrian, Amer. Journ. of Semit. Lang. and Lit.,* 1923; R. Harris, *Hadrian's Decree of Expulsion of the Jews from Jerusalem, Harv. Theol. Rev.* XIX, 1926; W. Stinespring, *Hadrian in Palestine, Amer. Orient. Soc.* LIX, 1939. See also, apart from the German works already cited, A. von Premerstein, *Alexandrinische und jüdische Gesandte vor Kaiser Hadrian,* in *Hermes,* LVII, 1922. In French, Renan's account of Hadrian's war in Palestine, in *L'Eglise Chrétienne,* 1879, is essential still." The passage on Hadrian at Pelusium (*MH* 360–361), summarized above, is based on the *Acts of the Pagan Martyrs,* esp. the *Acts of Paulus and Antoninus* (*CPJ* 158a = Musurillo 1954: 49–59 = Smallwood 1966: no. 517), to which the item from von Premerstein here refers. Yourcenar was influenced by the views of W.D. Gray, who argued for a visit to Alexandria by Hadrian shortly after his accession in "New Light." But whether the emperor in the *Acts of Paulus* is Hadrian or Trajan and whether Hadrian's putative visit to Alexandria can stand remain unresolved issues; see Horbury 2014: 215–22.

14 Grant 1956: 294–5 (it is in fact Ben Dama's uncle, Ismaël, who disallows the doctor's intervention).

15 Reinach 1884: 1–2; 16. The editors of *HZ* II refer to two works by Reinach: *Histoire des Israélites* and *Études d'histoire juive* (1883–1888). I have not seen the latter and cannot estimate the impact made. The florid summary of the war's events from Sachar (1968: 122–3) makes clear the importance of Rabbi Akiba as the paramount expounder of Jewish law in the early age of rabbinic scholarship, and his association with Bar Kokhba, but again lacks detail on Jewish sources. Yourcenar owned *The Babylonian Talmud in Selection. Edited and translated from the original Hebrew and Aramaic by Leo Auerbach* (Philadelphia 1944 [Bernier 2004: no. 3201]). It contains one citation from Rabbi Eleazar (possibly illustrating his conservatism) and several items from Rabbi Akiba, but nothing directly pertinent to Bar Kokhba.

16 The complex comprises Mishnah, *Taanith* IV 6; Jerusalem Talmud, *Taanith* IV 8, 68d–69b; Babylonian Talmud, *Gittin* 55a–58a; Midrash Rabbah, *Lamentations* II 4 (Horbury 2014: 29; cf. Hadas-Lebel 2006: 167–8). The Mishnah and Tosefta were redacted c. 200, the Talmuds belong, or are thought to belong, respectively to c. 400 and c. 600; and some elements of the tradition are much later still; see Schürer 1973: 76; 78–9; 90–1; Goodman and Alexander 2010: 91–3 (A. Tropper); 143–4; 147; 165 (S. Stern); Horbury 2014: 22–31.

17 Horbury 2014: 379; 388.

18 Herr 1971: 136, 138, 139; 1972: 87; cf. Schürer 1979: 377–8.

19 "La visite d'Akiba à Alexandrie s'appuie sur une supposition assez souvent faite par les historiens juifs; elle est plausible, sans plus."

20 Finkelstein 1981 [1936]: 264 (whether Yourcenar knew this work is unclear); Podro 1959: 115–16; see Herr 1971: 143 for the better context.

21 Renan 1879: 188–90. See Syme 1968: 60–5; 1971a: 17–29: the patriarch was Gamaliel of the age of Theodosius; but cf. Galimberti 2010.

22 Cf. Weksler-Bdolah 2020: 51.

23 Millar 1993: 372.

24 Schäfer 2003: VII–VIII, assuming that Hadrian did indeed "stumble" into war; Hadrian figures minimally in Schäfer's preface, as if incidental to the problems raised; cf. Birley 2006b: sceptical of the conference proceedings at large.

25 Horbury 2014. Consider, for example solely, the following: 1. Chronology: "The uprising ... probably began in late 132"; the arrival of Julius Severus in Judaea "may have been in the second half of 133 or in 134"; Bar Kokhba's death and the fall of Bethar "took place probably in the late summer of 135" (287, 388, 401). 2. Causes: (a) Hadrian's refusal to rebuild the Temple: "it seems unlikely that [Hadrian] or his advisers would have wished to allow the rebuilding of the temple"; (b) the *Historia Augusta*'s apparent reference to circumcision: "Probably ... a punitive ban introduced during the suppression of the revolt ... has been transmuted here into a cause" (316). 3. Events: (a) Nabataean support: "Other unrest in Arabia probably involved members of nomadic tribes, but it is not clear that there was a major revolt among the settled Nabataeans"; (b) Jerusalem's status: "It seems likely that Jerusalem itself ... remained in Roman hands" (338, 347). 4. Numismatic evidence: (a) Rabbi Eleazar of Modin is "a not unsuitable candidate" for "Eleazar the priest" named by the rebels' coins; (b) an apparent rosette above Bar Kosiba's name "will have been intended at least to enhance his dignity, but also ... probably evoked the nickname 'star' and its messianic associations" (357, 384).

26 Plans: see Poignault 1995: 670–1: the earlier visit to Jerusalem, with the appointment of Fidus Aquila as architect deriving from Epiph. *De mens. et pond.* 14, attributable to Renan 1879: 28–9 (mentioned in the *Notebook* in the list of modified facts, as is R.H. Lacey, *The Equestrian Officials of Trajan and Hadrian* [1927]); cf. Baker 2012; Horbury 2014: 229–30; 407; 425; Poignault 1995: 812: the sentence imitates the opening of Eusebius's account of the war: "The rebellion of the Jews once more progressed in character and extent."

27 Birley 1997a: 232–3; cf. 229; Boatwright 2000: 197; Horbury 2014: 308–11; and esp. Weksler-Bdolah 2020: ch. 3: archaeology suggests that the decision to rebuild Jerusalem was made and that construction began a decade or so before Hadrian's visit of 129/130, when the city was renamed; cf. Millar 2006: 188–9: the city's colonial constitution.

28 Helm p. 201[b–e] (trans. Horbury 2014: 291–2; cf. 293).

29 Schürer 1973: 554; Birley 1997a: 276 (despite Stinespring 1939: 364); cf. Poignault 1995: 814; note esp. Renan 1879: 223–4.

30 Herr 1972: 94–8; Hadas-Lebel 2006: 185–7.

31 Cf. Herr 1972: 95. Q. Tineius Rufus: *PIR*[2] T 227: *cos. suff.* 127 (in office on 1 May); governor of Thrace before appointment to Judaea; see Syme *RP* V 546; 594; Birley 1997a: 233; Eck and Weiss 2002: 482.

32 Cf. Joseph. *BJ* 1.88. Conflation: Gergely 1988: 50: critically regarded; cf. Poignault 1995: 812.

33 Tradition (followed by Renan 1879: 192): Herr 1972: 93 n.27; Oppenheimer 2003: 67–8; Eshel 2006: 124; Hadas-Lebel 2006: 183; cf. Rabello 1995: 196 n.65; Abusch 2003: 81–4. Perspective: e.g. Juv. 14.99; Tac. *Hist.* 5.5.

34 Smallwood 1959: 336; Schürer 1973: 537.

35 Herr 1971: 133–4; cf. *EJ*[2] vol. 1: 562–3.

36 See Smallwood 1959; Rabello 1995; cf. Poignault 1995: 814. Historians do not doubt the ban on circumcision, but whether it preceded or followed the outbreak of revolt is unknown; see Horbury 2014: 311–17 (summary of views). Directives: Cass. Dio 68.2.3; Suet. *Dom.* 7.1.

37 Millar 1993: 548–52: nos. 4, 8, 9, 12, 15 (= Smallwood 1966: no. 81), 17, 20, 23, 26 (variously transliterated as "Simeon").

38 Renan 1879: 547–8 denied the identity.

39 Cf. Mildenberg 1984: 80; Poignault 1995: 818–19; but see also Horbury 20014: 386: Jewish sources to the same effect.

40 See R. Marks 1994: 18: "The Bar Koziva legends … portray R. Akiba as believing that he has discovered the name "Kosiva" hidden within the word *kokhva* of Num. 24:17. His exegesis was a form of decoding that unlocked the secret message contained within the prophecy of Balaam"; cf. Schürer 1973: 543–4; Horbury 2014: 1. For the confusion between *kokhav* ("star") and *kozav* ("lie"), see R. Marks 1994: 14. Renan 1879: 199–201 provided the essentials.

41 Mildenberg 1984: 73–5 dismissed the notion of Akiba's proclamation, or ordination, of Bar Kokhba completely, though kept Akiba as his supporter. Schäfer 2003: 2–3 dismisses the tradition altogether.

42 See 2.d.

43 Schürer 1973: 549–50; Syme *RP* VI: 353–4; Birley 1997a: 272–3.

44 "The view has been followed here of historians who consider Hadrian to have spent two years in Palestine." The note is typed, but the word "ici" is crossed out and an illegible handwritten phrase added.

45 Renan 1879: 209.

46 R. Marks 1994: 23–6; Horbury 2014: 400–1; cf. Schäfer 2003: 6–7 (sceptical).

47 Renan 1879: 198; cf. Poignault 1995: 818–19.

48 R. Marks 1994: 26.

49 Ability: Schürer 1973: 546; Mildenberg 1984: 84. Letter: Birnbaum 1954
   (Bernier 2004: no. 3199) = Smallwood 1966: no. 81 = Millar 1993: 550: no. 15.

50 Healey 2009: no. 19 (trans).

51 R. Marks 1994: 14; Horbury 2014: 380; cf. Renan 1879: 207; Poignault 1995:
   819.

52 R. Marks 1994: 21; Mildenberg 1984: 73–5; Schürer 1973: 544.

53 Horbury 2014: 384–5, with Diod. Sic. 34.2.5–11.

54 Renan 1879: 206.

55 Renan 1879: 199 (citing no source): "He invested him in a certain way before
   the people, by solemnly handing him the baton of command, and by holding his
   stirrup when he mounted his horse to begin his reign as Messiah."

56 See Millar 2000: 127: from a "pseudohistorical narrative."

57 Schürer 1973: 544.

58 Horbury 2014: 356–7: the tradition, not introduced here (cf. Renan 1879: 198),
   that Eleazar of Modin was Bar Kokhba's uncle, is dubious. Mildenberg 1984:
   29–30 disputes the identification of the two Eleazars. Epispasm: cf. Renan 1879:
   198, with Celsus, *Med.* 7.25.1–2: less dangerous on a boy than on an adult.

59 Coinage: Mildenberg 1984: 31, 68. Assertion: Sachar 1968: 122–3; cf. *EJ*[2] vol. 3:
   159: "an altar may have been erected for sacred worship."

60 Cf. Renan 1879: 194. Mildenberg 1984: 79 dismisses the statement.

61 Horbury 2014: 347 n.260: doubtful, summarizing opinions. Contrast
   Mildenberg 1984: 62: the absence of rebel coin hoards in Jerusalem means the
   city did not fall, with Schürer 1973: 545: the coin legends mean that it did; cf. *EJ*[2]
   vol. 3: 159, 162: yes and no in two sections of an article by different authors.

62 Weber 1936: 314.

63 Horbury 2014: 391; Eck 1999: 81: some suggest that the legion was the second
   legion stationed in Judaea early in Hadrian's reign instead of Legion VI Ferrata,
   otherwise taken as based at Caparcotna to the north; cf. Keppie 2000: 225–32:
   sceptical of knowing the truth.

64 *IGRR* III 174 = *ILS* 8826 = Smallwood 1966 no. 216 = Sherk 1980: no. 164C
   ("when Publicius Marcellus, because of the revolt in Judaea, left Syria"), with
   Renan 1879: 205; cf. Eck 1999: 83; Horbury 2014: 334, 388.

65 Eck 1999.

66 Usfa: Smallwood 1959: 342; Herr 1972: 117; Schürer 1979: 331; 369; *EJ*[2] vol.
   20: 431–2; Horbury 2014: 403. Prohibition: Herr 1972: 94. Martyrdom: Herr
   1972: 113–25; Schürer 1973: 552; *EJ*[2] vol. 19: 640–1; Horbury 2014: 416–17.
   Sale: Horbury 2014: 401–2 ("Abraham's oak at Mamre"); cf. Renan 1879: 210.
   Ab: Schürer 1973: 551–2; Mildenberg 1980: 319 (= August, 135); Horbury
   2014: 401. At times the likely influence of individual academic resources can be
   traced: R. Harris concluded his paper on Hadrian's so-called expulsion decree,
   in the war's aftermath, as follows: "It is interesting to observe that the edict of

expulsion of the Jews from their holy place, under pain of death for a breach of the regulation, would be the exact inversion of their own prohibition publicly set up and inscribed, with regard to the entrance of foreigners within the Sanctuary" (1926: 205–6). Hadrian precedes his reference to the ninth day of Ab in a comparable way: "Une inscription placée sur le site de Jérusalem défendit aux Juifs, sous peine de mort, de s'installer à nouveau dans ce tas de décombres; elle reproduisait mot pour mot la phrase inscrite naguère au portail du temple, et qui en interdisait l'entrée aux incirconsis" (*MH* 480: "An inscription placed on the site of Jerusalem forbade the Jews, under pain of death, to re-establish themselves anew upon that heap of rubble; it reproduced word for word the interdict formerly inscribed on the temple door, forbidding entrance to the uncircumcised"). The date, more properly the ninth of Av, is the traditional date for commemoration of the destruction of both the First and Second Temples.

67 "L'ouverture d'écoles où s'enseignaient les lettres grecques scandalisa le clergé de la vieille ville; le rabbin Joshua, homme agréable et instruit, avec qui j'avais assez souvent causé à Athènes, mais qui s'efforçait de se faire pardonner par son peuple sa culture étrangère et ses relations avec nous, ordonna à ses disciples de ne s'adonner à ces études profanes que s'ils trouvaient à leur consacrer une heure qui n'appartiendrait ni au jour ni à la nuit, puisque la loi juive doit être étudiée nuit et jour" ("The clergy of the ancient city were scandalized by the opening of schools where Greek literature was taught; the rabbi Joshua, a pleasant, learned man with whom I had frequently conversed in Athens, but who was trying to excuse himself to his people for his foreign culture and his relations with us, now ordered his disciples not to take up such profane studies unless they could find an hour which was neither day nor night, since Jewish law must be studied night and day").

68 Podro 1959; Herr 1971: 138–9; 142–3; Schürer 1979: 373–4; *EJ*² vol. 11: 450–2; cf. Horbury 2014: 302–3; Batsch 2020: 79. In the Foreword to Podro 1959, Robert Graves wrote (8): "I can think of no historical parallel to the fact that Rabbi Joshua performed in rebuilding shattered national morale during the sixty-odd years between the first Revolt against Rome and the second. He contrived to restrain his people from foolish rebellion against the temporal power, while keeping faith with the eternal; practised no deception, avoided all suspicion of self-advancement, and though going as an ambassador of Israel to three Roman emperors – Vespasian, Trajan and Hadrian – remained all the while in the closest touch with the common people."

69 "Even in the rabbi Joshua, who had long been my counselor in Jewish affairs, I had felt irreconcilable differences under that compliance and desire to please, a point where two opposite kinds of thinking meet only to engage in combat."

70 Renan 1879: 23 (with n. 1); cf. Poignault 1994: 220.

71 Renan 1879: 246; Lieberman 1942: 16.

72 "Ismael, an important member of the Sanhedrin, who supposedly adhered to
the side of Rome, let his nephew Ben-Dama die rather than accept the services
of the Greek surgeon sent to him by Tineus Rufus."

73 *EJ*² vol. 10: 83–4; 300–1; cf. Finkelstein 1981 [1936]: 253.

74 "Our best agent, Elias Ben-Abayad, who played the role of informer and spy
for Rome, was justly despised by both camps; he was nevertheless the most
intelligent man in the group, a liberal mind but a man sick at heart, torn
between love for his people and his liking for us and for our culture; he too,
however, thought essentially only of Israel. Joshua Ben-Kisma, who preached
appeasement, was but a more timid, or more hypocritical Akiba."

75 *EJ*² vol. 6: 352–3; cf. Finkelstein 1981 [1936]: 77; 111; 164; 254–6; Horbury 2014:
413. Quotation: Podro 1959: 101.

76 "Joshua Ben-Kisma, leader of the so-called moderates, who had lamentably failed
in his role of peacemaker, succumbed at about that time to the last stages of a long
illness; he died calling down upon us foreign wars and victory for Parthia."

77 Supposed: cf. Blanckeman 2014a: 15; Célo 2014: 106–11.

78 9 September 1968 to Étienne Coche de la Ferté, on receipt of an exhibition
catalogue, *Israël à travers les Âges*.

79 Gergely 1988. Echoes: note Goodman 2003: 28.

80 Savigneau 1993: 383–6. Earlier: ch. 1.

81 Cf. *PV* 241 (from 1978–9): like all imperialists Hadrian thought he only had to
appear in Palestine to convince Israelites to accept Roman civilization; naivety
was involved.

82 Jesus: according to Origen (*C. Cels.* 2.14; 2.33; 2.59), Phlegon mentioned Jesus in the
thirteenth or fourteenth books of his *Chronicles*, attributing to him foreknowledge
of the future and recording an eclipse and earthquakes under Tiberius at the time of
the Crucifixion. Renan (1879: 41–2) took this to mean that Phlegon wrote of Jesus's
miracles (cf. Poignault 1994: 220 n.31), but this is not quite what Origen says.
Whether Phlegon and Hadrian had several conversations about Jesus, as Renan
asserted, is beyond proof. But Yourcenar has Hadrian instruct Phlegon to gather
information about Jesus, his victimization by intolerant Jews, and his Orphic-like
teachings (*MH* 457). Cf. *L* 562–3: 20 September 1977: Yourcenar's opposition to all
forms of religious intransigence and dogmatism.

83 Remarked: Stern 1976–80: nos. 72b, 72c, 72d, 75 (Varro); cf. 258 (Plutarch).
Mocked: Stern 1976–80: nos. 68 (Cicero), 129 (Horace), 186 (Seneca), 194
(Petronius), 230 (Quintilian), 240, 241, 243, 245 (Martial), 281 (Tacitus), 299,
301 (Juvenal).

84 "No people but Israel has the arrogance to confine truth wholly within the
narrow limits of a single conception of the divine, thereby insulting the
manifold nature of the Deity, who contains all; no other god has inspired his
worshipers with disdain and hatred for those who pray at different altars."

85 Cf. Di Méo 2014: 89–91; Célo 2014: 106–11.

86 Savigneau 1993: 383–6; Sarde 1995a: 261; 1995b.

87 See esp. the remark attributed to Michel: "«En voilà du moins qui peuvent se dire véritablement nobles, puisque leur généalogie remonte le cours des siècles!»" (*YO* 282: "at least some of them can truly call themselves noble, since their genealogies date back for centuries!"). Renan: Said 1994 [1979]: 133–4; 140–2; 149–51; 170; 231–2; 234; but see the historiographical comments of Horbury 2014: 72–4. In Edwardian England, even to his wife, Leonard Woolf was "my Jew" (Lee 1996: 308–9; cf. 669).

88 Cf. Goslar 1996: 81. See also *HZ* II 180; *HZ* III 207; *L* 298; *PV* 153.

89 E. Marks 1990: 212–13.

90 "And such a reader would mistake for a professional anti-Semite this aristocrat whose habitual irony towards Jews is a matter of caste."

91 E. Marks 1990: 219 n.3.

92 See Millar 1993: ch. 10 (emphatically).

93 For a balanced assessment, see esp. Terneuil 2006. For remarks beyond redemption, note Henderson 1968 [1923]: 221 (cf. Podro 1959: 111 n.2 on the bias throughout); Weber 1936: 314; cf. 1973 [1907]: 275.

94 Eck 1999; Eck and Foerster 1999; Eck 2003. Julius Severus: Birley 2005a: 129–32, with esp. *ILS* 1056 = Smallwood 1966: no. 217; Birley 2017: 59: exceptional transfer of an imperial legate from a three-legion to a two-legion province. Publicius Marcellus: Dąbrowa 2017: he perhaps moved from Syria in late summer 132. Tel Shalem: Bowersock 2003 dates the arch to 130, but there was no military victory then to commemorate.

95 Kloner and Zissu 2003.

96 Josephus: *BJ* 6.420; 7.23–4; 7.40; 7.96; 7.138, with Bradley 2004: 308–9.

97 Note esp. *HA Hadr.* 10.2, on food; for its conventionality, see Fündling 2006: 544.

98 *PV* 276 (from 1980): "découragement" of Hadrian's subsequent memory (cf. *MH* 486).

99 "an initial stage of hydropic heart."

100 "cette espèce de bouffissure des traits caractéristique des cardiaques."

101 Petrakis 1980: citing the relevant personality features: "competitive, achievement-oriented, involved in multiple activities with deadlines, impatient with slowness in others, like to set a rapid work pace, and tend to be hostile and aggressive" (90); cf. Birley 1994: 203; 1997a: 302, 357 n.6; Opper 2008: 57–9.

102 "Utiliser pour mieux comprendre un commencement de maladie de cœur" ("Make good use, the better to understand Hadrian's malady, of the first symptoms of a heart ailment").

103 1965: J.E. Howard 2018: 279 (quotation). Weakness: cf. *PV* 66 (from 1968); *YO* 224. 1985: Savigneau 1993: 424: heart attack on 18 September 1985; surgery in Bangor on 9 October 1985.

104 Mildenberg 1984: 97; cf. 107 n.308.

105 Syme *RP* VI 354, with the change of name from Judaea to Syria Palaestina an indication of "the personality or caprice of the ruler"; cf. Morwood 2013: 95: the Bar Kokhba war as an "anticipation of the holocaust"; accordingly, "[t]his genocidal process towards the end of Hadrian's life makes it impossible to ignore an uncompromisingly brutal aspect to his make-up."

106 Form: Šubert 2015. Fixation: cf. *DR* 209–10. "Manifesto": Brown 1967: 168; cf. 171. Most obvious: *Conf.* 2.4–10; 4.4–8; 8.6–12, with Lane Fox 2015: 140–3; 282. Questions: *Conf.* 3.2, with Lane Fox 2015: 71–4.

107 Consensus: Schürer 1973: 549–50; Millar 1993: 107; Birley 1997a: 272–3, with esp. n.38 (following Syme *RP* VI 353–4); cf. Fündling 2006: 676; Horbury 2014: 283–4 (uncertain). Q. Lollius Urbicus: *ILS* 1065 = Smallwood 1966: no. 220; cf. Birley 2005a: 138. Hadrian's request to the architect Apollodorus of Damascus for advice on the construction of siege engines in the *Poliorcita* attributed to him, if genuine (cf. Birley 1997a: 273; Migliorati 2003: 243), fits the context of the Jewish War (Millar 1964: 65–6; cf. Weksler-Bdolah 2020: 57–8), but does not require Hadrian's extended presence in Judaea. Note Birley 2003: 426 n.10: the senatorial despatch does not necessarily support Hadrian's presence at the front.

108 Eck, Holder, Pangerl 2010; *RMD* III 158, with Eck, Holder, Pangerl 2010: 197.

109 Illyricum: *AE* 1957: no. 135 = Smallwood 1966: no. 195 with Syme *RP* VI 355. Maroneia: (ch. 2): the inscription is very fragmentary; observe for possible consequence Jones 2011: 324: "As he returned from the Judaean war, he (*sc.* Hadrian) may have crossed from Asia via Samothrace and thence to Maroneia and Abdera, and so have learned of the plight which officials and private persons had imposed on these cities by their importunate demands." It may be that Hadrian did not remain in Judaea into early 133 (Birley 2006b: 680).

110 *IGRR* 1.149 = Oliver 1989: no. 86 (quoted in ch. 2). The promise was not fulfilled until nine years later by Antoninus Pius: *IGRR* 1.146 = Oliver 1989: no. 128; see Pleket 1973: 197; 208; 227; cf. Millar 1977: 457; Gordillo Hervás 2017: 86. Yourcenar seems not to have known *IGRR* 1.149; it is not listed among her inscriptional sources in the indices of Poignault 1995.

111 *AE* 2006.1403a–c = *SEG* 56 (2006): 1359. Games: Bowersock 1965: 83–4.

112 Schürer 1973: 549–50 supported Hadrian's early participation in the war and departure once Roman success seemed guaranteed. In contrast, Smallwood 1976: 450–1 supported a late appearance after 5 May 134, with Hadrian remaining until the end. Halfmann 1986: 209–10, omitting the Jewish material, rejected all arguments for Hadrian's participation. Poignault 1988b: 25–7 now requires revision.

113 Weber 1936: 313–14; 319; cf. 1973 [1907]: 275–6 (rejected by Syme *RP* VI 357).

114 Cf. Birley 1997a: 275: it was *"No doubt* Sextus Julius Severus ... to whom the dead leader was brought" (my emphasis).
115 *AE* 2006.1403 lines 28–32 (trans. Jones 2007). The statement follows a long history of Roman thought that penalties for crimes should be paid with the body. Voice: consistent with evidence cited in ch. 2.
116 *AE* 2006.1403a–c, on which see, with Jones 2007, Slater 2008: discussion of the original publication by G. Petzl and E. Schwertheim, *Hadrian und die dionysischen Künstler* (Bonn 2006). The inscription belongs to 134, but an effort has been made to assign it to 133 (Schmidt 2009, with the comments of Pleket in *SEG* 56 [2006] 1359): again, almost every item of evidence is open to question.
117 No indication: cf. Syme *RP* VI 354: a military diploma from September 134 (*CIL* XVI 79) also lacks the designation. Award: *ILS* 318 = Smallwood 1966: no. 117, conventionally dated 29 December 135; *SB* 6944 = Smallwood 1966: no. 462, dated 31 May 136; cf. Birley 1997a: 287; Eck and Pangerl 2015: 238: confident that reference to the second salutation began only in the early months of 137. Yourcenar converted the salutation into an actual triumph (*MH* 482).
118 Sibyl: *Sibylline Oracles* 12.165–75.

8. Rise and Fall

1 I quote here in (literal) translation only; see the *Endnote* for the French text.
2 *ER* 106–9 = *MH* 474–6. *ER* 102–3 has a footnote in which Yourcenar refers to the information from Jean Charbonneaux on indications in Hadrian's portraiture of heart disease and hypertension.
3 Quotation: Watt 2001 [1957]: 13: in relation to "the novelist's primary task."
4 Contrast with the concentration on the sole characteristic of "restlessness," invoked since at least Gibbon *Decline and Fall* I 36, is strong. Framework: cf. *SP* 806.
5 Carcopino: see *OR* 549–50, unflatteringly. Taken: the phrase "longues recherches" appears in the *Carnets* (*CNMH* 519). Alluded: "cette fameuse *Historia Augusta* aussi pleine de canulars que d'informations précieuses et dont Sir Ronald Syme vient de nous révéler que, contrairement aux opinions admises dont vous vous faites vous-même l'écho, elle est bien l'œuvre d'un seul auteur" (*DAF* 64: "that notorious *Historia Augusta*, a work as full of hoaxes as of trustworthy information, and which Sir Ronald Syme has just revealed to us, contrary to received opinions that you yourself echo, is indeed the work of a single author"). Syme's debt to Dessau went unmentioned.
6 Association: see the opening interview in Ledentu, de Chantal, Salamon eds. 2014. Secretary-General: Edmond 2017: 157–8.

7 *The Roman Revolution* was published on 7 September 1939, shortly after Britain's declaration of war against Germany. Specialists in the United States knew of it by the late 1940s. Lily Ross Taylor wrote to Syme from Bryn Mawr College on 20 March 1946 indicating that she had read the book, as had a visitor, Franz Neumann, who was speaking at Bryn Mawr on the revival of political life in postwar Germany. Similarly, J.H. Oliver wrote to Syme from the Johns Hopkins University on 12 February 1949, describing the work as "the most important political and social history of Rome since Mommsen." (Letters preserved in the Syme Archive of the Bodleian Library's Special Collections at Oxford [cf. Birley 2020: 2 n.3; cf. 12].)

8 Syme 1958: chs. IV, XXI, XXVI, XXVII (the proposal that Tacitus composed the *Annals* mostly under Hadrian was later withdrawn). Yourcenar made the episode of the consulars an occasion for a shrewd assessment by her Hadrian of the consequences involved (*MH* 362–5).

9 Topical studies: see ch. 1 n.67. Prosopography: see Bowersock 1994b: viii: Syme's deductions as "precise and scientific" (questionable in my view).

10 1958: 249; *RP* IV 46; V 551; VI 174 n.55: a "scabrous theme."

11 Quotation: *RP* I 57. Autocrat: observe Veyne 2005: 74 n.209: "En 1964, un colloque international sur les empereurs romains d'Espagne se réunit à Itálica. Comme l'un de nous demandait à Sir Ronald Syme son avis sur Hadrien, ce grand seigneur répondit en français: «Oh, Hadrien était un Führer, un Duce, un Caudillo.» Un jeune savant espagnol, à ces mots, sourit amèrement. Le lendemain, don García Bellido vint nous faire savoir discrètement de ne jamais parler de politique." The colloquium was the occasion for delivery of "Hadrian the Intellectual" (ch. 2).

12 *RP* VI 160 (no alternative structure was countenanced).

13 Quotation: *RP* VI 164 (making possible collocation with the preference of Augustus and Hadrian for Atticizing discourse in the promotion of "old" over "Asiatic" Greece [Spawforth 2012: 264–70]). Syme made his judgment as the holder of a degree in French literature (Bowersock 1994a: 542: M.A. in Latin and French in 1924 from the University of Auckland). The writing surely meets the tests of coherence and intelligibility (*RP* VI 179).

14 Syme's antipathy for Weber, due almost certainly to the latter's wartime Nazi affiliation (M.T. Griffin 2005: 37 n.73), his dismissal of Henderson, and his ridicule of Carcopino are all patent. Birley 1994: 177 n.6 is generous: the lecture "was aimed at correcting excessive credulity." Syme would not have appreciated Yourcenar's views on Weber: she commended his work highly in the *Note*, and hoped shortly after *Mémoires* was published to make grateful contact with him; he had died, however, before she could do so: she had come to know his works only in 1949 and was pleased to discover that his chapter in the first edition of the *Cambridge Ancient History* confirmed her own ideas (*OR* 549; *HZ* 108: 12 December 1951; 113–14: 28 December 1951); cf. Bruggisser 1994: 40–4.

15 *RP* VI 165–70 (quotations: 169). Pedanius is usually thought to have been put to death at the end of the reign on allegations of treason (see Birley 1997a: 291).

16 *RP* VI 168; 170–2; 178 (quotation: 171).

17 *RP* VI 172–3; 176–7; 179.

18 *RP* VI 178 (quoting Gibbon); 180.

19 *RP* VI 162.

20 Cf. *RP* VI 178: reference to the second edition of the *Oxford Classical Dictionary*.

21 Biographer: Savigneau 1993: 382, 439. Legal name: see ch 1. M.T. Griffin 2005: 25–6 = 2018: 332 thought Syme "amused" by the nom de plume, which hardly explains his "waspish description" of her. I see nothing inherently sinister in the adoption of a pen name. Contrast Syme's habit of referring to himself in the third person (e.g. *RP* VI 182), "a somewhat unnerving habit, whether in literature or in life" (Harold Bloom, *Shakespeare: The Invention of the Human* [New York 1988: 445]). Pseudonym: *PV* 229 (from 1978–9): "Et j'avais déjà publié un livre, et je portais déjà, presque exclusivement, le nom de Marguerite Yourcenar, qui est un pseudonyme, comme vous savez, mais qui est devenu légal entre-temps" ("And I had already published a book, and I already used, almost exclusively, the name of Marguerite Yourcenar, which is a pseudonym, as you know, but which meantime became legal"): in reply to a question about her early career.

22 Syme refers to *Mémoires* as a work from 1951 (e.g. *RP* VI 163), which I take to mean the original Plon edition. The quotations bear this out, as does the *Note*'s size cited (*RP* VI 163). He gave Yourcenar's description of the life of Hadrian there as "l'un des textes les plus solides" in the *Historia Augusta*, but she later changed this to "l'un des meilleurs textes de cette collection" (*OR* 546). In 1951 Plon had disallowed a longer *Note*.

23 *RP* VI 162 n.14; 174 n.54; the only other item registered on Yourcenar's background was a slight newspaper article, "Memories of a History Woman" (*The Observer*, 29 April 1984), apparently read a few days before delivery of the lecture (*RP* VI 165 n.20).

24 Recognized: *RP* VI 165. Imperfect: no knowledge for instance of *TGS* on the Spanish clan. The remarks at *RP* VII 619 n.87 are especially sharp. Inadequacies: Gibson 2018: n.94.

25 Plon 1951: 311; *OR* 543; Frick: 312–13.

26 Revisions: Yourcenar frequently refers to corrections necessary from printing errors, due either to her or to her printer. The former could be explained by inattention or fatigue (e.g. *HZ* IV 183). Syme was likewise alert to "inadvertence" (a favoured word). The revisions can admittedly lead to perplexity. Yourcenar knew the reference in Apuleius's *Apology* 11.3 to Hadrian and the poet Voconius (cf. Poignault 1995: 591–2: Voconius's funeral oration

in *Mémoires* derives from this text), but Apuleius's name does not appear in any French version of the *Note* that I have seen. It does, however, appear in the English translation (Frick 302). Attianus: *RP* VI 165 (with n.19).

27 Graindor 1934: 1 (see *OR* 548); cf. *HZ* II 68: she followed Bardon in *Les Empereurs et les lettres latines* in assigning Juvenal's exile to Hadrian's reign. On Plotina and the Epicurean inscriptions, see ch. 5; and on Arrian's wife (*RP* VI 165), see ch. 9. Syme *RP* VI: 168–9 maintained that Yourcenar's trust was excessive in the report of Trajan's resistance to the marriage to Sabina and of Plotina's involvement; it originated, he divined, from Hadrian's autobiography (*RP* VI 402).

28 *RP* VI 166. (Picard, incidentally, did not challenge Italica as the birthplace.)

29 *RP* VI 167; cf. *ER* 103.

30 *RP* VI 165.

31 *RP* VI 167.

32 *RP* VI 175; 179.

33 *RP* VI 169, with Cass. Dio 69.1. That documents were sometimes produced for public consumption on political matters is not in question (e.g. the Tiberian *Senatus Consultum de Cn. Pisone patre* [on which see M.T. Griffin 1997 = 2018: ch. 15]); it is the assumption of habitual practice and unattested examples that is problematic.

34 *RP* VI 170; 172; 173; 174.

35 Wiseman 1998: crediting Syme with an almost mystical knowledge of the Roman past; cf. Pelling 2015: 233–4: approvingly. Quotations: *RP* VI 165.

36 *RP* VI 164.

37 *RP* VI 171 n.42.

38 Watt 2001 [1957]: 176.

39 Pronouncement: Syme 1999: 93. Consequence: cf. M.T. Griffin 2005 = 2018: 325–8. Yourcenar's poetic self-affirmation, "quelqu'un qui est «en contact»" (*YO* 209), was also overlooked.

40 Savigneau 1990: 393 (from 1957): a fictional fact on this view can claim authenticity.

41 Syme 2013: 134.

42 Summary: but see Syme 1968: 219: "The criterion … is the probable (and provisional)." Stylist: Sherwin-White (1959: 140) notably called Syme's *Tacitus* "a contribution to literature rare in the writing of professional history." Quotation: *RP* VI 180.

43 *RP* VI 262; VI 392; III 927; cf. *RP* II 526: "Revolutionary leaders tend to collect partisans of dubious morality or excessive in their pretensions"; IV 312: "Ambiguity is normally inherent in the comportment of an emperor towards the actions and policy of his predecessor." For the idiom, cf. Gibbon *Decline and Fall* VI 145: "The observation, that in every age and climate ambition

has prevailed with the same commanding energy, may abate the surprise of a philosopher; but while he condemns the vanity, he may search the motive of this universal desire to obtain and hold the sceptre of dominion."

44 Syme 1958: 233–4 (cf. *RP* II 673); *RP* VI 103; IV 295; V 571.

45 Quotation: Syme *RP* III 949. Question: a personal factor may have been involved. A friendship with Jacqueline de Romilly, doyenne of Thucydidean studies, may date from the time of Syme's appointment to the Conseil international (Edmond 2017: 157–8). She herself spoke of him as a friend first encountered through meetings of the Fédération Internationale des Études Classiques (de Romilly and Grandazzi 2003: 21). In 1988 she became the second woman to enter the Académie française (Brémond 2019: 132–3; cf. de Romilly and Grandazzi 2003: 29). G.W. Bowersock has suggested to me (pers. comm.) that Syme's assault was motivated by annoyance that Yourcenar preceded her. Yourcenar mentioned her in 1979 in answer to a question about a woman's entry into the Académie, noting her admission already into the Académie des Inscriptions et Belles-Lettres (*RC* 131; see Peyroux 2011).

46 The lecture has had no obvious impact on Yourcenarian criticism, whether literary (e.g. Hébert 2012, Dezon-Jones 2014, Brochard and Pinon 2014) or historical (e.g. Poignault 2007a). See Bonali Fiquet 1994: 65; Saint 1994; Calandra, Adembri, Giustozzi 2013: 83 n.9; Poignault 2000 for awareness but no engagement. Note Goslar 1998: 171 n.217: "Spartien est un des auteurs de *L'Histoire Auguste*, il a également écrit *Vita Hadriani* et *Vita Aelii Caesaris*"; T.D. Allman in Deprez 2012: 148: "érudition méticuleuse"; Fréris 2019: 282: "une érudition qui ne fait aucun doute."

47 Syme 1983: 12 (and often elsewhere). As far as I know, M.T. Griffin 2005 = 2018: 325–38 is the only classical scholar to have written on the essay.

48 Quotation: Balsdon 1954–5: 467. Poem: quoted below.

49 Several items: *HZ* 245: March 21, 1953; *HZ* 268: 23 May 1953; *HZ* 508: 25 January 1956. The letter to Mozzillo continued that few historians trust Spartianus completely, but he had to be used and was generally superior to most of the other authors ("quasi barbares") of the collection.

50 Magie I: xxxii.

51 In theory: cf. Poignault 2007b: 266: doubtful. Dedicatee: "Hermanno Dessau DDLM Editor."

52 Magie II xxxii–xxxvi (cf. xiiii–xv: Mommsen). The groups are as follows: A: major lives: Hadrian, Pius, Marcus Aurelius, Commodus, Pertinax, Didius Julianus, Septimius Severus, Caracalla; B: minor lives: Aelius, Verus, Avidius Cassius, Pescennius Niger, Clodius Albinus, Geta; C: the lives of Elagabalus and Severus Alexander; D: the lives of the Maximini, the Gordians, Maximus and Balbinus; E: the lives attributed to the author "Pollio"; F: the lives attributed to the author "Vopiscus."

53 "two centuries of confused arguments about the authors and respective dates of the groups A, B, C, D, E, F."

54 *HZ* II 99–100, with Poignault 2007b: 265–9 (essential). Yourcenar gave the date of publication of Bardon's book in the *Note* (from first to last editions) as 1944, and spelled his first name "Henri" (both still in the Pléiade: *OR* 548). A second revised and corrected edition appeared in 1968, a copy of which she owned (Bernier 2004: no. 3022). She admired his later work, *La Littérature latine inconnue* (e.g. *HZ* II 335), and had copies of both its volumes (Bernier 2004: nos. 3058, 3059). Orengo became a lifetime friend.

55 In 1963 she referred to the subject of her essay as "les historiens de l'*Historia Augusta*" (*HZ* III 293: 19 January 1963), and in 1964 still spoke of the authors of the *Historia Augusta* in the plural (*HZ* IV 46: 15 February 1964). In 1967 she wrote that three months of intense work had been necessary before she could write her essay, despite having thought herself adequately prepared from her preparations for *Mémoires* (*HZ* IV 478: 13 January 1967). I wonder whether the 1954 impression of Magie's third Loeb volume was acquired in 1957 in connection with the new project.

56 "the slow political and cultural disintegration of the ancient world." Note also "l'histoire d'un monde qui s'en va" ("the history of a disappearing world"), wording that reappears in the essay itself.

57 27 November 1957.

58 Cf. *Chronologie* XXVII.

59 21 March 1959; 2 May 1959.

60 Confusion is apparent: P.K. Marshall in L.D. Reynolds ed. 1988 [1983]: 354 dates the Bambergensis, a page of which is illustrated in Opper 2008: 27 fig. 12, to the later ninth century; it was "written at Fulda" and copied from the Palatinus. Magie (I: xxv) dates the Bambergensis to "the ninth or tenth century" and (I: xxviii) mentions that the Palatinus was in Heidelberg in the late sixteenth century until sent to Rome. Perhaps this is the source of Yourcenar's remarks. Perhaps the reference to Munich has something to do with the Murbach manuscript, also from the ninth century, only a fragment of which now survives, as Marshall states. Whether Yourcenar studied Hohl's preface summarizing his earlier studies of the manuscript tradition is unclear; cf. Poignault 2007b: 268.

61 See *HZ* II 270–1: 13 October 1958 to Noël; *HZ* II 276: 19 October 1958 to Jaffé; *HZ* II 296: 11 March 1959 to Moras; *HZ* II 299: 21 March 1959 to Moras; *HZ* II 300: 31 March 1959 to Noël; *HZ* II 313: 9 April 1959 to Moras; *HZ* II 322–4: 13 April 1959 to Noël; *HZ* II 328: 2 May 1959 to Noël; *HZ* II 354: 17 June 1959 to Noël; *HZ* II 421–2: 4 December 1959; *HZ* II 449: 15 March 1960 to Moras.

62 bMS Fr 372 (41), 26 January 1956; 29 December 1956; 1 March 1957.

63 *HZ* II 335: 8 May 1959; *HZ* IV 132–3: 17 August 1964; cf. *HZ* II 405–7.

64 Names: *SBI* 6, 7, 8, 10, 11, 16. Qualified: *SBI* 7, 12. Quotations: "Spartianus, or the biographer who assumes this name"; "Spartianus, or the anonymous author who borrows that name."

65 Matters of debate: *SBI* 6–8, 11, 16 (reading "IIᵉ" for "IIIᵉ"). Quotation: "error and mendacity."

66 "almost a total imposture."

67 Bardon 1956: 270 with n.1; 272 n.1.

68 Bardon 1964: 320, where *Mémoires* is warmly commended. Syme was dismissive of Bardon (1971a: 249; 271; 289; 1983: 79; 95; 213), but he appears not to have pursued the reference in *Crépuscule* to Yourcenar's essay, which appeared twenty years later in Italian translation as the introduction to Soverini 1983.

69 "The essay, separated from the volume for which it is due to serve as preface, should be called *Reflections on the Historia Augusta* or, quite simply, *The Historia Augusta*. It is about 5000 words. As you will see, the subject is taken from antiquity, but in some respects it has an interest for the present moment, and for all time." Yourcenar thanked Noël for sending two copies of the issue of *Le Figaro littéraire* in which the essay appeared (*HZ* II 354: 17 June 1959). Characteristically, she noted a small misprint and lamented the title used. The editors of *HZ* II (271 n.1) write that the essay was divided into two parts spread over three pages with the heading "Marguerite Yourcenar, author of *Memoirs of Hadrian*" (cf. *HZ* II 370) and the sub-heading, chosen by the editor, "When does history tell the truth? Historians from century to century transform the image ("visage") of great men." Subsequent page headings were "History and truth," and "Can justice be rendered to men of the past?" Yourcenar disapproved. The article also had four illustrations apparently submitted by her to be chosen from portrait busts of Caracalla, Antoninus Pius, Julia Domna, and the baths of Caracalla or Diocletian. She approved the German title, *Betrachtungen zur Historia Augusta*, on 15 March (*HZ* II 449).

70 Note the date specified at *HZ* II 296: "le recueil de chroniques du IVᵉ siècle" ("collection of fourth-century chronicles").

71 "And yet it is impossible for modern historians of Antiquity to ignore the *Historia Augusta*; the very same people who deny its value are obliged to make use of it regardless" (anticipating the later comment to Mozzillo).

72 Import: cf. *HZ* III 109: 12 August 1961 to Noël. Relevance: *HZ* II 323: 13 April 1959 to Noël: "la constante comparaison entre la crise du IIIᵉ siècle et les dangers qui planent sur notre monde" ("the constant comparison between the third century crisis and the dangers that overhang our world"). For critical discussion, see esp. Vergniolle de Chantal n.d.; Poignault 1991, 2000: technical issues of incidental interest alone; Saint 1994: 74–6: Yourcenar's awareness of the text's shortcomings; Hébert 2012: 244–59 (assigning the *Historia Augusta* to the third century).

73 Contrast Hébert 2012: 244: Yourcenar more sensitive to the idea of historical transition (rather than rupture) than I see myself.

74 "it is less in the statement of facts than in the interpretation made of the facts that error and mendacity often flourish in the *Historia Augusta*."

75 Quotation: "the world had so altered as to render the great Antonines' way of life and of thought virtually impenetrable." But cf. Poignault 2000: 200: access was possible to Marius Maximus and Syme's Ignotus. Revolution: the rise of Christian Latin literature is unconsidered: the names of Ambrose, Jerome, and Augustine are conspicuously absent.

76 "this cultivated man, devoted to the cause of religious tolerance, friend and protector of the great Plotinus, preserving certain bygone refinements in an age of anarchy, seems to have been even more misunderstood, if possible, than calumniated by his mediocre portraitist."

77 "A dreadful odor of humanity rises from this book"; "the man-in-the-street and the man-on-the-backstairs."

78 Cf. Bardon 1964: 31: "L'histoire quotidienne de Rome s'agite sous nos yeux. Costumes, cuisine, hygiène, parfums, jeux de cirque, défilés, distributions de blé au peuple, d'argent à l'armée, tout vient à nous pêle-mêle, mais ce brassage est celui de la vie" ("The daily history of Rome unfolds before our eyes. Dress, cuisine, hygiene, perfumes, circus games, processions, grain distributions to the people, donatives to the army, everything comes to us *pêle-mêle*, but this is the hotch-potch of life").

79 Poetic: cf. Saint 1994: 76. Quotation: "the emperor in military garb, his African complexion blanched by disease and the northern climate." (Yourcenar knew of course that Severus died at York on 4 February 211.)

80 "Hadrian's countenance at once judicious and dreamy, his nervous mouth and his features soon swollen by the advance of dropsy."

81 Tel Shalem: see ch. 1; British Museum: Opper 2008: fig. 124. Contrast E. Clark 2015 [1952]: a repulsive face.

82 Boatwright 1987: 243–6.

83 Veil: cf. Syme *RP* I 57; II 742; III 1170; 1389; cf. 1958: 10–18 (Nerva's adoption of Trajan). Contrast Saint 1994: 81: Yourcenar missed the humour of the *Historia Augusta* (following Syme). Quotation: "to shoulder the wheel, to submit, or to struggle."

84 Gibbon's French title is *Décadence et chute de l'empire romain*.

85 "study of Roman decadence" (14 January 1962).

86 *SBI* 7, 19, 20, 21.

87 Bann 2002: 56–7: a Yourcenarian "preoccupation with the activist aspects of English aestheticism." Movement: defined by Jusdanis 1987: 34–7.

88 Essay: revised 1982; see Poignault 1995: 480: possible influence of Dorian Gray; cf. Hayashi 2014: Yourcenar's strictures on British hypocrisy; Fréris 2004: 188; 2019: *décadence* as a loss of humanism, and eventually as physical and emotional decline, influenced by Cavafy.

89 4 September 1963 to Claude Chevreuil; cf. *L* 211: 10 October 1964: critical of Pater's *Marius*. An aesthetic reference occurs in a different context, a definition of the age of Hadrian as the last age of Greek "romanticism," with its tastes for the archaic in language and aesthetic mysticism ("mysticisme esthétique"), its combination of passion and melancholia, and its appetite for the exotic (*HZ* 567: 18 July 1956).

90 "We must avoid making Hadrian a kind of insipid Des Esseintes"; cf. *HZ* III 427: "un constructeur" not "un décadent."

91 "Catastrophe and ruin will come; disorder will triumph, but order will too, from time to time." Cycle: Gaudin 2007: 27; Hébert 2012: 252–9; Blanchet-Douspis 2014 (with reference to statements on Western decline in the essays *Diagnostic de l'Europe* and *Improvisation sur Innsbruck* [*EM* 1649–55; 450–9]); cf. Morley 2005. Stoic view: Vergniolle de Chantel n.d.; cf. Body 1995; Hébert 2012: 246, 249: possible *Annaliste* influence.

92 The extract, which has no version in her *Journal*, is ambiguous in its use of the word "man" to mean both humankind and Hadrian himself; if intended as a comment on what might be called Hadrian's spirituality, it requires much elaboration.

93 Gustave Flaubert, *Correspondance* III ed. J. Bruneau (Gallimard: Pléiade 1991): 191 = F. Steegmuller ed., *The Letters of Gustave Flaubert 1857–1880* (Cambridge MA 1982): 20. Lucretius: note Julien 2014b: 232 n.5.

94 "in the pure mirror of humanism."

95 Hopkins 1999. For challenges, see esp. Liebeschuetz 1979; MacMullen 1981; Wardman 1982; Price 1984; Turcan 1996 [1989].

96 Flaubert's sentence was quoted by Jean d'Ormesson at Yourcenar's reception into the Académie (*DAF* 64), and has a continuing appeal in critical scholarship (Sanz 1994: 211; Medeiros 1994: 200; 1996: 82; Hörmann 1996: 6; Julien 2002: 155–6); see in contrast *YO* 267–8.

97 Cf. *L* 220: 3 February 1965 to Lidia Storoni Mazzolani; see Blanchet-Douspis 2008: 388–9; 2014; Bardon comparably remarked that the *Historia Augusta* is the best witness both to a moribund Rome and "la tragédie d'une civilisation qui est la nôtre" (1964: 36).

98 Mussolini's name is omitted from the Préface of *DR* (163), but appears in the English translation's Afterword (172).

99 Instability: but see J.E. Howard 2018: 136–8: financial resources on arrival not deficient.

100 "I confess to you … that the state of the world has thrown me into a crisis of despair from which I have not yet recovered" (4 February 1957 to Julia Tissameno); see Savigneau 1993: 242–3, with *SP* 736–7; Hébert 2012: 264–71.

101 "a period when all ideologies and all systems are in disgrace" (29 November 1957 to Carmen D'Aubreby).

102 "The situation is everywhere (and especially perhaps in France) so serious that one can only pray, with whatever conviction or belief there may be, for those who govern to be 'inspired' in the sense of justice, wisdom, and simply common sense. It is in this way, and in this way only, that I pray for the government of de Gaulle" (26 June 1958); cf. *HZ* II 392: 7 October 1959 to Constantin Dimaras.

103 "my goal was to demonstrate that the evils that cause a civilization to die are not the scandals or the novelettish crimes that popular history seizes on, but a certain baseness, a certain inertia, a certain insensible debasement of the public spirit and of culture."

104 12 August 1961; 19 November 1961; 8 January 1963; cf. *PV* 232–3 (from 1978–9).

105 "on the veracity of the historians of the *Historia Augusta* and what they teach us – in spite of themselves, as it were – about the civilization of their own time" (I think "véracité" here means the truth not of factual accuracy but of human behaviour); "the eternal tragedy of history: our inability to resist the evils from which we are dying, or even to recognize them clearly." The extract continues: "Les critiques ne s'y trompent pas, qui citent souvent cet essai dans des articles sur la politique de ce temps" ("Critics are not wrong when often citing this essay in articles on contemporary politics").

106 "la continuelle attaque contre la mégalomanie de l'homme moderne" (8 October 1970). Discipline: *L* 359: "Assurément, l'imagination et la sympathie (ou l'antipathie) jouent et doivent jouer partout leurs rôles, mais en matière d'histoire et de critique un rôle *controlé*, soumis non seulement à la nécessité de faire vrai, qui s'impose aussi au romancier, mais sous une forme un peu différente, mais de ne rien avancer qui ne soit authentique ou prouvable" ("To be sure, imagination and sympathy [or antipathy] play and must play their roles everywhere, but in a historical and critical context a *controlled* role, subject not only to the need to write truthfully, which the novelist is also obliged to do, though in a rather different form, but to propose nothing that is not authentic or provable").

107 Cf. Gaudin 1994: 97–8; 2007: 27–8: occasional notes of optimism in the essay.

108 "Bien plus, ils auraient même le droit de prend ombrage de cette attitude de franc-tireur" ("Indeed, they could rightly take offence at this irregular stance." Full extract quoted in ch. 4). Syme's undisputed eminence aside, the Bryce lecture must be acknowledged as a curiosity irrelevant to any estimation of *Mémoires*.

109 Bradley 2022.

110 Shown in the Petite Plaisance Trust's guide to the house (*Petite Plaisance: Marguerite Yourcenar 1903–1987*: 10).

111 The poem appeared first as one of six poems collectively entitled "Recoins du cœur" in *Le Manuscrit autographe* no. 31 (January 1931): 103–5; it was essentially unchanged when republished in *Les Charités d'Alcippe et d'autres poèmes* (Liège 1956) and *CA*; see Halley 2005: 385, 558; for English translation see *The Alms of Alcippe, Translated by Edith R. Farrell* (New York 1982): 40.

112 Stone: Goslar 1998: 210 (photograph). Companion: cf. Koelb 1998: 111–14: one of the "master-texts" on which *Mémoires* is built (dubious in my view).

9. The Isle of Achilles

1 Arr. *Peripl. M. Eux.* 21.1–23.4 (trans. Liddle); see Stadter 1980: 32–9; Bosworth 1993: 242–53. Temple: Rusyaeva 2003: literary and archaeological evidence. Allusion: Stadter 1980: 38; Silberman 1993: 302; Birley 1997a: 264.

2 The introductory sentence alone shows invention: *"Conformément aux ordres reçus, j'ai terminé la circumnavigation du Pont-Euxin"* (*MH* 499: *"I have completed the circumnavigation of the Black Sea, in conformity with the orders received"*); see Poignault 1995: 433–9: probable use of the translation by A. Baschmakoff, *La Synthèse des Périples Pontiques* (Paris 1948), a copy of which Yourcenar owned (Bernier 2004: no. 3264). Implied: *HZ* 474–6: 24 July 1955 to Constantin Coukadis (see below).

3 Responds: *MH* 500–1 (quoted below). Thought: Burgess 2009: 126–31; Rood 2011: 152. Understood: *CNMH* 534: "discrète allusion aux amours perdues" ("discreet allusion to a lost love"); cf. Poignault 1995: 439.

4 Woolf: Lee 1999 [1996]. Comparable examples: e.g. (of literary figures) Booth 2014; Parker 2016; Greene 2021.

5 See Wardle 2014: 424–5, on Suet. *Aug.* 66.1; cf. *Iul.* 72.1; *Tit.* 7.2.

6 "I belong assuredly among the friends; indeed I feel for him this extraordinary friendship born of the understanding that comes from the attempt to follow a man in every incident of his life and of listening to his thoughts; which comes also from the fact that I would never have taken Hadrian as the model for this portrait had he not belonged to the type of men I most admire."

7 *HA Hadr.* 4.2: the senators Sosius, Papus, and Platorius Nepos, and the equestrians Attianus, Livianus, and Turbo (text restored as in Birley 2005a: 248 n.78, following H.-G. Pflaum); that is: Q. Sosius Senecio (*cos bis.* 107), Aemilius Papus, A. Platorius Nepos (*cos. suff.* 119), P. Acilius Attianus, T. Claudius Livianus, Q. Marcius Turbo (Fündling 2006: 355 marks the passage "fiktiv"; cf. 360–71 for individual details). *HA Hadr.* 15.1–8: Attianus, Nepos, Turbo (from the first list); Septicius Clarus, Eudaemon, Polyaenus, Marcellus, Heliodorus, Titianus, Ummidius Quadratus, Catilius Severus, Servianus; that is: the senators T. Atilius Titianus (*cos.* 127), L. Catilius Severus (*cos. bis* 120), C. Publicius Marcellus (*cos.* 120), C. Ummidius Quadratus (*cos.* 118), L. Julius

Servianus (*cos. ter* 134); the equestrians C. Septicius Clarus, Valerius Eudaemon, C. Avidius Heliodorus; Polyaenus is otherwise unknown (cf. Fündling 2006: 738–56). *HA Hadr*. 9.7 credits Hadrian with a commendable general affability towards his friends, commonly issuing and accepting dinner invitations and assiduously visiting the sick in the manner seen earlier as described by Aulus Gellius (ch. 2); he thereby met the expectations of a "good emperor" (Talbert 1984: 163).

8 Birley 1997a: 24; 67; 84; 102; 122; 124; 132; 134; 173; 202; 2005b: 119–24; cf. Fündling 2006: 1013–14; Tomlin 2018: 90; 91.

9 Speech: see ch. 2.

10 Similar reconstructions: see Birley 1997a: 62–3: C. Julius Antiochus Epiphanes Philoppapus (*cos*. 109), a grandson of the last king of Commagene, but also a Roman citizen known, a little after his consulship, to have resided in Athens: "Hadrian could easily have got to know Philopappus at Rome in the summer of 109" – that is during his consulship – "and could well have been invited to stay with him in Athens … It is a fair bet that their friendship began, if not in 109, then at the latest about the year 111, when Hadrian … first came to Athens." The common prosopographical assumption that all members of a family maintained identical personal relations lies behind Birley 1997a: 84; 180; 189: a further suggestion of friendship between Hadrian and Q. Pompeius Falco (*cos*.108), the son-in-law of Sosius Senecio, so that when in Sicily in the year 125, Hadrian lodged at the family estate at Centuripae. Individuals identified as friends in *Mémoires* other than during the accession crisis include L. Licinius Sura and Q. Marcius Turbo (*MH* 340), the lawyer L. Neratius Priscus (*MH* 315, 342), the literary friend Victor Voconius (*MH* 368–9), and eventually Antoninus Pius (*MH* 504), all obviously authentic figures.

11 "Arrian of Nicomedia, one of the best minds of our time, likes to recall to me the beautiful lines of ancient Terpander, defining in three words the Spartan ideal (that perfect mode of life to which Lacedaemon aspired without ever attaining it): *Strength, Justice, the Muses.*"

12 Quotation: trans. Campbell, with a fragment from Plut. *Lyc*. 21.3, though the final phrase appears in Arrian alone (Bosworth 1993: 259); cf. Poignault 1995: 440. *Tactica*: see Stadter 1978, 1980: 42–3; Bosworth 1993: 253–64; its date is inferable from Arrian's reference to Hadrian's twentieth regnal year. Yourcenar's knowledge of the *Tactica* is confirmed by an entry in the *Notebook*, "all[usion] au *De Tactica*" (cf. also Alexander 1938: 175).

13 Career: Halfmann 1979: no. 56; Stadter 1980: 6–12; Bosworth 1993: 226–33; Syme *RP* IV 21–49; Poignault 1995: 559–62; Liddle 2003: 2–13. *Mémoires* nowhere includes reference to Arrian's consulship, though its tenure in 130 is recorded in the *Notebook*'s list of imagined and modified facts. Croisets: Yourcenar, recall, owned their *Histoire de la littérature grecque*, the final

volume of which gives details on Arrian. Parthian war: Arrian was to write its history (ch. 5).

14 Estimate: Bosworth 1993: 227–8; cf. Stadter 1980: 55 and Appendix 5. Hunting: see ch. 3. Military exercises: ch. 2 (the year is 128 though not specified directly).

15 Years of study: Bosworth 1993: 228–9; Long 2002: 38–9. Regard: see Birley 1997a: 58–62; cf. Long 2002: 11.

16 New Xenophon: Bosworth 1993: 272–5. *Bithyniaca*: Stadter 1980: 152–61; contra Poignault 1995: 562: composed after Hadrian's death, following the Croisets.

17 Pliny: Sherwin-White 1966: 525–55; Millar 2004: 23–41; cf. Birley 1997a: 66. (Thoughts of a literary design in *Ep.* 10 [Gibson and Morello 2012: 252–3; 258] seem to me beyond belief.) Cornutus Tertullus: *PIR²* I 273. Julius Severus: *PIR²* I 573; Halfmann 1979: no. 62; Sherk 1988: no. 164c; Mitchell 1995 [1993] I 154–5.

18 Poignault 1995: 562.

19 "I authorized the use of native speech for commands, and encouraged the soldiers in their national war cries."

20 Knew: above n.12.

21 Presence: Birley 1997a: 205: Arrian possibly in Hadrian's entourage. Judged: Busetto 2013: direct influence of Hadrian's speeches on the *Tactica*.

22 Birley 1997a: 262–3.

23 Quotation: Stadter 1980: 17. Remark: "Anyone who has been initiated into the mysteries of the Two Goddesses at Eleusis is aware that the altar of Eudanemos is in the plain" (*Anab.* 3.16.8); see Bosworth 1980: 317: initiation dates to Arrian's time with Epictetus. The *Anabasis* was one item to justify calling the age of Hadrian an age of "Greek romanticism" (*HZ* 567). Kerykes: Poignault 1995: 560 n.141, citing P. Graindor, *Marbres et textes antiques d'époque impériale* (Gand 1922): 51–2. Birley 1997a: 263–4 suggests receipt of the *Periplus* during the Athenian visit.

24 The *Notebook* includes the Athenian episode in the list of modified and imagined facts.

25 Dated: Syme *RP* III 1438; Braund 1991: 211; 212 n.25; Birley 1997a: 224–5; cf. Bosworth 1977: 228: 131 preferred. Gifts: Syme *RP* III 1442–4: the material at *HA Hadr.* 17.11–12 dismissed as fiction; contrast Braund 1991: 214–17: one of Hadrian's gifts was perhaps a silver vessel portraying Antinous, with reasons to supply Pharasmenes with a military garrison.

26 Cf. Cass. Dio 69.15.2: Vologaeses brought charges against Pharasmenes through an embassy to Hadrian (apparently), who produced a response after consultation with the senate. The obscurity of the episode cannot be overstated, and fictions result (Juntunen 2013). Whether Dio's excerpts belong to Hadrian's reign or that of Antoninus Pius is, in fact, uncertain; see Braund 1991: 217.

27 Developments: Bosworth 1977: 228–30; Syme *RP* III 1438–41; Braund 1991; Birley 1997a: 225–6; 287–8.

28 *Ectaxis*: Stadter 1978; 1980: 45; Bosworth 1977: 232–55; 1993: 264–72. Bosworth 1977: 247 and Birley 1997a: 288 see the *Ectaxis* as connected with an official report on military action Arrian sent to Hadrian. Some scholars: see Braund 1991: 212 n.25; cf. Weber 1973 [1907]: 234 n. 844: firmly against.

29 Cf. Poignault 1997: 180–4.

30 "To find this tone again in correspondence between a man of education and a prince one has to await the Renaissance." See the *Endnote* for the full text.

31 She was not the first to do so: see Pelham 1911: 213: "the intimate friend of Hadrian" (cf. 215; 216). The *Periplus* is the only pertinent evidence, and leaves unanswered the question of when the friendship began and how intimate it actually became. Syme approved Yourcenar's position in the Bryce lecture (*RP* VI 164), and proposed an identical view when studying Arrian's career (*RP* IV 21–49 [contesting Stadter 1980]): Hadrian initiated the long-lasting relationship with a "kindred soul" perhaps before his accession; it was based on a shared devotion to Epicurus; no reference was made to the *Periplus*. Rival supposition: Syme proposed as Hadrian's "special friend" C. Bruttius Prasens *cos. bis* 139 (*RP* V 563–78). The case centres on a presumed Epicurean communion with Hadrian that leads to circularity of argument and relies on a sequence of guesses. The hypothesis quickly became a fact (Birley 1997a: 70, 78, 154, 198, 296).

32 24 July 1955 to Constantin Coukidis, reaffirming belief in the authenticity of Arrian's authorship of the *Periplus* communicated earlier to the Abbé Vincent, despite the doubts of an unnamed German scholar. Yourcenar wondered whether a doubting American geographer had confused the work with the *Periplus of the Red Sea,* and commented that in both recent and older works (she specified F.H. Sandbach and Croiset) she had found nothing to suggest inauthenticity; as far as she could judge its style and vocabulary allowed the *Periplus* to be ascribed to the second century (*HZ* 335–6: 8 March 1954). Rostovtzeff: whether *Iranians and Greeks in South Russia* (Oxford 1922) supports Yourcenar is unclear: I find no specific reference there to the *Periplus*, and only one mention of "The White Island of Achilles" (36), where Rostovtzeff described Greek traditions relevant to his introduction of Cimmerians and Scythians in South Russia of the seventh to fifth centuries BC. But Yourcenar rightly distinguished Achilles's association with Leuce from his association in Greek mythology with Skyros, as also the heroic Patroclus from the Ptolemaic navarch commemorated on an island at Cape Sunion (she relied here on autopsy and found the reality a source of irritation). For Arrian's faulty geography, see Birley 1997a: 264; Liddle 2003: 128. Müller: for the *Periplus*, see *Geographi Graeci Minores* I (Paris 1855): 370–401. Translated: in the *Notebook*

("Mentions d'Auteurs Grecs contemporains d'Hadrien"), Yourcenar remarked that Arrian's "volumineux rapport" alluded to the *Periplus*.

33 26 March 1956; cf. Poignault 2007a: 147–8, 149. *TGS* 295 admits a doubt on the *Periplus*'s authorship.

34 The draft reads: "En vérité, j'ai vécu à Tibur; j'y mourrai, peut-être, comme Hadrien dans l'ile [*sic*] d'Achille" ("In truth, I have lived at Tibur; I shall perhaps die there, like Hadrian in the Isle of Achilles").

35 MacDonald and Pinto 1995: 89; the identification is uncertain.

36 *"And the shade of Patroclus appears at Achilles' side."*

37 The *Notebook* has no preparatory page for this entry. According to the *Chronologie* (XXIV), Yourcenar was in Italy in the winter of 1951. J.E. Howard 2018: 191 dates arrival in Rome in late February 1952 for a stay of two months. I assume this was the period of revisiting to which the final entry in the *Carnets* refers. It repeats the version first published in the *Mercure de France* of November 1952, one irrelevant detail apart.

38 Bernier 2004: nos. 3254, 3220, 3147, 3146.

39 Gifts: Bardon: Bernier 2004: nos. 3108, 3059 (*La Littérature latine inconnue* I [1952] = Bernier 2004: no. 3058). Note also G.W. Bowersock, *Julian the Apostate* (1978) (Bernier 2004: no. 3150), with elaborate handwritten Latin dedication.

40 Earlier: ch. 7. Clippings: respectively dated November 1975, March 1977 (the *subligaria* have a wide appeal; Yourcenar also kept a visitor's pamphlet from Vindolanda); January 1978; August 1979. Lifelong: cf. *PV* 91 (from 1971): "comme j'avais lu … plus ou moins toute ma vie."

41 Piranesi: *CNMH* 522–33. Lampshade: ch. 8.

42 Compared: *HZ* 483: 15 August 1955 to Alexis Curvers and Marie Delcourt. Sailed: *Chronologie* XIX (of the 1930s); cf. Savigneau 1993: 98–9; 473 n.3; J.E. Howard 2018: 52.

43 *HZ* 152: 24 May 1952; *HZ* III 20: 18 April 1962.

44 Wall: *HZ* II 296–7: 25 January 1954. Temple: *PV* 35 (from 1954). Carlisle: *HZ* II 243: 12 May 1958. Hope Antinous: *HZ* II 297: 12 March 1959. Shrewsbury: *HZ* II 242: 12 May 1958. Ainwick: *L* 236: 6 January 1966. Gaul: *L* 317: 7 May 1969.

45 Slippage: relevant to Blanckeman 2014b: an existential reading of Yourcenar's letters.

46 Earlier: ch. 6.

47 Gibbon for instance follows the practice of Suetonius: *Decline and Fall* V 240–2 (Justinian); VI 92 (Julian); VII 183 (Robert Guiscard).

48 See ch. 7.

49 Cass. Dio 69.22.1–4; *HA Hadr.* 24.8; 24.12–13. On suicides in Yourcenar's writings, see Castellani 2011: 245–57.

50 "If ever I am to undergo torture (and illness will doubtless see to that) I cannot be sure of maintaining the impassiveness of a Thrasea, but I shall at least have the resource of resigning myself to my cries."

51 Euphrates: Sherwin-White 1966: 746. Quotation: "I have never been opposed to voluntary departure from life, and had considered it as a possible end in my hour of crisis before Trajan's death. The problem of suicide which has obsessed me since seemed then of easy solution."

52 "sur la pente ascendante de son destin"; see *MH* 412, with *HA Hadr.* 13.3; cf. Poignault 1995: 455–6.

53 In 111/112: see Birley 1997a: 57–65: Hadrian's first visit to Greece, separate from *Mémoires'* educational visit with Isaeus.

54 Byzantine historian: Syncellus 659D. See Poignault 1995: 547–9, with Swain 1991.

55 Jones 1971: 56; Birley 1997a: 62 ("surely"); cf. Bowie 1997: investigation of Hadrian's relationship with Favorinus that concludes *non liquet.*

56 "Yes, but very young, at age thirty, when Plutarch was eighty. It's moving to think of this encounter, which had a great influence on the emperor."

57 "Antinous himself moreover was without doubt rather uncomplicated" (14 June 1952).

58 *PV* 162 (from 1955); *PV* 92 (from 1971); *L* 539: 23 March 1977; *PV* 242 (from 1978).

59 *PV* 144; 239; 367; 223 (from 1978 [quotation]); *YO* 279 (Jews); see also *PV* 168–9 (from 1975); 221 (from 1978–9): Roman civilization to be in decline but to subsist for several generations.

60 *HA Hadr.* 11.7; 23.10; *Ael.* 5.1; cf. *MH* 369; 488.

61 Cf. the virtually definitive long passage cited at the beginning of ch. 8.

62 "surely knew love"; "it must have been very important … in Hadrian's life."

63 "He was highly intelligent in everything … far closer to us than the Roman emperors depicted in the works of Suetonius or in popular movies and novels; in a sense he was a Renaissance man." (Dismissal of popular novels is delicious.)

64 "the great moment" (cf. Syme *RP* VI 174: in agreement).

65 The interview transcript is reconstituted; see *PV* 353 n.1.

66 See *HZ* IV 48: 15 February 1964 to Jean-Louis Côté; *HZ* IV 177–8: 10 November 1964 to Wells Hively on Perowne 1966 [1960]: a mediocre effort badly written by a writer lacking cultivation and literary sensibility who was not a serious historian, who relied on second- and third-hand material, was ignorant of classical antiquity and its literature, and had plagiarized *Mémoires* to boot; the book was detestable.

67 Early date: *HZ* 78: 7 October 1951 (before publication): "*de ce qui n'est qu'une fois*"; "cet extraordinaire mélange de volonté et de tempérament, de hasard et de destin, qu'est une personnalité d'homme." Aimed: *HZ* III 281: 14 January 1963; *PV* 242 (from 1978–9); cf. 296 (from 1981); *PV* 103 (from 1971).

68 Bust: *PV* 123 (from 1971). Novel: *HZ* II 36: 8 January 1957. Distinction: *PV* 160 (from 1975). Voice: *YO* 71, 238–9.

69 Meditation: *PV* 369 (from 1986–7): "Hadrien médite sur sa vie"; *HZ* IV 73: 27 March 1964: "une méditation historique"; cf. *HZ* IV 313–14: 26 October 1965; *YO* 198. Method: *HZ* 241: 20 March 1953; characterized to Christian Murciaux

394 Notes to pages 292–7

as the product of the pleasure that came from the art attributed to Hadrian, almost a duty, of enjoying soul and body together (*HZ* 135; cf. *PV* 108–9 [from 1971]; *PV* 221–2 [from 1978–9]).

70 Combination: Blanchet-Douspis 2008: 407–32: Stoic associations, connections to (Epicurean) *ataraxia*, Buddhist influence (but the segment title *Patientia* is not used in a technical Stoic sense); Cordonnier 2019. Condition: *PV* 46–7 (from 1956). Wisdomed ("assagi"): *PV* 111 (from 1971); cf. 196–7 (from 1977); 276 (from 1980); see also *HZ* II 256: 28 June 1958; *PV* 54 (from 1956). For the authorial transference involved, see Hörmann 1996: 123–52.

71 Poignault 1995: 907–34. For a different perspective, see J.E. Howard 1992: 4–5: *Mémoires* is "fundamentally mythic because it undertakes that return to the origins that is the foremost characteristic of myth."

72 "une méthode de vie et d'une *maniere d'être*"; "le risque de didactisme"; "à vue de propagande" (8 January 1957). Propaganda: cf. *HZ* III 117: its dangers.

73 "In a sense, every life that is recounted is offered as an example; we write in order to attack or to defend a view of the universe, and to set forth a system of conduct which is our own."

74 "He is useful if he clarifies the reader's thinking, rids him of timidity or prejudice, or makes him see and feel things that he would not otherwise have seen or felt" (cf. *YO* 327: a traveller is likely to consult a passerby to learn where he has come from and where he thinks he is headed; in response to Galey's observation that readers tended to look to her books as guides to life). "I simply find it interesting to see what others have done, whether they have made as many mistakes as we have, or otherwise.

75 Jefferson 2007: 19–22.

76 Ingredient: Litchfield 1914; Walsh 1970: 20–109; Chaplin 2000: 1–31. Livy: 1 *praef.* 9–10. Tacitus: *Hist.* 1.3; *Ann.* 3.65. Plutarch: Duff 1999: ch. 1. Pliny: Bradley 2010b.

77 Savigneau 1993: Frick responsible for the copies and preservation of letters; Brami 2019: 51–3: Yourcenar's desire to create a self-portrait "beyond the tomb."

78 25 September 1961; cf. *YO* 63. *Les Visages* again confirms the technique.

79 *PV* 202 (from 1978–9); *YO* 89; 324; 274; *PV* 256 (from 1978–9); cf. technically Lodge 2011: ch. 2.

80 *YO* 327; *PV* 66 (from 1966); *YO* 155; 224; *PV* 299 (from 1981); *ER* 64; cf. *PV* 182 (from 1976); *HZ* II 37; *YO* 107; *L* 83–84; *HZ* III 424.

81 *YO* 226–7, with *MH* 304–5; *YO* 317–18, with *MH* 293–4; *YO* 76–7, with *MH* 295. Historians: ch. 4. The sentence, "J'en suis là moi aussi" (*L* 459: 28 May 1975), in reference to *Animula vagula blandula*, has wide application.

82 See *EM* 597–8 ("Note de l'éditeur"). The lecture notably contains several allusions to Cavafy, whose poems were seemingly always in her consciousness. Imperially: Ughetto 2009: 254.

83 *L* 464: 25 July 1975; *L* 598: 27 December 1978 ("«d'entendre»"); cf. *YO* 71.
84 Admitted: *HZ* 246; *PV* 30; cf. *HZ* III 463: "pouvoir suprême." Pragmatism: *YO* 155–6 (cf. *HZ* II 251: a rhetorical question whether dictatorship could ever remedy an evil situation).

10. Residue

1 Earlier accounts: see Momigliano 1969c [1950]: 2 on "derivative authorities": "historians or chroniclers who relate and discuss events which they have not witnessed but which they have heard of or inferred indirectly from original authorities." The Bardon factor is all-pervasive.
2 Lewes 1863: 115.
3 Selective: R. Williams 1973: 18.
4 Images: despite *PV* 368–9, Yourcenar in my view underestimated their force; note *MH* 373 on Caligula, following from an early date *TGS* 284: "L'Empereur dément souhaitait que l'univers n'eût qu'une seule tête, afin de la trancher" ("That mad emperor wished that the world had only one head, so that he could cut it off"), with Suet. *Calig.* 30.2 taken at face value. Quotation: Lewes 1863: 116. Josephus (*AJ* 20.154) and Suetonius (*Ner.* 9–19.2) notably preserve elements of favourable estimates of Nero.
5 Cf. MacDonald 1975: 76: "To say with any precision what the Pantheon meant to Hadrian and his contemporaries will probably never be possible." A remark of much wider applicability.
6 Sources: the importance of Poignault 1995 cannot be overstated. Inferences: Lee 2009: 136.
7 Sense: cf. *TGS* 275: "Un cycle nouveau commence."
8 1922: *YO* 86–7; *PV* 140; *AN* 1035–6; *Chronologie* XVI. Indications: Savigneau 1993: 133–8, with Appendix 4 ("Self-Commentary"); J.E. Howard 2018: 86–7: clear account of Yourcenar's movements in 1939, with reference to the sole claim of Belgian nationality.
9 Statements: *YO* 133; *PE* 535–6; Brami 2019: 55–60, quoting from an unpublished letter of 22 September 1970: "Il m'a été assez dur, d'abord, d'exister dans un endroit en marge de l'histoire" ("It has been hard enough for me for one thing to exist in a place on the fringe of history").
10 *ACB* 24–5.
11 *ACB* 217: "Il est difficile, à distance, de s'imaginer ce qu'a été l'atmosphère des années d'occupation; il est impossible de savoir quelle figure on aurait faite, ou évité de faire, au sein d'une telle confusion, si comme tant d'autres on s'y était trouvé."
12 *SBI* 35–6: from «Les Tragiques» d'Agrippa d'Aubigné; cf. *HZ* III 96.
13 Watt 2001 [1957]: 134. For Watt's horrific experiences as a Japanese prisoner-of-war, see MacKay 2018: ch. 2.

14 And not at all photographic: cf. *HZ* IV 222 (from 1965), in reference to *L'Œuvre au Noir*.

15 "There is no past or future, only a series of successive presents, a road perpetually destroyed and continued, upon which we all go forward" (from 1931).

16 Bate 2015: 18.

17 "Plus récemment encore, j'ai revu mon père, auquel je pense pourtant assez peu. Il était couché dans son lit de malade, dans une pièce de notre maison d'Italica, que j'ai quittée sitôt après sa mort. Il avait sur sa table une fiole pleine d'une potion sédative que je l'ai supplié de me donner. Je me suis réveillé sans qu'il ait eu le temps de me répondre" ("More recently still I have seen my father, though I think of him rather seldom. He was lying on his sick bed in a room of our house in Italica, where I ceased to dwell soon after his death. On his table he had a phial full of a sedative potion which I begged him to give me. I awoke before he had time to reply"). Cf. *HA Hadr.* 26.10.

18 Quotation: Wilson Knight 2002 [1930]: 184. "Impression": "ce qui est le but de tout écrivain: transmettre une impression qu'on n'oubliera plus."

19 "Récit": *YO* 198. Evocation: Syme *RP* VI 164. Defined: "A meditation on the life of a man from another age, largely conditioned by ideas and customs different from ours, but having much in common with our life in many respects" (26 October 1965).

20 Pocock 2003: 19.

21 "one errs *more or less.*"

22 "The human substance and structure hardly change: nothing is more stable than the curve of a heel, the position of a tendon, or the form of a toe. But there are periods when the shoe is less deforming than in others. In the century of which I speak we are still very close to the undisguised freedom of the bare foot."

23 Expectation: Eagleton 2005: 17. Plutarch: *Alex.* 1.3: τὰ τῆς ψυχῆς σημεῖα.

BIBLIOGRAPHY

Citations of books with two dates, the second in square brackets, indicate dates of editions used and original dates of publication. E. Gibbon, *The History of the Decline and Fall of the Roman Empire* (1776–1788) is cited as *Decline and Fall* from the eight volumes of the fifteenth printing of the Folio edition (London 2006).

Classical Antiquity

Abusch, R. 2003. "Negotiating Difference: Genital Mutilation in Roman Slave Law and the History of the Bar Kokhba Revolt." In Schäfer ed. 2003: 71–91.

Alexander, P. J. 1938. "Letters and Speeches of the Emperor Hadrian." *Harvard Studies in Classical Philology* 49: 141–77.

Anderson, J.K. 1985. *Hunting in the Ancient World.* Berkeley.

André, J.-M. 1993. "Hadrien littérateur et protecteur des lettres." *Aufstieg und Niedergang der römischen Welt* II 34.1: 583–611.

Ansel, C. 2020. "Auguste/Tibère et Trajan/Hadrien: la difficulté d'être le successeur de *l'optimus princeps*." In Benoit et al. eds. 2020: 31–43.

Aymard, J. 1951. *Essai sur les chasses romaines des origines à la fin du siècle des Antonins.* Paris.

Baker, R. 2012. "Epiphanius, *On Weights and Measures* §14: Hadrian's Journey to the East and the Rebuilding of Jerusalem." *Zeitschrift für Papyrologie und Epigraphik* 182: 157–67.

Balsdon, J.P.V.D. 1934. *The Emperor Gaius.* Oxford.

Balsdon, J.P.V.D. 1954–1955. "The Aesthete as Emperor." *Yale Review* 44: 466–9.

Bardon, H. 1952. *La Littérature latine inconnue. Volume I.* Paris.

Bardon, H. 1956. *La Littérature latine inconnue. Volume II.* Paris.

Bardon, H. 1964. *Le Crépuscule des Césars: Scènes et visages de l'*Histoire Auguste. Monaco.

Bardon, H. 1968. *Les Empereurs et les lettres latines d'Auguste à Hadrien.* Paris (second edition; first edition 1940).

Barnes, T.D. 1978. *The Sources of the* Historia Augusta. Brussels.

Barnes, T.D. 1989. "Trajan and the Jews." *Journal of Jewish Studies* 40: 145–62.

Barnes, T.D. 2011. *Constantine: Dynasty, Religion and Power in the Later Roman Empire.* Malden MA.

Barrett, A.A. 2015. *Caligula: The Abuse of Power* (second edition). London.

Batsch, C. 2020. "Les «amphores hadriennes». Mémoires juives des empereurs Trajan et Hadrien." In Benoit et al. eds. 2020: 71–82.

Bazzana, G.B. 2010. "The Bar Kokhba Revolt and Hadrian's Religious Policy." In Rizzi ed. 2010: 85–109.

Beckmann, M. 2007. "Trajan and Hadrian." In W.E. Metcalf ed. *The Oxford Handbook of Greek and Roman Coinage* (Oxford 2007): 405–22.

Behr, C.A. 1968. *Aelius Aristides and* The Sacred Tales. Amsterdam.

Belayche, N. 2019. "Antinous divinisé: Des mots grecs pour l'écrire." *Metis* 17: 267–90.

Bellissime, M., and B. Berbessou-Brouset. 2016. "L'*Histoire romaine* de Zonaras." In Fromentin et al. eds. 2016: I 95–108.

Bennett, J. 1997. *Trajan* Optimus Princeps*: A Life and Times.* London.

Benoit, S., A. Gautier, C. Hoët-van Cauwenberghe, R. Poignault eds. 2020. *Mémoires de Trajan, mémoires d'Hadrien.* Villeneuve d'Ascq.

Berbessou-Brouset, B. 2016. "Xiphilin, abréviateur de Cassius Dion." In Fromentin et al. eds. 2016: I 81–94.

Bettini, M. *The Portrait of the Lover.* Berkeley.

Betz, H.D. 1992. *The Greek Magical Papyri in Translation* (second edition). Chicago.

Bidwell, P. 2022a. "Themed Section: Hadrian's Progress through the North-Western Provinces in A.D. 121–122." *Britannia* 53: 3–4.

Bidwell, P. 2022b. "Hadrian's Frontiers in Northern Britain." *Britannia* 53: 99–124.

Bird, H.W. 1994. *Aurelius Victor: De Caesaribus.* Liverpool.

Birley, A.R. 1976. *Lives of the Later Caesars: The first part of the* Augustan History, *with newly compiled* Lives of Nerva and Trajan. London.

Birley, A.R. 1987. *Marcus Aurelius.* New Haven.

Birley, A.R. 1994. "Hadrian's Farewell to Life." *Laverna* 5: 176–205.

Birley, A.R. 1997a. *Hadrian: The Restless Emperor.* New Haven.

Birley, A.R. 1997b. "Marius Maximus: The Consular Biographer." *Aufstieg und Niedergang der römischen Welt* II 34.3: 2678–757.

Birley, A.R. 1997c. "Hadrian and Greek Senators." *Zeitschrift für Papyrologie und Epigraphik* 116: 209–45.

Birley, A.R. 2000. *Onomasticon to the Younger Pliny: Letters and Panegyric*. Munich.

Birley, A.R. 2003. "Hadrian's Travels." In de Blois et al. eds. 2003: 425–41.

Birley, A.R. 2005a. *The Roman Government of Britain*. Oxford.

Birley, A.R. 2005b. "Hadrian, *De Vita Sua*." In M. Reichel ed. *Antike Autobiographien: Werke – Epochen – Gattungen* (Cologne 2005): 223–35.

Birley, A.R. 2006a. "Rewriting Second- and Third-Century History in Late Antique Rome: The *Historia Augusta*." *Classica, Belo Horizonte* 19: 19–29.

Birley, A.R. 2006b. "Hadrian, Circumcision, and the Bar Kokhba War." *Journal of Roman Archaeology* 19: 671–81.

Birley, A.R. 2012. "Early Life: Family, Youth and Education." In M. van Ackeren ed. *A Companion to Marcus Aurelius* (Malden MA 2012): 139–54.

Birley, A.R. 2014. "Two Governors of Dacia Superior and Britain." In V. Iliescu, D. Nedu, A.-R. Barbos eds. *In Memoriam Vasile Lica* (Galati 2014): 241–59.

Birley, A.R. 2017. "*Viri Militares* Moving from West to East in Two Crisis Years (AD 133 and 162)." In E. Lo Cascio and L.E. Tacoma eds. *The Impact of Mobility and Migration in the Roman Empire* (Leiden 2017): 55–79.

Birley, A.R. 2020. ed. *Select Correspondence of Ronald Syme, 1927–1939. History of Classical Scholarship Supplementary Volume 1*. Newcastle.

Birnbaum, S.A. 1954. "Bar Kokhba and Akiba." *Palestine Exploration Quarterly* 86: 23–32.

Blanchard-Lemée, M., M. Ennaïfer, M. Slim, and L. Slim. 1996. *Mosaics of Roman Africa: Floor Mosaics from Tunisia*. London.

Blois, L. de, P. Erdkamp, O. Hekster, G. de Kleijn, S. Mols eds. 2003. *The Representation and Perception of Roman Imperial Power*. Amsterdam.

Boatwright, M.T. 1987. *Hadrian and the City of Rome*. Princeton.

Boatwright, M.T. 1991. "The Imperial Women of the Early Second Century AD." *American Journal of Philology* 112: 513–40.

Boatwright, M.T. 1994. "Hadrian, Athens and the Panhellenion." *Journal of Roman Archaeology* 7: 426–31.

Boatwright, M.T. 2000. *Hadrian and the Cities of the Roman Empire*. Princeton.

Bollansée, J. 1994. "P. Fay. 19, Hadrian's Memoirs, and Imperial Autobiography." *Ancient Society* 25: 279–302.

Bonner, S.F. 1969 [1949]. *Roman Declamation*. Liverpool.

Bonner, S.F. 1977. *Education in Ancient Rome*. Berkeley.

Bosworth, A.B. 1977. "Arrian and the Alani." *Harvard Studies in Classical Philology* 81: 217–55.

Bosworth, A.B. 1980. *A Historical Commentary on Arrian's History of Alexander Volume I*. Oxford.

Bosworth, A.B. 1983. "Arrian at the Caspian Gates: A Study in Methodology." *Classical Quarterly* 33: 265–76.

Bosworth, A.B. 1988. *From Arrian to Alexander: Studies in Historical Interpretation.* Oxford.

Bosworth, A.B. 1993. "Arrian and Rome: The Minor Works." *Aufstieg und Niedergang der römischen Welt* II 34.1: 226–75.

Bowersock, G.W. 1965. *Augustus and the Greek World.* Oxford.

Bowersock, G.W. 1969. *Greek Sophists in the Roman Empire.* Oxford.

Bowersock, G.W. 1991. "Momigliano's Quest for the Person." *History and Theory* 30: 27–36.

Bowersock, G.W. 1994a. "Ronald Syme 1903–1989." *Proceedings of the British Academy* 84: 539–63.

Bowersock, G.W. 1994b. "Introduction." In G.W. Bowersock and T.J. Cornell eds. *A.D. Momigliano: Studies in Modern Scholarship* (Berkeley 1994): vii–xi.

Bowersock, G.W. 1998. "*Vita Caesarum*: Remembering and Forgetting the Past." In W.W. Ehlers ed. *La Biographie antique. Entretiens sur l'antiquité classique XLIV* (Geneva 1998): 193–210.

Bowersock, G.W. 2003. "The Tel Shalem Arch and P.Nahal Hever/Seiyal 8." In Schäfer ed. 2003: 171–80.

Bowersock, G.W. 2009. *From Gibbon to Auden: Essays on the Classical Tradition.* New York.

Bowie, E.L. 1997. "Hadrian, Favorinus, and Plutarch." In J. Mossman ed. *Plutarch and His Intellectual World* (London 1997): 1–11.

Bowie, E.L. 2002. "Hadrian and Greek Poetry." In Ostenfeld ed. 2002: 172–97.

Bradley, K.R. 1986. "Approaches to the Roman Empire: A Perspective." *International History Review* 8: 89–106.

Bradley, K.R. 1991a. "The Imperial Ideal in Suetonius' *Caesares*." *Aufstieg und Niedergang der römischen Welt* II 33.5: 3701–32.

Bradley, K.R. 1991b. *Discovering the Roman Family.* New York.

Bradley, K.R. 1998. "Introduction." In J.C. Rolfe ed. and trans. *Suetonius Volume 1* (Loeb Classical Library, Cambridge MA): 1–34.

Bradley, K.R. 2004. "On Captives under the Principate." *Phoenix* 58: 298–318.

Bradley, K.R. 2008a. "Hadrian, Yourcenar, Syme." *Mouseion* 8: 39–53.

Bradley, K.R. 2008b. "Apuleiana." *Phoenix* 62: 363–78.

Bradley, K.R. 2010a. "Freedom and Slavery." In A. Barchiesi and W. Scheidel eds. *The Oxford Handbook of Roman Studies* (Oxford 2010): 624–36.

Bradley, K.R. 2010b. "The Exemplary Pliny." In C. Deroux ed. *Studies in Latin Literature and Roman History XV* (Brussels 2010): 384–422.

Bradley K.R. 2011. "B.W. Henderson, Fellow of Exeter College 1901–1927." *Exeter College Register* 2011: 28–30.

Bradley K.R. 2012a. "Recovering Hadrian." *Klio* 94: 130–55.

Bradley, K.R. 2012b. "The Birthplace of Hadrian: Pursuing Ghosts." In C. Deroux ed. *Studies in Latin Literature and Roman History XVII* (Brussels 2012): 582–613.

Bradley, K.R. 2012c. *Apuleius and Antonine Rome: Historical Essays.* Toronto.

Bradley, K.R. 2016a. "Yourcenar's Suetonius: Grasping for the Wind." *Phoenix* 70: 147–69.

Bradley, K.R. 2016b . "Yourcenar, Apuleius, Petronius: Slender Threads." *Ancient Narrative* 13: 1–16.

Bradley, K.R. 2017a. "Allusive Syme." *Mouseion* 14: 125–38.

Bradley, K.R. 2017b. "Learning Virtue: Aeneas, Ascanius, Augustus." *Latomus* 76: 324–45.

Bradley, K.R. 2019. "Publilius Syrus and the Anxiety of Continuity." *Mouseion* 16 Supplement 1: 65–89.

Bradley, K.R. 2020. "Nero: Suspension of Disbelief." *Journal of Roman Archaeology* 33: 605–12.

Bradley, K.R. 2022. "Five Exquisite Lines." In W. Eck, F. Santangelo, K. Vössing eds. *Emperor, Army, and Society: Studies in Roman Imperial History for Anthony R. Birley* (Bonn 2022): 429–39.

Braund, D. 1991. "Hadrian and Pharasmenes." *Klio* 73: 208–19.

Breeze, D.J. 2006. *J. Collingwood Bruce's Handbook to the Roman Wall* (fourteenth edition). Newcastle.

Brennan, T.C. 2018. *Sabina Augusta: An Imperial Journey.* New York.

Brown, P.R.L. 1967. *Augustine of Hippo: A Biography.* London.

Brown, P.R.L. 1988. "Arnaldo Dante Momigliano." *Proceedings of the British Academy* 74: 405–42.

Brown, P.R.L. 2012. *Through the Eye of a Needle: Wealth, the Fall of Rome, and the Making of Christianity in the West, 350–550 AD.* Princeton.

Brunt, P.A. 1975. "The Administrators of Roman Egypt." *Journal of Roman Studies* 65: 124–47.

Brunt, P.A. 1977. "*Lex De Imperio Vespasiani.*" *Journal of Roman Studies* 67: 95–116.

Brunt, P.A. 1980. "On Historical Fragments and Epitomes." *Classical Quarterly* 30: 477–94.

Brunt, P.A. 2012. "Hugh Macilwain Last." *Athenaeum* 100: 435–45.

Brunt, P.A. 2013. *Studies in Stoicism.* Oxford.

Bruun, C. 2016. "Remembering Anniversaries at Roman Ostia: The *dies natalis* of Antinous, Hero and Divine Being." *Phoenix* 70: 361–80.

Burgersdijk, D. 2013. "Pliny's *Panegyricus* and the *Historia Augusta.*" *Arethusa* 46: 289–312.

Burgersdijk, D. 2016. "*Qui vitas aliorum scribere orditur.* Narratological Implications of Fictional Authors in the *Historia Augusta.*" In K. de Temmerman and K. Demoen eds. *Writing Biography in Greece and Rome: Narrative Technique and Fictionalization* (Cambridge 2016): 240–56.

Burgess, J.S. 2009. *The Death and Afterlife of Achilles*. Baltimore.

Burnand, Y. 1975. "Sénateurs et chevaliers romains originaires de la cité de Nîmes sous le haut-empire: Étude épigraphique." *Mélanges de l'École française de Rome: Antiquités* 87: 681–791.

Burns, B.E. 2015. "Sculpting Antinous: Creations of the Ideal Companion." In R. Blondell and K. Ormand eds. *Ancient Sex: New Essays* (Columbus OH 2015): 285–307.

Burton, G.P. 2002. "The Roman Imperial State (A.D. 14–235): Evidence and Reality." *Chiron* 32: 249–80.

Busetto, A. 2013. "Linguistic Adaptation as Cultural Adjustment: Treatment of Celtic, Iberian and Latin Terminology in Arrian's *Tactica*." *Journal of Ancient History* 1: 230–41.

Calandra, E. 2010. "Villa Adriana scenario del potere." In Rizzi ed. 2010: 21–50.

Cameron, A. 2011a. *The Last Pagans of Rome*. New York.

Cameron, A. 2011b. "*Antiquus Error/Novus Error*: The *HA*, Nichomachus Flavianus, and the 'Pagan Resistance'." *Journal of Roman Archaeology* 24: 835–46.

Cameron, A. 2014. "Momigliano and the *Historia Augusta*." In T.J. Cornell and O. Murray eds. *The Legacy of Arnaldo Momigliano* (London 2014): 147–64.

Cameron, A. 2016. Review of Ratti 2016a. *Bryn Mawr Classical Review* 2016.09.10.

Campbell, J.B. 1984. *The Emperor and the Roman Army 31 BC – AD 235*. Oxford.

Campbell, J.B. 1993. "War and Diplomacy: Rome and Parthia, 31 BC – AD 235." In Rich and Shipley eds. 1993: 213–40.

Capponi, L. 2010. "Hadrian in Jerusalem and Alexandria in 117." *Athenaeum* 98: 489–501.

Capponi, L. 2020. "Trajan dans les *Acta Alexandrinorum*: un portrait contradictoire." In Benoit et al. eds. 2020: 187–204.

Carcopino, J. 1934. "Lusius Quietus l'homme de QWRNYN." *Istros. Revue roumaine d'archéologie et d'histoire ancienne* 1: 5–9.

Carroll, M. 2006. *Spirits of the Dead: Roman Funerary Commemoration in Western Europe*. Oxford.

Carson, R.A.G. 1990. *Coins of the Roman Empire*. London.

Champlin, E. 1980. *Fronto and Antonine Rome*. Cambridge MA.

Champlin, E. 2003. *Nero*. Cambridge MA.

Chaplin, J.D. 2000. *Livy's Exemplary History*. Oxford.

Chastagnol, A. 1994. *Histoire Auguste: Les Empereurs romains des IIe et IIIe siècles*. Paris.

Claridge, A. 2013. "Hadrian's Succession and the Monuments of Trajan." In Opper ed. 2013: 5–18.

Clark, E. 2015 [1952]. *Rome and a Villa*. New York.

Clark, P.A. 1993. *The Balance of the Mind: The Experience and Perception of Mental Illness in Antiquity*. PhD diss. University of Washington.

Clark, P.A., and M.L. Rose (unpublished). "Celsus and the Somatic Interactions of Mental Illness."

Claytor, W.G., and A. Verhoogt eds. 2018. *Papyri from Karanis. The Granary C123 (P.Mich. XXI)*. Ann Arbor.

Coarelli, F. 2007. *Rome and Environs: an Archaeological Guide*. Berkeley.

Cohen, D., and R.P. Saller. 1994. "Foucault on Sexuality in Greco-Roman Antiquity." In J. Goldstein ed. *Foucault and the Writing of History* (Oxford 1994): 35–59.

Collingwood, R.G., and J.N.L. Myres. 1968 [1937]. *Roman Britain and the English Settlements*. Oxford.

Cornell, T.J. 1993. "The End of Roman Imperial Expansion." In Rich and Shipley eds. 1993: 139–70.

Cornell, T.J. 2013. "*Historia Augusta*." In Cornell ed. 2013: 1: 74–80.

Cornell, T.J. ed. 2013. *The Fragments of the Roman Historians* (3 Vols.). Oxford.

Cortés Copete, J.M. 2017a. "Governing by Dispatching Letters: The Hadrianic Chancellery." In C. Rosillo-López ed. *Political Communication in the Roman World* (Leiden 2017): 107–36.

Cortés Copete, J.M. 2017b. "Hadrian among the Gods." In Muñiz Grijalvo et al. eds. 2017: 112–36.

Cotton, H.M. 2003. "The Bar Kokhba Revolt and the Documents from the Judaean Desert." In Schäfer ed. 2003: 133–52.

Cramer, F.H. 1954. *Astrology in Roman Law and Politics*. Philadelphia.

Cribiore, R. 2001. *Gymnastics of the Mind: Greek Education in Hellenistic and Roman Egypt*. Princeton.

Crook, J.A. 1955. Consilium Principis: *Imperial Councils and Counsellors from Augustus to Diocletian*. Cambridge.

Crook, J.A. 1956/1957. "Suetonius *ab epistulis*." *Proceedings of the Cambridge Philological Society* n.s. 4: 18–22.

Dąbrowa, E. 2017. "Hadrianic Governors of Syria: A Reappraisal." *Zeitschrift für Papyrologie und Epigraphik* 201: 285–91.

Danziger, N., and N. Purcell. 2005. *Hadrian's Empire: When Rome Ruled the World*. London.

Davenport, C., and C. Mallan. 2014. "Hadrian's Adoption Speech in Cassius Dio's Roman History and the Problems of Imperial Succession." *American Journal of Philology* 135: 637–68.

Davidson, J. 2001. "Dover, Foucault and Greek Homosexuality: Penetration and the Truth of Sex." *Past & Present* 170: 3–51.

Davis, P.J. 2006. *Ovid and Augustus: A Political Reading of Ovid's Erotic Poems.* London.

Debevoise, N.C. 1938. *A Political History of Parthia.* Chicago.

Demougin, S. 1997. "*Procuratores Monetae.*" *Revue numismatique* 152: 41–5.

Den Hengst, D. 2002. "The Discussion of Authorship." In *Historiae Augustae Colloquium Perusinum. Historiae Augustae Colloquium Nova Series* VIII (Bari 2002): 187–95.

Dessau, H. 1889. "Über Zeit und Persönlichkeit der S.H.A." *Hermes* 24: 337–92.

Dickey, E. 2012. *The Colloquia of the Hermeneumata Pseudodositheana Volume 1.* Cambridge.

Dickey, E. 2015. *The Colloquia of the Hermeneumata Pseudodositheana Volume 2.* Cambridge.

Dickie, M.W. 2001. *Magic and Magicians in the Greco-Roman World.* London.

Dillon, J. 1996. *The Middle Platonists: A Study of Platonism 80 B.C. to A.D. 220.* London.

Dodds, E.R. 1970 [1965]. *Pagan and Christian in an Age of Anxiety: Some Aspects of Religious Experience from Marcus Aurelius to Constantine.* New York.

Dolansky, F. 2011a. "Honouring the Family Dead on the Parentalia: Ceremony, Spectacle, and Memory." *Phoenix* 65: 125–57.

Dolansky, F. 2011b. "Celebrating the Saturnalia: Religious Ritual and Roman Domestic Life." In B.M. Rawson ed. *A Companion to Families in the Greek and Roman Worlds* (Chichester 2011): 488–503.

Dolansky, F. 2019. "Nocturnal Rites to Appease the Untimely Dead: The Lemuria in Its Socio-Cultural Context." *Mouseion* 16 Supp. 1: 37–64.

Dover, K. 1978. *Greek Homosexuality.* London.

Downey, G. 1961. *A History of Antioch in Syria from Seleucus to the Arab Conquest.* Princeton.

Drinkwater, J.F. 2019. *Nero: Emperor and Court.* Cambridge.

Duff, T.E. 1999. *Plutarch's Lives: Exploring Virtue and Vice.* Oxford.

Dunbabin, K.M.D. 1978. *The Mosaics of Roman Africa: Studies in Iconography and Patronage.* Oxford.

Duncan-Jones, R.P. 2005. "Implications of Roman Coinage: Debates and Differences." *Klio* 87: 459–87.

Durry, M. 1932. "Le Règne de Trajan d'après des monnaies: À propos d'un livre récent." *Revue historique* 169: 316–27.

Eck, W. 1999. "The Bar Kokhba Revolt: The Roman Point of View." *Journal of Roman Studies* 89: 76–89.

Eck, W. 2003. "Hadrian, the Bar Kokhba Revolt, and the Epigraphic Transmission." In Schäfer ed. 2003: 153–70.

Eck, W., and G. Foerster. 1999. "Ein Triumphbogen für Hadrian im Tal von Beth Shean bei Tel Shalem." *Journal of Roman Archaeology* 12: 297–313.

Eck, W., P. Holder, and A. Pangerl. 2010. "A Diploma for the Army of Britain in 132 and Hadrian's Return to Rome from the East." *Zeitschrift für Papyrologie und Epigraphik* 174: 189–200.

Eck, W., and A. Pangerl. 2015. "Fünf Bürgerrechtskonstitutionen für die Auxiliareinheiten von Moesia Superior aus traianisch-hadrianischer Zeit." *Zeitschrift für Papyrologie und Epigraphik* 194: 223–40.

Eck, W., and P. Weiss 2002. "Hadrianische Konsuln. Neue Zeugnisse aus Militärdiplomen." *Chiron* 32: 449–89.

Eliav, Y.Z. 1997. "Hadrian's Actions on the Temple Mount according to Cassius Dio and Xiphilini Manus." *Jewish Studies Quarterly* 4: 125–44.

Else, G. 1957. *Aristotle's Poetics: The Argument*. Cambridge MA.

Eshel, H. 2003. "The Dates Used during the Bar Kokhba Revolt." In Schäfer ed. 2003: 93–105.

Eshel, H. 2006. "The Bar Kochba Revolt, 132–135." In S.T. Katzel ed. *The Cambridge History of Judaism Volume IV* (Cambridge 2006): 105–27.

Everitt, A. 2009. *Hadrian and the Triumph of Rome*. New York.

Evers, C. 1994. *Les Portraits d'Hadrien: Typologie et ateliers*. Brussels.

Evers, C. 1995. "Les Portraits d'Antinous." *Journal of Roman Archaeology* 8: 447–51.

Evers, C. 2013. "Images of a Divine Youth: The Brussels Antinous and Its Workshop." In Opper ed. 2013: 89–102.

Feeney, D. 2007. *Caesar's Calendar: Ancient Time and the Beginnings of History*. Berkeley.

Ferrill, A. 1991. *Caligula: Emperor of Rome*.

Festugière, A.-J. 1932. *L'Idéal religieux des Grecs et l'Évangile*. Paris.

Finkelstein, L. 1981 [1936]. *Akiba: Scholar, Saint and Martyr*. New York.

Finley, M.I. 1975. *The Use and Abuse of History*. London.

Fittschen, K. 2010. "The Portraits of Roman Emperors and Their Families: Controversial Positions and Unsolved Problems." In B.C. Ewald and C.F. Noreña eds. *The Emperor and Rome: Space, Representation, and Ritual. Yale Classical Studies* 35: 221–46.

Fraser, P.M. 1972. *Ptolemaic Alexandria I-III*. Oxford.

Freisenbruch, A. 2007. "Back to Fronto: Doctor and Patient in His Correspondence with an Emperor." In R. Morello and A.D. Morrison eds. *Ancient Letters: Classical and Late Antique Epistolography* (Oxford 2007): 235–55.

French, D. 2003. *Roman, Late Roman, and Byzantine Inscriptions of Ankara*. Ankara.

Frend, W.H.C. 1984. *The Rise of Christianity*. London.

Fromentin, V., E. Bertrand, M. Coltelloni-Trannoy, M. Molin, and G. Urso eds. 2016. *Cassius Dion: Nouvelles lectures*. Bordeaux.

Fuduli, L., and G. Salamone 2015. "*Hadrianus Restitutor Siciliae*: documenti monetali ed evidenza archeologica." *Mélanges de l'École française de Rome: Antiquités* 127: 201–15.

Fuks, A. 1961. "Aspects of the Jewish Revolt in A.D. 115–117." *Journal of Roman Studies* 51: 98–104.

Fündling, J. 2006. *Kommentar zur* Vita Hadriani *der* Historia Augusta *I–II*. Bonn.

Galimberti, A. 2007. *Adriano e l'ideologia del principato*. Rome.

Galimberti, A. 2010. "The Pseudo-Hadrianic Epistle in the Historia Augusta and Hadrian's Religious Policy." In Rizzi ed. 2010: 111–20.

Galimberti, A. 2013. "Adriano e Giovenale." *Mediterraneo antico* 16: 87–99.

Galimberti, A. 2017. "*P.Oxy.* 471: Hadrian, Alexandria, and the Antinous Cult." In Muñiz Grijalvo et al. eds. 2017: 98–111.

Galimberti, A., and M. Rizzi. 2020. "Trajan et Hadrien dans la *Chronographie* de Jean Malalas." In Benoit et al. 2020: 205–20.

Garnsey, P.D.A., and R.P. Saller. 2015. *The Roman Empire: Economy, Society and Culture* (second edition). Berkeley.

Gatz, B. 1967. *Weltalter, goldene Zeit und Sinnverwandte Vorstellungen*. Hildesheim.

Geiger, J. 2016. "The Bar-Kokhba Revolt: The Greek Point of View." *Historia* 65: 497–519.

Gergel, R.A. 1991. "The Tel Shalem Hadrian Reconsidered." *American Journal of Archaeology* 95: 231–51.

Gibson, R.K. 2018. "A Newly Discovered 'Dialogue'." In A. König and C. Whitton eds. *Roman Literature under Nerva, Trajan and Hadrian* (Cambridge 2018): 402–21.

Gibson, R.K. 2020. *Man of High Empire*. Oxford.

Gibson, R.K., and R. Morello. 2012. *Reading the Letters of Pliny the Younger: An Introduction*. Cambridge.

Giroire, C., and D. Roger. 2007. *Roman Art from the Louvre*. New York.

Gleason, M.W. 1995. *Making Men: Sophists and Self-Presentation in Ancient Rome*. Princeton.

Goodman, M. 2003. "Trajan and the Origins of the Bar Kokhba War." In Schäfer ed. 2003: 23–9.

Goodman, M., and P. Alexander eds. 2010. *Rabbinic Texts and the History of Late-Roman Palestine* (*Proceedings of the British Academy* 165). Oxford.

Gordillo Hervás, R. 2017. "Trajan and Hadrian's Reorganization of the Agonistic Associations in Rome." In Muñiz Grijalvo et al. eds. 2017: 84–97.

Gowing, A.M. 2005. *Empire and Memory: The Representation of the Roman Republic in Imperial Culture*. Cambridge.

Graf, D.F. 2018. "The Silk Road between Syria and China." In A. Wilson and A. Bowman eds. *Trade, Commerce, and the State in the Roman World* (Oxford 2018): 443–529.

Graf, F. 1997. *Magic in the Ancient World*. Cambridge MA.

Graindor, P. 1934. *Athènes sous Hadrien*. Cairo.

Grenier, J.-C., and F. Coarelli. 1986. "La Tombe d'Antinoüs à Rome." *Mélanges de l'École française de Rome: Antiquités* 98: 217–53.

Griffin, J. 1985. *Latin Poets and Roman Life*. London.

Griffin, M.T. 1984. *Nero: The End of a Dynasty*. New Haven.

Griffin, M.T. 1997. "The Senate's Story." *Journal of Roman Studies* 87: 249–63 = M.T. Griffin 2018: 229–47.

Griffin, M.T. 2000. "Nerva to Hadrian." *Cambridge Ancient History*² XI: 84–131.

Griffin, M.T. 2005. "'Lifting the Mask': Syme on Fictional History." In Tomlin ed. 2005: 16–39 = M.T. Griffin 2018: 325–38.

Griffin, M.T. 2014. "The Prince and His Tutor: Candour and Affection." *Scripta Classica Israelica* 33: 67–85 = M.T. Griffin 2018: 707–21.

Griffin, M.T. 2018. *Politics and Philosophy at Rome: Collected Papers* (ed. C. Balmaceda). Oxford.

Gualandi, G. 1963. *Legislazione imperiale e giurisprudenza* I–II. Milan.

Gunderson, E. 2003. *Declamation, Paternity and Roman Identity*. Cambridge.

Hadas-Lebel, M. 2006. *Jerusalem against Rome*. Leuven.

Hägg, T. 2012. *The Art of Biography in Antiquity*. Cambridge.

Haley, E. 2005. "Hadrian as Romulus or the Self-Representation of a Roman Emperor." *Latomus* 64: 969–80.

Halfmann, H. 1979. *Die Senatoren aus dem östlichen Teil des Imperium Romanum bis zum Ende des 2. Jahrhunderts n. Chr.* Göttingen.

Halfmann, H. 1986. *Itinera Principum: Geschichte und Typologie der Kaiserreichen im Römischen Reich*. Stuttgart.

Hallett, C.H. 2005. *The Roman Nude: Heroic Portrait Statuary 200 BC – AD 300*. Oxford.

Halliwell, S. 1987. *The* Poetics *of Aristotle: Translation and Commentary*. Chapel Hill.

Hannestad, N. 1988. *Roman Art and Imperial Policy*. Aarhus.

Harker, A. 2008. *Loyalty and Dissidence in Roman Egypt: The Case of the* Acta Alexandrinorum. Cambridge.

Harris, R. 1926. "Hadrian's Decree of Expulsion of the Jews from Jerusalem." *Harvard Theological Review* 19: 199–206.

Harris, W.V. 2010. "History, Empathy and Emotions." *Antike und Abendland* 56: 1–23.

Harris, W.V. 2013. "Thinking about Mental Disorders in Classical Antiquity." In W.V. Harris ed. 2013: 1–23.

Harris, W.V. ed. 2013. *Mental Disorders in the Classical World*. Leiden.

Harris, W.V. 2016. *Roman Power: A Thousand Years of Empire*. Cambridge.

Harrison, S.J. 2000. *Apuleius: A Latin Sophist*. Oxford.

Hauken, T., and H. Malay. 2009. "A New Edict of Hadrian from the Province of Asia Settling Regulations for Requisitioned Transport." In R. Haensch ed. *Selbtsdarstellung und Kommunikation: Die Veröffentlichung staatlicher Urkunden auf Stein und Bronze in der römischen Welt* (Munich 2009): 327–48.

Hawkins, C. 2016. *Roman Artisans and the Roman Economy*. Cambridge.

Healey, J.F. 2009. *Aramaic Inscriptions and Documents of the Roman Period*. Oxford.

Heilen, S. 2005. "The Emperor Hadrian in the Horoscopes of Antigonus of Nicaea." In G. Oestmann, H.D. Ruttkin, and K. von Stuckrad eds. *Horoscopes and Public Spheres: Essays on the History of Astrology* (Berlin NY 2005): 49–67.

Hekster, O., L. Claes, E. Manders, D. Slootjes, Y. Klaassen, and N. de Haan. 2014. "Nero's Ancestry and the Construction of Imperial Ideology in the Early Empire. A Methodological Case Study." *Journal of Ancient History and Archaeology* 11: 7–27.

Henderson, B.W. 1920. *The Study of Roman History*. London.

Henderson, B.W. 1968 [1923]. *The Life and Principate of the Emperor Hadrian A.D. 76–138*. Rome (London).

Herr, M.D. 1971. "The Historical Significance of the Dialogues between Jewish Sages and Roman Dignitaries." *Scripta Hierosolymitana* 22: 121–50.

Herr, M.D. 1972. "Persecution and Martyrdom in Hadrian's Days." *Scripta Hierosolymitana* 23: 85–125.

Hetland, L.M. 2015. "New Perspectives on Dating the Pantheon." In Mander and Wilson Jones eds. 2015: 79–98.

Highet, G. 1957. *Poets in a Landscape*. London.

Hingley, R. 2012. *Hadrian's Wall: A Life*. Oxford.

Holford-Strevens, L. 1988. *Aulus Gellius*. London.

Honoré, T. 1981. *Emperors and Lawyers*. London.

Hopkins, K. 1983. *Death and Renewal: Sociological Studies in Roman History Volume 2*. Cambridge.

Hopkins, K. 1999. *A World Full of Gods: Pagans, Jews and Christians in the Roman Empire*. London.

Hopkins, K. 2018 [2005]. "How to Be a Roman Emperor: An Autobiography." In Tomlin ed. 2005: 72–85 = K. Hopkins, *Sociological Studies in Roman History* (ed. C. Kelly) (Cambridge 2018): ch. 14.

Horbury, W. 2014. *Jewish War under Trajan and Hadrian*. Cambridge.

Howley, J.A. 2014. "'Heus tu, rhetorisce': Gellius, Cicero, Plutarch, and Roman Study Abroad." In J.M. Madsen and R.D. Rees eds. *Roman Rule in Greek and Latin Writing: Double Vision* (Leiden 2014): 163–92.

Hübner, S.R., and D.M. Ratzan 2009. "Fatherless Antiquity? Perspectives on "Fatherlessness" in the Ancient Mediterranean." In S.R. Hübner and D.M. Ratzan eds. *Growing Up Fatherless in Antiquity* (Cambridge): 3–28.

Humfress, C. 2005. "Law and Legal Practice in the Age of Justinian." In M. Maas ed. *The Cambridge Companion to the Age of Justinian* (Cambridge 2005): 161–84.

Husquin, C. 2018. "Les deux corps du prince: Corporalités impériales et traitement littéraire à travers l'exemple d'Hadrien." *Annales de Janua – Les Annales no. 6.* Publié en ligne le 13 avril 2018. http://09-edel.univ-poitiers.fr /annalesdejanua/index.php?id=1855.

Husquin, C. 2020. "Corps du prince, réputation et postérité entre politique et pathologie: L'Exemple de Caligula." In A. Gangloff and B. Maire eds. *La Santé du prince: Corps, vertus et politique dans l'antiquité romaine* (Grenoble 2020): 135–52.

Hutchinson, G.O. 2013. *Greek to Latin: Frameworks and Contexts for Intertextuality.* Oxford.

Israelowich, I. 2012. *Society, Medicine and Religion in the* Sacred Tales *of Aelius Aristides.* Leiden.

Jarrett, M. 1976. "An Unnecessary War." *Britannia* 7: 145–51.

Jones, C.P. 1971. *Plutarch and Rome.* Oxford.

Jones, C.P. 1978. *The Roman World of Dio Chrysostom.* Cambridge MA.

Jones, C.P. 1996. "The Panhellenion." *Chiron* 26: 29–56.

Jones, C.P. 1998. "A Constitution of Hadrian Concerning Cyrene." *Chiron* 28: 255–66.

Jones, C.P. 1999. "A Decree of Thyatira in Lydia." *Chiron* 29: 1–25.

Jones, C.P. 2004. "A Speech of the Emperor Hadrian." *Classical Quarterly* 54: 266–73.

Jones, C.P. 2006. "A Letter of Hadrian to Naryka (Eastern Locris)." *Journal of Roman Archaeology* 19: 151–62.

Jones, C.P. 2007. "Three New Letters of Hadrian." *Zeitschrift für Papyrologie und Epigraphik* 161: 145–56.

Jones, C.P. 2009. "A Petition to Hadrian of 129 CE." *Chiron* 39: 445–61.

Jones, C.P. 2010. *New Heroes in Antiquity.* Cambridge MA.

Jones, C.P. 2011. "An Edict of Hadrian from Maroneia." *Chiron* 41: 313–25.

Jouanna, J. 2013. "The Typology and Aetiology of Madness in Ancient Greek Medical and Philosophical Writing." In W.V. Harris ed. 2013: 97–118.

Juntunen, K. 2013. "Pharasmanes and the Iazyges: The Date of the Two Embassies in Cassius Dio 69.15.2*." *Historia* 62: 108–28.

Karivieri, A. 2002. "Just One of the Boys: Hadrian in the Company of Zeus, Dionysus and Theseus." In Ostenfeld ed. 2002: 40–54.

Karivieri, A. 2019. "«*Varius, multiplex, multiformis*»: Greek, Roman, Panhellenic." In J. Russi ed. *Gender, Memory, and Identity in the Roman World* (Amsterdam 2019): 283–300.

Kaster, R.A. 2005. *Emotion, Restraint, and Community in Ancient Rome.* Oxford.

Kemezis, A.M. 2014. *Greek Narratives of the Roman Empire under the Severans.* Cambridge.

Keppie, L. 2000. *Legions and Veterans: Roman Army Papers 1971–2000.* Stuttgart.

Kleiner, D.E.E. 1992. *Roman Sculpture.* New Haven.

Kloner, A., and B. Zissu. 2003. "Hiding Complexes in Judaea: An Archaeological and Geographical Update on the Area of the Bar Kokhba Revolt." In Schäfer ed. 2003: 181–216.

Lambert, R. 1988 [1984]. *Beloved and God: The Story of Hadrian and Antinous.* Don Mills ON.

Lane Fox, R. 1990. "Ancient Hunting: Homer to Polybios." In G. Shipley and J.B. Salmon eds. *Human Landscapes in Classical Antiquity: Environment and Culture* (London 1990): 119–53.

Lane Fox, R. 2015. *Augustine: Conversions to Confessions.* New York.

Lapini, N. 2020. "L'Arc de Trajan à Bénévent: la conquête de la Mésopotamie vue par Hadrien." In Benoit et al. eds. 2020: 45–56.

Lassus, J. 1969. "Antioche en 459, d'après la Mosaïque de Yakto." In J. Balty ed. *Actes du colloque Apamée de Syrie* (Brussels 1969): 137–47.

Lear, A. 2014. "Ancient Pederasty: An Introduction." In T.K. Hubbard ed. *A Companion to Greek and Roman Sexualities* (Oxford 2014): 106–31.

Lear, A., and E. Cantarella. 2008. *Images of Ancient Greek Pederasty: Boys Were Their Gods.* London.

Lecocq, F. 2020. "Deux faces du phénix impérial: Trajan et Hadrien sur les *aurei* de 117/118 apr. J.-C." In Benoit et al. eds 2020: 57–70.

Lepper, F.A. 1948. *Trajan's Parthian War.* Oxford.

Lepper, F.A., and S.S. Frere. 1988. *Trajan's Column: A New Edition of the Cichorius Plates.* Gloucester.

Levick, B.M. 1976. *Tiberius the Politician.* London.

Levick, B.M. 2015. *Claudius* (second edition). New York.

Levick, B.M. 2017. *Vespasian* (second edition). New York.

Lewes, G.H. 1863. "Was Nero a Monster?" *Cornhill Magazine* 8: 113–28.

Lewis, R.G. 1993. "Imperial Autobiography, Augustus to Hadrian." *Aufstieg und Niedergang der römischen Welt* II 34.1: 629–706.

Liddle, A. 2003. *Arrian: Periplus Ponti Euxini.* Bristol.

Lieberman, S. 1942. *Greek in Jewish Palestine: Studies in the Life and Manners of Jewish Palestine in the II–IV Centuries C.E.* New York.

Liebeschuetz, J.H.W.G. 1979. *Continuity and Change in Roman Religion.* Oxford.

Lightfoot, C.S. 1990. "Trajan's Parthian War and the Fourth-Century Perspective." *Journal of Roman Studies* 80: 115–26.

Lindsay, H. 2009. *Adoption in the Roman World.* Cambridge.

Litchfield, M.W. 1914. "National *exempla virtutis* in Roman Literature." *Harvard Studies in Classical Philology* 25: 1–71.

Long, A.A. 2002. *Epictetus: A Stoic and Socratic Guide to Life*. Oxford.

Longden, R.P. 1931. "Notes on the Parthian Campaign of Trajan." *Journal of Roman Studies* 21: 1–35.

Longden, R.P. 1954 [1936]. "The Wars of Trajan." *Cambridge Ancient History*[1] XI: 223–52.

Lyne, R.O.A.M. 1980. *The Latin Love Poets*. Oxford.

MacDonald, W.L. 1975. *The Pantheon: Design, Structure, Space*. London.

MacDonald, W.L., and J.A. Pinto. 1995. *Hadrian's Villa and Its Legacy*. New Haven.

MacMullen, R. 1981. *Paganism in the Roman Empire*. New Haven.

MacMullen, R. 1990. *Changes in the Roman Empire: Essays in the Ordinary*. Princeton.

MacMullen, R. 2003. *Feelings in History, Ancient and Modern*. Claremont CA.

Madsen, J.M. 2016. "Criticising the Benefactors: The Severans and the Return of Dynastic Rule." In C.H. Lange and J.M. Madsen eds. *Cassius Dio: Greek Intellectual and Roman Politician* (Leiden 2016): 136–58.

Mallan, C.T. 2013. "The Style, Method, and Programme of Xiphilinus' *Epitome* of Cassius Dio's *Roman History*." *Greek, Roman and Byzantine Studies* 53: 610–44.

Mander, T.A., and M. Wilson Jones eds. 2015. *The Pantheon from Antiquity to the Present*. Cambridge.

Marañón, G. 1956. *Tiberius: A Study in Resentment*. London.

Marks, R.G. 1994. *The Image of Bar Kokhba in Traditional Jewish Literature: False Messiah and National Hero*. University Park PA.

Mattern, S.P. 2013. *The Prince of Medicine: Galen in the Roman Empire*. New York.

McLynn, N. 1996. "The Fourth-Century Taurobolium." *Phoenix* 50: 312–30.

Meiggs, R. 1982. *Trees and Timber in the Ancient Mediterranean World*. Oxford.

Meyer, H. 1991. *Antinoos: Die archäologischen Denkmäler unter Einbeziehung des numismatischen und epigraphischen Materials sowie der literarischen Nachrichten. Ein Beitrag zur Kunst- und Kulturgeschichte der hadrianisch-frühantonininischen Zeit*. Munich.

Migliorati, G. 2003. *Cassio Dione e l'impero romano da Nerva ad Antonino Pio: alla luce dei nuovi documenti*. Milan.

Mikesell, M.W. 1969. "The Deforestation of Mount Lebanon." *Geographical Review* 59: 1–28.

Mildenberg, L. 1980. "Bar Kokhba Coins and Documents." *Harvard Studies in Classical Philology* 84: 311–35.

Mildenberg, L. 1984. *The Coinage of the Bar Kokhba War*. Aarau.

Millar, F.G.B. 1964. *A Study of Cassius Dio*. Oxford.

Millar, F.G.B. 1977. *The Emperor in the Roman World*. London.

Millar, F.G.B. 1993. *The Roman Near East 31 BC – AD 337*. Cambridge MA.

Millar, F.G.B. 1996. "Sir Ronald Syme." In C.S. Nicholls ed. *The Dictionary of National Biography 1986–1990* (Oxford 1996): 442–4.

Millar, F.G.B. 2000. *A Greek Roman Empire: Power and Belief under Theodosius II 408–450*. Berkeley.

Millar, F.G.B. 2004. *Rome, The Greek World, and The East Volume 2: Government, Society, and Culture in the Roman Empire*. Chapel Hill.

Millar, F.G.B. 2006. *Rome, The Greek World, and The East Volume 3: The Greek World, The Jews, and The East*. Chapel Hill.

Mitchell, S. 1995 [1993]. *Anatolia: Land, Men, and Gods in Asia Minor*. 2 Vols. Oxford.

Mitchell, S. 2013. "Trajan and the Cities of the East." In I. Piso and R. Varga eds. *Trajan und seine Städte* (Cluj-Napoca 2013): 225–32.

Mitford, T.B. 2018. *East of Asia Minor: Rome's Hidden Frontier*. Oxford.

Molin, M. 2016. "Biographie de l'historien Cassius Dion." In Fromentin et al. eds. 2016: II 431–46.

Momigliano, A.D. 1949. Review of Lepper 1948. *Rivista Storica Italiana* 61: 124–7 = *Quinto contributo alla storia degli classici e del mondo antico* II (Rome 1975): 1003–7.

Momigliano, A.D. 1968/1969. "Ammiano Marcellino e la Historia Augusta (A proposito del libro di Ronald Syme)." *Atti della Accademia delle scienze di Torino. Classe di scienze morali, storiche e filologiche* 103: 423–36 = *Quinto contributo alla storia degli studi classici e del mondo antico* (Rome 1975): I 93–103.

Momigliano, A.D. 1969a [1954]. "An Unsolved Problem of Historical Forgery: The 'Scriptores Historiae Augustae'." In A.D. Momigliano, *Studies in Historiography* (London 1969): 143–80 (expanded version, first published in *Journal of the Warburg and Courtauld Institutes* 17 [1954]: 22–46).

Momigliano, A.D. 1969b. Review of Syme 1968. *English Historical Review* 84: 566–9 = *Quinto contributo alla storia degli studi classici e del mondo antico* (Rome 1975): I 104–8.

Momigliano, A.D. 1969c [1950]. "Ancient History and the Antiquarian." In A.D. Momigliano, *Studies in Historiography* (London 1969): 1–39.

Momigliano, A.D. 1971. *The Development of Greek Biography*. Cambridge MA.

Momigliano, A.D. 1973. Review of Syme 1971a. *English Historical Review* 88: 114–15 = *Sesto contributo alla storia degli studi classici e del mondo antico* (Rome 1980): 714–16.

Momigliano, A.D. 1984. Review of Syme 1983 and *RP* III. *Times Literary Supplement* October 12, 1984 = *Ottavo contributo alla storia degli studi classici e del mondo antico* (Rome 1987): 392–8.

Momigliano, A.D. 1985. "Marcel Mauss and the Quest for the Person in Greek Biography and Autobiography." In M. Carrithers, S. Collins, and S. Lukes eds. *The Category of the Person: Anthropology, Philosophy, History* (Cambridge 1985): 83–92.

Montserrat, D. 1996. *Sex and Society and Græco-Roman Egypt*. London.

Morgan, T. 1998. *Literate Education in the Hellenistic and Roman Worlds.* Cambridge.

Mortensen, S. 2004. *Hadrian: Eine Deutungsgeschichte.* Bonn.

Morwood, J. 2013. *Hadrian.* London.

Muñiz Grijalvo, E., J.M. Cortés Copete, and F. Lozano Gómez eds. 2017. *Empire and Religion: Religious Change in Greek Cities under Roman Rule.* Leiden.

Murray, O. 1991. "Arnaldo Momigliano in England." *History and Theory* 30: 49–64.

Musurillo, H. 1954. *The Acts of the Pagan Martyrs:* Acta Alexandrinorum. Oxford.

Mynott, J. 2018. *Birds in the Ancient World: Winged Words.* Oxford.

Noreña, C.F. 2011. *Imperial Ideals in the Roman West.* Cambridge.

Oliver, J.H. 1989. *Greek Constitutions of Early Roman Emperors from Inscriptions and Papyri.* Philadelphia.

Oppenheimer, A. 2003. "The Ban on Circumcision as a Cause of the Revolt: A Reconsideration." In Schäfer ed. 2003: 54–69.

Opper, T. 2008. *Hadrian: Empire and Conflict.* London.

Opper, T. ed. 2013. *Hadrian: Art, Politics and Economy.* London.

Osborne, R. 2018. "Imaginary Intercourse." In D. Allen, P. Christensen, and P. Millett eds. *How to Do Things with History: New Approaches to Ancient Greece* (Oxford 2018): 314–38.

Osgood, J. 2011. *Claudius Caesar: Image and Power in the Early Roman Empire.* Cambridge.

Ostenfeld, E.N. ed. 2002. *Greek Romans and Roman Greeks: Studies in Cultural Interaction.* Aarhus.

Paribeni, R. 1926. *Optimus Princeps: Saggio sulla storia e sui tempi dell'imperatore Traiano.* Vol. 1. Messina.

Paribeni, R. 1927. *Optimus Princeps: Saggio sulla storia e sui tempi dell'imperatore Traiano* Vol. 2. Messina.

Parkin, T.G. 1992. *Demography and Roman Society.* Baltimore.

Paschoud, F. 2012. "On a Recent Book by Alan Cameron: «The Last Pagans of Rome»." *Antiquité tardive* 20: 359–88.

Peachin, M. 1986. "The *Procurator Monetae.*" *Numismatic Chronicle* 146: 94–106.

Pelham, H.F. 1911. *Essays in Roman History.* Oxford.

Pelling, C.B.R. 1997. "Biographical History? Cassius Dio on the Early Principate." In M.J. Edwards and S. Swain eds. *Portraits: Biographical Representation in the Greek and Latin Literature of the Roman Empire* (Oxford 1997): 117–44.

Pelling, C.B.R. 2009. "The First Biographers: Plutarch and Suetonius." In M.T. Griffin ed. *A Companion to Julius Caesar* (Oxford 2009): 252–66.

Pelling, C.B.R. 2015. "Rhetoric of *The Roman Revolution.*" *Syllecta Classica* 26: 207–47.

Penella, R.J. 2014. "Libanius' *Declamations.*" In L. van Hoof ed. *Libanius: A Critical Introduction* (Cambridge 2014): 107–207.

Perkins, J. 1995. *The Suffering Self: Pain and Narrative Representation in the Early Christian Era.* London.

Perowne, S. 1996 [1960]. *Hadrian.* New York.

Petrakis, N.L. 1980. "Diagonal Earlobe Creases: Type A Behavior and the Death of the Emperor Hadrian." *Western Journal of Medicine* 132: 87–91.

Pleket, H. 1973. "Some Aspects of the History of the Athletic Guilds." *Zeitschrift für Papyrologie und Epigraphik* 10: 197–227.

Plett, H.F. 2012. *Enargeia in Classical Antiquity and the Early Modern Age: The Aesthetics of Evidence.* Leiden.

Podro, J. 1959. *The Last Pharisee: The Life and Times of Rabbi ben Hananyah.* London.

Pöhlmann, E. 2019. "The Hymn of Mesomedes on Antinous (Inscription of Courion, Mitford No. 104). *Greek and Roman Musical Studies* 7: 128–39.

Pomeroy, S.B. 1999. "Reflections on Plutarch, *A Consolation to His Wife.*" In S.B. Pomeroy ed. *Plutarch's* Advice to the Bride and Groom *and* A Consolation to His Wife: *English Translations, Commentary, Interpretive Essays, and Bibliography* (New York 1999): 75–81.

Potter, D.S. 1991. "The Inscriptions on the Bronze Herakles from Mesene: Vologeses IV's War with Rome and the Date of Tacitus' *Annales.*" *Zeitschrift für Papyrologie und Epigraphik* 88: 277–90.

Power, T., and R.K. Gibson eds. 2014. *Suetonius the Biographer: Studies in Roman Lives.* Oxford.

Price, S.F.R. 1984. *The Roman Imperial Cult in Asia Minor.* Cambridge.

Price, S.F.R. 1987. "From Noble Funerals to Divine Cult: The Consecration of Roman Emperors." In D. Cannadine and S.F.R. Price eds. *Rituals of Royalty: Power and Ceremonial in Traditional Societies* (Cambridge 1987): 56–105.

Rabello, A.M. 1995. "The Ban on Circumcision as a Cause of Bar Kokhba's Rebellion." *Israel Law Review* 29: 176–214.

Raepsaet-Charlier, M.-T. 1987. *Prosopographie des femmes de l'ordre sénatorial: Ier–IIe siècles.* Louvain.

Ratti, St. 2007. "Nicomaque senior auteur de l'Histoire Auguste." In G. Bonamente and H. Brandt eds. *Historiae Augustae Colloquium Bambergense* (Bari 2007): 305–17.

Ratti, St. 2010. *Antiquus Error. Les Ultimes feux de la résistance païenne.* Turnhout.

Ratti, St. 2012. *Polémiques entre païens et chrétiens.* Paris.

Ratti, St. 2016a. *L'Histoire Auguste: Les Païens et les Chrétiens dans l'antiquité tardive.* Paris.

Ratti, St. 2016b. Reply to Cameron 2016. *Bryn Mawr Classical Review* 2016.09.22.

Rawson, B.M. 2003. *Children and Childhood in Roman Italy*. Oxford.

Rawson, E. 1991. *Roman Culture and Society: Collected Papers*. Oxford.

Reinach, T. 1884. *Histoire des Israélites*. Paris.

Renan, E. 1879. *L'Église chrétienne*. Paris.

Reynolds, J. M. 2000. "New Letters of Hadrian to Aphrodisias: Trials, Taxes, Gladiators and an Aqueduct." *Journal of Roman Archaeology* 13: 5–20.

Reynolds, L.D. ed. 1988 [1983]. *Texts and Transmissions: A Survey of the Latin Classics*. Oxford.

Rich. J., and G. Shipley eds. 1993. *War and Society in the Roman World*. London.

Richlin, A. 2006. *Marcus Aurelius in Love*. Chicago.

Rivet, A.F.L. 1988. *Gallia Narbonensis*. London.

Rizzi, M. 2010. "Hadrian and the Christians." In Rizzi ed. 2010: 7–20.

Rizzi, M. ed. 2010. *Hadrian and the Christians*. Berlin.

Rodrigues, N.S. 2014. "«Morte no Nilo» Antinoo: Sacrifício, Acidente ou Assassínio?" In F. de Oliveira, M. de Fátima Silva, and T.V.R. Barbosa eds. *Violência e transgressão: uma trajetória da Humanidade* (Coimbra 2014): 265–78.

Rohrbacher, D. 2016. *The Play of Allusion in the* Historia Augusta. Madison WI.

Roller, M. 2001. *Constructing Autocracy: Aristocrats and Emperors in Julio-Claudian Rome*. Princeton.

Roman, Y. 2008. *Hadrien: L'Empereur virtuose*. Paris.

Romeo, I. 2002. "The Panhellenion and Ethnic Identity in Hadrianic Greece." *Classical Philology* 97: 21–40.

Rood, T. 2011. "Black Sea Variations: Arrian's *Periplus*." *Cambridge Classical Journal* 57: 137–63.

Rostovtzeff, M.I. 1957. *The Social and Economic History of the Roman Empire* (second edition revised by P.M. Fraser). Oxford.

Rudd, N. 1976. *Lines of Enquiry*. Cambridge.

Russell, D.A., and N.G. Wilson eds. 1981. *Menander Rhetor*. Oxford.

Rusyaeva, A.S. 2003. "The Temple of Achilles on the Island of Leuke in the Black Sea." *Ancient Civilizations from Scythia to Siberia: An International Journal of Comparative Studies in History and Archaeology* 9: 1–16.

Rutherford, R.B. 1989. *The* Meditations *of Marcus Aurelius*. Oxford.

Sachar, A.L. 1968. *A History of the Jews* (fifth edition). New York.

Sallares, R. 1991. *The Ecology of the Ancient Greek World*. London.

Saller, R.P. 1994. *Patriarchy, Property and Death in the Roman Family*. Cambridge.

Šašel Kos, M. 2009. "Antinous in Upper Moesia: The Introduction of a New Cult." In M.G. Angeli Bertinelli and A. Donati eds. *Opinione pubblica e forme di communicazione a Roma: il linguaggio dell'epigrafia* (Faenza 2009): 177–88.

Savino, E. 2017. *Ricerche sull'Historia Augusta*. Naples.

Savo, M.B. 2009. "Tito Statilio Critone: medico letterato e storico delle guerre daciche." In E. Lanzillotta, V. Costa, and G. Ottone eds. *Tradizione e tramissione degli storici greci frammentari. In recordi di Silvio Accame* (Tivoli 2009): 499–540.

Scarborough, J. 1985. "Criton, Physician to Trajan: Historian and Pharmacist." In J.W. Eadie and J. Ober eds. *The Craft of the Historian: Essays in Honor of Chester G. Starr* (Lanham MD): 387–405.

Schäfer, P. 2003. "Bar Kokhba and the Rabbis." In Schäfer ed. 2003: 1–22.

Schäfer, P. ed. 2003. *The Bar Kokhba War Reconsidered: New Perspectives on the Second Jewish Revolt against Rome.* Tübingen.

Scheid, J. 1998. *Recherches archéologiques à la Magliana. Commentarii Fratrum Arvalium Qui Supersunt. Les copies épigraphiques des protocoles annuels de la confrérie arvale (21 av.-304 ap. J.-C.).* Rome.

Schmidt, St. 2009. "Zum Treffen in Neapol und den *Panhellenia* in der Hadriansinschrift aus Alexandria Troas." *Zeitschrift für Papyrologie und Epigraphik* 170: 109–12.

Schulz, V. 2019. *Deconstructing Imperial Representation: Tacitus, Cassius Dio, and Suetonius on Nero and Domitian.* Leiden.

Schürer, E. 1973. *The History of the Jewish People in the Age of Jesus Christ (175 B.C. – A.D. 135). A New English Version Revised and Edited by Geza Vermes & Fergus Millar.* Volume I. Edinburgh.

Schürer, E. 1979. *The History of the Jewish People in the Age of Jesus Christ (175 B.C. – A.D. 135). A New English Version Revised and Edited by Geza Vermes & Fergus Millar.* Volume II. Edinburgh.

Shahar, Y. 2003. "The Underground Hideouts in Galilee and Their Historical Meaning." In Schäfer ed. 2003: 217–40.

Sherk, R.K. 1980. "Roman Galatia." *Aufstieg und Niedergang der römischen Welt* II 7.2: 954–1052.

Sherk, R.K. 1988. *The Roman Empire: Augustus to Hadrian: Translated Documents of Greece and Rome 6.* Cambridge.

Sherwin-White, A.N. 1959. "Review and Discussion of R. Syme, *Tacitus.*" *Journal of Roman Studies* 49: 140–6.

Sherwin-White, A.N. 1966. *The Letters of Pliny: A Historical and Social Commentary.* Oxford.

Sidebottom, H. 2007. "Severan Historiography." In S. Swain, S. Harrison, and J. Elsner eds. *Severan Culture* (Cambridge 2007): 52–82.

Silberman, A. 1993. "Arrien, 'Périple du Pont Euxin': Essai d'interprétation et d'évaluation des données historiques et géographiques." *Aufstieg und Niedergang der römischen Welt* II 34.1: 276–311.

Slater, W.J. 2008. "Hadrian's Letters to the Athletes and Dionysiac Artists Concerning Arrangements for the 'Circuit' of Games." *Journal of Roman Archaeology* 21: 610–20.

Smallwood, E.M. 1959. "The Legislation of Hadrian and Antoninus Pius against Circumcision." *Latomus* 18: 334–47.

Smallwood, E.M. 1966. *Documents Illustrating the Principates of Nerva, Trajan and Hadrian*. Cambridge.

Smallwood, E.M. 1976. *The Jews under Roman Rule: From Pompey to Diocletian*. Leiden.

Smith, R.R.R. 2018. *Antinous: Boy Made God*. Oxford.

Soverini, P. 1983. *Scrittori della Storia Augusta. Volume primo*. Turin.

Spawforth, A.J.S. 1999. "The Panhellenion Again." *Chiron* 29: 339–52.

Spawforth, A.J.S. 2012. *Greece and the Augustan Cultural Revolution*. Cambridge.

Spawforth, A.J.S., and S.Walker. 1985. "The World of the Panhellenion I: Athens and Eleusis." *Journal of Roman Studies* 75: 78–104.

Spawforth, A.J.S., and S. Walker. 1986. "The World of the Panhellenion II: Three Dorian Cities." *Journal of Roman Studies* 76: 88–105.

Speidel, M. 2006. *Emperor Hadrian's Speeches to the African Army: A New Text*. Mainz.

Speller, E. 2003. *Following Hadrian: A Second-Century Journey through the Roman Empire*. Oxford.

Stadter, P.A. 1976. "Xenophon in Arrian's *Cynegeticus*." *Greek, Roman and Byzantine Studies* 17: 157–67.

Stadter, P.A. 1978. "The *Ars Tactica* of Arrian: Tradition and Originality." *Classical Philology* 73: 117–28.

Stadter, P.A. 1980. *Arrian of Nicomedia*. Chapel Hill.

Ste Croix, G.E.M. de. 1975. "Aristotle on History and Poetry." In B.M. Levick ed. *The Ancient Historian and His Materials* (Farnborough, Hants. 1975): 45–58.

Ste Croix, G.E.M. de. 1981. *The Class Struggle in the Ancient Greek World from the Archaic Age to the Arab Conquests*. London.

Stern, M. 1976. *Greek and Latin Authors on Jews and Judaism. Volume One: From Herodotus to Plutarch*. Jerusalem.

Stern, M. 1980. *Greek and Latin Authors on Jews and Judaism. Volume Two: From Tacitus to Simplicius*. Jerusalem.

Stinespring, W.F. 1939. "Hadrian in Palestine, 129/130 A.D." *Journal of the American Oriental Society* 59: 360–5.

Storoni Mazzolani, L. 1972. *The Idea of the City in Roman Thought from Walled City to Spiritual Commonwealth*. Bloomington.

Stover, J. 2020. "New Light on the *Historia Augusta.*" *Journal of Roman Studies* 110: 167–98.

Swain, S. 1991. "Plutarch, Hadrian, and Delphi." *Historia* 40: 318–30.

Swain, S. 1996. *Hellenism and Empire: Language, Classicism, and Power in the Greek World AD 50–250.* Oxford.

Syme, R. 1939. *The Roman Revolution.* Oxford.

Syme, R. 1956. "Foreward" to Marañón 1956.

Syme, R. 1958. *Tacitus.* 2 vols. Oxford.

Syme, R. 1968. *Ammianus and the Historia Augusta.* Oxford.

Syme, R. 1971a. *Emperors and Biography.* Oxford.

Syme, R. 1971b. *The* Historia Augusta: *A Call of Clarity.* Bonn.

Syme, R. 1971c. *Danubian Papers.* Bucharest.

Syme, R. 1978. *History in Ovid.* Oxford.

Syme, R. 1979. *Roman Papers* I–II (ed. E. Badian). Oxford.

Syme, R. 1983. *Historia Augusta Papers.* Oxford.

Syme, R. 1984. *Roman Papers* III (ed. A.R. Birley). Oxford.

Syme, R. 1986. *The Augustan Aristocracy.* Oxford.

Syme, R. 1988. *Roman Papers* IV–V (ed. A.R. Birley). Oxford.

Syme, R. 1991. *Roman Papers* VI–VII (ed. A.R. Birley). Oxford.

Syme, R. 1999. *The Provincial at Rome* and *Rome and the Balkans 80 BC–AD 14* (ed. A.R. Birley). Exeter.

Syme, R. 2013. "Tacite et Proust." *Histos* 7: 128–45.

Talbert, R.J.A. 1984. *The Senate of Imperial Rome.* Princeton.

Temporini, H. 1979. *Die Frauen am Hofe Trajans: Ein Beitrag zur Stellung der Augustae im Prinzipat.* Berlin.

Temporini-Gräfin Vitzthum, H. 2002. "Die Familie der «Adoptivkaiser» von Traian bis Commodus." In H. Temporini-Gräfin Vitzthum ed. *Die Kaiserinnen Roms: Von Livia bis Theodora* (Munich 2002): 188–213.

Thumiger, C. 2013. "The Early Greek Medical Vocabulary of Insanity." In W.V. Harris ed. 2013: 61–95.

Tomlin, R.S.O. 2018. *Britannia Romana: Roman Inscriptions and Roman Britain.* Oxford.

Tomlin, R.S.O. ed. 2005. *History and Fiction: Six Essays Celebrating the Centenary of Sir Ronald Syme (1903–1989).* London.

Toner, J. 2009. *Popular Culture in Ancient Rome.* Cambridge.

Toohey, P. 2013. "Madness in the *Digest.*" In W.V. Harris ed. 2013: 441–60.

Toomer, G.J. 1984. *Ptolemy's* Almagest. New York.

Townend, G.B. 1967. "Suetonius and His Influence." In T.A. Dorey ed. *Latin Biography* (London 1967): 79–111.

Toynbee, J.M.C. 1934. *The Hadrianic School: A Chapter in the History of Greek Art*. Cambridge.

Toynbee, J.M.C. 1971. *Death and Burial in the Roman World*. Baltimore.

Traiana, G. 2017–18. "Trajan and the Earthquake of Antioch (115 AD)." In E. Amato, P. De Cicco, and T. Moreau eds. *Canistrum ficis plenum. Hommages à B. Lançon* (*Revue des études tardo-antiques* Suppl. 5): 417–28.

Treadgold, W. 2007. "The Byzantine World Histories of John Malalas and Eustathius of Epiphania." *International History Review* 29: 709–45.

Treggiari, S.M. 1991. *Roman Marriage: Iusti Coniuges from the Time of Cicero to the Time of Ulpian*. Oxford.

Treggiari, S.M. 1998. "Home and Forum: Cicero between 'Public' and 'Private'." *Transactions and Proceedings of the American Philological Association* 128: 1–23.

Treggiari, S.M. 2007. *Terentia, Tullia and Publilia: The Women of Cicero's Family*. London.

Tuori, K. 2016. *The Emperor of Law*. Oxford.

Turcan, R. 1996 [1989]. *The Cults of the Roman Empire*. Oxford.

Turcan, R. 2008. *Hadrien: Souverain de la romanité*. Dijon.

Vanacker, W. 2013. "Ties of Resistance and Cooperation: Aedimon, Lusius Quietus and the Baquates." *Mnemosyne* 66: 708–33.

van Bremen, R. 2005. "«Plotina to All Her Friends»: The Letter(s) of the Empress Plotina to the Epicureans in Athens." *Chiron* 35: 499–532.

Veyne, P. 2001 [1991]. *La Société romaine*. Paris.

Veyne, P. 2005. *L'Empire gréco-romain*. Paris.

Vidman, L. 1982. *Fasti Ostienses*. Prague.

Villetard, M. 2020. "Les *Auditoria* d'Hadrien dans la topographie urbaine des forums impériaux." In Benoit et al. eds. 2020: 83–95.

Vout, C. 2003. "A Revision of Hadrian's Portraiture." In de Blois et al. eds. 2003: 442–57.

Vout, C. 2005. "Antinous, Archaeology and History." *Journal of Roman Studies* 95: 80–96.

Vout, C. 2007. *Power and Eroticism in Imperial Rome*. Cambridge.

Vout, C. 2010. "Hadrian, Hellenism, and the Social History of Art." *Arion* 18: 55–78.

Wallace-Hadrill, A.F. 1983. *Suetonius: The Scholar and His Caesars*. London.

Walsh, P.G. 1970. *Livy: His Historical Aims and Methods*. Cambridge.

Wardle, D. 1998. "Suetonius and His Own Day." In C. Deroux ed. *Studies in Latin Literature IX*. (Brussels 1998): 425–47.

Wardle, D. 2014. *Suetonius:* Life of Augustus. Oxford.

Wardman, A. 1982. *Religion and Statecraft among the Romans*. London.

Watson, A. ed. 1985. *The Digest of Justinian*. Philadelphia.

Weber, W. 1954 [1936]. "Hadrian." In S.A. Cook, F.E. Adcock, and M.P. Charlesworth eds. *The Cambridge Ancient History*¹ XI: 294–324 (with XII: 325–6).

Weber, W. 1973 [1907]. *Untersuchungen zur Geschichte des Kaisers Hadrianus*. Hildesheim.

Weinstock, S. 1971. *Divus Julius*. Oxford.

Weksler-Bdolah, S. 2020. *Aelia Capitolina-Jerusalem in the Roman Period in Light of Archaeological Research*. Leiden.

Westfall, R., and F. Brenk 2011. "The Second and Third Century." In G. Marasco ed. *Political Autobiographies in Antiquity: A Brill Companion* (Leiden 2011): 363–416.

White, P. 1967. "The Authorship of the *Historia Augusta*." *Journal of Roman Studies* 57: 115–33.

Whitehorne, J.E.G. 1977. "Was Marcus Aurelius a Hypochondriac?" *Latomus* 36: 413–21.

Whitmarsh, T. 2004. "The Cretan Lyre Paradox: Mesomedes, Hadrian and the Poetics of Patronage." In B.E. Borg ed. Paideia: *The World of the Second Sophistic* (Berlin 2004): 377–402.

Willers, D. 1990. *Hadrians panhellenisches Programm: Archäologische Beiträge zur Neugestaltung Athens durch Hadrian*. Basel.

Williams, C.A. 1999. *Roman Homosexuality: Ideologies of Masculinity in Classical Antiquity*. New York.

Williams, W. 1976. "Individuality in the Imperial Constitutions: Hadrian and the Antonines." *Journal of Roman Studies* 66: 67–83.

Wilson Jones, M. 2015. "Building on Adversity: The Pantheon and Problems with Its Construction." In Mander and Wilson Jones eds. 2015: 193–230.

Winterling, A. 2011. *Caligula: A Biography*. Berkeley.

Wiseman, T.P. 1998. "Late Syme: A Study in Historiography." In T.P. Wiseman, *Roman Drama and Roman History* (Exeter 1998): 135–52.

Woolf, G. 1993. "Roman Peace." In Rich and Shipley eds. 1993: 171–94.

Woytek, B.E. 2012. "System and Product in Roman Mints from the Late Republic to the High Principate: Some Current Problems." *Revue belge de numismatique et de sigillographie* 158: 85–122.

Yadin, Y. 1971. *Bar-Kokhba: The Rediscovery of the Legendary Hero of the Last Jewish Revolt against Imperial Rome*. London.

Yavetz, Z. 1996. "Caligula, Imperial Madness and Modern Historiography." *Klio* 78: 105–29.

Zahrnt, M. 1988. "Antinoopolis in Äegypten: Die hadrianische Gründung und ihre Priviligien in der neueren Forschung." *Aufstieg und Niedergang der römischen Welt* II 10.1: 669–706.

Zanker, P. 1988. *The Power of Images in the Age of Augustus*. Ann Arbor.

Zetzel, J.E.G. 2018. *Critics, Compilers, and Commentators: An Introduction to Roman Philology, 200 BCE – 800 CE*. New York.

Zissu, B., R. Porat, B. Langford, and A. Frumkin 2011. "Archaeological Remains of the Bar Kokhba Revolt in the Te'omim Cave (Mŭhâret Umm et Tûeimîn), Western Desert Hills." *Journal of Jewish Studies* 62: 262–83.

Modern Literature and Criticism

Adler, A. 2014. "«Le Graphique d'une vie humaine»." In Blanckeman ed. 2014: 21–33.

Armstrong, E. 1954. *Robert Estienne, Royal Printer: An Historical Study of the Elder Stephanus*. Cambridge.

Auden, W.H. 1989. *Forewords and Afterwords*. New York.

Babington, P.L. 1925. *Bibliography of the Writings of John Addington Symonds*. London.

Backscheider, P.R. 1999. *Reflections on Biography*. Oxford.

Bann, S. 2000. "Versions of Antinous: Symonds between Shelley and Yourcenar." In Pemble ed. 2000: 136–53.

Bann, S. 2002. "Pater's Reception in France: A Provisional Account." In L. Brake, L. Higgins, and C. Williams eds. *Walter Pater: Transparencies of Desire* (Greensboro NC 2002): 55–62.

Basch, M.F. 1983. "Empathetic Understanding: A Review of the Concept and Some Theoretical Considerations." *Journal of the American Psychoanalytical Association* 31: 101–26.

Bate, J. 2003. *John Clare: A Biography*. New York.

Bate, J. 2009. *Soul of the Age: A Biography of the Mind of William Shakespeare*. New York.

Bate, J. 2015. *Ted Hughes: The Unauthorised Life*. New York.

Beaton, R. 1983. "The History Man." *Journal of the Hellenic Diaspora* 10: 23–44.

Benedict, R. 1946. *The Chrysanthemum and the Sword*. Boston.

Benedict, R. 1989 [1934]. *Patterns of Culture*. Boston.

Bennett, A. 2015. "'It's readable all right, but it's not history': Robert Graves's *Claudius* Novels and the Impossibility of Historical Fiction." In A.G.G. Gibson ed. *Robert Graves and the Classical Tradition* (Oxford 2015): 21–41.

Benoit, C. 1994. "Le Personnage yourcenarien: de l'individuel à l'universel." In Vásquez de Parga and Poignault eds. 1994: I 61–70.

Bernier, Y. 2004. *Inventaire de la bibliothèque de Marguerite Yourcenar: Petite Plaisance*. Clermont-Ferrand.

Blanchet-Douspis, M. 2008. *L'Influence de l'histoire contemporaine dans l'œuvre de Marguerite Yourcenar*. Amsterdam.

Blanchet-Douspis, M. 2014. *L'Idéologie politique de Marguerite Yourcenar d'après son œuvre romanesque*. Amsterdam.

Blanckeman, B. ed. 2007. *Les Diagonales du temps: Marguerite Yourcenar à Cerisy*. Rennes.

Blanckeman, B. 2014a. "Introduction." In Blanckeman ed. 2014: 9–15.

Blanckeman, B. 2014b. "«En faveur de l'exact et du nu»: *Mémoires d'Hadrien* dans la correspondance de Marguerite Yourcenar." In Blanckeman ed. 2014: 255–74.

Blanckeman, B. ed. 2014. *Lectures de Marguerite Yourcenar:* Mémoires d'Hadrien. Rennes.

Body, J. 1995. "Marguerite Yourcenar et l'école des Annales: Réflexions sur le 'Possibilisme'." In Delcroix and Delcroix eds. 1995: 49–57.

Bonali Fiquet, F. 1994. *Réception de l'œuvre de Marguerite Yourcenar: Essai de bibliographie chronologique (1922–1994)*. Tours.

Booth, J. 2014. *Philip Larkin: Life, Art and Love*. London.

Brami, J. 2019. "Marguerite Yourcenar dans ses lettres et les Lettres: Touches pour un autoportrait d'outre tombe." In Poignaut ed. 2019: 49–66.

Brémond, M. 2012. "Marguerite Yourcenar ou la lutte pour les droits de l'auteur." *Société Internationale d'Études Yourcenariennes* Bulletin 33: 145–212.

Brémond, M. 2019. *Marguerite Yourcenar, une femme à l'académie: malgré eux, malgré elle* ... Paris.

Brochard, C. and E. Pinon. 2014. *L'Extase lucide: Étude de* Mémoires d'Hadrien. Rouen.

Bruggisser, P. 1994. "«Patience» d'un impatient: Hadrien à l'approche de la mort, de l'*Histoire Auguste* à Marguerite Yourcenar." *Historiae Augustae Colloquium Bonnense* (Bonn 1994): 39–69.

Caine, B. 2010. *Biography and History*. Basingstoke, Hants.

Calandra, E., B. Adembri, and N. Giustozzi eds. 2013. *Marguerite Yourcenar: Adriano, l'antichità immaginata. Tivoli, Villa Adriana, Antiquarium del Canopo 28 marzo – 3 novembre 2013*. Verona.

Castellani, J.-P. 2011. *Je, Marguerite Yourcenar: D'un Je à l'autre*. Paris.

Castellani, J.-P. 2015. "Examen stylistique de la correspondance de Marguerite Yourcenar." In M. Chehab ed. *Le(s) style(s) de Marguerite Yourcenar* (Clermont-Ferrand 2015): 209–24.

Castellani, J.-P., and R. Poignault eds. 1990: *Marguerite Yourcenar et l'art. L'art de Marguerite Yourcenar*. Tours.

Célo, J.-Y. 2014: "Guerre et paix dans *Mémoires d'Hadrien*." In Blanckeman ed. 2014: 99–111.

Chabot, A. 2015. "De l'histoire du roman: la «magie sympathique»." *Société Internationale d'Études Yourcenariennes* Bulletin 36: 93–117.

Chevallier, R. 1990. "Echos de l'iconographie antique dans *Mémoires d'Hadrien*." In Castellani and Poignault eds. 1990: 87–97.

Cliche, E. 1994. "Yourcenar, une écriture transversale." In Vásquez de Parga and Poignault eds. 1994: I 175–84.

Cliche, E. 2000. "La Réécriture du texte Woolfien, *The Waves* (1931), dans la traduction (1937) de Marguerite Yourcenar." In Poignault and Castellani eds. 2000: 323–32.

Cordonnier, V. 2019. *La Sagesse d'Hadrien selon Yourcenar.* La Plaine Saint-Denis.

Counihan, F., and B. Deprez eds. 2006. *Écriture de pouvoir, pouvoir de l'écriture. La Réalité sociale et politique dans l'œuvre de Marguerite Yourcenar.* Brussels.

Crick, B. 2019 [1980]. *George Orwell: A Life.* Toronto.

DeJean, J. 1989. *Fictions of Sappho 1546–1937.* Chicago.

Delcroix, S., and M. Delcroix eds. 1995. *Roman, histoire et mythe dans l'œuvre de Marguerite Yourcenar.* Tours.

Demanze, L. 2014. "«Un homme qui lit»." In Blanckeman ed. 2014: 143–55.

Deprez, B. 2003. *Marguerite Yourcenar: Écriture, maternité, démiurgie.* Brussels.

Deprez, B. 2009. "Ce qu'il importait précisément à l'auteur de dire. La correspondance comme paratexte: une stratégie de plus." In A.-A. Morello ed. *La lettre et l'œuvre. La correspondance de Marguerite Yourcenar* (Paris 2009): 33–47.

Deprez, B. 2012. *Marguerite Yourcenar et les États-Unis: Du nageur à la vague.* Paris.

Dezon-Jones, É. 2014. "Marguerite Yourcenar ou la politique du texte brûlé." In Blanckeman ed. 2014: 245–54.

Di Méo, N. 2014. "L'Empire dans *Mémoires d'Hadrien*." In Blanckeman ed. 2014: 85–98.

Doody, M.A. 1997. *The True Story of the Novel.* New Brunswick NJ.

Dowling, L. 1994. *Hellenism and Homosexuality in Victorian London.* London.

Eagleton, T. 2005. *The English Novel.* Malden MA.

Edel, L. 1957. *Literary Biography.* Bloomington.

Edel, L. 1984. *Writing Lives: Biographica Principia.* New York.

Edmond, M. 2017. *The Expatriates.* Wellington.

Ellmann, R. 1987. *Oscar Wilde.* New York.

Elton, G.R. 1992. "Thomas More and Thomas Cromwell." In G.R. Elton, *Studies in Tudor and Stuart Politics and Government* Vol. 4 (Cambridge 1992): 144–60.

Evangelista, S. 2007. "Platonic Dons, Adolescent Bodies: Benjamin Jowett, John Addington Symonds, Walter Pater." In G. Rousseau ed. *Children and Sexuality: From the Greeks to the Great War* (New York 2007): 206–30.

Evangelista, S. 2015. "Towards the Fin de Siècle: Walter Pater and John Addington Symonds." In N. Vance and J. Wallace eds. *The Oxford History of Classical Reception in English Literature Vol. 4: 1790–1880* (Oxford 2015): 643–68.

Filaire, M.-J. 2012. "Le Centaure et le faon: Antinoüs et l'animalité dans les *Mémoires d'Hadrien*." *Société Internationale d'Études Yourcenariennes* Bulletin 32: 61–74.

Filaire-Ramos, M.-J. 2014. "Antinoüs, es-tu là? Présence, résonance et sens de l'absence." In Blanckeman ed. 2014: 183–97.

Forster, E.M. 1927. *Aspects of the Novel*. London.

Forster, E.M. 1972 [1951]. *Two Cheers for Democracy*. London.

Fort, P.-L. 2014. "«Appartenir au même règne»." In Blanckeman 2014: 199–209.

Foucault, M. 1976. *Histoire de la sexualité* t. 1–3. Paris = *The History of Sexuality* vols. 1–3. New York 1978–86.

Fréris, G. 2000. "Décadence et conception de l'histoire de Cavafy dans *Mémoires d'Hadrien*." In Poignault and Castellani eds. 2000: 65–75.

Fréris, G. 2004. "L'Esprit décadent du XIXᵉ siècle et l'angoisse du XXᵉ siècle dans *Mémoires d'Hadrien*." In G. Fréris and R. Poignault eds. *Marguerite Yourcenar écrivain du XIXe siècle?* (Clermont-Ferrand 2004): 183–91.

Fréris, G. 2019. "Cavafy-Hadrien fait le bilan d'un moi et d'un empire." In Poignault ed. 2019: 277–92.

Funke, J., and R. Langlands. 2015. "The Reception of Rome in English Sexology." In J. Ingleheart ed. *Ancient Rome and the Construction of Modern Homosexual Identities* (Oxford 2015): 109–25.

Furbank, P.N. 2004. "On the Historical Novel." *Raritan* 23: 94–114.

Gaudin, C. 1994. *Marguerite Yourcenar à la surface du temps*. Amsterdam.

Gaudin, C. 2007. "Contre la décadence, le réenchantement du monde." In Blanckeman ed. 2007: 23–38.

Gellhorn, M. 2018 [1959]. *The Face of War*. New York.

Gergely, T. 1988. "La Mémoire suspecte d'Hadrien." In Nysenhole and Aron eds. 1988: 45–50.

Goslar, M. 1996. *Les Voyages de Marguerite Yourcenar*. Brussels.

Goslar, M. 1998. *Yourcenar, biographie, «Qu'il eût été fade d'être heureux»*. Brussels.

Goslar, M. 2007. *Antinoüs, de la pierre à l'écriture de* Mémoires d'Hadrien. Brussels.

Grant, F.C. 1956. "Hadrian's Memoirs." *Anglican Theological Review* 38: 290–9.

Greene, R. 2020. *The Unquiet Englishman: A Life of Graham Greene*. New York.

Grodent M. 1988. "L'Hellénisme vivant de Marguerite Yourcenar." In Nysenhole and Aron eds. 1988: 55–67.

Grosskurth, P. 1965. *The Woeful Victorian: A Biography of John Addington Symonds*. New York.

Grosskurth, P. 1984. *The Memoirs of John Addington Symonds*. London.

Guppy, S. 1988. "An Interview with Marguerite Yourcenar." *Paris Review* 106: 228–49 = "Une Interview de Marguerite Yourcenar" (PV 378–99).

Halley, A. 2005. *Marguerite Yourcenar en poésie*. Amsterdam.

Hammett, B. 2011. *The Historical Novel in Nineteenth-Century Europe: Representations of Reality in History and Fiction*. Oxford.

Harrington, A. 2001. "Dilthey, Empathy and *Verstehen*: A Contemporary Reappraisal." *European Journal of Social Theory* 4: 311–29.

Hayashi, O. 2014. "Marguerite Yourcenar et Yucio Mishima: le miroir d'Oscar Wilde." In R. Poignault and V. Torres eds. *Les Miroirs de l'altérité dans l'œuvre de Marguerite Yourcenar* (Clermont-Ferrand 2014): 39–48.

Hazareesingh, S. 2020. *Black Spartacus: The Epic Life of Toussaint Louverture.* New York.

Hébert, J. 2012. *L'Essai chez Marguerite Yourcenar: Métamorphoses d'une forme ouverte.* Paris.

Hoberman, R. 1987. *Modernizing Lives: Experiments in English Biography.* Carbondale IL.

Holliday, P.J. 2000. "Symonds and the Model of Ancient Greece." In Pemble ed. 2000: 81–101.

Holroyd, M. 2005 [1995]. *Lytton Strachey: The New Biography.* New York.

Hörmann P.A. 1996. *La Biographie comme genre littéraire:* Mémoires d'Hadrien *de Marguerite Yourcenar.* Amsterdam.

Houssais, Y. 2014. "*Mémoires d'Hadrien* ou le pari de l'éternité." In Blanckeman ed. 2014: 125–38.

Howard, D.R. 1987. *Chaucer: His Life, His Works, His World.* New York.

Howard, J.E. 1992. *From Violence to Vision: Sacrifice in the Works of Marguerite Yourcenar.* Carbondale IL.

Howard, J.E. 2018. *We Met in Paris: Grace Frick and Her Life with Marguerite Yourcenar.* Chicago.

Hynynen, A. 2005. "La Femme parfaite dans *Alexis ou le Traité du vain combat, Anna soror …, Mémoires d'Hadrien* et *L'Œuvre au Noir.*" In Ledesma Pedraz and Poignault eds. 2005: 285–99.

Jacquiot, J. 1990. "Les Œuvres d'art evoquées dans *Mémoires d'Hadrien.*" In Castellani and Poignault eds. 1990: 73–89.

Jamison, K.R. 2017. *Robert Lowell: Setting the River on Fire: A Study of Genius, Mania, and Character.* New York.

Jefferson, A. 2007. *Biography and the Question of Literature in France.* Oxford.

Jeffreys, P. 2009. *The Forster-Cavafy Letters: Friends at a Slight Angle.* Cairo.

Jouanny, S. 2014. "D'une œuvre à l'autre, une traversée." In Blanckeman ed. 2014: 215–29.

Julien, A.-Y. 2002. *Marguerite Yourcenar ou la signature de l'arbre.* Paris.

Julien, A.-Y. 2014a. *Marguerite Yourcenar et le souci de soi.* Paris.

Julien, A.-Y. 2014b. "Les Carnets de Notes de «Mémoires d'Hadrien»." In Blanckeman ed. 2014: 231–44.

Jusdanis, G. 1987. *The Poetics of Cavafy: Textuality, Eroticism, History.* Princeton.

Keeley, E. 1976. *Cavafy's Alexandria: Study of a Myth in Progress.* Cambridge MA.

Kendall, P.M. 1965. *The Art of Biography.* London.

Kermode, F. 2009. *Concerning E.M. Forster.* New York.

Kermode, F. 2019. *Pieces from the* London Review of Books. London.

Kiebunski, K. 2004. "Question of *Genre*: History and the Self in Marguerite Yourcenar's *Mémoires d'Hadrien.*" In J.H. Sarnecki and I.M. O'Sickey eds. *Subversive Subjects: Reading Marguerite Yourcenar* (Madison WI 2004): 148–65.

King, C. 2020. *The Reinvention of Humanity: How a Circle of Renegade Anthropologists Remade Race, Sex and Gender.* London.

Koelb, C. 1998. *Legendary Figures: Ancient History in Modern Novels.* Lincoln NE.

Kolbert, J. 1985. *The Worlds of André Maurois.* London.

Kohut, T.A. 2003. "Psychoanalysis as Psychohistory or Why Psychotherapists Cannot Afford to Ignore Culture." *Annual of Psychoanalysis* 31: 225–36.

Lebel, M. 1979. "Marguerite Yourcenar traductrice de la poésie grecque." *Études littéraires* 12: 65–78.

Ledentu, M., L. de Chantal, and G. Salamon eds. 2014. *Clio et ses disciples: Écrire l'histoire dans l'antiquité.* Paris.

Ledesma Pedraz, M., and R. Poignault eds. 2005. *Marguerite Yourcenar: La Femme, les femmes, une écriture-femme?* Clermont-Ferrand.

Lee, H. 1999 [1996]. *Virginia Woolf.* New York.

Lee, H. 2009. *Biography: A Very Short Introduction.* Oxford.

Lee, H. 2021. *Tom Stoppard: A Life.* New York.

Lejeune, P. 1975. *Le Pacte autobiographique.* Paris.

Lejeune, P. 1986. *Moi aussi.* Paris.

Lemaitre, G. 1968. *Maurois: The Writer and His Work.* New York.

Liddell, R. 1974. *Cavafy: A Critical Biography.* London.

Lindbergh, A.M. 1940. *The Wave of the Future: A Confession of Faith.* New York.

Lodge, D. 2011. *The Art of Fiction.* London.

Lukács, G. 1983 [1962]. *The Historical Novel.* Lincoln NE.

MacCulloch, D. 2019. *Thomas Cromwell: A Revolutionary Life.* New York.

MacKay, M. 2018. *Ian Watt: The Novel and The Wartime Critic.* Oxford.

Mackridge, P. 2009. "Introduction." In C.P. Cavafy, E. Sachperoglou, A. Hirst, and P. Mackridge. *The Collected Poems: With Parallel Greek Text.* New York.

Malinowski, B. 1944. *A Scientific Theory of Culture and Other Essays.* Chapel Hill.

Malinowski, B. 1945. *The Dynamics of Cultural Change: An Inquiry into Race Relations in Africa.* New Haven.

Manzoni, A. 1984. *On the Historical Novel: Del romanzo storico. Translated, with an Introduction by Sandra Bermann.* Lincoln NE.

Marcus, L. 2002. "The Newness of the 'New Biography'." In P. France and W. St. Clair eds. *Mapping Lives: The Uses of Biography* (Oxford 2002): 193–218.

Marks, E. 1990. "'Getting Away with Murd(h)er': Author's Preface and Narrator's Text. Reading Marguerite Yourcenar's *Coup de Grâce* 'After Auschwitz'." *Journal of Narrative Technique* 20: 210–20.

Massimilla, G. 2016a. "Suggestioni classiche in *Denier du rêve* di Marguerite Yourcenar." In M. Capasso ed. *Sulle orme degli antichi: Scritti di filologia e di storia della tradizione classica offerti a Salvatore Cerasuolo* (Lecce 2016): 403–34.

Massimilla, G. 2016b. "Marguerite Yourcenar lettrice dei classici: un Notturno in *Denier du rêve* e le traduzioni dei poeti greci in *La Couronne et la Lyre*." *Eikasmos* 27: 399–413.

Maurois, A. 1928. *Aspects de la biographie*. Paris = *Aspects of Biography* (Cambridge 1929).

McLoughlin, K. 2007. *Martha Gellhorn: The War Writer in the Field and in the Text*. Manchester.

McNeillie, A. ed. 2004. *The Essays of Virginia Wolf. Vol. IV 1925–1928*. London.

Medeiros, A.M. 1994. "L'Universalité dans *Mémoires d'Hadrien*." In Vásquez de Parga and Poignault eds. 1994: II 199–207.

Medeiros, A.M. 1996. *Les Visages de l'autre: Alibis, masques et identité dans* Alexis ou le traité du vain combat, Denier du rêve *et* Mémoires d'Hadrien. Bern.

Melzi d'Eril, F. 2009. "À la recherche d'un visage: Antinoüs dans la correspondance de Marguerite Yourcenar." In Morello ed. 2009: 203–13.

Mendelsohn, D. 2012. *C.P. Cavafy: Complete Poems*. New York.

Morello, A.-M. ed. 2009. *La Lettre et l'œuvre: Correspondances de Marguerite Yourcenar*. Paris.

Morley, N. 2005. "Decadence as a Theory of History." *New Literary History* 35: 573–85.

Mozzillo, A. 1955. "Adriano tra Gide e Spartiano." *Labeo* 1: 223–30.

Ness, B. 1994. *Mystification et créativité dans l'œuvre romanesque de Marguerite Yourcenar*. Chapel Hill.

Nisbet, G. 2013. *Greek Epigram in Reception: J.A. Symonds, Oscar Wilde, and the Invention of Desire, 1805–1929*. Oxford.

Nysenhole, A., and P. Aron eds. 1988. *Marguerite Yourcenar* (*Revue de l'Université de Bruxelles* 3–4). Brussels.

Parker, P. 2016. *Housman Country: Into the Heart of England*. London.

Pemble, J. ed. 2000. *John Addington Symonds: Culture and the Demon Desire*. Basingstoke.

Peyroux, M. 2011. *Jacqueline de Romilly, Marguerite Yourcenar, et la Grèce antique: Une passion commune*. Paris.

Peyroux, M. 2019. "Marguerite Yourcenar et la Pologne." https://paris.pan.pl/wp-content/uploads/2019/01/peyroux.pdf.

Picard, Ch. 1954. "L'Empereur Hadrien vous parle." *Revue archéologique* 43: 83–5.

Pocock, J.G.A. 2003. *Barbarism and Religion. Vol. 3: The First Decline and Fall*. Cambridge.

Poignault, R. 1988a. "Chronologie historique et chronologie du récit dans *Mémoires d'Hadrien*." In Nysenhole and Aron eds. 1988: 19–31.

Poignault, R. 1988b. "Du soleil de Lambèse aux boues du Nil." In C. Biondi and C. Rosso eds. *Voyages et connaissance dans l'œuvre de Marguerite Yourcenar* (Pisa 1988): 195–206.

Poignault, R. 1990. "Antinous: un destin de pierre." In Castellani and Poignault eds. 1990: 107–19.

Poignault, R. 1991. "Images de l'empereur Hadrien d'après l'*Histoire Auguste*, relue par Marguerite Yourcenar." *Revue des Études Latines* 69: 203–18.

Poignault, R. 1993. "Hadrien et les cultes antiques." In R. Poignaut ed. *Le Sacré dans l'œuvre de Marguerite Yourcenar* (Tours 1993): 177–96.

Poignault, R. 1994. "L'Empire romain figure de l'universel." In Vásquez de Parga and Poignault eds. 1994: II 209–23.

Poignault, R. 1995. *L'Antiquité dans l'œuvre de Marguerite Yourcenar: Littérature, mythe et histoire*. 2 vols. Brussels.

Poignault, R. 1997. "Deux amis d'Hadrien: Arrien et Plotine." In J.-P. Beaulieu, J. Demers, and A. Maindron eds. *Marguerite Yourcenar. Écriture de l'autre* (Montreal 1997): 179–90.

Poignault, R. 2000. "L'*Histoire Auguste* au carrefour du temps." In C. Biondi, F. Bonali Fiquet, M. Cavazzuti, and E. Pessini eds. *Marguerite Yourcenar Essayiste: Parcours, méthodes et finalités d'une écriture critique* (Tours 2000): 197–212.

Poignault, R. 2003. "L'Enfance dans *Mémoires d'Hadrien*." In M. Laurent and R. Poignault eds. *Marguerite Yourcenar et l'enfance* (Tours 2003): 63–77.

Poignault, R. 2005. "Matrones et amantes dans *Mémoires d'Hadrien*." In Ledesma Pedraz and Poignault eds. 2005: 301–20.

Poignault, R. 2006. "Le Pouvoir et les complots. Le Prince et le tyran." In Counihan and Deprez eds. 2006: 19–34.

Poignault, R. 2007a. "Marguerite Yourcenar et les spécialistes de l'Antiquité." In M. Chehab and R. Poignault eds. *Marguerite Yourcenar entre littérature et science* (Clermont-Ferrand 2007): 135–55.

Poignault, R. 2007b. "L'Antiquité dans la correspondance de M. Yourcenar (1951–1962) dans le sillage de *Mémoires d'Hadrien*." In Blanckeman ed. 2007: 257–71.

Poignault, R. 2010. *La Réception critique de l'œuvre de Marguerite Yourcenar*. Clermont-Ferrand.

Poignault, R. 2014. "L'Autre dans *Mémoires d'Hadrien*." In R. Poignault and V. Torres eds. *Les Miroirs de l'altérité dans l'œuvre de Marguerite Yourcenar* (Clermont-Ferrand 2014): 89–121.

Poignault, R. 2015. "Fabrique de «L'Écrivain devant l'Histoire»." *Société Internationale d'Études Yourcenariennes* Bulletin 36: 141–65.

Poignault, R. ed. 2019. *Marguerite Yourcenar et le monde des lettres.* Clermont-Ferrand.

Poignault, R., and J.-P. Castellani eds. 2000. *Marguerite Yourcenar. Écriture, réécriture, traduction.* Tours.

Portmann, T. 2001. "*Mémoires d'Hadrien* – Roman historique?" *Société Internationale d'Études Yourcenariennes* Bulletin 22: 89–104.

Rickman, H.P. ed. 1976. *Wilhelm Dilthey: Selected Writings.* Cambridge.

Robinson, C. 1988. *C.P. Cavafy.* Bristol.

Romilly, J. de, and A. Grandazzi. 2003. *Une certaine idée de la Grèce.* Paris.

Rowse, A.L. 1944. *A Cornish Childhood.* London.

Said, E.W. 1994 [1979]. *Orientalism.* New York.

Saint, N. 1994. "L'Écrivain et sa source: L'Essai sur l'*Histoire Auguste.*" *Société Internationale d'Études Yourcenariennes* Bulletin 13: 71–84.

Saint, N. 2000. *Marguerite Yourcenar: Reading the Visual.* Oxford.

Sanz, Y. 1994. "Littérature et construction du sujet universel chez Marguerite Yourcenar." In Vásquez de Parga and Poignault eds. 1994: I 205–14.

Sarde, M. 1995a. *Vous, Marguerite Yourcenar: La passion et ses masques.* Paris.

Sarde, M. 1995b. "Représentation des Juifs chez Marguerite Yourcenar." In C. Faverzani ed. *Marguerite Yourcenar et la Méditerranée* (Clermont-Ferrand 1995): 71–82.

Sarde, M., and É. Dezon-Jones. 2019. "Littérature et épistolarité chez Marguerite Yourcenar: Relation paradigmatique auteure-éditeur dans les lettres à Emmanuel Boudot-Lamotte." In Poignault ed. 2019: 69–80.

Savigneau, J. 1993. *Marguerite Yourcenar: Inventing a Life* (trans. J.E. Howard). Chicago = *Marguerite Yourcenar: L'Invention d'une vie* (Paris 1990).

Schueller, M., and R.L. Peters. 1968. *The Letters of John Addington Symonds. Vol. II: 1869–1884.* Detroit.

Strachey, L. 1918. *Eminent Victorians.* London.

Strachey, L. 1921 *Queen Victoria: A Life.* London.

Šubert, J. 2015. "Augustine's *Confessions* as Autobiography." *Eirene* 51: 171–85.

Symonds, J.A. 1879. *Sketches and Studies in Italy.* London.

Symonds, J.A. 1908. *A Problem in Greek Ethics: Being an Inquiry into the Phenomenon of Sexual Inversion Addressed Especially to Medical Psychologists and Jurists.* London.

Terneuil, A. 2006. "Réflexions sur la question juive chez Marguerite Yourcenar." In Counihan and Deprez eds. 2006: 107–17.

Terneuil, A. 2020. "«L'art magique capable d'évoquer un visage perdu». Mémoires des portraits de Trajan et Hadrien rêvés par Marguerite Yourcenar." In Benoit et al. eds. 2020: 407–21.

Ughetto, A. 2009. "*Mémoires d'Hadrien* dans la correspondance de Marguerite Yourcenar." In Morello ed. 2009: 243–55.

Vago, D. "Yourcenar, Flaubert, ou l'empathie par la prose." In Poignault ed. 2019: 389–401.

Van der Starre, E. 1995. "Entre roman et histoire." In Delcroix and Delcroix eds. 1995: 419–29.

Vásquez de Parga, M.-J. 1995. "L'Histoire mythifiée: Antinoüs." In Delcroix and Delcroix eds. 1995: 441–52.

Vásquez de Parga, M.-J., and R. Poignault eds. 1994. *L'Universalité dans l'œuvre de Marguerite Yourcenar*. 2 Vols. Tours.

Vergniolle de Chantal, H. n.d. "Les Visages de l'histoire dans *l'Histoire auguste*: De l'approche critique d'un texte à l'essai philosophique." Unpublished (Centre International de Documentation Marguerite Yourcenar, Brussels).

Vier, J. 1979. "L'Empereur Hadrien vu par Marguerite Yourcenar." *Études littéraires* 12: 29–35.

Wagner, F. 2014. "Hadrien, ou la première personne." In Blanckeman ed. 2014: 35–51.

Waquet, F. 2015. "Latin for Girls: The French Debate." *Yale Classical Studies* 37: 145–55.

Waters, S. 1995. "'The Most Famous Fairy in History': Antinous and Homosexual Fantasy." *Journal of the History of Sexuality* 6: 194–230.

Watt, I. 2001 [1957]. *The Rise of the Novel: Studies in Defoe, Richardson and Fielding*. Berkeley.

Weitzman, A. 1998. "Présence de Cavafy dans *Mémoires d'Hadrien*." *Société Internationale d'Études Yourcenariennes* Bulletin 19: 85–97.

Whatley, J. 1980–1. "*Mémoires d'Hadrien*: A Manual for Princes." *University of Toronto Quarterly* 50: 221–37.

Williams, R. 1973. *The Country and the City*. Oxford.

Wilson, A.N. 2014. *Victoria: A Life*. New York.

Wilson, A.N. 2015. *The Book of the People: How to Read the Bible*. London.

Wilson, A.N. 2017. *Charles Darwin: Victorian Mythmaker*. New York.

Wilson, A.N. 2020. *The Mystery of Charles Dickens*. New York.

Wilson Knight, G. 2002 [1930]. *The Wheel of Fire: Interpretations of Shakespearean Tragedy*. London.

Womersley, D. 1988. *The Transformation of "The Decline and Fall of the Roman Empire."* Cambridge.

Woolf, V. 1994 [1927]. "The New Biography." In A. McNeillie ed. *The Essays of Virginia Woolf. Vol. IV 1925–1928* (London 1994): 473–80.

Woolf, V. 2011 [1939]. "The Art of Biography." In S.N. Clarke ed. *The Essays of Virginia Woolf. Vol. VI 1933–1941 and Additional Essays 1906–1924* (London 2011): 181–9.

Wyss, A. 1995. "Auteur, narrateur, personnage: quelle historiographie pour *Mémoires d'Hadrien*?" In Delcroix and Delcroix eds. 1995: 483–91.

Young, G.M. 1948. *Today and Yesterday: Collected Essays and Addresses*. London.

Young, M.W. 2011. "Malinowski's Last Word on the Anthropological Approach to Language." *Pragmatics* 21: 1–22.

INDEX

PHOENIX SUPPLEMENTARY VOLUMES